LIBRARY

RESOURCES FOR THE FUTURE, INC.

To Choose a Future

To Choose a Future

Resource and Environmental Consequences
of Alternative Growth Paths

Ronald G. Ridker and
William D. Watson

Published for RESOURCES FOR THE FUTURE
By The Johns Hopkins University Press
Baltimore and London

Copyright © 1980 by Resources for the Future
All rights reserved
Manufactured in the United States of America

Library of Congress Catalog Card Number 79-3643
ISBN 0-8018-2354-4

Library of Congress Cataloging in Publication data will be found on the last printed
page of this book.

RESOURCES FOR THE FUTURE, INC.
1755 Massachusetts Avenue, N.W., Washington, D.C. 20036

Board of Directors: M. Gordon Wolman, *Chairman,* Charles E. Bishop, Harrison Brown, Roberto de O. Campos, Anne P. Carter, Emery N. Castle, William T. Coleman, Jr., F. Kenneth Hare, Franklin A. Lindsay, Charles F. Luce, George C. McGhee, Ian MacGregor, Vincent E. McKelvey, R. W. Manderbach, Laurence I. Moss, Janez Stanovnik, Charles B. Stauffacher, Russell E. Train, Franklin Williams

Honorary Directors: Horace M. Albright, Erwin D. Canham, Edward J. Cleary, Hugh L. Keenleyside, Edward S. Mason, William S. Paley, John W. Vanderwilt

President: Emery N. Castle

Secretary-Treasurer: John E. Herbert

Resources for the Future is a nonprofit organization for research and education in the development, conservation, and use of natural resources and the improvement of the quality of the environment. It was established in 1952 with the cooperation of the Ford Foundation. Grants for research are accepted from government and private sources only if they meet the conditions of a policy established by the Board of Directors of Resources for the Future. The policy states that RFF shall be solely responsible for the conduct of the research and free to make the research results available to the public. Part of the work of Resources for the Future is carried out by its resident staff; part is supported by grants to universities and other nonprofit organizations. Unless otherwise stated, interpretations and conclusions in RFF publications are those of the authors; the organization takes responsibility for the selection of significant subjects for study, the competence of the researchers, and their freedom of inquiry.

This book is a product of RFF's Renewable Resources Division, which is under the direction of Kenneth D. Frederick. Ronald G. Ridker is a senior fellow in the Renewable Resources Division. William D. Watson, formerly at RFF, is an economist with the U.S. Geological Survey.

The figures were drawn by Art Services, Inc. The book was edited by Charlene Semer.

RFF Editors: Joan R. Tron, Ruth B. Haas, Jo Hinkel, and Sally A. Skillings

We cannot absolutely prove that those are in error who tell us that society has reached a turning-point, that we have seen our best days. But so said all who came before us, and with just as much apparent reason. . . . On what principle is it that, when we see nothing but improvement behind us, we are expected to see nothing but deterioration before us?

—Macaulay, 1830

In the space of one hundred and seventy-six years the Lower Mississippi has shortened itself two hundred and forty-two miles. That is an average of a trifle over one mile and a third per year. Therefore, any calm person, who is not blind or idiotic, can see that in the old Oolitic Silurian Period, just a million years ago next November, the Lower Mississippi River was upward of one million three hundred thousand miles long. . . . By the same token any person can see that seven hundred and forty-two years from now the Lower Mississippi will be only a mile and three-quarters long. . . . There is something fascinating about science. One gets such wholesale returns of conjecture out of such a trifling investment of fact.

—Mark Twain

Contents

Foreword   xi

Acknowledgments   xiii

Explanatory Notes and Units of Measure   xv

1. Approaching the Task   1

Nature of the Problem   2
Method and Approach   5
Precursors   9
The Nature of the Results   11

2. Assumptions and Scenarios   15

Population   16
Labor Force and Labor Productivity   21
   Labor Force; Labor Productivity
Style of Living and Composition of Private Expenditures   30
Geographic Distribution of Population
   and Economic Activities   32
Technological Change and the Resource Base   34
   Construction; Transportation; Communications Technology;
   Energy Extraction, Conversion, and Use; Primary Metals
   Production; Materials Substitutions; Resource Base
International Developments   41
   Population and GNP Projections; World Prices
Public Policy Alternatives   51
Other Assumptions   53
Summary of Scenarios   53

3. The National Economy   58

General Characteristics   58
Role of Major Determinants   69
   Population and Labor Productivity; Import Dependency;
   Nuclear Options; Oil Prices; Environmental Policy
Conclusions   92

4. Nonfuel Minerals   96

Concepts and Methods   97
   Resource Adequacy, Reserves, and Resources; Estimates of
   Reserves and Resources; Demand Projections
Resulting Projections   107
   Molybdenum, Titanium, and Vanadium; Chromium, Potash,
   Phosphate Rock, and Manganese; Nickel, Copper, and Cobalt;
   Aluminum; Iron; Lead; Sulfur; Tin; Tungsten; Zinc;
   Roles of Population, Economic Growth,
   and Other Determinants
Conclusions   148
Technical Note A: The Status of Other Minerals
   of Commercial Value   150
Technical Note B: Comparison with Other Estimates   152

5. Energy   157

Resources and Reserves   157
   Nonrenewable Resources; Renewable Resources
World Demands and Supplies   168
   Total Energy Consumption; Oil; Gas; Other Energy Forms
U.S. Demand and Supply   186
   Methodology; Price Assumptions; Implications for Aggregate
   Demand; Distribution by Fuels and Sectors
Cumulative Demand Compared with Resources   211

6. Agriculture   221

Methods and Assumptions   221
   Productivity Assumptions; Foreign Demand;
   Environmental Policy

Domestic Consumption   230
Domestic Production, Exports, and Prices   233
    Role of Population and Economic Growth; Role of Other
    Factors
Input Requirements   240
    Land; Fertilizers, Pesticides, and Energy
Conclusions   245

7. Pollution Costs and Control Benefits   250

Methods, Scope, and Limitations   251
Emissions and Concentration Levels   257
Pollution Damages   270
Benefit–Cost Analysis   274
    Case Studies; Effects of Alternative Assumptions
    on Water Pollution Results
Comparison of Alternative Scenarios   291
Conclusions   296
Technical Note A: Comparisons with Other Studies   298
    Base Year Emissions; Pollution Control Costs;
    Urban Runoff and Runoff Control Costs
Technical Note B: Regional Pollution Damages   307

8. Other Environmental Concerns   325

Land Resources   327
    Power Plants; Solid Wastes; Mining; Erosion
Water Resources   346
Climate   355
Radiation   359
Toxic Chemicals and the Oceans   364
Common Characteristics   366

9. Summary and Prospects   372

Base Case   372
    Population and the GNP; Nonfuel Minerals; Energy;
    Agriculture, Forestry, and Fisheries; The Environment

Other Scenarios   387
The Difficult Case; Nuclear Phaseout; Other Policies;
Lower Population and Economic Growth Assumptions;
Scenario Comparisons Using an Index of Economic Welfare
Some Broader Considerations   405
The United States in the Next Fifty Years; Coping with
Uncertainties and Risks; Role of Population and Economic
Growth

Appendix   411

The SEAS/RFF Model   411
The National System; The Regional System
The Models in Detail   414
The National Economic Forecasting Model (FORECAST);
Inforum; The Energy Use Model (ENERGY); The Solid
Waste/Recycling Model (SOLRECYC); The Regionalization
Model (REGION); The Regional Transportation Residuals
Models (PTRANS and FTRANS); The Regional Municipal
Agricultural and Mining Runoff Model (RUNOFF); Air and
Water Ambient Models (AQUALITY and WQUALITY);
The Damages and Benefit–Cost Model (BENEFITS)

Epilogue   456

Index   460

Foreword

To Choose A Future is the culmination of an ambitious attempt to assess the resource and environmental problems that the United States may face over the next fifty years. The consequences of alternative population and economic growth rates, technological change, and trade, environmental, and nuclear policies are examined using large-scale, computer-based models, as well as more conventional methods.

The authors suggest that their study should be viewed as one step in the continual assessment of the longer-run impacts of given actions and events. Indeed, this study makes a notable contribution to developing a methodology that can help society to make better choices regarding the future. In terms of the richness of detail, discussion of the data and assumptions, and scenario development, Ridker and Watson have moved well beyond previous large-scale modeling efforts. Furthermore, when the results are viewed broadly, *To Choose a Future* represents a comprehensive, quantitative, and persuasive refutation of the more pessimistic of the "limits to growth" projections.

The methodology is geared to the long run, for which it is assumed that profit considerations and educated guesses regarding physical stocks and technological changes will determine the use and availability of resources. As is conventional in such studies, there is little allowance for the influence of political or institutional disruptions such as war or cartels, which recent history suggests can have important impacts on at least the short- and medium-term availability of resources. Thus the results do not offer direct policy guidance. The study does provide, however, useful insights as to the longer-term implications of policies such as phasing out nuclear power, setting energy prices at various levels, and establishing alternative environmental standards and levels of agricultural exports. But the results are not forecasts; rather, they are highly conditional projections dependent at times on controversial data and on the assumptions and judgments of the authors.

There is always the possibility that research results will be taken out of context and used inappropriately. The danger of such misuse is especially great for a study such as this which deals with issues of current importance to society but utilizes a methodology and a time perspective that abstracts from many of the factors of immediate concern to policymakers such as income distribution and instability stemming from political considerations. In view of the potential for misuse—and since *To Choose A Future* covers nearly the entire range of energy, resource, and environmental issues normally covered by Resources for the Future—perhaps it is appropriate to reemphasize that publication does not represent an institutional endorsement of the results, the assumptions, or the methodology. RFF's publication of this study reflects a belief that it makes a major contribution to the literature on long-term projections, that the scholarship is excellent, that the book pulls together and organizes a wealth of information that will be of use to others, and that the results provide useful qualitative insights as to the impact of specific assumptions on the long-term resource and environmental problems that will be encountered by society.

Kenneth D. Frederick, Director
Renewable Resources Division
Resources for the Future

Washington, D.C.
October 1979

Acknowledgments

This book has grown out of a four-year project involving contributions by a number of persons and funding institutions.

Harry Perry provided an early draft of much of what is now the energy chapter. Many of the critical assumptions pertaining to energy—resource estimates, rates of increase in capacity, costs of alternative energy sources and the like—are based on his recommendations.

William Vogeley developed the mechanism for estimating U.S. demands for nonfuel minerals and provided an early draft of materials in chapter 4. Wesley C. Pickard and Lee Dymond also provided draft materials plus many helpful comments.

Leroy Quance served as principal investigator of a project undertaken by the Economic Research Service of the U.S. Department of Agriculture which provided a report that serves as the basis of chapter 6 on agriculture. He was assisted by a team that included William Crosswhite, Anthony Rojko, and Allen Smith.

Virginia Hendry worked up the basic materials for chapter 8 and provided an early draft. In addition, as a research assistant throughout this project, she was a member of its core research team. Particularly important was her careful, accurate, indefatigable help with the computer derivation of quantitative estimates and their display for analysis.

As a research associate throughout this project, Adele Shapanka was closely associated with all its phases. In particular, however, she was responsible for most of its technological assumptions and their entry and use in the dynamic input–output model underlying much of this project ("Long-Range Technological Forecasts for Use in Studying the Resource and Environmental Consequences of U.S. Population and Economic Growth: 1975–2025," RFF Discussion Paper D-31, 1978).

Jack Alterman, in addition to developing the basic labor force and labor productivity projections ("Projections of Labor Force, Labor Productivity, Gross National Product and Households; Methodology and Data," RFF Discussion Paper, 1976), helped us think through many of the more difficult analytical issues linking energy and the environment to the economy.

Donna Nowicki served as a research assistant through an extended and particularly difficult period. Chris Sandburg, Phil Glaessner, and Mark Sobel helped in similar ways during shorter periods. Louanne Sawyer, Marcia Mason, and Doris Sofinowski provided expert programming assistance. John Mankin deserves special recognition for his steadfastness, perseverance, and accuracy in typing numerous versions of this difficult manuscript. Charlene Semer provided excellent editorial assistance.

Among others, the comments and advisory inputs of the following are especially noteworthy: Jack Schanz on chapters 4 and 5; Fred Sanderson, Ken Frederick, and Pierre Crosson on chapter 6; Henry Peskin and Leonard Gianessi on chapter 7; Sam Schurr, Hans Landsberg, and Milton Russell on chapter 5; Sterling Brubaker on chapter 8; and Robert Ayres on technological change. In the early stages of this project Clopper Almon and his associates helped us gain a working knowledge of the INFORUM model, which stands at the core of the system of models we have utilized.

The Center for Population Research of the National Institutes of Health provided the major portion of the financial support for this project. Other assistance critical to the completion of this project was provided by the Environmental Protection Agency and the Department of Energy.

R. G. R.
W. D. W.

Explanatory Notes and Units of Measure

Symbols used in the tables:

Three dots (. . .) indicate that data are not available or are not separately reported.

A dash (—) indicates that the amount is nil or negligible.

A blank space in a table indicates that the item is not applicable.

Quads = 10^{15} Btu

Weights:

One metric ton = 1.102 short tons; 1 long ton = 1.20 short tons.

Conversion factors:

Crude oil—1 barrel = 0.136 metric tons = 0.150 short tons
Uranium—1 short ton (U_3O_8) = 0.769 metric tons of uranium

One million barrels of oil per day equals:

2.1 quads (2.1 $\times$ 10^{15} Btu) per year
2.2 exajoules (10^{18} joules) per year
530 $\times$ 10^{12} kilo calories per year
50 million metric tons oil per year
76 million metric tons coal per year
57 billion cubic meters natural gas per year = 5.9 billion cubic feet per day
620 terawatt hours (10^9 kWh) per year

Approximate heat content of various fuels and electricity:

Crude oil: 1 barrel = 5.8 million Btu
Natural gas: 1 cubic foot = 1,030 Btu
Coal—1 short ton = 24 million Btu
U_3O_8—1 short ton = 120 million kWh(th) = 409.4 billion Btu (gross)
Electricity: 1 kWh = 3,412 Btu

Energy accounting conventions:

Coal, natural gas, petroleum—Reported at Btu content of fuel

Hydroelectric and geothermal power—Reported at 10,748 Btu/kWh(e) initially, decreasing to 7,745 Btu/kWh(e)

Fossil-fuel electric power generation—Reported at 10,241 Btu/kWh(e) initially, decreasing to 7,282 Btu/kWh(e)

Nuclear electric power generation—Reported at 10,929 Btu/kWh(e) initially, decreasing to 8,415 Btu/kWh(e)

Gasified coal—Includes conversion loss equal to 20 percent of synthetic natural gas produced

Shale oil—Includes conversion loss equal to 20 percent of synthetic crude oil produced

I

Approaching the Task

Human history could usefully be written by tracing the growth of the impacts people have on the world around them. In the beginning, humans were a negligible factor. Their number was small, and they had precious few bits of knowledge and capital with which to alter their surroundings. If they had disappeared from the earth at that stage in history, few traces of their presence would have remained after a few years. Today, the consequences of human actions stretch over vast areas of space and time. The most obvious and dramatic example is the power to send sufficient destructive power from one side of the globe to the other to destroy regional, if not global, ecological balances for centuries to come. But this is a potential impact; the majority of examples have to do with long-term, pervasive influences that occur on a daily basis: the accumulation of capital and knowledge along with that of carbon dioxide and carcinogens; the dedication of land on a more or less permanent basis to such uses as dams, cities, power plants, and nuclear storage sites; the increasing density of population per unit of land; and the depletion of low-cost energy and mineral deposits. All such results of human activities, for better and for worse, are part of the increasingly important bequest we leave to future generations.

Although these impacts have undoubtedly grown over time, the ability to take them into account in making decisions has not grown apace. Some would explain this growing gap by the human's tendency toward shortsightedness and indifference to events of less than immediate concern. Others would emphasize the inability to control the collective actions of the species. But the principal problem must be ignorance, the sheer inability to assess the longer run impacts of a given action in any realistic way. Without such knowledge, meaningful concern and effective efforts at control are not possible.

This book is devoted to developing and presenting a method for attacking this problem. It does so in large part by illustration, by applying this approach to specific sets of problems. This has the advantage of concreteness, and it permits deriving some policy implications from this study. Though we believe we have delineated the general range within which some longer run implications of current actions fall, we have taken only a small step, one that will have to be repeated many times by other groups of researchers. This study should be viewed as part of a process, a continual quest for answers that, someday, will make it possible for people more rationally to choose a future for themselves.

More specifically, this book is concerned with the resource, environmental, and related economic problems the United States may face during the next fifty years. How will population growth, economic growth, and other major developments during the next half-century affect the demand for resources? What environmental pressures will changes in these various factors cause? Will resources in the United States and the rest of the world prove adequate to meet these demands without substantial price increases? If not, what adjustments and accommodations are likely? In the adjustment process, how dependent is the United States likely to become on the rest of the world? How costly will it be to adjust to these resource and environmental changes; in particular, what effect will such adjustments have on economic growth?

Nature of the Problem

It can be argued that because the future is essentially unknowable, the best that can be done is to base answers to these questions on general principles. This is not a very useful approach. True, the earth is finite and subject to the laws of entropy (see, for example, Boulding, 1966, and Georgescu-Roegen, 1971). But when will this finiteness catch up with us? In twenty years, two hundred years, or two thousand years? The answer to that question makes an enormous difference for policy. It is also true that, so far in history, technological and institutional innovations not only have put off the point at which diminishing returns would otherwise have set in but also have provided us with increasing returns in many areas (see, for example, Beckerman, 1974; Kahn, Brown, and Martel, 1976;

and Simon, 1977). But by what act of faith can we convince ourselves that such a state of affairs will continue in the future? It can be argued that the way to handle such uncertainty is to dampen population and economic growth, giving ourselves more time to find technological and other solutions to problems appearing on the horizon (Meadows, Meadows, Randers, and Behrens, 1972). But how can this be done, and who will compensate the poor, who do not have the luxury of waiting? In any event, are there not less general and drastic ways to cope with uncertainty? Such generalizations do not help much when it comes to choosing among specific, concrete policies.

To answer in a useful way future resource and environmental problems, we must become highly specific, quantitative, and empirical. There are too many trends operating in different directions to say much on a general level. In particular, at least three characteristics about this problem area must be kept in mind in selecting an approach to answering these questions.

First, the resource and environmental problems the United States is likely to face differ greatly among the various materials, sectors of the economy, and regions of the country. As income increases and tastes and technology change over time, the composition of output will change. Because each sector uses a different mix of resources and generates a different mix of residuals—and because technological change and other factors also affect these mixes—the composition of resources and residuals cannot be expected to remain the same or to maintain the same relationship with aggregate output as they have in the past. In addition, the geographic distribution of population, economic activities, and hence associated environmental impacts, will not remain constant over time. In these circumstances, aggregate analysis may yield highly misleading results. Despite its greater cost, data requirements, and analytic complexity, a substantial degree of disaggregation is an absolute necessity.

Second, both the nature of the problems and the importance of various determinants of these problems differ depending on the time period one has in mind. During the next five years or so, the predominant problems will be those caused by marketing arrangements, production bottlenecks, public resistance to certain types of developments, and business cycles. The effects of changes in population and secular changes in per capita incomes, tastes, and technology to a large extent can be ignored. But as the time horizon is lengthened, these more fundamental determinants grow in importance, and questions of resource adequacy, as opposed to adequacy of production facilities and marketing arrangements, come to the fore.

A fifty-year time horizon was selected for this study in order to ensure that the effects of different rates of population growth can be observed. It is almost the shortest time period that can be used for this purpose, but it is probably the longest period over which we can maintain even a modicum of faith in our results. This focus requires emphasizing the more fundamental determinants of resource and environmental pressures. However, we also have some interest in longer run transition problems, for example, the transition to a post-petroleum world, which will be completed or well on its way toward completion by 2025. But a complete analysis of such issues would involve a range of considerations so large that they could not be accommodated with the scope of a single study. As a compromise, this study focuses on longer run, more fundamental determinants, considering shorter run issues, such as resistance to change, political conflicts, and production bottlenecks, only when there is good reason to believe they will not be resolved during a five- or ten-year period.

Third, on top of these complexities, there are a vast number of interdependencies to reckon with. If technology or tastes change so that producing a unit of output requires more or less of a particular resource, the effect of population growth on demand for that resource also will have changed. If restrictions are placed on nuclear power, some other form of energy—perhaps coal with all its environmental problems—must be substituted. If restrictions are placed on the use of the automobile, another form of transportation, with its own array of resource requirements and pollutants, must be substituted. If wastes from economic activities are not emitted into the air, they will show up in liquid or solid form. More generally, if a particular resource becomes scarce, its price will increase, inducing a search for substitutes—in both consumption and production—which eventually could replace the resource altogether. But these are examples of interdependencies only between sectors of the economy and physical resource and environmental flows. In truth, everything—from migration patterns and attitudes toward work and leisure to economic and political developments in the rest of the world—is related to everything else and can change in important ways during the next fifty years.

There is no way within the scope of one study to account adequately for all these complexities. That is why this study must be viewed as part of a continuing process of searching for answers to the questions posed. Nevertheless, maintaining an awareness of these difficulties and trying to take them into account will more nearly achieve the goal than ignoring or circumventing them by using overly simple analytical devices.

Method and Approach

We have attempted to cope with these complexities in four ways: by using a scenario approach, by applying a series of mathematical–economic models, by developing a number of special studies, and by choosing a particular style of presentation.

Chapter 2 begins by specifying a set of eight important determinants of future resource and environmental problems. It then projects the way each of these determinants might develop over time. For those cases in which the consequences of alternative possibilities are of particular interest, a plausible range of projections is specified. These alternatives are then combined into sets of projections, or scenarios, for study in the remaining chapters. Each scenario, then, is a set of assumptions about the fundamental determinants of resource and environmental pressures.

Different scenarios are useful for different purposes. To demonstrate that a particular resource is adequate, the appropriate scenario is one that generates the largest reasonably possible demand for resources and that uses reasonably conservative estimates of developments on the supply side. To demonstrate that a particular technological change will not be sufficient to solve a given problem, the scenario ought to incorporate a reasonably optimistic assessment of how rapidly this technology is likely to be developed and applied. Studying the effects of alternative population growth rates requires two scenarios that are the same in all respects other than these growth rates (and closely associated changes). In other words, the scenarios have been selected to help prove or disprove various hypotheses or propositions. As such, none of them necessarily represents what is most likely to occur. Rather, they should be viewed as collections of assumptions about the future which, after their resource and environmental consequences are studied, permit certain lessons to be drawn.

These consequences were derived through a series of models and special studies. The latter are particularly important. They provided a basis for selecting and building scenarios; the data and changes in parameters necessary to feed the models; materials to supplement the modeling results for specific sectors and with respect to adjustment mechanisms in which the models are weak; and a means of checking, and if necessary changing, results derived in more mechanical ways. But since other chapters will indicate the content and use of these studies in some detail, the remainder of this section focuses on the models.

The system of models this analysis uses has been dubbed SEAS/ RFF (Strategic Environmental Assessment System/Resources for the Future). The core of this package is a model called INFORUM, a dynamic input–output model of the U.S. economy, developed over a series of years by Clopper Almon and his students at the University of Maryland (Almon, Buckler, Horowitz, and Reimbold, 1974). Other models— some developed in the original SEAS project sponsored by the Environmental Protection Agency and later modified by Resources for the Future (RFF), and others added by RFF—include components involving physical and monetary variables associated with energy, nonfuel minerals, transportation, and the environment (pollution, abatement costs, and environmental quality).

The system includes 185 economic sectors delivering commodities to each other and to various final consumers.[1] In addition to measures of these commodities in dollars, the model uses physical estimates for all major fuels, some twenty nonfuel minerals, and forty-two pollutants. The system has the capacity to distribute population, economic activities, and pollution emissions across regions specified in a variety of ways (for example, by economic and metropolitan areas and by air and watersheds). By applying region-specific dispersion models, ambient pollution concentrations can be estimated by regions. All coefficients in the model are subject to change over time, some on the basis of econometrically fitted equations with time trends or lagged variables but most on the basis of exogenously specified changes in population and labor force characteristics, technology, tastes, and so on; these changes are derived from the special studies. The appendix to this volume provides a brief analytical description of this system and references to more detailed, technical descriptions.

In its present form this system requires a number of iterations involving interactions between the user and the models before usable results can be derived. Though a more self-contained package could have been

---

[1] In addition, there are 364 side equations dealing with product and technology mixes within these sectors. The purpose of these side equations is to provide more detail for forecasting energy use, residuals, and abatement costs. They can be used, for example, to reestimate automatically the composition of residuals from the electric power-generation sector when the composition of fuels purchased by this sector changes.

developed—and it is always possible to run a model in a completely mechanical way, naïvely trusting that the results are satisfactory—this approach deliberately was avoided in order to force at every stage consideration of the reasonableness, not only of the outputs, but also of the inputs, the intermediate products, and the parameters entering into the relationships between the inputs and outputs at different points in time. Thus, few results can be described as falling out of the models in any direct, simple fashion.

Although SEAS/RFF is only one of several tools that were used in this analysis, it is an important tool, especially in a project of this magnitude and complexity, for three reasons. First, it serves as an accounting device that provides both a classification scheme to keep track of the enormous body of data this study required and a set of definitional equations that must be satisfied to maintain consistency between projections of individual components. Second, it serves as a flexible mnemonic device that stores the data in easily accessible cells of the accounting structure. Taken together, these features force explicit recognition of what information is required and actually used in making a particular projection, and they permit the easy absorption of new data. Third, it permits carrying out sensitivity analyses, studies of the impacts of one or more changes when other things are held constant. Such analyses would be virtually impossible without a computerized model.

The principal criticisms of these models clarify further the way the models are used. One criticism is that large-scale, multipurpose models of this type are too large and complex for most purposes—that questions about specific sectors are better answered by special-purpose models, and broader, general questions are better answered by simpler models that incorporate only a few aggregated variables. But special-purpose models do not permit interactions and feedbacks between sectors not explicitly included. An energy model, for example, does not permit studying interactions with the economy or the environment.

As a compromise, it is sometimes suggested that models should be detailed with respect to the principal sector under investigation and aggregated with respect to others. The problem with such models, or with any aggregated model of these complex relationships, is one of acquiring useful information about their parameters. The only way to obtain reliable information on relationships among aggregate variables is through statistical analysis of historic movements in these variables. But relationships derived in this way cannot be used for projections beyond a few years. The farther into the future one attempts to project, the more one must rely on judgments of knowledgeable experts; that is the only way that deviations from past trends can be taken into account. Such experts are far more capable of providing useful judgments about changes in small, concrete items than about changes in synthetic aggregates of such items, however. It is much easier, for example, to make a reasonable judgment about the saturation level for ownership of private autos and about the material content of future autos than it is to make similar judgments about what is likely to happen to aggregate consumption. Thus, even if it were possible to derive some useful conclusions by using an aggregate consumption function, it is not appropriate in the present case because of the importance of compositional changes in explaining resource demands and environmental pressures. This purpose is better served by an aggregate built up from judgments about major components than by one derived some other way.

A closely related argument against models of the SEAS/RFF type pertains to the inadequacy of the data base required to support detailed descriptions of many sectors and relationships. But lying behind any projection, no matter how simple the methodology, is a host of implicit assumptions about all the factors that might influence the situation; a detailed model simply forces more explicit recognition of what is being assumed. That cannot be bad. It is better to know that the coefficients in an equation relating use of construction materials to buildings are being held constant than to ignore that fact by using methods that do not force one to spell out such simplifying assumptions wherever used.

Another, in some ways opposite, argument against the use of such models is that they encourage a false sense of accuracy and confidence in their results, whereas in fact they are overly simple, leaving out factors and relationships that cannot be quantified or fitted into the procrustian bed of a given computational algorithm. Anyone who confuses models with reality does so at his own risk; there is nothing in the mechanism that forces one to believe that answers are accurate to ten digits,[2] that factors left out of a model are less important than those included, that the structure of the model is going to remain constant for a fifty-year period, or that simplifications introduced for computational convenience are anything more than just that. It is for this very reason that our analysis relies upon special studies and judgments in deriving conclusions.

---

[2] The number of digits presented in a given number is not necessarily an indication of how accurate we believe it to be. Frequently, we have carried along more digits than are warranted to make it easier to check for computational errors.

A final criticism is that such models seldom are validated against past history. Certainly the SEAS/RFF package has not been so validated except in the sense that it is designed to produce nearly correct outputs for its base period, 1971. An historical analysis would require a study as detailed and complex as this one, and it would not prove much, because projections of future developments still must be based on reasoned judgments about deviations from past trends. In any event, the value of the accounting structure, memory capabilities, and capacity to help with sensitivity analysis do not depend on the ability to track past history.[3]

There is one difficulty with this study's eclectic approach: the results cannot be replicated easily, certainly not as easily as would be possible if the models were more self-contained and run in a more mechanical fashion. The only way to compensate for this shortcoming is to provide detailed documentation and justifications for all the extra modeling assumptions and judgments that have been made. The problem here is a practical one: to present a complete account of what was done would result in an extremely long-winded, tedious text. As a compromise—one that explains our particular style of presentation—we decided to present these materials on three different levels. The level in this volume is the most general and, we hope, the least tedious. It presents the study's principal conclusions, qualitative and quantitative, and the principal justifications for them. It is not excessively detailed about methodological specifics, data sources, and so on. It also contains references to a second level of materials that goes into more analytical detail; these materials all have been published or are available upon request from RFF. The third level of detail is available as computer code and data sets stored on computer tape, available from RFF at cost to those with the capacity, stomach, and patience to make reasonable use of it.

Precursors

Although other studies have been concerned with many of the same questions this study poses, none has taken the same approach in all

---

[3] More detailed discussions of the pros and cons of such large, multisector, long-term models can be found in Hoos (1969), Arthur and McNicoll (1955), Clark and others (1975), and Rodgers, Wery, and Hopkins (1976). For a more specific evaluation of the original SEAS model (an evaluation not fully applicable to SEAS/RFF because of improvements made in many of the original data sets, among other reasons), see SEAS Review Panel (1975).

dimensions. Most are less comprehensive. *Resources in America's Future* (Landsberg, Fishman, and Fisher, 1963) and its predecessors limited their projections to energy and nonfuel minerals,[4] taking as given various different scenarios about the national economy; environmental and regional problems and feedbacks among these various components were not covered. In addition, the methodology used in these studies made it difficult to study the impacts of different assumptions about individual determinants or to know whether appropriate account was taken of indirect resource requirements. More recently, several studies have focused on the energy sector and on interactions between that sector and the national economy.[5] Although some are more detailed and sophisticated with respect to energy than earlier studies, none covers environmental, regional, and other economic dimensions with as much care and detail as does this study. In addition, of course, there have been a vast number of studies focused on individual resources or environmental problems and pollutants. The present study has drawn upon many of these to develop a more comprehensive analysis than any one of them provides.

A few recent studies are even more comprehensive and ambitious than this one in that they attempt to answer questions about resource adequacy and environmental carrying capacity for the globe as a whole and for a longer period of years. For the most part, what they gain in generality, they lose in specificity and plausibility. *The Limits to Growth* (Meadows and coauthors, 1972) skirts data problems by aggregating to an outrageous degree (one composite industrial output, one nonrenewable resource, one "pollutant," and one geographic unit—the world as a whole). It also contains few of the important adjustment mechanisms that have helped the world avoid catastrophe so far in history and incorporates highly pessimistic assumptions about technological progress, future reserves of nonrenewable resources, the ability to control and absorb pollution, and the extent of future population growth. The Mesarovic and Pestel study (1974) divides the world into ten regions and uses a better economic model than *The Limits to Growth,* but it ignores most environmental problems, gives short shrift to technological progress and many adjustment mechanisms, and relies upon questionable data sources. The study of the world economy by Leontief, Carter, and Petri (1977), by

---

[4] See p. 9 of Landsberg and coauthors (1963) for a brief description of such predecessors.

[5] Many of these studies are referenced in chapter 5. In addition, a comparison of the results of applying five different models, one of which is SEAS/RFF, to a common problem can be found in Hitch (1977).

far the most detailed, sophisticated, and carefully executed of these studies, is forced to fill in data gaps by applying to other regions coefficients relevant for the United States and Europe and to make questionable assumptions about adjustment mechanisms. Herman Kahn's recent book, *The Next 200 Years* (1976), circumvents all difficulties by applying a heady blend of *chutzpa* and *hubris*. It is nevertheless useful in stretching the imagination. All too often, these studies reach pessimistic conclusions about the future simply because it is easier to see problems resulting from a continuation of current trends than to imagine how those trends will change.

Such studies can be influential at times in significantly changing general attitudes toward the future. Certainly that has been the case with *Limits to Growth,* which initiated a significantly heightened concern about what we are doing to the world around us and where we are going with our lemminglike pursuit of economic growth. But with the possible exception of the Leontief study, few of the quantitative projections and specific policy recommendations these studies offer can be taken seriously.

Perhaps the study closest in scope and approach to the present one is one RFF undertook for the President's Commission on Population Growth and the American Future (Ridker, 1972). Indeed, that can be considered a predecessor study in the sense that it extended and elaborated an earlier version of the INFORUM model for the purpose of resource and environmental analysis and focused on the resource and environmental impacts on the United States of alternate rates of growth of population. The present study differs in that it uses a vastly improved and detailed data base, pays more attention to international and technological developments, includes a more sophisticated analysis of the energy and environmental sectors and the effects of population growth, and examines a much wider range of possible scenarios.

The Nature of the Results

It is not possible to make many useful predictions about the long-term future in any absolute sense. The future will be determined by new discoveries and inventions, new ideological movements and institutional arrangements, and perhaps at times by the decisions of willful, impetuous individuals who happen to be strategically placed. Such discontinuities in human history have never been amenable to prediction. There is nothing in recent methodological advances in futurology, computer simulation models, or more traditional disciplines that has changed this situation. What can be done is to spell out some of the implications of different courses of action when they occur within specific contexts. Thus, this study's results—like all others involving the future—must be taken not as forecasts but as highly conditional projections, projections that cannot be used intelligently to evaluate alternate courses of action without understanding all the conditions assumed in their development.

In addition, it is important to remember that these results are perishable. By the time this book is published, much of the data on which they are based, and perhaps some of the scenarios as well, may be obsolete. Although this is true of all empirical studies, it is particularly so in this case because of the inordinate speed with which practically everything pertaining to resources, energy, and the environment is changing. Again, this is a reason this study must be viewed as part of a process of developing answers to questions about the resource and environmental future we face. These results are viewed most usefully as illustrations of a method, an approach which we hope will be applied several times over so that more dependable quantitative answers begin to emerge.

For the most part, the changes we investigate are assumed to occur within a fairly familiar, surprise-free environment: no major wars, no dramatic shifts in international power balances or ways of living, and no massive new discoveries or innovations. This approach, though perhaps not very imaginative, does have the virtue of leading to the question of whether and to what extent things can continue in this way for much longer. Also, to allow large, exogenous changes would permit us to prove virtually anything we wished.

The focus in this study is on physical and economic changes: numbers of people, where and how they live, resources they demand and supply, units of economic production, and physical measures of environmental quality. The social and political determinants and consequences of these changes, which will certainly be important during this time period, are not discussed or analyzed except in passing. Thus, the strongest conclusions concern economic, resource, and environmental developments that might occur, assuming that social and political factors do not stand in the way except to the extent indicated by the scenario being studied.

The study's results are presented at different levels of generality. Many of the more interesting and useful results arise in the course of discussing a particular sector or scenario. Such materials are presented in chapters that focus on individual topics, and to that extent at least, these chapters should be viewed as somewhat independent, self-contained essays. More general results, particularly those cutting across sectors, cannot be fully discussed until all the pieces have been developed. The concluding chapter, which combines the results of the analyses of various sectors, is reserved for this more comprehensive, cross-cutting discussion. That final chapter also offers a summary and conclusion. This conclusion cannot be understood properly, however, without also understanding the steps that led to its derivation.

References

Almon, Clopper, Jr., M. B. Buckler, L. M. Horowitz, and T. C. Reimbold. 1974. *1985: Interindustry Forecasts of the American Economy* (Lexington, Mass., Lexington Books).

Arthur, W. Brian, and Geoffrey McNicoll. 1975. "Large-scale Simulation Models in Population and Development: What Use to Planners," *Population and Development Review* vol. 1, no. 2 (December) pp. 251–265.

Beckermann, Wilfred. 1974. *In Defense of Economic Growth.* (London, Jonathan Cape Ltd.).

Boulding, Kenneth E. 1966. "The Economics of the Coming Spaceship Earth," in Henry Jarrett, ed., *Environmental Quality in a Growing Economy* (Baltimore, Md., Johns Hopkins University Press for Resources for the Future).

Clark, John, and others. 1975. *Global Simulation Models* (London, Wiley).

Georgescu-Roegen, N. 1971. *The Entropy Law and the Economic Process* (Cambridge, Mass., Harvard University Press).

Hitch, Charles J., ed. 1977. *Modeling Energy-Economy Interactions: Five Approaches* (Washington, D.C., Resources for the Future).

Hoos, Ida. 1969. *Systems Analysis in Social Policy* (Berkeley, Institute of Economic Affairs, University of California).

Kahn, Herman, William Brown, and Leon Martel. 1976. *The Next 200 Years* (New York, William Morrow and Co.).

Landsberg, Hans H., Leonard L. Fischman, and Joseph L. Fisher. 1963. *Resources in America's Future, Patterns of Requirements and Availabilities, 1960–2000* (Baltimore, Md., Johns Hopkins University Press for Resources for the Future).

Leontief, W., A. Carter, and P. Petri. 1977. *The Future of the World Economy* (New York, Oxford University Press for the United Nations).

Meadows, Donella H., Dennis L. Meadows, Jørgen Randers, and William W. Behrens. 1972. *The Limits to Growth* (New York, Universe Books for Potomac Associates).

Mesarovic, Mihajlo, and Eduard Pestel. 1974. *Mankind at the Turning Point* (New York, E. P. Dutton).

Ridker, Ronald G., ed. 1972. *Population, Resources, and the Environment,* vol. III of *Research Reports of the Commission on Population Growth and the American Future* (Washington, D.C., GPO).

Rodgers, Gerry B., Rene Wery, and Michael J. D. Hopkins. 1976. "The Myth of the Cavern Revisited: Are Large-Scale Behavioral Models Useful?" *Population and Development Review* (September–December) vol. 2, no. 3–4.

SEAS Review Panel. 1975. "Quality Review of the Strategic Environmental Assessment System (SEAS)," Report to the Executive Committee of the Science Advisory Board, U.S. Environmental Protection Agency.

Simon, Julian. 1977. *The Economics of Population Growth* (Princeton, N.J., Princeton University Press).

2

Assumptions and Scenarios

There are many ways to classify sources of resource and environmental pressures. The simplest starts from the proposition that these pressures relate to the throughput of materials in the economy, which is largely determined by total output. Total output, in turn, can be broken down into population and per capita output, giving us two principal determinants of resource and environmental pressures. But the composition of output, the way the output is produced, the way it is used, and where it is used can play equally important roles. Surely, a population that produces throwaway bottles, prefers single-family suburban homes, and relies heavily on private automobiles places vastly more pressure on the environment than one that places less emphasis on packaging and more on apartment living and mass transportation. Moreover, behind these factors are more fundamental ones, like tastes, technology, and labor productivity.

A useful classification of such determinants involves eight different categories. First, of course, are a number of *demographic variables* such as the size of the population; its rate of growth; its age, sex, and racial structure; and the number and size of households. Such factors can influence the amount and composition of consumption goods purchased, as well as the level of economic activity. Second is *output per capita* and its principal determinants, labor force participation rates and labor productivity. A third factor might be called the *style of living,* in particular, preferences for various kinds of goods and ways of using them. The *geographic distribution* of both population and economic activities is the fourth determinant. The more concentrated economic activities are, the more difficult it is for pollution to be absorbed and assimilated through natural environmental processes; on the other hand, a more dispersed economy requires more resources for transport, housing, and social overhead capital. Next on the list are the *technological methods* used at each

15

stage of economic activity, for example, from mining and energy conversion through transport and production to emission and treatment of effluents. In the past, changes in such methods have dramatically altered the character and magnitude of the problems consequent to population and economic growth; there is no reason to believe they will not continue to do so in the future. Closely related are changes in the *resource base*— more accurately, in the amounts of resources that can be obtained at different costs. These changes are likely to occur as a consequence of depletion on the one hand and new discoveries and technological advances on the other. A seventh set of factors involves *international relations,* in particular the terms on which the United States can acquire resources and finished commodities from abroad. Finally, all these factors are influenced by *institutions and policies*—by the way markets work, by rules and regulations governing the management of residuals and land use, by import policies with respect to fuels and minerals, by decisions made with respect to location of public investments, and so on.

This chapter is concerned with selecting assumptions about the way each of these determinants changes over time and with selecting scenarios—groups of assumptions about these determinants—for use in remaining chapters. The focus here is on the general nature of these assumptions and on the rationale for choosing them; details, for the most part, are deferred to the specialized chapters that follow. Population, labor force, and labor productivity, however, are discussed in more detail in this chapter because they involve assumptions common to all subsequent chapters.

For the most part, we use 1975 as the base year and project to the years 1985, 2000, and 2025. Because of time and budget constraints, some events that have occurred since 1975 have not been factored into the analysis. Given our interest in long-run projection, little is lost by not keeping completely up to date. But the reader should bear this limitation in mind in order to avoid confusion when the text refers to projections for the 1975–80 period.

Population

During the decade of the sixties and well into the seventies, almost all measures show a decline in the growth and anticipated growth of the U.S. population. In the fifties, the population growth rate averaged 1.7

percent annually; in the first half of the seventies, it averaged 0.8 percent. The crude birthrate, after reaching a peak of 25.3 per 1,000 population in 1957, has fallen steadily to 14.7 in 1974, where it remained through 1976. The total fertility rate,[1] which averaged 3.69 children per woman between 1955 and 1959, has fallen continuously to 1.86 in 1974 and to 1.76 in 1976, well below the population replacement level of 2.1 per woman. Birth expectations data, based on periodic surveys of wives eighteen to twenty-four years old, have also shown a decline, from 2.9 children per wife in 1967 to 2.2 in 1974; thereafter, through 1977, it remained between 2.1 and 2.2. Although the median age at first marriage has not increased by more than one year, from 20.3 to 21.3 between 1960 and 1976, during that same period, the percentage of unmarried women younger than thirty-five has increased from 37.6 percent to 45.3 percent; the most dramatic increase has been for twenty to twenty-four year olds—from 28.4 percent to 42.6 percent unmarried (Census Bureau, 1977a).

These trends have led to continuous downward revisions in population projections. From 1969 to 1972, for example, the Census Bureau used four projection series, incorporating assumptions about lifetime births per woman that ranged from 3.10 to 2.11. In late 1972, the bureau dropped the highest of these series and added a lower series that assumed an average ultimate fertility of 1.8 births. In late 1975, the bureau settled on three series based on ultimate fertility assumptions of 2.7, 2.1, and 1.7 children per woman (Census Bureau, 1975).[2] Recent changes in the roles of women, the family, and sexual attitudes and behavior, plus concerns about overpopulation, all can be used to argue that these trends will continue for some time. But before accepting the lowest of the recent population projections as the most likely, a number of other factors should be taken into account.

First, fertility rates and attitudes toward marriage and reproduction have fluctuated considerably in the past. Figure 2–1 provides rather dramatic evidence on this score so far as the total fertility rate is concerned.

---

[1] The total fertility rate is an estimate of the average number of children that 1,000 women would have if they passed through their reproductive years at the age-specific fertility rates of a particular year. Here, however, this rate is expressed on a per woman basis.

[2] In July 1977, these projections were further revised to update their base and take account of recent declines in mortality rates. The net effect was a further, though small, decline in the projections for the series incorporating the higher fertility assumptions but a slight increase for the series incorporating the lowest of the fertility assumptions.

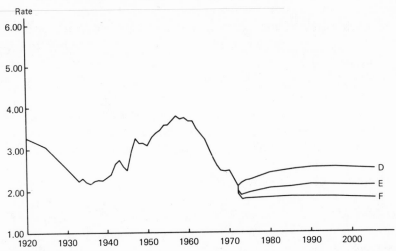

Figure 2–1. Total fertility rates, 1920–2025. The 1972 data are taken from Michael Teitelbaum, "International Experience with Fertility at or Near Replacement Level," in *Research Reports of U.S. Commission on Population Growth and the American Future:* vol. 1, *Demographic and Social Aspects of Population Growth* (Washington, D.C., GPO) pp. 648–649. The data for 1972 and later years are taken from Census Bureau, *Current Population Reports* ser. P-25, no. 493 (Washington, D.C., GPO, December 1972).

One explanation is that couples who find economic conditions good relative to those they experienced as children tend to have more children than did their parents; but their children, faced with more competition from their peers, react by having fewer children. Another possibility is that observing the problems of an older generation with many children, prompts the current generation to have fewer; conversely, observing the loneliness of people with few or no children, inspires others to have more. Yet another explanation links these trends with business cycles and the proportion of women who work (Butz and Ward, 1977). Some reversal of current fertility behavior and attitudes therefore would not be surprising.

Second, the decline in fertility rates in the sixties appears to have been caused both by a reduction in the number of unwanted children among older age groups because of the use of better contraceptives and easier access to abortions and by the later marriage and postponement of childbearing among women now reaching childbearing age. As these younger women grow older, they will have to decide whether to remain childless or to make up for lost time. It is unlikely that they will all decide to make the postponement permanent. Indeed, there is some preliminary evidence that supports the contention that childbearing simply will be undertaken later in the life cycle (Sklar and Berkov, 1975).

Third, attitudes expressed in recent surveys of birth expectations are not consistent with those reported in surveys of other attitudes, which indicate an aversion to childless marriages and the one-child family, a preference for those years when there are small children in the house, and a tolerance for large families. One explanation for this inconsistency is the possibility that the recent public attention given to the problems of population growth has induced respondents to report they expect to have one or two children without causing any fundamental change in personal preferences (Blake, 1974).

Fourth, mortality projections tend to be conservative in the sense that they do not take into account medical breakthroughs that could significantly improve trends in life expectancy. Certainly there are enough possibilities in the areas of cancer, heart disease, and the general retardation of aging so that this factor should not be ruled out altogether.[3] Increasing environmental hazards could work in the opposite direction, of course, a factor that will be discussed in chapters 7 and 8.

Finally, and perhaps most important, illegal immigration appears to be both sizable and on the rise.[4] This factor imparts a downward bias to standard population estimates and projections, which could be substantial. If, for example, 800,000 illegal immigrants (a commonly quoted figure that is twice the number of legal immigrants assumed by Census Bureau projections) were to enter the country each year *and* to remain on a permanent basis, the long-run effect on population size would be roughly equivalent to shifting the total fertility rate upward from 2.1 to 2.7; instead of having a population of 304 million in the year 2025, the United States might have closer to 368 million people. But no one knows the

---

[3] Indeed, as indicated in footnote 2, the Census Bureau has recently revised its projected mortality rates downward. This has been largely because of the dramatic drop in deaths from heart disease among the middle-aged and elderly.

[4] According to the U.S. Immigration and Naturalization Service, the number of illegal immigrants apprehended was 110,000, 345,000, and 767,000 in the fiscal years 1965, 1970, and 1975, respectively, even though there were only minor increases in surveillance staff and improvements in methods. In addition, the number of nonimmigrant admissions (some of whom later fail to leave when scheduled) was 2.1 million, 4.4 million, and 7.1 million in the same years. There are, however, no good figures on exits. According to a report to the Immigration and Naturalization Service (Lesko Associates, 1975), there are more than 8 million illegal residents in the United States, more than 5 million of whom are Mexicans.

actual numbers of immigrants, how long they stay, or whether it is appropriate to apply standard U.S. fertility and mortality rates to them.

Given the uncertainties in this situation, this study uses a range of population projections—for convenience, the Census Bureau projection series D, E, and F.[5] The E series, which was adopted as the baseline projection, assumes that the groups of women just entering the reproductive years will have a completed fertility rate of 2.1 births per woman. The D series, which assumes an average of 2.5 births per woman, comes closest of the three to reflecting a continuation of the trends of the last fifty years, and series F, which assumes 1.8 births per woman, is not too far removed from what might happen if trends during the last five years were to continue.[6] The narrowness of this range reflects a judgment that, though some rise in birthrates is possible, we are unlikely to return to anything like the high rates of the twenties and fifties; but the range may not prove to be wide enough to take into account all of the demographic factors listed above, particularly the last two.[7]

As can be seen in figure 2–2, all three projections imply substantial continued growth in population during the next half-century. Even in the case of the low projection, the population will increase by some 24 percent between 1975 and 2025, an amount more than twice the present population of Canada. But after 2025, growth quickly ceases under this low projection, while it would continue under the other two projections. Indeed, if the high projection prevailed, the U.S. population would double before the middle of the twenty-first century.

The Census Bureau's *Current Population Reports* also provide population, age, and sex distributions for the same three projections. These distributions, household projections, and other pertinent information are used to estimate various components of consumption and the labor force. Some of these data are given in table 2–1. Future changes in racial and urban–rural distributions are not taken into account in projecting consumption patterns (except insofar as the latter breakdown affects trans-

---

[5] These series can be found in Census Bureau (1972). The newer series, published in 1975, came along too late for use in this study, but they are quite close in concept and magnitudes to the D, E, and F series.

[6] Between 1925 and 1975, the U.S. population increased by 68 percent, approximately 1 percent a year. According to series D, it will increase by 72 percent during the next fifty years, averaging 1.08 percent a year. During the last five years, the average annual rate of increase has been 0.8 percent a year compared to a projected rate for series F of 0.4 percent during the half-century.

[7] All three series assume a constant immigration rate of 400,000 per year and use a common set of age- and sex-specific mortality rates.

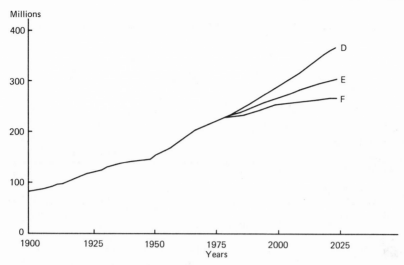

Figure 2–2. Population of the United States, 1900–2025. Data are taken from Census Bureau, *Statistical Abstract of the U.S. 1976* (97 ed., Washington, D.C., GPO, 1976), and *Current Population Reports,* ser. P-25, no. 493 (Washington, D.C., GPO, December 1972).

portation and housing requirements); the assumption is that birthrates and consumption patterns for these groups at the same income levels will have converged completely by the next decade or so.

Labor Force and Labor Productivity

Although output per capita clearly is related to resource and environmental pressures, it is determined by such a large number of factors that it is not useful to make direct assumptions about its future growth rates. Instead, we will concentrate on specifying assumptions about two of its principal determinants, the labor force and labor productivity.

Labor Force

Changes in the labor force are influenced not only by the size of certain age groups, but also by changes in labor force participation rates for different ages and sexes. The figures on the labor force presented in table 2–1 were derived under the assumption that average annual changes in

Table 2–1. Selected Demographic and Labor Force Indicators, 1975, 2000, and 2025

| | | Projection series | | | | | |
| | | 2000 | | | 2025 | | |
Indicator	1975	D	E	F	D	E	F
Population (millions)	213.9	286.0	264.4	250.7	367.5	303.8	264.9
Age distribution (%)							
School, 0–19 years	34.9	34.2	30.5	27.6	34.0	27.8	23.7
Working, 20–64 years	54.6	55.7	58.6	60.9	52.9	56.3	58.1
Young, 20–44 years	(34.2)	(35.4)	(36.5)	(37.6)	(33.3)	(33.5)	(32.7)
Old, 45–64 years	(20.4)	(20.4)	(22.0)	(23.2)	(19.6)	(22.8)	(25.4)
Retired, 65 years or more	10.5	10.1	10.9	11.5	13.1	15.8	18.2
Median age (years)	28.8	31.1	34.0	35.8	31.1	36.8	41.7
Households (thousands)	71.6	105.1	103.1	102.1	138.7	124.0	114.4
Household size (persons)	3.0	2.7	2.6	2.5	2.6	2.4	2.3
Labor force (millions)[a]	94.8	128.1	124.3	122.3	161.3	139.1	125.1
Percentage female[b]	39.1	38.9	39.2	39.5	38.6	39.1	39.4
Median age, male (years)	35.6	37.8	38.3	38.7	37.6	38.7	40.9
Median age, female (years)	35.8	38.1	38.8	40.2	37.8	39.3	41.5
Percentage of population	44.4	44.8	47.0	48.8	43.9	45.8	47.2

Sources: Census Bureau, *Current Population Reports*, ser. P-25, no. 493 (December 1972), and ser. P-20, no. 306 (January 1977) (Washington, D.C., GPO); and Jack Alterman, "Projections of Labor Force, Labor Productivity, Gross National Product, and Households: Methodology and Data" (Washington, D.C., Resources for the Future, 1976).

[a] Civilian noninstitutional labor force plus armed forces.

[b] The projected figures were based on trends up to 1972, when this percentage was 37.2; the comparable figure for 1970 was 36.7. Based on later data, our projections for this variable appear low. However, as text footnote 8 explains, the effect of this possible underestimation for our purposes is small.

participate rates for men of different ages and for women of different ages with and without children under the age of five continue in the future but at diminishing rates until the changes virtually cease by 2020.

The result, comparing 2025 with 1975, is a slower decline in the rate of growth of the labor force than of the population as a whole for series E and F. In part, this outcome results from the fall in the percentage of population in younger age groups, but it is also associated with the increase in the number of women in the labor force as fertility drops. Series D, with its higher fertility rates, results in a slight decline in the percentage of the population in the labor force.[8]

During this fifty-year period, the population will become significantly older, the median age rising from twenty-nine to thirty-seven years (assuming series E). Some commentators have suggested that this will mean a significantly older and less innovative labor force. But the average age of those in the labor force would increase only from thirty-six to thirty-eight years. The principal changes are to be found in the dependent portions of the population. Persons younger than nineteen will account for 28 rather than 35 percent of the population and the percentage older than age 64 will increase from 10 to 16 percent. In absolute numbers, these figures mean a slight increase in the younger age group but a full doubling in the size of the older group. As a consequence, there may be a significant shift in the composition of goods and services, public as well as private, demanded by this population, for example, fewer schools and more medical services.[9] As table 2–1 shows, this change in the age profile of the population, and hence in its dependency structure, is similar for all three projection series, albeit the shift is somewhat more dramatic in the case of series F and somewhat less so in the case of series D.

Labor Productivity

As used here, labor productivity means average annual hours worked per employee times output per worker-hour. The latter, in particular, is determined by a wide variety of factors: labor force characteristics such as its age, sex, and educational and occupational composition; the availability of other inputs into the production process (capital, raw materials, and land); and technology—that is, the recipe by which these

---

[8] Data for 1975 and thereafter suggest a more rapid increase in female entrants to, and older male retirements from, the labor force. The net effect is to increase the size of the labor force somewhat more rapidly than assumed here. But there is a larger proportion of part-time workers in the former group, so the net effect on total labor days available is small.

[9] An important implication of this shift is the need for significantly increased transfer payments between various age groups. By 2025, social security recipients per 100 workers could rise from 30 to well above 40. To finance payments to this group, social security tax rates will have to more than double. But because of our emphasis on resource and environmental issues, fiscal problems of this kind are set aside.

inputs are combined with labor to produce output. This section focuses on changes in hours worked per year and in the characteristics of the labor force, assuming for the moment that other factors progress more or less as they have in past. These other factors are discussed in remaining sections and additional adjustments in labor productivity introduced where appropriate.

AVERAGE HOURS AND UNEMPLOYMENT. For most of the post–World War II period, average hours worked per year declined by about 0.50 percent annually in the farm sector and about 0.35 percent in the private nonfarm sector. Average hours in the public sector declined much more rapidly during the late 1950s and 1960s as a result of the increase in part-time employment of women and teenagers. But with the more complete absorption of women into the labor force and the decline in the proportion of teenagers in the population, this rate of decline in work hours is likely to slow to that of the private nonfarm sector. With employment in the farm sector declining in importance, it will have less weight in the average reduction in work hours. As a consequence, work hours are projected in this study to decline by 0.34 percent a year between 1975 and 1985, the same rate as that used by the Bureau of Labor Statistics for this time period, and by 0.30 percent thereafter. If the decline results from a shorter workweek, it would mean that work hours per employee, which averaged about thirty-eight a week in 1970, would have declined to thirty-three by 2025.

If recent experience is used as a guide, an unemployment rate higher than the 4 to 4.5 percent typically assumed in long-term projection studies would be assumed. While it averaged 4.6 percent during most of the period following World War II, between 1970 and 1977 it averaged 6.3 percent and never fell below 4.9 percent. But two points of importance for the future should be kept in mind. First, we have just passed a peak in the rate of growth of the labor force. Between 1950 and 1955, the percentage increase in the labor force was about 4.5 percent. During the next five-year period, it rose to 7 percent and remained at this level through 1965. In the 1970–75 period, the labor force increased nearly 12 percent. But that is likely to be the highest labor force growth rate the economy will experience for some time to come. These five-year rates of growth can be expected to recede nearly as fast in the future as they have increased in the past: to 9 percent between 1975 and 1980, 6 percent between 1980 and 1985, 5 percent during the next five years, with even lower growth rates thereafter.[10] Thus, the pressure to absorb rapidly increasing numbers of labor force entrants—a factor of significance in accounting for recent difficulties in reducing unemployment rates—is nearly over.

Second, apart from this transition problem, there is little likelihood of any significant downward pressure on the labor market as a consequence of long-term demographic changes. A crude index of this pressure is the percentage of the total population that is in the labor force. In 1975 this index was 44 percent; its projected increase would be most rapid under the series F assumptions, but even then, it would rise only to 47 percent in 1985 and 49 percent in 2000 and then fall back to 47 percent in 2025. A more refined index, which takes into account the possibility that the goods and services demanded by the elderly may be more labor-intensive than those demanded by the young, would indicate even less downward pressure on the labor market and might even indicate a slight upward pressure.[11] Even if the net effect is downward, it cannot be so great as to increase significantly the government's difficulty in maintaining full employment.

On the basis of these considerations, all runs of the model used in this study assume that the unemployment rate, which stood at 8.5 percent at the end of 1975, returns to between 4 and 4.5 percent by 1980 and remains within that range thereafter.[12] Events up to the end of 1978, when the unemployment rate was 5.8 percent, suggest that this assumption may be a bit too optimistic about the duration of the transition period but probably not by more than two or three years.

WORKER-HOUR PRODUCTIVITY.   Projections of worker-hour productivity are determined by a wide variety of factors—changes in labor force characteristics, such as age, sex, and educational and occupational composition, as well as changes in the quality and availability of other

[10] A large part of the recent influx to the labor force represents low-skilled teenagers, products of the post–World War II baby boom. Once this cohort completes its entry into the prime working years, this structural problem will decline in importance. Another part of this influx is young women who have decided to work rather than to have babies. Unless fertility rates continue declining, which we do not assume, the rate of increase in female labor force participation rates will also decline.

[11] See Wachter and Wachter (1978) for a more comprehensive discussion of related points.

[12] On the average for the whole period, the economy undoubtedly will be at a higher unemployment rate, but this assumption will tend to make the study err on the high side, if at all, so far as use of resources and environmental pressures are concerned.

inputs (capital, land, and raw materials), the rate of technological progress, and levels of economic activity in different sectors. Two methods have been used to project worker-hour productivity. The first reflects the changing importance of different economic sectors, and assumes that productivity within those sectors continues to progress more or less on trend. The second gives more weight to changes in the character and quality of the labor force and assumes that productivity within each character and quality class continues to progress more or less on trend.

The first approach is built into the INFORUM model in the form of sector-by-sector productivity equations, each derived from econometric studies of historical trends. Although it would have been simple to adopt this mechanism, it was decided instead to use productivity estimates derived mainly by applying the second approach. The principal reason for this decision is the long-run nature of this study. The fact that productivity in the construction sector has been rather stagnant for the past twenty years does not mean that rapid advance is not possible given anticipated technological improvements such as factory production of component parts and service modules; the fact that agricultural productivity doubled in the last fifty years does not necessarily mean it will double again. Correcting for such changes in trend requires sector-by-sector judgments that are almost impossible to make with any confidence. Although the alternate approach also uses extrapolation, it has the advantage of taking explicitly into account changes in the character of the labor force, it does not have to be applied on a sector-by-sector basis, and it does not lead to implausible results when extrapolated for a quarter- to a half-century.

The method adopted for this study includes aspects of both approaches. It involves three steps. First, basic trends in worker-hour productivity for private nonfarm and farm sectors of the economy are established and projected forward. Then, these trends are weighted together using employment projections for these two sectors plus the public sector to obtain an overall, first approximation. In the second step, this estimate is modified by projected changes in the education, age, and sex composition of the labor force. A final modification is introduced in a few special cases in which we believe that an important change is in progress that would alter the secular trends used in the first two steps.

Many studies have used the 1948–68 period as a basis for establishing a basic, long-term trend (BLS, 1974). But the slowdown in productivity growth since 1968 has raised doubts about whether this trend is still appropriate, doubts that have been reinforced by the increases in energy prices since 1973. This study, therefore, is based on two alternative projections. The high-growth projection assumes that worker-hour productivity returns by 1980 to the trend line of the 1948–68 period. The low-growth projection assumes that after 1968 the long-term growth rate in labor productivity shifted downward by 0.3 percent per year and that only half of the shortfall from this new trend is made up by 1980. The latter assumption appears to be the more plausible one for the next five to ten years and is therefore used in the base case.

The projected reduction of 0.3 percent per year in labor productivity could result either from a lower rate of increase in output per worker-hour or from a more rapid rate of decline in hours worked per employee. Interpreted the latter way, it represents a doubling of the trend rate of decline in hours worked a year. If the average number of weeks worked in a year remain the same, average weekly workhours would then decline from thirty-eight in 1970 to twenty-eight in 2025, rather than to thirty-three as indicated above. Alternatively, if the workweek were to decline to thirty-two hours a week (a four-day workweek) and the remainder of the decline were taken in fewer workweeks a year, this would mean an average workyear of forty instead of forty-six weeks by 2025. Such a reduction in annual workhours is compatible with the concept of midcareer retraining, which some analysts have projected for the future.

The final, more judgmental adjustments in secular trends must, of course, be introduced with circumspection. What constitutes a sufficiently important change that is not more or less built into the historic trend? Raw material stocks are always being depleted; new technological changes and discoveries are always coming along. Will the advent of fusion, for example, signal a departure from trend, or will it merely offset the deterioration in productivity that would otherwise occur as a result of the depletion of oil and gas stocks? There is no way to answer such questions for all the factors likely to buffet the trend in upward and downward directions during the next quarter- to half-century. On the other hand, if no such adjustments were introduced or at least tested to determine whether they make much difference, the study will have ignored the more interesting events that may affect our future.

Two likely sources of trend modification were considered. The first pertains to the effect on the downward trend in energy used per unit of output—the Btu/GNP ratio—resulting from the increase in energy prices that started with the OPEC oil embargo of 1973–74.

Despite the steady fall in energy prices prior to 1973, the Btu/GNP ratio has fallen during the last fifty years, rapidly during the first half of

Table 2–2. Average Annual Growth Rates of GNP Per Employee, 1948–2025 (in percentages)

Case	1948–1968	1968–1975	1975–1980	1980–1985	1985–2000	2000–2025
High-growth case (DH)						
(a) No adjustments	2.42	0.75	4.32	2.30	2.28	2.09
(b) Adjusted for energy conservation	2.42	0.75	3.47	1.87	2.28	2.09
(c) Adjusted for energy conservation, depletion, and synthetics	2.42	0.75	3.47	1.83	2.26	2.09
Low-growth case (EL)						
(a) No adjustments	2.42	0.75	2.40	2.00	1.98	1.79
(b) Adjusted for energy conservation	2.42	0.75	1.57	1.57	1.98	1.79
(c) Adjusted for energy conservation, depletion, and synthetics	2.42	0.75	1.57	1.54	1.96	1.79

this period and slowly during the second. Although the latter half of this trend is factored into the long-run productivity trend, the likely acceleration in this decline brought on by the increases in energy prices since 1973 has only just begun. Unless technological developments also accelerate, this factor will have a dampening effect on the rate of improvement in labor productivity. There is no good basis upon which to estimate the extent of this effect, but it may not be very large given the adaptive capacity and conservation potential of the American economy. To account for this factor, the assumption was made that for each 1 percent greater decline in the Btu/GNP ratio than a continuation of the pre-1973 trend would have produced, labor productivity will be 0.2 percent less than it would have been.[13] Table 2–2 summarizes the effect of this assumption.

The second case involves more-rapid-than-normal depletion of natural resources and accelerated production of synthetic fuels. These features are built into scenarios designed to investigate the effects of attempts

---

[13] The Btu/GNP ratio for the base case was estimated by methods described in chapter 5. For an estimate of what the trend would have been, we accepted the projection of the Btu/GNP ratio given for the "Historical Growth" scenario in *A Time to Choose* (Ford Foundation, 1974). By the year 2000, our procedure implicitly assumes that technological developments and the replacement of less with more energy-efficient capital would have caught up sufficiently so as to eliminate this dampening effect; thereafter, the rate of growth in labor productivity is assumed to proceed at its old, long-term rate, though from a lower level than it would otherwise have.

to reduce dependence on imported petroleum and natural gas. In the base case, the productivity effects of depletion and the development of substitute fuels are ignored because it is assumed that depletion of domestic supplies continues more or less on trend and no special efforts are instituted to bring substitutes on-stream faster than warranted by commercial considerations. But if special efforts are made to reduce imports, depletion and the development of substitutes will occur more rapidly. Such an acceleration is likely for conventional petroleum and natural gas drilling, shale oil development, coal liquefaction and gasification, electricity production from low Btu gas and nuclear sources, and construction of solar heating units. A variety of adjustments in these cases has been introduced, the effect of which can also be observed in table 2–2.[14]

NET EFFECTS ON GNP PER EMPLOYEE.   Table 2–2 summarizes the net effects of these assumptions on annual growth rates of GNP per employee. Assuming no adjustments for energy conservation, depletion, or accelerated introduction of synthetics—that is, considering only changes in labor force characteristics and the composition of output—the annual rate of growth in GNP per employee, which averaged 2.42 percent during the 1948–68 period, would have to increase by 4.32 percent a year between 1975 and 1980 to return to trend. Thereafter, even under the high-growth assumptions, it would fall to 2.30 percent during the next five-year period, 2.28 percent between 1985 and 2000, and 2.09 percent during the next twenty-five years. If the low-growth assumptions prevail, which seems more likely at the present time, the annual growth rate for the 1975–80 period would be 2.40 percent, and the rates for later years would be scaled down correspondingly so that after the turn of the century the annual average growth rate of GNP per employee would be 1.79 percent.

---

[14] A third possible case pertains to environmental legislation that, in effect, requires that additional inputs of labor (and capital) be devoted to pollution abatement on a scale not built into the long-run productivity trend. After investigation, however, we decided not to introduce any adjustment for this factor because the amount of labor is so small. The amount of capital involved is not insignificant, but this factor is taken care of in another way as will be seen in chapter 3.

In large part, this issue involves an accounting problem. If pollution control equipment is produced by one sector for sale to another, GNP increases to the extent of that sale, and labor productivity is unaffected. If it is maintained and operated by the purchasing sector, the output-per-employee ratio of this sector is adversely affected. If it is maintained and repaired by a service sector, as in the case of automobile afterburners, GNP increases by the extent of the increased revenues of the service sector; but this implies a shift in the composition of output away from higher productivity sectors towards the lower productivity service sector. In all these cases, the changes—and certainly the net effects—are small.

Thus, quite apart from possible shifts in technological trends and resource problems, some long-run deceleration in the rate of growth of labor productivity should be expected. The introduction of special adjustments lowers this rate even further, particularly during the 1975–85 period when most of the accommodations to higher energy prices will be made.

A number of writers have predicted a slowdown in economic growth rates on other grounds—in particular, changes in social and cultural values such as a growing preference for risk aversion, leisure, localism, and health and environmental protection; a growing distaste for growth, industrialism, and the puritanic values that have fostered them; and simple satiation with material possessions. It is interesting to note, however, that a significant slowdown in economic growth rates can be projected without reference to these speculative and difficult-to-measure factors. Though some of them—for example, a growing preference for leisure—are built into the trends in workhours and labor force participation rates, most of these factors probably are better handled by considering their impacts on the composition of output.

Style of Living and Composition of Private Expenditures

Broadly interpreted, the style of living people select for themselves influences most of the other determinants of resource and environmental pressures: demographic trends, male and female labor force participation rates, working hours, geographic distribution of population and economic activities, and public policies with respect to issues such as environmental controls, highway construction programs, and education and health expenditures. Here, the concern is with the use people make of their disposable incomes, with how much they save and how much they spend on various categories of goods and services.

So far as personal savings are concerned, past savings rates have been quite stable despite all the changes that have occurred during the last twenty-five years,[15] and future trends may go either way. They could rise if, with growing opulence and fewer children, we become sated with

---

[15] During this period, personal savings remained between 5 percent and 9 percent of personal disposable income, and most of this variance can be explained by business cycles rather than secular trends.

goods and services or if we channel increasing portions of our incomes into housing (for example, second homes). But the expectation of increased economic security, guaranteed by extensions of old age pensions and unemployment and health insurance, is likely to dampen individual incentives to save. So, too, would the continuation of inflationary trends and increased leisure, which would increase consumption of recreational goods and services with no offsetting increase in incomes. But whatever the net effect of these factors, it can be offset by business and government savings, as has happened in the past (Paul and Scadding, 1974; and Denison, 1976). Accordingly, it was assumed that personal savings remain a constant fraction of personal disposable income and that the growth rate in personal disposable income is dampened to make room for more business and government savings whenever that seems necessary to finance required investments.

Projecting the composition of consumer expenditures is somewhat more complicated. The consumption equations in the INFORUM model (Almon and coauthors, 1974) specify that per capita expenditure on a given item changes over time as a consequence of a linear combination of changes in per capita income, relative prices, the age composition of the population, and a time trend reflecting autonomous changes in tastes. Two problems discouraged using these equations here without modification. First, it is not reasonable to assume that the coefficients of these equations will remain constant for the next quarter-century, let alone the next half-century. For example, constant coefficients imply that meat and poultry consumption will increase from 4.5 pounds a person a week, already one of the highest rates in the world, to 8.9 pounds a week by 2025; a more reasonable figure probably is no more than 5.5 pounds. Air travel is likely to exhibit an income elasticity of demand that increases as income rises during the next half-century. And if it is true that telecommunication is about to become a far more effective and inexpensive way to communicate, projections based on past trends in expenditures on communications and transportation will not be useful beyond the next ten years or so. To take saturation, taste, and technological changes of this kind into account, the coefficients of these consumption functions were changed in such a way that independent judgments play a larger and larger role as we move farther out in time.

The second class of problems arises from our interest in resource and environmental pressures as opposed to expenditure levels. Used without care, the model implies that a doubling of the number of dollars that consumers spend on furniture or cars means a doubling of the quantities of wood, plastic, metal, and other resources consumed. But it is more likely that as income rises an increasing proportion of expenditures will be used to purchase a better quality rather than a greater quantity of goods. Building in comfort, appearance, durability, versatility, and other quality characteristics often requires more labor and significant changes in the material composition of goods. Two examples will illustrate the way this study dealt with this problem. In the case of furniture, in which better quality generally means better workmanship rather than very significant changes in materials, we multiplied the entire materials input column to the furniture sector by a factor that starts at unity and becomes smaller over time. Thus, as expenditures on furniture increase, this factor dampens material inputs per dollar of expenditure in order to make way for the increased labor content. In the case of motor vehicles, in which it is somewhat easier to identify shifts in specific materials and components that are likely to contribute to increasing unit cost in the future, the input coefficients were altered individually.

On the whole, these changes have been introduced on the assumption that expenditure patterns will change slowly over time, in ways that would appear quite conservative and comfortable to the average person today. The housing mix is assumed to continue shifting toward medium- and high-density construction. The private automobile is assumed to remain the preferred mode of transportation for short- and medium-distance trips. But purchases of automobiles, as well as those of a number of other durables, semidurables, and basic foods are assumed to be subject to saturation in terms of physical units. Automobile ownership, for example, is expected to increase until it reaches an average of one car for each person of driving age, even though per capita expenditures are expected to increase almost three times between 1975 and 2025, nearly as fast as per capita disposable income. As the proportion of total expenditures that is devoted to these items falls, the proportion spent on recreation, medical and other services, plus some newer goods, will expand to absorb the slack.

Geographic Distribution of Population and Economic Activities

Three broad groups of factors will influence the future geographic distribution of population and economic activities. One is that a larger proportion of the population will have more freedom of choice in location than has been the case in the past. There are a growing number of retired, unemployed, and part-time workers who are relatively free from the constraints of having a certain employment location. For them, as well as for many fully employed persons, noneconomic factors, such as climate, scenery, safety from crime, and recreational opportunities, are likely to weigh relatively heavily in locational decisions. Moreover, the shift in the industrial composition of employment away from agriculture, mining, and manufacturing toward trade and services, the completion of the interstate highway system, and the increasing reliance on electronic communications has made and will continue to make businesses more footloose, with the consequence that a larger number of jobs will follow people than has been the case in the past. This set of factors, by itself, supports some continued movement on a national scale from North to South and from East to West, plus some further spreading and evening out of densities within metropolitan areas.

At the same time, there are several factors that might lead to a slowdown in the rate of migration or even a reversal of recent trends. One is the fact that the young adult population, the group most prone to migrate, will become a smaller fraction of the total population. Another is that if the trend toward two-paycheck families continues, migration will become somewhat harder. And more pervasively, there are a variety of countervailing mechanisms that tend to operate, at least in the long run, to bring depressed areas into favor. As a preferred region fills up, opportunities for continued growth begin to disappear, site costs and perhaps other input costs begin to rise, and the social and environmental amenities become fewer. Frequently, the reasons for the region's initial growth will be lost, and efforts will be made to discourage future growth. In the less preferred region, the converse may occur, eventually making the area relatively more attractive and reinforcing efforts to encourage growth. The result is likely to be an ebb and flow of population and economic activities among regions, which helps spread the benefits and costs of growth throughout the country, though the time lags appear to vary greatly among regions and to be virtually impossible to predict.

Changes in the relative importance of various resources also will have an independent influence on migration. Fuel price increases discourage greater dispersion of metropolitan areas, though the consequences for the distribution of population on a national scale are difficult to predict. These effects, however, are not likely to be very great. Coal mining activities will increase in all locations having good deposits and reasonable shipping costs; this probably means expansion in a variety of areas, though perhaps somewhat more in the West than in the East. Uranium mining, now located mainly in Colorado, Utah, and parts of Arizona, will expand and begin shifting to nonsandstone sources located mainly in Wyoming, Nevada, and Texas. Oil shale, which may come into substantial use after the year 2000, is located primarily in Colorado and Utah. Because plants for converting coal to oil and gas must take into account the location of markets, coal, water, and existing facilities such as pipelines and railroads, a large fraction of them are likely to be located in the Ohio, Tennessee, and upper and lower Mississippi river basins. Similar considerations will affect the location of coal-fired power plants. Nuclear plants, because they are somewhat more footloose, are likely to fill in where coal-fired plants would be more expensive to locate—on the seacoasts, for example, which tend to be long distances from coal fields but have water available for cooling. Government policies with respect to such factors, as well as with respect to the environment, water development, and the location of military and space facilities, also will play important roles.

These crosscurrents make it exceedingly difficult to project locational changes with any confidence. Certainly there is no model that captures enough of these factors to provide much guidance. In these circumstances, this study's approach has been somewhat eclectic. For a number of purposes, it relied on the share files built into the original SEAS package (see the appendix); for others, it used special studies plus judgments with respect to the types of factors discussed in the previous paragraph (see relevant portions of chapters 7 and 8, as well as Stevens and Trainer, 1978). What resulted were small shifts in the distribution of population, manufacturing, and agricultural activities, and somewhat more significant shifts in mining and energy conversion and generation facilities in the directions indicated above.

Technological Change and the Resource Base

There are two possible approaches to introducing technological change into the analysis. One is to assume that current trends in efficiency improvements and substitutions among materials and processes continue. This approach ignores the fact that some such changes will give way to new technologies that take the economy in somewhat different directions. The second is to introduce changes of any kind, whether evolutionary or revolutionary, but only if they can be specifically identified and justified. The first approach is the simplest to implement because it can rely on statistically estimated trends, but the results rapidly lose plausibility over a fifty-year period. The second approach overcomes this problem for the specific list of items the analysis includes, but of necessity that list must be very short compared to the vast array of changes that are always taking place. This approach, then, can result in substantial understatement of technological change in the economy as a whole.

The procedure we used combines features of both approaches. Improvements in labor productivity, agricultural yields, and energy efficiency were handled in fairly broadbrush ways; the trends were justified with reference to past history, the experience of other countries, and, wherever possible, anticipated qualitative developments that might support such trends. In addition, we have introduced a variety of specific, detailed changes that can have a significant impact on the composition of resources used or residuals generated. In general, these changes are introduced on the assumption that technology continues changing in evolutionary ways: substitution processes already under way continue to some limit, best practice slowly becomes average practice, and processes and products now in the pilot or demonstration stage come into commercial use. In a few cases in which it could be important in our time frame, techniques still in the experimental or laboratory stage are brought on-stream with appropriate time lags. This material is then translated into changes in specific input-output coefficients, taking care to make these changes in sets when links between them can be established. With a few exceptions spelled out later, only one full set of such changes was developed and used in all scenarios.

The study emphasizes specific technological changes in six main areas of importance for resource and environmental developments: construction, transportation, communications, energy production and use, primary metals production, and materials substitution.[16]

Construction

Three general currents will influence the mix of materials this sector uses. The first is the expected increase in the relative prices of land and timber, which will cause the construction costs of single-family dwelling units to rise more rapidly than that of multifamily units. The second is

[16] A more complete discussion of these changes, along with numerical details and a description of methods, can be found in Shapanka (1978).

the development and public acceptance of new materials (wood products, metals, plastics, and improved types of cements) and of factory-
produced components (structural elements, cabinets, and bathroom
modules). The third is the shift in the construction mix from single-
family to multifamily units, a result of the increasing number of smaller
households, of the increasing cost of single-family units, and of increasing
population densities in suburban areas. The result for materials used in
housing, per dollar of construction cost, is likely to be a decline in the use
of wood (by some 75 percent) and increases in the use of aluminum (by a
factor of 5), steel (by 2.5 times), concrete (by 10 times) and plastics (by
5.5 times). Changes in the mix of materials for commercial construction
are likely to be less dramatic but in similar directions—concrete, aluminum, and plastics substituting for wood and steel.

Transportation

The changes assumed in this sector are more modest than many expect and hope. Automobiles and airplanes are assumed to continue
dominating intercity travel, and air travel, with its high income elasticity,
gradually will increase its share. The personal automobile is assumed to
continue dominating local travel, mass transit making only small inroads.
Increasing affluence, the development of more efficient and less polluting
automobiles, and the increasing dispersion of urban development, abetted
by future communications technology, support this assumption.

The principal change is likely to be the eventual replacement of
gasoline-powered cars by electric ones as the dominant intra-urban
private vehicle. Eventual increases in the price of liquid fuels, improvements in the efficiency of electricity generation, growing urban air pollution problems, and the likelihood of substantial improvements in the
electric storage battery all point in this direction. But such developments,
particularly in batteries, are unlikely to occur before the turn of the century, and even then they are unlikely to be so dramatic as to replace—at
least for long trips—the internal combustion engine, which in the meantime will experience substantial improvements in energy efficiency. Accordingly, it was assumed that only 1 percent of the cars sold in 1990 will
be electric and that this figure will rise to 30 percent by 2025, at which
time about 15 percent of the vehicle stock would be electric.

The mandated elimination of lead from gasoline and the likelihood
that lead will not be used in whatever new batteries are developed will
result over time in a significant decline in the demand for lead. Other

likely materials changes associated with the automobile, many initiated to save weight, are the substitution of aluminum for copper in radiators, aluminum for steel in motor blocks, and aluminum and plastics for steel in panels and some structural parts.

For commodity transport, railroads and pipelines are expected to increase their share substantially, with air freight gaining slightly and water transport and motor freight losing (though not absolutely). Improvements in energy efficiency and modest changes in materials use are also expected in this sector.

Communications Technology

Dramatic changes can be envisioned in future telecommunications. Many of these changes will center around new devices for video communications, in particular the use of optical fibers for transmission purposes. Taken together, these changes will make possible adding high-quality visual communications to existing oral communications systems while dramatically reducing the costs of all types of electronic communications, record keeping, and information processing. Because the costs, especially in terms of time, of transporting people and documents probably has bottomed out, these developments could result in a significant degree of substitution of telecommunications for travel, mail, and conventional banking services. Intercity travel to business meetings to coordinate plans and exchange well-understood information is likely to be the first type of travel affected, but eventually daily intracity business travel also may be affected. If this happens on a large scale, it could affect commuting arrangements and the structure of urban areas.

All this is unlikely to happen rapidly. Optical transmission is undergoing field tests now and commercial applications are expected to begin in the early 1980s, but, even if all goes well, it will take considerable time to perfect optical transmission devices and to convert from copper and coaxial to optical cable. It was assumed that 25 percent of business travel and 30 percent of the total volume of mail will be eliminated by 2025. In addition, of course, these changes will affect the demand for copper and several other materials.

Energy Extraction, Conversion, and Use

In a controversial article in *Foreign Affairs,* Amory Lovins (1976) argued that there are two quite different technological paths available for future energy development: a "hard technology" option, in which dependence on fossil fuels and nuclear power produced by large-scale, capital-intensive methods increases, and a "soft technology" option, which relies on solar energy, conservation technologies, the replacement of electricity (with its high conversion and transmission losses) with more direct consumption of fuels in some uses, and more decentralized production and consumption. It would be interesting to investigate the economic, resource, and environmental consequences of these two, conceptually neat, alternatives. But this study examines only one major technological path into future energy patterns, a path that relies on hard technology supplemented by a few, slowly developing soft technologies, a mixed picture, which, at the present time appears, for better or worse, most likely. Two alternatives involving less use of nuclear power are considered, however. Because this topic is treated in detail in chapter 5, only a brief sketch of the energy assumptions are provided here.

Our assumptions about fossil fuels and electricity are as follows: (1) advanced recovery techniques and higher prices will make it possible to recover economically about 25 percent more petroleum than is now possible (but no more natural gas because recovery rates are already high); (2) the real costs of producing oil from shale, tar sands, heavy oils, and coal, and high-Btu gas from coal, thought to average about twice the cost of imported petroleum today, will fall slowly because of efficiency improvements to roughly half that level by about 2010 (however, a more difficult case in which these costs do not fall is also explored); (3) the efficiency of producing electricity both from fossil and from nuclear sources will improve substantially;[17] and (4) in some scenarios, breeder reactors will be available for economical production of electricity in some parts of the country by 2000, and fusion reactors about a decade later. The assumptions about breeder and fusion reactors may be too optimistic for a variety of political, economic, and technological reasons discussed in Shapanka (1978). In the case of fusion, at least, this makes little difference in the results, because it is expected to remain so small a percentage of total electric production that it could easily be replaced by other forms of nuclear- or fossil-fueled plants. Because of the uncertainties in this field, and because it is useful to consider what would happen if such

---

[17] Such improvements could arise in the case of fossil fuel plants because of the development of gas turbine topping cycles, closed-cycle alkali metal vapor turbines, and fluidized-bed combustion, and in the case of nuclear power because of the development of new materials permitting higher operating temperatures and pressures. As a consequence, we assume that power plant efficiency for fossil fuel plants will increase from 33 to 47 percent and that for nuclear plants from 31 to 41 percent during the next fifty years.

developments did not occur, scenarios in which the use of nuclear power is restricted were also developed.

Largely because of cost considerations, other sources of energy are not expected to develop rapidly until after the turn of the century. It is assumed that geothermal energy eventually will play a role similar to that of hydroelectric power, important in some local areas but not contributing more than perhaps 2.4 percent to total energy production during this fifty-year time frame. Solar energy, it is assumed, will be economical primarily for water heating and space conditioning in new dwellings. Solar electric, other solar forms, such as winds and tides, and possible technological developments in storage and efficiency of collection that could make retrofitting more economical are assumed to play a limited role within the fifty-year time frame. These assumptions may be too pessimistic. But at the present time, unless government intervention on behalf of solar energy development increases substantially, cost considerations are against more rapid advances.[18]

The principal technological advance that is introduced on the energy consumption side involves replacing electric heating with heat pumps in many climates, a development that could save as much as 50 percent of the electricity used in space heating. This substitution, plus improved building design and added insulation, is assumed to reduce energy consumption for space conditioning by 20 percent compared to what it otherwise would have been in 2025. Other improvements in energy efficiency and aspects of conservation are discussed in chapter 5.

Primary Metals Production

Declining ore grades, increasing energy costs, environmental controls, and increasing competition, both from abroad and from other materials, appear to be strongly influencing the directions of technological developments in the primary metals sector. In the copper industry, continuous smelting processes, which reduce energy requirements by as much as 50 percent and significantly reduce the cost of sulfur recovery, has already begun to replace more conventional smelting operations. But this

---

[18] Within the limited area of space heating and cooling, however, our projections result in solar energy contributing about 40 percent of net energy use in the residential sector and only a little less in the commercial sector. But this is not where the economy uses the bulk of the energy, so this contribution amounts to only 4 percent of energy use in 2025. To press beyond this amount, other applications will have to be found, and that is unlikely without significant technological and possibly scientific advances.

is likely to be an interim technology because of the advent of hydrometal-lurgical methods, which make it economical to recover copper from ores of lower grade while significantly reducing the emission of both air and water pollutants. The projections assume that conventional smelting methods will be phased out completely by 2025 and that hydrometallurgy will account for 90 percent of production and continuous smelting for the remainder. These changes signal shifts in the purchases of the copper sector away from fossil fuels toward electricity and industrial chemicals, and reductions in pollution emission coefficients.

In the aluminum industry, the Bayer–Hall process is likely to be replaced by the Bayer–Alcoa and nonelectrolytic processes because of the dramatic savings in energy that would result. At the same time, non-bauxitic materials are likely to be used in increasing quantities, particularly after the turn of the century. Similarly, the iron and steel industry is likely to be forced to use direct reduction methods and electric arc furnaces in order to cope with environmental problems and reduce costs so it can compete with foreign steel producers and domestic producers of substitutes such as concrete, aluminum, and plastics. As a consequence, the projections for the fifty-year period call for a reduction by half in the use of coke per unit of steel produced, a doubling per unit in the use of electricity, and a quadrupling for natural or synthetic gas.

Materials Substitution

A number of materials substitutions have already been mentioned. In summary, they include those of lighter metals for heavier, of plastics for metals, wood, and glass in a variety of end products, and of concrete for metals and wood in construction. For example, the use of aluminum and plastics (materials and resins) per dollar of total output is projected in the base case to grow between 1975 and 2025 by 57 percent and 53 percent, respectively, and use of steel, copper, and veneers and plywoods per dollar of output is expected to decline by 46 percent, 55 percent, and 34 percent, respectively.

Resource Base

Estimates of the quantities of energy, nonfuel minerals, land, water, and environmental carrying capacity are so critical for this study that they are discussed in some detail in later chapters. Suffice it to say here that the goal was to develop reasonably realistic figures, but figures which, if anything, err on the conservative side. For example, estimates are made of the extent to which current reserves are likely to be augmented during the next fifty years; but to ensure that the final figures are still conservative, these estimates do not include any resources that are termed speculative by the Bureau of Mines, assume only very modest changes in technology, and with only one or two exceptions do not embody price changes or estimates for regions where no published data exist. Needless to say, it would be a mistake to place a great deal of confidence in the resulting estimates. In the attempt to compensate for this, at critical junctures we have investigated the differences that would result from using alternative estimates.

International Developments

If this study had been conducted a half-century ago, it might have ignored international developments on the grounds that interrelations between the U.S. population and economy and its resource and environmental bases were not significantly affected by what happened abroad or at least that we were capable of keeping foreign events from affecting us if we so desired. No import or export was sufficiently important to our economy as a whole that a sizable change in international markets could make much difference to domestic developments. Indeed, most such changes were likely to emanate *from* this dynamic and massive economy. Even the effects of international wars could be set aside on grounds that they were unlikely to alter long-run population and economic growth rates or the availability of resources, provided this country could keep the conflict outside its borders. All this is changing, of course, and the changes in store for the United States during the next half-century will eliminate the last vestiges of this relatively sanguine picture.

At a minimum, we must consider likely developments with respect to three classes of internationally traded goods: energy (which essentially means petroleum), nonfuel minerals, and food. For each, projections of demand and supply for the rest of the world must be developed to play off against those developed for the United States. To do so without excessively complicating this study, we have based demand estimates for the rest of the world on exogenous projections of population and GNP per capita, and supply projections on independent judgments about resource availabilities and likely rates of exploitation. Some of these projections may turn out to be incompatible with each other because they did not take explicitly into account interactions among various countries' economic growth rates and feedbacks from resource and environmental pressures to population and GNP growth rates. But incorporating such interactions would have greatly extended and complicated the analysis. In the end, however, possible inconsistencies between assumed rates of population and economic growth on the one side and material and environmental resource constraints on the other can be identified; indeed, that is one of the main purposes of the study.

The chapters on nonfuel minerals, energy, and agriculture develop international demand and supply projections for these commodities. Other aspects of international relations—for example, the likelihood of embargoes or export quotas and their effects—are treated by special scenarios discussed in these chapters.

Population and GNP Projections

The global population projections provided in tables 2–3 and 2–4 reflect judgments about the range within which actual world population figures are likely to fall, assuming no major catastrophies. Because population growth rates in the industrial countries are already quite low and likely to fall further, there is little difference between the high and low projections. For the less developed countries (LDCs), the range is much larger. The high projections assume that current rates of decline in birth and death rates continue, and the low projections assume that breakthroughs in family planning induce substantially higher rates of decline in birthrates; this rate of improvement is within the range of feasibility but probably not without greater efforts than are being expended today (or more rapidly improving economic conditions than currently appear likely).

The GNP projections are based on a division of countries into four groups, each occupying a somewhat unique position in the world economy. The first group consists of the relatively developed, industrialized countries (OECD members, South Africa, Eastern Europe, and USSR), where economic growth is largely a matter of maintaining growth in labor productivity and full employment of the labor force. Although economic growth is affected by export earnings and the cost of imports, these countries have a greater capacity than those in any other group to adjust to changes originating abroad. Moreover, the foreign exchange earnings, capital inflows, and hence the growth rates in all other non-OPEC countries depend very heavily on the economic activities of this first group.

Projections for the United States are derived from runs of the SEAS/RFF model. Projections for other countries in this category begin by applying assumptions about growth rates in GNP per capita (an approximation for labor productivity) to the population projections (an approximation for the labor force). The projections are then modified to take into account the effects of higher petroleum and other import prices. After about a five-year period of adjustment to the new price regime, growth will resume for awhile at slightly less than historic rates, but during the last half of the fifty-year period covered by these projections it will slow down again. This long-run slowdown is assumed to occur for several reasons: structural changes similar to those shown in table 2–2 that will cause a slowdown in the U.S. growth rate, the elimination of the technological gap between countries like Japan and the United States, which had enabled the former to grow rapidly on the basis of technological transfers;[19] the beginning of capital repatriation by OPEC countries; and further increases in petroleum prices. The low-growth variant is derived by assuming a longer period of adjustment to the new energy situation and a slower rate of growth in productivity thereafter.

The second group of countries consists of the principal oil exporters (OPEC members). Income growth in this group during the next fifteen to twenty-five years will depend largely on earnings from petroleum exports; thereafter, it will depend on returns from investments made with these earnings and the degree of success the developed countries have in finding substitutes for imported petroleum. Growth in demand for resources and finished goods, however, depends on absorptive capacity, which varies by country depending on the amount of oil revenues, the size of the population, the extent to which other resources are available, and the level of skills and administrative capacity. The rates of growth assumed for these countries imply estimates of the speed with which this absorptive capacity is likely to increase.

Implicit in this approach is the assumption that the portion of income not consumed or invested domestically will be invested abroad,

---

[19] An interesting discussion of the institutional factors that have led to the rapid rate of economic progress in Japan during the last two decades and which will serve to inhibit growth in the future as this technological gap is eliminated, unless creativity and inventiveness can be stimulated, can be found in an article by Ohmae (1975).

mainly in the first group of countries. The amount invested will be more or less in line with what the first group requires to finance petroleum imports. This investment is what helps to maintain the growth rates in the GNP—more accurately, the gross domestic product (GDP)—of the developed countries.

The third group comprises countries whose growth rates are strongly dependent on foreign trade earnings in volatile international markets; for the most part, these countries are the principal nonfuel mineral exporters (see notes to table 2–4). Their growth rates are assumed to begin at somewhat lower levels than those of OPEC countries and to return to lower, more sustainable, levels more rapidly. The low variant is chosen to be compatible with the low-growth assumptions for their chief customers, the first group of countries.

The last group of countries consists of the resource-poor LDCs. Growth in these countries is highly dependent on three factors over which they have no control: petroleum prices, growth rates in developed countries, and capital inflows. If petroleum prices remain high and if growth rates in developed countries, plus capital inflows to the LDCs, are low, the per capita incomes of some countries in this group may actually fall. These conditions form the basis for the low variant for these countries. The high variant assumes that after a period of adjustment these countries will receive sufficient export earnings and capital inflows from either the developed or the OPEC countries to return more or less to the trends of the past decade. China is an exception to this pattern because it is assumed to be more independent of external factors.

Table 2–3 provides for the world as a whole four different projections: high population and high economic growth, low population and low economic growth, and two intermediate cases. At the present time, the most likely case appears to be the low economic growth variants in all countries, combined with the low population growth assumptions for the developed countries (with series E for the United States and high population growth assumptions for all others. This mixed case, the "Standard Case," is presented for a number of regional breakdowns in table 2–4.

Not too much should be made of these figures. They are based on simple extrapolation procedures supplemented by judgments that do not take into account efforts to change past trends—or the likelihood of success of these efforts. But it is interesting to note that the only group of LDCs to achieve a GNP per capita of $2,000 or more—a minimum level for being considered "developed" in 1972—is Latin America and then only after the year 2015 or so; individual countries in other groups, such

Table 2-3. World Population, GNP, and GNP Per Capita, Amounts and Annual Growth Rates, 1972–2025

Growth assumption	Growth rate (%) (1960–72)	Amount[a] (1972)	Growth rate (%) (1972–80)	Amount[a] (1980)	Growth rate (%) (1980–85)	Amount[a] (1985)	Growth rate (%) (1985–2000)	Amount[a] (2000)	Growth rate (%) (2000–25)	Amount[a] (2025)
High population and high economic growth										
Population	2.17	3,799.1	1.94	4,431.7	1.98	4,888.5	1.91	6,492.2	1.52	9,472.5
GNP	5.75	3,871.0	4.80	5,637.1	4.64	7,071.5	4.36	13,400.1	4.14	36,983.4
GNP per capita	3.50	1,018.9	2.81	1,272.0	2.61	1,446.6	2.40	2,064.0	2.58	3,904.3
High population and low economic growth										
Population	2.17	3,799.1	1.94	4,431.7	1.98	4,888.5	1.91	6,492.2	1.52	9,472.5
GNP	5.75	3,871.0	3.95	5,277.8	4.01	6,424.3	3.70	11,077.2	3.41	25,598.2
GNP per capita	3.50	1,018.9	1.97	1,190.9	1.99	1,314.2	1.76	1,706.2	1.86	2,702.4
Low population and high economic growth										
Population	2.17	3,799.1	1.55	4,297.6	1.46	4,621.0	1.26	5,574.8	0.75	6,725.3
GNP	5.75	3,871.0	4.81	5,636.1	4.68	7,084.2	4.22	13,172.5	3.97	34,843.8
GNP per capita	3.50	1,018.9	3.20	1,311.4	3.18	1,533.0	2.93	2,362.9	3.19	5,181.0
Low population and low economic growth										
Population	2.17	3,799.1	1.55	4,297.6	1.46	4,621.0	1.26	5,574.8	0.75	6,725.3
GNP	5.75	3,871.0	3.99	5,296.5	4.10	6,475.5	3.57	10,961.9	3.21	24,155.5
GNP per capita	3.50	1,018.9	2.40	1,232.4	2.60	1,401.3	2.28	1,966.3	2.44	3,591.7

Source: These projections were derived by aggregating projections by country and region developed from the sources listed in table 2–4.
[a] Population in millions of people, GNP in billions of 1971 dollars, GNP per capita in 1971 dollars.

Table 2–4. Population, GNP, and GNP Per Capita for Selected Regions of the World, Standard Case, 1972, 1985, 2000, and 2025

Projection and region	1972[a]	1985	2000	2025
Population (millions)				
United States	208.8	235.7	264.4	303.8
Canada	21.9	23.1	26.3	30.5
Western Europe[b]	369.3	382.8	403.3	424.4
Oceania	19.0	20.9	23.4	26.0
Latin America	299.4	421.9	597.5	877.9
Japan	107.0	121.2	130.6	136.8
Other non-Communist Asia	1,223.7	1,716.9	2,489.2	4,040.1
Africa	374.3	499.2	726.2	1,218.5
USSR	263.7	282.8	302.5	321.0
Eastern Europe	109.0	116.4	123.8	132.1
China (People's Republic)	803.0	1,043.0	1,358.9	1,853.0
Total world	3,799.1	4,863.9	6,446.1	9,364.1
Gross national product (billions of 1971 US$)				
United States	1,158.0	1,574.6	2,428.5	4,243.4
Canada	97.1	146.8	249.2	451.5
Western Europe[b]	896.2	1,294.5	1,910.2	3,434.4
Oceania	47.1	89.0	174.5	325.9
Latin America	180.6	354.3	732.6	2,262.8
Japan	247.9	481.4	805.3	1,482.1
Other non-Communist Asia	238.4	439.3	971.8	3,624.5
Africa	77.7	174.5	424.0	1,780.4
USSR	612.5	1,145.0	1,966.0	4,142.3
Eastern Europe	180.0	331.4	572.5	1,183.4
China (People's Republic)	135.5	245.9	475.9	1,268.7
Total world	3,871.0	6,276.7	10,710.5	24,199.4
GNP per capita (1971 US$)				
United States	5,395	6,680	9,185	13,968
Canada	4,434	6,354	9,476	14,803
Western Europe[b]	2,427	3,382	4,736	8,092
Oceania	2,479	4,258	7,457	12,535
Latin America	603	840	1,226	2,578
Japan	2,317	3,972	6,167	10,834
Other non-Communist Asia	195	256	390	897
Africa	208	350	584	1,461
USSR	2,323	4,049	6,499	12,904
Eastern Europe	1,651	2,847	4,620	8,958
China (People's Republic)	169	236	350	685
Total world	1,011	1,290	1,662	2,584

Note: Regional groups include the following countries:

Western Europe—all countries in the categories Western, Northern, and Southern Europe as established in Frejka (1973).

Eastern Europe—Czechoslovakia, Hungary, and Poland.

Latin America—OPEC, Equador and Venezuela; mineral producers, Bolivia, Chile, Jamaica; other, Peru, Argentina, Colombia, and Uruguay, among others.

Other non-Communist Asia—OPEC, Saudi Arabia, United Arab Emirates, Kuwait, Qatar, Iran, Iraq; mineral producers, Syria, Turkey, Israel, Lebanon, Jordan; other, Philippines, South Korea, Taiwan, Malaysia, Burma, Afghanistan, and Thailand, among others.

as Korea and Taiwan in the non-Communist Asia group, also cross this threshold, however. This continuing low level of per capita GNP occurs despite the fact that per capita GNP in all the LDCs at least quadruples between 1972 and 2025, a much faster growth rate than for most developed regions. Thus, though there is substantial absolute growth everywhere, these projections imply increasing polarization between rich and poor and declining numbers of "in-between" countries.

World Prices

Some explicit assumptions must be made about world prices, but there are only the roughest of principles and empirical observations upon which to base them. The magnitude of the problem can be reduced by agreeing to ignore the effects of general inflation, both worldwide and within each country. Changes in relative prices are most important for present purposes, and it is not unreasonable to assume that in the long run inflation will have little effect on such prices. Wages, interest rates, or other prices that tend to lag behind the rise in commodity prices eventually will catch up so that the same package of resources can be purchased as would have been purchased had the inflation not occurred. A further simplification is to concentrate on changes in the relative prices of the three groups of commodities most important for this analysis: energy, nonfuel minerals, and food.

OIL AND OTHER ENERGY PRICES. For several years after 1974, many believed that the OPEC cartel could not maintain the fourfold increase in the price of petroleum it imposed on the world in 1973–74.

Africa—OPEC, Libya, Nigeria, Algeria; mineral producers, Liberia, Morocco, Zaire, Zambia; West Africa, Ghana, Ivory Coast, Cameroon, Senegal, Sierra Leone; Southern Africa, Republic of South Africa, Rhodesia; other, Egypt, Tunisia, Uganda, Kenya, Tanzania, Ethiopia, Sudan, and Mali, among others.

Sources: Population—United States, Census Bureau, *Current Population Reports,* ser. P-25, no. 493 (Washington, D.C., GPO, December 1972); other countries, data for 1972 and *ex post* growth rates from IBRD, *World Bank Atlas* (Washington, D.C., 1974); future rates selected from Thomas Frejka, *The Future of Population Growth: Alternative Paths to Equilibrium, Reference Tables* (New York, Population Council, 1973).

GNP—United States, chapter 3, this study; other countries, *ex post* data from IBRD, *Prospects for Developing Countries,* Report 477 (Washington, D.C., 1974); and AID, *GNP.* Report RC-W-138 (Washington, D.C., AID, 1974).

[a] Based on preliminary data that have subsequently been revised. The largest discrepancy is for the USSR, whose population and GNP per capita are now estimated by the World Bank to have been 247.5 million and $1,530, respectively.

[b] Includes Albania, Greece, and Yugoslavia.

Once development plans and foreign investment channels were established, revenue needs would grow rapidly and major oil-producing countries would increasingly resist cutting back production to maintain an agreed-to price (Moran, 1978). At the same time, the high price would slowly dampen growth in demand and stimulate the development of new supplies. Such changes should not be expected very rapidly—it takes time for habits and customs to change, for legislation to be passed, for new energy sources to be found and brought into production, and for oil-using capital to wear out and be replaced by more appropriate capital. Eventually, however, the cumulative impact of these changes should be substantial. Thus, unless political or military factors intervene, OPEC members could find growing difficulties in agreeing on the allocation of sufficiently stringent output restrictions to keep the price of petroleum rising in line with inflation, at least for the next decade or two.

Price movements since 1974 lend some credence to this viewpoint. As figure 2–3 indicates, the dollar price of petroleum deflated by the U.S. GNP deflator declined by 15 percent between January 1, 1974, and April 1, 1979; and the real price decline was greater for countries whose currencies have appreciated against the dollar.[20] In June 1979, OPEC raised the market price to about $20 per barrel. In deflated dollars, this represents a 40 percent increase during the first half of 1979 but only a 20 percent increase over the January 1974 price. Continued inflation and further depreciation of the dollar could wipe out much of this increase if the price is not raised again before the end of the year.

After the overthrow of the Shah of Iran in December 1978, this viewpoint was replaced by a far more pessimistic perspective. That event, plus continuing political turmoil and reduced oil export levels in Iran, have taught other OPEC countries two lessons, it is now argued. One is that more revenue can be obtained, at least in the near term, by collectively reducing production, thereby forcing the price up, than by expanding production. The second is that too rapid a rate of internal development may be politically destabilizing. At the same time, unhappiness about the Egyptian–Israeli peace treaty and the U.S. role in bringing it about have stiffened the resistance of Middle Eastern producers to arguments in favor of increasing output. If these new perceptions lead OPEC producers to reduce investment in production capacity and if non-OPEC capacity

---

[20] For example, if we translate the current benchmark price into German marks and deflate by the German consumer price index, the decline between January 1, 1974, and January 1, 1979 is 29 percent.

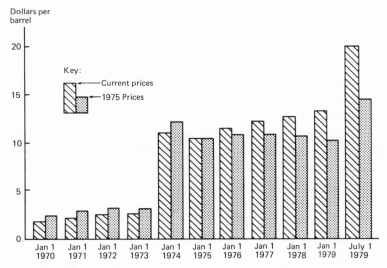

Figure 2–3. OPEC benchmark prices, current and deflated, 1970–79. Current price through January 1979 is for benchmark or marker light oil sold by Saudi Arabia. The July 1979 price is roughly the midpoint of the benchmark price of $18 and maximum of $23.50 agreed to at the OPEC meeting of June 1979. Actual market prices can vary substantially. Deflated price is the current price deflated by GNP deflator using 1975 = 100.

does not expand rapidly enough to compensate,[21] supplies could remain tight and prices rise faster than the general rate of inflation for a considerable period of time.

Given these uncertainties, we have decided to work with a variety of assumptions. The one used in most scenarios is that petroleum and nonpetroleum prices follow each other upward at roughly the same rate until depletion of petroleum resources makes it impossible for production to keep up with the growth in demand without a relative increase in petroleum prices. The analysis in chapter 5 indicates that this point is likely to occur around 2010. Accordingly, the first assumption is that the world price of petroleum in real terms remains at its 1975 level of $12 a barrel until 2010, after which it rises to $16 to $24 a barrel, depending on a number of other assumptions.

[21] Suppose, for example, that Mexico and other producers decide to gear petroleum production to internal development needs rather than to petroleum needs in the rest of the world and that Communist bloc countries become net importers of petroleum either because they cannot solve their production problems or for political reasons.

As a second case, we assume that the world price of petroleum, relative to other prices, doubles between 1980 and 2010 and reaches a peak of $32 a barrel in 2025. The analysis in chapter 5 suggests that this result would occur if, in contrast to the standard case, we assume more severe constraints on production and international trade, higher long-run costs for producing substitutes, and somewhat less favorable income and price elasticities of demand for petroleum.

A final case investigates what would happen if the price remained constant in *nominal* terms while worldwide inflation continues, again until production can no longer keep up with demand. This case is approximated by assuming that the real price falls to $6 a barrel by 1985, remains constant until the latter half of the 1990s, and then (according to the analysis of chapter 5) rises rapidly to more than $40 a barrel by 2020.

Assumptions for the world price of natural gas are similar. International coal prices are assumed to remain more or less constant in real terms and comparable uranium prices to rise slowly over time. The production costs of synthetics and other energy sources are based on the technological considerations outlined above. All this is discussed in more detail in chapter 5.

NONFUEL MINERALS.   In contrast to fossil fuel deposits, other mineral deposits tend to be spread more evenly across the earth's surface, in more continuous gradations and concentrations. In the past, this fact plus steady technological progress has permitted using relatively low-grade ores with reasonably stable long-term prices, albeit with substantial cyclical fluctuations because of periodic market disturbances. The establishment of producer cartels could change this picture, but as Stern and Tims (1976) point out in a comprehensive survey of such possibilities, the prospects for doing so in fields other than oil are generally not propitious over the long haul. Perhaps the best that such cartels might accomplish is to smooth out cyclical fluctuations. These considerations, plus the analysis of long-run demand and supply prospects in chapter 4, have led us to assume in all scenarios constant long-term prices for nonfuel minerals as a group.

FOOD.   Analytically, the simplest assumption about food prices is that the United States is a price-setter rather than a price-receiver in world markets. Because we are a principal exporter of most major grains, this assumption may not be too far from the mark. Accordingly, the price changes that are used result from the analysis presented in chapter 6, which indicates a range (depending on the scenario) extending from approximately a 20 to 25 percent increase to virtually no increase or a slight decrease during the fifty-year period. An important swing variable here is agricultural exports, a factor heavily dependent on government policy.

Public Policy Alternatives

It is difficult to think of a public policy issue that does not have some resource or environmental consequences. Here, only those policies with fairly direct consequences are considered. For the most part, the cases that are developed permit one to compare a policy that represents something like a continuation of current trends with one or more alternatives. Other policies and variations are taken up in relevant chapters.

For oil and gas, we assume gradual decontrol of domestic prices so that after 1980 for oil and 1985 for gas these prices follow world prices. Government policies with respect to prices of other resources are assumed to remain unchanged.

We make two alternative assumptions with respect to import policy. In the base case, oil is imported to the extent needed and no special efforts are made (except the modest ones built into the energy bill of 1975, which might come about as a consequence of the price increases anyway) to increase supplies of or decrease demands for oil. This case is contrasted with one in which a serious attempt is made to reduce U.S. vulnerability to embargoes and exorbitant prices by stockpiling and encouraging more rapid development of domestic substitutes. More specifically, we acquire gradually between 1975 and 1980 a petroleum stockpile amounting to 80 percent of six months' imports (the other 20 percent to come from emergency conservation measures) and maintain it thereafter.[22] At the same time, we undertake vigorous measures to develop domestic substitutes, primarily by subsidizing the development of coal liquefaction, coal gasification, and shale oil operations more rapidly than market prices would otherwise stimulate. Natural gas is stockpiled also and domestic production encouraged according to the same formula as oil. There are no special policies for nonfuel minerals, because their strategic stockpiles are already large enough in most cases to cover more than six months' imports.

[22] The choice of a six-month period for this purpose is based on the judgment that a cessation in international trade of petroleum would not last anywhere near this long without armed intervention to start the flow again.

Two additional scenarios with respect to energy involve alternative assumptions about nuclear developments. The first assumes a moratorium on the production of additional nuclear plants; this results in a phaseout of nuclear power by 2015 or so, when current plants (plus those under construction, which are allowed to be completed) wear out. Such a moratorium could result either from domestic pressures to halt further investments in nuclear power or from an international agreement aimed at limiting the spread of nuclear materials that could be diverted into weapons. Although such possibilities appear unlikely, delays in obtaining local approval for construction could result in something similar. In any event, this case is instructive because it indicates the importance of nuclear power and the economic and environmental tradeoffs that could be involved. The second scenario permits using all forms of nuclear power except breeders and other forms involving plutonium recycling, which are especially hazardous on both environmental and security grounds.

In the agricultural sector, the principal policy alternative considered pertains to exports. Although shortfalls from plans and needs abroad are an important determinant of U.S. food exports, it is unlikely that the U.S. government would permit exports of such a magnitude that they would seriously harm domestic consumers. Accordingly, the low-export case assumes that other countries experience no significant shortfalls from their plans, and the high-export case assumes an upper limit on the level of exports that might be permitted in case serious shortfalls occurred.[23]

The base case for environmental policy can be characterized as one in which there are some delays in implementing legislated federal pollution control standards. For example, implementation of automotive standards is delayed from 1975 to 1981, and best practicable technological standards for water pollution are delayed from 1977 to 1980. The contrasting case is one in which no slippage is permitted and the regulations become more stringent over time as needed to keep concentrations below certain target levels. Thus, by 2000 all facilities meet new source performance standards at removal efficiencies of 65 to 98 percent, and by 2025 such efficiency levels are increased to 85 to 100 percent. In addition, breeders and other forms involving plutonium recycling are assumed to be incompatible with stringent environmental standards and are not permitted. Chapter 8 considers the details of both these cases as well as other variants.

---

[23] In the end, as chapter 6 spells out, the alternate export projections were selected in a somewhat different way, which resulted in an average growth rate that may be too low and a range of about 20 percent between high and low exports.

The only case in which policy alternatives were not developed is that of public expenditures and taxes. Generally, they are assumed unchanged from current trends, varying only with respect to population and GNP per capita. Expenditures on education, for example, follow a secular trend of increasing expenditures per pupil, though the total is dampened by the declining numbers of school-age children projected in the different population series. Similarly, health expenditures increase as a consequence both of higher health standards and of an aging population. Some deviations from trends are introduced in special cases, for example, for highway construction, in which expenditures cease their rapid growth after completion of the interstate system. Military expenditures are assumed to grow at an elasticity of 0.8 with respect to per capita GNP, the presumption being that in the long run a rich nation will treat defense much as a rich individual treats insurance, purchasing more than lower income individuals but not quite in proportion to the differences in income. Assumptions such as these are held constant across scenarios, and alternatives are introduced in only a few cases in which special but limited points are to be made.

Other Assumptions

There are, of course, many other assumptions implicit in this analysis: no major wars, blockades, or disastrous political or bureaucratic mistakes; no colonization or importation of resources from outer space; no change for better or worse in the general behavior patterns of economic, political, and administrative institutions; no dramatic changes in domestic or international power balances. Thus, on the whole, the assumptions are conservative and conventional. This is deliberate in order to determine whether resource and environmental pressures can be managed in these circumstances. If the answer is no, or if serious pressures build up, it will be a strong sign that conventional trends of this kind cannot continue.

Summary of Scenarios

Given the number of permutations that could be involved, it is impossible to consider the effects of changes in each of the determinants and

Table 2-5. Summary of Principal Scenarios

Scenario	Characteristics
Base case	
EL	Population series E; low-productivity growth rate; no import restrictions or stockpiling; relaxed pollution control policy; constant real price of oil until 2010; trend agricultural exports
Difficult cases	
DH	Population series D; high-productivity growth rate; subsidies to develop domestic substitutes for imported energy; development of a petroleum stockpile; strict pollution control policy, including no breeder; constant real price of oil until 2010; expansion of agricultural exports
DHNU	Same as DH except that nuclear power is phased out
DHP1	Same as DH except continuously rising price of oil
Alternative cases	
DHP2	Same as DH except that oil prices decline between 1980 and 1985 and subsidies for domestic energy production are removed
DHRE	Same as DH except relaxed environmental control policy and breeder permitted
FH	Same as DH except slow population growth (series F) is assumed
DL	Same as DH except slow economic growth (low-productivity series) is assumed
FL	Same as DH except series F and low-productivity series are assumed

subdeterminants discussed above; nor would it be very instructive to do so, because in reality many of these changes depend on each other. Accordingly, the assumptions were grouped with respect to these determinants into a limited number of scenarios, each of which should be internally consistent. Three sets of scenarios have been developed. The first includes just one scenario called the base case, the second includes several particularly difficult cases; and the third comprises scenarios that relax, generally one at a time, the difficulties of the scenarios in the second set. Table 2-5 summarizes the characteristics of these scenarios. Other scenarios and variations on individual variables are described and analyzed in subsequent chapters.

Our goal in constructing the base case, scenario EL, was to develop, based on trends and policies up to about 1975, a "most likely" or "surprise-free" benchmark against which to observe the effects of conditions that might develop in the future. This case is not in all dimensions a simple extrapolation of trends, however. This would have led to many surprises indeed by 2025: two cars for each person of driving age, a doubling of per capita meat consumption, too low a price for energy and too high a rate of energy consumption, and so on. All along the line, judgmental adjustments were required to make this case internally consistent and reasonable.

The other distinguishing feature of the base case is the assumption that no special efforts are made to restrict energy imports. The decontrol of domestic oil and gas prices, assumed in all scenarios, will dampen the growth in demand for energy and stimulate production somewhat, but in EL whatever gap is present is filled with imports. Thus, an important outcome of this case is an indication of the extent of our dependence on the rest of the world if we continue more or less as we have so far.

The difficult case (scenario DH) places maximum pressure on the U.S. resource base but at the same time tries to minimize environmental deterioration. The same evolutionary technological developments and the same material-intensive pattern of consumption occur as in the base case, but population and economic growth are higher. So too is the growth in agricultural exports. At the same time, we try to achieve stringent environmental standards and to reduce dependence on imported petroleum and natural gas. This movement toward self-reliance is assumed to be accomplished by subsidizing the production of domestic substitutes rather than by raising domestic prices, so there is no additional dampening of demand over the base-case price projections (other than what occurs as a consequence of lowering disposable income to provide the subsidy).

The definition of stringent environmental policy rules out the use of breeder reactors, but fission reactors are permitted. To see what difference it would make if all nuclear power were ruled out, a second version of this case—scenario DHNU—adds a nuclear moratorium to these difficulties. A third version—scenario DHP1—assumes that petroleum prices in real terms, instead of remaining constant until anticipation of exhaustion forces them up, increase continuously, doubling between 1980 and 2010.

The remaining scenarios are designed to ascertain the effects of relaxing these difficulties. What would be the effect of a fall in oil prices (scenario DHP2)? What difference would it make if there were a lower population growth rate (FH), a lower economic growth rate (DL and FL), or a relaxation of environmental controls (DHRE)? The answers to such questions indicate the relative importance of the various determinants and thereby develop a basis for deriving policy implications from this study.

References

Agency for International Development (AID). 1974. *GNP,* Report RC-W-138 (Washington, D.C.).

Almon, Clopper, Jr., M. B. Buckler, L. M. Horowitz, and T. C. Reimbold. 1974. *1985: Interindustry Forecasts of the American Economy* (Lexington, Mass., Lexington Books).

Alterman, Jack. 1976. "Projections of Labor Force, Labor Productivity, Gross National Product, and Households: Methodology and Data" (Washington, D.C., Resources for the Future).

Blake, Judith. 1974. "Can We Believe Recent Data on Birth Expectations in the United States?" *Demography* vol. II, no. 1 (February) pp. 25–44.

BLS. See U.S. Bureau of Labor Statistics.

Butz, William P., and Michael P. Ward. 1977. "The Emergence of Counter-cyclical U.S. Fertility," Rand Corporation monograph R-1605-NIH (Santa Monica, Calif., Rand Corporation).

Census Bureau. 1972. *Current Population Reports* series P-25, no. 493 (December) (Washington, D.C., GPO).

———. 1974. *Current Population Reports* series P-20, no. 271 (October) (Washington, D.C., GPO).

———. 1975. *Current Population Reports* series P-25, no. 601 (October) (Washington, D.C., GPO).

———. 1976. *Statistical Abstract of the U.S. 1976* (97th Edition) (Washington, GPO).

———. 1977a. *Current Population Reports* series P-20, no. 306 (January) (Washington, D.C., GPO).

———. 1977b. *Current Population Reports* series P-25, no. 704 (July) (Washington, D.C., GPO).

Denison, Edward F. 1974. *Accounting for U.S. Economic Growth, 1929–1969* (Washington, D.C., Brookings Institution).

———. 1976. "The Contribution of Capital to the Postwar Growth of Industrial Countries," in *U.S. Economic Growth from 1976 to 1986: Prospects, Problems, and Patterns,* vol. 3—*Capital.* Study prepared for the use of the Joint Economic Committee, 94 Cong., 2 sess., November 15 (Washington, D.C., GPO).

Ford Foundation. 1974. *A Time to Choose.* Final Report of the Energy Policy Project of the Ford Foundation (Cambridge, Mass., Ballinger).

Frejka, Tomas. 1973. *The Future of Population Growth: Alternative Paths to Equilibrium, Reference Tables* (New York, Population Council).

International Bank for Reconstruction and Development (IBRD). 1974a. *World Bank Atlas* (Washington, D.C.).

———. 1974b. *Prospects for the Developing Countries,* Report 477 (Washington, D.C.).

Lesko Associates. 1975. "Basic Data and Guidance Required to Implement a Major Illegal Alien Study During Fiscal Year 1976." Report to the Immigration and Naturalization Service (October 15) (Washington, D.C.).

Lovins, Amory. 1976. "Energy Strategies: The Road Not Taken," *Foreign Affairs* (October).

Moran, Theodore H. 1978. *Oil Prices and the Future of OPEC: The Political Economy of Tension and Stability in the Organization of Petroleum Exporting Countries.* Research Paper R-8 (Washington, D.C., Resources for the Future).

Ohmae, Kenichi. 1975. "Yokkakari: The Cycle of Dependence in the Japanese Corporation," *Technology Review* vol. 77, no. 3 (January) pp. 41–47.

Paul, David A., and John L. Scadding. 1974. "Private Savings Ultrarationality and 'Denison's Law'," *Journal of Political Economy* vol. 82, no. 2, pt. 1 (March/April) pp. 225–249.

Shapanka, Adele. 1978. "Long-Range Technological Forecasts for Use in Studying the Resource and Environmental Consequences of U.S. Population and Economic Growth: 1975–2025," Discussion Paper D-31 (Washington, D.C., Resources for the Future).

Sklar, June, and Beth Berkov. 1975. "The American Birth Rate: Evidence of a Coming Rise," *Science* vol. 189, no. 4204 (August 29) pp. 693–700.

Stern, Ernest, and Wouter Tims. 1976. "The Relative Bargaining Strengths of the Developing Countries," in R. G. Ridker, ed., *Changing Resource Problems of the Fourth World* (Washington, D.C., Resources for the Future).

Stevens, Benjamin H., and Glynnis A. Trainer. 1978. "Distribution of Population and Economic Activity Among Regions of the United States in the Year 2025," in *Regional Perspectives on Population, Resources, and the Environment,* vol. II of *Resource and Environmental Consequences of Population and Economic Growth* (Washington, D.C., Resources for the Future).

Teitelbaum, Michael. 1972. "International Experience with Fertility at or Near Replacement Level," in *Demographic and Social Aspects of Population Growth,* vol. I of *Research Reports of U.S. Commission on Population Growth and the American Future* (Washington, D.C., GPO).

U.S. Bureau of Labor Statistics (BLS). 1974. *Population & Labor Force Projections* bulletin 1809 (Washington, D.C., GPO).

Wachter, M. L., and S. M. Wachter. 1978. "The Fiscal Policy Dilemma: Cyclical Savings Dominated by Supply Side Constraints," in Thomas J. Espenshade and William J. Serow, eds., *The Economic Consequences of Slowing Population Growth* (New York, Academic Press).

3

The National Economy

This chapter will examine the economic implications of the assumptions and scenarios developed in the previous chapter. First, it will trace how the economy unfolds over time. The general range of projections is reviewed, but the focus is on the base case (scenario EL). The chapter then turns to the differences that are introduced in future years by applying different scenarios.

General Characteristics

Given the assumptions common to most of our scenarios—in particular, that the U.S. economy returns to an unemployment rate of 4 to 4.5 percent and is able to maintain it from about 1980 onwards and that resource supplies are not interrupted in any major way by such events as wars, embargoes, or self-imposed limitations—the average annual rate of growth in GNP is likely to fall within the range of 2.5 and 3.5 percent. The rate should be more than 3 percent during the first half of the fifty-year period under investigation and less than 3 percent during the second half. This range brackets historic rates of growth—specifically, 3.1 percent from 1925 to 1975 and 3.3 percent from 1950 to 1975—but it is substantially less than the 4 percent rate that was considered the norm during the fifties and sixties or even the 3.6 percent rate estimated to be the potential growth rate between 1965 and 1977 (CEA, 1977, and Rasche and Tatom, 1977). The expected slowdown from recent decades results from the combined impacts of changes in the rate of growth of the population, and hence the labor force; changes in labor productivity arising from shifts in the composition of the labor force and of output; and a number of transitional factors related to higher energy and environmental clean-up costs.

This range of growth rates is sufficient to bring the GNP in 2025 to a level between 3.5 and 5.6 times that of 1975 and to support a standard of living (personal consumption per capita) some 2.7 to 3.7 times larger. If the world economy progressed along the lines indicated in table 2–4, the United States would still account for 17.5 percent of the world's GNP in 2025, compared with 29 percent in 1972. Thus, while the U.S. economy is unlikely to be as big or as rich as analysts thought just a few years ago, its growth and size during the next fifty years would still be impressive if these scenarios come to pass.

Table 3–1 compares selected GNP projections from this study with others, and table 3–2 provides a more detailed picture of the way the economy would evolve over time if the base case assumptions prevailed. It is the changes in such aggregates over time and the differences between scenarios at the same point in time, not the absolute values of the aggregates, that is of principal interest in these tables. This is because the official U.S. national accounts have been revised and because there are definitional differences between these accounts and some sectors in the model. Although the GNP figure used in the model is only 1.5 percent less than the officially defined GNP in 1971, and there is no reason to believe that this relationship will change significantly in the future, the discrepancy for components of the GNP could be greater.[1]

As can be seen for the base case shown in table 3–2, between 1975 and 2025 the fractions of GNP devoted to personal consumption expenditures, imports, and exports all increase, while that devoted to government expenditures decreases; but all such changes are small and slow by historical standards. Imports grow more rapidly than GNP mainly because of the increase in oil imports. Exports grow in line with imports, but this is an artifice imposed on the system exogenously as a way to indicate the long-run cost of imports in terms of the goods and services forgone to pay for them.[2]

---

[1] The discrepancy observed in table 3–1 between the model's estimate of GNP and the national accounts number for 1975 is larger (2.7 percent), but this is because the official figures for 1975 were themselves projections at the time the model runs were developed.

[2] These estimates of required exports are not strictly correct because they are based on 1971 prices; that is, the terms of trade are assumed implicitly to remain constant, an assumption roughly compatible with other assumptions until 2010 or so in all scenarios except for DHP1 and DHP2.

Table 3–1. Selected GNP Projections

(billions of 1971 dollars)

Source	1975[a]	1980	1985	1990	2000	2020	2025
This study							
EL (base case)	1,108	1,386	1,575	1,820	2,429	3,869	4,243
DH (difficult case)	1,108	1,508	1,743	2,042	2,924	5,354	6,212
FH	1,108	1,480	1,778	2,081	2,814	4,328	4,766
DL	1,108	1,391	1,561	1,811	2,507	4,334	4,907
FL	1,108	1,406	1,589	1,833	2,385	3,637	3,859
Annual growth rate from 1975							
4 percent	1,139	1,386	1,686	2,051	3,036		8,095
3.1 percent	1,139	1,327	1,546	1,801	2,443		5,241
Other studies							
Energy Policy Project (1973)	1,442		2,064		3,345		
Data Resources, Inc. (1976)		1,468	1,716	2,002			
Wharton (1976)		1,349	1,589				
BLS (1976)		1,525	1,817				
National Energy Outlook (1976)	1,121	1,467	1,746	2,002			
OBERS (1972)		1,546		2,142	2,978	5,278	
INFORUM (1976)	1,152	1,399	1,559				
National Planning Association (1976)	1,150	1,378	1,691				
Bureau of Mines (1974)			1,813		2,972		

Sources:

Energy Policy Project [Ford Foundation, *A Time to Choose* (Cambridge, Mass., Ballinger, 1973)].

Data Resources, Inc. ["The Economic Outlook Trend 1975–1990," *U.S. Long-Term Bulletin* (New York, Data Resources, Inc., 1976)].

Wharton [Wharton EFA, Inc., "Wharton Annual and Industry Forecasting Model, July 20, 1976" (Philadelphia, Pa., 1976)].

BLS [U.S. Bureau of Labor Statistics, "Projections to 1980 and 1985," *Monthly Labor Review* (March 1976)].

National Energy Outlook [U.S. Federal Energy Administration, *National Energy Outlook*, FEA N-75/713 (Washington, D.C., GPO, February 1976)].

OBERS [U.S. Department of Commerce, "1972 OBERS Projections, Regional Activities in the U.S. Series E Population," *Concepts, Methodology, and Summary Data* (Washington, D.C., GPO, 1972)].

INFORUM [University of Maryland, Bureau of Business and Economic Research, College Park, Md., computer print-out for January 1976 meeting].

Bureau of Mines [Bureau of Mines, Reference Macro Projections and Base Data," in *Mineral Facts and Problems* (Washington, D.C., Bureau of Mines, 1975)].

[a] Numbers for 1975 differ because of differences in the date at which the projections were made and slight differences in definition. The figure $1,139 billion is based on the official national accounts estimate.

[b] Used as the medium price projection in the National Energy Plan II (NEP-II, 1979), except that it starts from 1978 and projects only to 2000.

The fall in government's share—from 21 to 18 percent of the GNP over the fifty-year period—arises from the fact that a number of important government sectors, especially defense, education, and public construction, grow less rapidly than the GNP. Defense expenditures grow more slowly because of the assumptions specified in chapter 2, and education and public construction, among other reasons, because of the slowdown in the rate of population growth and the completion of the federal highway system. This decline does not necessarily indicate a reduction in the economic importance of the government sector because these data do not include transfers, which are likely to become more important over time. Indeed, the growth of transfers partly accounts for the increased share of GNP devoted to personal consumption expenditures over time.

Projected changes in the composition of private consumption for this case are given in table 3–3. The low income elasticities for most non-durable necessities and the continued slowdown in population growth explain the continuing decline in the share of the consumer's dollar spent on food, clothing, household furnishings, and the like. The decreasing share (in constant prices) spent on fuel and power reflects the lagged effect of higher energy prices. The rapid increase in the share spent on other transportation is a consequence of growing affluence and changes in tastes (increased travel by air, off-the-road vehicles, and so forth). The relative increase in communications expenditures results from technological changes projected for the communications sector. Increased expenditures on recreation, medical care, and education are a result of the aging of population and the increasing time spent in leisure and retirement, and of the high income elasticities attached to expenditures on these items. Private expenditures on education and health do not, of course, represent the total amount the economy devotes to these uses. The lower portion of table 3–3 shows assumed public plus private expenditures on these items.

The changes in shares do not mean that absolute expenditures in any category will fall. Even in the scenario with the lowest rate economic growth (FL), per capita expenditures on food, the slowest growing category, increase more than 85 percent between 1975 and 2025. This does not necessarily mean that the physical qualities consumed will increase in proportion to expenditures, however. Virtually all of the expenditure increase in the case of food, for example, involves shifts to higher cost, processed foods rather than any significant increase in pounds or calories of food purchased (see table 6–4).

Table 3–2. Principal Economic Indicators, Scenario EL, 1975–2025

Indicator	Absolute figures				Percentage of total			
	1975	1985	2000	2025	1975	1985	2000	2025
GNP per capita (1971$)	5,180	6,680	9,184	13,968				
Consumption per capita (1971$)	3,203	4,051	5,852	9,150				
GNP (billions of 1971$)	1,108	1,575	2,429	4,243	100.0	100.0	100.0	100.0
Personal consumption expenditures	685	955	1,547	2,780	61.8	60.6	63.6	65.5
Investments	167	286	380	665	15.1	18.1	15.6	15.7
Equipment	(86)	(174)	(219)	(416)	(7.8)	(11.0)	(9.0)	(9.8)
Construction	(81)	(112)	(161)	(249)	(7.3)	(7.1)	(6.6)	(5.9)
Government expenditures	237	317	488	759	21.4	20.1	20.0	17.9
Defense	(71)	(97)	(141)	(225)	(6.4)	(6.1)	(5.8)	(5.3)
Nondefense (federal)	(26)	(33)	(44)	(65)	(2.3)	(2.1)	(1.8)	(1.5)
Education	(50)	(64)	(117)	(179)	(4.5)	(4.1)	(4.8)	(4.2)
Health, welfare	(7)	(14)	(26)	(47)	(0.6)	(0.9)	(1.1)	(1.1)
Safety	(2)	(3)	(5)	(9)	(0.1)	(0.2)	(0.2)	(0.2)
State and local (general)	(47)	(66)	(104)	(166)	(4.2)	(4.1)	(4.3)	(3.9)
Public construction	(34)	(41)	(51)	(88)	(3.1)	(2.6)	(2.1)	(1.6)
Exports	96	129	207	445	8.6	8.1	8.5	10.4
Imports	75	121	205	423	6.7	7.7	8.4	9.9
Inventory change	3	9	11	18	0.3	0.6	0.5	0.4

Total output	1,808	2,632	4,049	7,241	100.0	100.0	100.0	100.0
Agriculture	71	83	102	139	3.9	3.2	2.5	1.9
Mining	29	28	30	42	1.6	1.1	0.7	0.6
Construction	58	80	118	188	3.2	3.0	2.9	2.5
Manufacturing	756	1,111	1,639	2,957	41.8	42.2	40.5	40.8
Paper	(27)	(37)	(53)	(90)	(1.4)	(1.4)	(1.3)	(1.2)
Industrial chemicals	(21)	(34)	(57)	(120)	(1.1)	(1.3)	(1.4)	(1.7)
Petroleum refining	(31)	(38)	(51)	(84)	(1.7)	(1.4)	(1.3)	(1.2)
Steel	(35)	(42)	(51)	(74)	(1.9)	(1.6)	(1.3)	(1.0)
Motor vehicle	(52)	(92)	(142)	(243)	(2.9)	(3.4)	(3.4)	(3.4)
Transportation	70	105	159	279	3.9	4.0	3.9	3.9
Communication	31	56	110	238	1.7	2.1	2.7	3.3
Electric utilities	35	59	93	161	1.9	2.2	2.3	2.2
Other utilities	23	24	24	32	1.3	0.9	0.6	0.5
Trade	240	358	576	1,116	13.3	13.6	14.2	15.4
Finance	224	332	551	970	12.3	12.6	13.6	13.4
Services	180	267	438	770	9.9	10.1	10.8	10.6
Other	87	127	208	349	4.8	4.8	5.1	4.8

Table 3-3. Composition of Consumption Expenditures, Scenario EL

Expenditure category	Billions of 1971$			Percentage of total		
	1975	2000	2025	1975	2000	2025
Private consumption expenditures						
Food	71	112	188	10.6	7.3	6.8
Beverage and tobacco	21	28	40	3.1	1.8	1.5
Clothes and footwear	25	54	86	3.7	3.6	3.1
Gross rent and real estate	101	251	435	15.0	16.4	15.8
Fuel, power and gas	34	51	64	5.1	3.3	2.3
Household operations, furniture, appliances, etc.	38	83	139	5.7	5.4	5.0
Medical care	50	147	281	7.4	9.6	10.2
Motor vehicles, parts, tires, repairs	42	89	176	6.2	5.8	6.4
Other transportation and communications	25	85	192	3.7	5.6	7.0
Recreation	21	48	89	3.1	3.1	3.2
Private schools	23	73	128	3.5	4.7	4.6
Other commodities	5	14	23	0.7	1.0	0.9
Other services	217	495	916	32.3	32.4	33.2
Total	673	1,530	2,756	100.0	100.0	100.0
Private and public expenditures on education and health						
Education						
Per capita (1971$)	367	743	1,040			
Per pupil (1971$)	1,333	3,190	4,914			
Percentage of GNP	7.1	8.1	7.4			
Health						
Per capita (1971$)	376	935	1,507			
Percentage of GNP	7.3	10.2	10.8			

The consequences of all these shifts in expenditures, plus the technological changes that affect input–output coefficients, are rather modest changes in the composition of output. Agriculture, mining, and construction, for example, which are already relatively small percentages of total output, continue to decline. Manufacturing just about holds its own (with steel becoming less and industrial chemicals somewhat more important). Communications, utilities, trade, finance, and services increase their shares. But all these changes are quite small and orderly.

The behavior of investment expenditures is something of an exception. Figure 3–1 shows investment, here defined to include public construction and inventory changes, as a share of GNP for four scenarios.[3]

[3] Scenarios DHNU, DL, FH, and FL are not included in figure 3–1 because they have investment rates equal to or just slightly higher than scenario DH and would have made the figure difficult to read.

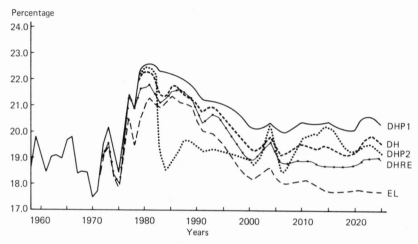

Figure 3–1. Investment as a percentage of the GNP, 1958–2025.

In the base case, the share increases from an average of less than 19 percent in the 1958–75 period to 21 percent in 1980; it remains near that level for another ten years, then slowly drops to something like a long-term equilibrium level of nearly 18 percent. The investment shares of the GNP in scenarios DH and DHP1 peak earlier, rise to higher levels, and do not settle down to as low a level by 2025.

A significant portion of the increase in investment (after allowing for recovery from the 1974–76 recession) is the result of additional expenditure on energy-saving and pollution-abatement equipment. Accelerated turnover of capital stock (to replace the existing stock with more energy-saving capital) plays an increasingly important role until 1985 and a decreasing role thereafter. A rough indication of the extent to which these expenditures explain additional aggregate investment expenditures can be gleaned from table 3–4, which compares the amounts that would have been spent in these directions had their shares remained the same as in 1971.

In 1985, the story is relatively simple. Total investment expenditures in the base case are 20 percent higher [55.9 ÷ (336.0 − 55.9) × 100] than they would have been had 1971 shares prevailed, and accelerated turnover of the capital stock accounts for practically all of the increase. By 2000 the picture changes. First, total investment is not much different from what it would have been. But this occurs because much of the increase in private fixed investment is offset by declines in public construction (relative to what would have occurred if the shares had remained constant). Additional energy-related investments account for 30

Table 3–4. Investments and Additions to Investments for Special Purposes Under Alternative Assumptions for Selected Years

Assumption and investment	1975		1985		2000		2025	
	Projected	Difference from 1971 shares[a]	Projected	Difference from 1971 shares[a]	Projected	Difference from 1971 shares[a]	Projected	Difference from 1971 shares[a]
EL								
Total investment as % of GNP	17.8[b]		21.3		18.2		17.7	
Total investment (billions of 1971$)	197.5	0.4	336.0	55.9	441.9	9.9	750.8	−4.1
Private fixed	167.0	5.7	286.0	56.7	379.9	26.3	665.0	47.1
(Energy)	(20.4)	(0.2)	(31.7)	(3.0)	(52.1)	(7.9)	(98.7)	(21.5)
(Abatement)	(5.4)	(3.1)	(8.1)	(4.8)	(15.6)	(10.5)	(31.8)	(22.9)
(Accelerated turnover)	(0)	(0)	(41.8)	(41.8)	(0)	(0)	(0)	(0)
Public construction	33.6	0.6	41.1	−5.8	50.7	−21.7	68.1	−58.3
Inventory change	−3.1	−5.7	8.9	5	11.3	5.3	17.7	7.1
DH								
Total investment as % of GNP	18.4		21.7		19.4		19.4	
Total investment (billions of 1971$)	204.0	15.4	378.3	63.6	566.5	42.4	1,206.3	106.7
Private fixed	171.5	17.0	322.8	65.0	490.9	61.6	1,080.0	179.2

(Energy)	(21.3)	(1.4)	(39.9)	(6.7)	(86.6)	(31.3)	(207.1)	(91.1)
(Abatement)	(12.6)	(7.2)	(14.2)	(5.2)	(33.2)	(18.2)	(80.1)	(48.9)
(Accelerated turnover)	(0)	(0)	(46.1)	(46.1)	(0)	(0)	(0)	(0)
Public construction	36.1	4.6	44.9	-7.7	58.9	-28.6	92.3	-91.4
Inventory change	-3.6	-6.2	10.6	6.3	16.7	3.5	34.0	22.4
DHP1								
Total investment as % of GNP	18.4		22.3		20.1		20.2	
Total investment (billions of 1971$)	204.0	15.4	388.3	73.6	579.1	55.0	1,229.3	129.7
Private fixed	171.5	17.0	332.8	75.0	504.5	75.2	1,105.7	204.9
(Energy)	(21.3)	(1.4)	(44.9)	(11.7)	(95.5)	(40.2)	(227.5)	(111.5)
(Abatement)	(12.6)	(7.2)	(14.2)	(5.2)	(32.8)	(17.8)	(78.3)	(47.1)
(Accelerated turnover)	(0)	(0)	(51.1)	(51.1)	(10.0)	(10.0)	(25.0)	(25.0)
Public construction	36.1	4.6	44.9	-7.7	58.1	-29.4	90.3	-93.4
Inventory change	-3.6	-6.2	10.6	6.3	16.5	3.3	33.3	21.7

a Projected amount minus the amount that would occur if the expenditure item had remained the same percentage of the GNP as it was in 1971. For example, given the level of the GNP projected for scenario EL in 1985, total investment would have been $280.1 billion had it remained 17.9 percent of GNP, the percentage that prevailed in 1971; instead, scenario EL projects a level $55.9 billion higher. Additional energy investments, over what a constant share of GNP would have projected, explain $3 billion of this increase, additional abatement investments $4.8 billion, and so on.
b In 1971 total investment as a percentage of GNP was 17.9 percent.

percent, and additional pollution-abatement investments for 40 percent, of the increase in private fixed investment. After 2000, public construction continues to grow less rapidly than the GNP, so that by 2025 the difference between our projection and a constant-share projection offsets a similarly calculated difference in private fixed investments.[4] Energy and abatement investments explain practically all of the additional private fixed investment.[5]

The situation is similar for scenario DH except that energy and abatement investments increase even more rapidly relative to the GNP than in the base case because of efforts to reduce energy imports and enforce stricter environmental standards. Scenario DPH1 differs from DH in that the continuously rising price of petroleum and natural gas results in slightly less abatement investment (because of lower energy consumption) and substantially more investment because of accelerated turnover of the capital stock.

Implicit in our procedure for entering these additional investment requirements into the model is the assumption that aggregate savings will increase to the extent necessary to finance this investment.[6] Thus, a period of capital shortage is ruled out by assumption. But this assumption may be unrealistic at least for the decade of the eighties, when the investment share of the GNP must remain above 21 percent in all scenarios except DHP2 (to be discussed later). Since World War II, an investment rate (again defined to include public construction and inventory accumulation) reaching 21 percent was achieved in only two years, 1950 and 1951.

----

[4] Later work not incorporated into these runs suggests that these estimates for public construction may be too low. If public construction were to maintain its 1971 share of the GNP, total investment as a percentage of the GNP would be about 19 percent from 2000 onwards in scenario EL and more than 20 percent from 2000 onwards in scenario DH. The actual figures are more likely to fall between these and those recorded in table 3–4.

[5] In 2025, for scenario DH, additional energy and abatement investments add up to more than additional private fixed investments because other components of that total are less than what constant shares would have predicted.

[6] Additional investment requirements were introduced by increasing appropriate investment coefficients. This is equivalent to assuming that the first round effects on the economy come at the expense of consumption rather than other, "normal" investments. Once consumption declines, "normal" investments also decline so that in the end both give way to allow for the new investment requirements; but the bulk of the effect is captured in the first round. This procedure allows us to assume as a first approximation that the GNP continues growing as it otherwise would have and requires us to judge the effect on the economy by observing how consumption and investment as percentages of total output deviate from the paths they otherwise would have taken.

The average was 19.2 percent in the fifties, 18.5 percent in the sixties, and 16 percent from 1970 through 1974.

If the investment rate cannot be increased to the required levels, the growth in labor productivity and hence in the GNP is likely to be less. A rough indication of the extent of the slowdown that might occur can be obtained by referring to an exercise developed for a different purpose in which the private fixed investment rate was held to a maximum of 18 percent of the GNP,[7] when the unconstrained runs required it to rise to 22 percent in 1985, 23 percent in 1990, 17 percent in 2000, and 20 to 21 percent from 2010 through 2025, roughly comparable to the situation in scenario DHP1. The result was a reduction in GNP in 2025 of between 8 and 24 percent, depending on the way the model is run (Ridker, Watson, and Shapanka, 1977). Scenarios EL and DH are not as severe (the private investment rate rises above 18 percent only during the decade of the eighties), but investment requirements for public construction may have been underestimated. In any event, much will depend on the way monetary and fiscal policy is managed. The only conclusion is that a substantial period of capital shortage, constrained economic growth, and accelerated inflation cannot be ruled out if the assumptions of these scenarios, particularly DHP1, prevail.

Role of Major Determinants

Now that the prominent features of the economy have been sketched for the fifty-year period under consideration, we turn to a comparison of scenarios that will indicate the role played by major economic determinants.

Population and Labor Productivity

Scenarios DH, FH, DL, and FL can be used to compare the impacts of changes in population and labor productivity because they incorporate the same assumptions about all other factors that might influence the

---

[7] A rate surpassed in only one year (1950) in the last fifty and never on a sustained basis.

Table 3–5. Macroeconomic Indicators for Scenarios with Alternative Population and Economic Growth Rates

		1985			
Indicator	1975	DH	FH	DL	FL
Population (millions)	213.9	243.9	230.9	243.9	230.9
Labor force (millions)	93.8	106.5	108.2	106.5	108.2
GNP (billions 1971$)	1,108	1,743	1,778	1,561	1,589
GNP per capita (1971$)	5,180	7,146	7,770	6,400	6,921
Private consumption per capita (1971$)	3,202	4,320	4,680	3,872	4,172
Percentage of GNP					
Private consumption	61.8	60.5	60.8	60.5	60.6
Private investment	14.8	19.1	19.3	19.1	19.1
Government expenditure	21.4	20.4	20.1	20.3	20.1
Net exports	2.0	0.1	0.2	0.1	0.2

situation.[8] Table 3–5 summarizes the principal macroeconomic impacts of changes in population and labor productivity, and figure 3–2 provides time trends for consumption per capita.

As one would expect to find within the range of changes being investigated, the decline in population growth (compare DH with FH, for example) results initially in a somewhat larger GNP because women are released from child rearing to enter the labor force. But later, once the labor force age groups begin to be affected by declining population growth

[8] These four scenarios differ from EL, the base case, in that they incorporate restrictions on energy imports, a higher level of agricultural exports, and more stringent environmental controls. On the other hand, they make the same assumptions as does EL with regard to technology, aggregate savings rates, and the ability of the government to maintain full employment. Although it can be argued that these factors are not independent of changes in population and labor productivity, within the range of the population and productivity estimates and over the time period being considered, we do not believe any other assumption is more defensible.

For example, it is sometimes argued that innovation is more rapid with a higher rate of turnover of the labor force, that the need to care for and educate children induces parents to work harder and save more than they would with fewer children, and that it is easier to maintain full employment when aggregate demand is buoyed up by increases in population growth and demand for labor is not being whittled away by rapid growth in productivity. But empirical evidence to support these arguments is weak; some counterarguments can be advanced; and in any case, it is difficult to believe that, within our time frame, whatever negative effects there might be would be so large that they could not easily be offset by appropriate government action. A discussion of many of these issues, particularly as they relate to the effects of changes in population growth rates, can be found in Espenshade and Serow (1978) and, within that volume, of most relevance to this study, Ridker (1978).

2000				2025			
DH	FH	DL	FL	DH	FH	DL	FL
286.0	250.7	286.0	250.7	367.5	264.9	367.5	264.9
128.1	122.3	122.3	122.3	161.3	125.1	161.3	125.1
2,904	2,814	2,507	2,385	6,212	4,766	4,907	3,859
10,154	11,225	8,766	9,513	16,903	17,992	13,352	14,568
6,356	7,102	5,423	6,002	10,750	11,790	8,488	9,651
62.2	63.3	61.9	63.1	63.6	65.5	63.6	66.3
17.4	17.1	17.6	17.2	17.9	17.2	18.2	17.0
20.3	19.6	20.1	19.6	18.5	17.6	18.3	17.6
0.2	0.1	0.4	0.1	0.0	0.3	0.0	0.8

rates, GNP is smaller. In all periods, the level of per capita output and consumption is higher with lower population growth rates. These results stem from changes in the size of the labor force relative to that of the population, operating in a model that includes no significant economies of scale.[9]

The table also shows that consumption as a percentage of the GNP increases with a shift from higher to lower population assumptions, whether labor productivity grows rapidly or slowly. Compositional shifts in consumption, and hence in output, are also present, but they are not as great as those observed over time, as shown in tables 3–2 and 3–3. The effect of population growth on investment's share of GNP is small and ambiguous, differing between 2000 and 2025 and between high- and low-productivity assumptions. In contrast, the effects of a decline in labor productivity (compare DH and DL, for example) is to reduce both GNP and GNP per capita. The effect of this decline on the shares of GNP devoted to consumption and investment is small and ambiguous.

These results can be interpreted as providing a prima facie case in favor of a policy to slow down population growth. As first approximations, per capita GNP—more accurately, per capita consumption—can be taken as a measure of material welfare, conventionally defined, and total GNP can be taken as a rough index of the throughput of resources

[9] The possibility of scale effects is present because of all the parameter changes introduced over time, but these changes are partly offsetting and apparently not large enough, on net, to produce significant scale effects.

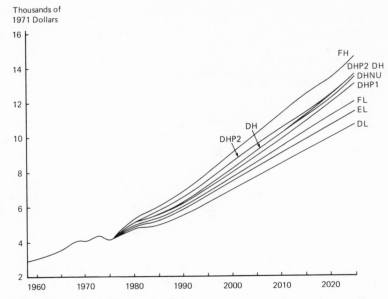

Figure 3–2. Consumption per capita.

and residuals that must eventually be disposed of in the environment. Since the scenarios incorporating lower population growth rates eventually result in higher levels of per capita and lower levels of total GNP and consumption, they are clearly superior. But two qualifications must be kept in mind. First, if parents prefer larger families than are compatible with the lower population assumptions, there is a welfare loss to be balanced against these material gains resulting from a decline in population growth. Second, the savings in resources and environmental depletion resulting from a slowdown in population growth rates are not necessarily proportional to changes in GNP; indeed, they may be much smaller. Much depends on changes that occur over time in factors linking resources and the environment to individual economic sectors and, through these sectors, to population and GNP. In several important instances, this qualification turns out to be important.

In general, so far as macroeconomic variables are concerned, the farther into the future one projects, the more important are changes in assumptions about population and labor productivity relative to changes in assumptions about policy. At least this is true for the types of policy changes considered here. In contrast, policy changes appear to affect timing and specific, sector-related variables, as we shall see below.

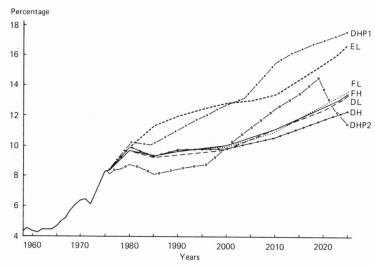

Figure 3–3. Imports as a percentage of the GNP. All prices are assumed to be constant except world prices for oil and natural gas, which follow the pattern outlined in figures 5–3 and 5–4 and tables 5–10, 5–12, and 5–13.

Import Dependency

One of the most important characteristics of the base case is the growing dependency on imports, especially petroleum and natural gas. As figure 3–3 indicates, total imports as a percentage of the GNP rose in the 1960s from 4 to 6 percent, and by 1975 it was well over 8 percent. The major items accounting for this increase, roughly in order of importance, were petroleum, natural gas and fuel oil, steel, consumer durables (such as radios, televisions, and motor vehicles), two categories of nondurables (meat products and apparel), and one category of services (international travel, especially air travel). If no special efforts are made to restrict imports (scenario EL), the import percentage of the GNP is likely to rise above 14 percent during the next fifty years. The largest factor accounting for this increase is petroleum and natural gas, as table 3–6 indicates, but airlines, iron ore, industrial chemicals, and some nonferrous metals are also important. Beyond 2025, however, the import percentage of the GNP should begin dropping rapidly (much as occurs in scenario DHP2 a few years earlier) because of exhaustion of petroleum and natural gas and the development of domestically produced synthetics.

Table 3–6. Oil and Gas Imports in Base and Difficult Cases

Import	Actual 1975	EL 1975	EL			
			1985	2000	2010	2025
Quantities imported, net (quads)[a]						
Petroleum	12.4	13.9	26.3	38.1	43.1	47.2
Natural gas	0.9	0.7	4.9	4.1	8.5	13.1
Total	13.3	14.6	31.2	42.2	51.6	60.3
Percentage of total merchandise imports						
Petroleum	27.0	30.0	36.9	43.4	38.4	41.8
Natural gas	1.1	0.8	9.3	6.4	10.1	12.1
Total	28.7	30.8	46.2	49.8	48.5	53.9
Percentage of domestic requirements[b]						
Petroleum	37.9	40.8	61.4	77.3	73.5	66.4
Natural gas	4.5	3.2	22.2	25.5	47.0	68.2

Source: Data for Actual 1975 imports based on Bureau of Mines, News Release, March 14, 1977; and Energy Information Administration, Department of Energy, *Statistics and Trends of Energy Supply, Demand and Prices*, vol. III, DOE/EIA-0036/3 (Washington, D.C., DOE, 1977).

A slow, general rise in imports as a share of the GNP does not necessarily pose a problem: it would not happen if it could not be paid for. But an increased dependency on specific commodities could weaken the economy or its strategic position if the commodity is essential for the country, if no reasonably priced substitutes exist, and if foreign suppliers are capable of determining the quantity (and hence the price) of what is sold to the United States. It is difficult to think of commodities that meet all these criteria simultaneously. Either there are multiple suppliers so that collusion is difficult, or domestic sources or substitutes could be developed at reasonable cost and within a reasonable period, or existing stockpiles would allow the United States to forgo purchases for longer than exporters can forgo revenues.[10] The exceptions, of course, are petroleum and natural gas, as recent history so vividly indicates. These commodities, then, merit particular attention.

The situation with respect to petroleum is particularly dramatic. In 1965 the United States imported 21 percent of its liquid petroleum requirements; just ten years later, this figure was close to 35 percent, and if the base case assumptions prevail, it could reach 77 percent by the turn of the century. During the next twenty-five years, this percentage would fall somewhat because rising world petroleum prices and falling costs of producing synthetics would stimulate domestic production of liquid fuels from coal, tars, and shale (see chapter 5). But given the time lags in-

[10] See Stern and Tims (1976) and chapter 4 of this volume.

DH				DHP1				DHP2			
1985	2000	2010	2025	1985	2000	2010	2025	1985	2000	2010	2025
24.6	26.2	41.5	57.2	24.3	20.2	28.5	36.5	36.4	71.8	66.0	38.1
1.8	0	6.9	13.0	1.7	0.0	2.5	8.6	8.0	20.6	20.1	13.5
26.4	26.2	48.4	70.2	26.0	20.2	31.0	45.1	44.8	92.4	86.1	51.6
37.2	42.2	38.1	40.6	41.4	54.5	57.4	54.9	25.5	34.7	45.0	36.4
2.2	0.0	5.1	5.8	2.0	0.0	4.0	7.5	4.5	8.5	7.5	5.8
39.4	42.2	43.2	46.4	43.4	54.5	61.4	62.4	30.0	43.2	52.5	42.2
52.0	49.8	59.3	57.3	51.5	42.6	47.5	44.5	68.8	86.5	71.0	44.3
7.6	0	22.0	33.7	7.2	0	9.2	25.2	31.7	58.2	49.8	32.8

[a] One quad = 10^{15} BTU = 173 million barrels of crude oil equivalent.
[b] Requirements for liquids and gases from all sources including conversion losses.

volved in bringing such plants onstream, plus the expected growth in demand during the period, the United States would still have to import more than 66 percent of its liquid fuels in 2025. This result occurs despite the assumption, built into this case, of a substantial shift into nuclear and other forms of energy. After 2025, however, the petroleum import dependency rate would fall rapidly; indeed, as chapter 5 indicates, there is even a possibility that the United States would begin to export synthetic fuels during 2030–35.

The situation with respect to gaseous fuels is similar but does not occur as soon. The United States can take care of a larger share of its requirements from domestic sources for a longer period, and world production of natural gas is likely to peak later. As a result, the stimulus for production of synthetics does not become significant until close to the end of the fifty-year time horizon.

One of the main characteristics of the difficult case is the introduction of a program meant to reduce energy import dependency to more acceptable levels. This program involves subsidies to stimulate more rapid production from domestic sources than would otherwise be the case and stockpiles to provide a minimum of six months' supply in case of an embargo, both starting in 1980. The program does not include efforts to raise domestic prices or to induce conservation legislatively to a greater extent than already built into the base case.

The benefits of such a policy can be observed by comparing the base case (EL) with the difficult case (DH) in table 3–6 (see also figure

3–3).[11] The maximum effect on imports would be felt in about the year 2000, when oil imports would be 50 rather than 77 percent of domestic requirements and there would be virtually no natural gas imports; thereafter, these dependency rates would begin growing again, however, particularly dramatically in the case of natural gas, until sometime after 2025 when domestic capacity to produce synthetics is sufficiently enlarged.

The costs of this policy of reducing imports can be seen in table 3–7. The annual costs (ignoring the costs and carrying charges of the stockpile) would grow to $10.5 billion in 2000. After 2010, they would begin to fall as international oil and gas prices rise and the costs of synthetic production decline. Compared to a GNP of $2.9 trillion and a military budget of $165 billion in 2010, these subsidies do not appear excessively large. But neither are the benefits, particularly so far as petroleum is concerned. Even in scenario DHP1 (a case in which petroleum and natural gas prices rise continuously and the cost of producing synthetics does not fall over time), dependence on imported oil is not reduced below 42 percent in 2000. The program could be expanded, but only by increasing the likelihood of a capital shortage, inflation, and a further slowdown in economic growth.

There are a variety of reasons for these results. In particular, they reflect our assumptions about the effects of the subsidy in stimulating more rapid extraction of remaining supplies of petroleum and natural gas, (for example, from offshore fields and secondary recovery), the specific patterns of exhaustion of these sources, the pattern of expansion of synthetic capacity, and numerous judgments about costs and prices (all discussed in chapter 5). Needless to say, many of these judgments may prove far from the mark. But if they are anywhere near correct, a subsidy program to rapidly develop a synthetic fuels industry using currently available technologies should be approached with caution. At the present time, a better alternative may be to subsidize research and development, including perhaps one or two pilot plants of minimum commercial size, and to place greater emphasis on efforts to substitute other energy forms for liquids in consumption as well as on across-the-board conservation.

11 Although these two cases are identical in most relevant respects—in particular their assumptions about price, legislated conservation, and technological developments—scenario DH incorporates a higher growth rate in energy demand. This tends to overstate the reduction in imports as a percentage of the GNP, understate the reduction in oil and gas imports as a percentage of requirements, and overstate the costs of the stockpile and production subsidy program. But as will be seen below when considering the impact of different rates of growth in population and economic activity on these dependency ratios, the extent of these biases are not so great as to change the general conclusions.

Table 3–7. Cost of Energy Stockpiles and Production Subsidies in Scenarios DH and DHP1

Scenario and cost item	1980	1985	2000	2025
Scenario DH				
Stockpiles of petroleum and natural gas[a]				
Quantity (quads)	11.5	11.3	10.9	27.9
Value (billion 1975$)	25.9	25.4	24.5	81.5
Production subsidies (billions 1975$)				
Annual	0	6.5	10.5	0
Cumulative (1980–2010)				
Coal to gas				140.0
Coal to oil				12.4
Shale				73.3
Total				225.7
Scenario DHP1				
Stockpiles of petroleum and natural gas[a]				
Quantity (quads)	11.5	10.7	8.4	17.9
Value (billion 1975$)	25.9	28.4	29.4	106.5
Production subsidies (billion 1975$)				
Annual	0	10.9	15.4	
Cumulative (1980–2010)				
Coal to gas				210.0
Coal to oil				18.6
Shale				120.9
Total				349.5

[a] Over and above normal commercial inventories.

The effects of changes in the import share of the GNP as population and economic growth rates change are also of interest. Figure 3–3 compares these percentages for the DH, DL, FH, and FL runs, which differ from each other only with respect to these two variables. The larger the overall size of the economy, the smaller are imports as a percentage of the GNP; because larger economies tend to be more self-sufficient than smaller ones, this result is not unreasonable. But the situation is reversed with respect to imports of oil, gas, and other minerals approaching exhaustion within this time span. The following comparison of oil and gas (imports as a percentage of requirements) for 2025 is indicative of the relationship of these imports to the size of the economy:

	Percentage of requirements			
Import	DH	DL	FH	FL
Oil	58.2	57.5	57.1	55.8
Gas	35.3	32.3	31.6	21.4

The increase in these percentages as the size of the economy increases would be greater were it not for the fact that the capacity to produce synthetics also increases with the size of the economy; here, we assume this capacity is proportional to GNP across runs. In absolute terms, of course, differences between these runs are more significant. In contrast to oil imports in 1975 of 6 million barrels per day and gas imports of 0.4 in equivalent units, the 2025 figures are:

	Million barrels a day or equivalent			
Import	DH	DL	FH	FL
Oil	29	23	22	17
Gas	7	5	4	3

Nuclear Options

Two levels of restraints on the use of nuclear power were considered. The first, incorporated into scenario DH, eliminates the use of plutonium recycling even for light-water reactors and assumes that the United States will not use breeder technology. The second, incorporated into scenario DHNU, permits nuclear electric facilities under construction to be completed and existing plants to be used but prohibits additional construction or replacement. This results in an increase of nuclear plants [assuming an average of 1,000 megawatts (MW) each] from twenty-three in 1975 and fifty-eight in 1980 to seventy-eight in 2000, and a reduction to nearly zero by 2020. Judging the overall impact of these scenarios requires bringing together and considering all the effects involved: economic, resource, and environmental, a task left to the summary chapter; here, the concern is solely with the economic impact.

For the first of these cases, the economic impact cannot be very large. On the one side, eliminating the breeder reactor will increase the cost of nuclear fuel. Not only would more uranium have to be used, but the United States would have to turn sooner to imports and lower-grade domestic sources. As a consequence, the cost of nuclear fuel as a percentage of electricity-generating costs would increase from about 9 percent today to about 30 percent in 2025 (table 5–11). On the other side, capital costs should be less, because best judgments today suggest that these costs are likely to prove higher for the breeder reactor than for other types. Although the net effect of these two changes is uncertain, the delivered cost of electricity probably will not change much.

To reflect this situation in the model, the current and capital account coefficients in relevant sectors were adjusted, but the level of GNP and consumer prices was left unchanged. The effects of these changes on specific sectors and on the environment are discussed in chapters 5 and 7.

A phaseout of all nuclear power could be more serious, particularly for those sections of the country where nuclear power is now cheaper than coal-fired electricity. The most likely substitute fuel for producing electricity is coal, which the United States has in relative abundance. But to expand its use would increase electricity costs principally for transportation to move the coal from the mine to generating plants that now operate with nuclear fuel and for additional pollution-abatement equipment.[12] There would also be some increase in the cost of coal as more is produced, but not, it is estimated, until after 2010 or so; and there would, of course, be some savings from the elimination of investments in reactors and related capital for mining, waste disposal, and so on.

As indicated in chapter 5, the best judgment is that the busbar cost of electricity in the Northeast, Southeast, and California, where nuclear power is currently the more economical alternative, would be 4.5 percent higher if this alternative were not available in 2000 and 73 percent higher in 2025; the latter figure is equivalent to a 57 percent increase in the delivered cost. For the country as a whole, the impact is significantly less: the busbar cost would be 1.5 percent higher in 2000 and 22 percent in 2025, and the delivered cost in 2025 would be 17 percent greater.

Judged this way, the economic costs of phasing out nuclear power, though significant, are smaller for the nation as a whole than one might expect. Additional private investment expenditures associated with converting power plants to coal begin increasing in 1980 and reach $96.7 billion per year in 2025, which makes the total investment costs for electricity about 50 percent higher than in scenario DH.[13] Approximately half of these expenditures are for additional production facilities, and the other half are for extra pollution-abatement equipment. Assuming, as is done here, that the full-employment GNP level is the same in both cases, resources to cover these additional investments must come from private and public consumption and the investment required to support this consumption.[14] The net effect, shown in table 3–8, is a reduction in private consumption plus government expenditures of $55 billion, or $150 per capita, in 2025. Investment, of course, increases by less than the additional cost

[12] Sufficient additional abatement equipment was added to ensure that pollution damages from associated residuals are equal in scenario DH and DHNU. In the case of nuclear power, a comparison of abatement and safety equipment is figured into the design of the plant and hence does not appear as a separate figure.

[13] The discounted value of this additional expenditure stream through 2025 is $192.7 billion if discounted back to 1985, using a 9 percent rate.

[14] The mechanism for implementing these changes in SEAS/RFF is to lower personal disposable income. As this is done, the demand for state and local government services also declines because demands for many of these services, as well as private consumption, are a function of disposable income.

Table 3–8. The Economy in Scenarios DH and DHNU for Selected Years

GNP component	1975		1985	2000		2025	
	Actual	DH	DHª	DH	DHNUᵇ	DH	DHNUᵇ
GNP (billions of 1971$)	1,192	1,108	1,743	2,924	2,919	6,212	6,196
Private consumption	770	685	1,054	1,818	1,813	3,951	3,905
Private investment	138	164	333	508	509	1,114	1,151
Government	261	237	355	593	592	1,146	1,137
Net exports	23	21	1	5	5	1	3
Percentage of GNP							
Private consumption	64.6	61.3	60.5	62.2	62.1	63.6	63.0
Private investment	11.6	15.1	19.1	17.4	17.4	17.9	18.6
Government	21.9	21.6	20.4	20.3	20.3	18.5	18.4
Net exports	1.9	2.0	—	0.1	—	—	—

ª Estimates for scenario DHNU are almost identical to those of scenario DH.
ᵇ The total GNP differs slightly between Scenarios DH and DHNU because GNP targeting is stopped when the model produces a GNP that is within 1 percent of the desired level. This is done to reduce computation costs.

of the shift to coal because of declines in other sectors.[15] The aggregate economic effects of not using nuclear power might have been even less had we allowed some environmental deterioration to occur and included additional adjustments in the analysis. In particular, some adjustments to the higher cost of electricity and more concerted shifts toward the development and use of solar and other options—which undoubtedly would go hand in hand with a decision to forego nuclear development—would have further dampened these effects. The economic repercussions would have been smaller yet if the nuclear phaseout case were run in conjunction with any of the other scenarios. In the base case, for example, which incorporates smaller growth rates in population and labor productivity and no restrictions on petroleum imports, the requirements for nuclear power are 55 percent less (see table 5–19).[16]

On the other hand, the value of forgone consumption and government services between 1985 and 2025, discounted to 1985 at 9 percent, is $113 billion, not an insignificant figure by present standards. In addition, we are assuming that sufficient savings will be forthcoming to finance the additional investment requirements; though these requirements, in themselves, are not large, they come on top of the unprecedented level of investments the other scenarios require. Finally, the burden on specific regions that are forced to substitute coal for nuclear fuel, if not offset by other policies, would be substantially higher than the national average. Thus, such a policy would make little sense unless it had substantial advantages on other grounds. These issues will be addressed in subsequent chapters.

Oil Prices

Although the effects of different oil price assumptions have been discussed in passing, their importance warrants more detailed treatment. Chapter 5 explains how energy prices were projected and used in the model. Suffice it to say here that such price changes influence the model

---

[15] It might be noted that we have not included scenario DHNU on figure 3–1 because the scale is too small to distinguish it from scenario DH. Investment (defined to include public construction) as a percentage of the GNP for this case is 19.47 instead of 19.38 percent in 2000 and would slowly rise to 20.06 percent as compared with 19.42 percent in 2025.

[16] Similar conclusions have been reached in other recent studies of the nuclear–coal tradeoff, even when a more rapid phaseout of nuclear power has been assumed. See, for example, the papers in Hitch (1977).

through judgmentally determined elasticities and time lags that are used
to change unit demands for fuels by different sectors of the economy and
different final demand purchasers.[17]

The assumptions of the standard case imply that the world price of
oil in constant dollars will remain at its 1975 price of $12 per barrel until
about 2010, after which production can no longer keep up with demand
without an increase in price. During the next twenty years, the price might
rise to a peak some 60 percent higher, but it would eventually fall back
to the long-run cost of producing synthetic liquids and gases, which by
that time would have come down into the $14 to $16 range. If, on the
other hand, there were more severe constraints on production, no fall over
time in the costs of producing synthetic fuels, and a somewhat higher income elasticity and a lower price elasticity of demand for energy—the
assumptions of scenario DHP1—the price of petroleum would slowly rise
from $12 to $35 per barrel by 2025 (all prices in 1975 dollars) and then,
during the next ten years, fall to about $24 as the capacity to produce
substitutes expands.

The quantitative effects on the U.S. economy are difficult to judge.
If the high investment requirements (figure 3–1) and the more costly
imports (see figure 3–3) of scenario DHP1 can be financed, an implicit
assumption of this analysis, the depressing effects on consumption per
capita (see figure 3–2) and GNP (table 3–9) are likely to be modest. If
they cannot, the GNP and eventually consumption per capita will be
lower, quite possibly by substantial margins in later years if the numerical
exercise of limiting investments to 18 percent of the GNP is any guide.
Note, however, that this analysis fails to take account of the fact that the
United States has sufficient coal, shale, and tar sands to become eventually
a net *exporter* of fuels in the form of synthetic liquids and gases. But there
are too many unknowns to warrant a guess about quantitative impacts of
these changes.

Scenario DHP2, a case in which the price of petroleum in real terms
falls from $12 to $6 by 1985, is included for its heuristic value. As chapter

---

[17] Second-round effects—that is, the effect of increased energy prices on the
prices and demands for other goods and services—have not been taken into account
(except in a general way through assumptions about the effects on capital requirements and labor productivity as explained in chapter 2). In scenarios in which oil
prices in real terms remain constant until 2010, the neglect of second-round effects
is of little consequence until close to the end of the fifty-year time horizon because
of time lags built into the analysis. In cases in which oil prices increase (decrease)
for a significant portion of the period, this omission introduces a slight overestimate
(underestimate) of demand for nonenergy goods and services.

Table 3-9. The Economy in Scenarios DH, DHP1, and DHP2 for Selected Years

GNP component	1975		1985			2000			2010			2025		
	Actual	DH	DH	DHP1	DHP2	DH	DHP1	DHP2	DH	DHP1	DHP2	DH	DHP1	DHP2
GNP (billions of 1971$)	1,192	1,110	1,743	1,743	1,743	2,924	2,886	3,038	4,049	3,985	4,163	6,212	6,075	6,167
Private consumption	770	680	1,054	1,047	1,095	1,818	1,780	1,915	2,536	2,472	2,621	3,951	3,826	3,947
Private investment	138	168	333	343	286	508	521	520	720	738	744	1,114	1,139	1,076
Government	261	240	355	352	364	593	580	613	783	765	797	1,146	1,109	1,135
Net exports	23	21	1	1	−2	5	5	−10	10	10	1	1	1	9
Percentage of GNP														
Private consumption	64.6	61.3	60.5	60.1	62.8	62.2	61.7	63.0	62.6	62.0	63.0	63.6	63.0	64.0
Private investment	11.6	15.1	19.1	19.7	16.4	17.4	18.0	17.1	17.8	18.5	17.9	17.9	18.7	17.4
Government	21.6	21.6	20.4	20.2	20.9	20.3	20.1	20.2	19.3	19.2	10.7	18.5	18.3	18.4
Net exports	1.9	2.0	—	—	—	0.1	0.2	−0.3	0.3	0.3	—	—	—	0.1

5 indicates, the price could not remain at the $6 level for more than another ten to fifteen years, after which it would rise rapidly, reaching perhaps $44 before being forced down again by synthetic production. Because investment and import requirements would be significantly lower in this scenario than in DH and DHP1 between 1980 and 2000, the intermediate-run effects as well as the long-run effects—once export earnings from the production of synthetics is factored in—are likely to be positive for the U.S. economy. Economic growth rates for countries that do not have good feedstocks for producing synthetics would also be somewhat higher between 1980 and 2000, but they would be substantially lower during the next twenty-five years. Indeed, for some countries these rates might even become negative. If not mitigated by other factors, this latter period could range from serious to disastrous for many countries, and possibly for world peace. Given the disruptions to the world economy this course of events implies, this scenario is not one that ought to be preferred by the United States or any other country with adequate alternative sources of energy.

Environmental Policy

We are concerned primarily with two environmental policy packages: a strict enforcement case in which existing and prospective federal regulations are fully enforced with no slippage, and a case in which these standards are relaxed somewhat, permitting some slippage both in implementation dates and in control levels. Chapter 7 considers the consequences of additional cases, in particular one that introduces uniform standards that would minimize the sum of national control and damage costs. To assess these consequences, we estimate both the benefits and the costs of pollution control and resulting levels of environmental quality. This chapter is concerned only with the narrowly defined economic consequences of these policy alternatives. In particular, what economic costs do these policies impose on the national economy and on specific sectors that must bear the brunt of the costs?

In chapter 7, abatement costs are defined to include costs of controlling air pollution (from stationary and mobile sources) and water pollution and of treating municipal waste water, including costs of collector and trunk sewer lines, treatment facilities, and combined sewer overflow facilities. These activities are the subjects of the benefit–cost analysis contained in that chapter. Here, the costs of water cooling for electric utilities, containment, and storage of radioactive waste products from power generation, solid waste disposal, and land reclamation are also considered.[18]

Table 3–10 presents figures for abatement costs broken down by these categories for scenarios DH and DHRE.[19] Even in DHRE, expenditures would grow from $13 billion in 1975 to almost $135 billion in 2025 (both in 1971 dollars). Although $135 billion is a large figure by today's standards, it is only 2.1 percent of the GNP in 2025. Even in the more stringent case (DH), these expenditures are only 3.1 percent of GNP.

Total costs expressed as a percentage of the GNP for other scenarios are presented in figure 3–4.[20] The scenario with the highest level of abatement expenditures is DHNU, the nuclear phaseout case. As a percentage of the GNP, for example, these expenditures reach 3.6 percent in 2025. Taken at face value, this suggests that the environmental problems of coal are more costly to control than those of nuclear power. This is somewhat misleading because most environmental controls associated with coal are counted separately from other investment and operating expenses, whereas some of those associated with nuclear power are incorporated into the design of the plant. Nevertheless, the overall level of investment (which includes both production and abatement capital) is higher in the nuclear phaseout scenario (compare DHNU with DH in table 3–8). Changes in assumptions about population and economic growth, holding policy constant (scenarios DL, FL, and FH), appear to alter abatement expenditures more or less in proportion to the size of the economy. As percentages of GNP, then, abatement expenditures are not appreciably affected by growth rate differences.

Figure 3–4 also indicates that abatement expenditures are not spread smoothly over time. In scenario DH, for example, as a percentage of the GNP, they rise from 1975 to a peak in 1979 of more than 2.6 percent,

---

[18] Left out of both chapters is an estimate of enforcement costs, that is, the legal fees, monitoring costs and other administrative expenses incurred in implementing and enforcing environmental regulations (as well as in attempting to resist such implementation and enforcement).

[19] See Table 7–1 for the definitions of strict and relaxed enforcement built into these cases.

[20] This figure presents resource costs, that is, operating costs plus the costs of the capital put in place in a given year, whereas table 3–8 presents annualized costs, that is, operating costs plus capital consumption allowances in a given year. Resource costs are more useful to indicate whether expenditures tend to be bunched up in certain years, and annualized costs are useful to indicate the general burden of these costs over a number of years.

Table 3–10. Annualized Abatement Costs in Scenarios DH and DHRE for Selected Years (billions of 1971 dollars)

	Actual[a] 1975	DH				DHRE			
		1975	1985	2000	2025	1975	1985	2000	2025
Air pollution	5.3	4.1	15.7	24.5	52.1	3.7	12.4	19.9	43.5
(Mobile)	⋯	(1.2)	(8.0)	(13.3)	(14.5)	(1.2)	(8.0)	(12.8)	(12.7)
(Electric utilities)	⋯	(1.1)	(3.9)	(4.2)	(6.9)	(1.0)	(1.6)	(1.8)	(6.1)
Water pollution	3.9	9.3	31.4	44.6	131.8	7.7	18.4	30.0	83.8
Industrial point sources	1.8	5.2	15.1	22.1	94.0	4.8	9.4	16.8	63.1
(Electric utilities)	0.1	0.3	0.7	1.0	2.7	0.2	0.4	0.5	0.9
Municipal waste water	1.9	3.7	12.7	17.5	31.3	2.8	7.9	10.3	16.2
(Urban runoff)	⋯	⋯	(2.3)	(4.6)	(9.6)	⋯	(0.9)	(2.8)	(5.3)
Nonpoint sources[a]	⋯	⋯	2.3	3.0	3.6	⋯	0.2	1.4	2.3
(Agricultural sediment)	⋯	⋯	(1.1)	(1.1)	(1.3)	⋯	(0)	(0)	(0)
(Construction sediment)	(0.2)	⋯	(0.4)	(0.4)	(0.6)	⋯	(0.2)	(0.4)	(0.6)
(Forestry sediment)	⋯	⋯	(0.1)	(0.3)	(0.6)	⋯	(0)	(0.2)	(0.6)
(Acid mine sediment)	⋯	⋯	(0.8)	(1.2)	(1.2)	⋯	(0)	(0.8)	(1.2)
Thermal pollution	⋯	0.4	1.3	2.0	2.9	0.1	0.9	1.5	2.2

Solid waste[b]	3.3	0.6	1.2	1.9	3.3	0.6	1.2	1.9	3.3
Sulfur sludge	…	0	0.5	0.4	0	0	0.3	0.3	0
Land reclamation	…	0.4	0.3	0.4	0.9	0.4	0.3	0.4	0.9
Radiation	…	0.1	0.2	1.4	3.0	0.1	0.2	1.4	3.0
(Onsite)	…	(—)	(—)	(0.1)	(0.1)	(—)	(—)	(0.1)	(0.1)
(Offsite)	…	(—)	(0.2)	(1.3)	(2.9)	(0.1)	(0.2)	(1.3)	(2.8)
Total	12.5	14.5	49.5	73.2	191.1	12.5	32.8	53.9	134.5
Percentage of GNP	1.1	1.3	2.8	2.5	3.1	1.1	1.9	1.9	2.1

Source: Figures in column 1 adapted from Segel and Dreiling, "Pollution Abatement and Control Expenditures, 1972–76," *Survey of Current Business* vol. 58, no. 2 (February 1978). The numbers listed here omit expenditures for regulation, monitoring, research, and development and are annualized by multiplying capital account and durable goods by 0.12 and deflated to 1971$ using the GNP deflator.

Differences between projected 1975 and actual 1975 arise because (a) the model begins implementing the assumed policy prior to 1975, (b) there has been substantially more slippage from regulations in the case of industrial and municipal water pollution control than we expected or built into DHRE, (c) the model's coverage differs from that of the Segel-Dreiling study (for example, solid waste is more narrowly defined, but land reclamation and radiation-related expenditures are included).

[a] Costs for 1985 and thereafter are incremental to those existing in 1975, the value for which is unknown.

[b] Projections include only urban wastes. The Segel-Dreiling figures include solid waste disposal costs for manufacturing. The Segel-Dreiling estimates for state and local governments ($1,171.6 million) should be comparable to our projections.

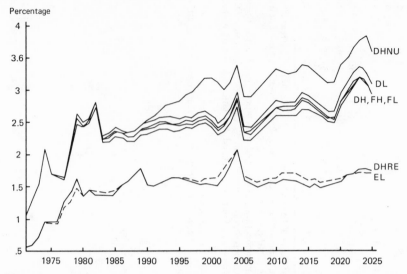

Figure 3–4. Abatement resource costs as a percentage of the GNP. Actual figures for 1971–75 are indicated by the lower line. The 1975 figure differs from that indicated in table 3–10 because these are resource, not annualized, costs.

and they remain high until 1983 when they fall to 2.2 percent. This period, during which the majority of the legislated standards must be met, involves the most rapid rate of expansion of abatement expenditures during the fifty-year period covered by this study, and these expenditures explain a substantial portion of the increased investment requirements for this period. Thereafter, abatement expenditures grow more or less along a trend line except for peaks above trend in 2003, 2013, and 2023, and troughs in 2005 and 2018; the timing of additional regulations and equipment replacement cycles accounts for these fluctuations.

These percentages never become so large that they would be difficult to finance in the aggregate, but their impact on individual sectors could be quite substantial. This can be seen in table 3–11, which assumes that legislated standards will be met by certain dates and that the capital for this purpose will be put in place over a four-year period prior to these dates.

The sharp sectoral impacts of abatement requirements is apparent in the year-to-year investment expenditures for some sectors. Abatement investment requirements in the industrial chemicals sector, for example, are likely to reach a series of peaks during the next twenty-five years, following the pattern shown in figure 3–5A. Given strict enforcement,

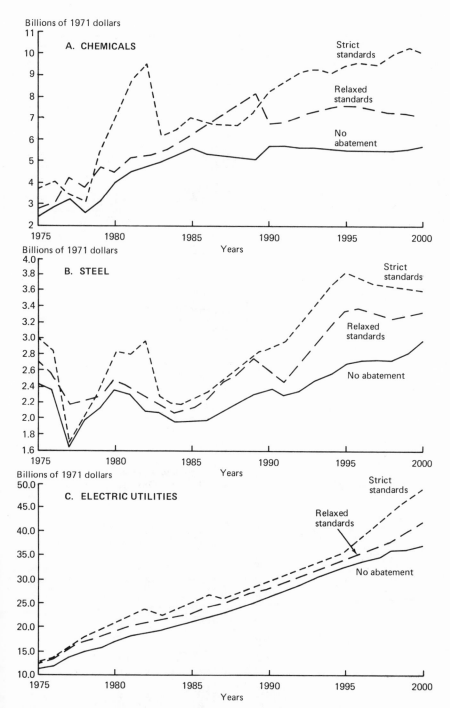

Figure 3–5. Investments for selected industrial sectors, Scenario EL, 1975–2000. *A*, chemicals; *B*, steel; and *C*, electric utilities.

Table 3–11. Abatement Investment as a Percentage of Total Investment for Selected Purposes, Base Case, 1976–2025

Industry	Control standard[a]	1976–80	1981–85	1986–90	1991–95	1996–2000	2001–05	2006–10	2011–15	2016–20	2021–25
Average for the economy[b]	R	3.4	2.6	3.1	2.8	3.1	4.4	3.6	4.2	3.9	4.3
	S	4.8	4.9	3.7	4.7	5.9	5.9	6.5	7.9	7.3	8.1
Transportation[c]	R	1.4	2.6	2.4	2.3	2.2	2	1.9	1.8	1.8	1.8
	S	2.3	2.6	2.6	2.5	2.2	2	1.8	1.7	1.7	1.7
Electric utilities	R	10.7	9.3	8.1	5.4	8.2	13.3	7.1	6.3	5.6	5.4
	S	15	16.6	10.7	8.8	19.8	15.2	9.5	7.8	6.9	8.3
Municipal water treatment[d]	R	27	21.9	1.2	0.7	1.1	1.4	1.7	1.5	12	7.2
	S	34.8	27.4	11.6	10.6	10.8	10.9	11	21.7	17.7	10.8
Industrial chemicals	R	21	9.2	27.5	22.1	24.7	27.6	31.9	33.6	36.7	42.3
	S	31	33.9	26.4	37.8	44	38.9	49.3	57.1	56.1	56
Petroleum refining	R	24.9	8.4	20.2	35.8	26.9	80.8	51	60.6	47.4	50.6
	S	28.6	22	27	49.6	38.6	87	67.2	68.5	66.7	80.1
Steel	R	10.7	5.9	13	15.3	16	12.5	14.2	25	22.1	23.3
	S	12	16.8	14.7	27.4	24.6	18.5	30.4	46.3	40.1	40.3

Aluminum	R	9.4	4.4	7.5	11.2	20.9	16.7	14.2	14	18.4	15.6
	S	10.1	8.3	11.3	18.6	28.5	22.8	20.8	22.1	26.3	23.3
Cement, concrete, and gypsum	R	14.7	4	12.4	14.1	15.5	17.8	17.5	30.6	31.7	28.7
	S	13.3	10.8	20.1	26.9	25.6	26.2	37.3	50.8	51.7	47.6
Paving plus asphalt	R	75.6	33	48.4	98.5	94	34	96.3	95	100	98.9
	S	78.6	49.3	65	99.1	95.8	49	98.6	97.6	100	99.6
Pulp mills	R	28.7	11.8	18.6	62.2	40.5	27.2	56.4	85.3	59.2	57
	S	28.1	19.5	41.2	81.5	54.8	46.8	82.6	92.8	73.7	75.4
Grain mill products	R	38.1	9.3	22.4	47.7	36.9	32.6	69.6	62	50.5	69.4
	S	39.5	23.4	30.9	60	47.7	49.6	85.1	78.2	71.5	85.5
Grain handling	R	9.4	2	14.9	10.4	10.1	14.7	7.4	26.6	14.9	20.8
	S	9.8	5.6	23.8	12.8	18.6	18.8	18.4	46.8	26	43

[a] R = relaxed pollution control standards; S = strict pollution control standards.

[b] Total abatement investment as percent of total investment in the economy.

[c] Total investment for this sector is the value of all transport equipment produced in the indicated period plus investment for abatement.

[d] Total investment for this sector is the expenditures on water treatment to meet the standards in force up to 1972 plus investment for controls above 1972 levels.

the 1976 peak occurs because of efforts to apply "best practicable technology" (BPT) standards; the 1982 peak happens when this sector moves from BPT to "best available technology" (BAT) standards on all equipment; and the expenditure increases starting in 1990 reflect replacement of earlier abatement investments plus the cost of converting to coal for process heat. Under relaxed enforcement, the 1976 peak is delayed until 1979; the 1982 peak is shifted to 1989, and it is smaller because only new plants are involved; and the increases starting after 1990 also are delayed and smaller. The large increase in abatement investments after 1990 results from the assumption that both the strict and relaxed standards will have to be upgraded over 1985 levels by 2000 and that this turn of the screw will be quite expensive.

Steel industry investments, shown in figure 3–5B, have a similar pattern. In this case, the increases after 1990 are accentuated by the upgrading and replacement of the large investment made for air pollution control equipment prior to 1975. Similar investment patterns for electric utilities are less dramatic but involve very large expenditures for pollution abatement.

Had abatement investments been added along with other investments in the normal course of expanding capacity, a less erratic and more easily managed pattern would have been observed. But the benefits to companies of delaying implementation as long as possible are so large that this outcome is as unlikely in the future as it has been in the past. Indeed, given loopholes built into current legislation and judging from recent trends, we are likely to observe substantially greater delays in implementing standards than those built into scenario DHRE.[21] To avoid this, new ways will have to be found to force compliance or to help industries over these transition problems.

Conclusions

This chapter has three purposes: to lay the economic foundation for estimating resource requirements and environmental pressures, to

---

[21] One such loophole involves grandfather clauses that exempt certain categories of plants in operation from having to meet more stringent standards in the future. The result is likely to be some delay in retiring such plants, which would reduce short-run costs but leave the sector in a less favorable competitive position in the long run. In sectors, such as electric utilities, in which future regulations require expensive stack-scrubbing equipment, it could pay a company to delay retiring old plants for substantial periods of time, possibly more than a decade.

indicate the economic consequences of changes in major determinants, and to search for economic problems that might be inherent in the assumptions of the various scenarios, problems that might be so severe as to invalidate one or more of the scenarios. To serve the first purpose, projections were developed of aggregate economic output and its composition.

The second purpose was accomplished by comparing the economic results of applying different scenarios. The most important long-run determinants of per capita GNP and consumption are population and labor productivity. Of the two, labor productivity plays the more important role. There are two reasons for this. First, although the immediate impact of a smaller population is a decline in the denominator of the ratio of GNP to population, the longer-run impact involves a reduction in the numerator as well (because of declines in the labor force); accordingly, a change in population size will have a smaller impact on GNP per capita than an equal percentage change in labor productivity, which affects only the numerator. Second, labor productivity was assumed to change more than population during the fifty-year period being studied. Some compositional changes were also noted; though these are significant for some individual commodities, the effects on broad aggregates are small and sometimes ambiguous.

Scenarios involving policy differences indicate that these changes have less effect in the long run than population and productivity on broad aggregates and more effect on timing and on specific, sector-related variables, particularly in the shorter run. Even in the short run, it is somewhat surprising to observe how small the macroeconomic effects sometimes are—or stated differently, how large and drastic a policy change must be to have very sizable economic impacts. This is certainly the case with respect to policies aimed at reducing petroleum imports and at eventually eliminating the use of nuclear power. Large changes in the world petroleum price could have more profound impacts, but even here the effects are smaller than we would have guessed before undertaking the analysis.

The principal economic problem that was identified is one that cuts across all scenarios, though it tends to be worse in the more difficult of the cases investigated. This has to do with the sizable run-up in investment requirements as a consequence of efforts to adjust to energy price increases and to complete the emplacement of adequate environmental controls. These requirements could be sufficiently large, particularly in the eighties, to exacerbate inflationary tendencies and slow down the overall rate of economic growth. For the purpose of projecting resource and environmental pressures, the analysis will proceed on the assumption that such a slowdown will not occur. In the concluding chapter, after other problems with these growth rates have been identified, this issue will be reexamined.

References

BLS. See U.S. Bureau of Labor Statistics.

Bureau of Mines. 1974. "Reference Macro Projections and Base Data," for use in 1975 edition of *Mineral Facts and Problems.*

Council of Economic Advisors (CEA). 1977. *Economic Report* (Washington, D.C., GPO).

Data Resources, Inc. 1976. "The Economic Outlook Trend 1975–1990," *U.S. Long-Term Bulletin* (New York, Data Resources, Inc.).

Espenshade, T. J., and W. J. Serow, eds. 1978. *The Economic Consequences of Slowing Population Growth* (New York, Academic Press).

FEA. See U.S. Federal Energy Administration.

Ford Foundation. 1973. *A Time to Choose* (Cambridge, Mass., Ballinger) p. 498 (historic growth path).

Hitch, Charles J., ed. 1977. *Modeling Energy–Economy Interactions: Five Approaches* (Washington, D.C., Resources for the Future).

INFORUM. 1976. University of Maryland, Bureau of Business and Economic Research, Computer Print-out for January 1976 Meeting, College Park, Md.

National Planning Association. 1976. *Looking Ahead* vol. 2, no. 2 (April) (Washington, D.C., NPA).

OBERS. See U.S. Department of Commerce.

Rasche, R., and J. Tatom. 1977. "Energy Resources and Potential GNP," *Federal Reserve Bank of Saint Louis Review* (June) (Saint Louis, Mo.).

Ridker, Ronald G. 1978. "The Effects of Slowing Population Growth on Long Run Economic Growth in the U.S. During the Next Half Century," in T. J. Espenshade and W. J. Serow, eds., *The Economic Consequences of Slowing Population Growth* (New York, Academic Press).

————, William D. Watson, Jr., and Adele Shapanka. 1977. "Economic, Energy and Environmental Consequences of Alternative Energy Regimes: An Application of the RFF/SEAS Modeling System," in Charles J. Hitch, ed., *Modeling Energy-Economy Interactions: Five Approaches* (Washington, D.C., Resources for the Future).

Segel, Frank W., Frederick J. Dreiling. 1978. "Pollution Abatement and Control Expenditures, 1972–1976," *Survey of Current Business* vol. 58, no. 2 (February) (Washington, D.C., GPO).

Stern, E., and W. Tims. 1976. "The Relative Bargaining Strengths of the Developing Countries," in Ronald G. Ridker, ed., *Changing Resource Problems of the Fourth World* (Washington, D.C., Resources for the Future).

U.S. Bureau of Labor Statistics (BLS). 1976. "Projections to 1980 and 1985," *Monthly Labor Review* (March) Basic Series.

U.S. Federal Energy Administration (FEA). 1976. *National Energy Outlook,* FEA N-75/713 (February) (Washington, D.C., GPO).

U.S. Department of Commerce. 1972. "1972 OBERS Projections, Regional Activities in the U.S. Series E Population," *Concepts, Methodology, and Summary Data* (Washington, D.C., GPO).

Wharton (Wharton EFA, Inc.). 1976. "Wharton Annual and Industry Forecasting Model, July 20, 1976" (Philadelphia, Pa.).

4

Nonfuel Minerals

This chapter on nonfuel minerals and the next on energy concern the issue of long-term resource adequacy. Are resources likely to be available during the next fifty years in the quantities necessary to satisfy projected demands without substantial increases in prices? If not, what price increases are likely to be necessary to close the gap between supply and demand, and what are the effects of those increases likely to be? In addition, how sensitive are these answers to different assumptions about population and economic growth rates and, especially in the case of energy, certain policy and technological options?

Resource shortages can occur for several reasons. Ore deposits may become depleted. There may be restrictions for environmental or other reasons on using some deposits. Investment in capacity to produce from usable, high-quality deposits may be inadequate. Short-term disruptions, such as strikes or business cycles, may occur. Government or cartel actions may impose constraints on trade. The emphasis here is on longer term reasons for shortages, in particular, the possibility of depletion. Accordingly, year-by-year comparisons between supply and demand are of less concern than are comparisons between the stock of resources available and the cumulative demand for them over a series of years. Nevertheless, supply bottlenecks and production problems cannot be completely ignored; particularly in the case of energy, these problems do figure importantly in parts of the analysis.

The first section of this chapter begins by discussing several basic concepts, and the terms adequacy, exhaustion, reserves, and resources are defined, as well as various breakdowns of the last term that are used to describe degrees of availability. It then reviews what is known about the quantities of various nonfuel minerals likely to be available in the future, discusses the estimates this study uses, and presents the methods developed to project demand in major regions of the world. The chapter's second section presents and compares the cumulative demand and supply projections, the third section discusses the role of various determinants of demand, and the final section develops overall implications. Because price increases for nonfuel minerals are unlikely to be very great compared to other price increases, the effects of price changes on the economy have not been considered in any detailed way. This considerably simplifies the analysis compared to that of energy, in which such price increases and reactions to it must be treated with more care.

Concepts and Methods

Resource Adequacy, Reserves, and Resources

If the world's resources were known with certainty, if markets operated under more or less competitive conditions, and if there were no technological changes, the mineral deposits costing the least to bring to market would be mined first. As the most favorable deposits are exhausted, prices would begin to rise, making it profitable to bring lower grade deposits to market and encouraging conservation and the search for substitutes to reduce demand. Eventually, the price would rise to a point where demand is reduced to zero. Because this point will be reached before actual physical exhaustion occurs, the question of resource adequacy should be posed in terms of costs and prices, not in terms of when the world or a particular country will "run out." Indeed, the concept of "running out" is incorrect in two important senses: first, because increasing costs of production will shut off demand long before the pool of available resources is empty; and second, because these resources are not literally consumed but are transformed by what we call consumption into waste products, many of which can be recycled, though at a cost that someday could be too great to pay.

This kind of reasoning has led to historic investigations of scarcity or resource adequacy by studying materials costs relative to other price movements. If materials are increasing in scarcity, their prices relative to other prices ought to be rising over time. But the classic study of this type, by Barnett and Morse (1963), which covered the period from 1870 to 1957, found that nonrenewable minerals in general had become available to society at decreasing or constant, not increasing, real cost. Later studies found that this same situation prevailed through 1970 (National Commission on Materials Policy, 1973; and Nordhaus, 1974).[1] The reasons for these price declines are not difficult to find. Clearly, they are related to new discoveries, improvements in knowledge, and technological changes that have kept costs from rising as they otherwise might have done.

It is very difficult to apply this same approach to assessing resource adequacy in the future, however. Not only does it require projecting resource availability and demand as functions of geological knowledge and growth in population and GNP per capita, it also requires knowing how these estimates will affect and be affected by changes in prices. To simplify the task, we first ask, What would happen to resource availability if prices were to remain constant (and in some cases if there were no foreign trade)? In this artificial context, the answer can be couched in terms of years to resource exhaustion. This is useful because it helps weed out the minerals that are unlikely to cause problems within a given time frame; those remaining can be examined to see what is likely to happen if these simplifying assumptions are relaxed.

At any given time, the minerals available for use consist of known deposits that can be exploited economically given existing technology and prices of already mined materials in stockpiles and above-ground inventories and of scrap (waste materials in the production process and materials embodied in finished goods no longer in use) that can be recycled economically. In this study, stockpiles and inventories are assumed to be unchanged, and recycled materials are subtracted from total or gross demand. Thus, the demand to be discussed and compared with resource availability is that for primary mineral resources, which must be mined or imported.

Known deposits of ore that can be commercially exploited with existing technology and prices are commonly known as reserves. Over time, they are depleted by mining activities and replenished by new discoveries, technological advances, and price increases; the latter two factors make it possible to exploit less favorable deposits economically. Thus, there is no compelling reason to expect reserves to fall over time. Indeed, if anything, one might predict that they would increase more or less in proportion to mineral production, so long as prices do not change, because business firms will find it in their interest to increase their exploratory and research activities in order to replenish reserves at about

---

[1] Smith (1977), using more sophisticated statistical techniques, concluded that the trend is downward over certain periods but not others.

Table 4–1. Changes in World Reserves and Cumulative Production of Selected Minerals, 1950–70

(thousands of metric tons)

Ore	Known reserves in 1950	Cumulative production 1950–70	Known reserves in 1970	Percentage increase in known reserves 1950–70
Iron	19,000,000	9,355,000	251,000,000	1,221
Manganese	500,000	194,000	635,000	27
Chromite	100,000	82,000	755,000	675
Tungsten	1,903	630[a]	1,328	−30
Copper	100,000	80,000	279,000	179
Lead	40,000	48,000	86,000	115
Zinc	70,000	70,000	113,000	61
Tin	6,000	3,800[b]	6,600	10
Bauxite	1,400,000	505,000	5,300,000	279
Potash	5,000,000	216,000	118,000,000	2,360
Phosphates	26,000,000	1,011,000	1,178,000,000	4,430
Oil[c]	75,000,000	180,727,000	455,000,000	507

Source: National Commission on Supplies and Shortages, *Government and the Nation's Resources*, Report of the National Commission on Supplies and Shortages (Washington, D.C., GPO, 1976).

[a] Production of tungsten was estimated from production of tungsten concentrates.

[b] 1950–52 production estimated from an average of 1953–57 production.

[c] Thousand barrels.

the same rate as they draw upon them. Somewhere between ten and twenty years' worth of reserves at current production rates appears to be typical, but for a given mineral this factor can vary considerably because of time lags, uncertainties, and discontinuities attached to exploration, research, changes in policy, and so on.

Table 4–1 provides dramatic support for this description of the situation. Reserves of all but two of the minerals listed in the table increased by quite large amounts between 1950 and 1970. Because this was a period of constant or falling real prices for most minerals and no major changes in market structure, new discoveries and technological advances probably account for the bulk of these increases. This is not, of course, a situation that can continue forever, but it does illustrate two of the means by which reserves have been replenished over time.

The third means, price increases, is illustrated in figure 4–1 by a curve that traces estimates of the amount of copper that can be economically recovered from U.S. sources at different prices. For prices between the dotted lines, a 10 percent increase in price is estimated to increase re-

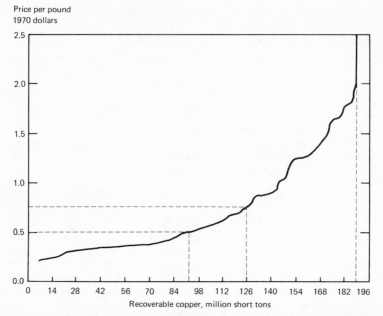

Figure 4–1. Total domestic recoverable copper resources. Price is calculated using a 6 percent rate of return. From National Academy of Sciences, *Mineral Resources and the Environment* (Washington, D.C., NAS, 1975) p. 178.

serves by about 7 percent. At higher prices, this elasticity is much lower, and eventually it falls to zero. But new discoveries and technological improvements, which in effect shift this curve to the right and downward, can postpone this day for a long time.

Additions to reserves come from the larger body of minerals called resources. This term and its various subdivisions have taken on such a variety of meanings that it is wise to establish a common set of definitions for use in this study.[2] Figure 4–2, a modified version of the classification of resources used by the U.S. Geological Survey (1973, page 4) is helpful. The most comprehensive category is the *resource base*, typically taken to be the mineral content of the earth's crust to a depth of one kilometer or one mile. Obviously, far less than this amount will ever be exploited by man. The term *resources* frequently is applied to the amount that ever could be used, but at times it is interpreted as the amount available given the technologies and prices expected to prevail during a specified period of time. This latter meaning of the word resources is adopted here because of its greater specificity.

[2] A good review of such definitions is given in Schanz (1975).

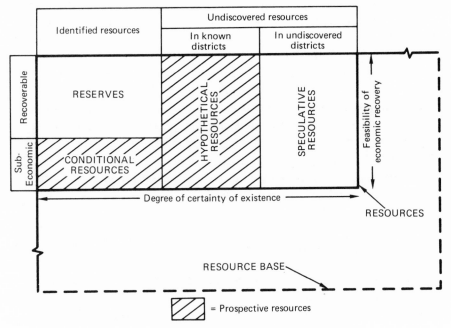

Figure 4–2. Classification of mineral resources used in this volume.

Resources are subdivided along two dimensions, one pertaining to the degree of certainty of existence and the other to the feasibility of economic recovery. The broadest breakdown according to degree of certainty is into *identified* and *undiscovered resources,*[3] and the latter category is subdivided into *hypothetical resources* (unknown deposits in known districts) and *speculative resources* (deposits in unknown districts whose existence has been postulated on the basis of geological principles). The second dimension, economic feasibility, is here broken into *recoverable resources* (recoverable at current technology and prices) and *subeconomic resources* (additional resources expected to become available because of technological and price changes likely to occur within a given time frame).[4]

---

[3] Frequently, identified resources are subdivided into proved, probable, and possible. Our analysis is complicated enough without adding these categories.

[4] Sometimes a threefold breakdown is used: recoverable, paramarginal, and submarginal. Paramarginal means recoverable at a price (or an equivalent technological change) that is a specified amount above current levels. This classification is most useful when resources are taken to mean ultimately recoverable resources, that is, defined without a time dimension. Because we are defining resources to mean what might be exploited given technological and price changes likely to occur within a fifty-year time horizon, this added category is not required.

The U.S. Geological Survey, which defines resources as the amount ultimately recoverable, uses the term *potential resources* for the difference between resources and reserves, that is, for the amount that ultimately might be added to reserves (USGS, 1973). Because we are defining resources as what might be available for exploitation during the next half-century, the term *prospective reserves,* meaning the amount that might be added to reserves during the next half-century given expected changes in technology and prices is used to denote the difference between resources and reserves.[5]

In practice, existing estimates seldom fit these neat categories. Nevertheless, this framework is useful as a basis for interpreting and using these estimates in appropriate ways.

Estimates of Reserves and Resources

Our estimates of reserves are taken from *Mineral Facts and Problems* (Bureau of Mines, 1975). Although they are the best estimates available, they do not warrant a great deal of confidence for several reasons: there are frequent differences of opinion about what is commercially exploitable and what is not; most public knowledge about such reserves must be gathered from their owners, who generally have more incentive to influence the market or the government than to provide the most accurate data; and for some countries, no published data exist.

The situation is far worse, however, when it comes to estimates of resources that may be added to reserves in the future. Estimating the amount of a mineral that might be discovered must rely on extrapolation from better explored minerals or regions; estimating the amount that might be added at different levels of production costs requires highly detailed information from a variety of fields, including geology, engineering, and economics. These data are always difficult and sometimes impossible to assemble, and technological change is obviously hard to predict. More times than not, these problems, combined with the experts' natural tendency toward caution, result in omitting estimates for some regions and understating those for others.

To date, three approaches to estimating prospective reserves (and related concepts) have been used. The first, used to estimate ultimately

---

[5] With due apologies to those who prefer other terms or use this term in different ways.

recoverable petroleum resources, extrapolates from past rates of growth in production, proved reserves, and discovery per foot of drilling over time (see, for example, Hubbert, 1969 and 1972). As McKelvey (1973) has pointed out, these variables are strongly influenced by economic, political, and other factors that bear no relation to the amount of a mineral in the ground; moreover, the method makes no allowance for shifts in trends that might occur because of technological breakthroughs or major discoveries. The only value of this method is to project the status of the relevant variables over a short period of time on the assumption that current trends will continue.

The second approach extrapolates from better explored to less explored minerals and regions. Although there are many variants of this method, none appears to have postulated a relationship between one mineral or region and others that both can be tested and proves out well in such tests. Moreover, even if one of these postulated relationships were accepted without test, applying such approaches requires using very poor proxies for the desired variables.[6]

The third approach relies on expert judgment and, in principle at least, ought to be better than any mechanical approach because it can take into account detailed, specialized information not incorporated in general theories. This is essentially the approach the U.S. Geological Survey (USGS, 1973) and the Bureau of Mines (1975) use. But the care with which analysts assemble their facts, their varying degrees of

---

[6] The approach developed by Erickson (1973) can be used to explain these points. He begins by assuming that the ratio between deposits of grades appropriate for inclusion in the reserve category and concentrations in the earth's crust is the same for a wide variety of minerals. He then selects as a minimum estimate of that ratio the largest ratio observed between reserves of a mineral and its crustal abundance on the assumption that that mineral will be the one most fully explored. For the United States, that mineral turns out to be lead, which provides Erickson with the equation, $R = 2.45A \times 10^6$ (where R means reserves and A means crustal abundance measured in parts per million). Extrapolation to the world involves multiplying these estimates by 13.5, the ratio of the land area of the world to that of the United States.

This method can be improved upon in several ways, for example, by taking current reserves plus past production as the dependent variable. But either way it leaves much to be desired. It suggests, for example, that the United States has large prospective reserves of tin, though very little tin has ever been mined commercially in the United States. It also suggests very large prospective reserves of molybdenum in the rest of the world, though most geologists think the United States is especially well endowed with molybdenum compared to the rest of the world. More important, it ignores the fact that the cutoff grade for inclusion in the reserve category, and therefore the quantities of reserves (and past production), differ from mineral to mineral, across regions, and over time depending on technologies in use, prices, and other factors having little or nothing to do with crustal abundance.

cautiousness or myopia, and the way they interpret their assignments can significantly affect the outcome. Typically, for example, they provide estimates of identified, hypothetical, and speculative resources without specifying the technological or price assumptions they are using implicitly.

This study relies on expert judgments, taking its cues from estimates provided primarily by the USGS and the Bureau of Mines (plus other sources which are especially important in the case of energy). There are two reasons for doing so. First, none of the mechanical approaches is value- or judgment-free; the difference is that they require broad sweeping judgments that are easier to make explicit but do not take into account exceptions and detailed, specialized knowledge. At least the opportunity for taking such materials into account is present if experts in different areas are asked to pool their information and judgments. Second, interviews with these experts can overcome some of the problems that such an approach has by furnishing a notion of what they had in mind and how they interpreted their assignments. For example, discussion with these experts suggests that if excessive optimism has crept in anywhere, it is in their estimates of future discoveries. To guard against this possibility, the study excludes estimates of speculative resources. In contrast, these experts are likely to have underestimated the subeconomic resources that might become economic in the next fifty years; though they were asked to think in terms of ultimately recoverable resources, they were also asked to ignore price changes and to think conservatively about technological change. In addition, where estimates were not available for some regions of the world, the figure implicitly entered is zero. On net, this treatment probably means that the estimates used here are excessively conservative. Except for the case of uranium, discussed in the next chapter, there was no attempt to correct this bias.

Demand Projections

The projection procedure for the United States began with gross domestic demand (that is, demand excluding exports that can be satisfied from primary production, secondary production, or imports). In those cases in which the SEAS/RFF model includes a specific sector that can be associated with a specific mineral—aluminum, copper, iron, lead, or zinc —the demand projections are derived directly from the model. In all other cases, information from the Bureau of Mines (1975) on unit requirements (and changes in unit requirements over time) for each major mineral-using sector was combined with projections of the output of these sectors. With the exception of the fertilizer sector (a major user of phosphate rock, potash, and sulfur), for which projections were developed by the methods indicated in chapter 6, sector projections were derived from the model. Secondary production, estimated by assuming that the percentage of demand satisfied by recycling remains the same as in the base period (roughly, the 1971–74 average), was then subtracted from these gross demand projections.[7] Though recent developments have tended to raise the cost of primary production relative to that of secondary production, there is no basis on which to estimate the effects on the extent of recycling over time.[8] Thus, on this ground at least, the procedure tends to overstate the demand for primary production.

In developing projections for the rest of the world, we must rely on more general relationships that can be formulated between mineral consumption on the one side and population and economic growth on the other. At least two broad sets of factors appear to be operating. One is the impact of per capita income, which influences not only the quantities but also the composition of commodities a country produces and consumes.[9] The other is a country's factor proportions and available technology,

[7] This procedure pertains to the United States. For the rest of the world, the consumption numbers in the base year are for total consumption, primary and secondary. As indicated below, global projections are based on U.S. projections. Thus, if no U.S. recycling is assumed for those minerals, none is assumed for the rest of the world. In those cases that assume constant recycling percentages for the United States, the projection method for the rest of the world implies that their recycling percentages start at zero but increase and become the same as those for the United States at the point in time when per capita GNP in other regions catches up to that of the United States.

[8] Primary producers have tended to be hurt more than secondary producers by increasing energy costs (because their operations tend to be more energy-intensive), by more restrictive environmental regulations, and by increasing difficulties, at least in the United States, in finding sites for their operations that do not run into local opposition. In addition, many governments, attempting to enlarge their shares of the revenues generated by domestic mining operations, have increased royalty charges and taxes on primary producers; and there is a possibility that the U.S. government may eliminate some of the tax advantages it currently provides to primary producers.

[9] Malenbaum (1972), for example, has found what he believes to be a general tendency for the intensity of use (consumption per dollar of the GNP) of a given mineral to rise and then fall with the level of development. Presumably, the reason for this tendency is the change in the composition of production as development occurs. In early stages, emphasis typically is placed on heavy industry and construction, while in later "postindustrial" stages, the importance of services increases. But Vogely (1976) has challenged the assumption that services are less material-intensive and has suggested that at least part of the curvilinearity is more apparent than real, resulting from substitutions of one mineral for another over time as relative factor prices and technology change.

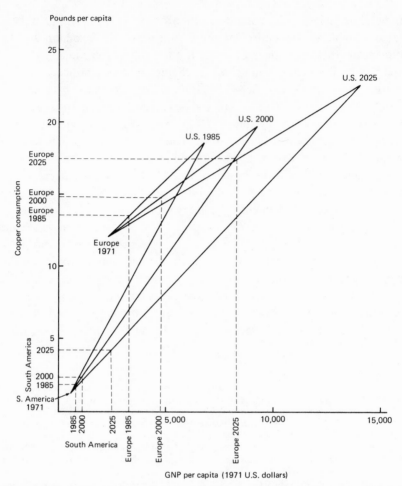

Figure 4–3. Consumption estimation technique: Copper in Europe and South America.

which influence the selection from among minerals that can be substituted for each other in the production of commodities.

Figure 4–3 illustrates the procedure used to capture these two factors. This procedure assumes that mineral consumption per capita is a function of GNP per capita, but that this function changes over time as GNP per capita increases. As a guide to estimating the direction of change, the assumption is made that the relationship for other regions approaches that for the United States, though it never reaches it until the

GNP per capita of the subject country catches up to that of the United States.

For convenience, the projections were made from four points in time, starting with historic data for 1971 for the region in question. A straight line was drawn from this first point through a point representing the projected relationship between consumption per capita and GNP per capita for the United States in 1985. The relationship for the region (Europe or South America, in figure 4–3) in 1985 is then found by locating its 1985 GNP per capita (developed in chapter 2) on that straight-line segment. The same procedure is repeated using the U.S. relationship in the year 2000 and then again in the year 2025. These estimates are then multiplied by population and cumulated on the basis of interpolations made between them.[10]

This approach is intuitively appealing because other countries do appear to be following U.S. consumption patterns and using U.S. technological methods to the extent that their incomes permit. It is, of course, recognized that factor proportions and relative prices differ greatly among countries. These facts are implicitly taken into account by starting the analysis with the position of the country in 1971 and permitting it to move toward the U.S. position only with what amounts to very substantial time lags, lags that are much longer for poor than for rich countries.

Resulting Projections

There are about seventy-seven materials with significant commercial value at the present time. Of these, the twenty-five listed below will not be discussed because they are clearly adequate in supply, without further exploration or technological developments given likely demands at current prices.

[10] The same procedure could have been followed using single-year segments, but as we are only interested in estimates for 1985, 2000, and 2025, we used the simpler procedure. Another option is to start new line segments for Europe from future years, rather than rotating the line segments around the 1971 base. This procedure was not followed because of concern that too much weight would then be placed on estimates derived from estimates with an increasingly weak foundation in fact. As things have turned out, however, the results would not have been greatly affected.

Minerals in Relative Abundance

Argon	Iodine
Bromine	Lithium
Calcium	Mica
Chlorine	Oxygen
Clays	Perlite
Corundum and emery	Pumice
Industrial diamond	Quartz crystals
Diatomite	Sand and gravel
Garnet	Sodium
Gem stones	Stone
Graphite	Strontium
Gypsum	Vermiculite
Magnesium	

Another group of minerals includes important, less abundant ferrous, nonferrous, and nonmetallic minerals. A complete adequacy analysis has been undertaken for these seventeen minerals, along the lines indicated in the previous section, and the results are presented here. The remaining minerals are of lesser economic importance; they are discussed in less quantitative detail in technical note A.

Tables 4–2 through 4–18 summarize comparisons of cumulative demand and resources for the seventeen important, scarce minerals for the world and its major regions. In all cases, the standard case was used for assumptions about population and economic growth (see chapter 2). The figures in the column for 1974 of these tables provide estimates of reserves and prospective reserves for that year.[11] Estimates of demand for each region, assuming no imports or exports of the mineral in question and no price changes, are subtracted first from reserves and then, when reserves become zero, from prospective reserves. A negative figure for prospective reserves indicates the extent to which imports are needed to fill the gap.[12] The world totals are derived by adding up these positive and negative figures; consequently, they indicate what would happen if free trade occurred among the regions. The last column in each table summarizes this material by indicating when the indicated reserves or prospective reserves would be exhausted *if* there were no price changes. Although these tables conveniently summarize the cumulative demand and resource estimates and identify resources for which no foreseeable

[11] In all cases, these are derived from the Bureau of Mines (1975) and USGS (1973).

[12] Demand estimates to 2025 are derived by the methods described in the previous section. After 2025, it is assumed that demand continues to grow at the annual rate projected for the 2015–2025 period.

problem exists, they can give a misleading picture of the situation unless their footnotes and the discussion in the text are kept in mind.

Molybdenum, Titanium, and Vanadium

Tables 4–2 to 4–4 indicate that reserves plus prospective reserves of molybdenum, titanium, and vanadium are more than sufficient to satisfy world demand; comparable deposits in the United States are sufficient to satisfy its requirements until sometime beyond the year 2100. This is true even in the scenario incorporating the highest demand projections. These three minerals, therefore, can be set aside without further discussion.

Chromium, Potash, Phosphate Rock, and Manganese

World resources of chromium, potash, phosphate rock, and manganese are also adequate at least to the year 2100, but U.S. resources are not (see tables 4–5 to 4–8). Apart from deposits in Brazil, most chromium resources are located in the Eastern Hemisphere (in order of importance, southern Rhodesia, South Africa, USSR, Turkey, and India), where long supply lines could be disrupted in times of emergency. As a consequence, the U.S. government stockpiles chromium; in 1976, these stockpiles held the equivalent of a four-year supply at current consumption levels. In the long run, technological developments that lower the cutoff grade for economic recovery appear likely, in which case world resources would be extended and spread over a larger geographic area.

Without imports and with no price increase, U.S. reserves and prospective reserves of potash would not last beyond 2025. Imports are growing, and are expected to continue growing, because supplies elsewhere are available and are cheaper than in the United States. Ninety-five percent of U.S. imports originate in Canada from enterprises having strong participation by U.S. investors, and Canadian resources are vast, more than adequate through the twenty-first century even with a high rate of export to the rest of the world.

More than 80 percent of mined phosphate rock is used to produce fertilizer, and no adequate substitute is available for it. If adequate supplies of this mineral were ever to become difficult to obtain, food production could be affected seriously. But the figures in table 4–7 suggest

Table 4–2. Remaining Molybdenum Resources, Standard Case, 1974–2050, and Year of Exhaustion if No Price Increase (thousands of short tons)

Region	1974	1985	2000	2025	2050	Year of exhaustion
United States						
Reserves	3265	2916	2259	662	0	2033
Prospective reserves	514300	514300	514300	514300	512640	[a]
North America (excluding U.S.)						
Reserves	1050	1027	959	699	230	2060
Prospective reserves	60300	60300	60300	60300	60300	2587
South America						
Reserves	1025	946	769	95	0	2028
Prospective reserves	52525	52525	52525	52525	51365	2323
Europe						
Reserves	5	0	0	0	0	1975
Prospective reserves	5645	5504	5081	3684	1317	2061
USSR						
Reserves	1000	794	320	0	0	2008
Prospective reserves	380300	380300	380300	379178	376796	2687

						Year
Asia						
Reserves	26	0	0	0	0	1978
Prospective reserves	121665	121590	121274	119697	116456	2291
Africa						
Reserves	0	0	0	0	0	1975
Prospective reserves	100	87	29	−408	−1417	2004
Oceania						
Reserves	13	3	0	0	0	1987
Prospective reserves	5213	5213	5180	5066	4886	2285
Antarctica						
Reserves	0					
Prospective reserves	50					
World (excluding U.S.)						
Reserves	3119	2541	989	0	0	2007
Prospective reserves	625798	625798	625798	620885	609984	2380
Total world						
Reserves	6384	5457	3248	0	0	2014
Prospective reserves	1140098	1140098	1140098	1133846	1122624	2480

Note: Apportionment of figures for prospective reserves for Asia and USSR provided by authors.
[a] After the year 2700.

Table 4-3. Remaining Titanium Resources, Standard Case, 1974–2050, and Year of Exhaustion if No Price Increase (thousands of short tons)

Region	1974	1985	2000	2025	2050	Year of exhaustion
United States						
Reserves	31600	24295	10377	0	0	2009
Prospective reserves	403100	403100	403100	377605	324344	2138
North America (excluding U.S.)						
Reserves	56700	56415	55258	50086	40233	2108
Prospective reserves	387600	387600	387600	387600	387600	2330
South America						
Reserves	69500	69257	68029	58951	38355	2080
Prospective reserves	215300	215300	215300	215300	215300	2169
Europe						
Reserves	43000	40360	31666	743	0	2026
Prospective reserves	135800	135800	135800	135800	82806	2077
USSR						
Reserves	25200	22527	13907	0	0	2014
Prospective reserves	127400	127400	127400	110173	55380	2069
Asia						
Reserves	132000	130399	124481	91124	20407	2056
Prospective reserves	210000	210000	210000	210000	210000	2097
Africa						
Reserves	22800	22500	21175	11068	0	2039
Prospective reserves	984600	984600	984600	984600	972394	2303
Oceania						
Reserves	19600	19392	18623	16051	11931	2097
Prospective reserves	124000	124000	124000	124000	124000	2312
World (excluding U.S.)						
Reserves	368800	360851	333139	210796	0	2048
Prospective reserves	2184700	2184700	2184700	2184700	2158407	2153
Total world						
Reserves	400400	385147	343516	185301	0	2043
Prospective reserves	2587800	2587800	2587800	2587800	2482750	2151

Note: Apportionment among regions, where required, provided by authors.

Table 4–4. Remaining Vanadium Resources, Standard Case, 1974–2050, and Year of Exhaustion if No Price Increase (thousands of short tons)

Region	1974	1985	2000	2025	2050	Year of exhaustion
United States						
Reserves	100	0	0	0	0	1985
Prospective reserves	9900	9897	9703	9221	8521	2198
North America (excluding U.S.)						
Reserves	0	0	0	0	0	1975
Prospective reserves	11000	10995	10978	10907	10774	2457
South America						
Reserves	300	246	139	0	0	2013
Prospective reserves	1500	1500	1500	1314	778	2076
Europe						
Reserves	100	40	0	0	0	1990
Prospective reserves	2800	2800	2693	2241	1505	2085
USSR						
Reserves	8000	7941	7801	7367	6649	2162
Prospective reserves	4000	4000	4000	4000	4000	2204
Asia						
Reserves	100	55	0	0	0	1994
Prospective reserves	1300	1300	1233	691	−377	2045
Africa						
Reserves	2000	1947	1840	1481	847	2074
Prospective reserves	19000	19000	19000	19000	19000	2289
Oceania						
Reserves	200	197	186	152	98	2082
Prospective reserves	1900	1900	1900	1900	1900	2335
World (excluding U.S.)						
Reserves	10700	10422	9771	7553	3674	2068
Prospective reserves	41500	41500	41500	41500	41500	2177
Total world						
Reserves	10800	10419	9574	6874	2295	2060
Prospective reserves	51400	51400	51400	51400	51400	2180

Note: Prospective reserves include only conditional resources because no estimates are available for hypothetical resources. Most vanadium is re-covered as a byproduct of other mineral production which complicates estimation and interpretation.

Table 4–5. Remaining Chromium Resources, Standard Case, 1974–2050, and Year of Exhaustion if No Price Increase (thousands of short tons)

Region	1974	1985	2000	2025	2050	Year of exhaustion
United States						
Reserves	0	0	0	0	0	1975
Prospective reserves	2164	−4273	−17156	−50685	−100778	1979
North America (excluding U.S.)						
Reserves	56	0	0	0	0	1975
Prospective reserves	5234	4485	2543	−4122	−15658	2012
South America						
Reserves	2643	1752	0	0	0	1998
Prospective reserves	2364	2364	1772	−9445	−32296	2007
Europe						
Reserves	3883	0	0	0	0	1978
Prospective reserves	1993	−7337	−28079	−74747	−138849	1979
USSR						
Reserves	7645	464	0	0	0	1986
Prospective reserves	8030	8030	−3998	−36908	−87506	1996

						Year
Asia						
Reserves	10418	0	0	0	0	1985
Prospective reserves	8953	8352	−14157	−85793	−208015	1992
Africa						
Reserves	687960	681822	669896	633345	572159	2162
Prospective reserves	1072960	1072960	1072960	1072960	1072960	2274
Oceania						
Reserves	0	0	0	0	0	1975
Prospective reserves	0	−322	−1143	−3642	−7552	1975
Undistributed resources						
Reserves	891					
Prospective reserves	891					
World (excluding U.S.)						
Reserves	713496	673926	601151	393005	56599	2054
Prospective reserves	1100425	1100425	1100425	1100425	1100425	2104
Total world						
Reserves	713496	667489	581831	340156	0	2048
Prospective reserves	1102589	1102589	1102589	1102589	1056244	2095

Note: The prospective reserve figures include only conditional resources. In addition, there are another 45 million tons classified as "hypothetical or speculative resources," one million of which are estimated to be located in the United States. No estimates are available for Oceania; the negative numbers indicated, therefore, are cumulative demand estimates for this region.

Table 4-6. Remaining Potash Resources, Standard Case, 1974–2050, and Year of Exhaustion if No Price Increase (thousands of short tons)

Region	1974	1985	2000	2025	2050	Year of exhaustion
United States						
Reserves	200000	133826	21837	0	0	2003
Prospective reserves	200000	200000	200000	-7586	-286334	2025
North America (excluding U.S.)						
Reserves	5000000	4957897	4885379	4720175	4500158	2277
Prospective reserves	69000000	69000000	69000000	69000000	69000000	a
South America						
Reserves	10000	0	0	0	0	1983
Prospective reserves	27000	22524	-9398	-114383	-294346	1997
Europe						
Reserves	4715000	4603109	4429574	4089258	3688034	2201
Prospective reserves	4790000	4790000	4790000	4790000	4790000	2327
USSR						
Reserves	800000	770471	696078	495934	201709	2064
Prospective reserves	1000000	1000000	1000000	1000000	1000000	2115
Asia						
Reserves	245000	213398	134862	0	0	2015
Prospective reserves	1005000	1005000	1005000	857844	354861	2064
Africa						
Reserves	20000	9189	0	0	0	1992
Prospective reserves	95000	95000	78790	-20340	-206479	2022
Oceania						
Reserves	10000	5452	0	0	0	1996
Prospective reserves	10000	10000	7111	-11161	-33795	2011
World (excluding U.S.)						
Reserves	10800000	10555040	10090397	8880330	7073155	2113
Prospective reserves	75926976	75926976	75926976	75926976	75926976	2388
Total world						
Reserves	11000000	10688866	10112234	8672747	6586823	2104
Prospective reserves	76126976	76126976	76126976	76126976	76126976	2368

Note: Prospective reserves include only conditional resources. Hypothetical and speculative resources are believed to be very large.
a After the year 2700.

that these resources will be adequate well beyond this time horizon.[13] More important, these figures do not include identified subeconomic resources for the People's Republic of China or hypothetical and speculative resources for any region. Various estimates of these excluded categories suggest that economically usable ores may be at least ten times greater than the figures in table 4–7,[14] though environmental considerations could restrict their use in some countries, particularly the United States.

The U.S. appears to have no resources of manganese ore containing more than 35 percent of this metal, the cutoff grade at current prices. Though technological improvements during the next quarter-century should make it economical to exploit the 74 million tons estimated to be contained in ores of lesser quality, in the absence of trade and assuming constant prices, these resources would be exhausted during the first decade of the next century. This assessment does not include sea-bed sources, however, which are expected to become available at close to present prices well before the turn of the century. As of now, however, the United States is dependent on foreign supplies, mostly in the forms of ore from Brazil, Gabon, Australia, and South Africa and of alloy from South Africa and France. Government stockpiles are estimated at about 3.1 million short tons of contained manganese, about two and one-half times the current rate of annual consumption.

Thus, for all practical purposes, U.S. access to these minerals is sufficiently well assured that they can also be set aside as clearly adequate without significant price increases.

Nickel, Copper, and Cobalt

These minerals are best treated as a group because, along with manganese, the prospect of profitably extracting them from deep-sea nodules throws their reserve and prospective reserve figures into doubt.[15]

[13] This would not be so for the United States if it continues exporting 40 percent more than it now consumes. In that event, the U.S. resource estimates in table 4–7 would last until 2054 instead of 2076, as they would in the absence of trade.

[14] For an interesting discussion of these estimates and of various demand projections and likely adjustments in the event that serious depletion were ever to occur, see Wells (1975). Also, see Turbeville (1977).

[15] Nodules in prime areas of the Pacific are estimated to contain (in dry weight) 25 percent manganese, 6 percent iron, 1.5 percent nickel, 1.2 percent copper, 0.25 percent cobalt, 0.15 percent molybdenum, 0.11 percent vanadium, and 0.8 percent zinc (Leipziger and Mudge, 1976; and Mero, 1965), but the most likely candidates for profitable exploitation in the near future and the ones likely to have the greatest impact on mineral markets are manganese, nickel, copper, and cobalt.

Table 4–7. Remaining Marketable Phosphate Rock Resources, Standard Case, 1974–2050, and Year of Exhaustion if No Price Increase (thousands of short tons)

Region	1974	1985	2000	2025	2050	Year of exhaustion
United States						
Reserves	2500000	2078064	1310282	0	0	2021
Prospective reserves	4500000	4500000	4500000	4210380	2287178	2076
North America (excluding U.S.)						
Reserves	2000	0	0	0	0	1975
Prospective reserves	2000	−83468	−260106	−721902	−1391492	1975
South America						
Reserves	80000	48570	0	0	0	1994
Prospective reserves	420000	420000	370573	−80551	−967462	2022
Europe						
Reserves	30000	0	0	0	0	1976
Prospective reserves	70000	−179335	−803957	−2364789	−4522810	1979
USSR						
Reserves	800000	258605	0	0	0	1990
Prospective reserves	3200000	3200000	2617358	947157	−1021298	2038

Asia					
Reserves	340000	145437	0	0	0	1991
Prospective reserves	2000000	2000000	1639298	−230211	−3588789	2023
Africa					
Reserves	12840000	12702635	12411384	11431442	9718392	2127
Prospective reserves	53960000	53960000	53960000	53960000	53960000	2317
Oceania					
Reserves	1120000	1095331	1042883	920105	765563	2136
Prospective reserves	2030000	2030000	2030000	2030000	2030000	2274
World (excluding U.S.)					
Reserves	15212000	13915779	11325440	4209230	0	2036
Prospective reserves	61682000	61682000	61682000	6182000	54982112	2125
Total world					
Reserves	17712000	15993843	12635718	3919593	0	2034
Prospective reserves	66182000	66182000	66182000	66182000	5269328	2120

Note: Later figures published by the Bureau of Mines [*Mineral Commodity Profiles: Chromium—1977, Cobalt—1977, Copper—1977, Manganese—1977, Phosphate—1977,* and *Nickel—1977* (Washington, D.C., GPO)] shift about 10 billion short tons from the identified subeconomic category (here listed as prospective reserves) into the reserve category for Africa and make other changes that result in a reserve figure of 27,792 million and a prospective reserve figure of 54,232 million. No prospective reserve estimate is included for the Peoples' Republic of China, and estimates for hypothetical and speculative resources, believed to be very large, also are not included.

Table 4–8. Remaining Manganese Resources, Standard Case, 1974–2050, and Year of Exhaustion if No Price Increase (thousands of short tons)

Region	1974	1985	2000	2025	2050	Year of exhaustion
United States						
Reserves	0	0	0	0	0	1975
Prospective reserves	103600	86022	53506	−34361	−173025	2017
North America (excluding U.S.)						
Reserves	2200	792	0	0	0	1990
Prospective reserves	90100	90100	87053	71824	43433	2076
South America						
Reserves	44100	43399	40348	17201	0	2035
Prospective reserves	94000	94000	94000	94000	57910	2069
Europe						
Reserves	5300	0	0	0	0	1983
Prospective reserves	3000	668	−21053	−99376	−239830	1986
USSR						
Reserves	750000	743381	723151	646210	504740	2103
Prospective reserves	1500000	1500000	1500000	1500000	1500000	2191
Asia						
Reserves	47300	44185	31725	0	0	2014
Prospective reserves	106800	106800	106800	58710	−117749	2035
Africa						
Reserves	1004500	986420	951667	846202	670266	2108
Prospective reserves	1417600	1417600	1417600	1417600	1417600	2182
Oceania						
Reserves	160100	159609	157832	151519	140837	2191
Prospective reserves	30300	30300	30300	30300	30300	2210
World (excluding U.S.)						
Reserves	2013500	1975454	1877622	1492390	765708	2069
Prospective reserves	3241800	3241800	3241800	3241800	3241800	2123
Total world						
Reserves	2013500	1957876	1827528	1354429	489084	2061
Prospective reserves	3345400	3345400	3345400	3345400	3345400	2112

Note: Prospective reserves equal the "other identified" figures of the USGS plus the hypothetical resource figures of the Bureau of Mines that assumes 30 percent metal content in ore. No sea-bed resources are included.

If adequacy is judged strictly from land-based resources, as is done in tables 4–8 to 4–11, of these four minerals only reserves and prospective reserves of manganese are sufficient to satisfy global demand through the next century, and the United States has virtually no reserves of manganese, nickel, and cobalt.[16] If sea-bed sources are included, world reserve figures for these three minerals could increase by one order of magnitude. Because the United States is further advanced in exploration and development, its deficiency in these minerals—assuming political and other barriers to exploitation can be overcome—would disappear.

At the present time, it is not useful to attempt to quantify the increases in reserves and prospective reserves that sea-bed sources would permit. First, the quantities estimated from the few explorations that have been made so far are so vast that they overwhelm the cumulative demand projections during this time period. Holser (1976), for example, estimates that prime areas of the ocean floor contain 29 billion dry tons of nodules (7.25 billion tons of manganese, 435 million tons of nickel, 348 million tons of copper, and 72.5 million tons of cobalt). Second, because nodules are forming all the time, they are more like a renewable resource. An often-cited estimate is that they are forming at the rate of 10 million tons per year, though only a fraction of this increase occurs at likely mining sites (Bureau of Mines, 1975, page 738). Third, although some experts expect production of these minerals in prime areas to begin in less than ten years, there are many uncertainties at present. The technology is too new and untested to inspire confidence in the cost estimates, though most look favorable,[17] and some unresolved problems in hoisting large quantities of nodules from the seabed remain; environmental problems may be present, though they are not expected to be serious; the impact of nodule production on relevant markets and hence on prices and reserves is difficult to judge;[18] and the timing of these developments is in

[16] However, in each case there are believed to be large quantities of lower grade, land-based materials distributed irregularly throughout the world. Their quantities and qualities have not been fully assessed, but they could move into the reserve category during the next twenty-five years if projected technological improvements materialize.

[17] According to Leipziger and Mudge (1976), by 1985 a seven-metal recovery process is likely to yield a pretax rate of return between 82 and 112 percent and a three-metal recovery system could produce a comparable rate of 45 to 85 percent, compared to a 27 percent pretax rate of return in 1974 for land-based operations. On the basis of such projections, at least four consortia of major mining enterprises are currently engaged in exploration and development activities.

[18] If production were set on the basis of what is appropriate for the nickel market, the output of manganese and cobalt could be so large relative to land-based production that prices would fall, raising the cutoff grade for profitable exploitation

doubt because of uncertainties about international control and regulation of such activities. These latter uncertainties are likely to be difficult to resolve because of the high stakes involved, particularly for countries dependent on land-based mining of these minerals for foreign exchange earnings.

All these uncertainties surrounding sea-bed exploitation are likely to be resolved in the next ten to fifteen years, well within this study's time horizon. Thus, though we cannot provide quantitative estimates, it seems reasonable to conclude that adequacy of these four minerals is ensured for the foreseeable future without significant price increases. The one possible exception is copper, because nodules may not contribute greatly to its supply for some time (see footnote 18). But here, technological advances, in particular the introduction of hydrometallurgy on the supply side and aluminum and glass fiber substitutes on the demand side, are likely to extend land-based resources considerably (see Shapanka, 1978). Short-term disruptions in supply certainly could arise, but at least as far as the United States is concerned, existing stockpiles should be adequate to take care of such problems.[19]

Aluminum

The figures on reserves and prospective reserves of aluminum given in table 4–12 refer only to bauxite resources.[20] If there were no international trade and no increase in price, major consuming regions of the world quite soon would exhaust their holdings of bauxite (the United

---

of land-based reserves, and the output of copper may not be great enough relative to land-based production to have any significant effect on its price. Thus, nodule production could generate excess supplies of some minerals while not significantly offsetting shortages of others.

[19] As indicated above, U.S. government stockpiles of manganese in 1977 were 3.1 million short tons (more than one year's requirements). Comparable figures for cobalt as of the end of 1976 were 41.7 million pounds (two years' requirements). As of October 1977, there was no strategic stockpile of nickel, but the government has set a goal to accumulate about one year's requirement. Government stocks of copper at that date included 20,400 short tons, but a goal of 1,299,000, equivalent to about one-half year of consumption, was set.

[20] Although the prospective reserve figures include what the Bureau of Mines terms speculative resources, it is still a conservative figure because it does not include estimates for a number of unexplored but promising areas in South America, Africa, and Asia and because it excludes identified, lower grade deposits, for example, 200–500 million tons in the United States in areas where mining may be restricted because of environmental considerations such as proximity to population or scenic areas.

Table 4-9. Remaining Nickel Resources, Standard Case, 1974–2050, and Year of Exhaustion if No Price Increase (thousands of short tons)

Region	1974	1985	2000	2025	2050	Year of exhaustion
United States						
Reserves	200	0	0	0	0	1976
Prospective reserves	15000	12821	8113	-4776	-24798	2018
North America (excluding U.S.)						
Reserves	14000	13724	13042	10561	6128	2075
Prospective reserves	27200	27200	27200	27200	27200	2143
South America						
Reserves	1100	986	508	0	0	2007
Prospective reserves	1500	1500	1500	-1436	-9252	2018
Europe						
Reserves	0	0	0	0	0	1975
Prospective reserves	0	-2934	-8303	-22851	-45533	1975
USSR						
Reserves	5700	3953	209	0	0	2001
Prospective reserves	4300	4300	4300	-7424	-27736	2012
Asia						
Reserves	6200	4532	500	0	0	2002
Prospective reserves	7900	7900	7900	-8492	-41312	2016
Africa						
Reserves	800	668	158	0	0	2003
Prospective reserves	4200	4200	4200	525	-8312	2028
Oceania						
Reserves	31500	31393	31100	30147	28592	2229
Prospective reserves	3500	3500	3500	3500	3500	2243
World (excluding U.S.)						
Reserves	59300	52322	37214	0	0	2020
Prospective reserves	48600	48600	48600	31730	-66724	2035
Total world						
Reserves	59500	50143	30327	0	0	2014
Prospective reserves	63600	63600	63600	26954	-91522	2032

Note: Prospective reserves include only conditional resources. Hypothetical resources from land-based deposits are believed to be large but have not been quantified. In addition, no estimate is included for sea-bed resources, though they too are believed to be large.

Table 4-10. Remaining Copper Resources, Standard Case, 1974–2050, and Year of Exhaustion if No Price Increase (thousands of short tons)

Region	1974	1985	2000	2025	2050	Year of exhaustion
United States						
Reserves	90000	67957	31689	0	0	2012
Prospective reserves	211000	211000	211000	166313	68631	2065
North America (excluding U.S.)						
Reserves	60000	55505	46680	23570	0	2044
Prospective reserves	91000	91000	91000	91000	80517	2092
South America						
Reserves	130000	127132	120116	92807	41802	2065
Prospective reserves	156000	156000	156000	156000	156000	2106
Europe						
Reserves	20000	0	0	0	0	1981
Prospective reserves	70000	54653	−323	−110936	−246534	2000
USSR						
Reserves	40000	22971	0	0	0	1997
Prospective reserves	50000	50000	41901	−30908	−131819	2016
Asia						
Reserves	30000	9577	0	0	0	1989
Prospective reserves	20000	20000	−13891	−150695	−380934	1996
Africa						
Reserves	60000	58540	54074	30608	0	2042
Prospective reserves	100000	100000	100000	100000	81480	2077
Oceania						
Reserves	20000	18386	15581	9409	1490	2055
Prospective reserves	33000	33000	33000	33000	33000	2126
World (excluding U.S.)						
Reserves	360000	276763	124137	0	0	2010
Prospective reserves	520000	520000	520000	243854	−364997	2037
Total world						
Reserves	450000	344721	155826	0	0	2010
Prospective reserves	731000	731000	731000	410166	−296364	2041

Note: In addition to these resources, the USGS [U.S. Geological Survey, United States Mineral Resources, Geological Survey Professional Paper 820 (Washington, D.C., GPO, 1973)] lists as speculative resources 120 million short tons in the United States and an additional 200 million tons in the rest of the world. No estimate of copper resources is available for China, and no estimate of sea-level deposits is included.

Table 4-11. Remaining Cobalt Resources, Standard Case, 1974–2050, and Year of Exhaustion if No Price Increase (thousands of short tons)

Region	1974	1985	2000	2025	2050	Year of exhaustion
United States						
Reserves	0	0	0	0	0	1975
Prospective reserves	842	715	462	−239	−1385	2019
North America (excluding U.S.)						
Reserves	565	536	479	298	0	2050
Prospective reserves	1039	1039	1039	1039	1032	2102
South America						
Reserves	0	0	0	0	0	1975
Prospective reserves	151	121	54	−231	−794	2008
Europe						
Reserves	25	0	0	0	0	1978
Prospective reserves	0	−71	−280	−966	−2166	1978
USSR						
Reserves	225	165	1	0	0	2001
Prospective reserves	0	0	0	−622	−1785	2001
Asia						
Reserves	0	0	0	0	0	1975
Prospective reserves	216	52	−294	−1529	−3792	1988
Africa						
Reserves	1147	921	494	0	0	2012
Prospective reserves	3	3	3	−726	−2693	2013
Oceania						
Reserves	740	735	721	670	582	2136
Prospective reserves	35	35	35	35	35	2140
World (excluding U.S.)						
Reserves	2702	2093	808	0	0	2007
Prospective reserves	1444	1444	1444	−2032	−9580	2016
Total world						
Reserves	2702	1966	428	0	0	2004
Prospective reserves	2286	2286	2286	−2272	−10965	2016

Note: The prospective reserve figures include only conditional resources. No estimates for hypothetical, speculative, or sea-bed resources are available, though they are believed to be large.

Table 4-12. Remaining Aluminum Resources, Standard Case, 1974–2050, and Year of Exhaustion if No Price Increase (thousands of short tons)

Region	1974	1985	2000	2025	2050	Year of exhaustion
United States						
Reserves	10000	0	0	0	0	1976
Prospective reserves	40000	−34899	−227029	−843076	−1887387	1982
North America (excluding U.S.)						
Reserves	270000	262628	240157	136357	0	2043
Prospective reserves	110000	110000	110000	110000	41685	2054
South America						
Reserves	780000	773984	751096	576045	171279	2058
Prospective reserves	680000	680000	680000	680000	680000	2082
Europe						
Reserves	270000	204607	44653	0	0	2003
Prospective reserves	120000	120000	120000	−427405	−1505299	2010
USSR						
Reserves	30000	0	0	0	0	1983
Prospective reserves	30000	15733	−115302	−666964	−1721164	1988
Asia						
Reserves	200000	164107	53093	0	0	2005
Prospective reserves	620000	620000	620000	20101	−1397615	2026
Africa						
Reserves	1270000	1265658	1245851	1062399	621548	2073
Prospective reserves	540000	540000	540000	540000	540000	2088
Oceania						
Reserves	1010000	1006072	994140	948717	868211	2170
Prospective reserves	330000	330000	330000	330000	330000	2199
World (excluding U.S.)						
Reserves	3830000	3662789	3183688	879262	0	2031
Prospective reserves	2430000	2430000	2430000	2430000	−1371360	2044
Total world						
Reserves	3840000	3587891	2916659	0	0	2025
Prospective reserves	2470000	2470000	2470000	2466184	−3258759	2038

Note: Includes only aluminum available in bauxite. The U.S. figure excludes 200 to 250 million tons of low-grade bauxite for which mining may be restricted because of environmental considerations such as their proximity to population or scenic areas.

States by 1982, the USSR by 1988, and Europe by 2010); if free trade were possible, the resource estimates for the world would be exhausted in 2038 (in the high-demand case, 2028; in the low-demand case, 2047).

But bauxite is far from the only source of aluminum. Indeed, the average aluminum content from all sources in the earth's crust is 8.3 percent, making it the most abundant of the structural metals. Presently, somewhere between a 20 and an 80 percent increase in the price of bauxite (the higher price would be equivalent to a 10 percent increase in the price of aluminum) would be required to justify switching to nonbauxitic sources using existing technology. This cross-over price is likely to fall significantly over time, however, certainly before bauxite resources are exhausted.[21] Once such cost reductions are achieved, these reserve and resource figures will change dramatically. For example, in 1967 the Bureau of Mines (1967) estimated that the United States had 166 million dry tons of alumina (Al_2O_3) in anorthosite, clays, laterite, and shale, compared to 140 million tons of alumina in bauxite ores. All this amount will not become economical, in part because comparable supplies in other parts of the world could still prove to be cheaper to exploit but also because of environmental restrictions on use. Nevertheless, it is not impossible to imagine that the United States might move from its current position of almost total dependence on imports to virtual self-sufficiency within the next fifty years.

At the present time, the world price of aluminum is strongly influenced by the International Bauxite Association, whose members in 1975 controlled 85 percent of total non-Communist world bauxite production. This cartel, formed in 1974, imposed tax levies during the first two years of its existence that increased the FOB price of bauxite from about $8 to $12 a ton to around $20 to $30 a ton. These increases, plus energy price increases, have resulted in a significant increase in the price of the refined metal. Further real price increases are possible in the short run, but for several reasons they are unlikely to be sustainable over any significant time period. First, the increase in bauxite prices has stimulated the development of new capacity. Brazil, for example, may have the

---

[21] This estimate of the required price increase comes from Pindyck (1977). The higher figure assumes U.S. natural gas prices will double (roughly equivalent to deregulation and in line with the assumption we make in chapter 5). Because natural gas is used in aluminum production for generating steam, it should be possible to substitute coal, which would reduce the extent of the necessary price increase somewhat. More important, Pindyck's estimates assume existing technology. As footnote 20 indicates, a number of significant energy-saving changes are in the pilot stage of development.

capacity to produce some 4.4 million short tons of bauxite a year at a cost of about $1.06 per ton by 1982 (Pindyck, 1977). Second, the increases in both bauxite and energy prices have aroused interest in developing new processes to produce alumina from abundant and widely dispersed nonbauxitic sources and to reduce it to aluminum by more energy-efficient means. Several promising possibilities are in the pilot stage of testing.[22] Third, although the rapid growth in demand for aluminum is likely to continue if its price does not rise significantly, the availability of close substitutes—particularly steel, copper, and plastics, all of which are less energy-intensive in production—will act as an additional constraint on price increases. Finally, Australia, which has about one-fourth of world bauxite reserves and which could increase its current profits by leaving the cartel, is likely to resist efforts at further price increases.[23]

Thus, a simple comparison of the resource and cumulative demand estimates for aluminum is misleading. Taking other factors into account, the adequacy of aluminum supply seems well assured for periods substantially beyond our time horizon; indeed, U.S. aluminum import dependency may even recede over time as technological changes move nonbauxitic materials into the reserve category.

Iron

Iron is one of the most abundant elements, comprising 5 percent of the earth's crust. The resource figures given in table 4–13 clearly are underestimates because they do not include estimates for hypothetical and speculative resources, which the USGS believes to be enormous but does

[22] A European producer, Pechiney Ugine Kuhlmann, has in the pilot stage of development an "H-plus" process for extracting alumina from clay, shale, and other nonbauxitic materials. The Superior Oil Company is developing a process that produces oil, alumina, and other valuable minerals from shale. The Toth Aluminum Co. is working on a chemical process to be applied to Georgia clay. Alcoa recently announced plans to build a pilot plant to test a direct reduction process for making an aluminum-silicon alloy directly from aluminum ores, using coal in place of electricity. Alcoa also has developed a technique that may replace the Hall process for reducing alumina and result in a 30 percent savings in electricity (see Shapanka, 1978).

[23] Pindyck (1977) estimates that the optimal cartel price of bauxite, with Australia in the cartel, is $22 a ton, that it will fall to about $21 a ton and then rise for the next few decades by no more than 0.2 percent a year. He also estimates that if Australia left the cartel, an act that "could nearly double its profits," the price would fall initially by $3 to $4. These estimates do not take account of the impending technological changes, which could conceivably result in a fall in price over time.

Table 4–13. Remaining Iron Ore Resources, Standard Case, 1974–2050, and Year of Exhaustion if No Price Increase (thousands of short tons)

Region	1974	1985	2000	2025	2050	Year of exhaustion
United States						
Reserves	4000000	2938601	1049788	0	0	2007
Prospective reserves	14000000	14000000	14000000	10614578	4418783	2065
North America (excluding U.S.)						
Reserves	12100000	11924517	11553628	10467408	8741649	2124
Prospective reserves	17500000	17500000	17500000	17500000	17500000	2211
South America						
Reserves	19400000	19207792	18759248	17016816	13746230	2109
Prospective reserves	31600000	31600000	31600000	31600000	31600000	2188
Europe						
Reserves	8500000	6843204	4166274	0	0	2019
Prospective reserves	3100000	3100000	3100000	1358984	-6556880	2030
USSR						
Reserves	31000000	29844144	27943264	23496400	17214736	2099
Prospective reserves	26000000	26000000	26000000	26000000	26000000	2150
Asia						
Reserves	11300000	9516472	5943895	0	0	2016
Prospective reserves	7500000	7500000	7500000	2762320	-14763424	2030
Africa						
Reserves	3300000	3199959	2917700	1423634	0	2038
Prospective reserves	4700000	4700000	4700000	4700000	2971651	2067
Oceania						
Reserves	10200000	10115831	9967379	9611126	9114662	2252
Prospective reserves	10800000	10800000	10800000	10800000	10800000	2383
World (excluding U.S.)						
Reserves	95800000	90651920	81251376	55536848	15168752	2058
Prospective reserves	101200000	101200000	101200000	101200000	101200000	2098
Total world						
Reserves	99800000	93590512	82301168	52151424	5587488	2053
Prospective reserves	115200000	115200000	115200000	115200000	115200000	2094

Note: Prospective reserves exclude hypothetical and speculative resources, believed to be very large.

not quantify (USGS, 1973, page 304). In addition, lower grade ores than those included in the USGS subeconomic category may become economical because of new technological methods such as flotation and magnetic separation processes (Shapanka, 1978). Presently, however, many of the higher grade U.S. deposits have been depleted, and lower cost sources can frequently be found abroad. Partly as a consequence, the United States imports one-third of its total iron consumption even though it could rely exclusively on domestic sources for many years if necessary. Foreign sources of supply are numerous and widely distributed geographically, so strategic problems are unlikely to arise from relying on imports. An Association of Iron Ore Exporting Countries was formed in 1975, but it probably cannot affect the world price of iron to any significant extent.

Lead

Given the assumptions inherent in table 4–14, world resources of lead would last until about 2016 and U.S. resources until 2040. But there are several reasons to believe that little if any price increase would be necessary to close the gap between demand and supply when these dates are reached. First, the USGS (1973, page 326) estimates that if all speculative and conditional resources were included, the total figure for world lead resources could be as high as 1.5 billion short tons; any significant decline in reserves or rise in price is likely to stimulate exploratory activities and move some of these speculative resources into the reserve category. Second, the rest of the world is behind the United States in shifting away from lead-based paints, gasoline additives, and piping and cable-covering materials. In addition, the U.S. projections incorporate the assumption that nonlead acid batteries will be developed and used after 1990 (Shapanka, 1978), an assumption not directly incorporated in the projections for the rest of the world. The projection method used in this study assumes that lead consumption per dollar of the GNP in the rest of the world will decline and slowly converge toward the U.S. rate, and any increase in price would speed up this process. Third, good substitutes are present for major dissipative uses of lead, and secondary recovery can be applied to a greater extent than it has been so far with only modest increases in cost.

The price of lead may increase, however, particularly in the United States during the next five to ten years because of increased efforts to

Table 4–14. Remaining Lead Resources, Standard Case, 1974–2050, and Year of Exhaustion if No Price increase
(thousands of short tons)

Region	1974	1985	2000	2025	2050	Year of exhaustion
United States						
Reserves	59000	46693	25416	0	0	2015
Prospective reserves	60000	60000	60000	36328	−30368	2040
North America (excluding U.S.)						
Reserves	25000	22596	17722	4188	0	2031
Prospective reserves	26000	26000	26000	26000	9443	2060
South America						
Reserves	6000	4279	14	0	0	2001
Prospective reserves	6000	6000	6000	−11507	−45042	2012
Europe						
Reserves	25000	3131	0	0	0	1987
Prospective reserves	25000	25000	−5869	−76903	−167278	1998
USSR						
Reserves	18000	9095	0	0	0	1994
Prospective reserves	18000	18000	9551	−36397	−104992	2007
Asia						
Reserves	9000	29	0	0	0	1986
Prospective reserves	9000	9000	−11434	−83680	−212786	1993
Africa						
Reserves	5000	3863	650	0	0	2002
Prospective reserves	9000	9000	9000	−6896	−41406	2018
Oceania						
Reserves	18000	17046	15364	11411	6047	2073
Prospective reserves	12000	12000	12000	12000	12000	2109
World (excluding U.S.)						
Reserves	106000	60039	0	0	0	1996
Prospective reserves	105000	105000	78997	−161784	−544016	2010
Total world						
Reserves	165000	106732	0	0	0	2000
Prospective reserves	165000	165000	164413	−125457	−574385	2016

Note: The prospective reserve figures exclude source subeconomic resources. If speculative and sub-economic resources, such as the Kupferschiefer beds of Central Europe, are included [U.S. Geological Survey, *United States Mineral Resources*, Geological Survey Professional Paper 820 (Washington, D.C., GPO, 1973), p. 326], estimates are that the world total resources of lead could be as high as 1.5 billion short tons.

control toxic emissions from mining and smelting operations. Techno-logical improvements that reduce such emissions are likely, but if they induce price increases they could speed up the substitution of other materials for lead.

Sulfur

A comparison of cumulative demand and resource estimates for sulfur is misleading. Not only is there no prospective reserve estimate for Africa, but the figures in table 4–15 exclude hypothetical as well as spec-ulative sources, both considered to be vast.[24] In addition, the increased use of coal for direct combustion and for the production of synthetic liquids and gases, combined with environmental restrictions on sulfur emissions from combustion, will greatly increase the supplies of sulfur.[25] The United States is currently self-sufficient in sulfur and could purchase more from Canada and Mexico if this situation were to change.

Tin

The United States produces negligible quantities of tin, and if we relied on domestic resources, they would be exhausted in two or three years. Even world resources will not last beyond 2030, given the assump-tions on which table 4–16 is based. Adding speculative resources, esti-mated to be 8.4 million tons, would extend these resources by less than five years. An increase in price to close the gap between demand and supply appears necessary shortly after the end of the fifty-year time hori-zon.

Primary supplies of tin may not be very elastic with respect to a change in price. Tin is one of the more well-explored metals, so increased search efforts may not greatly alter the long-run resource situation. Some

---

[24] If ever needed, gypsum and anhydrite deposits could be used as an "al-most unlimited sulfur resource" according to the Bureau of Mines (1975), though some improvements in technology or price increases or both would be necessary to justify their use.

[25] Identified coal resources of the U.S. are estimated to contain over 20 billion tons of sulfur and those of the world over 80 billion tons. Methods for economically recovering sulfur from combustion products captured by scrubbers are in the process of development. But a more likely source is the sulfur removed in the process of producing synthetic liquids and gases from coal and shale, which can much more easily and economically be recovered with existing technology. As indicated in chapter 5, in the base case the production of such fuels would begin in 2010 and utilize 400 million tons of coal, containing about 8 million tons of sulfur, per year. By comparison, the U.S. demand for sulfur in 2025 would be about 28 million tons.

Table 4-15. Remaining Sulfur Resources, Standard Case, 1974–2050, and Year of Exhaustion if No Price Increase (thousands of short tons)

Region	1974	1985	2000	2025	2050	Year of exhaustion
United States						
Reserves	257000	121161	0	0	0	1994
Prospective reserves	448000	448000	322919	−272806	−1102318	2015
North America (excluding U.S.)						
Reserves	566000	540727	487885	334901	94599	2058
Prospective reserves	1300000	1300000	1300000	1300000	1300000	2132
South America						
Reserves	34000	19524	0	0	0	1995
Prospective reserves	34000	34000	13422	−175777	−556471	2004
Europe						
Reserves	386000	275770	47335	0	0	2003
Prospective reserves	879000	879000	879000	311553	−612495	2035
USSR						
Reserves	168000	109382	0	0	0	1996
Prospective reserves	504000	504000	450161	−72393	−931304	2023
Asia						
Reserves	779000	731203	591864	0	0	2024
Prospective reserves	632000	632000	632000	594478	−644857	2039
Africa						
Reserves	23000	10440	0	0	0	1991
Prospective reserves	0	0	−26232	−224405	−643576	1991
Oceania						
Reserves	28000	18868	750	0	0	2001
Prospective reserves	11000	11000	11000	−34753	−100717	2008
World (excluding U.S.)						
Reserves	1984000	1705913	1027184	0	0	2014
Prospective reserves	3360000	3360000	3360000	2033615	−2094826	2039
Total world						
Reserves	2241000	1827074	902105	0	0	2010
Prospective reserves	3808000	3808000	3808000	1760810	−3197157	2036

Note: Prospective reserves exclude hypothetical and speculative resources, including deposits contained in coal and shale. No prospective reserve figure is available for Africa.

Table 4-16. Remaining Tin Resources, Standard Case, 1974–2050, and Year of Exhaustion if No price Increase (thousands of short tons)

Region	1974	1985	2000	2025	2050	Year of exhaustion
United States						
Reserves	46	0	0	0	0	1975
Prospective reserves	93	−586	−1830	−4950	−9614	1977
North America (excluding U.S.)						
Reserves	29	0	0	0	0	1977
Prospective reserves	31	−103	−423	−1331	−2764	1979
South America						
Reserves	1783	1660	1371	173	0	2028
Prospective reserves	5642	5642	5642	5642	3487	2076
Europe						
Reserves	326	0	0	0	0	1978
Prospective reserves	2420	1580	−270	−4471	−10330	1998
USSR						
Reserves	695	342	0	0	0	1992
Prospective reserves	1009	1009	489	−2304	−7078	2006
Asia						
Reserves	7297	6477	4756	0	0	2022
Prospective reserves	11413	11413	11413	10413	295	2051
Africa						
Reserves	789	716	518	0	0	2016
Prospective reserves	1816	1816	1816	1245	−1090	2040
Oceania						
Reserves	211	152	51	0	0	2007
Prospective reserves	336	336	336	135	−236	2036
World (excluding U.S.)						
Reserves	11130	8373	3031	0	0	2007
Prospective reserves	22667	22667	22667	9501	−17716	2035
Total world						
Reserves	11176	7694	1109	0	0	2003
Prospective reserves	22760	22760	22760	4552	−27330	2030

Note: World (U.S.) figures exclude 8,405 (78) million short tons classified as speculative.

improvements can be expected in the percentage of tin recovered during mining operations, which now is not very high in the average operation. A significant increase could be achieved in the percentage of demand satisfied by recycling (now 20 percent in the United States), but it would require collecting and detinning tin cans, a costly activity not practiced in the United States except during wartime emergencies.

On the other hand, there are good substitutes for tin in most of its major uses. This fact is attested to by events of the last decade (1964–74), a period during which the price of tin in constant dollars increased by more than 50 percent. During that period, U.S. consumption not only ceased growing but actually declined by more than 20 percent. The principal reason for this decline was the substitution of aluminum, tin-free steel, and other metallic and nonmetallic materials in containers and construction. But other changes have also played important roles—examples are the substitution of aluminum, copper-based alloys, and plastics for bronze; miniaturized, integrated electronic circuits for wired circuits; and the development of epoxy resins and tinless or low-tin solders as metal-joining media. Such changes are still in process in the United States and have hardly begun in poorer countries.[26] An increase in tin prices would certainly encourage them and in the process push the time of severe depletion of this resource much further into the future than the numbers in table 4–16 indicate.

The price of tin is influenced by an international agreement between producing and consuming countries. Buffer stock purchases and export controls agreed to by these countries are partly responsible for the recent runup in tin prices. Malaysia, Indonesia, Thailand, and Bolivia produce more than 60 percent of world output, and the remainder comes mainly from the USSR, China, Australia, Nigeria, and Zaire. In 1977 the United States had 227,000 short tons stockpiled, equivalent to roughly three years' consumption.

Tungsten

The reserve and prospective reserve figures for tungsten shown in table 4–17 are far from certain, particularly for the Communist countries, where information is outdated, incomplete, and difficult to evaluate, but where the bulk of the world's resources are thought to exist. If these data are anywhere near correct, however, tungsten supply could become a

---

[26] Unfortunately, these changes are not adequately captured in our cumulative demand projections, particularly for the rest of the world.

Table 4-17. Remaining Tungsten Resources, Standard Case, 1974–2050, and Year of Exhaustion if No Price Increase (thousands of short tons)

Region	1974	1985	2000	2025	2050	Year of exhaustion
United States						
Reserves	119	18	0	0	0	1987
Prospective reserves	360	360	185	−299	−1020	2012
North America (excluding U.S.)						
Reserves	240	209	149	0	0	2024
Prospective reserves	355	355	355	343	95	2058
South America						
Reserves	65	58	35	0	0	2011
Prospective reserves	143	143	143	42	−254	2030
Europe						
Reserves	13	0	0	0	0	1978
Prospective reserves	38	−10	−156	−610	−1366	1984
USSR						
Reserves	175	81	0	0	0	1993
Prospective reserves	350	350	261	−204	−935	2016
Asia						
Reserves	1300	1212	1015	288	0	2032
Prospective reserves	2375	2375	2375	2375	1324	2068
Africa						
Reserves	12	0	0	0	0	1983
Prospective reserves	15	11	−28	−219	−612	1991
Oceania						
Reserves	39	36	25	0	0	2020
Prospective reserves	108	108	108	98	42	2065
World (excluding U.S.)						
Reserves	1844	1544	897	0	0	2013
Prospective reserves	3384	3384	3384	2113	−1705	2041
Total world						
Reserves	1963	1562	722	0	0	2009
Prospective reserves	3744	3744	3744	1814	−2726	2037

Note: Prospective reserves exclude hypothetical and speculative resources, for which no estimates are available.

problem. Without a price increase, U.S. resources are inadequate to satisfy its demand beyond 2012, and world resources would last barely two decades beyond.

There are no estimates of the extent to which tungsten reserves may respond to a price increase, but it does appear that a number of technological improvements in exploration, mining, and beneficiation will be necessary to increase supplies significantly. Recycling, already satisfying one-third of U.S. demand, can be increased somewhat, but not without incurring substantial additional costs. In addition, the demand may be quite inelastic: not only is the cost of tungsten a small fraction of final product prices, but it is commonly believed that there are few satisfactory substitutes available that do not cost significantly more. Moreover, because of its unique properties, demand for tungsten is likely to grow with the growth of modern industry. Nevertheless, because the cost of tungsten is such a small fraction of the cost of final goods, even a quadrupling of its price—the same increase that occurred for oil in 1973–74—is unlikely to be disruptive. At that level of cost, few would dispute the contention that substantial additional resources and substitutions on both the demand and supply sides will be found.[27]

A sudden cutoff of supply is unlikely in the near future, because tungsten now is produced in countries that differ widely, both geographically and politically, and the United States imports concentrates or ferrotungsten from more than a dozen of them. In any event, the U.S. government maintains a large stockpile, equivalent in 1977 to 110 million pounds of contained tungsten, more than six and one-half years' worth of consumption.

Zinc

As table 4–18 indicates, without trade or price increases, domestic resources of zinc would last until shortly after 2040, and world resources

---

[27] Ayres and Noble (1972) review the substitution possibilities and find many more materials with similar properties (for example, molybdenum and ceramics) and processes to accomplish similar tasks (for example, electrical and electrochemical substitutions for milling tools) than is commonly believed. They also review the experience of the Korean war, when supplies from China were suddenly cut off and the world price more than quadrupled. Within three years, U.S. consumption fell from 14 million pounds to 4 million pounds per year with no significant effect on the economy or war effort. Two of the ways this was accomplished were to substitute molybdenum for tungsten in steel alloys and tungsten carbide tips for solid forged steel alloy cutting tools. The demand for tungsten in these uses did not recover after imports became available again, and the price returned to its earlier level.

Table 4-18. Remaining Zinc Resources, Standard Case, 1974–2050, and Year of Exhaustion if No Price Increase (thousands of short tons)

Region	1974	1985	2000	2025	2050	Year of exhaustion
United States						
Reserves	30000	11828	0	0	0	1991
Prospective reserves	180000	180000	158930	79914	−32829	2044
North America (excluding U.S.)						
Reserves	38000	35255	29285	11111	0	2036
Prospective reserves	0	0	0	0	−18469	2036
South America						
Reserves	10000	8064	2793	0	0	2005
Prospective reserves	0	0	0	−22386	−73540	2005
Europe						
Reserves	22000	0	0	0	0	1984
Prospective reserves	0	−4241	−47831	−148110	−287304	1984
USSR						
Reserves	12000	378	0	0	0	1986
Prospective reserves	0	0	−24643	−96957	−212631	1986

Asia						
Reserves	12000	0	0	0	0	1983
Prospective reserves	0	−5110	−42476	−171374	−400453	1983
Africa						
Reserves	7000	5395	720	0	0	2002
Prospective reserves	0	0	0	−25306	−81090	2002
Oceania						
Reserves	18000	16371	13648	7193	0	2046
Prospective reserves	0	0	0	0	−1863	2046
Undistributed resources						
Reserves	0					
Prospective reserves	1661000					
World (excluding U.S.)						
Reserves	119000	56112	0	0	0	1993
Prospective reserves	1661000	1661000	1592496	1215171	585650	2068
Total world						
Reserves	149000	67940	0	0	0	1993
Prospective reserves	1841000	1841000	1751427	1295084	552822	2065

Note: Because prospective reserves have not been distributed by region, except for the United States, the zeros and negative numbers attributed to regions are misleading and the dates indicate when regions run out of reserves. Protpective reserves exclude subeconomic undiscovered resources estimated to be 2,679 thousand short tons, of which 223 thousand are attributed to the United States. These figures also exclude sea-bed resources of zinc.

(assuming trade) would last until 2065. It is likely, however, that long before these dates are reached technological improvements will move other deposits into these reserve categories. More than 2.6 million short tons of zinc are believed to be available for exploitation if there are even small improvements in technology or increases in price, and an unknown but probably large amount more is available in sea-bed nodules. In addition, secondary recovery, which now meets about 5 percent of demand—in part because of the many dissipative uses of zinc—can be increased, and substitutes, particularly aluminum and plastics, are available for some major uses at modestly higher prices. Accordingly, little price increase should be necessary to close the gap between demand and supply should one develop in the foreseeable future.

During the last decade, imports of zinc metal and ore provided between one-third and one-half of total U.S. demand. Canada and Mexico provided about 40 percent of total imports, with at least ten other countries accounting for the remainder. The U.S. government maintains a stockpile estimated at 373,000 short tons in 1977, about three months' consumption.

Roles of Population, Economic Growth, and Other Determinants

Up to this point, the analysis has been based on one set of assumptions about population, economic growth, and other factors that determine the adequacy of resources. This section varies these assumptions in order to determine their influence on resource outcomes. The focus is on the United States because of the sketchiness of the analysis for the rest of the world, though the impact of changes in U.S. demand on global resource adequacy will be considered.

Table 4–19 presents data on rates of growth in gross domestic demands for various minerals (that is, domestic demand, excluding exports, that is satisfied by primary production, secondary production, or imports) and compares them to rates of growth in U.S. population, GNP per capita, and total GNP for groups of years from 1955 to 2025. Base case assumptions are used throughout. Four points can be made on the basis of these data. First, there is substantial variation among rates of growth of different minerals, which makes generalization somewhat difficult. This variation is explained by changes in the composition of the economy and substitutions among minerals over time. Second, the rates

Table 4–19. Rates of Growth in U.S. Mineral Demands and Selected
Economic Indicators, Scenario EL
(coverage annual percentages)

Indicator and mineral	1955–70	1971–85	1986–2000	2001–25
Population	1.40	0.93	0.74	0.56
GNP per capita	2.49	1.98	2.15	1.63
GNP	3.88	2.91	2.90	2.19
Aluminum	7.03	4.83	3.21	2.81
Chromium	−0.72	3.01	2.20	1.92
Cobalt	3.66	3.40	1.63	2.54
Copper	2.42	2.15	1.07	0.99
Iron in ore	2.07	1.18	1.55	1.46
Lead	1.93	1.78	1.74	1.35
Manganese	1.24	2.37	1.83	2.32
Molybdenum	3.50	2.20	1.61	1.76
Nickel	3.16	3.17	2.32	2.16
Phosphate rock	3.37	3.38*	1.74*	0.82*
Potash	6.36	2.37*	1.33*	0.87*
Sulfur	4.27	1.97*	2.29*	1.62*
Tin	−0.28	2.16	1.61	1.93
Titanium	1.07	2.26	2.17	1.90
Tungsten	5.52	3.90	1.63	1.87
Vanadium	5.97b	2.89	1.95	1.72
Zinc	2.49	2.36	1.55	1.66

Note: Demand is gross domestic demand, that is, demand satisfied by primary plus secondary production plus net imports (imports minus exports). Most of the growth rates in this table are based on log-linear regressions through all the data for the years listed. The exceptions, which result from absence of annual data, are based on data for the beginning and end of the period indicated; they are indicated by an asterisk attached to the numbers.

of growth experienced during the 1955–70 period may lead to overestimation of future rates of growth for many minerals.[28] The reasons for not following past trends more closely have to do with the belief that certain substitutions are petering out—certainly the negative rates and those close to zero are unlikely to continue much longer if the GNP continues to grow at postulated rates—and we have not introduced many other substitutions to take their place.[29] Third, most of the rates of growth in de-

[28] The cases in which the 1971–85 growth rates are significantly lower than the 1955–70 rates are special. In the 1955–70 period, aluminum was just beginning to be used in a big way. So far as sulfur and potash are concerned, had the time series been extended to 1975 or 1976, the historic rates of growth would have appeared to be much smaller. The same is true in the case of vanadium.

[29] Only a few, clearly identifiable technological changes have been introduced, certainly nothing like the volume of large and small adjustments that have occurred in the past (see Shapanka, 1978).

mand are lower than that of GNP; this suggests that the material intensity of GNP is falling over time. Fourth, most of these demand growth rates fall over time,[30] a phenomenon explained in part by the slowdown in population and economic growth that occurs during this period. In addition, there appears to be a tendency for the rates to fall slightly faster than those of the GNP, per capita GNP, and population. These last two points are explained by changes in composition, substitutions from these minerals to other materials not on this list such as cement, plastics, glass and paper, and improved economies in the use of materials.

Table 4–20 provides a different view of this situation, one that permits somewhat better separation of the various determinants. The first three columns indicate differences in demand for various minerals in the year 2025 under alternate assumptions with respect to population and economic growth (that is, growth in labor productivity). As can be seen, lower population growth (the shift from DH to FH) and lower labor productivity (the shift from DH to DL) happen to make roughly the same difference in GNP for 2025. But the difference in annual demand for nonfuel minerals is somewhat larger and the difference in cumulative demand for these minerals is somewhat smaller (with three exceptions) when the lower level of GNP results from a lower rate of population growth rather than a smaller rate of productivity improvement. This suggests that in most years the impact of the shift in population assumptions is less than that of a shift in labor productivity assumptions, but that the importance of population growth grows over time and eventually surpasses that of productivity improvement. The exceptions are for minerals associated with fertilizer production, for which the effect of population change is always larger by a sizable amount.

The effects on cumulative demand, however, are more important in judging resource adequacy. As one would expect, the impacts of shifting assumptions about population and economic growth rates on cumulative demand are substantially less than they are on annual demand. To generate any really significant savings in resources, both population and economic growth rates must be lower (compare FL with DH).

The last two columns of table 4–20 can be used to indicate the impacts of recycling and net imports in the special case where their per-

[30] This is certainly the case comparing 1985–2000 or 2000–25 with 1971–85. The fact that a few rates of growth are higher in 2000–25 than in one of the earlier periods is in part due to the conservative nature of the technological changes we have introduced: the farther out we project, the fewer changes we can foresee and the more likely is the growth rate to converge on the average for the sectors which constitute the principal purchasers of the mineral in question.

Table 4–20. Percentage Differences in U.S. Mineral Demand in 2025, Alternate Scenarios

	Reduction in annual demand, 2025			Reduction in cumulative demand, 1975–2025			Reduction in demand from:	
	DH to FH	DH to DL	DH to FL	DH to FH	DH to DL	DH to FL	Re-cycling[a]	Net imports[a]
Population	27.9	0	27.9	...	...	...	...	...
GNP per capita	(8.8)[b]	20.5	11.0	...	...	...	...	...
GNP	21.6	20.5	35.8	...	...	...	...	...
Aluminum	25.0	20.8	40.8	14.6	16.7	29.0	4.6	85.0
Chromium	24.0	21.3	39.8	12.0	16.4	26.2	10.0	90.0
Cobalt	25.2	20.5	40.8	13.4	16.1	27.4	1.0	99.0
Copper	25.5	21.2	41.5	11.5	15.5	25.3	20.0	10.0
Iron in ore	25.6	21.1	41.8	12.5	15.7	26.5	0.0	30.0
Lead	23.7	21.2	39.2	11.0	16.0	25.0	34.0	25.0
Manganese	23.2	19.2	38.2	12.3	15.1	25.3	0.0	97.0
Molybdenum	24.1	21.4	39.6	11.5	15.5	24.5	0.0	−130.0
Nickel	24.6	21.5	41.0	12.8	16.6	27.3	30.0	64.0
Phosphate rock	20.1	4.8	20.6	13.1	5.6	13.5	0.0	−40.0
Potash	20.9	5.0	21.4	13.9	6.1	14.4	0.0	45.0
Sulfur	22.4	16.1	33.0	12.4	12.0	20.8	0.0	−4.0
Tin	24.6	19.9	39.5	12.3	15.5	25.9	19.9	81.0
Titanium	23.7	21.2	39.0	11.6	16.2	25.4	0.0	55.0
Tungsten	24.5	21.0	40.3	12.3	15.7	25.9	4.0	39.0
Vanadium	24.1	21.2	39.7	11.7	15.9	25.5	0.0	25.0
Zinc	24.9	21.3	41.0	12.2	16.2	26.4	6.0	58.0

Note: Demand is gross domestic demand, that is, demand satisfied by primary plus secondary production plus net imports (imports minus exports). Recycling as percentage of demand is secondary production as percentage of gross domestic demand. Net imports as percentage of demand is (imports minus exports plus changes in government and private inventories) as percentage of gross domestic demand.

[a] These figures are rough averages of the percentage of demand satisfied by recycling and net imports during the 1972–74 period, assumed to be constant over time for the purpose of this exercise. They were derived from various chapters in the U.S. Bureau of Mines, *Mineral Facts and Problems*, Bureau of Mines Bulletin 667 (Washington, D.C., GPO, 1975).

Reductions in demand caused by these two factors are to be compared with a hypothetical case in which no recycling or net imports are present.

[b] Increase.

centages of gross demand are held constant during the whole fifty-year period. For example, secondary production provides 4.6 percent of the aluminum supply and imports provide 85 percent; thus, only 10 percent of gross demand is satisfied by domestic production. Clearly, secondary production and imports can have large impacts on the rates of exhaustion of domestic resources. Undoubtedly, these sources can and will play even larger roles in the future.

These points are more clearly summarized in table 4–21, which presents dates when domestic resources would be exhausted in a number

Table 4-21. Year When Specified Resources Categories for the United States Equal Zero, Assuming Constant Prices, Alternative Scenarios

Mineral	DH			FH			DL			FL		
	No recycling, no imports	Recycling, no imports	Recycling and imports	No recycling, no imports	Recycling, no imports	Recycling and imports	No recycling, no imports	Recycling, no imports	Recycling and imports	No recycling, no imports	Recycling, no imports	Recycling and imports
Aluminum												
Reserves	1976	1976	1985	1976	1976	1985	1976	1976	1986	1976	1976	1986
Prospective reserves	1981	1981	2006	1981	1981	2007	1981	1982	2008	1981	1981	2009
Chromium												
Reserves	1975	1975	1975[a]	1975	1975	1975[a]	1975	1975	1975[a]	1975	1975	1975[a]
Prospective reserves	1978	1979	Never[b]	1978	1978	Never[b]	1978	1979	Never[b]	1978	1979	Never[b]
Cobalt												
Reserves	1975	1975	1975[a]	1975	1975	1975[a]	1975	1975	1975[a]	1975	1975	1975[a]
Prospective reserves	2013	2014	Never[b]	2015	2016	Never[b]	2017	2017	Never[b]	2020	2020	Never[b]
Copper												
Reserves	2001	2006	2009	2002	2007	2011	2004	2009	2012	2004	2009	2013
Prospective reserves	2034	2042	2048	2040	2051	2058	2041	2051	2057	2051	2066	2075
Iron in ore												
Reserves	2002	2002	2009	2003	2003	2011	2004	2004	2012	2004	2004	2013
Prospective reserves	2042	2042	2057	2051	2051	2069	2050	2050	2067	2063	2063	2088
Lead												
Reserves	2001	2010	2022	2001	2011	2026	2004	2014	2028	2004	2015	2033
Prospective reserves	2017	2029	2047	2019	2035	2057	2022	2036	2056	2025	2043	2070
Manganese												
Reserves	1975	1975	1975	1975	1975	1975	1975	1975	1975	1975	1975	1975
Prospective reserves	2012	2012	2197	2014	2014	2251	2015	2015	2226	2018	2018	2287
Molybdenum												
Reserves	2024	2024	2004	2028	2028	2005	2029	2029	2007	2035	2035	2007
Prospective reserves	2659	2659	2425	2800+	2800+	2571	2790	2790	2509	2800+	2800+	2700

Nickel												
Reserves	1975	1976	1985	1975	1976	1984	1975	1976	1985	1975	1976	1985
Prospective reserves	2005	2012	2105	2006	2014	2132	2008	2016	2124	2009	2018	2158
Phosphate rock												
Reserves	2018	2018	2008	2022	2022	2011	2020	2020	2010	2023	2023	2011
Prospective reserves	2065	2065	2046	2082	2082	2058	2068	2068	2049	2082	2082	2058
Potash												
Reserves	2002	2002	2018	2004	2004	2023	2003	2003	2020	2005	2005	2203
Prospective reserves	2021	2021	2046	2027	2027	2058	2024	2024	2049	2027	2027	2059
Sulfur												
Reserves	1992	1992	1992	1993	1993	1992	1993	1993	1993	1994	1994	1993
Prospective reserves	2011	2011	2010	2013	2013	2012	2014	2014	2013	2016	2016	2015
Tin												
Reserves	1975	1975	Never[b]	1975	1975	Never[b]	1975	1975	Never[b]	1975	1975	Never[b]
Prospective reserves	1976	1977	Never[b]	1976	1977	Never[b]	1976	1977	Never[b]	1976	1977	Never[b]
Titanium												
Reserves	2006	2006	2024	2006	2006	2028	2009	2009	2030	2010	2010	2035
Prospective reserves	2103	2103	2167	2130	2130	2215	2122	2122	2197	2154	2154	2233
Tungsten												
Reserves	1986	1986	1992	1986	1986	1992	1987	1987	1994	1987	1987	1994
Prospective reserves	2007	2008	2020	2008	2009	2023	2010	2011	2024	2011	2012	2028
Vanadium												
Reserves	1985	1985	1987	1984	1984	1987	1985	1985	1988	1985	1985	1988
Prospective reserves	2143	2143	2169	2184	2184	2219	2169	2169	2200	2200	2200	2263
Zinc												
Reserves	1989	1990	2005	1989	1990	2006	1990	1991	2008	1990	1991	2008
Prospective reserves	2028	2030	2067	2033	2036	2083	2034	2036	2080	2040	2043	2103

Note: It is assumed that reserves are exhausted before using prospective reserves. Recycling and net import percentages are taken from table 4–20 and held constant over time.

a Demand for primary production is zero; resources are zero.
b Demand for primary production is zero; resources are greater than zero.

of carefully specified sets of circumstances if prices were not to rise. As the mineral-by-mineral discussion of the previous section makes clear, prospective reserve estimates are too uncertain and in general too incomplete to place any confidence in individual dates. But more confidence can be placed in differences between exhaustion dates resulting from changes in specific assumptions.

It is interesting to note how small these differences are when assumptions about population and economic growth are changed. In the absence of recycling and trade, the extent of the differences depends on the amount of resources relative to cumulative demands. In cases in which reserves plus prospective reserves are small relative to demand (for example, for aluminum and cobalt), resources are used up quickly regardless of population and economic growth assumptions. For somewhat more abundant resources (copper, iron, and zinc, for example), lower population growth (compare FH with DH) or economic growth (compare DL with DH) extends the date of hypothetical exhaustion by five to ten years. Only in cases in which exhaustion would occur much later in time (for example, molybdenum, titanium, and vanadium) are the differences between these scenarios significantly enlarged.

The introduction of recycling at current rates makes little difference in these exhaustion dates—lead, for which the recycling rate is 34 percent, is exhausted only eight or nine years later than if it were not recycled. The introduction of net imports along with recycling, of course, makes a more significant difference. For example, if 64 percent of nickel requirements were imported each year (as has been the case in recent years), it would reduce the demand for primary production sufficiently to extend U.S. resources by 90 to 140 years. The introduction of trade in phosphate rock, which is now exported, means that exhaustion of the resource figures given in table 4–7 would occur some twenty to twenty-five years earlier.

What difference would various rates of growth in the United States and the rest of the world have on world adequacy? Assuming the standard case for the rest of the world, if scenario DH were to hold for the United States instead of EL, the dates of hypothetical exhaustion would occur, on the average, five years later (excluding molybdenum, for which the date shifts by twenty-five years, the range is from one year, for cobalt, to ten years, for titanium and vanadium). This picture is not changed by basing the comparison on FL instead of EL. A shift in assumptions about world population and economic growth has a more sizable effect on global resource adequacy. If, for example, the high population and economic growth case (DH) is substituted for the standard case, the dates of hypothetical exhaustion would average some nineteen years earlier (excluding molybdenum for which the date would be shifted by more than one hundred years). This would mean that aluminum, copper, nickel, and tungsten would join cobalt, lead, sulfur, and tin in having hypothetical exhaustion dates of 2030 or earlier.

Finally, how sensitive are these results to changes in resource and demand estimates? The problem in answering this question is to choose estimates that lie within a reasonable range, for obviously there are combinations of estimates that will dramatically affect the results. Because our resource estimates are more likely to be too low than too high, suppose we increased them across the board by 50 to 100 percent. If these increases occurred only in the United States and if this country were to rely on its own resources (with recycling held constant), the hypothetical exhaustion dates would be postponed by some eighteen years for a 50 percent increase in resources and thirty-two years for a 100 percent increase.[31] If these resource increases occurred throughout the world, a 50 percent increase in resources would extend their exhaustion dates by twenty-two years,[32] and a 100 percent increase would lengthen the period by about forty years.

On the demand side, a convenient procedure is to accept the range of estimates used by the Bureau of Mines (1975). In addition to projecting a "probable" demand for the year 2000, its analysts were asked to specify "low" and "high" demand estimates, differing from the probable not because of different estimates of end uses (for example, construction or transport) but only because of different estimates of requirements per unit of end use (for example, aluminum per unit of construction or transport). Applying these high/low ranges (specified as percentages of the probable estimates) to our demand estimates yields alternate projections that can be used to specify a range of dates when hypothetical exhaustion might occur for each mineral. For the standard case, this procedure results in a range averaging about thirteen years for the United States and fourteen years for the world (excluding molybdenum). In the case of manganese, for example, the probable estimate for exhausting U.S. sources

[31] This is a weighted average that excludes molybdenum and includes two years for aluminum and chromium, twenty to twenty-two years for copper, iron, and phosphate rock, thirty-seven or more years for titanium and vanadium, and seven to twelve years for the remainder.

[32] Again excluding molybdenum. This weighted average includes five years for aluminum, cobalt, and lead, thirty years or more for phosphate rock, potash, titanium, and vanadium, and eight to twenty years for the remainder.

(assuming no trade) is 2017, with a range between 2011 and 2020. World resources would be exhausted some time between 2097 and 2121.

Obviously, it would be possible to select combinations of such assumptions—for example, a conservative estimate of resources, the upper end of the demand range, and a scenario incorporating rapid rates of growth in population and economic activities—that would require within the given time frame significant price rises to balance demand and supply. But with equal logic combinations could be selected that would postpone the need for such price increases by many decades. Changing one variable at a time, however, as was done here, does not significantly alter the general nature of the overall conclusions.

Conclusions

The principal goal of this chapter has been to estimate whether reserves and resources for major nonfuel minerals are adequate to satisfy cumulative demand projections without significant increases in real prices during the fifty-year time horizon. Prices of only a few minerals—lead, tin, tungsten, and (given the discussion of technical note A) perhaps fluorine and mercury—might increase for this reason during the next fifty years, and there are only one or two for which the price increases might be described as being more than modest—more than, say, 50 percent during the whole period.[33] These special cases are tungsten and perhaps fluorine and mercury, which may have relatively inelastic demand or supply curves. Because the cost of these elements is typically a small percentage of the cost of the final goods or services into which they are incorporated, and because most of these final goods and services are difficult to describe as essential to the safety and welfare of society, even a fourfold price increase would not disrupt the economy much. In addition, there are other minerals—particularly some of those associated with deep-sea nodules—whose prices may well fall over time. Given the assumptions of this analysis, therefore, there is no reason to expect a *general* increase in nonfuel mineral prices relative to other prices.

Two important factors support this conclusion. First, it is a conclusion that is not very sensitive to changes in assumptions. Of course, this

---

[33] We are talking here about long-run trends in real prices, not shorter run fluctuations, which are quite likely to be greater than 50 percent.

statement can only hold for the specific variations in assumptions we have selected, but we believe that our range of alternatives is reasonably broad and representative of what might happen. Second, we are more likely to have erred by underestimating reserves and resources and overestimating growth rates in demand than the other way around. Only a few of the many technological changes and substitutions that are likely to occur on the supply and demand sides of the market have been incorporated. Certainly, there are many more opportunities for adjustments in the event that excess demand pressures do develop. Estimates of speculative, and in many cases hypothetical, resources have been left out, as have some estimates for whole continents. The percentage of gross demand met by recycling has been held constant, even though there are some reasons to believe it will increase over time.[34]

It should be emphasized that the only price increases considered here are those resulting from physical depletion. Long-run price increases may also result from more or less permanent restrictions on the ability to mine certain lands or purchase resources in any desired amounts from certain countries, or from increases in production costs resulting from environmental regulations or higher energy prices. Moreover, nothing in this analysis suggests that short-run disruptions in production and trade will occur with less frequency or severity than they have in the past.

This last qualification need not be a serious one, because the U.S. government holds sizable stockpiles of most minerals. These stockpiles are meant for strategic purposes, but at times they have been used to achieve economic goals. If this policy continues, the stockpiles should be sufficient to cope with most short-run contingencies. So far as environmental constraints are concerned, chapter 3 suggested that though some sectors may experience significant cost increases if fiscal relief is not provided, in the aggregate, relative to the size of the economy as a whole, these increases are not very large. Energy prices and availability are considered in the next chapter, and problems of land and water use are discussed, to the extent possible, in chapter 8.

---

[34] Technical note B compares our projections of demand with others and finds them to be on the low side. But the principal reason for this is the lower rate of growth in GNP assumed in scenario EL, the case used as a basis of comparison. Had comparable rates of growth in GNP been used, our projections would have been much closer. See technical note B for a discussion of other reasons.

Technical Note A: The Status of Other Minerals of Commercial Value

A number of other minerals were reviewed as part of this study, but detailed demand and supply projections were not made for them.[35] The results are summarized briefly here.

ASBESTOS.   The primary use of asbestos is in construction; among others, cement products, floor tile, paper products, paints, and caulking contain asbestos. World production in the decade 1964–73 increased at an annual rate of approximately 4 percent a year. Known reserves of asbestos are quite large, sufficient to sustain the historical rate of growth in production for forty years. Continued increases in consumption of asbestos are unlikely, however. It has been identified as a major health hazard because its fibers in the atmosphere can cause cancer of the lungs. There are a large number of substitutes in virtually all of its uses, and some of them, such as fiberglass, are based on materials in inexhaustible supply.

BARIUM.   The major use of barium is as a weighting agent for oil and gas drilling muds. Known reserves are about thirty times greater than current world production. Although barium is the choice for drilling muds in oil and gas, there are many substitutes that are not significantly higher in price. Further, the cost of the mud is an extremely small proportion of the cost of oil and gas drilling. There was a technological change in drilling technology in the mid-fifties that substantially reduced the barium requirements per foot drilled. Even though known reserves of barium are a relatively small multiple of current production, the availability of this mineral should not cause any significant problems.

BORON.   The use of boron increased rapidly in the decade 1964–73. World production has increased at an annual rate of almost 8 percent per year. Boron is an abundant material, but there are few commercially attractive deposits known. Reserves in these deposits, however, are more than two-hundred times the current rate of production. A problem that appears to be developing is the rapid rate of growth in boron consumption, which, if continued, would exhaust these resources in thirty-seven years. The major uses of boron have been in ceramics and glass; con-

[35] This review is taken from the analysis provided by Vogely (1976).

sumption in these uses has been increasing at a rate of almost 11 percent a year. Many substitutes are available for boron in most other uses, such as in soaps and detergents, but unless technology can discover substitutes for boron in ceramics and glass, it is possible that toward the end of the fifty-year period a shortage problem could arise for the production of some of these products. Boron is such an abundant element that long before this shortage occurs exploration efforts should find new deposits as required. Presently, these efforts are being retarded by the presence of very large known reserves.

FELDSPAR.   Currently known reserves of this mineral are sufficient to sustain production increases for more than seventy-five years at the annual growth rate experienced during the decade 1964–75.

FLUORINE.   This mineral is one of the most versatile and useful of the elements. It is used in steel and aluminum production, and it is very important in the fluorocarbon chemicals, such as refrigerants, plastics, solvents, aerosols, lubricants, coolants, and in other industrial products. Demand for fluorine has been growing rapidly during the past decade, at an annual rate of 7.55 percent. If this rate of use is sustained for the next fifteen years, known reserves would be exhausted. But these factors make this result very unlikely. First, fluorine can be recycled, even though now it is not, from the aluminum pot lines in which it is used as a flux in the electrolytic cells. Second, there are substitutes available for fluorine in steel making: bauxite and high-alumina clays, both in large supply. Third, the use of fluorine in aerosols, a large and rapidly growing use, is undergoing severe environmental challenge because of the effect of fluorine on the ozone in the atmosphere.

This commodity must be flagged as potentially troublesome. It should be noted, however, that the total value of its consumption is less than $200 million, and even very large price rises, if needed to develop new supplies, would have minimal impact on the economy.

TALC.   On a worldwide basis, demand for talc has been increasing 4.6 percent a year during the past decade. At this rate of increase, known reserves are adequate for only thirty years, but there are good, relatively abundant substitutes for talc in virtually every one of its uses.

OTHER NONFERROUS METALS.   There are many other nonferrous metals that have very limited uses in our industrial economy. Adequacy is no problem for most of these, including: arsenic, beryllium, bismuth, cadmium, cesium, gallium, germanium, gold, hathium, indium, radium, rare earths, scandium, selenium, silver, tellurium, thallium, yttrium, and zirconium. A few deserve some discussion, however. *Antimony* is fairly widely used as a fire retardant in railroad products, chemicals, glass, and ceramics. Its total world production in 1973 was 76 thousand tons, and there was very little growth during the past decade. Known reserves are 5.6 million tons, adequate for about seventy-five years. *Mercury* has recently been flagged as a problem resource. Cook (1976), for example, states that mercury is exhausted within the United States and is in a period of rapidly rising cost. However, Goeller and Weinberg (1976) examine mercury by use and conclude that

> Acceptable alternatives are now known for all major uses of mercury, except possibly for high-performance electric batteries (which would require other scarce materials such as cadmium and silver) or electric switches. For minor uses, such as pharmaceuticals or laboratory uses, which amount to less than 1 to 5 percent each of the total, alternatives have not been sought very seriously because the amount of mercury is small. We can hardly imagine society collapsing or even being impeded in the long-run if we have to do without mercurial pharmaceuticals or mercury batteries.

PLATINUM GROUP. These metals are extremely rare and have very important uses in the industrial sector as catalysts. Like gold and silver, platinum metals are virtually 100 percent recyclable. The resource supply is ample to handle foreseeable requirements.

OTHER FERROUS METALS. Four remaining ferrous metals can be mentioned in passing: columbium, lithium, silicon, and tantalum. Present consumption of these minerals is very low, and resources are very large.

Technical Note B: Comparison with Other Estimates

It is impossible to summarize here all the resource demand and supply estimates made by others and to explain completely the reasons for the differences between these estimates and ours. It is useful to point out, however, that our estimates of demand are generally on the low side. The principal reason for this is the difference in assumptions about GNP. As can be seen in table 4–22, scenario EL uses a figure for the U.S. GNP in

Table 4-22. Comparisons with Other Demand Estimates for the Year 2000

Indicator and mineral	United States			World			
	Scenario EL	National Commission	Bureau of Mines[a]	Standard case	National Commission	Bureau of Mines[a]	Leontief
Population (millions)	286	318	264	6,446	6,430	6,430	6,300
GNP per capita (1971 US$)	9,187	9,537	11,225	1,662	1,788	1,788	2,196
GNP (billions of 1971 US$)	2,429	3,033	2,968	10,711	11,495	11,495	13,833
Minerals (thousands of short tons)							
Aluminum	16,493	28,400	22,960	60,965	51,545	72,760	44,400
Chromium	1,107	1,260	1,240	2,016	...	6,010	...
Cobalt	19	13	22	123	...	83	...
Copper	3,265	9,700	6,000	16,418	21,708	30,000	28,200
Iron in ore	140,789	220,000	129,000	864,583	1,086,000	1,130,000	1,900,400
Lead	2,420	2,730	2,430	10,974	...	11,650	16,900
Manganese	2,458	2,360	2,130	10,765	...	22,100	...
Molybdenum	49	...	97	181	...	293	...
Nickel	525	550	550	2,122	...	2,210	2,617
Phosphate rock	57,272	...	69,000	263,027	...	456,000	...
Potash	8,151	...	12,000	44,134	...	60,000	...
Sulfur	18,966	...	25,760	76,192	110,697	123,200	...
Tin	114	146	90	582	...	452	...
Titanium	1,073	2,090	1,450	3,580	...	5,635	...
Tungsten	15	38	26	69	...	88	...
Vanadium	15	31	33	69	...	90	...
Zinc	2,616	3,200	3,200	12,819	14,824	13,300	20,700

Sources: Other demand estimates were taken from National Commission on Materials Policy, Towards a National Material Policy—Basic Data and Issues, An Interim Report (Washington, D.C., GPO, 1972); and Material Needs and the Environment: Today and Tomorrow, Final Report of the National Commission on Material Policy (Washington, D.C., 1973); Wilfred Malenbaum, "Materials Requirements Abroad in the Year 2000," (Washington, D.C., National Committee on Materials Policy, 1972); Bureau of Mines, Mineral Facts and Problems, Bulletin 667 (Washington, D.C., GPO); Wasily Leontif, Ann Carter, and Peter Petri, The Future of the World Economy (New York, Oxford University Press, 1977). Estimates from these sources were converted to the same units used in this study.

[a] "Probable" estimates.

the year 2000 that is some 20 percent lower than those of the National Commission on Materials Policy (1972) or the Bureau of Mines (1975). But even after accounting for this difference, the demand figures here are significantly lower than those sources for aluminum, copper, lead, molybdenum, potash, tungsten and vanadium, and they are significantly higher for iron and some alloying elements.

On a general level, the most likely explanation of these differences is that our procedures allow for more changes in the composition of demand and output and more substitutions, not just among items in this list, but also among items like glass, plastics, and cement that are not on the list of minerals [see Shapanka (1978) for a discussion of these substitutions]. This is the most likely explanation because neither the National Commission nor the Bureau of Mines used a detailed, dynamic model; as a consequence, their procedures may involve more rigid linkages to national aggregates like GNP or GNP per capita and to historic time trends.

At the world level, the differences in GNP again account for the bulk of the differences among demand estimates; our standard case uses a global GNP some 7 percent lower than that of the Bureau of Mines and 23 percent lower than the UN target used by Leontief and coauthors (1977). Leontief's procedure at the global level is the most sophisticated in the sense that it uses input–output tables specific to various regions of the world; also, for better or worse, his procedure for changing consumption patterns over time is quite different from ours.

References

Ayres, Robert U., and Stedman Noble. 1972. "Substitution Possibilities for Tungsten," in *Materials Scarcity and Substitution,* Part B. IRT-302-R, International Research and Technology Corp. for the Conference Board.

Barnett, Harold J., and Chandler Morse. 1963. *Scarcity and Growth: The Economics of Natural Resource Availability* (Baltimore, Md., Johns Hopkins University Press for Resources for the Future).

Bureau of Mines. 1967. *Potential Sources of Aluminum,* Information Circular 8335. U.S. Department of Interior (Washington, D.C., GPO).

———. 1975. *Mineral Facts and Problems,* Bureau of Mines Bulletin 667, U.S. Department of Interior (Washington, D.C., GPO).

———. 1977. Mineral Commodity Profiles: *Chromium—1977, Cobalt— 1977, Copper—1977, Manganese—1977, Phosphate—1977,* and *Nickel—1977.* U.S. Department of Interior (Washington, D.C., GPO).

Cook, E. 1976. "Limits to Exploitation of Non-Renewable Resources," *Science* vol. 191, no. 4227 (February) pp. 677–682.

Council on International Economic Policy, Executive Office of the President. 1974. *Special Report, Critical Imported Materials* (December) (Washington, D.C., GPO).

Erickson, Ralph L. 1973. "Crustal Abundance of Elements and Mineral Reserves and Resources," in U.S. Geological Survey, *United States Mineral Resources* (Washington, D.C., GPO).

Goeller, H. E., and A. M. Weinberg. 1976. "The Age of Substitutability," *Science* vol. 191, no. 4228 (February) pp. 683–688.

Holser, Alexander. 1976. "Manganese Nodule Resources and Mine Site Availability." (Washington, D.C., Ocean Mining Administration, U.S. Department of Interior).

Hubbert, M. King. 1969. "Energy Resources," in National Academy of Science, *Resources and Man* (San Francisco, W. H. Freeman) pp. 157–242.

————. 1972. *U.S. Energy Resources, A Review as of 1972*. Committee on Interior and Insular Affairs, U.S. Senate (Washington).

Leipziger, Danny, and James Mudge. 1976. *Seabed Mineral Resources and the Economic Interests of Developing Countries* (Cambridge, Mass., Ballinger).

Leontief, Wasily, Ann Carter, and Peter Petri. 1977. *The Future of the World Economy* (New York, Oxford University Press).

Malenbaum, Wilfred. 1972. "Materials Requirements Abroad in the Year 2000," research report for the National Commission on Materials Policy (Washington, D.C.).

McKelvey, V. E. 1973. "Mineral Resource Estimates and Public Policy," in U.S. Geological Survey, *United States Mineral Resources* (Washington, D.C., GPO).

Mero, John. 1965. *The Mineral Resources of the Sea* (New York, Elsevier).

National Academy of Sciences (NAS). 1975. *Mineral Resources and the Environment* (Washington, D.C., NAS).

National Commission on Materials Policy. 1972. *Towards a National Material Policy—Basic Data and Issues,* An Interim Report (Washington, D.C., GPO).

————. 1973. *Material Needs and the Environment: Today and Tomorrow,* Final Report of the National Commission on Materials Policy (Washington, D.C., GPO).

National Commission on Supplies and Shortages. 1976. *Government and the Nation's Resources,* Report of the National Commission on Supplies and Shortages (December) (Washington, D.C., GPO).

Nordhaus, William D. 1974. "Resources as a Constraint on Growth," in *Papers and Proceedings of the American Economic Review* vol. 64, no. 2 (May).

Pindyck, R. S. 1977. "Cartel Pricing and the Structure of the World Bauxite Market," *The Bell Journal of Economics* vol. 8, no. 2 (Autumn).

Schanz, John J., Jr. 1975. *Resource Terminology: An Examination of Concepts and Terms and Recommendations for Improvement* (Palo Alto, Calif., Electric Power Research Institute, 1975).

Shapanka, Adele. 1978. "Technological Assumptions and Their Use in Studying the Resource and Environmental Consequences of Population and Economic Growth in the U.S." (Washington, D.C., Resources for the Future).

Smith, V. Kerry. 1977. "Measuring Natural Resource Scarcity: Theory and Practice," Resources for the Future Discussion Paper D-11 (November) (Washington, D.C., Resources for the Future).

Turbeville, W. J., Jr. 1977. "New Sources of Phosphate Rock," *Industrial Minerals* (April) pp. 39–41.

U.S. Geological Survey (USGS). 1973. *United States Mineral Resources,* Geological Survey Professional Paper 820 (Washington, D.C., GPO).

Vogely, William A. 1976. "Non-Fuel Resources," a report to Resources for the Future (Washington, D.C.).

Wells, Frederick J. 1975. *The Long-Run Availability of Phosphorous* (Baltimore, Md., Johns Hopkins University Press for Resources for the Future).

5

Energy

The energy situation is more complex than that for nonfuel minerals because we cannot as easily set aside the possibilities of and reactions to price increases, cartel actions, and technological changes. The first section of this chapter reviews the energy resource and reserve figures for the world and major subdivisions, including the United States. This is followed by an analysis of demands for and supplies of energy and important fuels in major regions of the world and the consequences of this situation for world prices of petroleum and natural gas, the two internationally traded fuels that are likely to experience large price changes in the coming years. The analysis then centers on the U.S. situation. We first discuss our projection methods and assumptions with respect to elasticities and domestic prices, then set forth our results with respect to demand, production, and imports of different fuels. The final section compares estimates of cumulative energy requirements and resources for different scenarios.

Resources and Reserves

Here, as in chapter 4, *reserves* are defined as the portion of total resources that is known and economically recoverable on the basis of current prices and technology, *prospective reserves* are the portion likely to be added to reserves in the next fifty years, and *resources* are the sum of these two categories. Thus, prospective reserves include future discoveries that are likely to become economic because of expected price increases or technological improvements during the next fifty years. Estimates that are based on assumptions about such changes are so noted in the text.

Renewable resources are handled separately. There are three relevant categories here, depending on the resource in question: capacity in place, potential capacity that could be developed, and likely additions to current capacity. The context should make clear just which is meant.

Nonrenewable Resources

In 1972 nonrenewable energy sources supplied 97.7 percent of the world's energy consumption (United Nations, 1974). Virtually all these resources came from fossil fuels; nuclear fuels provided less than 1 percent in that year. Except for countries well endowed with hydroelectricity,[1] the principal renewable energy source, this general picture describes individual countries as well.

Table 5–1 presents different estimates of world reserves and resources for nonrenewable sources of energy. The wide range of these estimates reflects the uncertainty surrounding these figures. In the case of coal, the width of this range is of little consequence because even if the lowest of the estimates prevailed, resources would be adequate for more than 1,000 years at present consumption rates or more than 140 years at a 5 percent a year growth rate. This study uses a value approximately midway in this range.

Variations in estimates of reserves and prospective reserves for petroleum and natural gas are critical, because these estimates are small relative to anticipated demands during the next fifty years. Except for the Hubbert figures, which might include some prospective reserves in the reserve category, the reserve estimates are in reasonably close agreement. Our estimates were chosen deliberately to be on the conservative side.

The resource estimates vary somewhat more than those for reserves, but as a recent review (Lichtblau and Frank, 1978) makes clear, estimates of total, *ultimately* recoverable petroleum appear to center around the Moody and Esser (1975) estimate of 2,030 billion barrels or 1,711 billion barrels (9,924 quads) of *remaining* recoverable petroleum as of 1975. Even without any further increase in petroleum prices (in real terms), this figure is probably too low, because it does not include recoverable petroleum resources in unexplored regions, particularly in less

[1] Norway, Sweden, Portugal, Finland, and New Zealand.

developed countries.[2] If the price rises substantially, as is likely, the recovery rate (which is assumed to increase from 33 percent to 40 percent
because of technological improvements alone) ought to increase further,
and more costly sources of petroleum (oil from more expensive recovery
techniques, smaller fields, deeper wells, and more viscous oils) will come
into use.[3] These factors eventually should increase the resource figure by
25 percent, to 12,500 quads.

Our estimate for natural gas resources is higher than others cited in
table 5–1, but the other estimates appear to be excessively conservative.
Until recently, there was very little world trade in natural gas and no
great incentive to explore for it; indeed, most of the gas that is presently
being consumed was discovered as a by-product of petroleum exploration. Some countries have not published estimates of their natural gas
resources. The estimate used here begins with the World Energy Conference Survey figures for natural gas and adjusts them for countries that did
not report.[4] It was not assumed that recovery rates would be higher in the
future, however, because present recovery rates for gas average around
80 percent.

The wide spread in the values shown in table 5–1 for oil shale and
tar sand resources is the result of several factors. First, only small quantities of these resources have been, and are expected in the next decade or
so to be, produced commercially. As a consequence, there has been little
incentive to invest in exploration. Second, deposits of shale vary greatly
in quality—from as little as 1 gallon or less per ton of shale up to 100 gallons or more per ton—and there are large variations in the geologic conditions under which they are found. Third, it is not clear just how costly
it will be to contain or correct the environmental problems associated
with shale. If in situ techniques can be used, environmental problems
could be small; if above-ground methods must be used, the costs could be

---

[2] Of the 600 sedimentary basins in the world where petroleum could exist,
there has been virtually no exploratory drilling in 200. Many of these are in South
America and Africa. They have not been explored because they are in remote areas
where infrastructure (roads, airfields, supply points, pipelines, and trained manpower) is lacking or in deep offshore waters, which have been too costly to explore
in the past, or because of political factors (Exxon, 1978; and IBRD, 1978).

[3] Heavy oils alone have been estimated to be at least equal to ultimately
recoverable petroleum resources, but recovery rates are likely to be substantially
lower.

[4] By some standards, the figure used in this study is still quite conservative.
For example, the U.S. Geological Survey provided an estimate of nearly 20×10^{18}
Btu for the world (USGS, 1965, p. 17).

Table 5–1. Comparison of Estimates of World Nonrenewable Energy Reserves and Resources (10^{18} Btu)

Source	This study	NAS 1975	ERDA 1976	Hubbert 1974	WEC 1974	WEC 1978	Moody and Esser 1975	Exxon 1978
Reserves								
Coal	24.0	...	14.3	47.0–178.0	14.3	17.2	...	...
Petroleum	3.5	3.6	4.1	10.1	4.1	4.2	...	...
Natural gas	2.0	2.1	2.4	...	1.9	2.2	...	...
Oil shale	2.0[a]	72.0	3.0	1.7	10.4	1.2	...	...
Tar sands		4.5[b]	...	2.2	...	0.6–1.2	...	...
U_3O_8	1.3[c]	...	0.2[b]	...	0.5[b]	1.0[b]	...	...
Resources								
Coal	172.5	220	120.0–160.0	...	237	254	...	...
Petroleum	10.0[d]	10.4	7.8–11.3	...	17.3	11.0[e]	9.9	12.2
Natural gas	10.0	7.0	3.1–6.1	...	9.8	10.3	...	...
Oil shale	15.8[f]	205.2	6.8–9.6	...	...	...	...	...
Tar sands	...	...	...	...	...	...	...	...
U_3O_8	8.2–40.9	...	2.0–2.7[b]	...	2.1[b]	2.0[b]	...	...

Sources:: NAS [National Academy of Sciences, Committee on Mineral Resources and the Environment, Mineral Resources and the Environment (Washington, D.C., February 1975) p. 98]; ERDA [U.S. Energy Research and Development Administration, *A National Plan for Energy Research and Development, and Demonstration: Creating Energy Choices for the Future*, vol. 1 (Washington, D.C., GPO, 1976) pp. 107 and 110]; Hubbert [M. Hubbert, "U.S. Energy Resources, A Review as of 1972." Report prepared for the Senate Committee on Interior and Insular Affairs, serial no. 93-40 (Washington, D.C., GPO, 1974)]; WEC [World Energy Conference, Survey of Energy Resources (New York, U.S. National Committee of the World Energy Conference, 1974) tables IV-1, IV-2, IV-3, III-12, VII-1, and IX-2]; *World Energy Resources 1985–2020* (New York, IPC Science and Technology Press, 1978) pp. 8, 15, 54, 60, and 116; Moody and Esser [J. D. Moody and R. W. Esser, "World Crude Resource May Exceed 1500 Billion Barrels," *World Oil* (September, 1975) pp. 47–56]. Estimated at 2030 billion barrels, 319 of which were consumed by the end of 1975, assuming 5.8 million Btu a barrel. Exxon (Exxon, "Exploration in Developing Countries." Paper presented at Aspen Institute, July 16–20, 1978.) Based on a poll of twenty-nine "experts" at the last World Energy Conference; the mean response was 2.1 trillion barrels.

This study—the above sources, plus the following: World Power Conference, *Survey of Energy Resources* (London, Central Office of World Power Conference, 1968); H. R. Linden, "Review of World Energy Supplies," in *U.S. Energy Resources: A Review as of 1972*, Committee Print 93-75, pt. 1, U.S. Senate Committee on Interior and Insular Affairs (Washington, D.C., 1974); U.S. Senate Committee on Interior and Insular Affairs, *Energy Research and Development: Problems and Prospects*, serial no. 93-21 (92-56) (Washington, D.C., 1973) pp. 117–121; *Oil and Gas Journal* (December 31, 1973) p. 86 and (December 27, 1976) p. 105; U.S. Nuclear Regulatory Commission, *Final Generic Environmental Statement on the Use of Recycled Plutonium in Mixed Oxide Fuel in Light Water-Cooled Reactors*, vol. 4, NUREG-002 (Springfield, Va., National Technical Information Service, 1976); and Nuclear Energy Policy Study Group, *Nuclear Power Issues and Choices* (Cambridge, Mass., Ballinger, 1977) chapters 2 and 3.

ª Known deposits recoverable under 1965 conditions and containing 10 to 100 gallons per ton of shale.

ᵇ Incomplete estimate.

ᶜ U_3O_8 up to $50 a pound (forward cost), assuming 120 million kWh (th) or 409.4 billion Btu a short ton.

ᵈ This estimate assumes a continuation of current prices in real terms. If prices rise substantially, this figure is assumed to increase to 12.5×10^{18} Btu, the number used in figures 5–3 and 5–4 and table 5–21.

ᵉ Remaining recoverable as of 1977 excluding deposits in deep offshore and polar regions.

ᶠ The value is for what are now marginal and submarginal known deposits containing 10 to 100 gallons per ton of shale. Total oil shale resources of grades from 5 to 100 gallons per ton in undiscovered and unappraised deposits could be as large as $13,000 \times 10^{18}$ Btu. Only 144×10^{18} Btu of this total is in the known or possible expansion of known deposits.

substantial, depending on geologic conditions. Because the second and third of these factors are important in determining the cost of producing shale oil, the assumptions used in establishing what will be "economic" are critical in estimating the quantities of both proved and prospective reserves. Estimates of oil shale resources of all kinds as large as 13,000 $\times$ 10^{18} Btu have been made. We estimate that 15.8×10^{18} Btu can be exploited by the year 2010 at costs only slightly higher than 1975 oil prices, given the technological changes expected to occur by that date. If these prices rise significantly, as may be expected after the turn of the century, this figure will prove far too conservative.

Published estimates of world uranium resources probably are understated by a wide margin. They are based on data derived from exploratory efforts, which have been quite small compared to those for other fuels. Even the United States, where the most exploration has occurred, is considered by many to be far from fully surveyed so far as this mineral is concerned. In addition, there is no published information for large regions of the earth, particularly the Soviet Union and the People's Republic of China, although there is little reason to believe occurrences there will be substantially less than elsewhere. To take this uncertainty into account, we have developed both a low and a high estimate, using for extrapolation purposes data primarily from the United States.

In 1976, the U.S. Energy Research and Development Administration (ERDA, 1976b) estimated U.S. resources of uranium oxide at 3.7 million tons, recoverable at $30 or less a pound (forward cost of ore). For several reasons, this estimate is unsatisfactory for our purposes. First, it is likely that the estimate will prove to be too conservative in the long run. Until very recently, the demand for uranium could be satisfied from easily found deposits of high-grade ores. Thus, there was virtually no exploratory activity directed toward finding lower grade ores, and the result is a severe lack of knowledge that tends to bias most estimates downward (NEPS, 1977). For example, more than 90 percent of the ERDA estimates are for uranium recovery from sandstone, although there appears to be a reasonable probability that large deposits of somewhat lower grade exist in other formations like the Rossing deposit (NRC, 1976). Second, the estimate extends only up to the forward cost figure of $30 a pound, but it is likely that higher cost categories will become economic within the fifty-year time frame. Third, the cost categories are based upon the concept of "forward cost," which is misleading in that it includes less than full costs of recovery, and these may be as much as 50 to 100 percent greater than forward cost.

Table 5–2. Nuclear Regulatory Commission Estimates of U.S. Uranium Resources

(thousands of tons of U_3O_8)

Forward cost	Proved reserves	Prospective reserves[a]			Total resources
		Probable	Possible	Speculative	
Contiguous United States ($/lb U_3O_8)					
$10	270	440	420	500	1,630
$10–$15	160	215	255	500	1,130
$15–$30	210	405	595	1,000	2,210
$30–$50	200	400	600	1,000	2,200
Subtotal	840	1,460	1,870	3,000	7,170
By-product	140	—	—	—	140
Total conterminous United States					7,310
Alaska					1,400
Total United States					8,710

Source: U.S. Nuclear Regulatory Commission, *Final Generic Environmental Statement on the Use of Recycled Plutonium in Mixed Oxide Fuel in Light Water Cooled Reactors*, vol. 4, NUREG-002 (Springfield, Va., National Technical Information Service, 1976).

[a] Called potential reserves by the Nuclear Regulatory Commission.

To adjust for these problems, we began with estimates made by the Nuclear Regulatory Commission (reproduced in table 5–2), because they include estimates for a forward cost category of $30 to $50 a pound (NRC, 1976). From these estimates, we subtracted the two most questionable figures—1 million tons described as speculative in the $30 to $50 range and 1 million tons indicated for Alaska, where virtually no exploration has yet taken place. Then, the cost categories were revised, using factors given in the NRC report, to reflect more nearly the estimated total recovery cost. This procedure yields the following estimates for all categories of resources, from proved to speculative reserves:

Total recovery cost per ton (1975$)	U_3O_8 resources (thousands of short tons)
$16 or less	270
$16–35	2,480
$35–75	2,210
$75–100	1,210
Subtotal	6,170
By-product	140
Total	6,310

This total is equivalent to 2,583 quads of energy in the form of electricity at 120 million kWh(th) a ton.[5] It could, of course, be incorrect by a wide margin. The best estimate of the CONAES uranium resource subpanel (Silver, 1977) is 1.76 million tons, but it does not include ore above $30 a pound forward cost, does not include either possible or speculative reserves in prospective reserve figures, and is based on a much smaller figure for by-product recovery. If the NRC is correct about the size of Alaskan reserves and speculative reserves in the $30 to $50 (forward cost) range, the resource estimate would be 8.71 million tons.

We tried two different methods in order to arrive at a similar estimate for the entire world. The first assumes (1) that proved reserves for the non-Communist world other than the United States, estimated to be 1.8 million tons (NEPS, 1977), would be in the same ratio to prospective reserves as they are in the United States, and (2) that total resources in Communist countries bear the same relationship to land area as they do in the non-Communist world excluding the United States. This approach yields an estimate of 20 million tons, or 8,188 quads, of uranium oxide recoverable at a cost of $100 a ton or less for the world excluding the United States. Because this method is a function of the level of exploratory efforts in the rest of the non-Communist world, which have been substantially less than that in the United States, these figures are undoubtedly too low. Nevertheless, this method does have the virtue of making use of all available information in a conservative fashion.

The second estimating technique ignores all but the U.S. figures and simply assumes that recoverable uranium resources in the rest of the world (including the Communist nations) bear the same relationship to land area as they do in the United States. The estimate arrived at in this fashion is 100 million tons, or 40,940 quads.

It is impossible to say whether these figures are likely to be too low or too high. Both methods assume that finds will be in proportion to land mass, which is known to be a poor approximation in the cases of fossil fuels and many minerals. In addition, both methods ignore Alaska, Antarctica, and ocean areas, and base extrapolations on areas that have been far from fully explored. As a consequence, we decided to use a range of estimates for this fuel source.

Table 5–3 shows the geographic distribution of energy resources. Most of the world's coal resources are found in the USSR (35 percent), the People's Republic of China (35 percent), and the United States (19

[5] One quad equals 10^{15} Btu or 173.8 million barrels of oil. A kilowatt-hour is equal to 3,412 Btu.

Table 5-3. World Nonrenewable Energy Resources, by Region
(10^{18} Btu)

Region	Coal	Petroleum	Natural gas	Oil shale and tar sands	U_3O_8[a]
North America (excluding the United States)	1.2	0.40	0.48	2.0	...
Western Europe	5.3	0.40	0.32	0.4	...
Oceania	4.2	0.03	0.05	0.9	...
Latin America	0.6	0.70	1.21	1.9	...
Japan	—	—	—	—	...
Other non-Communist Asia[b]	2.1	4.00	4.08	2.5	...
Africa	1.0	0.80	1.31	3.3	...
USSR	60.0	2.00	2.67	0.5	...
Eastern Europe	6.0	0.01	—	—	...
China (People's Republic)	60.0	0.80	0.07	2.5	...
Subtotal (excluding United States)	140.4	9.15	10.18	14.0	8.2–40.9
United States	32.1	0.85	0.92	1.8	2.6
Total world	172.5	10.0	11.10	15.8	10.8–43.5
Total amount (in units indicated)	(6,522 billion metric tons)	(1,724 billion barrels)	(10,571 trillion cubic feet)	(2,724 billion barrels)	(26.4–106.3 million short tons)[c]

Sources: For the U.S. oil and gas estimates see USGS, *Geological Estimate of Undiscovered Recoverable Oil and Gas Resources in the United States*, Circular 725 (Washington, D.C., GPO, 1975). For all other estimates, see sources for table 5-1.

[a] At a forward cost of $50 or less per pound of U_3O_8, equivalent to $100 or less total recovery cost.

[b] Includes the Middle East oil-producing countries.

[c] At 120 million kWh(th) per ton and 3412 Btu per kWh.

percent).[6] Petroleum resources are even more unevenly distributed. The Middle East ("Other non-Communist Asia"), contains about 40 percent, the Communist countries about 30 percent, and most of the remainder is divided roughly equally among the United States, Latin America, and Africa.[7]

There are, of course, many competing estimates for petroleum resources. Even in the United States, where there is relatively good agreement among geologists, the range of recent estimates for prospective reserves of petroleum is 55 to 90 billion barrels (0.3 to 0.5 × 10^{18} Btu)

[6] ERDA's estimates of the regional distribution of *proved reserves* for coal shows the United States with 34 percent, the USSR with 23 percent, and Communist Asia with 16 percent (ERDA, 1976a).

[7] ERDA's estimates of the regional distribution of *proved reserves* for oil shows 57 percent in the Middle East and 12 percent in the USSR (ERDA, 1976a).

and of natural gas is 374 to 704 trillion cubic feet (0.39 to 0.74 $\times$ 10^{18} Btu) (NAS, 1975). Table 5–4 summarizes the most recent U.S. Geological Survey estimates. These estimates—142.1 billion barrels, or approximately 0.85 $\times$ 10^{18} Btu, of oil and 921.8 trillion cubic feet, or 0.92 $\times$ 10^{18} Btu, of natural gas—are the basis for the U.S. figures shown in table 5-3.

High-grade oil shale and tar sands are more evenly distributed around the world, although Japan and Eastern Europe have negligibly small deposits. It is likely that the same holds for uranium oxide, but too little is known about this mineral to be certain.

There are, of course, other nonrenewable energy sources that may someday be tapped. Nonrecovered petroleum, heavy oils and tars, and methane in geopressured reserves and coal mines are cases in point. Each has been estimated to include more energy than all the petroleum that has ever been or is likely to be produced at current prices and technology. Although higher prices or improvements in technology or both are required to make their use economical, it is important to note their existence in order to characterize appropriately the energy resource estimates presented in tables 5–1 and 5–3. These estimates of nonrenewable energy sources are consciously conservative. If time proves them wrong, the price of energy will rise to the point at which some of these additional sources will come into use. Thus, there is reason for confidence that the total energy resource estimates are conservative, even if the estimates for some individual fuels are not.

Renewable Resources

In addition to the energy resources already discussed, there are at least four others of actual or potential importance: hydroelectric, geothermal, solar (including, for example, wind, biomass, and ocean thermal gradients), and fusion energy. They are classified as renewable because, for all practical purposes, depletion of these resources can be ignored for a period substantially beyond this study's time horizon. Of these four sources, hydroelectricity is by far the most widely used today; geothermal and solar energy presently are used to a limited extent; and fusion technology is yet to be proved. Commercial use of tidal energy is minuscule and almost certain to remain so.

The most comprehensive estimate of hydroelectric potential (capacity now installed plus the potential of sites that are yet to be developed) comes from a 1962 study of the National Academy of Sciences

Table 5–4. U.S. Geological Survey Median Estimates of U.S. Reserves and Prospective Reserves of Petroleum and Natural Gas

Source	Reserves			Prospective reserves		
	Onshore	Offshore	Total	Onshore	Offshore	Total
Petroleum (billion barrels)						
Conterminous states	39.0	5.9	44.9	44.0	11.0	55.0
Alaska	15.0	0.2	15.2	12.0	15.0	27.0
Total	54.0	6.1	60.1	56.0	26.0	82.0
Natural gas (trillion cubic feet)						
Conterminous states	288.0	103.2	391.2	345.0	63.0	408.0
Alaska	46.4	0.2	46.6	32.0	44.0	76.0
Total	334.4	103.4	437.8	377.0	107.0	484.0

Source: USGS, *Geological Estimate of Undiscovered Recoverable Oil and Gas Resources in the United States,* Circular 725 (Washington, D.C., GPO, 1975).

(NAS, 1962). It places the maximum U.S. potential at 6.83 quads a year (of fossil fuel equivalent) and that for the rest of the world at 105 quads a year. Since that time, the rise in the price of other fuel sources undoubtedly has made a number of additional hydroelectric sites competitive; however, growing pressures to preserve environmental, scenic, and aesthetic values may prevent some economically attractive sites from being developed. Implicitly assuming that these two forces offset each other, and in the absence of more recent information, the Academy figures will be used in this study. In any case, since the rate of hydroelectric exploitation is likely to be slow and the total world potential is small compared to projected energy demands, it will remain a minor energy resource in all but a few especially well endowed countries.

Lack of data and differences in estimates about the cost of exploiting geothermal energy have led to considerable controversy about the size of this resource. But even the lowest estimates indicate a large potential. In the United States alone, identified hydrothermal systems with temperatures higher than 150°C are estimated at 1.65×10^{18} Btu, almost as large as our estimate of U.S. oil and gas resources. In addition, identified hot igneous sources, for which economic technologies are not yet available, are estimated to contain 100×10^{18} Btu, a value larger than all nonrenewable resources in the world other than coal (USGS, 1975b). There are no acceptable figures for the rest of the world, but there is no reason to believe the United States is exceptionally well endowed.

Geothermal potential is a long way from being realized, however. In 1974, only 1,400 kWe capacity (equivalent to about 86×10^9 Btu of fossil fuel) of geothermal energy were being used in the world. Technological breakthroughs to permit the commercial exploitation of dry hot rocks, the discovery of a large number of widely dispersed, conveniently located hot-rock deposits, or substantially higher energy prices or both will be necessary before much of this potential is exploited commercially. The projections in table 5–9 reflect the judgment that such exploitation will occur slowly.

The solar energy incident on the earth each day is more than 1,000 times the amount of commercial energy consumed daily. But the amount varies greatly from place to place, during different periods of the day and year, and with weather conditions. This great variability, together with the dilute nature of solar energy, creates difficult problems in using it. Both problems can be overcome—variability by providing storage and supplementary energy sources, and dilution by using concentrating devices—but only at costs that restrict current commercial applications to space and water heating in favorable locations. There are a variety of other ways that solar energy can be captured and used: marine or terrestrial farming, ocean thermal energy conversion, windmills, and generation of electricity either through the steam cycle or more directly through photovoltaic devices. Substantially higher fuel prices or technological breakthroughs or both will be necessary, however, before these methods will make a significant contribution to meeting the world's energy requirements.

The feasibility of controlled fusion reactions has not yet been proved, so it is impossible to make good judgments about when, if ever, and at what cost it will become available as an energy resource. Should fusion prove to be competitive with other energy forms, it would represent an almost unlimited resource, because the fuels that could be used (deuterium and tritium) can be made available in virtually any quantities. But even if its feasibility is proved, it cannot be developed quickly enough to play more than a minor role in the most advanced countries during the next fifty years.

World Demands and Supplies

Total Energy Consumption

The methods used for projecting world energy demands and supplies differ significantly between the United States and the rest of the

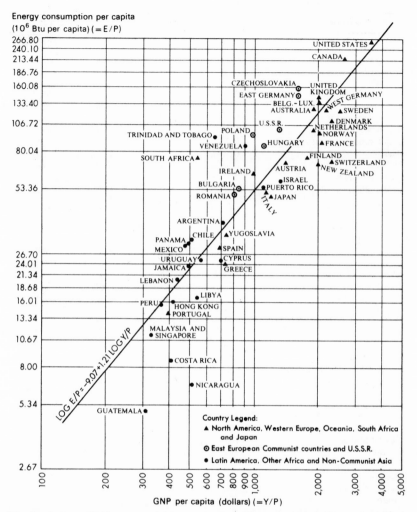

Figure 5–1.   GNP per capita, energy consumption per capita and per unit of GNP in forty-nine selected countries, 1965. From Joel Darmstadter, Perry Teitelbaum, and Jaroslav Polach, *Energy in the World Economy: A Statistical Review of Trends in Output, Trade, and Consumption Since 1925* (Baltimore, Md., Johns Hopkins University Press for Resources for the Future, 1972) page 34.

world. Our projections for the United States used the SEAS/RFF model. The method used for the rest of the world takes its cue from the fact that there is a good correlation between total energy consumption in an economy and the total size of that economy as measured by GNP or GDP. This correlation shows up clearly in figure 5–1, which plots 1965 data

Table 5-5. World Energy Consumption, Total, Per Capita, and Per Dollar of GNP by Major Regions, 1925–72

Region	1925	1950	1960	1972
Total energy consumption (10¹⁵ Btu)				
United States	20.1	34.2	44.8	71.9
Canada	0.9	2.7	3.9	8.7
Western Europe	14.5	17.5	26.1	44.7
Oceania	0.4	0.9	1.4	2.7
Latin America	0.7	2.4	4.9	9.1
Japan	0.9	1.7	3.7	10.7
Other non-Communist Asia	0.8	2.1	4.6	9.4
Africa	0.4	1.3	2.2	4.0
USSR	0.7	8.4	17.9	33.9
Eastern Europe	1.5	4.4	8.1	13.6
China (People's Republic)	0.7	1.2	6.6	13.8
Total world	41.6	76.8	124.2	222.5
Energy consumption per capita (10⁶ Btu per capita)				
United States	174	224	248	345
Canada	91	198	217	399
Western Europe	52	58	80	124
Oceania	48	73	90	134
Latin America	7	14	23	30
Japan	14	21	39	101
Other non-Communist Asia	2	3	5	7
Africa	2	6	8	11
USSR	4	47	84	137
Eastern Europe	22	49	82	127
China (People's Republic)	2	2	10	16
Total world	22	31	42	59
Energy consumption per dollar of GNP (10³ Btu per 1965 US$ of GNP)				
United States	101	87	83	81
Canada	81	101	98	117
Western Europe	...	61	57	56
Oceania	...	60	64	69
Latin America	...	51	65	63
Japan	36	60	51	45
Other non-Communist Asia	...	30	52	36
Africa	...	57	62	55
USSR	16	64	75	63
Eastern Europe	...	80	87	75
China (People's Republic)	...	36	77	99
Total world	...	70	71	65

Sources: For 1925, 1950, and 1960, see J. Darmstadter, P. Teitelbaum, and J. G. Polach, *Energy in the World Economy: A Statistical Review of Trends in Outputs, Trade, and Consumption Since 1925* (Baltimore, Md., Johns Hopkins University Press for Resources for the Future, 1971) pp. 10, 63, 70–71, 865, and 267; for 1950 and 1960, see J. Darmstadter, "Energy," in R. G. Ridker, ed., *Population, Resources, and the Environment*, vol. 3 of *Research Reports of the Commission on Population Growth and the American Future* (Washington, D.C., GPO) table 15, p. 129. Energy consumption for 1972: U.S. Bureau of Mines, *Energy Perspectives 2* (Washington, GPO, 1976). Figures for the rest of the world are from the United Nations, *World Energy Supplies,*

from forty-nine countries.[8] It is also indicated in table 5–5 by the relative constancy over time of the figures for energy consumption per dollar of GNP. This table also indicates slow, fairly steady shifts in this ratio over time, however. Such movements are related mainly to a country's stage of economic development. In poor countries, where commercial forms of energy are still being substituted for noncommercial forms, the ratio is rising. It is likely to continue rising in those economies so long as heavy industry and transport are becoming increasingly important. In later stages of growth, when energy-intensive sectors begin growing at slower rates relative to other sectors, the ratio falls again.

Shifts in the ratio of energy consumption to GNP undoubtedly also are related to long-term changes in the relative price of energy. Between 1925 and 1972, when such price trends were slightly downward, there was probably some upward pressure on these ratios in all countries; thereafter, especially given the fourfold increase in petroleum prices in 1973–74, the pressure ought to be downward. However, it is still too early to know what will be the full impact of this dramatic price change and succeeding developments.

We have tried to take these features into account by developing two sets of projections for each region and applying judgment in selecting the final value. Both sets use the population and GNP projections provided in chapter 2. The first method relies on cross-sectional information for major regions of the world and assumes that regions move up the regression line according to the speed of their economic development. The second method relies on time-series data for each region, projecting regions along a path established by their recent past.

The case of Japan can be used to illustrate these methods. If Japan has a population of 130.6 million and a GNP of $801 million (in 1971 dollars) in the year 2000, the cross-sectional data for 1972 suggest a figure of 35.2 quads, while time-series data yield an estimate of 27.4 quads (see figure 5–2). But, historically, as indicated in figure 5–1, Japan

---

[8] The correlation coefficient for the logs of these data is 0.87. Where hydroelectric energy consumption is subtracted and replaced by its fossil-fuel equivalent, the coefficient increases to 0.89. Applied to a division of the world into eleven regions, the coefficient is 0.98 for 1965 and 0.97 for 1972 data.

1971–75, series J, no. 21 (New York, UN, 1978), with hydro and nuclear electricity evaluated at 10,000 Btu per kilowatt hour. Population figures for 1972 are from the U.S. Department of Agriculture, *World Population by Country, 1950–74* (Washington, D.C., USDA Economic Research Service, June 1975); and United Nations, *Statistical Yearbook* (New York, UN, 1974 and 1975) table 18.

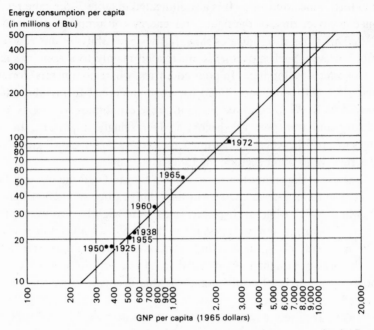

Figure 5–2.   GNP per capita and energy consumption per capita in Japan.

has used less energy per unit of GNP than is typical for a country at its level of GNP; in addition, neither approach reflects the effects of increased energy prices. To allow for these factors, a figure of 26 quads was selected for the year 2000. This number implies that per capita energy consumption will more than double but that energy consumption per unit of GNP will decline, though at a slower pace. A similar procedure was used to estimate values for 2025 and for other major consuming regions of the world (except the United States). In most cases, the estimate that was selected falls within the range prescribed by the two projection methods.

The results, presented in table 5–6, indicate a figure of 574 quads for total world consumption in 2000. This is for the standard case presented in table 2–4, a case in which developed countries have relatively slow population and economic growth rates, and developing countries have somewhat higher population growth rates than developed countries but still have quite low economic growth rates. Other reasonable assumptions about such rates of growth provide a range around this figure of 480 to 600 quads.

It is of interest to note that these projections imply an elasticity of energy demand with respect to GNP (the percentage change in energy

Table 5-6. Projected World Energy Consumption by Major Regions, Standard Case, 1972–2025

(quads of energy)

Region	1972	1985	2000	2025
Total energy consumption (10^{15} Btu)				
United States	72	93	114	171
Canada	9	11	16	26
Western Europe	45	53	73	127
Oceania	3	5	7	12
Latin America	9	22	57	155
Japan	11	17	28	50
Other non-Communist Asia	9	23	64	228
Africa	4	8	18	69
USSR	34	82	108	193
Eastern Europe	14	22	38	58
China (People's Republic)	14	25	51	112
Total world	224	361	574	1,201
Cumulative consumption from 1975		3,344	10,463	32,964
Energy consumption per capita (10^6 Btu per capita)				
United States	345	395	431	563
Canada	399	449	604	849
Western Europe	124	138	182	300
Oceania	134	198	317	478
Latin America	30	52	95	177
Japan	101	137	211	363
Other non-Communist Asia	7	14	25	56
Africa	11	15	24	57
USSR	137	289	357	599
Eastern Europe	127	187	308	439
China (People's Republic)	16	24	37	60
Total world	59	74	89	128
Energy consumption per dollar of GNP (10^3 Btu per 1971 US$ of GNP)				
United States	63	59	47	40
Canada	95	71	64	57
Western Europe	50	40	38	36
Oceania	45	47	42	38
Latin America	48	61	78	68
Japan	43	34	34	33
Other non-Communist Asia	40	52	66	63
Africa	54	43	42	39
USSR	56	72	54	47
Eastern Europe	79	65	66	49
China (People's Republic)	98	102	107	88
Total world	58	57	54	50

demand divided by the percentage change in GNP) for the world as a whole that falls over time and approaches that of the United States by the end of the period. In the 1975–80 period, this elasticity is 1.08; in the next two decades, it is 0.87 and 0.88, respectively, and for the period 2000–25, it is 0.85. These projections (and the figures in table 5–9, which extend to 2050) imply a gently falling energy–GNP ratio for the world as a whole starting in about 1985, with virtually no change between 1975 and 1985. This fall more or less continues the decline experienced prior to 1973.[9]

Most other projections of world energy demand have not gone beyond 1985 and have not always spelled out the assumptions on which they are based. Still, it is of interest to note that the figures presented in table 5–6 are within the range of estimates made by others. This comparison is presented in table 5–7.

Oil

These projections of total energy requirements must now be broken down into fuels and compared with projections of supply. The most critical fuels are, of course, the oils and gases. In 1925, these two fuels accounted for 13.3 percent and 3.2 percent, respectively, of total world consumption of commercial energy; hydroelectric power was responsible for 0.7 percent; and solid fuels accounted for the remainder (Darmstadter and coauthors, 1971, p. 13). These percentages have grown steadily until, in 1972, they reached 43.5 for oil and 21.6 percent for gas (with hydroelectricity accounting for 2.4 percent) (United Nations, 1974, pp. 6–29). The future, of course, may be quite different from the past because of the sharp increases in petroleum prices starting in 1973–74 and the likelihood of further price increases at some point in the future and because of technological and other changes. To indicate what might happen under different circumstances, we developed a simple model of the world oil and gas markets, which we used to explore a number of possible developments. Other fuels are treated as well, but in a more summary fashion.

Because the world price of petroleum is currently set by OPEC at a level far in excess of its cost of production, the range of uncertainty with respect to future prices is exceedingly large. Indeed, it is not difficult to

---

[9] The energy–GNP ratios of tables 5–5 and 5–6 are not strictly comparable because of the different price bases assumed for purposes of deflation.

Table 5-7. Comparison of Projections of World Energy Demand
(quads of energy)

Source	1980	1985	1990	2000
Total world				
This study	275	361	433	574
Department of Interior	296	351	417	...
National Energy Plan II[a]		300–354		
World excluding Communist countries				
This study	190	228	271	380
OECD (oil at $9 a barrel)	187	230	...	...
Energy Policy Project	230	299	...	...
Workshop on Alternative Energy Strategies		240–416		336–434

Sources: U.S. Department of Interior, *Energy Perspectives* (Washington, D.C., 1975) and *Energy Perspectives II* (Washington, D.C., 1976); U.S. Department of Energy, *National Energy Plan II* (Washington, D.C., DOE, 1979); Organisation for Economic Co-operation and Development, *Energy Prospects to 1985*, vol. II (Paris, OECD, 1975); Ford Foundation, *A Time to Choose*, Final Report of the Ford Foundation Energy Policy Project (Cambridge, Mass., Ballinger, 1974); and Workshop on Alternative Energy Strategies, *Energy: Global Prospects 1985–2000* (New York, McGraw-Hill, 1977).

[a] *National Energy Plan II* growth rates of 2.4 to 4.1 percent annually applied to this study's figure of 237 quads of consumption in 1975.

imagine various circumstances under which the world price of petroleum, relative to all other prices, would rise, fall, or remain constant during the next ten to twenty years. At some point thereafter, however, unless technological advances of unexpected magnitudes and types occur, the price will have to rise, for eventually production of petroleum will not be able to keep up with the growth in demand without such a rise. To model these alternatives, we have developed three cases: a standard case, a case in which the real price of petroleum rises, and a case in which this price temporarily falls.

THE STANDARD CASE

1. In the standard case, the world price of petroleum is assumed to remain at its 1975 level of approximately $12 a barrel in real terms, just keeping pace with inflation, until forced up by excess demand. The world is assumed to consist of a single market for petroleum, all countries being willing to buy and sell in this market in such a way that this price pattern is validated.

2. It is assumed that in anticipation of declining ability to maintain production levels and higher costs of production, the price begins rising ten years in advance of the time when, without such a rise, primary resources of oil would be exhausted. This assumption represents a

time horizon that is substantially longer than that of most business and government planners today, although it is not unknown in the petroleum industry where there can easily be a ten-year lag between exploration of and production from a new oil field.

3. Between 1975 and 2025, world GNP grows according to the standard case assumptions, averaging 3.6 percent a year. Thereafter, it grows at 3.3 percent a year.

4. The elasticities of demand for oil are taken to be 0.9 with respect to GNP and −1.0 with respect to price. The first of these values is implicit in the projections presented in the previous section. The second represents a long-run elasticity reflecting judgments about possibilities for substituting other fuels and replacing energy-using producer and consumer capital.[10]

5. At $12 per barrel or less, the remaining recoverable petroleum resources for the world amount to 10,000 quads, assuming a 40 percent recovery rate. If petroleum prices rise to $16 (in 1975 dollars) or more, the recovery rate will increase and more costly sources of petroleum will come into use, raising the recoverable resource figure to 12,500 quads.

6. The cost of producing synthetic liquids (from coal, tar, shale, or other sources) will be in the neighborhood of $24 a barrel in 1980 and will decline over time until it reaches $12 a barrel in 2010 (all prices in 1975 dollars); thereafter, it will rise along with the price of coal. Such a cost reduction during this time period is in line with what has been experienced in other capital-intensive industries.[11] In addition, how-

---

[10] Kennedy (1974) reports cross-country price elasticities for various petroleum products that range from −.17 to −1.05. Griffin and Gregory (1976), using cross-country data, report energy own-price elasticities of about −.80 and elasticities of substitution between capital and energy of about 1.0. We have chosen a value near the higher end of this range because of the long-run character of this analysis.

[11] Between 1939 and 1968, innovations in petroleum-cracking processes resulted in cost reductions of 25 percent per volume of gasoline produced (expressed in constant dollars), equivalent to reductions in capital and operating costs of about 60 percent (Fisher, 1968). A study by Enos (1958) of four major petroleum process innovations reports that capital costs per unit of capacity were halved during a five-year period. Hirsch (1952) found that unit costs in the machine tool industry were reduced by 20 percent for each doubling of cumulative output. And as a consequence of evolutionary innovations and economies of scale, the real cost of electricity declined approximately 70 percent in the thirty years between 1940 and 1970. Based on these experiences, our assumption that synthetic fuel, which has not yet been produced on a commercial scale, can experience a cost reduction of 50 percent in thirty-five years appears to be a reasonable possibility.

ever, when synthetics enter international trade, an average of $1.20 a barrel must be added to cover transportation costs.

7. There is an upper limit on the speed with which the capacity to produce synthetic liquids can be expanded. It is assumed that after fifteen years of production a maximum of 100 quads per year can be produced. Thereafter, up to 70 additional quads of production capacity can be added each year. These assumptions are based on an extrapolation of projections developed for the United States.[12]

Once the point is reached at which (according to assumption 2) the price must begin to rise, the model selects a time path of future prices, and hence demands, such that the world's remaining petroleum resources are not exhausted before the capacity to produce synthetic liquids has expanded sufficiently to take over the market. Figure 5–3 indicates the outcome. The area under the petroleum production curve represents total petroleum resources. If the price of liquid fuels were not to increase, demand would continue growing along the path established in the 1975–2010 period. But synthetics cannot come onstream fast enough to fill the gap left by the declining petroleum curve, so the price of oil must rise, as it does in this case starting about 2010. Once the cost of synthetics becomes low enough to cross this price curve, synthetics production begins.[13] Because synthetic production capacity is constrained for a time, however,

---

[12] See Senate Committee on Interior and Insular Affairs (1973). This study concluded that with adequate incentives (but something short of a wartime crash program) thirty-six plants producing 7 quads per year could be constructed in the United States during an eleven-year period by starting construction of six plants at a time in the first year and building up to ten starts a year in the sixth year. A continuation of the expansion at the rate of twelve starts a year, reached in the eighth year, would result in 14 quads of output a year at the end of the fifteenth year. During this period—1973–83—the United States is assumed in this study to have an average GNP of $1.5 trillion in 1971 dollars. To extrapolate to the world, we assume that the relationship between the capacity to produce synthetic plants and GNP established in this study holds for other countries so long as they possess adequate quantities of coal, shale and/or tar sands and have a GNP per capita at least equal to that of the United States in 1973. The average GNP for the fifteen-year period starting in 2010 (when, according to our assumptions, synthetic liquids would begin coming onstream) for those regions possessing the largest coal, shale and tar deposits (Western and Eastern Europe, USSR, Communist China, and the United States) is $11.5 trillion (1971 dollars). All but Communist China would have per capita GNPs of at least $5,500 to 2010, but the centrally planned character of China should permit greater expansion of this special sector if high priority is given to this task. Assuming the same relationship as in the United States, we get $14 \times 11.5/1.5 =$ 107 quads Btu, a figure rounded to 100 for entry into the simulation model.

[13] In the figure, the cost curve for synthetics includes a margin for international transport. This explains why production, which would initially be for the domestic market, is seen to begin somewhat before the two curves cross.

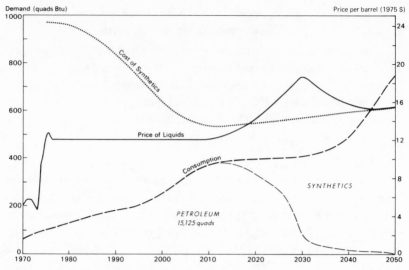

Figure 5–3.   World liquid fuels market, standard case. The cost of synthetics equals the cost of production plus international transport.

the price of oil does not fall to the long-run cost of producing synthetics until, in this case, about 2040. Thus, in this illustration, the transition from natural to synthetic liquids takes about twenty-five years starting in 2010, and the price of liquids rises during this period about 50 percent above its historic level.

RISING PRICE CASE.   A number of other studies predict shortages and rising petroleum prices much sooner than implied by the standard case. Differences in demand and resource estimates account for some of this difference in results, but the principal discrepancy is in the production estimates. The Organisation for Economic Co-operation and Development (OECD, 1977) based its conclusions on judgments about OECD import requirements, OPEC production capacity, and OPEC's desired production level (assumed to be substantially less than capacity); the rest of the world was more or less ignored despite the fact that supplies in the rest of the world could grow faster than demands for several decades. A study by the Central Intelligence Agency (CIA, 1977) based its conclusion on the projection that the USSR will soon become a major importer of petroleum, not because it does not have the petroleum, but because it cannot solve its production problems in a timely fashion. The Workshop on Alternative Energy Strategies (1977) assumed that there is a minimum reserve-to-production ratio and that when that ratio is reached, production can increase only as fast as reserves; reserves are assumed to increase arithmetically up to a point at which increments to reserves must taper off because of the approach of complete exhaustion; and the reserve-to-production ratio for the world is assumed to be 15, despite the fact that the present ratio in the United States is 10 and is likely to fall farther as exhaustion is approached. That study group also assumed there is no trade with Communist countries, and in some scenarios it placed a ceiling well below capacity on OPEC production. In addition to making a number of assumptions similar to those of the Workshop on Alternative Energy Strategies, the National Energy Plan II (DOE, 1979) assumes that the cost of producing substitutes does not fall over time as one might expect because of technological improvements or economies of scale.

If we impose similar production constraints, but no other changes— more specifically, if global production cannot increase beyond 190 quads in 2000 and 200 quads in 2025[14]—the model indicates that oil prices would begin rising in 1987. But because petroleum reserves would last longer and synthetic production would be induced to come on-stream more rapidly, the model also indicates that the price would rise slowly to a maximum of 40 percent above the present level, which it would reach only after 2020, and then would equally slowly fall until it approached the long-run cost of producing synthetics.

To simulate a case in which the real price of oil rises continuously from its present level, additional assumptions were necessary. In this rising price case, we assumed, in addition to the production constraints, that the cost of synthetic liquids remains at $24 a barrel (1975 dollars), that the GNP elasticity is 1, and the price elasticity is −.75. The principal results in this case are indicated in figure 5–4. The price of oil starts rising in 1980 and reaches $24 a barrel in 2010, at which point synthetic production begins. The price continues to rise, reaching $34 in 2025, by which time the production of synthetics is sufficient to begin pulling the price of oil down toward the long-run cost of production, $24, which is reached in 2034.

[14] These figures assume that production from various political regions of the world might be limited to something like the following (in quads):

Region	1975	1985	2000	2025
OPEC countries	56	70	70	70
Communist countries	23	30	60	70
Rest of world	33	45	60	60
Total	112	145	190	200

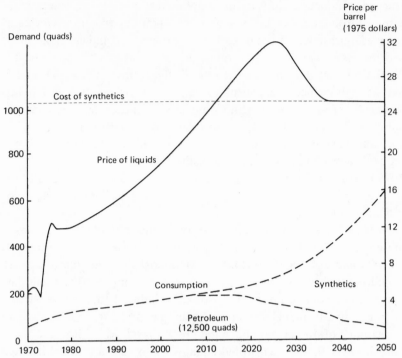

Figure 5–4.   World liquid fuels market, rising price case. The cost of synthetics equals the cost of production plus international transport.

FALLING PRICE CASE.   Although at the present time there appears to be little likelihood of the price of oil falling, figure 5–5 illustrates a case in which the real price falls from \$12 to \$6 a barrel between 1980 and 1985, a result that could occur if the market price of oil should remain constant while inflation (and devaluation of the dollar) proceeds at present rates. Because of the more rapid growth in demand, the transition would begin about ten years earlier than in the standard case, last longer, and have a much higher peak price for liquid fuels. Far more serious, the rate of growth in consumption of liquids, instead of merely slowing down, as in the standard and the rising price cases, would actually become negative for a time. This probably would not occur without a significant fall in GNP in a number of countries,[15] a decline that would limit the extent of

[15] All these runs treat the growth of GNP as exogenous. In fact, however, if the prices of oil were to fall, GNP would grow more rapidly during the 1980–2000 period and less rapidly—indeed, perhaps at a negative rate—for a period thereafter.

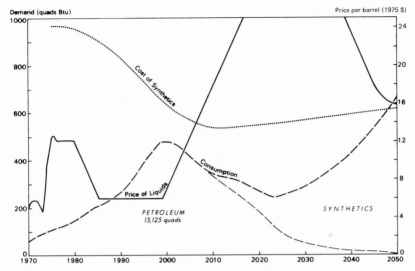

Figure 5–5. World liquid fuels market, price drop case. The cost of synthetics equals the cost of production plus international transport.

the price rise. Once the transition is completed, economic growth could resume, though from lower levels than in the other cases. It is unlikely that all our assumptions would hold for such a long period, but if they should, this transition would be exceedingly difficult, particularly for poor nations and for those without adequate sources of other fuels.

Still other possibilities are listed in table 5–8. As can be seen, a longer planning horizon, less of a constraint on the growth of synthetic production capacity, a larger resource base, or a lower rate of growth would smooth out the transition, while opposite assumptions or a higher long-run cost of producing synthetics would make it worse. The possibilities are many.

Gas

A model similar to that for oil was developed to project the future course of events for gas. The critical assumptions for the standard case are:

1. The world price for natural gas follows the petroleum price assumptions for the same number of Btu (that is, it is $2 per million Btu when a barrel of oil costs $12), until such a time as production can no longer keep up with demand.

Table 5-8. World Oil Market Transition, Various Assumptions

	Maximum price				Crude production			Synthetic production	
					Maximum		60 quads	Be-	Half of con-
Assumption	Rise begins (year)	1975 U.S.$ a barrel	Year	Equilibrium price reached (year)[a]	Quads	Year	Year	ginning year	sumption (year)
1. Standard case	2010	19.3	2030	2042	314	2010	2029	2011	2027
2. Rising price case	1980	34.0	2025	2035	200	2025	2050	2010	2029
3. Temporary price fall	1997	42.0	2019	2044	401	1996	2022	2007	2018
4. Petroleum resources doubled	2029	14.0	2053	2053	385	2032	2053	2011	2042
5. Petroleum resources doubled and price falls to $6	2011	32.5	2039	2062	642	2010	2039	2023	2038
6. Twenty years' foresight	2000	16.1	2033	2040	273	2008	2033	2008	2028
7. High GNP growth[b]	2005	25.1	2024	2043	347	2006	2024	2007	2023
8. High synthetic limits[c]	2010	16.1	2029	2036	317	2010	2029	2011	2027
9. Low synthetic limits[d]	2010	19.7	2029	2042	313	2010	2029	2011	2028

Note: All assumptions are the same as those for the standard run, listed in the text, except for the item specified.
[a] Price declines from its peak to the long run cost of producing substitutes in the year specified. This price is $14 a barrel in all cases except the rising price case in which it is $24 a barrel.
[b] The average annual growth rate for the GNP during the period 1975–2025 is 4.3 percent for the high GNP growth case.
[c] Maximum of 150 quads Btu after fifteen years, maximum addition of 100 quads each year thereafter.
[d] Maximum of 60 quads Btu after fifteen years, maximum addition of 60 quads each year thereafter.

2. The price begins rising fifteen years in advance of the time exhaustion of natural gas would otherwise occur. The reason for this extended period is that the extent of remaining resources is known with more certainty than for oil because a higher percentage (80 percent) routinely is recovered and there is less possibility of enhanced recovery than in the case of petroleum (see assumption 5 below). Also, gas exhaustion is likely to occur after that of oil.

3. The assumptions about world GNP growth rates are the same as for oil.

4. The elasticity of demand with respect to the GNP starts at 0.80 in 1975 and rises to 0.85 by 2000. It is assumed to be slightly less than for oil because the transport and distribution networks for gas will probably develop more slowly. The elasticity of demand with respect to price is -0.5. It also is assumed to be lower than for oil because conversion from gas to other fuels is more expensive than conversion from oil to other fuels.[16] The cross-elasticity of demand for natural gas with respect to the petroleum price is assumed to be unity.

5. The ultimately remaining recoverable natural gas resources are assumed to be 11,100 quads at a primary recovery rate of 80 percent. No higher recovery rate is assumed to be feasible at the prices that are expected to prevail during the next fifty years.

6. The cost of producing synthetic gases is assumed to follow the same path as for synthetic liquids.

7. The ability to expand production of synthetic gases is the same as for liquids.

Given these assumptions, natural gas production would grow more slowly and peak fourteen years later than in the case of oil. Production of synthetics would begin on a significant scale in the rest of the world in 2029 (somewhat earlier in the United States because a more extensive transmission and distribution network is already in place). The price of gas would follow that of oil until 2010, when oil prices begin to rise; thereafter, it remains constant until 2023, when it begins rising, and reaches a peak in 2041 of $30 a barrel of oil equivalent. During the next decade, it falls to the long-run cost of producing synthetics.

---

[16] For example, storage for coal and pollution control equipment must be added when boilers are converted from gas to coal. In comparison, less extensive adjustments are needed when coal is substituted for oil. Here again, the outcome for the United States is not greatly affected by this assumption within the relevant range.

In the case where the price of oil rises throughout most of the period, the price of gas follows that of petroleum up to the cost of producing synthetics, $24 a barrel, but does not go above it because there is still sufficient natural gas to satisfy demand while synthetic capacity is being developed. In the case where oil and hence gas prices in 1985 are half their 1975 levels and then begin rising again around 1998, natural gas production would flatten out and remain almost level until it begins its precipitous decline around 2035, almost twenty years later than in the case of petroleum.

Other Energy Forms

Projections of development and use of other energy forms must be based on very rough judgments. Development of hydroelectricity has been slow in the past, and there is little reason to believe it will speed up appreciably in the future. Our projection, which assumes past trends continue along a path that is asymptotic to the potential remaining to be developed, results in a little more than half the U.S. hydroelectric potential and one-quarter of the world's potential being in operation in 2025. A continuation of this trend would result in roughly one-third of the world's potential being developed by 2050. Growth in the world use of geothermal capacity and solar energy is projected as a function of U.S. projections (discussed in a later section).[17] The rate of nuclear development is based on a rough judgment about the speed with which capacity can be increased; however, development in the rest of the world is assumed to occur more rapidly than in the United States because alternative fuels (especially coal) are less easily and cheaply available. If correct, these projections mean that 5,200 plants of 1,000 megawatts capacity would be in operation worldwide in 2025 and would supply 22 percent of world energy demand. Coal production was estimated as a residual.

The resulting projections for all types of energy are given in table 5–9. Hydroelectricity, solar energy, and geothermal energy are projected to grow steadily, but relatively slowly; they would represent 7.0, 1.0, and

[17] World use of geothermal potential is assumed to equal that in the United States times the ratio of the world's GNP to that of the United States, scaled down by a factor of 0.75 to reflect the judgment that development is likely to be slower in the rest of the world because of uncertainty about the size and location of this resource. A similar formula was used for global projections of solar energy use, but since we have no basis on which to indicate whether development will be more or less rapid than in the United States, the global figures were not scaled down.

Table 5–9. Projected World Energy Production, Standard Case, 1975–2050 (quads)

Energy source	1975	1980	1990	2000	2010	2025	2050
Hydro	15.7	21.1	30.3	40.7	50.8	62.4	69.1
Solar	—	—	1.9	5.6	27.4	60.3	237.0
Geothermal	—	—	1.4	4.1	11.3	22.1	32.0
Liquids							
Petroleum	112.3	127.3	166.4	222.6	313.7	217.0	25.5
Converted coal	—	—	—	—	2.5	50.0	378.0
Shale	—	—	—	—	2.5	50.0	378.0
Gas							
Natural gas	42.0	48.1	66.4	117.8	166.6	221.1	27.7
Converted coal	—	—	—	—	3.3	13.0	325.4
Coal (direct use)	69.6	87.2	137.6	125.5	105.0	229.2	102.9
Coal (total)	69.6	87.2	137.6	125.5	110.8	292.2	806.2
Nuclear	3.4	15.3	29.0	57.7	107.9	275.9	665.5
Total	243.0	299.0	433.0	574.0	791.0	1,201.0	2,241.0

0.7 percent, respectively, of total energy demand in 2000, and 5.2, 5.0, and 1.8 percent in 2025. It is not until 2050 that the share of solar energy becomes important (11 percent). This slow rate of diffusion results from our assumptions that solar-electric technology will not develop rapidly enough to be of commercial importance globally until after 2025 and that solar space heating and cooling devices will be installed primarily on new structures, thereby tying the rate of diffusion to the turnover of the building stock.[18] If the cost of other energy sources were to increase by substantially more than assumed in the standard case, our numbers are likely to be too small.

Petroleum and natural gas remain major sources of energy in 2025 (18 percent and 21 percent, respectively) but virtually disappear by 2050. Nuclear energy is projected to supply 23 percent of total energy requirements in 2025 and 30 percent in 2050, and a large portion is provided by either breeder reactors or fusion or both, depending on technological developments (see Shapanka, 1977). By 2050, coal (in the form of synthetic oil and gas), oil shale, and nuclear energy are the most important energy sources, followed closely by solar energy.[19]

[18] More recent assessments suggest that these assumptions may be far too pessimistic. In particular, see Solar Working Group (1978).

[19] Two additional comments on table 5–9 are useful. First, the split between synthetic liquids from oil shale and coal in which each is assigned one-half of the total synthetic production is arbitrary. Oil shale resources are better distributed around the world than coal, so more countries would be able to produce synthetic liquids from shale domestically. On the other hand, there is every reason to assume

U.S. Demand and Supply

The previous two sections of this chapter depicted the amounts of various energy resources, the global demands and supplies, and the resulting prices, at least for petroleum and natural gas, that might exist in the world during the next half-century. This picture provides the backdrop for the future U.S. energy situation.

Methodology

The first step was to run the SEAS/RFF model, incorporating all the assumptions of a particular scenario but assuming no changes in prices. This provided a first-cut estimate of total energy requirements plus breakdowns by fuels and major users for various years into the future.

An estimate of the time path of prices for individual fuels was then worked out. The model does not contain a mechanism for determining prices; this had to be done outside the model. In the case of energy prices, however, this is only a small drawback because domestic prices depend so heavily on government regulations, international prices, and the costs of producing various forms of energy at different points in time; all are factors that cannot be determined endogenously anyway.

The distribution of fuels by major users was then modified to take account of assumptions about fuel supply constraints and judgments about interfuel substitutions that are likely to occur as a consequence of the changes in relative fuel prices. No explicit cross-elasticities of demand were applied, although they are, of course, implicit in the procedure and could be derived after the fact.

The next step was to combine projected fuel prices with these new fuel-mix assumptions to obtain weighted averages of energy prices by

---

that countries with very large coal reserves would be willing either to export the coal or to convert it into liquids and transport it by low-cost methods to other countries, as is now done with crude oil.

Second, the apparent anomaly in which coal production is lower in 2000 and 2010 than in 1990 and 2025 is explained by the timing of nuclear growth and oil price changes. Up to 2000, the nuclear capacity is expected to grow slowly. During the next 10 years, in addition to a more rapid rate of growth in nuclear electric, there is still sufficient oil to supply other energy needs. The result is a temporary decline in coal production. But after 2010 petroleum production starts leveling off, prices start rising, and production of synthetic gas and liquids from coal becomes economical.

major users, that is, the residential, commercial, and transportation sectors, industrial users for raw material and feedstock purposes, other industrial users, and the electricity-generating and public (especially military) sectors. For the commercial and other industrial sectors, price elasticities were applied to the appropriate averages of energy prices.[20] The price elasticities of energy for raw material and feedstock uses and for the public sector are assumed to be zero. A more eclectic approach was used for the residential and transport sectors; this approach, explained in a later section, tries to take into account saturation effects, legislated energy efficiencies, and related influences.[21]

The coefficients associated with energy then were adjusted to reflect these changes. For example, if the share of oil used by industry for other than raw material purposes is projected to fall over time by 25 percent, oil-delivery coefficients for each sector within this group are decreased by this common percentage. However, such adjustments in coefficients are made after taking into account the fact that equal monetary units of two different fuels cannot be substituted for each other on a one-to-one basis; if for instance, petroleum costs 80 cents and coal costs 43 cents per million Btu and if petroleum were substituted for coal on an equal Btu basis, the petroleum coefficient would have to increase by 1.86 times the amount that the coal coefficient went down.

Next, the nonenergy coefficients were adjusted to reflect these changes. These adjustments are of two types. First, for energy-producing and -handling sectors, capital and current account coefficients were increased by an amount that reflects the assumed increase in the cost of producing different fuels. For example, synthetic liquid from coal is assumed to be available in 2000 at $3.50 per million Btu (excluding refining and distribution costs), compared with $2.00 for domestic crude. In model runs in which synthetic oil is produced in that year, the resulting increase in the average cost of oil is reflected in the model by increasing the capital and current account coefficients for the petroleum-producing

---

[20] The price change in a given time segment results in a deviation of demand from the course it would otherwise follow, according to a given response path; the deviations resulting from changes in prices in various time segments are added together to obtain the cumulative response. The long-run price elasticity for industrial uses other than for raw material and feedstock purposes is taken to be −0.7 with fifteen years required for the full response to occur. The comparable elasticity for commercial sectors is assumed to be −0.4 with a twenty-year lag.

[21] Second-round effects—effects of increased energy prices on the prices and demands for other goods and services—have not been taken into account. However, demands for these other goods are affected through changes in income.

sector. Another example is the adjustments made in the capital and current account coefficients of the electricity-generating sector to reflect
changes in fuel mix and differences in capital costs assumed for different
technologies.

The second type of adjustment pertains to the energy-consuming
sectors. In the short run, higher energy prices are likely to induce some
conservation and, where possible, substitution of labor and other variable
inputs for energy. In addition, the capital stock will be turned over more
rapidly, and the existing stock will be replaced by more energy-saving
capital. Though virtually nothing is known about the magnitude of such
effects, they cannot be ignored altogether, because their cumulative
effects could be significant during a fifty-year period, given the extent of
the price changes being considered. Accordingly, we have introduced the
somewhat arbitrary assumption that a doubling of energy prices will cut
the expected life of existing durable equipment by one-third in the industrial sector and by 23 percent in the commercial sector. This means that
during the time this capital stock is being replaced the level of investment
is higher than it otherwise would be.[22]

At this point, a new run of the model was made, and the results were
checked in a number of ways. One check ensures that no supply constraints are violated; another ensures that the Btu/output ratio for individual sectors remains within reasonable bounds. If problems were
encountered, the model was adjusted, and the above steps repeated as
required.

Price Assumptions

Table 5–10 summarizes the energy price projections used in scenarios EL and DH, assuming world prices are those indicated in the
standard case discussed earlier.[23] Scenario DH is the case in which efforts
are made to reduce dependence on imported oil and natural gas by subsidizing the development of domestic substitutes. Because these subsidies
are paid for from general revenues, prices in this case are assumed to be

---

[22] Short-run adjustments in other inputs and the possibility that the new capital stock is more expensive than the old are not introduced, with one exception. That
exception is for increased construction costs, to include better insulation and the use
of heat pumps (which, while saving energy, have higher capital costs than most
other space conditioning equipment) in residential and commercial buildings.

[23] All prices in this section are based on 1975 dollars.

Table 5–10. U.S. Energy Prices by Fuels, Scenarios EL and DH
(in 1975 dollars per 10⁶ Btu except for uranium oxide, which is dollars per
pound)

Fuel	1971	1975	1980	1985	2000	2010	2025
Prices at point of production							
Petroleum[a]	0.84	1.85	2.00	2.00	2.00	2.00	2.67
Natural gas (interstate)[a]	0.27	0.50	0.90	2.00	2.00	2.00	2.23
Coal	0.43	0.75	0.85	1.00	1.00	1.10	1.25
Uranium oxide	10.00	11.00	18.00	26.00	35.00	40.00	51.00
Electricity	4.49	5.83	6.00	7.50	6.90	6.81	6.68
Delivered prices[b]							
Petroleum[a]	2.31	3.32	3.47	3.47	3.47	3.47	4.14
Natural gas (interstate)[a]	0.74	0.97	1.37	2.47	2.47	2.47	2.70
Coal	0.62	0.94	1.04	1.19	1.19	1.29	1.44
Electricity	6.57	7.91	8.08	9.58	8.98	8.89	8.76

[a] Includes cost of transportation of imported oil and gas.

[b] Delivered prices are derived by adding downstream costs, such as refining and distribution, to the prices at point of production.

the same as in scenario EL. The extent of the subsidies per unit of energy produced can be judged by comparing assumed prices with the costs of producing synthetic liquids and gases.

For both liquids and gases, domestic prices are assumed to be decontrolled according to the pattern indicated in table 5–10.[24] This means that the price of petroleum increases to the world level of $2 per million Btu (equivalent to $12 a barrel) by 1980, and the price of natural gas follows suit within the next five-year period. Thereafter, these prices follow world prices. Between 1975 and 1985, coal prices are assumed to increase somewhat as environmental, health, and safety regulations are fully implemented; thereafter, they should remain roughly constant until after 2000, when there is some price increase as miners turn to more difficult-to-mine seams. The price of uranium oxide is assumed to increase substantially as high-quality deposits are depleted.[25]

The price of electricity must be derived by projecting fuel and other costs for different types of plants and weighting the estimates by the per-

[24] This pattern of decontrol is based roughly on the Energy Act of December 1975.

[25] Our price projection for uranium oxide between now and 2000 is very similar to that given in NRC (1976) for the situation in which spent fuel is reprocessed beginning in 1986, but no plutonium is recycled. The NRC expected U_3O_8 price in 2000 is $34.20 per pound, and its forecast does not go beyond 2000.

Table 5–11. Projected Cost of Electricity Generation
(mills per kWh, 1975 dollars)

Plant and cost type	1971	1985	2000	2025
Coal-fired				
Capital	8.4	12.0	11.5	11.0
Operating	1.0	2.2	1.9	1.6
Fuel	6.9	13.7	13.7	19.8
Total	16.3	27.9	27.1	32.4
Nuclear[a]				
Capital	...	16.5	15.4	13.5
Operating	...	2.0	2.0	2.0
Spent fuel and storage	...	0.4	0.4	0.4
Fuel	...	4.7	5.7	6.7
Total	...	23.6	23.5	22.6

[a] These figures pertain to fission reactors. The total cost of electricity for breeders is assumed to be the same, although, of course, the breakdown of costs will be different because fuel costs are lower and capital costs higher.

centage of electricity produced by each type. Table 5–11 provides estimates of the relevant costs for coal-fired and nuclear plants.[26] The 1985 estimates are based on a recent study of nuclear power (NEPSG, 1977). Capital and operating costs for coal-fired plants are adjusted downward in later years on the assumption that technical improvements in environmental control equipment will reduce these costs.[27] However, rising coal prices offset this decline and result in a net increase in the cost of electricity after 2000. Capital costs for nuclear plants are similarly adjusted to reflect projected refinements in this still-young technology. The projected increase in nuclear fuel costs after 2000 is only slight because of an assumed decrease in the real cost of enrichment of U_3O_8 with the introduction of gas centrifuge and possibly laser-enrichment technology.

The distribution of fuels used to produce electricity in the base case changes sharply during the fifty-year period (see table 5–18). The percentage of electricity generated from nuclear sources, which was 10.6 in 1975, is expected to rise to 18.0 in 1985 and to 52 in 2000 and 63 per-

[26] Oil, gas, and hydroelectric plants are also in use, but coal and nuclear fuels will dominate in the future.

[27] Stack-gas scrubbers for sulfur dioxide removal were developed in a great hurry in order to comply with regulatory deadlines. As a result, they were initially more expensive to install and operate than they will be when the technology is fully developed. Moreover, if the technology of fluidized-bed combustion of coal with limestone or dolomite is successfully commercialized, this will be a cheaper method of sulfur dioxide control than scrubbers.

Table 5–12. U.S. Energy Prices by Fuel, Scenario DHNU
(in 1975 dollars per 10^6 Btu except for uranium oxide, which is dollars per pound)

Fuel	1971	1975	1980	1985	2000	2010	2025
Prices at point of production							
Liquids[a]	0.84	1.85	2.00	2.00	2.00	2.00	2.67
Gas[a]	0.27	0.50	0.90	2.00	2.00	2.00	2.23
Coal	0.43	0.75	0.85	1.00	1.00	1.25	1.50
Uranium oxide	10.00	11.00	18.00	26.00	26.00	26.00	26.00
Electricity	4.49	5.83	6.00	7.50	7.53	7.98	8.65
Delivered prices[b]							
Liquids	2.31	3.32	3.47	3.47	3.47	3.47	4.14
Gas	0.74	0.97	1.37	2.47	2.47	2.47	2.70
Coal	0.62	0.94	1.04	1.19	1.19	1.44	1.69
Electricity	6.57	7.91	8.08	9.58	9.61	10.06	10.73

[a] Includes cost of transportation of imported oil and gas.
[b] Delivered prices are derived by adding downstream costs, such as refining and distribution, to the prices at point of production.

cent in 2025.[28] It should be noted that at the present time there is considerable uncertainty and controversy about the future relative costs of generating electricity from coal and nuclear fuels. This is the result of rapidly changing safety requirements for nuclear plants, the need for environmental controls for which some costs have not yet been firmly established, and the rapid escalation in construction costs at apparently differential rates for nuclear and coal plants. Several recent studies (Bupp, Derian, Donsimoni, and Treitel, 1975; and Scott, 1975) indicate that electricity generated at nuclear plants may become more expensive relative to coal-generated electricity, but many projections still show nuclear electricity with an increasing share of the market, which implies lower costs (Corey, 1976).

Table 5–12 lists the price assumptions for the nuclear-phaseout case (DHNU). In this scenario, only those nuclear plants already in operation (fifty-two plants with a combined capacity of 42,533 MW) and those on which actual construction has been started would continue operating over their normal life. The total installed nuclear generating capacity in 1985 would be about 107,000 MW, sufficient to produce (at 70 percent load

[28] Our figure of 18 percent for 1985 is lower than most other projections but about the same as that of the Department of Interior, made in 1975 (Dupree and Corsentino, 1975, p. 28). A recent projection for 1990 by the U.S. Department of Energy (1979) is 22 percent.

Table 5–13. U.S. Prices of Fuels, Scenarios DHP1 and DHP2 (in 1975 dollars per 10^6 Btu except for uranium oxide which is dollars per pound)

Scenario	1971	1975	1980	1985	2000	2010	2025
Scenario DHP1							
Prices at point of production							
Oil[a]	0.84	1.85	2.00	2.40	3.30	4.00	5.70
Gas[a]	0.27	0.50	0.90	2.40	3.30	4.00	4.00
Coal	0.43	0.75	0.85	1.00	1.00	1.10	1.25
Uranium oxide	10.00	11.00	18.00	26.00	35.00	40.00	51.00
Electricity	4.49	5.83	6.00	7.50	6.90	6.81	6.68
Delivered prices[b]							
Oil	2.31	3.32	3.47	3.87	4.77	5.47	7.17
Gas	0.74	0.97	1.37	2.87	3.77	4.47	4.47
Coal	0.62	0.94	1.04	1.19	1.19	1.29	1.44
Electricity	6.57	7.91	8.08	9.58	8.98	8.89	8.76
Scenario DHP2							
Prices at point of production							
Oil[a]	0.84	1.85	2.00	1.00	1.17	2.33	7.00
Gas[a]	0.27	0.50	0.90	1.00	1.17	2.33	7.00
Coal	0.43	0.75	0.85	0.90	0.90	1.00	1.10
Uranium oxide	10.00	11.00	18.00	26.00	35.00	40.00	51.00
Electricity	4.49	5.83	6.00	7.29	7.32	7.06	6.68
Delivered prices[b]							
Oil	2.31	3.32	3.47	2.47	2.64	3.80	8.47
Gas	0.74	0.97	1.37	1.47	1.64	2.80	7.47
Coal	0.62	0.94	1.04	1.09	1.09	1.19	1.29
Electricity	6.57	7.91	8.08	9.37	9.40	9.14	8.68

[a] Includes cost of transportation of imported oil and gas.

[b] Delivered prices are derived by adding downstream costs, such as refining and distribution, to the prices at point of production.

factor) 700×10^9 kilowatt hours of electricity that year. These plants would begin to be retired around 2000, and by 2020 no nuclear plants would be operating. Because this is a variant of the difficult case in which efforts are made to reduce energy imports, it is assumed that all of the shortfall in nuclear electricity is made up by coal-fired generating plants. These increased coal requirements account for the increases in coal prices over the base case starting in 2010. Electricity prices also increase for this reason, but a more important reason is the substitution of coal-fired plants, which are assumed to be more expensive to operate than nuclear plants in those regions like the Northeast, where nuclear plants are now used.

The prices utilized for scenarios DHP1 and DHP2 are indicated in table 5–13. Oil and gas prices are derived from the earlier discussion of these international markets. Coal prices are assumed to be a bit lower in scenario DHP2 than in the base case because of increased competition from oil and gas in earlier years. The price of U_3O_8 is the same as in the base case.

In addition to the prices based on natural fuels, the costs of synthetic liquids and gases must be specified. These are taken from the discussion of world oil and gas markets. In dollars per million Btu (1975 dollars) exclusive of international transport, these costs are:

Synthetic	1985	2000	2010	2025
Gas from coal	4.00	3.00	2.00	2.23
Oil from coal	4.50	3.50	2.00	2.23
Oil from shale	3.50	2.50	2.00	2.23

These costs are assumed to hold for all scenarios except DHP2, in which they remain constant at their 1985 level.

Implications for Aggregate Demand

BASE CASE. Table 5–14 and figure 5–5 present information on energy consumption and consumption–output ratios for the period 1920–70 and projections to 2025 using base-case assumptions. For roughly a half-century prior to 1973–74, the growth rate of energy consumption was less than that of GNP, but it has been accelerating. These movements, which are reflected in the rapid but decelerating decline in the energy–GNP ratio, occurred largely because of changes in the composition of output and technology. The rapid improvement in productivity made possible by the shift to electricity in many industrial sectors is an important example of such changes. It is noteworthy that the relative decline in the consumption of energy occurred despite the fact that energy prices were not rising relative to other prices during this period.[29] Even if energy prices had not increased after 1973, it is likely that the energy–GNP ratio would have declined anyway, although at a much slower rate than in the

[29] Indeed, in the case of electricity prices, the period from 1930 to 1970 was one of continuous and rapid decline. During that time, delivered electricity prices, deflated by the wholesale price index, fell by 75 percent. The trends in other energy prices similarly deflated were less clear. Those for natural gas (estimated at the wellhead) fell to about half their 1930 level by 1950 but then rose again to roughly their earlier level; and those for crude oil and bituminous coal rose slightly until 1950 and then receded a bit.

Table 5–14. U.S. Consumption of Energy by Sectors, 1950–70, and Base-Case Projections, 1975–2025

Item	1920	1950	1960	1970	1975[a]	1985	2000	2025
Total gross consumption (quads)	19.8	34.1	45.0	68.8	74.9	93.0	114.2	171.4
Growth rate (percentage)[b]	...	1.83	2.81	4.30	1.71	2.19	1.38	1.64
Total net consumption (quads)[c]	19.2	29.6	36.5	56.9	60.8	71.6	86.9	131.4
Industrial[d]	...	12.9	16.2	23.4	24.9	30.8	37.9	64.7
(Combustion)	...	...	...	...	(18.2)	(21.6)	(24.9)	(41.6)
(Raw material)[e]	...	...	...	...	(6.7)	(9.2)	(13.0)	(23.1)
Commercial ⎫	...	8.1	11.5	17.0	6.1	7.7	10.5	15.5
Residential ⎭					11.2	10.7	11.2	10.6
Transport	...	8.6	10.8	16.5	18.0	21.3	25.6	37.6
Other[f]	...	...	...	...	0.6	1.1	1.7	2.9
Percentage of total net consumption[e]								
Industrial[d]	...	43.6	42.1	41.1	41.0	43.0	43.6	49.2
(Combustion)	...	...	...	...	(29.9)	(30.2)	(28.7)	(31.7)
(Raw material)	...	...	...	...	(11.0)	(12.8)	(15.0)	(17.6)
Commercial ⎫	...				10.0	10.8	12.1	11.8
Residential ⎭	...	27.4	29.9	29.9	18.4	14.9	12.9	8.1
Transport	...	29.1	28.1	29.0	29.6	29.7	29.5	28.6
Other[f]	...	...	...	...	1.0	1.5	2.0	2.2

Electricity consumption

Gross								
Quads	0.8	5.1	8.4	17.0	20.8	32.2	43.6	64.8
Percentage of total gross	4.0	15.0	18.7	24.7	27.8	34.6	38.2	37.8
Net[g]								
Quads	0.2	1.1	2.6	5.2	6.7	10.9	16.2	27.6
Percentage of total net	1.0	3.7	6.8	9.1	11.0	15.2	18.6	21.0
Conversion loss (percentage of total gross)[h]	3.0	13.2	14.4	17.3	19.0	23.0	23.9	23.3

Source: 1920–70: Joel Darmstadter, "Energy," in Ronald G. Ridker, ed., *Population, Resources, and the Environment,* vol. 3, *Research Reports of the Commission on Population Growth and the American Future* (Washington, D.C., GPO, 1972) pp. 108 and 111.

[a] Projected by model.

[b] Annual growth rate from previous year listed.

[c] Figures for individual sectors are direct consumption of energy plus net electricity.

[d] Includes agriculture, mining, construction, and manufacturing.

[e] Includes energy used as feedstocks for chemicals, asphalt and paints, and coal for coking in the steel industry.

[f] Electricity consumed by electric utilities.

[g] Electricity delivered to consumers by utility sector, computed at 3,412 Btu per kWh.

[h] Includes losses from electricity generation and transmission, coal gasification and liquefaction, and shale oil retorting. In the period 1920–70, this figure also includes a small amount for miscellaneous and unallocated; in these cases, the proper figure for conversion loss is the difference between gross and net electric.

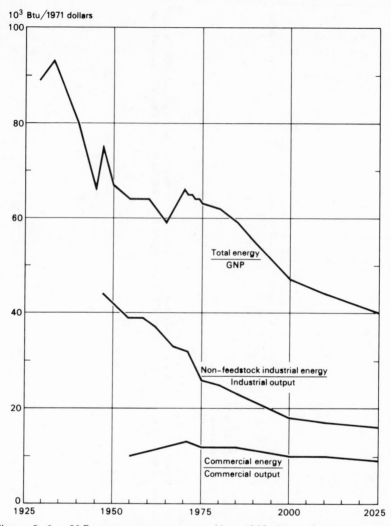

10^3 Btu/1971 dollars

Total energy / GNP

Non-feedstock industrial energy / Industrial output

Commercial energy / Commercial output

Figure 5–6. U.S. gross energy-output ratios, 1929–74, and base-case projections to 2025. Sources for historical data: Energy/GNP—in constant dollar GNP from Census Bureau, *Historical Statistics of the United States, Colonial Times to 1970* (Washington, D.C., GPO, 1975), table F1–5; energy consumption from Sam H. Schurr and Bruce C. Netschert, *Energy in the American Economy, 1850–1957: Its History and Prospects* (Baltimore, Md., Johns Hopkins University Press for Resources for the Future, 1960) table VII; industrial energy/output adapted from data from Conference Board, *Energy Consumption in Manufacturing,* report to the Ford Foundation Energy Policy Project (Cambridge, Mass., Ballinger) table 1–3; commercial energy/output, energy consumption from Schurr and Netschert, *Energy in the American Economy,* table B–9, page 596; commercial output from Clopper Almon, Jr., Margaret Buckler, Lawrence Horwitz, and Thomas Reimbold, *1973–1985 in Figures* (Lexington, Mass., Lexington Books, 1974).

196

past, because of continuing compositional changes and eventual saturation of demand in some markets. Because of these price increases, particularly the fourfold increase of 1973–74, this ratio should fall more
rapidly, especially during the next twenty-five years.[30] This decline, plus
the projected slowdown in the rate of growth of population and GNP, will
result in a distinct break with the trend of accelerating energy consumption growth rates prior to 1973.

Table 5–15 compares our projections of both total energy demand
and energy–output ratios with others. Our projections of total demand are
lower than most others, but the difference is explained largely by differences in GNP projections rather than in energy–output ratios, at least
before 2000.

The industrial sector's reduced demand for energy for combustion
purposes has been the principal component of the decline in energy consumption relative to output. Historically, this sector has been more sensitive to changes in energy prices than have other consumers; further, it has
considerable potential for additional energy savings through process
changes as old capital equipment wears out.[31] Most of the savings are
likely to be realized during the first half of the projection period, after
which time the incentive that the 1973–74 price increase provided to improve capital equipment and buildings will have petered out. In contrast,
the use of fuels as raw materials for products like plastics, asphalt, fertilizer, and drugs is projected to become increasingly important because
demand for these products is growing relatively rapidly and energy savings per unit of output are difficult to achieve. The net effect of these
offsetting changes will be to increase industry's share in total demand for
energy.

The commercial sector uses energy primarily for space conditioning
and lighting, so the extent of its use is determined to a great extent by the
characteristics of the building stock. This means there are fewer opportunities for improving efficiency of use in this sector than in the industrial

---

[30] Even so, this ratio is not projected to fall to current levels experienced by
Europe before 2000. Using the U.S. ratio in 1972 as a base of 100, other countries
had the following ratios in that year: France, 53.7; West Germany, 69.7; Italy, 61.8;
Netherlands, 85.9; United Kingdom, 75.7; Sweden, 71.8; and Japan, 57.4 (see
Darmstadter, Dunkerely, and Alterman, 1977).

[31] Fuel consumption by the primary aluminum industry in 1968, for example,
has been estimated to be about 7.5 times the theoretical minimum requirements.
Also, existing industrial plants in both Europe and Japan are significantly more
energy-efficient in many industries than are plants in the United States. See Gyftopoulos, Lazaridis, and Widmer, 1974.

Table 5-15. Comparison of Recent U.S. Energy Consumption Projections

Source	1971	1975	1980	1985	1990	2000	2010	2025
Total Energy Consumption (quads)								
This study, base case								
Gross	69.7	74.9	86.6	93.0	100.1	114.2	138.9	171.4
Net	57.9	60.8	68.2	70.5	75.4	85.2	105.2	128.4
DRI–Brookhaven								
Base case, gross				100.0	115.3	156.2		
Energy tax case, gross				93.5	97.8	117.9		
Energy policy project								
Historical growth, gross				116.1		186.7		
Technical fix, gross				91.3		124.0		
FEA–National Energy Outlook, 1977								
$13 a barrel, oil								
Gross				91.3	102.8			
Net				69.6	78.0			
Department of Interior								
Gross			87.1	103.5		163.4		
Net			68.9	77.5		110.2		
Institute for Energy Analysis								
Gross								
Low case				82.1		101.4	118.3	
High case				88.0		125.9	158.8	
National Energy Plan II, gross				90.0		119.0		

Energy/GNP ratio (10³ Btu/1971$)

This study, base case								
Gross	67	68	62	59	55	47	44	40
Net	55	55	49	45	41	36	34	31
DRI–Brookhaven								
Base case, gross				50		44		
Energy tax case, gross				49		39		
Energy Policy Project								
Historical Growth, gross				56		55		
Technical fix, gross				47		36		
FEA–National Energy Outlook, 1977								
$13 a barrel								
Gross				55	54			
Net				42	41			
Department of Interior								
Gross			56	57		55		
Net			45	42		37		
Institute for Energy Analysis								
Gross								
Low case				51		42	38	
High case				54		50	47	

Sources: Data Resources, Inc., and Brookhaven National Laboratory, *The Relationship of Energy Growth to Economic Growth Under Alternative Energy Policies.* Report prepared for the U.S. Energy Research and Development Administration (Washington, D.C., GPO, 1976); Ford Foundation, *A Time to Choose.* Final Report of the Ford Foundation Energy Policy Project (Cambridge, Mass., Ballinger, 1974); U.S. Federal Energy Administration, *Project Independence* (Washington, D.C., GPO, 1977) append. A1, pp. 37 and 38; W. G. Dupree, Jr., and John S. Corsentino, *United States Energy Through the Year 2000* (Washington, D.C., Department of Interior and GPO, 1975); Institute for Energy Analysis; *Economic and Environmental Implications of a U.S. Nuclear Moratorium, 1985–2010* (Oak Ridge, Tenn., IEA-Oak Ridge Associated Universities, 1976); and U.S. Department of Energy, *National Energy Plan II* (Washington, D.C., DOE, 1979).

sector.[32] The increase in the energy–output ratio for this sector during the period 1955–73 occurred largely because of the introduction of air conditioning. This change is now virtually complete, so future gains in efficiency will no longer be offset by this factor.

Per capita residential consumption of energy on a net basis has been growing at about 1 percent a year. This study's projections suggest an absolute decline in this use according to the following patterns (in 10^6 Btu annually):

Basis	1975	1985	2000	2025
Net	52.2	45.5	42.4	34.8
Gross	72.9	74.6	73.0	59.4

There are at least four reasons for expecting this turnabout. First, the trend toward smaller multifamily dwelling units is likely to pick up momentum. Second, fuel price increases, changes in building codes, and energy legislation all are likely to result in better insulation of existing and new homes. In addition, the trend toward use of electricity for space heating, which is assumed to be about 35 percent more efficient than is direct use of fuels, is expected to continue. Perhaps most important is that the average household appears to be approaching something like a saturation point in its use of energy for many purposes.[33]

As table 5–16 indicates, net energy use for transportation is projected to grow from 18 quads in 1975 to 37.6 quads in 2025, an average annual growth rate of 1.5 percent compared with more than 3 percent in earlier years. Of this 20-quad increase, only 1.5 quads will be attributable to automobiles. This is the net result of assumptions about the vehicle stock, vehicle miles driven, and especially fuel economy: (1) the personal vehicle stock will increase gradually to the extent that by 2025 there will be one car in operation per person of driving age (compared to 0.7 in 1974); (2) the annual miles driven per vehicle will remain constant rather than increase as in the past; (3) average fuel economy of the ve-

---

[32] Moreover, because the direct users of commercial energy, such as tenants of office buildings, do not generally pay directly for their use of energy, they have little incentive to conserve on its use. With time, this arrangement could be changed, of course.

[33] In 1968, 84 percent of household energy consumption was accounted for by the use of space heating (57 percent), water heating (15 percent), cooking (6 percent), and refrigeration (6 percent), none of which is likely to grow in the future. The remaining uses involve air conditioners and small appliances. Although energy use for air conditioning and small appliances is likely to continue expanding for a number of years, that expansion will be partially offset by improvements in efficiency mandated by new federal efficiency standards for such appliances (see Newman and Day, 1975).

Table 5–16. Projection of U.S. Energy Demand for Transportation, Base Case (10^{15} net Btu)

	1975	1980	1985	2000	2010	2025
Automobiles	9.1	9.4	9.0	8.7	9.04	10.6
Electric	0.0	0.0	0.0	—	0.08	1.2
Bus	0.1	0.1	0.2	0.3	0.3	0.4
Truck	3.8	5.0	5.5	6.9	8.4	10.2
Rail	0.5	0.7	0.7	1.0	1.3	1.6
Air	2.0	2.5	3.1	5.2	7.0	9.8
Pipeline	0.8	0.9	0.9	1.1	1.3	1.5
Water	0.5	0.6	0.6	0.7	0.8	1.0
Military	0.8	0.9	1.0	1.3	1.6	1.9
Other	0.3	0.3	0.3	0.4	0.5	0.6
Total	18.0	20.4	21.3	25.6	30.2	37.6

hicle stock will increase from about 12 miles per gallon (mpg) in 1975 to 25 mpg by 1990, a consequence of the new car standards mandated by the Energy Act of 1975, with further improvements to 30 mpg by 2000; and (4) electric cars will become 1 percent of the vehicle population in 2000, 3 percent in 2010, and 15 percent in 2025.

Passenger air travel is projected to increase at an annual rate of nearly 4.3 percent between 1975 and 2025 as operating costs decline and consumers have more leisure time and discretionary income to spend on travel. Rail travel is projected to increase by about 4.1 percent per year, with local transit systems growing at 3.3 percent per year, primarily as a result of the building of subway systems in several large cities. Trucks will use about 15 percent less energy per ton-mile by 2025 as a result of the replacement of gasoline engines by diesel engines. Airplanes will reduce their energy consumption by about 20 percent by means of improved design, lighter materials, and better engines. The rationale for all of these assumptions can be found in Shapanka (1977).

OTHER SCENARIOS. Table 5–17 compares projected total energy demands for all major scenarios of this study. The differences among results for the several scenarios raise some interesting points about the role of various determinants of the growth in energy requirements.

First, all scenarios are characterized by declining rates of growth in future energy demand. This is because rates of growth of population and GNP decline, even in the high-growth cases, and because compositional, technological, and other changes continue to depress the energy–GNP ratio, though at a slower pace than in the past.

Table 5–17. Projected Gross Energy Demands by Scenarios
(quads)

	1975	1985	2000	2010	2025	Percentage increase between 1975 and 2000	Percentage increase between 2000 and 2025
EL	74.9	93.0	114.2	138.9	171.4	152	150
DH	74.9	105.9	143.0	187.7	259.5	191	181
DL	74.9	96.9	127.1	161.8	214.7	170	169
FH	74.9	105.3	134.6	162.4	198.9	180	148
FL	74.9	98.3	121.7	143.4	166.2	162	137
DHNU	74.9	105.9	140.4	182.6	246.6	187	176
DHP1	74.9	105.4	133.9	171.0	230.5	179	172
DHP2	74.9	108.1	166.6	210.2	262.0	222	157
DHRE	74.9	103.5	141.0	185.0	257.2	188	182

Second, comparing across runs in a given year, a lower population growth rate (scenario FH instead of DH) results in higher energy requirements between 1975 and about 1990 or so; thereafter, it results in a decrease in energy requirements. This outcome is a consequence of the higher GNP resulting from increased female participation in the labor force associated with lower birth rates during early years before the smaller population size affects the size of the labor force. In contrast, slower economic growth (DL instead of DH or FL instead of FH) results in lower energy requirements during all periods.

However, the lower rate of population growth becomes more important over time, and its effect on energy requirements eventually surpasses that of the lower economic growth rate. The shift from DH to FH assumptions reduces energy requirements by 6 percent in 2000 and 23 percent in 2025, whereas the shift from DH to DL assumptions reduces energy requirements by 11 percent and 17 percent in these years.

Of course, these figures depend on the magnitude of the differences in assumptions among the scenarios. If the percentage differences among scenarios in energy requirements are divided by the corresponding percentage differences in population and GNP per capita, the importance of GNP per capita appears to be somewhat greater at all points in time. In 2000, a 1 percent difference in GNP per capita would change energy requirements by 0.81 percent, whereas a comparable difference in population would change energy requirements by 0.46 percent. In 2025, however, these elasticities are virtually equal, 0.83 for GNP per capita and 0.81 for population.

Third, over the fifty-year period, the impacts of changes in assumptions about population and economic growth are greater than those of any of the policy changes whose separate effects can be observed in the table. A consumption level of 260 quads, which occurs in scenario DH in 2025, would occur fourteen years later if the rate of population growth were as slow as that incorporated into scenario FH. A slowdown in economic growth rates (scenario DL instead of DH) would postpone the 260-quad level by nine years. In contrast, the oil price increase built into scenario DHP1 (a continuous rise, doubling in thirty years) would delay by five years reaching 260 quads of consumption. The principal impact of scenario DHP2, in which real oil prices fall, can be observed in 2000. Prior to 1990 or so, the economy will not have had sufficient time to adjust to the lower oil prices; thereafter, it is in the process of adjusting back again to much higher prices than those used in DH. The deviations from scenario DH caused by a shift from nuclear energy to coal in the production of electricity or by changes in environmental controls are negligible.[34]

If several of these changes were to occur together, their impacts would be more significant. A slowdown in both population and economic growth (scenario FL or EL instead of DH) would postpone a consumption level of 260 quads for more than twenty-five years; a slowdown in economic growth plus a price rise (what might be labeled scenario DLP1, not shown in table 5–17) would postpone this consumption level by nearly twenty years; and, of course, other policy changes can be imagined that would have still larger impacts.

The effects of efforts to reduce import dependency, incorporated into DH, cannot be judged easily from table 5–17 because the only case not including such efforts presented in that table is EL, which includes different assumptions about population and economic growth. A special run that removes these different assumptions indicates that the import reduction policy, by itself, would lead to a modest increase in energy requirements—2.2 quads in 2000 and 5.8 quads in 2025—because of the

---

[34] The small impact of environmental controls can be demonstrated in a more significant way by comparing DH with runs that incorporate no abatement activity. When such a run is made with a sufficient amount of additional economic activity inserted to maintain full employment, energy requirements in 2000 and 2025 are 136.9 and 248.5 quads, respectively. When such a run is made without returning the economy to full employment, the comparable figures are 135.6 and 245.8. Thus, if abatement activities were eliminated altogether, the energy savings over DH (which incorporates strict controls) would be between 4 and 4.5 percent.

energy needed for more domestic mining, conversion, and refining activities.

An additional result, not shown in the table, pertains to changes in energy requirements by major sectors over time and across scenarios. As table 5–14 for the base case indicates, the percentage of total net energy requirements for the industrial and commercial sectors, plus conversion losses, increases over time, and the percentage associated with transportation and residential uses goes down. This picture is not changed by more than a percentage point or so comparing scenarios but, a few of the changes are interesting. As a percentage of total requirements in 2025, residential requirements are slightly lower with lower population growth and higher for lower economic growth, the transport and commercial sectors follow the opposite pattern, and industrial requirements fall in both cases. Again, referring to 2025, the nuclear-phaseout case would induce some decline in residential and commercial use and a slight increase in use for transport and industry and in conversion losses, while the oil-price-decline case results in an increase in industrial and commercial requirements and a fall in transport and conversion requirements. However, except for the change in industrial requirements in this last case, all these differences are quite small and certainly insignificant in contrast to the changes that take place over time.

Distribution by Fuels and Sectors

BASE CASE.   Table 5–18 presents a breakdown of energy consumption and production by fuels and by sectors.[35] The most significant factor about the consumption figures is the extent of the increase in primary fuels devoted to electricity generation. In 1975, 27.8 percent of gross energy consumed went to this use; in 2000, this figure is expected to increase to 38.2 percent and to remain at roughly this level thereafter. This increase represents a slowdown from earlier rates of increase (see table 5–14), but it is still quite significant. The predominance of this use of

---

[35] Table 5–18 indicates that synthetic fuels from coal are produced only after 2000. However, in the scenarios like the base case in which natural gas prices are completely deregulated, gas even from coal may be less costly than electricity for space conditioning. An important consideration here, in addition to price deregulation, is the availability of gas-fueled heat pumps. If gas heat pumps become available at reasonable costs (as seems likely), then synthetic gas from coal will be supplied much earlier than 2000 (Ridker, Watson, and Shapanka, 1977).

Table 5–18. Energy Consumption and Production, by Fuel and by Sector, Scenario EL, 1975–2025
(quads)

Sector and fuel	1975[a]	1985	2000	2025
Consumption by sectors and fuels				
Industrial, excluding raw				
material/feedstock	18.2	21.1	34.9	41.6
Coal	2.1	2.3	4.3	7.4
Oil	4.7	6.6	8.5	14.3
Gas	8.8	8.7	6.5	10.9
Electricity	2.6	4.1	5.6	9.0
Raw material/feedstock uses	6.7	9.1	13.0	23.1
Coal	2.6	2.6	2.5	2.5
Oil	3.3	5.2	8.3	15.9
Gas	0.8	1.3	2.2	4.7
Commercial	6.1	7.7	10.5	15.5
Oil	2.4	3.0	4.0	3.1
Gas	2.4	2.5	2.0	1.2
Solar	—	—	0.6	3.2
Electricity	1.3	2.2	4.0	8.0
Residential	11.2	10.7	11.2	10.5
Coal	0.4	0.0	0.0	0.0
Oil	3.6	3.1	2.9	2.1
Gas	5.1	4.2	3.0	0.8
Solar	—	—	0.6	3.2
Electricity	2.1	3.5	4.8	5.5
Transportation	18.0	21.3	25.6	37.6
Oil	17.2	20.4	24.4	33.9
Gas	0.8	0.9	1.1	1.5
Electricity	0.0	0.0	0.2	2.1
Electricity generation	20.8	32.2	43.6	64.8
Coal	8.7	14.4	14.0	17.6
Oil	2.9	4.5	1.3	0.0
Gas	4.2	4.5	1.3	0.0
Hydro	2.9	3.0	3.2	3.3
Nuclear, LWR	2.2	5.8	20.2	19.7
Nuclear, breeder	0.0	0.0	2.5	16.5
Nuclear, fusion	0.0	0.0	—	4.7
Geothermal	—	—	1.1	2.9
Total domestic consumption				
Gross	74.9	93.0	114.2	171.4
Net	60.8	71.6	86.9	131.4
Production, imports and exports				
Production, gross	62.2	64.2	74.9	121.1
Coal, direct	15.5	21.7	23.7	37.5
Coal, liquefied	0.0	0.0	0.0	8.3
Coal, gasified	0.0	0.0	0.0	0.5
Petroleum	20.2	16.5	11.2	6.1
Natural gas	21.4	17.2	12.0	5.6
Shale oil	0.0	—	—	9.5
Hydro	2.9	3.0	3.2	3.3
Geothermal	—	—	1.1	2.9
Solar (space conditioning)	—	—	1.1	6.4
Nuclear, LWR	2.2	5.8	20.2	19.7
Nuclear, breeder	0.0	0.0	2.5	16.5
Nuclear, fusion	0.0	0.0	—	4.7

(continued)

205

Table 5–18. (Continued)

Sector and fuel	1975[a]	1985	2000	2025
Imports	15.3	31.9	43.1	61.4
(Petroleum)	(13.9)	(26.3)	(38.1)	(47.2)
(Natural Gas)	(0.7)	(4.9)	(4.1)	(13.1)
Exports	2.5	3.1	3.7	11.1
(Coal)	1.8	2.4	2.9	10.0
Electricity produced				
Gross	20.8	32.2	43.6	64.8
Net	6.7	10.9	16.2	27.6

[a] The figures for 1975 are derived from the model which uses 1971 as its base. They are, therefore, not identical with the actual figures for that year.

energy will continue, it is assumed, because of (1) the increasing importance of nuclear power, which during this time span is likely to be available only in the form of electricity;[36] (2) because of the decreasing importance of small-scale, onsite electricity generation;[37] and (3) because of continued decline in the price of electricity relative to that of oil and gas.[38]

Beyond 2000, most major markets for electricity, other than that for electric cars, will be saturated. In addition, the eventual development of capacity to produce synthetic liquids and gases from coal should begin to encroach on some markets that earlier had to turn to electricity because of the growing shortages of oil and gas. Other projections of energy consumed as electricity tend to be slightly lower than this one for 1985 but somewhat higher for 2000, the terminal year for most projections (see sources for table 5–15).

Solar energy is projected to provide only 4.3 percent of the nation's energy requirements in 2025. Although this may appear small, it represents nearly 40 percent of the net energy required for space conditioning and water heating in the residential sector. This means that nearly 60 percent of all residences, which represent virtually all single-family dwellings, would be equipped with solar collectors providing on the average

[36] Eventually, nuclear energy may also be used to generate hydrogen for use as a fuel.

[37] Our figures for electricity include only what is produced by electric utilities. This substitution is likely to occur because the shift from use of oil and gas to coal and nuclear power in the production of electricity will give an advantage to large-scale, remote power stations, which can handle environmental problems more easily.

[38] That is, taking into account the whole period from 1971 to 2000 and beyond, the price of electricity is expected to increase by less than the price of oil and gas (see table 2–10). This whole period is relevant because of time lags involved in replacing capital equipment associated with energy use.

about 60 percent of their requirements. Because the upper limit on the proportion of all residential space conditioning and water heating requirements that will be met by solar energy for the country as a whole appears to be around 50 percent, given current prices and modest improvements in technology, and because no major technological breakthroughs are projected, this level of use represents a substantial achievement (Shapanka, 1977).

It is of interest to note that in order to meet projected energy demands coal production in this base case must grow by 3.4 percent a year between 1975 and 1985, though thereafter the growth rates are substantially lower, averaging 2.2 percent a year for the fifty-year period. Such rates of growth ought to be feasible. But they result from the fact that this scenario is one in which nuclear developments are pushed rapidly and petroleum and natural gas imports are permitted to enter as needed to fill the gap.

In 1975, the United States had the equivalent of thirty-four operating nuclear plants averaging 1,000 MW in capacity. By 1985, this number is likely to rise to ninety. To validate this scenario, the United States must have 390 such plants in 2000 and 794 in 2025. On strictly technical and economic grounds, we believe these numbers are feasible; that is, there appears to be sufficient skilled labor, productive capacity, and sites available to permit this extent of nuclear development. Even if the technological problems of the breeder reactor and fusion are not solved after the turn of the century, as we have assumed, uranium resources appear adequate to run the nuclear program with light-water reactors.[39] But it remains to be seen whether these numbers of plants—let alone the even larger numbers implicit in some of the other scenarios— will be permitted to be built at the rate required.

The percentage of total liquid fuels consumed that is supplied by petroleum imports tells a large part of the story of future import dependency. In the base case, this percentage would rise from 41 percent of liquid fuel consumption in 1975 to 77 percent in 2000 (see table 5–18). Thereafter, it would remain at roughly this level for a time and then begin dropping as synthetics come on stream. In 2025, petroleum imports would still represent 69 percent of total consumption of liquid fuels, but from that point on they would decline rapidly. The remainder of the

[39] The projected breakdown by types of reactors was necessary to estimate uranium and other resource requirements, but uncertainties are so great that they must be considered little better than notional figures (see Shapanka, 1977).

Table 5–19. U.S. Energy Production, Net Imports, and Consumption, by Fuel and Scenario
(quads)

	1975	2000					
Fuel	EL	EL	DH	DL	FH	FL	DHNU
Petroleum							
Production	20.2	11.2	18.6	18.6	18.6	18.6	18.6
Net imports	13.9	38.1	26.2	20.5	23.8	18.9	26.8
Consumption	34.1	49.3	44.8	39.1	42.4	37.5	45.4
Natural gas							
Production	21.4	12.0	16.2	14.4	15.2	14.1	16.3
Net imports	0.7	4.1	0.0	0.0	0.0	0.0	0.0
Consumption	22.1	16.1	16.2	14.4	15.2	14.1	16.3
Coal (including use in synfuels)							
Production	15.5	23.7	31.9	28.4	29.8	27.3	60.9
Net imports	−1.8	−2.9	−2.9	−2.9	−2.9	−2.9	−2.9
Consumption	13.7	20.8	29.0	25.5	26.9	24.4	58.0
Hydroelectric	2.9	3.2	3.2	3.2	3.2	3.2	3.2
Solar	—	1.1	2.2	2.2	1.9	1.9	2.2
Geothermal	—	1.1	1.7	1.7	1.7	1.7	1.7
Shale oil	—	—	7.8	6.8	7.4	6.5	7.9
Nuclear	2.2	22.7	38.2	34.3	35.8	32.4	5.9
Total domestic use, gross	74.9	114.2	143.1	127.2	134.5	121.7	140.6
Oil imports as a percentage of consumption[a]	40.8	77.3	51.4	46.0	49.3	44.3	51.8

[a] Petroleum, liquefied coal, and shale oil.

story with respect to import dependency has to do with how this dependency varies by scenario and which countries the United States would find itself dependent on.

OTHER SCENARIOS.   Table 5–19 compares production, consumption, and net imports, by fuel, for the major scenarios that show significant differences in their energy results. The impacts of alternate population and economic growth assumptions on total energy use grow over time, so that by 2025 the savings in energy use resulting from differences in these assumptions become quite substantial. If, for example, the low population and low economic growth assumptions (FL) were to occur rather than the high assumptions (DH), 40 percent less petroleum would be consumed in that year. Imports also would be 40 percent less, and coal and nuclear electric production each would be 35 percent less. Import dependence would be somewhat less in FL than DH in 2025, but not by as much as in earlier years because by this time U.S. production of oil and natural gas would have fallen to quite low levels in all scenarios.

2000		2025							
DHP1	DHP2	EL	DH	DL	FH	FL	DHNU	DHP1	DHP2
18.6	11.2	6.1	2.9	2.8	2.7	2.9	2.9	2.9	6.1
20.2	71.8	47.2	57.2	45.7	43.2	34.6	57.8	36.5	38.1
38.8	83.0	53.0	60.1	48.5	45.9	37.5	60.7	39.4	44.2
13.3	12.0	5.6	3.8	3.8	3.8	3.8	3.8	3.8	5.6
0.0	20.6	13.1	13.1	9.7	8.8	6.7	13.3	8.6	13.5
13.3	32.6	18.7	16.9	13.5	12.6	10.5	17.1	12.4	19.1
31.5	20.7	46.3	75.1	62.4	58.3	49.5	135.1	72.9	97.4
−2.9	−2.9	−10.0	−10.0	−10.0	−10.0	−10.0	−10.0	−10.0	−10.0
28.6	17.8	36.3	65.1	52.4	48.3	39.5	125.1	62.9	87.4
3.2	3.2	3.3	3.3	3.3	3.3	3.3	3.3	3.3	3.3
2.2	1.1	6.4	8.1	7.7	6.0	5.4	8.1	8.1	9.0
1.7	—	2.9	4.5	4.5	4.5	4.5	4.5	4.5	4.5
8.6	—	9.5	27.5	22.4	21.4	17.6	27.9	30.2	23.1
37.7	29.0	40.9	74.0	62.4	56.8	47.9	—	69.6	71.4
133.9	166.7	171.4	259.5	214.7	198.5	166.2	246.7	230.5	262.0
44.3	86.5	69.0	61.4	60.6	60.4	58.9	61.4	57.4	48.0

The difficult case would entail less dependence on imported oil in 2000 than would the base case: 51 percent in DH compared with 77 percent in EL, but because this means that U.S. petroleum resources are used up at a faster rate, the difference in import dependence in 2025 is not that great (69 percent in EL compared with 61 percent in DH); thereafter, import dependence should fall rapidly as synfuels from coal, shale, and tar sands take over.

This reduction in import dependence is obtained by substantially increasing the annual rate at which coal production must grow, from 1.7 to 2.9 percent a year during the first twenty-five years, and from 2.2 to 3.2 percent a year over the whole fifty-year period. As can be seen in table 5–20, a sizable and growing fraction of this coal will be used to produce synfuels.[40] But the most dramatic increases in coal production occur in

[40] The figures for 1985 assume that efforts to develop domestic substitutes started in 1975. A shift to the policies outlined in scenario DH at the present time would not generate these levels of output by 1985.

Table 5–20. Net Production of Synthetic Fuels, Scenarios EL, DH, and DHP1 (10^{15} Btu)

Fuel and scenario	1980	1985	2000	2010	2025
Liquids from coal					
EL	0	0.0	0.0	2.5	7.5
DH	0	0.0	0.0	3.3	11.0
DHP1	0	0.0	0.0	3.3	11.0
High-Btu gas from coal					
EL	0	0.0	0.0	3.3	11.0
DH	0	1.8	7.4	11.3	17.4
DHP1	0	1.8	7.4	11.3	17.4
Shale oil					
EL	0	0.0	0.0	2.5	7.6
DH	0	1.8	6.2	11.3	22.0
DHP1	0	2.0	6.8	12.4	24.2

scenario DHNU (see table 5–19), in which the use of nuclear power is phased out; in this case, coal production must increase by 5.6 percent a year during the first twenty-five years and 4.4 percent during the whole period, and virtually all of the increase is used for electric power generation. Serious doubts can be raised about the feasibility of sustaining these rates of growth for such long periods and about the environmental impacts of using this much coal. Although there is no basis on which to judge the former issue, we can say something about the latter and will do so in chapter 7.

Exports of coal are assumed to continue at modest rates during the first thirty-five years, and then exports, in the form of synfuels, will begin growing as the United States becomes able to produce such products. If production, siting, or environmental problems become severe, these exports could be cut back; if these problems were solved, however, the United States could become a major exporter of such fuels.

Virtually all of this analysis has been based on the standard world case in which petroleum prices remain at their 1975 level (in real terms) until about 2010. If petroleum prices were to rise as in scenario DHP1, consumption and imports would both be about 35 percent less than in scenario DH by 2025. The ratio of imports to domestic consumption would fall, but only by a few percentage points because of declines in both the numerator and denominator of that ratio. The impact of rising prices on natural gas is similar though less dramatic. The impact on total energy use is much less because use of other fuels is roughly the same in both cases. If by 1985 these prices were to fall to half their 1975 level, petroleum and natural gas imports would soar, while domestic production

Table 5–21. World Cumulative Demand for Nonrenewable Energy Sources and Percentage of Resources Used, 2000 and 2025, Standard Case

	1975–2000		1975–2025	
Energy source	Cumulative demand (quads Btu)	Percentage of resources	Cumulative demand (quads Btu)	Percentage of resources
Coal	2,832	1.6	7,035	4.1
Petroleum	3,907	31.0[a]	10,567	85.0[a]
Natural gas	1,734	17.3	6,062	60.6
Uranium (U_3O_8)[b]	963	2.4–11.7	6,313	15.4–77.0
Oil shale and tar sands	—	—	625	4.0

[a] Assuming resources of 12,500 quads, that is, 10,000 quads from table 5–1 plus 25 percent additional for improvements in recovery rates and use of more costly sources.

[b] These figures are somewhat higher than cumulative production (of nuclear power) because they include estimates of fuel rods that must be kept in inventory.

of petroleum, natural gas, and coal would fall during the first twenty-five years (compare DHP2 with DH in 2000). By 2025, however, because of the dramatic runup in world prices (see figure 5–4), the situation is reversed.

Cumulative Demand Compared with Resources

Cumulative energy demand can now be compared with resources in order to determine whether energy resources in our different scenarios will be adequate in the long run. (Though short-run supply bottlenecks could arise, they are not discussed except in passing.) For nonrenewable energy resources, tables 5–21 and 5–22 present this comparison for the world and for the United States. No comparable analysis of renewable energy sources is necessary because it is clear that potentials for using such sources will be far from exhausted in 2025.

Resource adequacy obviously is well assured, both globally and domestically, in the case of coal, oil shale, and tar sands. If difficulties arise in meeting requirements for these resources, they will come from other directions, for example, from water shortages, siting conflicts, or pollution control. All we can say at this point is that inadequacy of resources proper will not be one of the constraints that must be considered for a substantial period beyond this study's time horizon.

It is of interest to note in table 5–22 that the smallest U.S. cumulative production figure for coal in 2025 occurs in the base case, scenario

Table 5–22. U.S. Cumulative Production of Nonrenewable Energy Sources and Percentage of Resources Used, Various Scenarios, 2000 and 2025

Energy source	1975–2000								
	EL	DH	DL	FH	FL	DHNU	DHP1	DHP2	DHRE
Coal									
Cumulative production (quads Btu)	544	698	645	682	639	903	694	532	684
Percentage of reserves	10.6	13.6	12.6	13.3	12.5	17.7	13.5	10.4	13.4
Percentage of resources	1.7	2.2	2.0	2.1	2.0	2.8	2.2	1.7	2.1
Petroleum									
Cumulative production (quads Btu)	404	511	509	509	509	510	511	404	510
Percentage of resources	47.5	60.0	59.7	59.7	59.7	59.9	60.0	47.4	59.9
Natural gas									
Cumulative production (quads Btu)	426	489	472	480	471	489	466	425	486
Percentage of resources	46.2	53.0	51.2	52.1	51.1	53.0	50.5	46.1	52.7
Uranium (U_3O_8)[a]									
Cumulative production (quads Btu)	337	490	441	480	435	26	485	405	474
Percentage of resources	13.0	18.9	17.0	18.5	16.8	10.2	18.7	15.6	18.3
Oil shale									
Cumulative production (quads Btu)	0	88	79	86	77	89	95	0	88
Percentage of resources	0	4.9	4.4	4.8	4.3	4.9	5.3	0	4.9

[a] These figures are somewhat higher than cumulative production (of nuclear power) because they include estimates of inventories of fuel rods that must be kept in inventory.

EL, not in scenario FL, which incorporates the smallest population and economic growth assumptions. The reason is that there is no attempt in this case to restrict imports of petroleum and natural gas. As expected, the largest cumulative production figure occurs in the case in which nuclear power is phased out; and it is large indeed, constituting by 2025 almost twice the amount of coal that would be used without such a restriction.

The situation with respect to uranium is surrounded by so much uncertainty, especially with global resources, that no firm conclusions should be drawn from the numbers presented. If forced to choose, the smaller of the depletion percentages shown in table 5–21 for the world

1975–2025								
EL	DH	DL	FH	FL	DHNU	DHP1	DHP2	DHRE
1,403	1,988	1,745	1,759	1,584	3,312	1,999	1,926	1,962
27.4	38.9	34.1	34.4	31.0	64.7	39.1	37.6	38.4
4.4	6.2	5.4	5.5	4.9	10.3	6.2	6.0	6.0
618	736	731	732	732	732	736	619	733
72.5	86.4	85.8	85.9	85.9	85.9	86.4	71.9	86.0
637	713	687	699	685	712	691	636	708
69.1	77.3	74.5	75.8	74.3	77.2	74.9	69.0	76.8
911	1,784	1,540	1,602	1,378	360	1,719	1,427	1,401
35.1	68.8	59.4	61.8	53.1	13.9	66.3	55.5	54.0
108	505	428	437	375	513	580	293	506
6.0	28.1	23.8	24.3	20.8	28.5	32.3	16.3	28.1

may be more nearly correct, simply because the larger of these percentages does not adequately take into account the fact that there has been so little exploration. The U.S. figures suggest a modestly comfortable situation, at least until 2025 or so, but it will be necessary to turn to higher cost sources even within this time frame. Whatever the case, all these figures, those for the United States and the world alike, are likely to change considerably in the next few years as recently intensified exploration efforts provide better information.

If the smaller of the uranium resource estimates incorporated into these figures should prove to be correct, there would be a strong argument in favor of the breeder reactor and other forms of plutonium recycling. But such methods, which are incorporated into scenarios EL and DHRE for the United States, make little difference in the depletion percentages for the United States during this time span. To a large extent, this is because the methods are not assumed to come into commercial use until 1990 to 2000. As a consequence, the difference in depletion percentages only begins to become significant after 2015 or so. In addition, however, there are other technological options that would conserve uranium but are not analyzed here. A promising one is laser enrichment, which would extract virtually all the uranium 235 from uranium ore instead of leaving 28 to 43 percent in tailings as current technology does. This by itself would increase recoverable uranium resources by about 50 percent. Another option is high-temperature, gas-cooled reactors that use a thorium fuel cycle. Even less is known about thorium than about uranium resources, but present knowledge suggests that these two resources are roughly equal in magnitude; this option, then, would double the resource base for nuclear fuels. Beyond 2025, if fusion becomes available at reasonable cost, it would eliminate the question of adequacy for at least the next century.

This leaves petroleum and natural gas as the two energy resources for which adequacy is least assured. Globally, by 2025, only 15 percent of petroleum resources and perhaps 40 percent of natural gas resources would remain according to this study's assumptions. In the standard world case depicted in figure 5–3, world resources of petroleum would be essentially exhausted by 2030–35, and those for natural gas shortly thereafter. In contrast to uranium, there is little likelihood that resource estimates for these two fuels are understated by a wide margin.

The petroleum situation is also more serious, at least for the United States and its political allies, because of the distribution of global resources and the likely sequence of their exploitation. As table 5–3 indicates, world petroleum resources can be roughly divided into thirds, slightly more than one-third controlled by OPEC, a bit less than one-third by the Communist countries, and the remainder by the rest of the world. This third category of countries represents the major oil consumers. If they use their resources first and turn to OPEC when their own are inadequate, as appears to be happening, a time will come when the principal remaining petroleum resources of the world will be controlled by the Communist countries.[41] The timing of this event depends on many things,

---

[41] This assumes, of course, that Communist countries will not have used up their petroleum resources before that time, an assumption that may seem strange

including (importantly) the extent to which OPEC restricts rates of production from its fields; the seriousness of this factor depends on whether the capacity to produce synthetic liquids and gases has been developed by the time it happens.

The most practical ways to deal with this situation are to force conservation and to develop synthetic liquids and gases at a more rapid pace than these scenarios assumed *and* to shift consumption from domestic to foreign sources in order to hold remaining domestic sources in reserve. This last move has not been part of recent energy policy proposals, ostensibly because of concerns about foreign dependency and the balance of payments in the next decade or two. But the risks involved in such short-run dependency can be minimized by stockpiling and diversifying sources of supply; in the long run diversification will not be possible, particularly if the present pattern of exploitation continues. And the balance of payments problem will be more difficult to handle after U.S. sources are depleted than they are now (unless, of course, synthetic liquids and gases become competitive before such difficulties begin growing). Most likely, all these methods of dealing with this situation will have to be pushed simultaneously if this long-run picture is to change much.

These projections of resources and cumulative demands for petroleum and natural gas undoubtedly are subject to wide margins of error, but results do not appear to be highly sensitive to changes in a number of the underlying assumptions. As can be seen by comparing lines 1, 4, and 5 of table 5–8, even a doubling of petroleum resources would postpone the transition to synthetic fuels by little more than a decade. Quite clearly, this is because of the large annual increments to world consumption by that time. Similarly, changes in assumptions about population and economic growth rates, at least within the ranges and over the time period studied, have relatively small effects. Although cumulative consumption of energy in all forms is somewhat sensitive to these factors, the cumulative use of petroleum alone is not. In experimenting with alternative population and economic growth rates for the world, we found that a shift from the high-

given recent projections that the Soviets will begin importing petroleum soon. But such projections are based on current production problems, not reserve estimates. In the long-run context of this study, it is more appropriate to assume that these production problems will eventually be solved and to include prospective as well as current reserves in the analysis. If this is done, and if at the same time we assume that oil consumption is the same percentage of total energy consumption as projected for the United States, these countries would have consumed only half of their petroleum resources by 2000 (estimated from tables 5-3, 5-6, and 5-18). But this percentage is substantially lower today than in the United States, and it is likely to remain lower during the next fifty years, especially in China.

est to the lowest of these growth rates would reduce cumulative energy consumption by about 25 percent, but it would reduce cumulative petroleum consumption by only 12 percent during the fifty-year period. Obviously, a decline in growth rates only for the United States would have an even smaller effect; indeed, it would save little more than a year's worth of global consumption in 2025.

The intermediate-run effects of various policy options on the U.S. resource situation are somewhat greater. If, for example, the United States does not attempt to restrict imports (scenario EL) or if the world price of oil were to fall in early years (DHP2), the United States would rely more heavily on resources from the rest of the world. This is reflected in lower U.S. depletion percentages for these cases in 2000. But given the price rises that would occur thereafter, this difference is all but eliminated by 2025.

On the other hand, changes in other factors, such as tastes and technology, could make an enormous difference in the outcome. In these respects, our assumptions reflect the state of present, or at least recent, conventional wisdom: continuation of trends in tastes (though with some saturation), continued shifts toward electric and nuclear power, a small role for solar energy until well after 2000, substantial though undramatic efforts at conserving energy and reducing imports, and a substitution of coal for nuclear energy in case the latter fails to grow as rapidly as projected. Our analysis covers a plausible and interesting range of possibilities, and—at least in terms of availability of energy resources—all of them seem feasible. Whether they are desirable is a separate question which must also take into consideration the environmental and other consequences of these scenarios.

References

Almon, C., Jr., M. B. Buckler, L. M. Horowitz, and T. C. Reimbold. 1974. *1985: Interindustry Forecasts of the American Economy* (Lexington, Mass., Lexington Books).

Bupp, I. C., J. Derian, M. Donsimoni, and R. Treitel. 1975. "The Economics of Nuclear Power," *MIT Technology Review* vol. 77, no. 4, pp. 14–25.

Central Intelligence Agency (CIA). 1977. *The International Energy Situation: Outlook to 1985.* ER77-102404 (April) (Washington, D.C., CIA).

Conference Board. 1974. *Energy Consumption in Manufacturing.* Report to the Ford Foundation Energy Policy Project (Cambridge, Mass., Ballinger) tables 1–3.

Corey, G. 1976. "A Comparison of the Cost of Nuclear vs. Conventional Electric Generation," *Nucleonics Week* (August 1).

Darmstadter, J. 1972. "Energy," in R. G. Ridker, ed., *Population, Resources, and the Environment,* vol. 3, *Research Reports of the Commission on Population Growth and the American Future* (Washington D.C., GPO).

———. 1979. *Energy Supply and Demand in the Midterm: 1985, 1990, and 1995,* DOE/EIA-0102/52 (Washington, D.C., GPO).

———, P. D. Teitelbaum, and J. G. Polach. 1971. *Energy in the World Economy: A Statistical Review of Trends in Outputs, Trade, and Consumption Since 1925* (Baltimore, Md., Johns Hopkins University Press for Resources for the Future).

———. 1977. J. Dunkerley, and J. Alterman, *How Industrial Societies Use Energy* (Baltimore, Md., Johns Hopkins Press for Resources for the Future).

Data Resources, Inc., and Brookhaven National Laboratory. 1976. *The Relationship of Energy Growth to Economic Growth Under Alternative Energy Policies.* Report prepared for the U.S. Energy Research and Development Administration (Washington, D.C., GPO).

DOE. See U.S. Department of Energy.

Dupree, W. G., and J. S. Corsentino. 1975. *United States Energy Through the Year 2000* (rev. December) (Washington, D.C., Department of Interior and GPO).

Enos, J. L. 1958. "A Measure of the Rate of Technological Progress in the Petroleum Industry," *Journal of Industrial Economics* vol. 6, no. 3 (June) pp. 180–197.

ERDA. See U.S. Energy Research and Development Administration.

Exxon. 1978. "Exploration in Developing Countries." Paper presented at Aspen Institute Energy Committee Seminar, July 16–20.

FEA. See U.S. Federal Energy Administration.

Fisher, H. W. 1968. "Innovations in a Large Company," in *The Process of Technological Innovation.* Report of a symposium sponsored by the National Academy of Engineering (Washington, D.C., National Academy of Engineering).

Ford Foundation. 1974. *A Time to Choose.* Final report of the Ford Foundation Energy Policy Project (Cambridge, Mass., Ballinger).

Griffin, J. W., and P. R. Gregory. 1976. "An Intercountry Translog Model of Energy Substitution Responses," *American Economic Review* vol. 66, no. 5 (December) pp. 845–857.

Gyftopoulos, E., L. Lazaridis, and T. Widmer. 1974. *Potential Fuel Effectiveness in Industry.* Report prepared for the Ford Foundation Energy Policy Project (Cambridge, Mass., Ballinger).

Hirsch, W. Z. 1952. "Manufacturing Progress Functions," *Review of Economics and Statistics* vol. 34 (May) pp. 143–155.

Hubbert, M. K. 1974. "U.S. Energy Resources, A Review as of 1972." Report prepared for the Senate Committee on Interior and Insular Affairs, Serial No. 93-40 (Washington, D.C., GPO).

IBRD. See International Bank for Reconstruction and Development.

Institute for Energy Analysis. 1976. *Economic and Environmental Implications of a U.S. Nuclear Moratorium, 1985–2010* (September) (Oak Ridge, IEA–Oak Ridge Associated Universities).

Interior Department. 1975. *Energy Perspectives* (Washington, D.C., GPO).

———. 1976. *Energy Perspectives II* (Washington, D.C., GPO).

International Bank for Reconstruction and Development (IBRD). 1978. "Petroleum and Gas in Non-OPEC Developing Countries: 1976–1985." World Bank Staff Working Paper No. 289 (Washington, D.C., IBRD).

Kennedy, M. 1974. "An Economic Model of the World Oil Market," *The Bell Journal of Economics and Management Science* vol. 5, no. 2 (Autumn) pp. 540–577.

Lichtblau, J. H., and H. J. Frank. 1978. *The Outlook for World Oil into the 21st Century with Emphasis on the Period to 1990* (Palo Alto, Calif., Electric Power Institute).

Linden, H. R. 1974. "Review of World Energy Supplies," in *U.S. Energy Resources: A Review as of 1972* Committee Print 93-75, pt. I, Senate Committee on Interior and Insular Affairs (Washington, D.C., GPO).

Moody, J. D., and R. W. Esser. 1975. "World Crude Resource May Exceed 1500 Billion Barrels," *World Oil* (September) pp. 47–56.

National Academy of Sciences (NAS). 1962. *Energy Resources: A Report to the Committee on Natural Resources* (Washington, D.C., NAS) tab. 3.

———. 1966. *Energy Resources: A Report to the Committee on Natural Resources* Publication 1000-D (Washington, D.C., NAS) p. 99.

———. 1975. Committee on Mineral Resources and the Environment. *Mineral Resources and the Environment* (February) (Washington, D.C., NAS).

NEPSG. See Nuclear Energy Policy Study Group.

Newman, D. K., and D. Day. 1975. *The American Energy Consumer*. Report to the Ford Foundation Energy Policy Project (Cambridge, Mass., Ballinger).

NRC. See U.S. Nuclear Regulatory Commission.

Nuclear Energy Policy Study Group (NEPSG). 1977. *Nuclear Power Issues and Choices*. Directed by the Mitre Corporation for the Ford Foundation (Cambridge, Mass., Ballinger) chap. 2 and 13.

OECD. See Organisation for Economic Co-operation and Development.

Oil and Gas Journal. 1973. "Worldwide Oil at a Glance," vol. 71, no. 53 (December 31) p. 86.

———. 1976. "Worldwide Oil and Gas at a Glance," vol. 74, no. 52 (December 27) p. 105.

Organisation for Economic Co-operation and Development (OECD). 1975. *Energy Prospects to 1985*, vol. II (Paris, OECD).

Ridker, R. G., and W. D. Watson, Jr., and A. Shapanka. 1977. "Economic, Energy, and Environmental Consequences of Alternative Energy Regimes, An Application of the RFF/SEAS Modeling System," in C. J. Hitch, ed., *Modeling Energy–Economy Interactions: Five Approaches* (Washington, D.C., Resources for the Future) pp. 135–198.

Schurr, S. H., B. C. Netschert, with V. F. Eliasberg, J. Lerner, and H. H. Landsberg. 1960. *Energy in the American Economy, 1850–1957: Its History and Prospects* (Baltimore, Md., Johns Hopkins University Press for Resources for the Future) tab. XXIII and XXIV, pp. 545–548.

Scott, R. E. 1975. "Projections of the Cost of Generating Electricity in Nuclear and Coal-Fired Plants." Paper from the Center for the Study of the Biology of Natural Systems (Saint Louis, Mo., Washington University).

Silver, L. T. 1977. "Problems of U.S. Uranium Resources and Supply to the Year 2010." Supplement to testimony before the House Subcommittee on Fossil and Nuclear Energy on the preliminary findings of the Committee on Nuclear and Alternative Energy Systems, National Academy of Sciences, 95 cong. 1 sess. (June 9, 1977).

Solar Working Group. 1978. *Solar Energy Research and Development: Program Balance* (DOE/IR-0004 (Washington, D.C., U.S. Department of Energy).

United Nations. 1974. Department of Economic and Social Affairs. *Statistical Yearbook, 1973* (New York, United Nations) tab. 18.

———. 1975. *Statistical Yearbook, 1974* (New York, United Nations) tab. 18.

———. 1977. *World Energy Supplies, 1969–1972* series J, no. 21 (New York, United Nations).

———. 1978. *World Energy Supplies, 1971–1975*, series J, no. 21 (New York, United Nations).

U.S. Bureau of Mines. 1976. *Energy Perspectives 2* (Washington, D.C., GPO).

U.S. Census Bureau. 1975. *Historical Statistics of the United States, Colonial Times to 1970* (Washington, D.C., GPO) tab. F 1–5.

U.S. Department of Agriculture (USDA). 1975. *World Population by Country, 1950–1974* (June) (Washington, D.C., USDA Economic Research Service).

U.S. Department of Energy (DOE). 1979. *National Energy Plan II* (Washington, D.C., DOE).

U.S. Energy Research and Development Administration (ERDA). 1975. *A National Plan for Energy Research and Development and Demonstration*, vol. 1, ERDA-48 (Washington, D.C., GPO).

———. 1976a. *A National Plan for Energy Research and Development and Demonstration: Creating Energy Choices for the Future* vol. 1 (Washington, D.C., GPO).

———. 1976b. *Statistical Data of the Uranium Industry* ERDA-GJO-100 (January 1) (Grand Junction, Colo., ERDA).

U.S. Federal Energy Administration (FEA). 1974. *Project Independence* (November) (Washington, D.C., GPO) append. AI, pp. 37 and 48.

———. 1976. *Energy Outlook.* (February) (Washington, D.C., GPO) append., p. F80.

———. 1977. *National Energy Outlook.* (Washington, D.C., GPO).

U.S. Geological Survey (USGS). 1965. *Resources of Oil, Gas, and Natural-Gas Liquids in the U.S. and the World,* USGS Circular 522 (Washington, D.C., USGS).

————. 1975a. *Geological Estimate of Undiscovered Recoverable Oil and Gas Resources in the United States,* USGS Circular 725 (Washington, D.C., GPO).

————. 1975b. *Assessment of Geothermal Resources of the United States,* USGS Circular 726 (Washington, D.C., GPO).

U.S. Nuclear Regulatory Commission (NRC). 1976. *Final Generic Environmental Statement on the Use of Recycled Plutonium in Mixed Oxide Fuel in Light Water Cooled Reactors* vol. 4, NUREG-002 (Springfield, Va., National Technical Information Service).

U.S. Senate, Committee on Interior and Insular Affairs. 1973. *Energy Research and Development: Problems and Prospects* serial no. 93-21 (92-56) (Washington, D.C.) pp. 117–121.

Workshop on Alternative Energy Strategies (WAES). 1977. *Energy: Global Prospects 1985–2000* (New York, McGraw-Hill) p. 90.

World Energy Conference. 1974. *World Energy Conference Survey of Energy Resources* (New York, U.S. National Committee of the World Energy Conference) tab. III-12, IV-1, IV-2, IV-3, VIII-1, and IX-2.

————. 1978. *World Energy Resources 1985–2020* (New York, IPC Science and Technology Press).

World Power Conference. 1968. *Survey of Energy Resources* (London, Central Office of World Power Conference).

6

Agriculture

In recent years, concerns have been voiced about the capacity of U.S. agriculture to continue meeting prospective increases in demand, foreign as well as domestic, without substantial increases in prices. Demand from abroad, which in 1976 absorbed 22 percent of U.S. agricultural production in terms of value, is likely to continue to expand rapidly. Domestic production may not grow as rapidly, however. Growth in yields has slowed markedly in recent years; the surplus of high-quality land, which can be called into production at little cost, no longer exists; and more intensive cultivation is likely to increase environmental costs. This chapter speaks to these concerns. It compares projections of foreign and domestic demand for U.S. agricultural production with projections of production potential. It also presents estimates of the land and other resource requirements that are likely to accompany efforts to meet future demand and considers the associated effects on relative prices.

Methods and Assumptions

This chapter's demand and production projections rest heavily on the results of a study undertaken for this project by the Economic Research Service (ERS) of the Department of Agriculture (USDA, 1977b). That study used specialized models of the agriculture sector, in particular the National Interregional Agricultural Projections (NIRAP) model (Jaski, 1977; and Rojko and Schwartz, 1976). The SEAS/RFF model contains materials on agriculture, but the ERS models have the advantage of being more detailed so far as foreign agricultural trade, domestic production trade, and prices are concerned.

The NIRAP model estimates constant-price demand at the farm gate as a function of disposable income per capita and population, and constant-price supply as a function of productivity changes; it then adjusts these estimates by the impact of the price changes necessary to eliminate the gap between demand and supply. Demand for fertilizers, pesticides, and land is then estimated on the basis of functions that include among their arguments these adjusted projections of the demand for agricultural products. Population assumptions are those provided in chapter 2, and disposable income per capita was derived from the SEAS/RFF model.[1]

Productivity Assumptions

Between 1950 and 1978, total agricultural productivity (total output divided by total inputs in constant dollars) increased at an average annual rate of 1.9 percent.[2] There are, however, a number of reasons for believing that this growth rate cannot be sustained for many more years.

First, there are some indications that decade-to-decade growth rates in productivity have fallen. Although the rate for the 1970–77 period is somewhat higher than that for the 1960s, table 6–1 indicates that it is substantially below that of the 1950s, so the overall trend is downward.[3] This table also shows these productivity figures adjusted for changes in the amount of idle land.[4] In addition, table 6–1 traces the rather dramatic drop in the rate of growth of crop yields. Other sources have indicated significantly diminishing returns to increasing levels of fertilizer use in

---

[1] Time and budget constraints made it impossible to match all the parameters of SEAS/RFF and the ERS models. As a consequence, the projections of expenditures on food derived from SEAS/RFF, presented in chapter 3, are not completely consistent with the detailed physical data presented here.

[2] The growth rates in this section and in table 6–1 were derived by fitting logarithmic regression lines through the data for the years indicated.

[3] The 1969–77 interval may be more representative than is 1970–78 because the figure for 1970 was depressed by the corn blight and the 1978 figure was only a preliminary estimate at the time of this writing.

[4] The standard productivity index includes in its denominator the rental value of all farmland, whether in use or not. Thus, when harvested acreage increases significantly, as it did from 1972 on, the productivity index increases at a rate that cannot be sustained once all idle land is in production. The adjusted figures include only the rental value of the land actually in use and are therefore more appropriate for long-term projection purposes. This is not, however, an ideal measure. No adjustment has been made for other inputs like equipment and buildings that also may not be fully utilized; and it was necessary to use figures for "cropland used for crops," a series that excludes pastureland. Available data do not permit avoiding these limitations.

Table 6–1. Average Annual Growth Rates in Productivity and Crop Yield
for U.S. Agriculture, 1950–77

Period	Productivity[a]		Crop yield[b]
	Standard	Adjusted	
1950–59	2.34	2.41	2.30
1960–69	1.52	1.44	1.70
1970–78	1.64	1.49	1.00
1969–77	1.59	1.27	0.76

[a] Farm output per unit of total input. The growth rates for the standard measure
were developed using a logarithmic least-squares fit through data taken from table
B-93 of the Council of Economic Advisors' *Economic Report of the President* (Washington, D.C., GPO, 1978). The adjusted rates were similarly derived from a series
provided by Donald Durost of the U.S. Department of Agriculture, which excludes
from the input series the rental value of land not used in farm production. This was
done by substituting a series on cropland used for crops in place of the series included
in the standard measure.
[b] Total crop production per acre of cropland used for crops, computed from variable
weights for individual crops produced each year. Growth rates were derived from
logarithmic least-squares fits through data taken from table B-93 of the Council of
Economic Advisors' *Economic Report of the President.*

recent years (see figure 6 of National Academy of Sciences, 1975, page
9). According to one explanation, these declining rates of productivity
growth reflect the fact that the potential to improve productivity made
possible by scientific and technological advances after World War II is
being used up and that few new advances have come along (National
Academy of Sciences, 1975). If this explanation is correct, it will take a
significant increase in expenditures on research and extension services—
expenditures which have lagged in recent years—to raise this rate of
growth, and even then there could be a substantial time lag involved.[5]

Second, a number of social, economic, and political changes are
likely to make rapid productivity growth in the agricultural sector more
difficult or costly. These changes include stricter environmental controls
(for example, removal of some pesticides from the market and more
difficult clearance requirements for others), opposition to using government lands in the West for grazing, increased competition for land and
water, increased energy and hence fertilizer prices, and a general loss of
the agricultural sector's political influence (National Academy of Sciences, 1975, chapter 5).

[5] Indeed, Lu (n.d.) found that, historically, a 1 percent increase in research
and extension expenditures has been associated with a productivity increase of 0.037
percent, this effect being spread over a fourteen-year period.

Third, there appear to be biological limits to the speed and efficiency with which plant and animal growth can occur. Though we are still far from these limits, as we approach them, the cost and difficulty of making additional productivity advances can increase dramatically (National Academy of Sciences, 1975, chapter 7).

Finally, two of the foundations on which productivity advances must rest—soil fertility and weather—may be deteriorating. Soil fertility may be declining because of the long-term failure to control erosion and loss of topsoil, and the weather may become less favorable because of long-run climate changes possibly associated with damage to the ozone layer (Schneider and Mesicrow, 1976).

But arguments can be raised against each of these points. The decline in the rate of growth of yields during the last twenty-five years could be the result of factors other than a slowdown in technological advances. In the fifties, many marginal farmers left the land, and because of acreage controls, those who remained had an incentive to adopt new technologies rapidly. In the early sixties, when farmers were paid to reduce acreage, they retired their least productive acreage first; by the end of that decade, however, it became increasingly difficult to substitute other inputs for land, and the rate of growth in productivity declined.

In the early seventies, because of crop failures abroad and the elimination of excess stockpiles of grains, there was a complete reversal in land-use policy. Now, farmers were asked to increase acreage, and somewhat less productive land was brought back into production. In addition, and perhaps more important, U.S. production was adversely affected by a series of problems, including an infestation of corn leaf blight in 1970, a drought that seriously affected feedgrain yields in the corn belt and plains states in 1974, and a near-doubling of fertilizer prices between 1973 and 1975. If these factors, rather than any basic slowdown in technological advances, account for the decline in productivity growth, a stabilization in acreage and prices and a return to the weather patterns of the sixties could raise the productivity growth rate significantly.

Along with the social, economic, and political factors that constrain agricultural production, there are others that could be positive influences. For example, there is a growing disenchantment with urban living and a preference for a rural lifestyle among many young adults, the status of agriculture as an occupation is improving, enrollments in agricultural colleges are increasing, and people are becoming aware that agricultural exports are an important means of paying for oil imports. Moreover, many of the constraints are likely to give way rather quickly if food prices should rise significantly.

Though energy and fertilizer prices have risen dramatically since 1972, it is not clear that future increases over and above that of general inflation will be very significant, at least during the next several decades. According to Dvoskin, Heady, and English (1978), even if energy prices were to double by 1985, energy would constitute only 5.6 percent of production costs in that year, compared with 3.1 percent without such a rise. But as indicated in chapter 5, once domestic prices have reached international levels, we do not anticipate that such a doubling in real prices would occur in less than twenty or thirty years, and then (if it occurs at all) only for oil and gas. So far as nitrogen fertilizer prices are concerned, they should be held down in coming decades by expansion of capacity, especially in OPEC countries where the basic feedstock is flared-off gas, currently a waste product, plus some technological changes that are likely to reduce production costs. And in the long run these prices should be held down by the cost of using coal as a feedstock.

Notions about the biological limits to plant and animal growth have changed dramatically as scientific knowledge has advanced, and there is no reason to believe they will not continue to change. Many of the research areas scientists consider most promising impinge on these limits: enhancement of photosynthetic efficiencies, the introduction of bioregulators in crop production, improvement of biological nitrogen fixation, new techniques for genetic manipulation, much more efficient methods for nutrient and water uptake, and twinning in beef cattle and sheep, to mention a few. With adequate support for research, many of these advances are quite likely to occur during our fifty-year time horizon. In the meantime, substantial improvements in productivity can occur as a result of further adoption of and marginal improvements in the same technologies that have boosted agricultural yields during the last twenty-five years. It is still the case that the top 10 percent of U.S. farmers routinely achieve yields 50 to 80 percent greater than the average farmer, a difference that is only partially explained by differences in land quality.[6]

Erosion, loss of topsoil, and possible weather changes are problems discussed in chapter 8. If appropriate policies are not implemented and enforced to reduce the present topsoil loss rate, there is little doubt that crop yields will be affected adversely at some point in the future, but there is no good evidence as to when and what extent. So far as weather

[6] An important part of the explanation is the economics of scale because of larger size of the farms in the top 10 percent that allows using more and better equipment, better management, vertical integration, and so forth. Thus, the cost of achieving some of these higher yields may be further consolidation of small into large farms.

changes are concerned, some scientists believe that adverse shifts in long-term trends are occurring, but others disagree. Moreover, there is no evidence as yet that changes in weather during the last several decades have induced long-run changes in crop yields (Luttrel and Gilbert, 1976). It has been shown that the exceptionally favorable weather from 1960 to 1973 helped lower the year-to-year variability of yields during that period, and this is not likely to happen again even in the absence of long-run climate deterioration (Thompson, 1975). There is no consensus on this issue.

These crosscurrents permit building plausible cases for a variety of future productivity growth rates. Prudence suggests using rates lower than the average of the past quarter-century, however. Accordingly, two rates have been selected for use in this study. The lowest, 0.9 percent annually, is used in most scenarios; a higher rate, which works out to 1.38 percent annually, is used in a special case to determine the extent of the difference higher productivity might make. Both in terms of past trends and future possibilities, neither of these rates can be considered excessively optimistic; indeed, those who stress the possibilities of technological breakthroughs relevant for agriculture are likely to consider them downright pessimistic.

Foreign Demand

Between 1950 and 1975, world grain production increased at an annual rate of 2.76 percent a year, while population increased 1.86 percent a year. These figures are not quite as favorable as they may seem on the surface, however. First, the large stockpiles of foodgrains of the fifties and early sixties have been eliminated. Stocks are building up again from their 1975 low, when they were equivalent to thirty-eight days' consumption, but they still are a far cry from the days when the United States initiated the PL 480 program and other deliberate efforts to curb grain production and reduce stocks. Second, year-to-year fluctuations in production have been severe. World grain production, for example, actually fell in 1961, 1965, 1972, and 1974 because of poor crops in either the Soviet Union, the Indian subcontinent, or China. Third, much of the growth in grain output—indeed, 47 percent of it between 1960 and 1975 —has occurred in the developed countries; within this group, 55 percent of the increase was from two regions, North America and Australia–New Zealand. Per capita production in less developed countries has increased by less than 0.3 percent a year, and within that group, food-deficit countries, in which a third of the world's population lives, experienced a slight fall in per capita production between 1960 and 1975. Finally, as a consequence of growing affluence, an increasing portion of world grain production is being fed to livestock. This improves the diets of the rich, but leaves less for the poor than the global production figures suggest.

These last two factors, plus changes in policies in the Soviet Union and the People's Republic of China that have led them to import grain in lean years rather than cut back on consumption and reduce livestock demand, have brought about very rapid growth in foreign trade, especially since 1971–72. World grain imports, for example, have grown at almost twice the rate of growth in grain production, from 12 percent of world production in 1961–62 to more than 16 percent in 1975–76. The United States supplied 32 percent of these imports in 1955 and 44 percent in 1961–62 and accounted for 51 percent of world grain trade in 1975–76; Canada and Australia–New Zealand accounted for most of the remainder.[7] Thus, import dependence has increased while exports have become increasingly concentrated.

What should we assume about the future, in particular about U.S. exports? One thing seems fairly certain, given our projections of world population and GNP per capita: the growth in demand for agricultural products is unlikely to slow down appreciably during the next fifty years. Population growth in poorer countries will ensure continued growth in direct demand for grains and other crops, while growth in per capita income in richer countries will continue to increase the demand for livestock products. But how much of this growth in demand will be translated into demand for U.S. exports depends on a host of variables, including not only population and economic growth rates, but trade policies, differential price developments, secular changes in weather patterns, and the success of agricultural development programs in poorer countries, particularly in parts of Africa and South America, which eventually could become major exporters.

Table 6–2 illustrates two of the many sets of circumstances with respect to world grain production and trade for the year 2000 that could lead to significantly different levels of U.S. exports. Alternative I assumes scenario EL for the United States, low population and economic growth

---

[7] Data in this and the preceding paragraph came from USDA (1960–77) and the Food and Agriculture Organization (1960–76). These data exclude production information on USSR and China, which is not available.

Table 6–2. World Grain Production, Trade, and Per Capita Use, 1969–71 Average and Two Alternatives for 2000

	Production and new imports (millions of metric tons)						Per capita use		
	Actual (1969–71 average)		Alternative I (2000)		Alternative II (2000)		Actual (1969–71 average)	Alternative I (2000)	Alternative II (2000)
Country	Production	Net imports	Production	Net imports	Production	Net imports			
Developed countries	401.7	−32.2	645	−52	710	−95	528	664	654
United States	208.7	−39.9	321	−86	348	−101	824	889	864
Canada	33.4	−14.9	65	−28	70	−34	880	1,407	1,200
Australia–New Zealand	15.0	−10.9	33	−20	37	−26	268	681	496
Centrally planned countries	401.1	5.2	:	18	:	18	361	:	:
USSR	165.0	−3.9	:	9	:	9	664	:	:
China (People's Republic)	163.9	3.0	:	4	:	4	220	:	:
Less developed countries	279.3	17.9	693	47	640	105	171	233	198
India	87.0	3.2	210	10	197	13	160	232	191
Other South Asia	23.7	2.4	53	5	45	14	152	206	173
Thailand	10.8	−3.2	29	−9	29	−7	205	347	270
Argentina	19.2	−8.2	39	−23	38	−22	455	494	480
Brazil	21.0	0.8	65	−1	62	6	230	358	343
World totals[a]	681.0	89.7	1,338	186	1,350	240	274	328	289
U.S. as percentage of world production	30.6		24.0		25.8				
U.S. as percentage of world exports		44.5		46.2		42.1			

[a] World production excludes production in centrally planned countries.

rates for the rest of the world, and reasonably successful efforts to increase agricultural output in the LDCs. Alternative II assumes scenario DH for the United States, higher population growth rates for the rest of the world than in Alternative I, and less success in agricultural development programs in LDCs. In this second case, increased output in developed countries is assumed to compensate for the lower production in LDCs, so that world production (excluding centrally planned countries) remains about the same in both cases. Production is assumed to grow at an average annual rate of about 2.3 percent, a rate that is within the general range others have projected for the year 2000.[8]

LDC imports in Alternative II are not sufficiently higher than in Alternative I to compensate for their lower level of production. As a result, per capita consumption levels for Alternative II increase only modestly during the thirty-year period, and in some South Asian countries, they actually fall slightly. In both cases, the U.S. contribution to world production (excluding centrally planned countries) falls slightly over time, and an increasing proportion of its production is exported. In Alternative I, this increase in exports is sufficient to increase the U.S. share of world trade, while in Alternative II, because of even greater increases in exports by other developed countries, this share falls somewhat. Needless to say, many other combinations of events, with yet other effects on U.S. exports, could also occur.

In the end, we selected two sets of constant-price foreign demand projections that more or less cover the range of past growth rates in U.S. exports. Once these foreign demand projections were entered into the NIRAP model, they were then modified to account for changes in U.S. agricultural prices. The runs with high foreign demand tend to be the ones in which prices increase the most, so they are also the runs in which U.S. export growth rates are dampened the most.[9] The result is a set of U.S. export projections with an average rate of growth lower than that experienced during the last quarter-century and a range of about 20 percent between the high and low rates (see table 6–7). Nevertheless, sub-

---

[8] On the high side, Leontief and coauthors (1977) projected growth rates of 3.08 and 3.42 percent and Strout (1975), 3.23 percent. On the low side, Blakeslee, Heady, and Framingham (1973) projected rates of 1.86 percent (from 1960 to 2000). Recent U.S. Department of Agriculture projections to 1985 cover the range 1.97 to 3.0 (USDA, 1976).

[9] This procedure probably dampens the higher foreign demand projections more than might occur in practice. For example, if other major exporters experience similar production cost increases, it would cancel out much of the impact that higher U.S. prices would have on U.S. exports.

stantially more than half U.S. wheat and rice production, a fifth of coarse grain production, and more than a third of soybean production will continue to be exported (see table 6–5).

Environmental Policy

The geographic dispersion of agriculture makes it possible for the environment to assimilate and dilute many of the waste products associated with the growing of food; it also makes environmental regulation difficult. As a consequence, environmental controls have been applied more slowly to agriculture than to manufacturing and processing operations. But increasing concerns about the environment and increasing intensity of land use in the future are likely to result in more stringent standards and more serious enforcement efforts as time goes by. To study the impacts that such changes may have, two alternative assumptions with respect to environmental policy have been developed.

The first assumes a continuation of present trends: current regulations continue, and farmers slowly adopt such practices as integrated pest management and containment and the processing of livestock wastes and then only on the largest of units. The second assumes that more stringent environmental controls are applied—for example, restrictions on quantities of plant nutrients and pesticides that can be used, limits to irrigation discharge, and the application of livestock waste disposal restrictions to much smaller units. The details of these policies are outlined in table 6–3. At this stage, we are not concerned with the likelihood that these policies can be implemented and enforced. Instead, we are asking a hypothetical question: if these policies were to operate as intended, what would be their economic and environmental effects?

Domestic Consumption

The question of what is likely to happen to domestic consumption of food in the future can be disposed of relatively quickly. If the prices of food products relative to all other products remained more or less constant, the principal determinants of consumption would be per capita income, taste, and population. The impact of changes in per capita income is already low and is likely to become smaller in the future because elasticities relating physical quantities of food consumed to changes in

Table 6–3. Alternative Environmental Control Scenarios

Pollutant	Current trends	Stringent controls
Sediment	Promotion of voluntary adoption of conservation and management practices to control erosion	Require the adoption of conservation and management practice to limit soil erosion to an average of 5 tons per acre
Plant nutrients	No restriction on use	Limit use to plant nutrient requirements of crop Use fertilizer formulation that minimizes mobility
Pesticides	Cancellation and suspension of selected pesticides Loss of specific uses during reregistration Loss of specific products during reregistration Loss of chemicals and products at five-year renewal periods Substitution of more environmentally acceptable pesticides for specific uses.	Ban on whole groups of pesticides for all uses Stringent control over application practices Alternate methods of pest management substituted for chemical pesticides Registration of custom operators
Salinity	More efficient water use in irrigation through such procedures as scientific irrigation scheduling	Absolute limits in quality and quantity or irrigation discharge by requiring: (1) all delivery systems to be lined and (2) all irrigation systems to be pressurized.
Animal waste	Zero discharge to waterways for feedlots of 1,000 animal units and larger from 1977 to 1984.	Zero discharge to waterways for all feedlots of 100 or more animal units Storage capacity from feedlot runoff from a twenty-five-year, twenty-four-hour storm Special penalties for violators

income are relatively low. Although they vary considerably among food items, a composite elasticity of 0.16 was found for the 1955–75 period.[10] For the 1975–85 period, when per capita disposable income is projected to be in the range of $4,000 to $5,400 (in 1971 dollars), assumptions

---

[10] This elasticity indicates the percentage change in an index of the physical quantity of food consumed per capita that is associated with a 1 percent change in per capita disposable income. For the historical period, it was calculated from USDA (1977a). For the 1955–65 period, this elasticity was 0.2, but the least squares fit was poor; for the 1955–75 period, it was 0.18, with a substantially better fit.

about responses for individual commodities imply an aggregate elasticity of 0.16; for the remainder of this century (for per capita incomes between $5,400 and $8,800), this elasticity falls to 0.04; thereafter (for per capita incomes higher than $8,800), it becomes 0.01.

In addition to this total income effect, tastes have been shifting away from dairy products, grains, and fish, toward meats, poultry, vegetables, and fruits. Within each food category, there have been shifts toward higher quality and more processed commodities. But many of these trends are close to having played themselves out. Between 1960 and 1973, consumption of meat by the average American increased from 147 pounds a year to 184 pounds, and consumption of poultry increased from 34.4 to 50 pounds. Considering that people in other countries at comparable incomes consume substantially lower quantities of meat and poultry and that concern about possible deleterious effects of high meat diets is increasing, it is difficult to believe that per capita consumption will increase at anything like this rate during the next fifty years. Conversely, consumption of dairy products declined in the sixties at a rate that cannot continue for the next half-century.[11] Thus, without significant price changes, there is likely to be little change in per capita consumption of physical quantities of food in the future, certainly much less than has occurred in recent decades. As a consequence, the principal determinant of total consumption is population, and its rate of increase is also slowing down.

Some price increases at the farm gate can be expected, particularly in those scenarios that combine high growth rates of demand and slower productivity increases. But by the time processing, trade, and transport margins are added, the impact on consumers is greatly dampened. Moreover, with the likely growth in such margins in the future, the relative impacts of changes in farm-gate prices will be even less at the retail level.

The projections for per capita consumption presented in table 6–4 reflect these trends. In the base case (EL), almost no change is projected from the 1972–74 average of 1,730 pounds of food consumed a year by the average person. The same is true for per capita consumption of calories, which increases by less than 4 percent from the average of 3,222

---

[11] The one trend that may continue during this period is the continued shift toward more processed foods, a trend that could increase expenditures even though physical quantities consumed do not increase by a significant amount. Such a trend is reflected in the projected changes in the composition of consumption expenditures presented in chapter 3. It is not, however, of relevance here, where our concern is to estimate physical input requirements for farm production.

Table 6-4. Per Capita U.S. Food Consumption Price Index, Scenarios EL and DH

Food	1960	1972–74 Average	EL			DH		
			1985	2000	2025	1985	2000	2025
Pounds a year[a]	. . .	1,730	1,746	1,756	1,737	1,759	1,806	1,775
Calories a day[a]	. . .	3,222	3,262	3,324	3,331	3,197	3,337	3,364
Selected commodities (lb/yr)								
Meat	147	184	203	216	223	194	204	208
Poultry	34	50	53	57	62	55	61	64
Eggs	42	39	36	34	32	36	34	31
Milk	653	552	514	488	451	520	499	442
Wheat	121	150	142	139	132	149	152	147
Potatoes	109	116	122	125	127	127	135	140
Fruits	140	130	219	224	234	214	230	238
Vegetables	200	206	241	245	245	248	262	265
Food price index (1972 = 100)[b]	71	115	131	131	130	133	135	136

[a] Includes only those commodities projected, 95 percent of total.

[b] In the NIRAP model, this index is based on a regression equation linking it to the farm price ratio. In 1977, it was 155. Because the model begins projecting in 1972–74 and assumes that input prices are constant thereafter (see footnote b of table 6–5), this inflationary increase is not captured.

calories a day recorded for 1972–74. Because some individual commodities have higher income elasticities than others, their consumption changes by greater amounts, but all of these changes are slower than they were during the preceding decade.

The food price index, after the runup from an index of 100 in 1972 to 131 in 1985, remains virtually constant thereafter given the conditions specified in this scenario. Even in the difficult case (DH), with its higher per capita income, larger export demands, and more stringent environmental controls, per capita food consumption levels and retail prices do not change much. Thus, the consumer is unlikely to be greatly affected by any of the circumstances envisioned by the scenarios this study postulates.

Domestic Production, Exports, and Prices

The picture changes when we look at farm output and price indexes for the base and difficult cases. As table 6–5 indicates, between 1972–74 and 2025 total farm output would increase by 57 percent in the base case

Table 6-5. Farm Output, Exports, and Prices, Scenarios EL and DH

Output	1960	1972–74 average	EL			DH		
			1985	2000	2025	1985	2000	2025
Farm output								
Indexes (1967 = 100)								
Total	91	109	123	144	171	127	159	201
Livestock and products	88	106	117	133	156	119	145	184
All crops	93	114	129	153	183	133	171	217
Selected commodities								
Wheat (million bushels)	1,355	1,682	1,941	2,329	2,743	1,923	2,442	3,068
Rice, rough (million cwt)	55	92	116	156	183	128	174	217
Coarse grains (million bushels)[a]	6,109	7,124	8,481	10,028	12,250	8,638	10,957	14,060
Soybeans (million bushels)	555	1,344	1,610	2,009	2,463	1,719	2,418	2,994
Exports								
Index (1967 = 100)	79	150	165	202	244	178	232	275
Selected commodities								
Wheat (million bushels)	662	1,125	1,058	1,340	1,628	963	1,281	1,592
Rice, rough (million cwt)	0.4	58	70	98	108	79	108	120
Coarse grains (million bushels)[a]	459	1,513	1,432	1,823	2,424	1,798	2,486	2,905
Soybeans (million bushels)	130	480	609	776	971	621	864	1,064
Farm price index (1972 = 100)[b]	109	111	112	112	107	122	131	134

a. Corn, grain sorghum, oats, and barley.
b. Same as farm price ratio (ratio of prices received to prices paid by farmers) assuming prices paid are constant during the projection period.

(EL). Rice and soybean production would more than double, while live-stock production would increase by about 45 percent. Although produc-tivity improves slowly in this case, growth in demand is also moderate, and as a consequence the farm price index (assuming constant input prices) would remain virtually stable from 1972–74 to 2000 and fall slightly thereafter. Rice prices would increase (by about 20 percent), while wheat, corn, and soybean prices would fall from their 1972–74 levels. Most of these changes would occur before 1985; thereafter, with the exception of rice, these prices do not change much.

In contrast, farm output in the difficult case (DH) would increase 84 percent between 1972–74 and 2025. Average grain prices would in-crease through the whole projection period, ending about 25 percent higher than in the base case, because of increases in domestic and foreign demand plus more stringent environmental controls. Wheat prices in this case show the strongest increase; in 2025 they would be almost 40 percent higher than in the base case. Thus, the changes over time and between scenarios are much more significant at the farm level than at the con-sumer's level.

Exports will be affected by these changes in domestic prices. Al-though foreign demand at any given price is higher in the difficult case, it is not as high as it would have been had domestic prices not risen. In-deed, as table 6–7 indicates, exports of wheat are actually lower in this case than in the base case, the result of the assumption that other sources of supply are available for which prices have not increased comparably. If foreign demand were not dampened by the domestic price increase, which might occur if other suppliers experienced the same price increase or if a substantial portion of U.S. grain exports were committed through intergovernmental agreements, the domestic price increase would have been some 5 to 10 percent greater.

Role of Population and Economic Growth

Tables 6–6 and 6–7 indicate the impacts of alternate population and economic growth rate assumptions. As can be seen by comparing the percentage differences between scenarios, the impact of changes in per capita GNP on farm output is small and falls over time, as one would expect because of declining income elasticities (compare DH and DL or FH and FL). In contrast, the impact of population is large and grows over time (compare DH and FH or DL and FL). The change in output is less

Table 6-6. Projections of Effect on U.S. Agriculture of Various Population and Economic Growth Assumptions, Base Case Assumption

	1972–74 average	DH 2000	DH 2025	FH 2000	FH 2025	DL 2000	DL 2025	FL 2000	FL 2025
Population (millions)	210.5	286.0	367.5	250.7	264.9	286.0	367.5	250.7	264.9
GNP per capita (1971$)	5,437.1	10,237.8	16,710.2	11,142.8	18,068.7	8,786.7	13,382.3	9,605.1	14,514.9
Farm output index (1967 = 100)	109	151	193	141	159	149	191	140	158
Export index (1967 = 100)	150	200	240	204	247	200	239	204	247
Farm price index (1972 = 100)[a]	111	118	122	109	99	117	121	108	98

Note: All scenarios in this table use the same productivity and export assumptions as does the base case (EL). Thus, scenario DH in this table is not the difficult case but the base case with series D population and the highs of the aggregate economic growth rate assumptions.

[a] Same as farm price ratio (ratio of prices received to prices paid by farmers) assuming prices paid are constant during the projection period.

Table 6-7. Percentage Difference Between Various Scenarios in Their Projected Impacts on U.S. Agriculture

Item	DH to FH 2000	DH to FH 2025	DL to FL 2000	DL to FL 2025	DH to DL 2000	DH to DL 2025	FH to FL 2000	FH to FL 2025
Population	−12.3	−27.9	−12.3	−27.9	0	0	0	0
GNP per capita	8.8	8.1	9.3	8.5	−14.2	−19.9	−13.8	−19.7
Farm output index	−6.6	−17.6	−6.0	−17.3	−1.3	−1.0	−0.7	−0.6
Export index	2.0	2.9	2.0	3.3	0	−0.4	0	0
Farm price index	−7.6	−18.9	−7.7	−19.0	−0.8	−0.8	−0.9	−1.0

Note: Percentage changes based on table 6-6.

than proportional to the change in population, however, because if population is lower in a given year, per capita income is higher and prices are lower. This is significant, not because of the effect on domestic demand, but because of the impact of prices on foreign demand. As can be seen, a shift from DH to FH increases exports by some 2 to 3 percent, thereby dampening the impact of the population change on output and prices.

This last point can usefully be stated the other way around. If the U.S. population were to begin growing more rapidly, there would be some diversion of farm sales from foreign to domestic markets, and in effect a portion of the burden of that population increase would shift to foreigners. Although the overall effect on exports would not be large, the impact on specific crops could be significant. For example, the 28 percent increase in U.S. population in 2025 implied by using population series D rather than F, would mean that the United States would consume 1,384 million bushels of wheat in that year instead of 951 million. Of that difference, 22 percent would come from a 6 percent decline in exports, and the remaining 78 percent from a 13 percent increase in domestic production.

Role of Other Factors

A comparison of the two scenarios in the productivity columns of table 6–8 indicates the impact of a change in assumptions about agricultural productivity. If productivity were to increase at the more rapid of the two rates, by 2025 it would be some 28 percent higher. This would cause farm output to be 5.5 percent greater and exports to be 6 percent higher. Prices received by farmers would be almost 20 percent lower, and retail prices, though not very different in any scenario, would settle at their base-case level. Thus, it is clear that farmers would share most of the productivity gain with others.

The two scenarios in the exports panel of table 6–8 indicate the impact of a change in assumptions about exports; both cases assume high population growth, high economic growth, and trend environmental policy. In 2025, farm output in the high-export case would be higher than in the low-export case by almost 6 percent. Most of this difference would be in crop output, for which exports would be higher by some 18 percent, with coarse grains exhibiting the most difference. Judging from the fact that farm-gate prices would be only 7 percent higher than in the low-export case, this case by itself would not put a great deal of strain on U.S. agriculture. But, as indicated above, the range of difference between these two assumptions about exports is narrower than it might be in practice.

Table 6–8. Impact on U.S. Agriculture of Alternative Assumptions About Productivity and Exports

Item	1972–74 average	Low productivity			High productivity			1972–74 average	Low exports			High exports		
		1985	2000	2025	1985	2000	2025		1985	2000	2025	1985	2000	2025
Farm output (1967 = 100)														
Total	109	127	159	201	127	161	212	109	125	151	193	128	161	204
Livestock and products	106	119	145	184	120	148	194	106	119	140	179	120	146	185
All crops	114	133	171	217	134	173	228	114	131	160	206	136	174	221
Exports (1967 = 100)	150	178	232	275	179	236	292	150	163	200	240	186	240	284
Farm price index[a]	111	122	131	134	120	122	108	111	114	118	122	118	127	130

Note: The panel showing productivity differences uses the difficult case (scenario DH); the panel on export differences uses scenario DH but with trend environmental policy.

[a] Same as farm price ratio (ratio of prices received to prices paid by farmers) assuming prices paid are constant in real terms).

Table 6–9. Percentage Difference in Likely Impacts on Production Costs and Yields of Specified Commodities Under Trend and Stringent Environmental Controls

	Trend controls		Stringent controls	
Output	Costs	Yields	Costs	Yields
Livestock[a]				
Beef	—	...	1	...
Swine	—	...	2	...
Dairy	1	...	4	...
Crops[b]				
Corn	3	—	11	−13
Soybeans	1	—	6	−8
Small grain	1	—	7	−13
Fruits and vegetables	3	−1	11	−13
Sorghum	—	—	2	−2

Note: Likely impacts are based on judgments of ERS experts assuming the environmental controls listed in table 6–3.

[a] Only the costs of meeting effluent guidelines for livestock firms were considered.

[b] Cost increases and yield decreases resulted mainly from assumed restrictions on soil losses and pesticide use.

The assessment of the economic impacts of a more stringent environmental policy than is likely to exist if current trends continue was undertaken on two levels. First, expert judgments were pooled to obtain indications of likely changes in costs and yields (USDA, 1977b). The results, presented in table 6–9, indicate that cost impacts for livestock producers as a whole are unlikely to be very great under either policy. Much of what is required, if current trends continue, is already in place; more stringent policies would mean, to a large extent, that smaller producers would have to meet the standards imposed on larger producers under current trends. The dairy sector would experience the largest cost increases because of the relatively large number of small farms in that sector. But these are average environmental control costs; the cost to individual farmers would vary greatly depending upon the climate, geographic concentration of livestock production, and size of unit. In general, the cost would be proportionately greater the smaller the production unit.

Although cost and yield impacts on crop producers will be small if current trends continue, they could become quite substantial if more stringent environmental controls are imposed. This is because of expected difficulties in limiting soil erosion to an average of 5 tons per acre and in meeting the rather stringent pesticide regulations.

Table 6–10. Impact on U.S. Agriculture of Alternative Assumptions About
Environmental Policy

Item	1972–74 average	Trend controls			Stringent controls		
		1985	2000	2025	1985	2000	2025
Farm output (1967 = 100)							
Total	109	128	161	204	127	159	201
Livestock and products	106	120	146	185	119	145	184
All crops	114	136	174	221	133	171	217
Exports (1967 = 100)	150	186	240	284	178	232	275
Farm price index[a]	111	118	127	130	122	131	134

Note: Both scenarios use the difficult case (scenario DH). For assumptions about
environmental policy, see table 6-3.

[a] Same as farm price ratio (ratio of prices received to prices paid by farmers) assuming
prices paid are constant in real terms.

Second, these expected cost and yield impacts were entered into the
NIRAP model to allow for market adjustments. Table 6–10 compares
production and price results for two scenarios that differ from each other
only with respect to environmental policy. In 2025, when the effects of
stringent controls are greatest, farm output would be about 1.5 percent
less that it would be under trend controls, and the bulk of the decline
would be in crops rather than livestock; exports would be 3 percent less,
and the farm price index would be 3 percent higher. These impacts seem
surprisingly small. But even if they were underestimated, it is unlikely
that environmental policy would ever be a significant factor in affecting
farm production and prices in the aggregate. For individual farmers and in
special situations the effect could be quite severe, however.

Input Requirements

During the twenty-five-year period, 1950–74, farm output increased 46 percent, while total inputs into farming remained relatively
fixed. This dramatic difference was the result of compositional changes in
inputs and productivity improvements. The most obvious shifts in inputs
were a decline in labor's share of total inputs, from 38 percent in 1950
to 15 percent in 1975, and an increase in the share for agricultural chemicals, from 3 percent in 1950 to 16 percent in 1975, most of which was
due to a fivefold increase in the use of chemical fertilizers. These trends,
particularly the substitution of chemicals for labor and land, cannot con-

tinue at this rate much longer; if the high-demand scenarios prevail, inputs of land will have to begin rising soon. This section discusses input requirements for land, fertilizer, pesticides, and energy; water requirements are discussed in chapter 8.

Land

The total cropland in the continental United States often is cited as 385 million acres, with an additional 80 to 90 million acres devoted to pasture. But a certain amount of this is not harvested each year because of crop failure or because it is set aside for summer fallow or soil improvement. Since World War II, the number of acres actually harvested has varied between 352 million (in 1949) and 287 million (in 1962). For the purposes of this chapter, we take the base of cropland that can be harvested on a regular basis to be 330 million acres.[12]

If additional acres are required, they could come from cropland used for pasture or soil improvement. But since other lands would then have to be found for these purposes, it is best to set these acres aside and assume that any additional land would come from the conversion of noncropland. By considering physical characteristics, regional land use problems, and cropland trend data, such land has been classified as having high, medium, or low potential for conversion.[13]

In the high-potential category are 95.7 million acres (68.2 million of which are grasslands in the Great Plains suitable for wheat and grain sorghum production, and pasture in the corn belt and lower Great Lakes regions) that could be converted relatively quickly, although yields are likely to be modest in the northern plains. The remaining acres in this category would require drainage and hence would take somewhat longer to convert. In the medium category are 57 million acres, 29.2 million of which (in the Texas–Oklahoma prairies and Coastal Plain and Piedmont regions) could be converted relatively quickly; the remainder would re-

---

[12] The agricultural land base for this study was derived from the estimate of total crop land acreage for all farms reported in the 1969 Census of Agriculture. To this base were added projected public and private irrigation developments in the seventeen western states and conversion of pasture and forestland in the eastern states. These figures were then reduced to reflect land shifted to urban and other nonagricultural uses.

[13] This summary of the potential for converting noncropland to cropland is based on the 1967 conservation needs inventory as analyzed by Frey and Otte (1975), and Cotner, Skold, and Krause (1975).

quire drainage. Much of the land requiring drainage in the North-Central region could probably be developed by individual, on-farm investments, but other areas would require public investment programs.[14]

The low-potential category includes some 111.8 million acres of land with some degree of physical limitation for cropping. Reasons for this low conversion potential vary. In the Appalachia–Ozark region, the fields are small and scattered, and operating costs are high (which probably explains the high abandonment rate in these areas). In the Northeast and Northern Great Lakes regions, the growing season is so short that only low-volume crops like hay can be produced economically; in addition, many of these fields are scattered and small. In the Rocky Mountains and Far West regions, water is a limiting factor and is likely to become more so in the future because of competing demands for energy and non-fuel minerals production. In all regions, lands with severe erosion problems, rough terrain, or high clearing costs are included in this category.

Because much of the land in the high-potential category now is used for grazing and forestry, converting it to crop production would affect beef and wood production. The effects on beef production could be mitigated by changing grazing locations, by using existing roughages more intensively, and by changing livestock production patterns, including more cow/calf operations in confinement. Although it would be somewhat more difficult to offset the effects of conversion on pulp and timber production, they are likely to be small relative to total timber output. In addition, in the long run, these effects can be mitigated by shifting forestry production to land of lower cropland value that still has good potential for forestry.

Table 6–11 provides estimates of cropland requirements for various scenarios. Currently available cropland is adequate to cover requirements in the base case; indeed, productivity appears to increase sufficiently relative to demand that less land would be required in 2025 than in 1975. The same situation holds for other scenarios incorporating series E or lower population projections. If, however, population series D were to prevail instead of series E or F, some pasture and forestland would have to be converted for crop use. This occurs with low as well as high economic growth rates and with accelerated as well as trend productivity growth.

---

[14] This assessment was based on the 1967 Conservation Needs Inventory. Since that time, some of the basic public investments in the Mississippi Delta have been put in place and estimates of land with high and medium potential have been revised. A 1975 survey by the Soil Conservation Service puts land in these two categories at 111 million acres. It is not clear, however, whether the definitions are the same as those used in the earlier study.

Table 6–11. Cropland Harvested and Required, Various Scenarios
(millions of acres)

Scenario	1972–74	1975	1985	2000	2025
Base case, EL					
Cropland harvested	311	331	304	310	318
Noncropland conversion required	—	—	—	—	—
Base case, DH[a]					
Cropland harvested	311	331	297	331	370
Noncropland conversion required	—	—	—	1	40
Base case, DL[a]					
Cropland harvested	311	331	321	327	366
Noncropland conversion required	—	—	—	—	36
Difficult case, DH					
Cropland harvested	311	331	341	376	412
Noncropland conversion required	—	—	11	46	82
Difficult case, DH with accelerated technology					
Cropland harvested	311	331	339	360	391
Noncropland conversion required	—	—	9	30	61
Difficult case, DHRE (DH with trend environmental controls)					
Cropland harvested	311	331	317	354	390
Noncropland conversion required	—	—	—	24	60

Notes: In all scenarios, irrigated cropland is assumed to increase from 34.8 million acres in 1969 (includes only the seventeen western states, three Delta states, and Florida), to 41.4 million acres in 1985, and to 45.2 million acres in 2025. See Water Resources Council, *1972 OBERS Projections, Regional Economic Activity in the U.S., Series E. Population*, vol. 1, *Concepts, Methodology, and Summary Data* (Washington, D.C., 1974). Also, the same complement of other inputs per acre is assumed in all scenarios in a given year.

The results in this table are based on runs of the NIRAP model for the base case (EL) and the difficult case (DH). Other cases are interpolated.

[a] These scenarios differ from the base case (EL) only with respect to population and economic growth assumptions.

The largest conversion requirements occur in scenario DH because of higher export demand and yield losses associated with a strict environmental policy. In all cases, however, there is sufficient noncropland with high conversion potential available so that the medium- and low-potential lands would not have to be used during our time frame. However, environmental problems may result from clearing even the high-potential lands.

Unfortunately, we do not have adequate estimates of conversion costs, additional inputs necessary to use converted land, or the effects on livestock and timber production. Some declines in yields and increased production costs are built into those cases that would require land conversion. For example, the difficult case has slightly more than 9 percent lower yields per acre than the base case in 2025.[15] But these estimates of declining yields and increasing costs as demand increases are likely to be too low, among other reasons, because they are based on data from the past when more high-quality land was available (Crosson and Frederick, 1977).

Our projections of cropland requirements may be overstated, however, because they assume that the same complement of other inputs is used on each acre across all scenarios in a given year. In reality, as demand increases, more fertilizer, pesticides, and so on are likely to be used per acre. According to one estimate, a 1 percent increase in output typically has been associated with a 0.28 percent increase in real estate (land, buildings, and land improvements) and a 0.74 percent increase in all other inputs (Tweeten and Quance, 1969). A recent study by Iowa State University concluded that, nationally, the marginal rate of substitution of fertilizer for land is 560 pounds of nitrogen for 1 acre of land under moderate-demand conditions and because more marginal land must be used, 830 pounds of nitrogen for 1 acre under high-demand conditions (Dvoskin and Heady, 1975). In addition, under high-demand conditions, further irrigation developments are likely. In 2025, 1 irrigated cropland acre would substitute for 1.4 nonirrigated acres in corn production, 2.0 nonirrigated acres in grain sorghum production, and 1.8 nonirrigated acres in wheat production, according to the ERS base-case yield projections. All such developments would reduce the projected land requirements, though perhaps by no more than 5 to 10 percent unless agricultural land prices were to rise sharply relative to those of other inputs.

In sum, the United States has adequate land to meet during the next fifty years any of the contingencies investigated. The exact extent of additional land requirements depends on productivity growth and the ability to develop and use other inputs such as irrigation and fertilizers. As long as high-quality land is available, resulting cost increases for agricultural and forestry products are likely to be modest. Beyond 2025, however, a continuation of these high-demand conditions would soon require converting land with moderate potential, a situation that could raise production costs and prices substantially. Even this case may not affect U.S. consumers to any great extent; they would simply pay a somewhat larger percentage of their very high (by world standards) incomes for food. But it certainly would affect the ability of the United States to continue serving as the breadbasket for much of the world.

---

[15] If productivity were to grow as fast as assumed in the accelerated productivity case, this decline would be fully offset.

Fertilizers, Pesticides, and Energy

As tables 6–12 and 6–13 indicate, the rate of increase in use of fertilizers, pesticides, and energy is expected to decline quite significantly compared to rates for the sixties. Partly, this is a function of the slowdown in the rate of growth of output. But in the case of pesticides and fuels, declining growth rates also result from decreasing intensities of use per unit of output, a consequence of already high use rates, environmental regulations, and rising prices. Fertilizer and electricity use per unit of output continues to rise but at slower rates than in the past.

The shift from trend to strict environmental controls would result in an increase in fertilizer and pesticide use, despite the fact that output is slightly lower. These controls would result in less use of chemicals per acre, but the increase in acres cultivated more than offsets this reduction in use rates. As we shall see in chapter 7, residuals from fertilizer and pesticides are significantly less in this case despite their increased consumption, because per acre application rates are lower and because sediment losses to streams, the principal carrier of these residuals, is substantially less.

Conclusions

From 1959 to 1972, the ratio of prices received to prices paid by farmers has fallen by about 10 percent, and grain exports have risen by 70 percent. Our analysis suggests that if domestic demand remains relatively strong, some reversal of these trends could be expected in coming years, but the extent of this reversal is unlikely to be dramatic. Even if both U.S. and foreign demand were to grow at the highest, and productivity at the lowest, of the rates assumed, and if at the same time strict environmental controls were imposed, farm prices in real terms would not have to increase by much more than 20 percent to balance projected demand and supply. Perhaps this statement should be modified to read 25 to 30 percent to take into account the possibility that export demand and cost and yield penalties associated with converting new land into cropland have been underestimated. But changes in this range are not of great significance when spread over a fifty-year time horizon, particularly because these are farm-gate prices, not consumer prices.

If the productivity growth rate were modestly higher (though still lower than the average for the past decade and well within the range of

Table 6–12. Fertilizer and Pesticide Use, Alternative Environmental Control Assumptions, Scenario DH

Chemical	1966	1971	Trend controls			Strict controls		
			1985	2000	2025	1985	2000	2025
Farm output (1967 = 100)[a]			128	161	204	127	159	201
Fertilizers (million tons)[a]								
Nitrogen	5.3	8.1	11.9	15.4	20.5	12.7	16.5	21.9
Phosphates	3.9	4.8	6.7	8.7	11.5	7.2	9.4	12.4
Potassium oxides	3.2	4.2	6.3	8.3	11.0	6.9	9.0	11.9
Total	12.4	17.1	24.9	32.4	43.0	26.8	34.9	46.2
Pesticides[b,c]								
Fungicides	33.2	41.7	48.1	56.5	68.2	53.7	62.2	74.6
Insecticides	148.9	169.8	192.4	233.4	272.6	215.6	260.7	303.3
Herbicides	115.3	227.9	452.5	601.5	741.4	500.9	667.2	822.4
Miscellaneous	55.8	54.7	85.7	110.2	133.8	95.2	122.4	148.4
Total	353.2	494.1	778.7	1,001.6	1,216.0	865.4	1,112.5	1,348.7

[a] Primary nutrient use. Historical data is taken from U.S. Department of Agriculture, *Agricultural Statistics 1977* (Washington, D.C., GPO, 1977).
[b] Active ingredients excluding sulfur and petroleum.
[c] Used by farmers. In 1971 farmers used 27 percent of fungicides, 63 percent of herbicides, and 58 percent of insecticides. Historical data are taken from the U.S. Department of Agriculture, *Agricultural Statistics 1977* (Washington, D.C., GPO, 1977).

Table 6–13. Farm Energy Requirements, Scenarios EL and DH

		Scenario EL			Scenario DH		
Energy use	1974	1985	2000	2025	1985	2000	2025
Farm output (1967 = 100)	109	123	143	171	127	159	201
Energy requirements							
Fuel (billion gallons)[a]	8.0	7.7	7.8	8.1	8.4	9.1	9.9
Nitrogen fertilizer							
(million tons)	8.2	10.8	13.0	16.1	12.7	16.5	21.9
Electricity (billion							
kilowatt hours)	32.0	55.2	88.8	152.1	58.2	108.4	212.0

[a] Includes gasoline, diesel, and LP fuels in gasoline equivalents.

what appears feasible considering the types of innovations likely to come along), little if any of this price increase is likely to occur. If at the same time the growth in demand is not as rapid—a likely prospect, particularly so far as U.S. demand is concerned—no net additions to cropland may be required and prices could well fall. Moreover, both productivity growth rates and exports are to a significant extent within our control, the former through expenditures on research and extension (see footnote 4) and the latter through price support and export control programs.

A continuation of the high rates of growth in demand beyond 2025, however, would require converting noncropland of lower potential and would greatly increase the likelihood of substantial and serious price rises. The difficulties could be severe in this event, especially for countries dependent on U.S. exports, which would have to bid output away from domestic consumers. Thus, our conclusion is sanguine only in the sense that there is more breathing space than many observers have thought.

In the agricultural sector of the economy, much depends on what happens abroad, particularly in less developed countries. If food-deficit countries are able to contain their population growth and modernize their agricultural sectors, and if countries such as Sudan, Brazil, and Argentina are able to enter the world export market in a substantial way, the United States could find its agricultural export markets weakening with a consequent downward pressure on domestic prices. If these developments do not occur, domestic prices could increase significantly. To a large extent, therefore, the outcome depends on how wisely this breathing space is used.

Two other problems should be mentioned. One pertains to variations in output around the smooth trend lines on which this analysis has been based. As recent history demonstrates, fluctuations, both on the up and on the down side, can be substantial. Because of declines both in stocks of food grains and in the availability of surplus farmland, the world is more vulnerable to such fluctuations, particularly on the down side, than it was just a decade ago. This situation can be improved through the development and adroit management of adequate reserve stocks and the development of sufficient new farmland to serve as a buffer in case of production shortfalls. But these are issues that lie beyond the scope of this analysis. The other problem pertains to environmental and ecological concerns associated with the projected levels of farm output and land use, topics to which we turn in the next two chapters.

References

Blakeslee, L., E. O. Heady, and C. F. Framingham. 1973. *World Food Production, Demand and Trade* (Ames, Iowa State University Press).

CEA. See Council of Economic Advisors.

Cotner, M. L., M. D. Skold, and O. Krause. 1975. *Farmland: Will There Be Enough?* ERS-584 (Washington, D.C., Economic Research Service, USDA).

Council of Economic Advisors (CEA). 1978. *Economic Report of the President* (Washington, D.C., GPO, January).

Crosson, P., and K. D. Frederick. 1977. *The World Food Situation,* Research Paper R-6 (Washington, D.C., Resources for the Future).

Dvoskin, D., and E. O. Heady. 1975. "U.S. Agricultural Export Capabilities Under Various Price Alternatives, Regional Production Variations, and Fertilizer Use Restrictions," CARD Report 63 (Ames, Center for Agricultural and Rural Development, Iowa State University, December).

————, and B. C. English. 1978. "Energy Use in U.S. Agriculture: An Evaluation of National and Regional Impacts from Alternative Energy Policies," CARD Report 78 (Ames, Center for Agricultural and Rural Development, Iowa State University, March).

Food and Agriculture Organization (FAO). 1960–76. *FAO Production Yearbook* (Annual) (Rome, UN).

Frey, H. T., and R. C. Otte. 1975. *Cropland for Today and Tomorrow,* Agricultural Economic Report no. 291 (Washington, D.C., USDA, July).

Jaski, M. R. 1977. "System Documentation of the Annual Version of NIRAP: National Interregional Agricultural Projections," working papers (Washington, D.C., USDA, Economic Research Service).

Leontief, W., A. Carter, and P. Petri. 1977. *The Future of the World Economy* (New York, Oxford University Press for the United Nations).

Lu, Y. C. n.d. "Agriculture in the Third Century: Productivity Growth and Emerging Technologies" (in process) (Washington, D.C., USDA, Economic Research Service).

Luttrell, C. B., and R. A. Gilbert. 1976. "Crop Yields: Random, Cyclical, or Bunchy?", *American Journal of Agricultural Economics* (August) vol. 58, no. 3, pp. 521–531.

National Academy of Sciences (NAS). 1975. Committee on Agricultural Production Efficiency, *Agricultural Production Efficiency* (Washington, D.C., NAS).

Rojko, A. S., and M. W. Schwartz. 1976. "Modeling the World Grain-Oilseeds-Livestock Economy to Assess World Food Prospects," *Agricultural Economics Research* vol. 28, no. 3 (July) pp. 89–98.

Schneider, S. H., and L. E. Mesicrow. 1976. *The Genesis Strategy: Climate and Global Survival* (New York, Plenum Press).

Strout, A. M. 1975. "World Agricultural Potential: Evidence from the Recent Past," in working paper prepared for W. Leontief and P. Petri, *The Future of the World Economy*. (mimeographed).

Thompson, L. M. 1975. "Weather Variability, Climatic Change, and Grain Production," *Science* vol. 188, no. 4188 (May 9) pp. 535–541.

Tweeten, L. G., and C. L. Quance. 1969. "Positivistic Measures of Aggregate Supply Elasticities: Some New Approaches," *American Journal of Agricultural Economics* vol. 51, no. 2 (May) pp. 342–352.

U.S. Department of Agriculture (USDA). 1976. *World Economic Conditions in Relation to Agricultural Trade*, WEC-10 (Washington, D.C., USDA, Economic Research Service).

―――. n.d. "National-Interregional Agricultural Projections (NIRAP) System Users Manual," working papers (Washington, D.C., USDA).

―――. 1960–77. "Foreign Agricultural Circular: Grains" (Washington, D.C., USDA, Foreign Agriculture Service).

―――. 1977. *Agricultural Statistics 1977* (Washington, D.C., GPO).

―――. 1977a. *Food, Consumption, Prices and Expenditures,* Agricultural Economic Report no. 138 (Washington, D.C., USDA, January).

―――. 1977b. *Food and Agriculture,* Report prepared for Resources for the Future (Washington, D.C., USDA, February).

U.S. Water Resources Council (WRC). 1974. *1972 OBERS Projections, Regional Economic Activity in the U.S., Series E Population* vol. 1 of *Concepts, Methodology, and Summary Data* (Washington, D.C. GPO).

7

Pollution Costs and Control Benefits

This and the next chapter are concerned with assessing the environmental impacts of the various scenarios developed in earlier chapters. This chapter focuses on the mass pollutants, such as particulate matter (PM) and suspended solids (SS), which have been the subject of environmental regulations during this decade; the next chapter discusses a wide variety of other environmental concerns. Together, they touch upon most of the potentially important environmental and physical side effects of economic activities during the next quarter- to half-century.

This chapter has an additional goal: to apply benefit–cost analysis to pollution problems in order to assess the appropriateness of various pollution policies over time. It must be emphasized that data weaknesses make it impossible to look upon the conclusions of this analysis with a high degree of confidence. The analysis and applications in this chapter should be taken as illustrations of what could be done with good data and what needs to be done in the future to develop more definitive policy analyses.

Our approach to this policy analysis differs from others in three ways. First, instead of estimating the impacts of different policies given the current state of the economy, we have extended the analysis several decades into the future. This is important because, as we shall show, a longer time horizon may lead to different policy conclusions. In addition, extending the analysis into the future permits us to discuss the impact of long-run changes, such as those in population and in the composition of output, as well as the effects of differences in the timing of policy implementation. Second, though we are interested in assessing national policies, we have tried wherever possible to take into account the fact that emissions, ambient concentrations, and the damages that result from them differ greatly among regions. To do so, these three factors were assessed at the regional level using 243 Air Quality Control Regions (AQCRs) for air pollutants and 101 Aggregated Sub-Areas (ASAs) for water pollutants (U.S. Water Resources Council, 1974a and 1974b). Third, we have tried to take quite explicitly into account the fact that pollution controls purchase not only a reduction in average damages but also a reduction in the probability of ever experiencing a high level of damages. As a consequence, it may be appropriate to have more stringent controls than would be appropriate if the sole objective were merely to minimize the sum of pollution control plus damage costs.

The next section provides a brief description of methods, the alternative pollution control policies being simulated, and limitations of the analysis. Remaining sections present results and analyses of results. The first of these sections provides projections of the physical quantities of emissions and the regional environmental quality resulting from alternative scenarios and control policies. Benefits and costs of alternative pollution control policies for scenario DH are analyzed in the second of these sections. Thereafter, we look across the various scenarios and control policies to determine the relative importance of various determinants of environmental quality. The final section draws policy implications and conclusions, and the technical notes to this chapter add details on abatement costs and regional breakdowns.

Methods, Scope, and Limitations

The analysis involves four steps: (1) projecting national economic activity, abatement costs, and pollution residuals; (2) assigning national point source residuals to regions; (3) estimating regional transportation residuals, urban runoff, agricultural, mining, and other nonpoint residuals; and (4) estimating regional air and water pollution damages as a function of regional ambient conditions.

The national components of SEAS/RFF were used to derive estimates of national economic activity. ABATE, a submodel within this system, estimates the investment and operating and maintenance costs associated with the control of pollution for 131 abating sectors.[1] These

---

[1] The estimates of abatement costs reported in this analysis are annualized costs in 1971 dollars unless otherwise noted.

costs create a demand for resources that modifies sector output levels. In turn, these revised output levels change emissions and abatement costs during the next year. Comparisons of ABATE's cost estimates with those of other studies are found in technical note A to this chapter.

Residuals are estimated by (1) applying residual coefficients to national output levels and then assigning national estimates to regions, or (2) using estimates of regional economic activity and regional coefficients to calculate regional residuals directly. The first method was used to calculate regional residuals from electric utilities, industrial plants, burning of residential and commercial fuels, and municipal sewage plants. The second method was used to estimate residuals from transportation, urban runoff, agriculture, mining, forestry, and nonurban construction. Residual coefficients were obtained from several published sources; details are provided in the appendix to this volume.

The procedures used to estimate regional air and water pollution damages are outlined in figure 7–1. Regional residuals are transformed

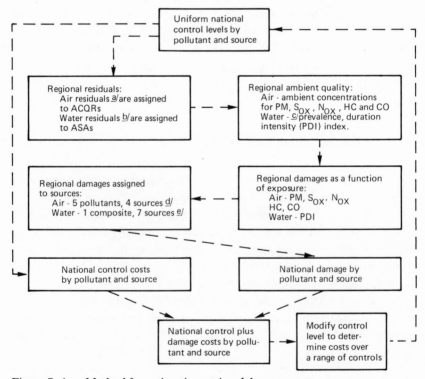

Figure 7–1.   Method for estimating regional damage costs.

into ambient concentrations by using dispersion models with appropriate transfer coefficients for each region; per capita average damages in dollars are calculated as a function of average per capita exposure. Per capita damages are multiplied by regional population and summed to obtain national damages for the sources and pollutants indicated in figure 7–1. National damages and control costs are added to obtain total environmental costs. Total national costs over a range of controls are obtained by changing assumed national control levels.[2]

Lying behind these procedures is a per capita regional pollution damage function that satisfies two properties. First, it assigns damages to regions almost in proportion to each region's share in total pollution exposures. The assignment of damages is not exactly proportional, because regions that have high average exposures receive proportionately more damages and those with small average exposures receive proportionately less; in other words, the regional damage function is concave upward. The slopes, or concavity, of the function are fixed by making them equal in a relative sense to the slopes of a few, existing, empirically estimated damage functions.[3] Second, the function assigns damages to regions so that, when estimated 1971 per capita damages are multiplied by regional populations and summed, the result agrees with published estimates of total national pollution damages for that year. Satisfaction of these two properties is just sufficient to determine a unique regional per capita damage function that can be used to forecast damages.

Both pollution control costs and damages are uncertain because of the incomplete state of information, measurement error, random error, and other factors. But uncertainty can be quantified, and by so doing one can estimate tradeoffs between total *expected* costs and risk avoidance. Procedures used to do this analysis are described in the appendix to this volume. The resulting tradeoff between total expected costs and risk avoidance is illustrated by figure 7–2.

---

[2] Both point and nonpoint sources of pollution are used to determine air and water pollution damages, but benefit–cost analysis is undertaken only for industrial point sources, feedlots and dairies, electric utilities, transportation, the burning of fuels by residential and commercial sectors, municipal sewage treatment, and urban runoff. For these sources, control benefits are calculated as damages avoided by reducing residuals from the indicated sources while residuals from other sources (mining, agriculture, nonurban construction, and forestry) are held constant.

[3] For example, if the empirical functions have slopes that increase by 50 percent as exposure goes from its median level to twice that amount, then the derived functions will also have the same relative change in slope over the same range of exposures relative to the median.

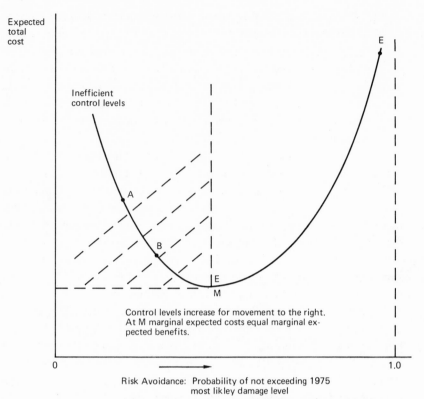

Figure 7–2.   Expected total costs and risk avoidance for alternative control levels.

Risk avoidance is defined as the probability that the damages associated with a given control level will not exceed the 1975 damage level in a given year. By this definition, control levels smaller than *M*, such as *A* and *B*, are inefficient because a move to M would reduce expected total costs *and* risk. The control levels higher than *M*, on *EE*, are efficient. A northeast move along *EE* raises total expected costs but reduces the probability of exceeding 1975 damage levels. That is, if society chooses controls that, like M, minimize expected total costs, over a long period of time pollution control and associated damage costs will be minimized. But in some years, damage costs may be very high, so high that society is willing to pay something extra in terms of control costs in order to reduce the frequency with which such levels are experienced. Thus, the control level that minimizes expected total cost is not necessarily the optimal one to choose. The optimum would certainly not be anything less than level

Table 7-1. Strict and Relaxed Pollution Control Policies

Element and policy	Standards[a]
Water	
Strict	BPT in 1977, BAT in 1983
Relaxed	BPT in 1980, BAT for construction begun on or after 1990
Air—mobile sources	
Strict	Federal standards for new cars starting in 1978
Relaxed	Federal standards for new cars starting in 1978, *plus* less stringent controls in the period after 2000
Air—stationary sources	
Strict	SIP standards by 1977; NSP standards for construction begun on or after 1980 *except* control of sulfur oxide for electric utilities to be implemented immediately for high-sulfur fuels and after 1980 for all fuels
Relaxed	SIP standards by 1978; NSP standards for construction begun on or after 1983 *except* control of sulfur oxide for electric utilities starting in 1976 for high-sulfur fuels and for all fuels by 1990, *plus* some relaxation in standards for some pollutants in some sectors

[a] Definitions of abbreviations: BPT, best practicable technology; BAT, best available technology; SIP standards, state implementation plan standards; NSP standards, new source performance standards.

M,[4] but it could be something greater, depending on the cost society is willing to pay to reduce the risks of high damage levels. The empirical analysis that follows will investigate whether simulated EPA controls are efficient in this sense.

Four alternative national pollution control policies are simulated: strict, relaxed, cost-minimizing, and efficient standards. The first two cases, outlined in table 7-1, reflect our assessment, as of 1975, of the possible range of future EPA regulations. The strict case is meant to simulate currently legislated federal regulations (except that we have not assumed that all discharges to water will be eliminated by 1985) and to reflect our judgment about what might constitute strict regulations in the future. The relaxed case is somewhat more in line with current practice, and over time it allows for some slippage in both stringency and timing.[5] In the cost-minimizing case, controls are set at the point where the sum

[4] So long as society is not concerned with reducing the risk of experiencing very large control costs.

[5] Since 1975, the EPA's regulatory program has undergone a number of revisions. For example, there has been a growing emphasis on controlling toxic and potentially harmful chemical substances in water. If this emphasis continues, actual regulations on dissolved solids may eventually exceed the strict end of our range. In most cases, however, our range is sufficiently wide to cover future policy options.

of expected pollution control and damage costs is minimum (point *M* in figure 7–2). The last case is a mixed strategy that imposes strict controls when they are within the efficient range but moves all controls that are in the inefficient range up to the point of minimum cost.[6]

This analysis is subject to a variety of limitations that should be kept in mind when assessing the results. First, the focus in this chapter is on currently well-known air and water pollutants. No attempt is made to identify pollutants that are ignored today but may become important in the future. No analysis is included of risks to the ecological system, for example, as a consequence of the accumulation of small, but widespread, interacting effects. For a complete assessment of environmental problems, such possibilities should also be studied.

The study uses five independent damage categories for air pollution and one total damage category for water pollution; synergistic and antagonistic interactions among and within these categories are ignored. There is some evidence that reducing health impacts would require reductions in both particulates and sulfur oxides, that fine particulates are more damaging to health than larger particulates, that sulfuric acid and sulfates are more damaging than sulfites, and that coliform estimates may be better than biochemical oxygen demand (BOD) and chemical oxygen demand (COD) loadings for measuring recreational damages to water bodies. Most such complexities had to be ignored, however, because of the absence of adequate data.

The pollution controls that are investigated are uniform national control levels that apply to every region, and no attempt was made to perform benefit–cost analysis for each region. We chose to emphasize uniform national controls because that is the context in which most environmental policy decisions currently are made. But there is little doubt that the appropriate level of control varies substantially among regions, and if regional controls were applied, it would reduce aggregate control

---

[6] In addition to these policies, assumptions had to be made about controls on pollutants from nonpoint sources not included in our benefit–cost analysis. For ore, coal, and minerals milling and mining, it is assumed that all facilities meet best practicable technology (BPT) standards by 1980 and best available technology (BAT) standards by 1985. The per unit sediment runoff from ore, coal, and minerals mining is assumed to be reduced to about one-half of its current level by 1985. Sediment runoff from nonurban construction (per unit of activity) is assumed to be one-half and one-fourth current levels by 1980 and 1985, respectively. Sediment runoff from forestry (per unit of activity) is assumed to be one-half and one-fourth current levels by 1985 and 2000, respectively. Acid mine drainage from abandoned coal mines is assumed to be one-half and one-fourth current levels by 1985 and 2000, respectively. Sediment runoff from agriculture on a per unit basis is assumed to be about two-thirds of its pre-1970 level beginning in 1975.

plus damage costs significantly below the amounts reported in this chapter.

Estimates of exposures are derived from simple models that capture few of the nuances of interdependent transport interactions and micro-scale exposure variations. Estimates of pollution damage and control cost, generally taken from studies completed before 1975, are replete with weaknesses that make it difficult to judge the overall direction of the biases inherent in them. For example, the control-cost estimates exclude transaction costs, such as legal fees and cost of monitoring and enforcement, and do not take into account the possibility that, over time, costs may rise for the use of such media as land and water into which pollution is discharged. In addition, the control-cost estimates are based on end-of-pipe treatment methods, whereas over time pollution controls will induce changes in production processes, and these could substantially lower control costs.[7] Finally, in some instances, data required for the analysis did not exist and had to be assigned on the basis of subjective judgments.

In a number of cases, we believed that our assumptions might be critical to the outcome and experimented with alternative values to determine the sensitivity of our results to these assumptions. Budget and time constraints made it necessary to limit such sensitivity tests to a few areas, and because the uncertainties are particularly large and important for the the analysis of water pollution, we chose to emphasize variations in assumptions pertaining to that area.

Emissions and Concentration Levels

This section provides an indication of the levels of emission discharges and concentrations upon which our pollution damage estimates are based. The focus here is on national or summary estimates; detailed regional materials from which the damage estimates were developed are presented in technical note B to this chapter.

We begin with estimates of national emissions in 1975 and in future years for each of four different control policies[8]—R (relaxed), S (strict),

---

[7] A review and assessment of the national damage estimates can be found in Waddell (1974) and Heintz, Hershaft, and Horak (1976); the first technical note to this chapter provides a comparison of our control-cost estimates with others.

[8] Comparisons with other studies are provided in technical note A to this chapter.

Table 7–2. National Emissions for Alternative Policies, Scenario DH
(millions of tons)

Emission and policy[a]	1975	1985	2000	2025
Particulate matter (PM)				
Gross[b]	98.2	167.7	188.1	383.2
Net R	23.9	13.1	2.9	3.3
S	19.6	3.0	2.1	2.4
E	6.6	2.8	2.0	2.0
M	6.7	6.1	2.2	2.2
Sulfur oxides (SO$_x$)				
Gross	50.9	69.7	66.5	118.6
Net R	37.4	42.8	31.4	30.0
S	32.3	18.4	11.3	11.0
E	15.6	9.6	7.7	7.1
M	15.6	9.7	8.0	7.1
Nitrogen oxides (NO$_x$)				
Gross	18.7	23.4	20.7	37.8
Net R	18.4	19.9	13.4	20.1
S	17.8	15.9	9.8	12.9
E	17.8	15.9	9.8	12.9
M	18.5	18.7	11.6	15.7
Hydrocarbons (HC)				
Gross	27.4	22.9	27.4	39.5
Net R	20.6	9.9	8.1	8.7
S	19.2	7.1	5.8	5.9
E	13.0	7.1	5.8	5.9
M	17.3	13.2	11.5	8.2
Carbon monoxide (CO)				
Gross	125.0	119.7	160.7	249.8
Net R	86.9	30.9	18.9	24.4
S	84.8	24.7	13.7	14.2
E	84.8	24.7	13.7	14.2
M	124.0	104.9	125.7	109.3
Biochemical oxygen demand (BOD)				
Gross	19.9	23.9	31.6	54.3
Net R	7.8	7.2	6.2	5.5
S	7.4	4.3	3.7	3.7
E	7.2	4.4	3.6	3.7
M	9.0	7.5	7.6	9.5
Chemical oxygen demand (COD)				
Gross	15.7	20.9	30.0	55.2
Net R	7.2	5.8	5.2	5.4
S	6.9	3.1	2.9	2.5
E	5.6	3.1	2.9	2.5
M	5.6	4.1	4.5	6.8
Suspended solids (SS)				
Gross	733.8	689.9	879.4	1,418.1
Net R	552.6	580.1	538.4	601.6
S	517.7	341.8	350.1	469.7
E	514.8	341.8	350.1	469.7
M	517.3	348.9	358.9	495.4

(continued)

Table 7–2. (Continued)

Emission and policy[a]	1975	1985	2000	2025
Dissolved solids (DS)				
Gross	367.3	362.1	476.6	799.8
Net R	300.9	334.5	255.5	296.1
S	285.6	162.6	164.3	217.3
E	284.1	261.2	264.3	217.3
M	285.4	165.0	170.3	226.4
Nutrients				
Gross	8.4	8.3	9.5	12.8
Net R	5.9	6.1	6.5	6.0
S	5.7	4.8	5.0	4.9
E	5.6	4.9	5.0	4.9
M	5.7	5.1	5.4	5.7
Other[c]				
Gross	5.9	7.3	9.9	17.2
Net R	4.9	3.4	2.1	3.0
S	4.8	1.9	1.3	1.9
E	4.7	1.9	1.3	1.9
M	4.7	2.5	1.4	2.7

[a] Emissions from point sources (industry, electric utilities, and municipal waste water treatment plants); urban runoff; point emissions and sediment runoff from minerals, ore, and coal mining and milling; and sediment runoff from nonurban construction, forestry, and agriculture.

[b] Gross emissions from mining and nonpoint sources (other than agriculture and urban runoff) are calculated as emissions that would have occurred assuming 1975 control levels in every year after 1975. Gross emissions for agricultural nonpoint sources are emissions that would have occurred if emission control measures in effect in 1975 and subsequent years were to be removed. Gross emissions for point sources and urban runoff are discharges assuming no control in any year.

[c] Includes acids, bases, oils, grease, heavy metals, and pesticides. The heavy metals included here are for ore, coal, and minerals mining, forestry, and nonurban construction. Heavy metals for other sources (including industrial point sources) are included in the suspended and dissolved solids estimates.

E (efficient), and M (cost-minimum)—assuming scenario DH prevails in all cases. Table 7–2 shows that under policies S and E substantially smaller emissions are generated than under R. The largest differences occur for PM, SO$_x$, COD, SS, and DS. Emissions under policies S and E are quite similar, and when they are equal, policy S is considered an efficient policy. This occurs for a large number of pollutants and sources. In cases in which policy S is not efficient—for example, control of PM and SO$_x$—emissions under policy E will be smaller than those under S. The cost-minimizing policy M has emissions that are usually somewhat larger than S and E but rarely larger than R. Notable exceptions are HC and CO from transportation sources, BOD from municipal sewage treatment plants and industrial sources, and COD from industrial sources.

Table 7–3. Sources of Air Pollution Emissions, Scenario DH

Emission and source	1975[a]	1985 R	1985 S	2000 R	2000 S	2025 R	2025 S
Particulate matter (PM), %							
Cement	30.0	28.1	3.5	5.7	5.9	7.2	8.1
Steel	9.1	8.5	8.9	14.6	12.6	6.9	5.0
Paving and asphalt	13.8	13.8	6.6	8.8	3.0		
Pulp mills	3.8	3.3	6.6	7.3	7.4	5.6	6.8
Petroleum refining				8.5	7.6	18.9	6.6
Fertilizers	4.6	4.2					
Industrial chemicals						3.0	3.8
Passenger transportation		3.8	16.4	6.5	8.9	5.0	6.8
Freight transportation			10.6	10.8	14.9	19.7	26.8
Residential and commercial fuel burning	5.3		18.6	11.8	14.5	17.2	10.7
Incineration			3.0	5.2	4.2	3.1	
Electric utilities	19.0	21.5	18.5	13.3	15.6	5.7	19.4
Net discharges (10⁶ tons)	23.9	13.1	3.0	2.9	2.1	3.3	2.4
Sulfur oxides (SO), %							
Petroleum refining	11.6	7.6	8.5	8.7	12.2	29.4	23.3
Cement		3.0	3.2	5.0	4.6	7.0	4.4
Pulp mills	3.0		4.1	4.8	8.2	6.9	9.0
Steel			3.2	4.7	5.7	4.9	5.0
Industrial chemicals	4.0	3.7	4.3	5.1	5.1	6.9	4.7
Fabrics							3.0
Copper	5.2	3.0					
Petroleum and natural gas extraction	3.5						
Coal processing						4.5	3.1
Freight transportation			3.4		5.9	4.6	12.5
Residential and commercial fuel burning	11.2	10.5	22.9	10.6	18.5	10.1	11.1
Electric utilities	53.5	63.7	44.4	52.9	30.2	20.4	13.5
Net discharges (10⁶ tons)	37.4	42.8	18.4	31.4	11.3	30.0	11.0
Nitrogen oxides (NO), %							
Petroleum refining	3.3	3.7	4.3	5.9	7.2	23.3	22.4
Steel				3.6	4.9	4.9	7.5
Cement				3.0	4.1	4.7	7.1
Pulp mills					3.0		
Industrial chemicals				3.6	3.5	5.8	5.6
Passenger transportation	39.6	25.8	32.5	19.0	26.0	12.2	15.8
Freight transportation	7.5	8.6	10.8	10.1	11.7	9.5	12.5
Residential and commercial fuel burning	7.7	8.2	10.1	9.3	12.5	8.4	11.4
Electric utilities	33.9	45.7	33.3	40.6	24.3	26.9	11.5
Net discharges (10⁶ tons)	18.4	19.9	15.9	13.4	9.8	20.1	12.9
Hydrocarbons (HC), %							
Paints	6.3	6.5	9.1	7.7	10.8	4.9	7.2
Petroleum refining	4.8	6.4	5.1	5.4	4.5	5.3	6.4
Industrial chemicals		3.0					
Solvent evaporation	23.1	32.6	17.9	37.1	20.5	21.9	12.9
Passenger transportation	43.7	28.5	39.9	23.6	32.7	34.6	32.2
Freight transportation	6.1	9.9	13.8	10.4	13.6	16.2	19.9
Incineration	8.4	4.5	6.3	6.7	9.3	8.4	12.2
Net discharges (10⁶ tons)	20.6	9.9	7.1	8.1	5.8	8.7	5.9

(continued)

Table 7-3. (Continued)

Emission and source	1975[a]	1985 R	1985 S	2000 R	2000 S	2025 R	2025 S
Carbon monoxide (CO), %							
Steel	6.2	13.2		19.1	4.7	9.1	
Petroleum refining	3.4	4.1				3.0	4.7
Plywood and veneer		3.0		5.5	3.6	6.0	3.9
Passenger transportation	76.1	58.3	72.9	44.2	60.7	52.4	56.7
Freight transportation	6.2	13.4	16.8	16.8	20.5	16.2	23.3
Incineration	5.1	3.2		7.8	4.6	9.0	4.2
Net discharges (10^6 tons)	86.9	30.6	24.7	18.9	13.7	24.4	14.2

Note: Blank entry indicates that discharges for sector are less than 3 percent of total discharges.

[a] Actual, as estimated by this study.

Tables 7-3 and 7-4 indicate the major sources of air and water pollutants under policies R and S. Sources accounting for at least 3 percent of total net residuals are reported as individual sectors. Most air pollutants are accounted for by eight sectors: transportation, electric utilities, fuel burning by residential and commercial sectors, cement, steel, petroleum refining, pulp and paper, and industrial chemicals. In the case of water pollution, only in the cases of BOD and COD are quantities originating from point sources larger than those from nonpoint sources. Nonpoint sources—especially agricultural runoff and mining—are particularly important in the cases of suspended and dissolved solids because these pollutants are associated with sediment discharges.

Table 7-5 shows national net emissions for alternative scenarios. Except for scenario EL, which incorporates the relaxed control policy, all scenarios assume strict pollution controls. Emissions differ little for the four scenarios with different population and economic growth rates (DH, FH, DL, and FL). FH compared to DH, and FL compared to DL, have higher air emissions in the period from 1975 to 1985. This occurs because the relatively low population growth in FH and FL results in higher labor force-participation rates by females than in DH and DL and hence higher GNP and emissions in earlier years. After 1985, this effect is swamped by the cumulative impact of lower population growth rates, which ultimately slows labor force growth and results in lower air emissions for FH and FL compared to DH and DL, respectively. In the period after 1985, scenario DHP1 has smaller emissions than DH because (among other reasons) the higher energy prices incorporated into DHP1 induce lower levels of energy consumption. In contrast, scenario DHP2

Table 7-4. Sources of Water Pollution Emissions, Scenario DH

Emission and source	1975	1985 R	1985 S	2000 R	2000 S	2025 R	2025 S
Biochemical oxygen demand (BOD), %							
Point sources	51.5	45.8	44.4	39.6	33.6	23.8	13.5
Pulp mills	(17.6)	(18.3)	(6.6)	(15.0)	(7.9)	(14.0)	(5.2)
Industrial chemicals	(6.9)	(5.4)					
Plastics and resins	(5.8)	(6.4)		(8.1)	(4.2)	(12.3)	(4.1)
Forestry and fishery products	(4.4)	(7.0)	(11.6)	(12.5)	(20.6)	(32.1)	(61.8)
Canned and frozen foods				(5.7)	(5.4)	(12.3)	(8.8)
Fabrics				(3.2)		(3.4)	
Meat products	(4.6)						
Livestock	(3.2)						
Municipal sewage treatment	(40.9)	(42.0)	(70.6)	(43.5)	(52.9)	(13.5)	(13.3)
Urban runoff	4.5	3.4	3.8	3.1	3.3	3.5	2.6
Agricultural runoff	31.3	34.5	38.9	43.6	48.9	53.8	55.9
Mining and other non-point sources[a]	12.7	16.3	12.9	13.7	14.2	18.9	28.0
Net discharges (10^6 tons)	7.8	7.2	4.3	6.2	3.7	5.5	3.7
Chemical oxygen demand (COD), %							
Point sources	54.3	61.3	51.9	65.9	61.6	67.5	65.4
Forestry and fishery products	(20.7)	(28.1)	(58.0)	(37.6)	(59.7)	(48.4)	(79.2)
Plastics and resins	(12.9)	(14.1)	(12.1)	(17.0)	(12.3)	(15.8)	(6.9)
Industrial chemicals	(20.9)	(20.5)	(11.9)	(19.3)	(11.6)	(17.6)	(6.1)
Fabrics	(12.5)	(12.9)	(8.8)	(13.2)	(8.1)	(9.5)	(3.2)
Livestock	(11.5)	(5.5)					
Textiles	(5.7)	(4.4)					
Noncellulosic fibers	(4.4)	(3.8)					
Knitting				(3.0)			
Urban runoff	45.7	38.7	48.1	34.1	38.4	32.5	34.6
Net discharges (10^6 tons)	7.2	5.8	3.1	5.2	2.9	5.4	2.5
Suspended solids (SS), %							
Point sources	2.0	1.4	0.5	0.6	0.3	0.2	0.1
Pulp mills	(6.2)	(7.3)	(8.5)	(11.9)	(9.5)	(17.8)	(13.8)
Paper mills						(3.0)	
Plastics and resins				(6.2)	(6.8)	(15.1)	(17.7)
Cement	(5.9)	(5.9)	(3.9)				
Forestry and fishery products		(3.1)	(4.0)	(6.7)	(5.3)	(13.1)	(9.1)
Steel	(13.8)	(12.1)		(17.0)		(6.9)	(3.3)
Aluminum	(22.0)	(21.6)					
Paving and asphalt	(19.2)	(19.7)					
Fabrics						(5.3)	(4.1)
Canned and frozen foods				(3.7)	(3.4)	(13.2)	(11.7)
Municipal sewage treatment	(15.9)	(17.5)	(74.9)	(40.0)	(64.8)	(15.6)	(30.7)
Urban runoff	1.1	0.7	0.8	0.6	0.6	0.5	0.3
Agricultural runoff	65.9	63.5	72.9	74.9	76.2	73.1	65.9

(continued)

Table 7–4. (Continued)

Emission and source	1975	1985 R	1985 S	2000 R	2000 S	2025 R	2025 S
Mining and other non-point sources[a]	31.0	34.4	25.8	23.9	22.9	26.2	33.7
Net discharges (10^6 tons)	552.6	580.1	341.8	538.5	350.1	601.6	469.7
Dissolved solids (DS), %							
Point sources	7.4	6.8	8.7	9.2	7.6	11.7	5.6
Industrial chemicals	(38.8)	(30.5)	(14.4)	(37.0)	(21.5)	(55.3)	(34.1)
Misc. chemicals	(3.3)						
Steel	(3.2)						
Electric utilities	(10.4)	(18.5)	(23.2)	(13.2)	(15.2)	(12.8)	(18.8)
Municipal sewage treatment	(42.7)	(46.2)	(62.4)	(48.8)	(63.3)	(31.8)	(47.1)
Urban runoff	1.3	0.8	1.1	0.8	0.8	0.7	0.5
Agricultural runoff	51.8	47.2	65.7	67.6	69.6	63.6	61.0
Mining and other non-point sources[a]	39.5	45.2	24.5	22.4	22.0	24.0	32.9
Net discharges (10^6 tons)	300.9	334.5	162.6	255.5	164.3	296.1	217.3
Nutrients, %							
Point sources	25.2	26.0	28.1	26.0	26.3	11.7	9.8
Industrial chemicals				(3.5)	(3.6)	(12.2)	(14.2)
Livestock	(3.8)						
Municipal sewage treatment	(93.5)	(95.2)	(96.7)	(95.9)	(95.9)	(87.7)	(85.7)
Urban runoff	1.2	0.8	0.7	0.6	0.5	0.6	0.4
Agricultural runoff	68.3	67.1	67.6	69.2	69.9	82.1	83.0
Mining and other non-point sources[a]	5.3	6.1	3.6	4.2	3.3	5.6	6.8
Net discharges (10^6 tons)	5.9	6.1	4.8	6.5	5.0	6.0	4.9
Other, %[b]							
Point sources	28.5	25.6	3.4	23.6	6.1	39.1	5.2
Steel	(40.4)	(44.3)	(13.3)	(40.9)	(10.1)		
Industrial chemicals	(25.4)	(24.9)	(48.7)	(12.9)	(55.4)	(10.6)	(71.3)
Meat products	(22.2)	(16.0)	(3.5)				
Forestry and fishery products			(23.9)	(4.3)	(22.4)		(21.8)
Canned and frozen foods			(6.2)	(3.0)	(6.6)		(3.4)
Electric utilities				(30.3)		(83.0)	
Textiles	(3.0)	(3.1)					
Urban runoff	2.0	1.7	2.0	2.2	2.2	1.5	1.2
Agricultural runoff	0.2	0.6	0.9	1.2	1.6	1.0	1.4
Mining and other non-point sources[a]	69.3	72.1	93.7	73.0	90.1	58.3	92.2
Net discharges (10^6 tons)	4.9	3.4	1.9	2.1	1.3	3.0	1.9

Note: Numbers in parentheses are percents of total point source discharges. Blank entry indicates that discharges from sector are less than 3 percent of total point source discharges.

[a] Point emissions and sediment runoff from minerals, ore, and coal mining and milling, and sediment runoff from nonurban construction, forestry, and acid coal mine drainage.

[b] Includes acid, bases, oil, grease, heavy metals, and pesticides. The heavy metals included here are for ore, coal, and minerals mining; forestry; and nonurban construction. Heavy metals for other sources (including industrial point sources) are included in the suspended and dissolved solids estimates.

Table 7–5. National Net Emissions for Alternative Scenarios, Strict Enforcement (millions of tons)

Emission and scenario	1975	1985	2000	2025
Particulate matter (PM)				
DH	19.6	3.0	2.1	2.4
DL	19.5	2.7	1.9	1.9
FH	19.6	3.0	2.0	1.8
FL	19.5	2.8	1.8	1.4
DHNU	19.6	3.0	2.2	2.4
DHP1	19.6	3.0	1.9	2.0
DHP2	19.4	3.2	3.1	2.2
EL[a]	23.9	12.0	2.9	2.6
Sulfur oxides (SO$_x$)				
DH	32.3	18.4	11.3	11.0
DL	32.1	16.7	9.8	8.7
FH	32.4	18.6	10.7	8.3
FL	32.2	17.0	9.3	6.7
DHNU	32.3	18.4	11.5	11.5
DHP1	32.3	18.3	10.3	9.1
DHP2	32.0	18.6	18.8	12.7
EL[a]	37.4	39.7	37.0	27.5
Nitrogen oxides (NO$_x$)				
DH	17.8	15.9	9.8	12.9
DL	17.6	14.2	8.5	10.2
FH	17.7	16.1	9.4	9.9
FL	17.7	14.6	8.2	8.0
DHNU	17.7	15.8	9.7	13.1
DHP1	17.8	15.8	8.9	10.7
DHP2	17.5	17.1	16.3	17.1
EL[a]	18.4	18.8	14.2	16.6
Hydrocarbons (HC)				
DH	19.2	7.1	5.8	5.9
DL	19.2	6.3	5.0	4.6
FH	19.1	7.2	5.6	4.6
FL	19.2	6.5	4.9	3.8
DHNU	19.2	7.1	5.9	6.0
DHP1	19.2	7.1	5.2	4.7
DHP2	18.8	7.8	8.0	6.3
EL[a]	20.6	9.7	6.9	6.3
Carbon monoxide (CO)				
DH	84.8	24.7	13.7	14.2
DL	85.0	21.6	11.6	11.0
FH	84.6	25.3	13.4	11.3
FL	85.0	22.6	11.6	9.2
DHNU	84.8	24.6	13.8	14.3
DHP1	84.8	24.6	12.2	11.4
DHP2	82.1	29.0	21.9	15.0
EL[a]	86.9	35.6	16.1	17.6
Biochemical oxygen demand (BOD)				
DH	7.4	4.3	3.7	3.7
DL	7.4	4.2	3.5	3.4
FH	7.4	4.1	3.3	2.8
FL	7.4	4.0	3.1	2.6
DHNU	7.4	4.3	3.7	3.8

(continued)

Table 7-5. (Continued)

Emission and scenario	1975	1985	2000	2025
DHP1	7.4	4.3	3.6	3.6
DHP2	7.4	4.3	3.7	3.7
EL[a]	7.8	6.8	5.5	4.5
Chemical oxygen demand (COD)				
DH	6.9	3.1	2.9	2.5
DL	6.9	2.9	2.6	2.1
FH	6.9	3.1	2.7	1.9
FL	6.9	2.9	2.4	1.7
DHNU	6.9	3.1	2.9	2.5
DHP1	6.9	3.1	2.8	2.4
DHP2	6.9	3.1	3.0	2.5
EL[a]	7.2	5.4	4.5	3.9
Suspended solids (SS)				
DH	517.7	341.8	350.1	469.7
DL	517.7	332.3	333.2	430.7
FH	517.7	327.0	312.0	352.9
FL	517.7	313.7	297.8	326.8
DHNU	517.7	341.9	351.5	474.5
DHP1	517.7	339.4	342.7	454.7
DHP2	517.7	342.4	352.0	468.2
EL[a]	552.6	561.0	482.5	490.1
Dissolved solids (DS)				
DH	285.6	162.6	164.3	217.3
DL	285.6	157.9	156.3	198.5
FH	285.6	155.9	146.7	163.0
FL	285.6	149.6	139.8	150.5
DHNU	285.6	162.7	165.9	221.5
DHP1	285.6	161.5	160.8	210.3
DHP2	285.6	162.0	164.3	216.9
EL[a]	300.9	318.1	229.3	241.6
Nutrients				
DH	5.7	4.8	5.0	4.9
DL	5.7	4.8	4.9	4.7
FH	5.7	4.6	4.4	3.7
FL	5.7	4.5	4.3	3.6
DHNU	5.7	4.8	5.0	4.9
DHP1	5.7	4.8	4.9	4.7
DHP2	5.7	4.8	5.0	4.9
EL[a]	5.9	5.9	5.8	6.1
Other[b]				
DH	4.8	1.9	1.3	1.9
DL	4.8	1.8	1.2	1.6
FH	4.8	1.9	1.3	1.6
FL	4.8	1.8	1.2	1.4
DHNU	4.8	1.9	1.3	1.9
DHP1	4.8	1.9	1.3	1.8
DHP2	4.8	1.9	1.3	1.9
EL[a]	4.9	3.3	1.8	1.7

[a] Scenario EL assumes relaxed rather than strict enforcement.
[b] Includes acids, bases, oil, grease, heavy metals, and pesticides. The heavy metals included here are for ore, coal, and minerals mining; forestry; and nonurban construction. Heavy metals for other sources (including industrial point sources) are included in the suspended and dissolved solids estimates.

Table 7-6. Ambient Pollution Concentrations for Alternative Policies, Scenario DH

Pollutant and policy	1975			1985			2000			2025		
	H	Mn	V	H	Mn	V	H	Mn	V	H	Mn	V
Particulate matter (PM)(μg/m³)[a]												
R	156.5	54.2	46	83.6	44.3	5	62.5	37.0	0	73.0	36.8	0
S	132.2	52.0	35	80.8	36.8	2	64.7	36.2	0	73.4	36.0	0
E	84.2	40.0	2	80.5	36.7	2	62.5	36.1	0	58.5	35.9	0
M	90.2	40.0	2	92.3	37.9	3	62.5	36.1	0	58.5	36.0	0
Sulfur oxides (SOx)(μg/m³)[b]												
R	140.8	12.4	35	160.8	11.2	36	112.7	8.0	5	229.8	7.5	5
S	171.2	11.9	38	138.5	7.0	9	84.8	5.0	1	105.9	4.6	1
E	81.3	6.5	1	85.5	4.5	1	45.8	4.0	0	60.7	3.7	0
M	81.4	6.5	1	85.5	4.7	1	49.0	4.0	0	60.7	3.7	0
Nitrogen oxides (NOx)(μg/m³)[c]												
R	108.1	26.8	2	104.3	26.6	1	73.9	24.1	0	89.3	23.8	0
S	108.1	26.7	2	90.1	25.8	0	60.0	23.2	0	64.3	22.6	0
E	108.1	26.7	2	90.1	25.8	0	60.0	23.2	0	64.3	22.6	0
M	108.1	26.8	2	103.5	26.3	1	71.5	24.1	0	69.4	23.0	0
Hydrocarbons (HC) (1975 = 100)[d]												
R	100.0	100.0		77.5	37.3		65.8	29.0		70.2	23.4	
S	116.2	104.8		57.5	37.8		45.9	28.9		44.7	20.5	
E	113.1	70.6		57.5	37.8		45.9	28.9		44.7	20.5	
M	131.4	87.2		117.0	51.3		101.5	43.8		69.3	24.3	

Carbon monoxide (CO) (mg/m³)[e]

R	34.7	3.1	59	13.6	2.4	3	8.3	2.2	0	10.2	2.3	1
S	35.9	3.1	57	15.5	2.3	3	9.5	2.2	0	9.8	2.2	0
E	35.9	3.1	57	15.5	2.3	3	9.5	2.2	0	9.8	2.2	0
M	45.5	3.5	65	44.8	3.2	63	51.4	3.4	65	39.9	3.2	61

Water pollution (PDI index)[f]

R	20.7	1.5	10	19.7	1.3	6	11.7	0.8	2	13.5	0.8	3
S	12.2	1.4	10	6.9	0.8	2	3.7	0.5	0	3.5	0.4	0
E	11.9	1.3	9	6.2	0.7	1	3.7	0.5	0	3.5	0.4	0
M	12.7	1.4	11	10.9	1.1	4	8.1	0.9	2	18.7	1.0	3

Note: Column heading abbreviations are: H, highest concentration over all regions; Mn, median concentration over all regions; V, number of AQCRs where primary standard is violated.

[a] Annual average concentration; primary standard is 75 $\mu g/m^3$.

[b] Annual average concentration; primary standard is 80 $\mu g/m^3$.

[c] Annual average concentration; primary standard is 100 $\mu g/m^3$.

[d] It is not possible to calculate violations for this measure.

[e] Eight-hour concentration; primary standard is 10 mg.

[f] The PDI (prevalence, duration, intensity) index measures ambient water quality based upon expert judgment [J. B. Truitt, A. C. Johnson, W. D. Rowe, K. D. Feigner, and L. J. Manning, "Development of Water Quality Management Indices," *Water Resources Bulletin*, vol. 11, no. 3 (June, 1975)]. Violations are the number of ASAs with PDIs in excess of 5.31. This value is the average PDI in 1975 plus one standard error when policy R is in effect.

Table 7-7. Ambient Pollution Concentrations for Alternative Scenarios Under Strict Enforcement

Pollutant and policy	1975			1985			2000			2025		
	H	Mn	V	H	Mn	V	H	Mn	V	H	Mn	V
Particulate matter (PM)(μg/m³)[a]												
DH	132.2	52.0	35	80.8	36.8	2	64.7	36.2	0	73.4	36.0	0
DL	132.1	52.0	34	75.4	36.7	1	60.8	36.1	0	65.6	35.8	0
FH	132.1	51.9	35	81.8	36.9	2	63.8	36.2	0	65.2	35.7	0
FL	132.2	52.0	34	77.2	36.7	2	60.3	36.1	0	60.0	35.6	0
DHNU	132.2	52.0	35	80.8	36.8	2	65.6	36.3	0	75.9	36.0	1
DHP1	132.2	52.0	35	80.4	36.7	2	58.7	35.8	0	60.8	35.6	0
DHP2	132.3	52.0	35	88.8	36.9	3	80.5	36.6	3	74.9	35.9	0
EL[b]	150.0	55.7	53	86.3	44.3	5	75.1	36.7	1	63.5	36.0	0
Sulfur oxides (SOx)(μg/m³)[c]												
DH	171.2	11.9	38	138.5	7.0	9	84.8	5.0	1	105.9	4.6	1
DL	171.3	11.9	37	123.9	6.6	8	73.6	4.6	0	77.7	4.1	0
FH	170.9	11.8	38	138.8	7.1	9	81.3	4.9	1	82.8	4.0	1
FL	171.3	11.9	37	127.4	6.7	6	71.1	4.5	0	68.2	3.7	0
DHNU	171.2	11.9	38	138.3	7.0	9	85.4	5.0	1	106.2	4.7	1
DHP1	171.2	11.9	38	137.8	7.0	9	77.0	4.5	1	87.7	3.7	0
DHP2	171.4	12.1	38	164.2	7.1	12	170.1	7.2	15	82.2	4.5	1
EL[b]	172.0	11.9	46	148.6	10.5	37	176.0	8.8	23	138.8	6.0	9
Nitrogen oxides (NOx)(μg/m³)[d]												
DH	108.1	26.7	2	90.1	25.8	0	60.0	23.2	0	64.3	22.6	0
DL	108.3	26.5	2	81.5	25.2	0	54.0	22.8	0	55.3	22.0	0
FH	108.0	26.5	2	91.8	25.9	0	59.2	23.2	0	52.9	22.0	0
FL	108.3	26.5	2	84.4	25.3	0	53.8	22.7	0	46.7	21.6	0
DHNU	108.1	26.7	2	90.1	25.8	0	61.1	23.3	0	64.6	22.6	0
DHP1	108.1	26.7	2	89.6	25.5	0	54.5	21.5	0	53.2	21.4	0
DHP2	105.8	26.4	2	100.6	26.1	1	81.9	24.9	0	109.8	23.8	1
EL[b]	108.7	26.7	2	90.9	26.2	0	74.7	24.6	0	72.0	23.3	0
Hydrocarbons (HC) (1975 = 100)[e]												
DH	100	100		57.5	37.8		45.9	28.9		44.7	20.5	
DL	100	100		51.4	33.5		39.9	24.7		35.6	16.2	

FH	100	100	58.1	38.5	44.2	28.0	0	34.3	16.1
FL	100	100	53.0	34.7	39.0	24.3	0	28.1	13.2
DHNU	100	100	57.4	37.8	46.6	29.1	0	45.0	20.9
DHP1	100	100	57.3	37.6	40.8	25.6	0	35.9	16.5
DHP2	100	100	60.6	40.9	54.0	38.3	1	94.0	21.5
EL[b]	100	100	70.7	48.6	50.6	31.9	0	35.9	20.7

Carbon monoxide (CO)[b] (mg/m³)[f]

	H	Mn	V	H	Mn	V	H	Mn	V	H	Mn
DH	35.9	3.1	57	15.5	2.3	3	9.5	2.2	0	9.8	2.2
DL	36.0	3.1	57	13.8	2.3	2	8.4	2.2	0	8.1	2.1
FH	35.8	3.1	57	15.8	2.3	3	9.3	2.2	0	8.2	2.1
FL	36.0	3.1	57	14.4	2.3	3	8.3	2.2	0	7.1	2.1
DHNU	35.9	3.1	57	15.5	2.3	3	9.6	2.2	0	10.1	2.2
DHP1	35.9	3.1	57	15.4	2.2	3	8.4	2.1	0	7.9	2.0
DHP2	35.7	3.1	57	17.6	2.4	9	12.9	2.3	1	9.8	2.2
EL[b]	36.2	3.2	57	18.1	2.5	16	9.2	2.2	0	10.1	2.2

Water pollution (PDI index)[g]

	H	Mn	V	H	Mn	V	H	Mn	V	H	Mn
DH	12.2	1.4	10	6.9	0.8	2	3.7	0.5	0	3.5	0.4
DL	12.2	1.4	10	6.7	0.7	1	3.5	0.5	0	3.2	0.4
FH	12.2	1.4	10	6.8	0.8	1	3.5	0.5	0	2.8	0.3
FL	12.2	1.4	10	6.5	0.7	1	3.3	0.4	0	2.6	0.3
DHNU	12.2	1.4	10	6.9	0.8	2	3.8	0.5	.0	3.7	0.4
DHP1	12.2	1.4	10	6.6	0.8	1	3.6	0.5	0	3.4	0.4
DHP2	12.2	1.4	10	6.9	0.8	2	3.6	0.5	0	3.4	0.4
EL[b]	12.5	1.5	12	9.4	1.3	5	5.7	0.7	1	4.8	0.6

Note: Column head abbreviations are: H, highest concentration over all regions; Mn, median concentration over all regions; V, number of AQCRs where primary standard is violated.

a Annual average concentration; primary standard is 75 µg/m³.
b Scenario EL has relaxed rather than strict enforcement.
c Annual average concentration; primary standard is 80 µg/m³.
d Annual average concentration; primary standard is 100 µg/m³.
e It is not possible to calculate violations for this measure.
f Eight-hour primary standard is 10 mg/m³.
g Violations are the number of ASAs with PDIs in excess of 5.31. This value is the average PDI in 1975 plus one standard error when policy R is in effect.

has lower energy prices, larger energy consumption, and larger emissions in comparison to DH.[9]

Emissions for scenarios DHNU and DH are virtually identical because we have forced scenario DHNU to have the same net discharges from coal-fired power plants as does DH. Thus, DHNU has higher pollution control levels and higher plant control costs in the electric utility sector. This was done to provide an upward bias to the estimate of the economic costs of a nuclear phaseout. Scenario EL, with its relaxed control policy, has substantially higher emissions than the other scenarios (except for DHP2 in some years). In an overall comparison, it would appear that pollution control policy could provide a much more flexible lever on residuals than would policies to encourage different economic and pollution growth rates.

Summary indicators of ambient environmental quality are shown in table 7–6 for alternative policies and in table 7–7 for alternative scenarios. Each table contains estimates of the highest pollution concentration over all regions, the median concentration, and the number of regions where standards are violated. The pattern in these tables follows that described above for emissions.

Pollution Damages

Tables 7–8 and 7–9 provide for alternative control policies, air and water pollution damage estimates based on the emission and concentration levels reported above. If controls were not to change from their 1975 levels, pollution damages would increase substantially over time, but the four control policies we have simulated all incorporate increasingly stringent regulations over time. The consequence is that damage estimates for air pollution actually fall over time no matter which policy is followed. Damage estimates for water pollution also fall over time for the strict and efficient policies. Although they rise under the relaxed and minimum-cost policies, they remain far below the levels that would have been experi-

[9] A more complete explanation is given in a later section, where we compare pollution damage costs for alternative scenarios.

Table 7–8. National Air Pollution Damages for Alternative Control Policies, Scenario DH

(most likely values, billions of 1971 dollars)

Year and pollution source	No control	1975 control	Policy[a]			
			R	S	E	M
1975						
Electric utilities	15.8	4.6	4.6	3.6	3.4	3.4
Industrial point sources	34.8	9.6	9.6	7.5	0.7	0.7
Residential/commercial fuels burning	1.8	1.8	1.8	1.7	1.6	1.6
Transportation	7.0	6.2	6.2	6.1	4.7	5.0
Total	59.4	22.2	22.2	18.9	10.4	10.7
1985						
Electric utilities	50.4	14.3	9.6	1.5	0.8	1.2
Industrial point scores	99.1	29.1	8.9	4.0	0.5	0.7
Residential/commercial fuels burning	3.2	3.2	2.8	2.7	2.7	2.8
Transportation	11.3	10.2	7.0	6.8	6.8	9.2
Total	164.0	56.8	28.3	15.0	10.8	13.9
2000						
Electric utilities	37.5	8.1	4.4	0.5	0.5	0.6
Industrial point sources	201.7	60.2	6.2	2.7	1.3	1.4
Residential/commercial fuels burning	2.7	2.4	1.3	1.3	1.2	1.3
Transportation	20.8	18.0	6.2	6.0	6.0	9.9
Total	262.7	88.7	18.1	10.5	9.0	13.2
2025						
Electric utilities	68.7	13.0	1.2	0.1	0.1	0.4
Industrial point sources	506.5	164.2	10.8	3.5	3.5	4.7
Residential/commercial fuels burning	4.9	4.0	0.7	0.5	0.5	0.5
Transportation	31.6	27.0	7.0	6.0	4.3	7.7
Total	611.7	208.2	19.7	10.1	8.4	13.3

[a] Column heading abbreviations are: R, relaxed; S, strict; E, efficient; and M, cost minimum. For all policies and in particular for R, S, E, and M, control costs and damages are total and not incremental; that is, they include amounts that would have occurred without the policy plus any additional amounts that occur because the policy is in place.

enced had 1975 controls been maintained. In all cases, the efficient policy leads to the lowest level of damages.

While industrial point sources do not in general contribute the largest proportion of emissions to water, this analysis suggests that they are responsible for a large share of the damage from water pollution. This result is plausible because industrial point sources result in relatively high concentrations in densely populated regions. It can be argued, however,

Table 7-9. National Water Pollution Damages for Alternative Control Policies, Scenario DH
(most likely values, billions of 1971 dollars)

Year and pollution source	No control	1975 control	Policy[a]			
			R	S	E	M
1975						
Electric utilities	1.2	0.4	0.4	0.4	0.4	0.5
Industrial point sources	19.8	5.1	5.1	4.0	4.0	4.0
Municipal sewage treatment	6.3	2.7	2.7	2.4	2.4	3.5
Urban runoff	2.9	2.9	2.9	2.9	1.6	1.6
Agriculture	...	1.0	1.0	0.9	0.9	0.9
Mining and other non-point sources	...	1.1	1.1	1.1	1.1	1.1
Total	30.2	13.2	13.2	11.7	10.4	11.6
1985						
Electric utilities	3.7	1.4	1.3	0.9	0.5	0.5
Industrial point sources	60.4	15.9	7.6	1.2	1.2	3.2
Municipal sewage treatment	12.8	5.5	4.7	3.7	3.6	6.8
Urban runoff	6.7	6.3	3.6	2.1	2.1	2.7
Agriculture	...	3.2	1.7	1.2	1.2	1.2
Mining and other non-point sources	...	2.1	1.2	0.8	0.8	0.8
Total	83.6	34.4	20.1	9.9	9.4	15.2
2000						
Electric utilities	2.9	1.1	0.9	0.6	0.6	0.8
Industrial point sources	107.7	28.8	6.6	1.6	1.6	3.2
Municipal sewage treatment	18.4	7.7	5.4	3.4	3.4	8.3
Urban runoff	10.0	9.1	3.2	1.8	1.8	4.1
Agriculture	...	4.2	2.0	1.4	1.4	1.4
Mining and other non-point sources	...	1.8	0.9	0.6	0.6	0.6
Total	139.0	52.7	19.0	9.4	9.4	18.4
2025						
Electric utilities	5.7	2.2	1.9	0.8	0.8	1.6
Industrial point sources	257.4	71.1	12.4	2.3	2.3	19.2
Municipal sewage treatment	30.5	12.6	5.1	2.3	2.3	9.0
Urban runoff	16.8	15.3	3.8	1.7	1.7	7.0
Agriculture	...	5.0	2.8	1.9	1.9	1.9
Mining and other non-point sources	...	3.2	1.7	1.2	1.2	1.2
Total	310.4	109.4	27.7	10.2	10.2	39.9

[a] Column heading abbreviations are: R, relaxed; S, strict; E, efficient; and M, cost minimum. For all policies and in particular for R, S, E, and M, control costs and damages are total and not incremental; that is, they include amounts that would have occurred without the policy plus any additional amounts that occur because the policy is in place.

272

that our methods lead to an understatement of damages assigned to agricultural runoff, mining, and other nonpoint sources. First, we may have underestimated emissions from these sources, a possibility discussed in technical note A to this chapter.[10] Second, our procedure and associated assumptions for allocating total water pollution damages between point and nonpoint sources may also lead to underestimation, a point that requires some explanation. A weight for sediment from agriculture was selected so that the damage model assigned $350 million of the $11.1 billion of national water pollution damages to agricultural sediments in 1971. This weight was applied to sediment from other nonpoint sources and held constant for projection purposes.[11] The figure of $350 million was selected for this purpose because it is roughly the middle of the range of damage estimates from agricultural sediment discharges reported by the best of the studies of this issue so far available (Wade and Heady, 1976). But that figure is only for damages associated with silting of reservoirs and alteration in stream flows; it does not include any estimate for damages to water-based recreation activities, which some believe to be sizable and others—on the basis of equally inadequate facts—believe to be negligible.

If a larger figure than $350 million had been used—which would have involved selecting a larger weight—less damages would have been assigned to point sources of water pollution and the conclusions of our benefit–cost analysis would be affected. For example, the weight used in our standard case, 0.0075, implies that an average of 29 percent of total water pollution damages are attributable to urban runoff, agriculture, mining, and other nonpoint sources. If instead a weight of 0.5 had been assigned, an average of 52 percent of water pollution damages would have been attributed to these sources and correspondingly less to industrial sources (see table 7–18 and the discussion associated with it). The maximum that can be attributed to these sources is 60 percent, the figure obtained when the weight is set at unity.

---

[10] If such emissions were 3.5 times larger, as suggested by Gianessi and Peskin (1978), damages from these sources might have been $3.4 billion rather than $2.1 billion in 1975; under policy S, they might be $5.3 billion instead of $3.1 billion in 2025.

[11] This procedure was used only for deriving damage estimates for suspended and dissolved solids, the two pollutants associated most directly with sediment runoff. Other pollutants from nonpoint sources are treated exactly like pollutants from any other source; in effect, they are assigned a weight of 1 for entry into the damage model.

Benefit–Cost Analysis

Expected cost–risk curves of the type illustrated in figure 7–2 were estimated for twenty-four different pollutants and sources. To demonstrate the use of this analytical device, five are discussed below in detail. The remainder are summarized in tables presenting principal implications of alternative national control policies. In all cases, scenario DH is assumed. A set of sensitivity tests is then presented to indicate the extent to which our conclusions are changed by altering the assumptions upon which they are based.

Case Studies

CARBON MONOXIDE AND NITROGEN OXIDES FROM TRANSPORTATION. Figure 7–3 shows expected total cost (control plus damage costs) and

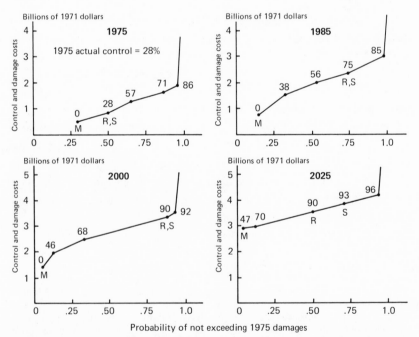

Figure 7–3.   Expected total costs and risks for carbon monoxide from transportation sources for alternative policies, Scenario DH. Note that numbers above the cost–risk line are percentage removal levels. The level indicated by *M* is the minimum expected total cost level calculated in this study.

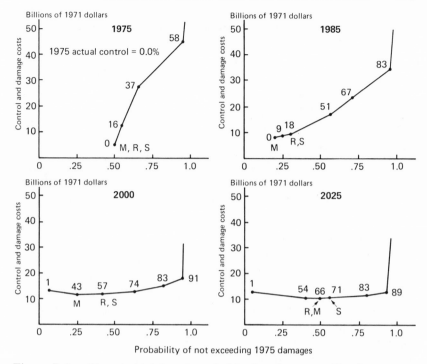

Figure 7–4. Expected total costs and risks for nitrogen oxides from transportation sources for alternative policies, Scenario DH. Note that numbers above the cost–risk line are percentage removal levels. The level indicated by *M* is the minimum expected total cost level calculated in this study.

associated risks for various levels of control of CO discharges from transportation sources. The simulated EPA policies, R and S, suggest that decision makers are willing to go well beyond the control levels at which expected marginal costs equal benefits (policy M) in order to increase the probability that future damages will not exceed 1975 levels. Figure 7–4 shows a similar outcome for control of NO_x from transportation sources.[12] However, in the years beyond 1985, the simulated NO_x control policies do draw closer to a least-cost policy.

As table 7–10 indicates, if policy M, the minimum-cost strategy, were followed instead of policy S, which simulates legislated EPA regulations, the costs of controlling CO emissions from transport during the next fifty years would be $133 billion less, but damage costs might be $60 billion more and the probability of avoiding damages as high as the 1975

[12] The curves in figure 7–4 appear to be flatter than those in 7–3 because of a different vertical scale.

Table 7–10. Cumulative Expected Costs of Emissions from Transportation, Alternative Policies, 1975–2025
(billions of 1971 dollars)

Emission and policy	Total costs	Control costs	Damage costs	X[a]
Carbon monoxide (CO)				
S	152.2	143.7	8.5	0.75
M	78.9	10.7	68.2	0.08
Nitrogen oxides (NO$_x$)				
S	507.2	270.9	236.3	0.44
M	474.4	182.6	291.8	0.35

[a] Weighted probability of not exceeding 1975 most likely damages.

levels would fall substantially, from 0.75 to only 0.08. The figures for NO$_x$ are smaller but move in the same direction.

This situation arises, we believe, because EPA is applying to the whole country a standard appropriate for regions with the greatest potential damages. Obviously, it is difficult administratively (especially in the case of transportation), as well as politically, to have different standards for different regions. But if such differential standards were possible, the cost of achieving comparable probabilities of avoiding damages as high as those experienced in 1975 would be significantly less. If control cost were cut, for example, in half, the expected savings associated with both pollutants would have been $430 million a year in 1975 and would rise to $5.6 billion a year in 2025.

SULFUR OXIDES FROM ELECTRIC POWER PLANTS. In his 1977 energy message, President Carter advocated that legislated standards for SO$_x$ from power plants and industrial boilers be strictly enforced. Our assessment supports this position. Indeed, figure 7–5 for power plants suggests that currently legislated standards (policy S) should, if anything, be tightened during the next twenty years or so, not relaxed or delayed as some have argued. The issue is significant, first because of the sizable cost figures involved, as evidenced in table 7–11, and, second, because the consequences of decisions made today will be with us for many decades, given the life-span of power plants.[13]

Because of data weaknesses, we cannot hold to our conclusions with a high degree of confidence, however, particularly with respect to

[13] This point can be seen in figure 7–5 by noting that it would take more than fifty years for policy R, if implemented today, to catch up with policies S or M, assuming that plants must wear out before efficient control equipment is installed.

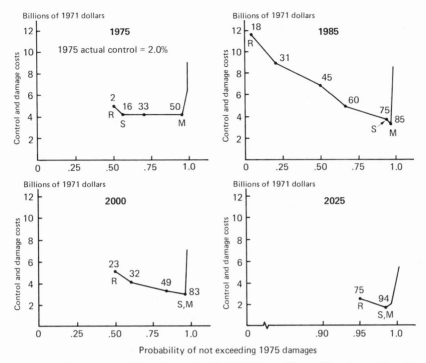

Figure 7–5. Expected total costs and risks for sulfur oxides from electric utilities for alternative policies, Scenario DH. Note that numbers above the cost–risk line are percentage removal levels. The level indicated by *M* is the minimum expected total cost level calculated in this study.

control costs and damage functions. To at least partially cope with these uncertainties, we have used relatively high cost figures for sulfur oxide pollution control equipment ($125 to $150 per kilowatt in 1975 dollars) and a wide range of estimates for damages. This range, derived from published estimates, extends from half the most likely value on the low side to three times that value on the high side in order to cover 96 percent of the frequency distribution of damages.

WATER POLLUTION FROM INDUSTRIAL POINT SOURCES. In its 1976 report, the National Commission on Water Quality (1976b) argued that a shift from BPT to BAT standards for industrial point sources would substantially increase control costs while producing few additional benefits. The reason given was that BAT requirements, though much more costly, would increase by only a few percentage points the percentage of pollution removed. Assuming for the moment that our assumption on the proportion of damages accounted for by sediments is correct, our analysis

Table 7–11. Cumulative Expected Costs of Sulfur Oxide Emissions from
Electric Utilities, Alternative Policies, 1975–2025
(billions of 1971 dollars)

Period and policy	Total costs	Control costs	Damage costs	X[a]
1975–2000				
R	234.2	7.3	226.9	0.24
S	96.5	46.7	49.8	0.90
M	89.6	66.0	23.6	0.99
2000–2025				
R	118.9	19.7	99.2	0.64
S	68.3	60.2	8.1	0.99
M	68.2	50.9	17.3	0.99
1975–2025				
R	353.1	27.0	326.1	0.44
S	164.8	106.9	57.9	0.94
M	157.8	116.9	40.9	0.99

[a] Weighted probability of not exceeding 1975 most likely damages.

disagrees with this argument. To demonstrate this, we have added policy
scenarios in which BPT and BAT standards, as they were expected to
evolve as of 1975, are assumed to be fully implemented starting in 1975.
This is in contrast to policies R and S, which phase these standards in over
time (see table 7-1). Our results differ in three respects from NCWQ's.

First, as indicated in table 7–12, our analysis suggests that a shift
from BPT to BAT standards would reduce quite substantially emissions
of BOD, COD, SS, and DS, and the extent of such reductions would grow
over time. This result is not affected by the weight assigned to agricultural
sediments in calculating damages.

Second, the incremental costs of reducing these emissions exceed
the benefits of doing so only in the years from 1975 to 1983. Thereafter
(and at least until close to the end of our time horizon[14]), the situation is
reversed, as indicated by the crossing of the total cost curves for BPT and
BAT in figure 7–6. This conclusion illustrates the importance of extending
the time horizon of typical benefit–cost analyses.

Third, our analysis suggests that a third strategy would be less costly
than either BPT or BAT. This is policy M in figures 7–6 and 7–7. It would
start at 72 percent removal in 1975, just 2 percent above actual control
policy in that year but substantially below both BPT and BAT removal
levels. Over time, it would rise slowly to 92 percent in 1985 and to 95
percent in 2000; because of changes in technology and the composition

[14] As figure 7–7 indicates, in 2025, BPT is somewhat less costly than BAT,
although the latter substantially reduces the probability of exceeding 1975 damage
levels.

Table 7–12. Discharges of Water Pollution from Industrial Sources Under Alternative Policies, Scenario DH
(millions of tons)

Pollutant and policy	1975	1985	2000	2025
Biochemical oxygen demand (BOD)				
Gross	8.0	11.6	17.0	34.3
BPT	1.3	1.9	2.8	1.6
BAT	0.4	0.6	0.6	0.4
R	2.4	1.9	1.4	1.1
S	2.2	0.6	0.6	0.4
M	2.2	1.0	0.9	3.0
Chemical oxygen demand (COD)				
Gross	12.5	17.3	25.8	49.5
BPT	2.1	3.5	6.9	5.4
BAT	1.1	1.6	1.8	1.7
R	3.9	3.5	3.4	3.7
S	3.6	1.6	1.8	1.7
M	3.6	2.3	2.2	5.4
Suspended solids (SS)				
Gross	51.0	83.2	126.7	258.1
BPT	4.9	6.8	3.7	1.3
BAT	0.3	0.5	0.4	0.1
R	9.3	6.8	1.8	0.9
S	8.7	0.5	0.4	0.1
M	8.7	4.0	2.7	19.8
Dissolved solids (DS)				
Gross	16.1	19.6	25.4	54.0
BPT	5.5	8.1	18.1	28.0
BAT	1.3	2.0	2.7	4.2
R	10.4	8.1	8.9	19.1
S	9.6	2.0	2.7	4.2
M	9.6	2.8	3.1	8.0
Nutrients				
Gross	0.7	1.0	1.4	2.4
BPT	0.05	0.08	0.1	0.1
BAT	0.03	0.04	0.05	0.07
R	0.1	0.08	0.07	0.09
S	0.09	0.04	0.05	0.07
M	0.09	0.08	0.08	0.3
Other[a]				
Gross	2.4	3.6	5.3	9.7
BPT	0.7	0.9	0.6	0.3
BAT	0.04	0.06	0.08	0.1
R	1.4	0.9	0.3	0.2
S	1.3	0.06	0.08	0.1
M	1.3	0.2	0.2	0.8

[a] Includes acids, bases, oil and grease.

of the economy after 2000, it would recede somewhat to 91 percent by 2025.

However, the second and third of these results are sensitive to a number of assumptions made in the course of our analysis.[15] If, for ex-

[15] The percentage reduction in residuals due to a shift from BPT to BAT is, of course, not affected by other assumptions.

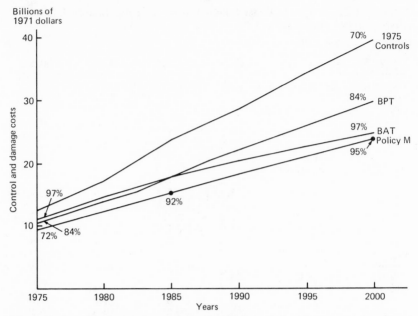

Figure 7–6.   Total costs for water pollution from industrial sources for alternative policies, Scenario DH. Note that the percentages are average removal rates for biochemical oxygen demand, chemical oxygen demand, suspended solids, dissolved solids, nutrients, oil and grease, acids, and bases.

ample, we had selected a weight of approximately 0.15 or greater for sediment from agriculture, mining, and other nonpoint sources, instead of 0.0075, or had estimated total water pollution damages in the base year at half the value actually used, the cost of BPT standards would be less than that of BAT in all years, and the cost savings involved in shifting to policy M would be less.[16] Thus, though we cannot hold to our conclusions with substantial confidence, it is important to remember that the NCWQ conclusions are based on equally tenuous—but in that case implicit— assumptions about these same factors. Far better data will be required to narrow this range of uncertainty and settle such issues.

URBAN NONPOINT SOURCES.   The Federal Water Pollution Control Act requires local jurisdictions to control urban runoff, which by our estimates amounts to between 20 and 40 percent of mass water pollutant

[16] These and similar points are discussed in detail in connection with table 7–18.

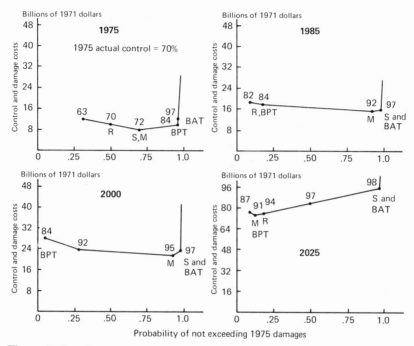

Figure 7–7. Expected total costs and risks for water pollution discharges from industrial sources for alternative policies, Scenario DH. Note that numbers above the cost–risk line are percentage removal levels. The level indicated by *M* is the minimum expected total cost level calculated in this study. Starting in 1985, S and BAT controls are equivalent.

loadings in urban areas. As figure 7–8 shows, policy R increases control from none in 1975 to 40 percent control in 1985, 60 percent in 2000, and 70 percent in 2025. This policy would be inefficient in all years except those around 2000. Policy S would cost only $30 billion more than R during the whole period ($120 billion more in control costs but $90 billion less in damage costs) and would increase the probability of not exceeding 1975 damages from 0.4 to 0.7 (see table 7–13).

OVERALL ASSESSMENT. The results of similar analyses for other pollutants and sources are summarized in table 7–14. Policies R and S are significantly more strict than is required for minimum cost (though not necessarily inappropriate because of the additional risk-avoidance they purchase) for controls on CO and HC from industry in all years and for HC and water pollutants from residential and commercial sources at least

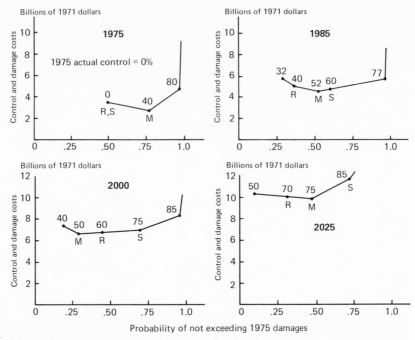

Figure 7–8.   Expected total costs and risks from urban nonpoint sources, alternative policies, Scenario DH. Note that numbers above the cost–risk line are percentage removal levels. The level indicated by *M* is the minimum expected total cost level calculated in this study.

up to 2000; policy S is significantly more strict in the same sense for NO_x and CO from electric power plants.

On the other hand, there are a number of cases in which control levels under policies R and S are clearly too low. Table 7–15 indicates the cumulative savings in total costs and the improvements in risk-avoidance that would accrue if all cases in which controls are inefficient in the

Table 7–13. Cumulative Expected Costs of Runoff Control for Urban Nonpoint Sources, Alternative Policies, 1975–2025
(billions of 1971 dollars)

Policy	Total costs	Control costs	Damage costs	X[a]
R	343.0	136.9	206.1	0.4
S	372.5	255.8	116.7	0.7
M	329.1	119.1	210.0	0.4

[a] Weighted probability of not exceeding 1975 most likely damages.

Table 7–14. Average Percentage of Pollutant Removed and Efficiency for Alternative Policies, Scenario DH

Source, pollutant, and policy	1975	1985	2000	2025
Electric utilities				
Particulate matter (PM)				
R	90.2 (I)	96.7 (I)	99.3 (E)	99.5 (E)
S	92.3 (I)	99.3 (E)	99.4 (E)	99.5 (E)
M	95.4	98.0	99.3	99.5
Nitrogen oxides (NO_x)				
R	1.0 (E)	13.8 (E)	17.2 (E)	45.6 (I)
S	11.8 (E)	49.9 (E)	63.8 (E)	85.0 (E)
M	1.0	13.8	17.2	65.3
Hydrocarbons (HC)				
R	0.0 (E)	0.0 (E)	0.0 (E)	0.0 (E)
S	0.0 (E)	0.0 (E)	0.0 (E)	0.0 (E)
M	0.0	0.0	0.0	0.0
Carbon monoxide (CO)				
R	0.0 (E)	0.0 (E)	0.0 (E)	3.0 (E)
S	0.0 (E)	26.5 (E)	36.0 (E)	50.0 (E)
M	0.0	0.0	0.0	0.0
Water pollution[a]				
R	58.5 (E)	58.9 (I)	57.8 (I)	55.3 (I)
S	59.4 (E)	68.2 (I)	73.0 (E)	80.0 (E)
M	51.8 (E)	82.1	62.8	63.5
Industry				
Particulate matter (PM)				
R	65.1 (I)	88.9 (I)	98.7 (I)	99.3 (E)
S	71.6 (I)	98.5 (I)	99.2 (E)	99.7 (E)
M	94.2	98.8	99.2	99.3
Sulfur oxides (SO_x)				
R	46.6 (I)	62.3 (I)	69.9 (I)	75.9 (I)
S	53.4 (I)	78.6 (I)	85.9 (I)	91.6 (I)
M	90.6	95.6	94.3	94.9
Nitrogen oxides (NO_x)				
R	3.0 (E)	12.3 (E)	17.6 (I)	34.0 (I)
S	3.0 (E)	20.2 (E)	25.7 (E)	51.1 (E)
M	3.0	12.3	21.6	42.5
Hydrocarbons (HC)				
R	26.0 (E)	49.7 (E)	65.8 (E)	82.7 (E)
S	39.0 (E)	76.1 (E)	82.2 (E)	90.2 (E)
M	1.0	19.8	41.6	77.6
Carbon monoxide (CO)				
R	49.3 (E)	77.3 (E)	88.2 (E)	93.2 (E)
S	59.0 (E)	95.1 (E)	96.5 (E)	97.3 (E)
M	1.0	48.1	72.6	78.7
Residential and commercial				
Particulate matter (PM)				
R	13.8 (I)	37.8 (I)	63.7 (I)	88.2 (I)
S	16.8 (I)	45.3 (E)	69.8 (I)	92.1 (I)
M	33.4	45.3	81.9	95.2
Sulfur oxides (SO_x)				
R	0.0 (E)	0.0 (E)	0.0 (E)	0.0 (E)
S	0.0 (E)	0.0 (E)	0.0 (E)	0.0 (E)
M	0.0	0.0	0.0	0.0

(continued)

Table 7–14. (Continued)

Source, pollutant, and policy	1975	1985	2000	2025
Nitrogen oxides (NO$_x$)				
R	0.0 (E)	0.0 (E)	1.0 (I)	15.9 (I)
S	0.0 (E)	0.0 (E)	3.0 (E)	17.8 (E)
M	0.0	0.0	3.0	17.8
Hydrocarbons (HC)				
R	3.7 (E)	23.4 (E)	28.4 (E)	41.2 (I)
S	4.6 (E)	26.3 (E)	33.5 (E)	48.0 (E)
M	0.0	0.0	0.0	48.0
Carbon monoxide (CO)				
R	0.0 (E)	16.1 (E)	23.4 (E)	34.4 (E)
S	2.7 (E)	49.0 (E)	63.4 (E)	80.7 (E)
M	0.0	0.0	0.0	0.0
Water pollution[b]				
R	53.7 (E)	57.5 (E)	62.9 (E)	77.5 (E)
S	54.4 (E)	63.6 (E)	74.5 (E)	88.2 (E)
M	37.6	39.2	45.4	66.9
Transportation				
Particulate matter (PM)				
R	13.9 (E)	23.5 (E)	61.8 (E)	65.9 (I)
S	13.9 (E)	23.5 (E)	61.8 (E)	66.3 (I)
M	13.9	23.5	61.8	79.7
Sulfur oxides (SO$_x$)				
R	4.0 (E)	11.0 (E)	40.3 (E)	46.8 (I)
S	4.0 (E)	11.0 (E)	40.4 (E)	47.3 (I)
M	4.0	11.0	40.4	78.9
Hydrocarbons (HC)				
R	23.5 (I)	61.9 (E)	77.0 (E)	76.1 (I)
S	23.5 (I)	61.9 (E)	77.5 (E)	83.6 (E)
M	69.3	61.9	77.0	79.8

Note: I and E indicate economically inefficient and efficient control, respectively.
[a] Percentage removed is the weighted average for BOD, COD, suspended solids, dissolved solids, nutrients, acids, bases, oils, and grease.
[b] Covers pollution control by municipal waste water treatment plants.

cost–risk sense were eliminated and replaced with controls set at the point of minimum cost. If cases in which policy R is inefficient were eliminated, it would save $625 billion in total costs and $1,069 billion in damages during the whole 1975–2025 period. Eliminating inefficient cases for S would save $142 billion in total costs and $268 billion in damages. Under policy S, more than 85 percent of these costs would be eliminated by tightening controls on SO$_x$ from industry, electric power plants, and transportation sources, and on particulates from industrial sources. The same is true for policy R except that also tightening water pollution controls could make a substantial additional difference in costs.

The same pattern of results can be seen in table 7–16, which provides a summary of the estimates of damages, costs, and benefits (com-

Table 7–15. Changes in Costs and Probabilities of Not Exceeding 1975
Damages If Inefficient Control Policies Were Changed to Policy M, 1975–2025
(billions of 1971 dollars)

Source, pollutant, and policy	Total costs	Damage costs	Probabilities[a]
Electric utilities			
Particulate matter (PM)			
R	−2.7	−5.7	0.14
S	−0.6	−1.4	0.04
Sulfur oxides (SO$_x$)			
R	−195.3	−285.2	0.55
S	−6.9	−26.2	0.05
Nitrogen oxides (NO$_x$)			
R	−0.2	−0.5	0.06
Water pollution			
R	−5.1	−21.6	0.11
S	−1.5	−5.9	0.10
Industry			
Particulate matter (PM)			
R	−74.1	−89.2	0.12
S	−18.9	−25.5	0.04
Sulfur oxides (SO$_x$)			
R	−265.2	−431.7	0.83
S	−97.7	−163.7	0.43
Nitrogen oxides (NO$_x$)			
R	−0.04	−0.8	0.01
Water pollution			
R	−51.4	−152.8	0.42
Residential and commercial			
Particulate matter (PM)			
R	−1.9	−4.0	0.10
S	−0.4	−1.7	0.04
Nitrogen oxides (NO$_x$)			
R	−0.06	−0.1	0.02
Hydrocarbons (HC)			
R	−0.04	−0.1	0.03
Transportation			
Particulate matter (PM)			
R	−2.0	−3.7	0.21
S	−0.5	−2.2	0.10
Sulfur oxides (SO$_x$)			
R	−10.1	−20.3	0.05
S	−7.4	−17.5	0.05
Hydrocarbons (HC)			
R	−5.3	−24.4	0.12
S	−3.8	−15.3	0.08
Urban nonpoint sources			
Runoff			
R	−11.1	−29.2	0.09
S	−3.8	−8.4	0.03
Total			
R	−624.5	−1,069.3	
S	−141.5	−267.8	

[a] Difference in weighted probability of not exceeding 1975 most likely damages.

285

Table 7–16. Discounted Expected Benefits and Costs, Scenario DH
(discount rate = 9 percent; in billions of 1971 dollars)

Source and pollutant	Benefits[a]	Policy R Costs Total	Damage	Control
Discounted to 1975 for the period 1975–2000				
Electric utilities				
Particulate matter (PM)	338.5	19.3	5.1	14.2
Sulfur oxides (SO$_x$)	23.6	93.5	91.2	2.3
Nitrogen oxides (NO$_x$)	0.4	2.5	2.2	0.3
Hydrocarbons (HC)	0.0	—	0.005	0.0
Carbon monoxide (CO)	—	—	—	0.01
Water pollution[b]	19.2	13.8	10.5	3.3
Industry				
Particulate matter (PM)	875.2	61.5	50.4	11.1
Sulfur oxides (SO$_x$)	191.9	82.7	69.5	13.2
Nitrogen oxides (NO$_x$)	0.2	1.7	1.3	0.4
Hydrocarbons (HC)	1.4	2.8	1.2	1.6
Carbon monoxide (CO)	0.07	0.1	0.02	0.08
Water pollution[b]	505.5	156.8	76.2	80.6
Residential and commercial				
Particulate matter (PM)	4.6	3.7	2.6	1.1
Sulfur oxides (SO$_x$)	0.01	23.3	21.4	1.9
Nitrogen oxides (NO$_x$)	0.004	0.8	0.7	0.05
Hydrocarbons (HC)	0.1	0.6	0.4	0.2
Carbon monoxide (CO)	0.001	—	0.01	0.01
Water pollution[b,c]	80.9	76.1	43.6	32.5
Transportation				
Particulate matter (PM)	4.4	8.2	3.0	5.2
Sulfur oxides (SO$_x$)	2.0	7.9	5.1	2.8
Nitrogen oxides (NO$_x$)	17.2	88.5	56.1	32.4
Hydrocarbons (HC)	32.5	45.8	23.9	21.9
Carbon monoxide (CO)	5.2	26.1	2.4	23.7
Urban nonpoint				
Water pollution[b]	30.5	50.5	42.3	8.2
Total	2,133.4	766.2	509.1	257.1
Discounted to 2000 for the period 2000–2025				
Electric utilities				
Particulate matter (PM)	511.4	30.6	0.3	30.3
Sulfur oxides (SO$_x$)	55.2	59.4	50.9	8.5
Nitrogen oxides (NO$_x$)	1.0	2.5	1.9	0.6
Hydrocarbons (HC)	0.0	—	0.005	0.0
Carbon monoxide (CO)	—	—	—	0.03
Water pollution[b]	26.4	21.2	14.4	6.8
Industry				
Particulate matter (PM)	3,312.4	59.8	3.9	55.9
Sulfur oxides (SO$_x$)	599.3	197.4	117.7	79.7
Nitrogen oxides (NO$_x$)	1.4	4.4	2.8	1.6
Hydrocarbons (HC)	4.4	6.2	1.0	5.2
Carbon monoxide (CO)	0.3	0.2	0.02	0.2
Water pollution[b]	1,636.9	423.9	98.3	325.6

	Policy S				Policy E		
		Costs				Costs	
Benefits[a]	Total	Damage	Control	Benefits[a]	Total	Damage	Control
337.0	19.2	2.2	17.0	337.0	18.9	1.1	17.8
103.9	42.4	27.8	14.6	117.6	33.0	12.2	20.8
1.1	2.9	1.5	1.4	1.1	2.9	1.5	1.4
0.0	—	0.005	0.0	0.0	—	0.005	0.0
—	0.3	—	0.3	—	0.3	—	0.3
21.6	13.3	7.6	5.7	24.3	12.7	5.3	7.4
908.9	36.2	22.2	14.0	929.3	21.6	2.3	19.3
196.0	67.0	49.1	17.9	240.1	31.8	3.8	28.0
0.4	1.8	1.2	0.6	0.4	1.8	1.2	0.6
1.8	3.5	0.9	2.6	1.8	3.5	0.9	2.6
0.08	0.1	0.01	0.1	0.08	0.1	0.01	0.1
552.6	139.2	27.2	112.0	552.6	139.2	27.2	112.0
5.2	3.2	1.9	1.3	6.1	3.1	1.5	1.6
0.01	23.3	21.4	1.9	0.01	23.3	21.4	1.9
0.01	0.8	0.7	0.06	0.01	0.8	0.7	0.06
0.1	0.7	0.4	0.3	0.1	0.7	0.4	0.3
0.004	—	0.008	0.03	0.004	—	0.008	0.03
89.4	86.9	36.0	50.9	89.4	86.9	36.0	50.9
4.2	7.5	2.2	5.3	4.2	7.5	2.2	5.3
1.9	7.8	4.8	3.0	1.9	7.8	4.8	3.0
17.6	88.9	55.6	33.3	17.6	88.9	55.6	33.3
32.7	45.7	23.6	22.1	40.6	51.3	15.7	35.6
5.2	26.3	2.4	23.9	5.2	26.3	2.4	23.9
41.9	49.5	30.8	18.7	49.3	46.6	24.2	22.4
2,321.8	666.3	319.5	346.8	2,418.7	609.0	220.4	388.6
510.3	31.1	0.3	30.8	510.3	31.1	0.3	30.8
125.0	37.8	4.3	33.5	125.0	37.5	4.3	33.5
2.4	3.4	0.8	2.6	2.4	37.5	0.8	2.6
0.0	—	0.005	0.0	0.0	—	0.005	0.0
—	1.2	—	1.2	—	1.2	—	1.2
34.4	22.5	7.0	15.5	34.4	22.5	7.0	15.5
3,314.9	63.4	1.6	61.8	3,314.9	63.4	1.6	61.8
655.1	160.8	40.8	120.0	678.5	158.4	13.9	144.5
2.1	4.9	2.2	2.7	2.1	4.9	2.2	2.7
4.9	8.4	0.6	7.8	4.9	8.4	0.6	7.8
0.3	0.3	0.005	0.3	0.3	0.3	0.005	0.3
1,702.9	473.4	21.3	452.1	1,702.9	473.4	21.3	452.1

(continued)

Table 7–16. (Continued)

Source and pollutant	Benefits[a]	Policy R Total	Policy R Damage	Policy R Control
		Costs		
		Total	Damage	Control
Residential and commercial				
Particulate matter (PM)	23.8	2.1	1.0	1.1
Sulfur oxides (SO$_x$)	0.08	13.3	11.7	1.6
Nitrogen oxides (NO$_x$)	0.05	1.1	1.0	0.07
Hydrocarbons (HC)	0.5	1.0	0.5	0.5
Carbon monoxide (CO)	0.009	—	0.01	0.03
Water pollution[b,c]	188.0	106.8	59.6	47.2
Transportation				
Particulate matter (PM)	28.3	7.7	2.0	5.7
Sulfur oxides (SO$_x$)	17.8	16.0	10.3	5.7
Nitrogen oxides (NO$_x$)	92.8	113.3	47.5	65.8
Hydrocarbons (HC)	94.4	56.7	22.1	34.6
Carbon monoxide (CO)	19.8	34.8	1.8	33.0
Urban nonpoint				
Water pollution[b]	109.1	82.4	42.8	39.6
Total	6,723.4	1,240.9	491.5	749.4

[a] Costs and benefits of policy indicated compared to no controls.
[b] Covers control of BOD, COD, suspended solids, dissolved solids, nutrients, acids, bases, oil, grease, heavy metals, and pesticides.

pared to no controls) by source and pollutant for policies R, S, and E, discounted for two time periods. The same pattern of results as discussed above can be seen. For example, policies E and S have substantially lower costs than policy R for SO$_x$ from electric utilities and industry, while policy R, compared with policies S and E, has (slightly) lower costs for NO$_x$ and CO from transport (but substantially higher costs than policy M, not shown in this table).

Table 7–17 provides another summary view, one that compares the costs in given years for various policies. It shows that damages would increase dramatically over time if there were no controls or if controls were held constant at 1975 levels. The other policies examined here hold damage costs to approximately 1975 levels and, although control costs are substantially larger, have significantly lower total costs. The major difference among these policies is that R has smaller control costs and more damages as compared with S and E. Policy M, the least-cost policy, tends to have lower control costs in all years and higher damage costs in later years than does policy R because in no case does it allow for efforts

	Policy S				Policy E		
		Costs				Costs	
Benefits[a]	Total	Damage	Control	Benefits[a]	Total	Damage	Control
25.7	2.1	0.8	1.3	28.7	2.0	0.4	1.6
0.1	13.1	11.5	1.6	0.1	13.1	11.5	1.6
0.1	1.0	0.9	0.1	0.1	1.0	0.9	0.1
0.5	1.1	0.5	0.6	0.5	1.1	0.5	0.6
0.02	0.1	0.005	0.09	0.02	0.1	0.005	0.09
217.3	118.9	34.2	84.7	217.3	118.9	34.2	84.7
27.2	8.0	2.3	5.7	28.6	7.8	1.8	6.0
17.0	15.4	9.7	5.7	22.9	13.4	5.0	8.4
94.1	116.1	45.8	70.3	94.1	116.1	45.8	70.3
97.9	56.4	18.6	37.8	100.0	56.2	16.5	39.7
20.1	35.9	1.5	34.4	20.1	35.9	1.5	34.4
134.1	93.4	21.4	72.0	134.1	93.4	21.4	72.0
6,986.6	1,268.5	225.8	1,042.7	7,022.3	1,263.7	191.3	1,072.4

[c] Includes pollution control for municipal waste water treatment plants.

to reduce risks by increasing controls beyond the point of minimum total cost.

Effects of Alternative Assumptions on Water Pollution Results

Although a wide variety of sensitivity tests would be of interest, the most crucial tests for our purposes are associated with water pollution. Table 7–18 summarizes the results obtained. The standard assumptions (first column) are scenario DH, national water pollution damages of $11.1 billion in the base year, an income–environment elasticity of 1.6 between 1975 and 1985 declining to zero by 2010, curvilinear damage functions, a weight for sediment that assigns about $350 million of $11.1 billion in damages to agricultural sediment in the base year, and an increasing average plant size that over time reduces unit capital abatement costs for industrial sources and municipal sewage plants.

Table 7–17. Most Likely Pollution Control and Damage Costs, Alternative
Policies, Scenario DH
(billions of 1971 dollars)

Cost and policy[a]	1975	1985	2000	2025
Damage costs				
Policy				
A	95.6	256.0	410.5	933.9
B	35.3	91.1	141.4	317.6
R	35.3	48.4	37.1	47.5
S	30.7	24.9	19.8	20.4
E	20.8	20.2	18.3	18.7
M	22.3	29.0	31.6	53.2
Control costs				
Policy				
A	0.0	0.0	0.0	0.0
B	11.3	16.9	20.2	48.5
R	11.3	29.9	48.3	125.1
S	13.0	45.8	67.1	181.0
E	16.8	47.7	67.8	181.9
M	12.5	28.5	45.4	111.0
Total costs				
Policy				
A	95.6	256.0	410.5	933.9
B	46.6	108.0	161.6	366.1
R	46.6	78.3	85.4	172.6
S	43.7	70.7	86.9	201.4
E	37.6	67.9	86.1	200.6
M	34.8	57.5	77.0	164.2

Note: Control costs and damages are total and not incremental; that is, they include
amounts that would have occurred without the policy plus any additional amounts
that result because the policy is in place.

    [a] Letter designations represent the following policies: A, no control; B, control at
1975 levels; R, relaxed control; S, strict control; E, efficient control; M, cost-minimizing
control.

The facts that we used damage functions that were curvilinear rather
than linear and that we changed average plant size over time makes little
difference to our results. The same is true for changes in the income–
environment elasticity, at least within the range tested. A shift from scenario DH to DL or FL does make some difference, particularly in later
years.

The most significant differences in results occur when the base-year
damage estimates or the weight assumed for sediment discharges is
changed. It is difficult to say whether the range of estimates for these two
parameters, which is very large in percentage terms, is reasonable in the
sense that the low and high estimates are very likely to be experienced.
But if they were to occur instead of the standard assumptions, the results

would have been significantly different. In particular, if a sediment weight between 0.15 and 0.5 had been selected, NCWQ recommendations to move to BPT instead of BAT standards to reduce total costs for industrial point sources would be validated. However, BPT standards would still be inefficient, and even lower total costs and risks could be achieved at more stringent, least-cost controls. For sediment weights above 0.5, BPT standards become efficient, but this would imply that more than 50 percent of water pollution damages must be accounted for by nonpoint sources, a percentage that seems quite high to us. In any event, it must be remembered that BAT standards imply lower probabilities of experiencing damages equal to or greater than 1975 levels. Thus, even if BPT proved to have lower total costs, society might still choose a somewhat more stringent standard in order to reduce this probability.

Comparison of Alternative Scenarios

Table 7–19 shows pollution control and damage costs by scenario, with each scenario having pollution control policy S. Comparisons of FH with DH and of FL with DL show that FH and FL, with smaller populations, have slightly larger pollution damages between 1975 and 1993. The reason is that, for a period, FH and FL have larger work forces than DH and DL would have (more female workers because there are fewer women with small children) and therefore larger GNPs and more environmental residuals. It is also clear in early years that the low economic growth scenarios, DL and FL, have an advantage in reducing damages, compared with DH and FH, respectively. From 1975 to about 2000, pollution control levels are relatively low (they are building up to the high levels to come after 2000), and the relatively low pollution loadings of DL and FL in this period are especially helpful in keeping damages (and thus total pollution costs) at relatively low levels. When pollution control reaches higher levels (after 2000), lower economic growth is less effective than lower population growth in reducing total costs and damage costs below the levels of scenario DH.

Damage costs under scenarios DHNU (nuclear phaseout) and DH are almost identical, but DHNU control costs are higher because of the extra effort required to maintain environmental quality when more coal is burned. It is important to note, however, that none of the damage estimates include environmental risks of radioactivity storage from nuclear

Table 7–18. Sensitivity of Water Pollution Results to Variations in Assumptions

Result	Standard assumptions	Base year national damages (bill. 71$)[a]		Income-environ-ment-elas-ticity = 1	Linear damage func-tions	Sediment weight[b]			Scenario		No change in average plant size
		$5.55	$20.2			1	0.5	0.125	DL	FL	
Percentage of pollution removed under policy M[c]											
Electric utilities											
1975	51.8	46.1	79.7	51.8	48.6	45.4	45.4	45.4	51.8	51.8	51.8
1985	82.1	58.9	82.1	77.0	77.0	46.3	56.5	71.8	77.0	77.0	82.1
2000	62.8	55.2	86.4	62.8	62.8	31.9	31.9	50.4	56.7	56.7	62.8
2025	63.5	51.1	75.8	70.1	63.5	30.7	30.7	50.4	56.9	43.9	63.5
Industry											
1975	72.4	72.4	72.4	72.4	72.4	54.2	54.2	68.7	72.4	72.4	72.4
1985	92.4	88.3	96.5	92.4	92.4	75.0	83.7	88.0	92.5	92.4	92.4
2000	95.5	92.0	97.2	95.5	95.5	81.3	90.7	95.5	95.5	95.5	95.5
2025	90.7	87.6	95.3	93.5	90.7	76.6	79.4	87.9	87.9	87.9	90.7
Municipal sewage treatment											
1975	37.6	37.6	42.4	37.6	37.6	37.6	37.6	37.6	37.6	37.6	37.6
1985	39.2	27.1	45.3	39.2	39.2	24.2	24.2	31.7	39.2	39.2	39.2
2000	45.4	33.7	62.9	45.4	41.7	37.9	37.9	37.9	37.9	37.9	45.4
2025	66.9	63.3	74.0	70.3	63.5	60.2	60.2	60.2	60.2	60.2	63.5
Urban runoff											
1975	40.0	0.0	40.0	40.0	40.0	5.7	17.1	22.9	40.0	40.0	40.0
1985	52.0	48.0	77.0	52.0	52.0	26.0	39.0	45.0	52.0	52.0	52.0
2000	50.0	50.0	75.0	45.5	45.5	31.8	45.5	45.5	45.5	45.5	50.0
2025	75.0	50.0	75.0	75.0	50.0	45.0	50.0	50.0	50.0	50.0	75.0

Alternative assumptions

Years when total costs for industry under BAT become less than those under BPT	1983	BPT costs always less	1976	1986	1984	BPT costs always less	BPT costs always less	BPT costs = BAT costs between 1992 and 2000	1990	1985	1983
Year after 1979 when industrial BPT controls become efficient	2025	2010	Never	Never	2025	1980	2005	2020	2015	2015	2025
Year after 1979 when industrial BAT controls become efficient	1980	1980	1980	1980	1980	1980	1980	1980	1980	1980	1980
Average percentage of water pollution damages attributed to non-point sources	29	25	29	27	29	60	52	40	28	28	26
Increase in cumulative costs 1975–2025 (billion 1971 $)[d]											
Electric utilities	0.0	4.7	8.1	1.3	0.3	19.5	13.7	3.8	1.4	2.5	0.07
Industry	0.0	59.6	89.4	18.6	0.0	210.3	108.6	17.4	7.4	13.1	0.0
Municipal sewage treatment	0.0	30.6	44.0	1.7	4.1	57.4	43.6	15.5	6.3	13.4	1.2
Urban runoff	0.0	36.8	36.5	0.2	4.8	65.9	48.1	20.1	11.1	14.0	0.0

[a] Out of the total of $11.1 billion in 1975, health-related damages are $1.6 billion. This last figure uses estimates of health care costs and foregone income taken from B. S. Cooper and D. P. Rice, "The Economic Cost of Illness Revisited," Social Security Bulletin, DHEW publication no. (SSA) 76-11703 (Washington, D.C., GPO, 1976). The implied value of life in the Cooper and Rice estimates is about $30,000. R. Thaler and S. Rosen, in "The Value of Saving a Life: Evidence from the Labor Market" (paper presented at the National Bureau of Economic Research conference (Washington, D.C., Nov. 30, 1973), using wage and occupational safety data, estimate a value per statistical life saved of about $200,000. Total health damages of $10.7 billion and total water pollution damages of $20.2 billion result when the health damages estimate is adjusted upward to agree with this $200,000 value.

[b] The weight given to sediment discharges from agriculture, mining, and other nonpoint sources. The standard assumption, derived by assuming that $350 million of the total water pollution damage figure of $11.1 billion in 1975 came from agricultural sediment, is 0.0075.

[c] Percentage removed is the weighted average for BOD, COD, suspended solids, dissolved solids, nutrients, acids, bases, oils, and grease.

[d] Equals cost for controls at the cost-minimizing levels (for point sources and urban runoff under the standard assumptions minus cost for controls at cost-minimizing levels under the alternative assumptions. Controls for nonpoint sources are set at the constant levels indicated previously.

Table 7-19. National Expected Pollution Costs Under Alternative Scenarios for Policy S
(billions of 1971 dollars)

Year	DH	DL	FH	FL	DHNU	DHP1	DHP2
Total costs							
1975	51	51	51	51	51	51	51
1985	78	67	78	68	77	77	81
2000	93	80	88	76	107	89	117
2010	127	110	112	96	153	121	147
2025	210	177	160	133	246	200	200
Control costs							
1975	14	14	14	14	14	14	14
1985	48	45	47	44	48	48	47
2000	70	64	66	60	84	69	72
2010	104	95	94	84	130	102	109
2025	186	162	146	124	222	182	176
Damage costs							
1975	37	37	37	37	37	37	37
1985	30	22	31	24	29	29	34
2000	23	16	22	16	23	20	45
2010	23	15	18	12	23	19	38
2025	24	15	14	9	24	18	24

wastes, diversion, and proliferation. The relevant tradeoff, then, is between the extra control costs of the DHNU scenario and the risk of having radioactive by-products and the other special problems of the nuclear fuel cycle. These issues are addressed more completely in chapter 8.

Damage costs under scenario DHP2 (reduced oil price) are larger than damages under DH. There are four reasons for this. First, GNP growth is higher in DHP2 than in DH because the dampening effects on GNP of higher energy prices is not present. Second, when energy is cheaper, more is consumed. Third, relatively more oil than coal is consumed, and oil has less stringent control requirements than does coal. Fourth, in the period 1980 to 2000, scenario DHP2 has less investment (because of lower energy prices) and more consumption than scenario DH, and consumption contributes more to residuals than does investment.[17] A clear implication is that DHP2 requires higher pollution control levels to maintain environmental quality. This is a good example of an extraneous event that makes a difference to the impacts that population and economic growth have.

---

[17] The difference in damage costs between scenarios DHP1 and DH is explained in similar fashion. But in this case, the impacts would be reversed in direction because the price of energy in DHP1 is higher than in DH.

Table 7–20. Expected Pollution Control and Damage Costs, Absolute Levels and Compared to Consumption (billions of 1971 dollars)

Scenario or policy	1975		1985		2000		2025	
	Level	% of con-sump-tion[a]	Level	% of con-sump-tion	Level	% of con-sump-tion	Level	% of con-sump-tion
Alternative scenarios, policy S								
DH	51	7.5	78	7.4	93	5.1	210	5.4
DL	51	7.5	67	7.1	80	5.3	177	5.8
FH	51	7.5	78	7.3	88	5.0	160	5.1
FL	51	7.5	68	7.0	76	5.0	133	5.1
DHNU	51	7.5	77	7.3	107	5.9	246	6.4
DHP1	51	7.5	77	7.4	89	5.0	200	5.2
DHP2	51	7.5	81	7.4	117	6.1	200	5.1
Alternative policies, scenario DH								
R	54	7.9	89	8.4	94	5.2	183	4.6
S	51	7.5	78	7.4	93	5.1	210	5.4
E	41	6.0	73	6.9	92	5.1	208	5.3
M	39	5.7	67	6.3	85	4.7	173	4.4

[a] Control and damage costs divided by total consumption times 100.

Table 7–20 displays pollution costs for alternative scenarios and for alternative control policies. The estimates of pollution costs as a percentage of total consumption are meant to indicate the extent to which pollution control and damage costs subtract from economic well-being. For any particular year, these percentages are fairly constant across alternative scenarios except for DHNU and DHP2, which have somewhat higher percentages in later years. In contrast, in the period from 1975 to 1995, the percentages vary among policies; they are much lower for policies S, E, and M than for R in scenario DH. It should be clear from this comparison that pollution control policy probably provides a much better lever on environmental quality, at least with respect to mass pollutants, than does policy directed toward changing economic and population growth rates.[18] Also, over time, the cost of strict, efficient, and cost-minimizing environmental controls added to that of environmental damages is less as a percentage of personal consumption than the present level of 7.9

[18] Other environmental impacts, such as land disturbed for mining and sites required for electric power plants, discussed in the next chapter, are probably more closely related to economic and population growth than to specific mitigating policies.

percent. Thus, in the future as controls rise above present level, total pollution costs would be relatively less burdensome.

Conclusions

If pollution policy develops over time as we think it might—somewhere between what we have called the relaxed and the strict cases—environmental damages resulting from the mass pollutants covered in this chapter are likely to remain the same or fall over time despite the growth in the economy and greater number of people at risk. They would rise somewhat if the relaxed policy were pursued while the economy grows at the most rapid of the rates considered, but they would fall under either the relaxed or the stringent policy if the rate of growth were lower. In all cases, after 1985 they fall over time on a per capita basis and as a percentage of consumption.

Pollution control costs, though never a large percentage of GNP, will increase over time relative to both population and economic growth in all scenarios. The net effect is that total costs (damage plus control costs) as a percentage of GNP or of consumption remain roughly the same or fall slowly over time. The result is similar for scenarios with high rates of population and economic growth and those with low rates of growth. Though the mass of pollutants to be treated differs significantly among scenarios, the appropriate level of controls to minimize total costs and the cost of control as a percentage of the GNP do not differ greatly. Clearly, control policy is central to achieving acceptable levels of environmental quality; indirect approaches that would alter population and economic growth can have little impact on their own.

The policies we have analyzed, and which we believe to be most likely, are based on uniform national emission standards. In fact, some regions will be "overcontrolled," while others could experience deterioration in environmental quality; and some industries will find the costs of meeting control regulations rising rapidly, while others are not seriously burdened. Differential standards for special regions and some means of easing the transition for especially hard-hit sectors and regions would be worthy of serious consideration.

A possible example of "overcontrol" in some regions may be regulations on CO and NO_x from transportation. Our analysis of these pollutants suggests that control levels may be set far above the point of minimum total cost for the nation as a whole. Such a policy could be justified as a means of reducing risks and insuring against unexpectedly large damages, but a more likely explanation in this case is that the uniform national controls have been set to be appropriate for the more vulnerable regions. This is not necessarily wrong given the administrative and political difficulties of applying region-specific standards, especially for nonstationary pollution sources, but the costs of regulating on the basis of the worst case are not small.

A possible example of "undercontrol," according to our analysis, is the regulation of SO_x from power plants and industries. In this case, we find that the relaxed policy implies a level of control that is well below one that would minimize total costs during the whole of our fifty-year time horizon and that the same is true for the strict policy during the first half of this period. This is an area in which evidence on both damage and control costs is very weak, however, and one in which large control costs for important industries justify substantial investments in acquiring better information.

The most serious problem posed by inadequate information is in the area of water pollution, particularly for those pollutants associated with sediment from nonpoint sources. If the damages from these pollutants are as small relative to those associated with point sources as our analysis indicates, this country should move quite soon to controls approaching the more stringent and costly BAT standards for point sources. But if other plausible values for certain parameters in our analysis prove to be correct, the whole thrust of policy should shift from point to nonpoint sources.

One way to cope with such uncertainties is to increase the level of controls beyond the point where total costs are at a minimum. At least that would reduce the risk that high levels of damages would ever be experienced. In the case of water pollution, for example, our analysis suggests that a 20 percent increase in total costs over the whole period might reduce from 0.6 to 0.3 the probability of ever experiencing damages as high as the 1975 level. A similar analysis of air pollution suggests that a cost increase of 6 percent would reduce this probability from 0.5 to 0.3. Economic analysis cannot determine whether such a tradeoff is socially desirable, but it can provide the data on which such judgments ought to be made. But the primary way to deal with such uncertainties is to acquire better information on damages and costs, and our analysis suggests that investing in better data could produce substantial gains in a number of specific areas.

Technical Note A: Comparisons with Other Studies

Base Year Emissions

Tables 7–21 and 7–22 compare the emission estimates of this study for 1975 with estimates from other studies. For air pollutant discharges, there is close agreement between this study's estimates and EPA estimates. In contrast, there are some large differences among the various estimates of water pollution emissions.

Two aggregates for water pollutant discharges are presented in table 7–22: emissions from electric utilities, industrial point sources, municipal waste water treatment plants, and urban runoff; and emissions from all other sources—agriculture, mining, and other nonpoint sources. For point sources and runoff, each of the studies compared used the same methodology to estimate discharges. For example, all three studies used estimates for urban runoff taken from a model developed by Heaney and coauthors (1977). A two-step procedure was followed to reach the estimates for point sources. First, pollutant discharge coefficients, based mainly upon data in EPA development documents, were estimated; then, they were multiplied by an estimate of output to obtain discharges. The estimates in this study used development documents issued prior to 1975; the DOE (Borko and coauthors, 1978) and Gianessi–Peskin (1978) estimates used more recent development documents. Because the data and coverage are sometimes sparse and uncertain, it was necessary to use some judgment in estimating pollutant coefficients and activity levels.

Considering the differences in base years, dates of data sources, and latitude in judgment, there is reasonable agreement among all the water pollution estimates except for dissolved solids. The discrepancy here arises from different interpretations of the same or similar data with the derived discharge coefficients being much lower for the DOE and this study. Also, fewer industries are covered in the DOE and this study's estimates.[19]

In the agriculture, mining, and other nonpoint source category, a substantial part of the difference between the estimates stems from using different data sources for sediment runoff from nonirrigated agriculture. This study used data from the Department of Agriculture (USDA, 1975) to obtain an estimate of 517 million tons of sediment discharged to water

---

[19] If we used the Gianessi–Peskin coefficients for dissolved solids, our benefit–cost analysis would swing toward higher controls for industrial point sources.

Table 7–21. Air Pollution Emission Estimates for 1975 (millions of tons)

Study	Particulate matter	Sulfur oxides	Nitrogen oxides	Hydro-carbons	Carbon monoxide
This study	23.9	37.4	18.4	20.6	86.9
EPA[a]	15.9	32.7	21.7	23.8	97.0

[a] U.S. Environmental Protection Agency, *1973 National Emissions Report* (1976).

Table 7–22. Water Pollution Emission Estimates for 1975

Pollutant and study	Point sources and urban runoff[a]	Agriculture, mining, and other nonpoint sources[b]
Biochemical oxygen demand (BOD)		
DOE[c]	3.2	—
This study	4.4	3.4
Gianessi and Peskin[d]	7.7	14.3
Suspended solids (SS)		
DOE	11.6	—
This study	17.1	535.5
Gianessi and Peskin	21.8	2,064.0
Dissolved solids (DS)		
DOE	11.7	—
This study	26.1	274.8
Gianessi and Peskin	118.9	946.4
Nutrients		
This study	1.6	4.3
Gianessi and Peskin	0.6	4.4
Other		
DOE	1.2	—
This study[e]	1.5	3.4
Gianessi and Peskin[f]	1.1	15.4

Note: — indicates emissions were not estimated.

[a] Includes emissions from electric utilities, industrial point sources, municipal waste water treatment plants, and urban runoff sources.

[b] Includes point emissions and sediment runoff from minerals, ore, and coal mining and milling, and acid mine drainage, and sediment runoff from nonurban construction forestry, and agriculture.

[c] Emissions as estimated by the Department of Energy's AEAR Model. Methods and data sources are provided in B. Borko, M. DeBolt, T. Piwowar, and B. Stokes, "Water Residuals Update for Non-Energy Sectors: Methodology and Data Book" (Mitre Working Paper WP-13026, 1978).

[d] L. P. Gianessi and H. M. Peskin, "Estimates of National Water Pollutant Discharges by Polluting Sector: 1972," app. B-1 (Washington, D.C., Resources for the Future, 1978). These estimates are for 1972 and include discharges from man-originated as well as natural sources. Their estimated discharges from natural sources are (in million tons): biochemical oxygen demand, 3.5; suspended solids, 522.0; dissolved solids, 231.0; nutrients, 1.1; other, 3.8.

These estimates should be subtracted from the agriculture, mining, and other non-point source estimates to obtain their estimate of man-originated discharges in that category. This allows their estimates to be directly compared with this study's estimates, which include only man-originated discharges. Gianessi's and Peskin's estimates from point sources and urban runoff are all of man-originated discharges.

[e] Includes emissions of acids, bases, oil, grease, pesticides, and heavy metals. The heavy metals included here are for ore, coal, and minerals mining; forestry; and nonurban construction. Heavy metals for other sources (including industrial point sources) are included in the suspended and dissolved solids estimates.

[f] Includes phosphorus and heavy metals.

from irrigated and nonirrigated agriculture in 1972. In contrast, Gianessi and Peskin used an estimate from a report prepared by the Midwest Research Institute (1975). That report estimated sediment delivered to water from nonirrigated agriculture as 1.8 billion tons. Gianessi and Peskin then applied fixed coefficients to this number to obtain estimates of various pollutant loadings from nonirrigated agriculture. As a point of comparison, Wade and Heady (1976) estimated that gross erosion from all agriculture, only a part of which gets into water, amounted to about 1.5 billion tons in the early 1970s. A recent estimate by the Soil Conserva-

Table 7–23. Estimated Total Pollution Control Expenditures, 1975–84 (billions of 1975 dollars)

Pollution type and source	1975		1984		1975–84	
	CEQ[a]	This study	CEQ[a]	This study	CEQ[a]	This study
Air pollution						
Public	0.2	—	0.8	—	6.0	—
Private						
Mobile	4.9	1.5	5.7	10.1	52.6	57.0
Industrial	4.5	2.0	10.5	5.1	74.3	40.7
Utilities	2.0	1.6	7.0	5.9	42.0	35.6
Fuel burning						
Commercial and in-						
stitutional air	—	0.4	—	0.6	—	5.2
(Subtotal)	(11.6)	(5.5)	(24.0)	(21.7)	(174.9)	(138.5)
Water pollution						
Public	10.1	8.5	21.6	19.1	157.9	139.2
Private						
Industrial	3.6	4.0	13.1	20.8	73.6	121.2
Utilities	1.0	0.3	2.2	1.4	16.8	7.8
(Subtotal)	(14.7)	(12.8)	(36.9)	(41.3)	(248.3)	(268.2)
Radiation						
Nuclear power plants	<0.05	0.06	<0.05	0.10	0.2	0.9
Solid waste	5.4	0.63	7.7	1.18	59.6	12.0
(Subtotal)	(5.4)	(0.69)	(7.7)	(1.28)	(59.8)	(12.9)
Land reclamation						
Surface mining	—	0.32	—	0.20	—	2.05
Noise	—	—	0.6	—	3.4	—
Electrical utilities/thermal	—	0.6	—	2.0	—	14.2
Total	31.7	19.9	69.2	66.9	486.4	435.9

Note: Estimated costs are the sum of annualized capital costs and operation and maintenance costs. The dash (—) indicates that the cost was not estimated.

[a] CEQ cost estimates are from Council on Environmental Quality, *Environmental Quality:* 1976 (Washington, D.C., GPO, 1976) p. 167.

Table 7–24. Estimated National Air Pollution Control Costs
(millions of 1975 dollars)

Source	Cumulative investment (1971–79)		Annualized costs (1979)	
	This study	EPA[a]	This study	EPA[a]
Mobile sources	15,056.8	28,906.9	5,277.4	9,234.9
Steam electric power	24,424.1	9,332.5	3,268.5	5,792.1
Commercial and industrial fuel burning	3,576.7	6,923.0	1,123.0	1,850.2
Fuel industries group	3,549.7	1,195.7	852.1	339.5
Chemical industries group	762.0	598.9	203.3	170.1
Metals industries group	5,973.5	5,215.4	1,458.4	1,903.6
Burning and incineration group	87.8	2,307.7	28.1	902.7
Quarrying and construction group	1,473.6	1,401.2	352.2	331.8
Food and forest products group	4,246.1	3,281.0	812.9	618.4
Total	59,150.3	59,162.3	13,375.9	21,143.3

[a] EPA cost estimates are from U.S. Environmental Protection Agency, *The Cost of Clean Air: Annual Report of the U.S. EPA to the Congress of the United States*, Document no. 93-122 (Washington, D.C., GPO, 1974) p. I-3. The EPA cost estimates, originally in 1973 dollars, have been adjusted to 1975 dollars using a price inflator of 1.251.

tion Service (USDA, 1978) places gross erosion from all agriculture at 2 billion tons in 1977.[20]

Pollution Control Costs

Table 7–23 compares aggregate cost estimates from this study with the estimates of the Council on Environmental Quality (1976). For each of the years, 1975 and 1984, there are notable differences between the two studies in pollution control costs, perhaps because the timing of control implementation differs. The cumulative expenditures during the 1975–84 period are in closer agreement, but even here this study has notably smaller air pollution expenditures and larger industrial water pollution expenditures.

Table 7–24 compares national air pollution control costs as estimated by EPA with those of this study. EPA has higher cumulative

[20] In our benefit–cost analyses, use of the larger estimates would increase the least-cost controls for nonpoint sources and leave minimum cost controls for point sources unaffected if damages for nonpoint sources only are adjusted upward.

Table 7–25. Capital Cost Estimates for Industry to Apply BPT and BAT Technology

(1973 production in millions of 1975 dollars)

Industry	BPT			BAT		
	NCWQ[a]	This study	NRDI[b]	NCWQ	This study	NRDI
Inorganic chemicals	520	361	564	247	411	147
Iron and steel	2,910	1,648	1,887	949	1,396	1,305
Organic chemicals[c]	4,450	12,732	3,046	3,926	12,471	2,355
Petroleum refining	1,050	947	673	1,180	893	1,286
Pulp and paper	2,640	870	1,831	798	1,015	643
Textiles	537	362	428	300	477	320
Fruits and vegetables	443	—	117	161	—	200
Fabricated metal[d]	14,628	4,080	296	14,113	3,299	74
Steam electric power	3,740	3,464	—	2,030	4,756	—
Feedlots	705	1,761	—	169	1,397	—
Food processing[e]	46	257	65	125	395	41
Leather tanning and fishing	120	14	89	73	19	17
Machinery and mechanical products	3,900	4,170	—	3,900	3,584	—
Water supply	1,200	—	—	100	—	—
Meat products and rendering	130	610	75	240	743	160
Dairy products	79	427	52	51	863	93
Grain mills	56	353	5	13	427	22
Cane sugar	153	10	36	170	9	40
Beet sugar	90	19	30	69	16	26
Building paper and board and paving and roofing materials	126	—	56	4	—	18
Fertilizer	64	—	118	60	—	95
Rubber processing	220	87	240	48	82	86
Nonferrous metals (bauxite, aluminum)	91	64	35	112	64	26
Glass, pottery, and related products	45	—	33	20	—	95
Cement, gypsum, and plaster	134	187	100	9	191	0
Asbestos	4	13	4	9	12	4
Fish hatcheries and farms	50	—	—	47	—	—
Timber products processing	14	—	—	25	—	—
Furniture and fixtures	8	—	—	0	—	—
Paint and ink formulation	23	—	—	0	—	—
Soap and detergent	10	—	—	2	—	—
Phosphate	73	—	—	14	—	—
Structural clay products	5	—	—	0	—	—
Insulation fiberglass	14	—	—	0	—	—
Laundries	25	—	—	21	—	—
(Subtotal)	(38,303)	(32,436)	(9,780)	(28,985)	(32,520)	(7,053)

(continued)

Table 7–25. (Continued)

Industry	BPT			BAT		
	NCWQ[a]	This study	NRDI[b]	NCWQ	This study	NRDI
Minerals extraction						
Ore mining and dressing	610	—	74	400	—	0
Coal mining	1,000	—	40	400	—	0
Petroleum and gas extraction	234	—	130	1,070	—	0
Minerals mining and processing	730	—	29	500	—	5
(Subtotal)	(2,574)		(273)	(2,370)		(5)
Total	40,877	32,436	10,053	31,355	32,520	7,058

Note: A dash (—) indicates that the cost was not estimated.

[a] NCWQ cost estimates are from National Commission on Water Quality, *Staff Report to the National Commission on Water Quality* (Washington, D.C., GPO, 1976a) p. II-82.

[b] NRDI cost estimates are from R. A. Luken, D. J. Basta, and E. H. Pechan, *The National Residuals Discharge Inventory* (Washington, D.C., National Research Council, 1976) pp. 67–68.

[c] Organic chemicals include plastics and synthetics and miscellaneous chemicals.

[d] Fabricated metal includes metal finishing, ferroalloy foundries, and nonferrous mill products.

[e] Food processing includes canned and preserved seafood and miscellaneous food and beverages.

investment estimates for mobile sources, commercial and industrial fuel burning, and incineration, and lower estimates for the other categories.

Table 7–25 compares water pollution control capital costs as estimated by the National Commission on Water Quality (1976b) and by the National Residuals Discharge Inventory system (Luken, Basta, and Pechan, 1976) with those of this study. Compared with this study, the National Commission on Water Quality (NCWQ) has much higher estimates for fabricated metals and much lower estimates for organic chemicals. The National Residuals Discharge Inventory, with a few exceptions, has substantially lower capital cost estimates than both the NCWQ's and this study's estimates.

Table 7–26 compares operation and maintenance costs from NCWQ with those of this study. This study has substantially higher estimates for iron and steel and substantially lower estimates for fabricated metals and steam electric power.

Table 7–26. Operation and Maintenance Costs to Achieve BPT Pretreatment and BAT Effluent Limitations

(1973 production in millions of 1975 dollars)

Industry	BPT		BAT	
	NCWQ[a]	This study	NCWQ	This study
Industries				
Inorganic chemicals	156	92	104	53
Iron and steel	229	1,679	64	841
Organic chemicals[b]	682	1,683	2,499	909
Petroleum refining	179	66	395	40
Pulp and paper	135	46	21	33
Textiles	88	50	29	31
Fruits and vegetables	39	—	16	—
Fabricated metal[c]	3,237	134	2,213	67
Steam electric power	1,420	15	260	10
Feedlots	43	60	1	30
Food processing[d]	13	25	13	22
Leather tanning and fishing	27	3	13	2
Machinery and mechanical products	390	314	390	157
Water supply	160	—	3	—
Meat products and rendering	13	54	14	37
Dairy products	6	30	3	39
Grain mills	4	4	1	2
Cane sugar	17	3	13	2
Beet sugar	17	2	5	1
Building paper and board, and paving and roofing materials	18	—	1	—
Fertilizer	36	—	16	—
Rubber processing	18	14	12	7
Nonferrous metals (bauxite, aluminum)	30	20	30	10
Glass, pottery, and related products	6	—	6	—
Cement, gypsum, and plaster	30	44	1	23
Asbestos	1	3	4	2
Fish hatcheries and farms	10	—	31	—
Timber products processing	1	—	8	—
Furniture and fixtures	3	—	0	—
Paint and ink formulation	22	—	2	—
Soap and detergent	1	—	0	—
Phosphate	9	—	1	—
Structural clay products	1	—	0	—
Insulation fiberglass	6	—	0	—
Laundries	4	—	1	—
(Subtotal)	(7,051)	(4,341)	(6,170)	(2,318)
Minerals extraction				
Ore mining and dressing	25	—	18	—
Coal mining	50	—	26	—
Petroleum and gas extraction	18	—	61	—
Minerals mining and processing	72	—	50	—
(Subtotal)	(165)		(155)	
Total	7,216	4,341	6,325	2,318

Table 7-27. Urban Runoff Generation and Runoff Control Costs, 1973 Conditions

Pollutant	This study	Luken
Runoff (millions of tons, before control)		
Biochemical oxygen demand (BOD)	0.35	1.6
Chemical oxygen demand (COD)	3.2	—
Suspended solids (SS)	5.8	30.0
Dissolved solids (DS)	3.8	—
Nutrients	0.07	—
Oil and grease	0.08	—
Runoff control capital costs (billion 1975$)	55 (85)[a]	126.2 (52)[a]

Note: — indicates residual not estimated.
Source: R. A. Luken, D. J. Basta, and E. H. Pechan, *The National Residuals Discharge Inventory* (Washington, D.C., National Research Council, 1976).
[a] Number in parentheses is the average removal efficiency at the indicated cost.

It is worth pointing out that the analyses of efficient pollutant controls in this study are done at the aggregate industrial level. Thus, errors for individual sectors can be averaged out when summing costs to obtain aggregate industrial control costs. However, any attempt to refine the analysis by disaggregating it would require reconciliation of the cost discrepancies noted in tables 7–23 through 7–26.

Urban Runoff and Runoff Control Costs

Estimates of urban runoff and runoff control costs have been made by Luken and coauthors (1976) and Heaney and coauthors (1977). This study used the latter to estimate urban runoff and runoff control costs. A comparison of estimates from Luken with those of this study is presented in table 7–27. It can be seen that this study's estimates are substantially lower.

For runoff generation, some of the discrepancy arises because the concentration of BOD and suspended solids in runoff in the Heaney study is much less than the concentrations used in Luken. The Heaney con-

---

Note: The dash (—) indicates that the cost was not estimated.
[a] NCWQ cost estimates are from National Commission on Water Quality, *Staff Report to the National Commission on Water Quality* (Washington, D.C., GPO, 1976a) p. II-82.
[b] Organic chemicals include plastics and synthetics.
[c] Fabricated metal includes metal finishing, ferroalloy foundries, and nonferrous mill products.
[d] Food processing includes canned and preserved seafood and miscellaneous food and beverages.

centrations are based on an empirical function that has gross population density as its explanatory variable. This function, which shows concentration increasing with population density, produces estimates of concentration that compare well with empirical data. The Luken concentrations are derived by averaging data for a number of cities (the precise number is not reported) and then applying these averages to all cities.

Another source of discrepancy between the two studies is their estimates of urban land acreages. The Heaney study appears to have fewer acres of urbanized land area, especially in the unsewered category. In contrast, more than 80 percent of residuals generation and runoff control costs in the Luken study are associated with unsewered areas. Luken and coauthors estimate land acreage by examining characteristics of counties and eliminating all counties not in SMSAs and all counties with a population density less than 0.6 persons per acre. This scheme could result in including counties with large parcels of undeveloped land, which satisfy the 0.6 persons per acre criterion because a small part of the county is densely populated, but which (except for their densely populated parts) are not really urbanized areas. In comparison, Heaney and coauthors regress the percentage of land undeveloped against gross population density for 106 cities (subject to the percentage undeveloped being 100 when population density is zero) and then use this relationship to determine the percentage of land undeveloped for all cities.

From these comparisons, it would seem that the Heaney study is somewhat more soundly based than the Luken study, and it was on the basis of this evaluation that the Heaney model was chosen to generate this study's runoff residuals and runoff control costs.

Technical Note B: Regional Pollution Damages

Regional air and water damages for alternative control policies are shown in figures 7–9 through 7–14.[21] Table 7–28 provides a list of Air Quality Control Regions that corresponds to the regions identified in figures 7–9 through 7–11; the aggregated subareas identified in figures 7–12 through 7–14 are listed in table 7–29. According to this study's estimates, most air pollution damages in 1975 occurred in the Northeast–Pennsylvania–Great Lakes industrial belt, along the Gulf Coast, in southern California, and in scattered metropolitan areas such as Saint Louis and Kansas City. Under control policies S and E, damages in these areas would fall by substantial amounts in the future.

In 1975, most water pollution damages, according to this study's estimates, were concentrated east of the Mississippi, principally in Florida, the middle Atlantic region, the Great Lakes region, the Ohio River basin and lower Mississippi River basin and also in the San Francisco Bay area, southern California, and the Houston–Galveston bay area. Damages in these areas would remain more or less constant in future years under policy S.[22] Policies R, and M in later years, would allow damage to rise somewhat.

---

[21] Base year estimates and forecasts of regional emissions and concentrations are available from the authors.

[22] For water pollution, control policies S and E are nearly identical.

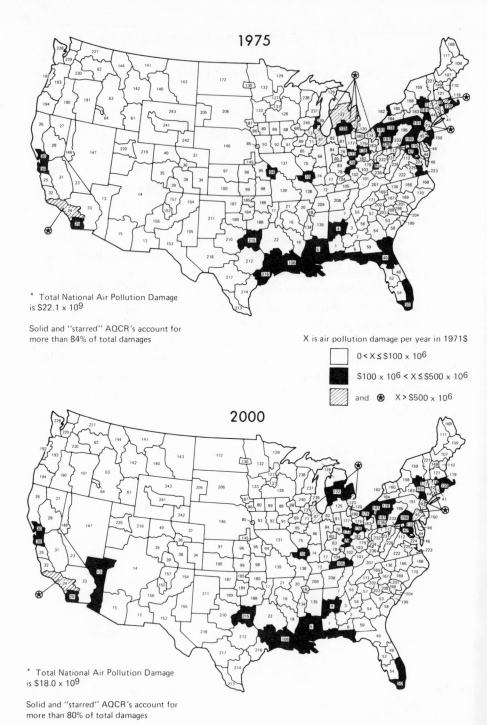

1975

* Total National Air Pollution Damage
is $22.1 x 10^9

Solid and "starred" AQCR's account for
more than 84% of total damages

X is air pollution damage per year in 1971$

$0 < X \leq \$100 \times 10^6$

$\$100 \times 10^6 < X \leq \$500 \times 10^6$

and ✹ $X > \$500 \times 10^6$

2000

* Total National Air Pollution Damage
is $18.0 x 10^9

Solid and "starred" AQCR's account for
more than 80% of total damages

Figure 7–9. Regional air pollution damages under relaxed enforcement,
Scenario DH.

308

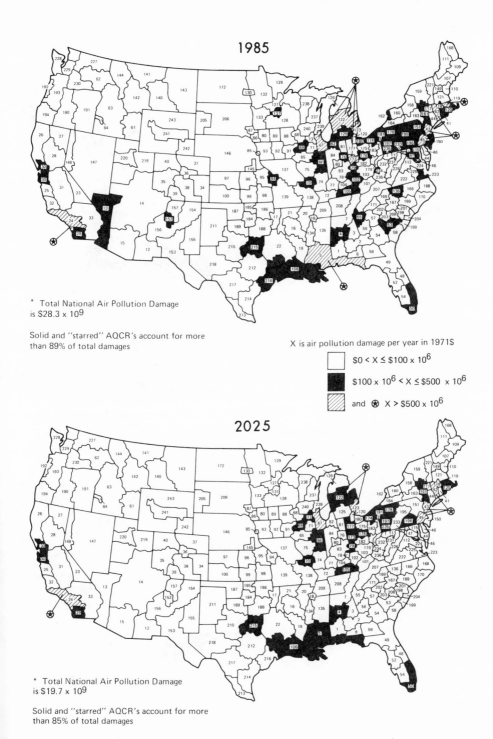

1985

* Total National Air Pollution Damage
is \$28.3 x 10^9

Solid and "starred" AQCR's account for more
than 89% of total damages

X is air pollution damage per year in 1971\$

$\$0 < X \le \$100 \times 10^6$

$\$100 \times 10^6 < X \le \$500 \times 10^6$

and ⊛ $X > \$500 \times 10^6$

2025

* Total National Air Pollution Damage
is \$19.7 x 10^9

Solid and "starred" AQCR's account for more
than 85% of total damages

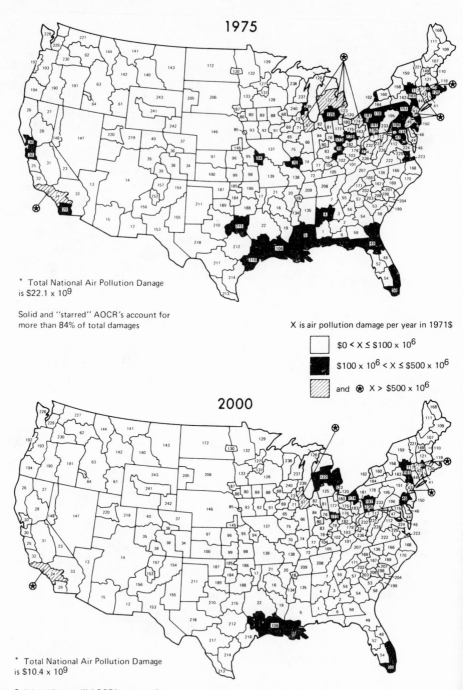

1975

* Total National Air Pollution Danage
is $22.1 × 10^9

Solid and "starred" AOCR's account for
more than 84% of total damages

X is air pollution damage per year in 1971$

$0 < X \leq $100 × 10^6

$100 × 10^6 < X \leq $500 × 10^6

and ⊛ X > $500 × 10^6

2000

* Total National Air Pollution Damage
is $10.4 × 10^9

Solid and "starred" AOCR's account for
more than 79% of total damages

Figure 7–10.   Regional air pollution damages under strict enforcement,
Scenario DH.

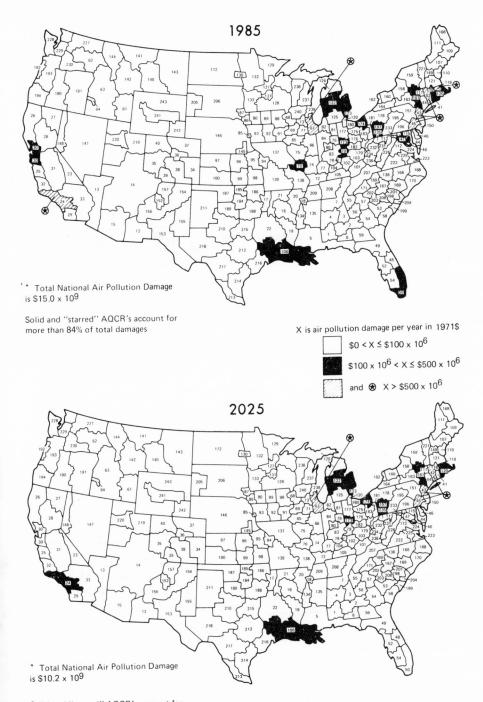

1985

'* Total National Air Pollution Damage
is 15.0×10^9

Solid and "starred" AQCR's account for
more than 84% of total damages

X is air pollution damage per year in 1971$

$0 < X \le 100×10^6

$100 \times 10^6 < X \le 500×10^6

and ⊛ X > 500×10^6

2025

* Total National Air Pollution Damage
is 10.2×10^9

Solid and "starred" AQCR's account for
more than 81% of total damages

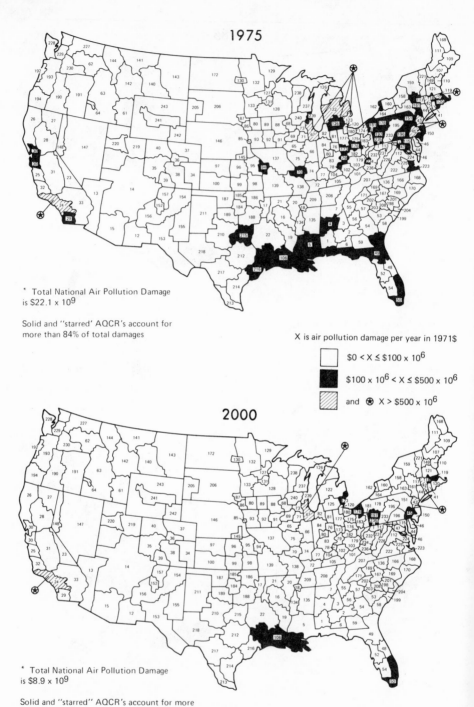

1975

* Total National Air Pollution Damage is 22.1×10^9

Solid and "starred" AQCR's account for more than 84% of total damages

X is air pollution damage per year in 1971$

☐ $0 < X \leq \$100 \times 10^6$

■ $\$100 \times 10^6 < X \leq \$500 \times 10^6$

▨ and ⊛ $X > \$500 \times 10^6$

2000

* Total National Air Pollution Damage is 8.9×10^9

Solid and "starred" AQCR's account for more than 78% of total damages

Figure 7–11. Regional air pollution damages under efficient enforcement, Scenario DH.

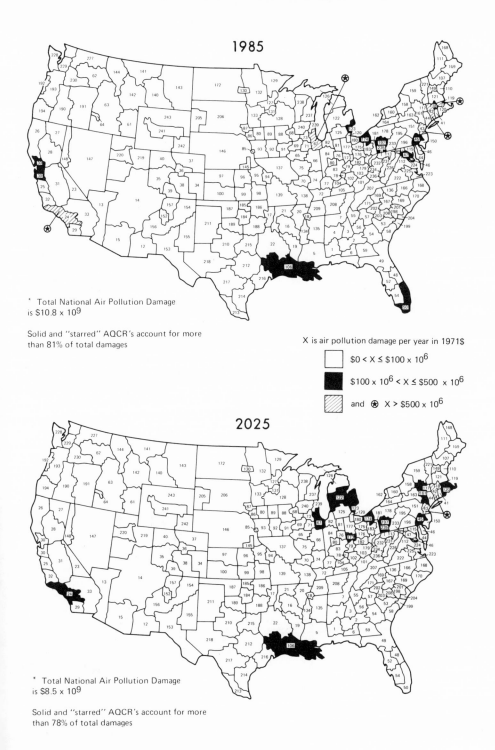

1985

* Total National Air Pollution Damage
is 10.8×10^9

Solid and "starred" AQCR's account for more
than 81% of total damages

X is air pollution damage per year in 1971$

☐ $0 < X \leq \$100 \times 10^6$

■ $\$100 \times 10^6 < X \leq \$500 \times 10^6$

▨ and ⊛ $X > \$500 \times 10^6$

2025

* Total National Air Pollution Damage
is 8.5×10^9

Solid and "starred" AQCR's account for more
than 78% of total damages

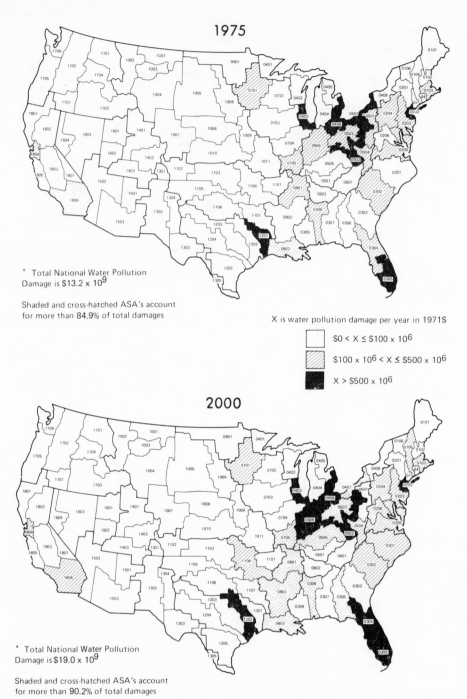

1975

* Total National Water Pollution
Damage is $13.2 x 10^9$

Shaded and cross-hatched ASA's account
for more than 84.9% of total damages

X is water pollution damage per year in 1971S

$0 < X \leq 100×10^6

$100 \times 10^6 < X \leq 500×10^6

$X > 500×10^6

2000

* Total National Water Pollution
Damage is $19.0 x 10^9$

Shaded and cross-hatched ASA's account
for more than 90.2% of total damages

Figure 7–12.   Regional water pollution damages under relaxed enforcement,
Scenario DH.

314

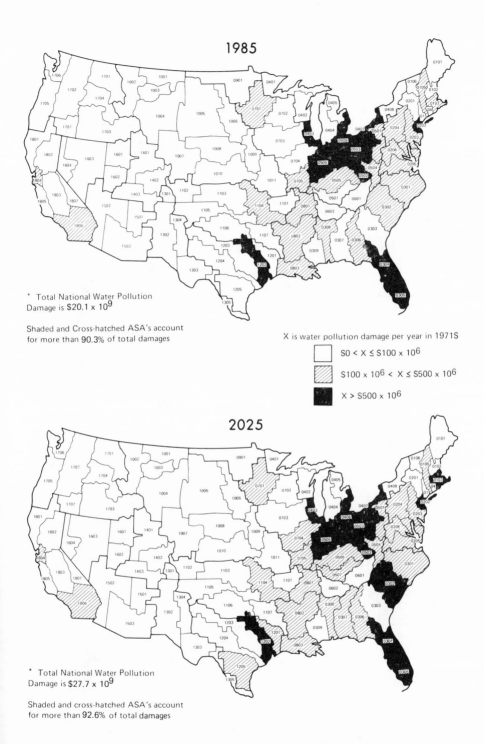

1985

* Total National Water Pollution
Damage is 20.1×10^9

Shaded and Cross-hatched ASA's account
for more than **90.3%** of total damages

X is water pollution damage per year in 1971$

$0 < X \leq \$100 \times 10^6$

$\$100 \times 10^6 < X \leq \$500 \times 10^6$

$X > \$500 \times 10^6$

2025

* Total National Water Pollution
Damage is 27.7×10^9

Shaded and cross-hatched ASA's account
for more than **92.6%** of total damages

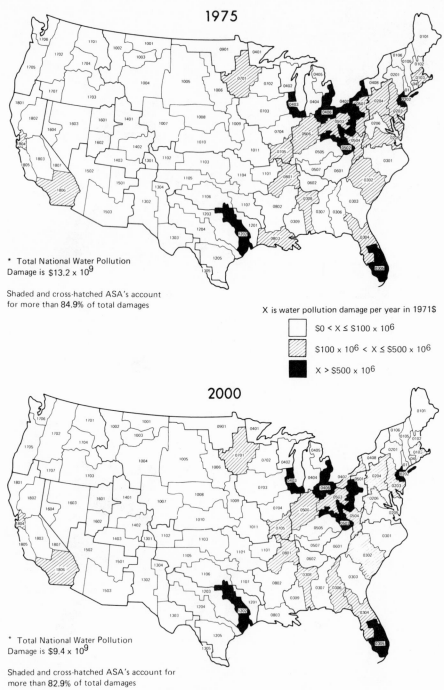

1975

* Total National Water Pollution
Damage is $13.2 x 10^9$

Shaded and cross-hatched ASA's account
for more than 84.9% of total damages

X is water pollution damage per year in 1971$

$\$0 < X \le \$100 \times 10^6$

$\$100 \times 10^6 < X \le \$500 \times 10^6$

$X > \$500 \times 10^6$

2000

* Total National Water Pollution
Damage is $9.4 x 10^9$

Shaded and cross-hatched ASA's account for
more than 82.9% of total damages

Figure 7–13. Regional water pollution damages under strict enforcement,
Scenario DH.

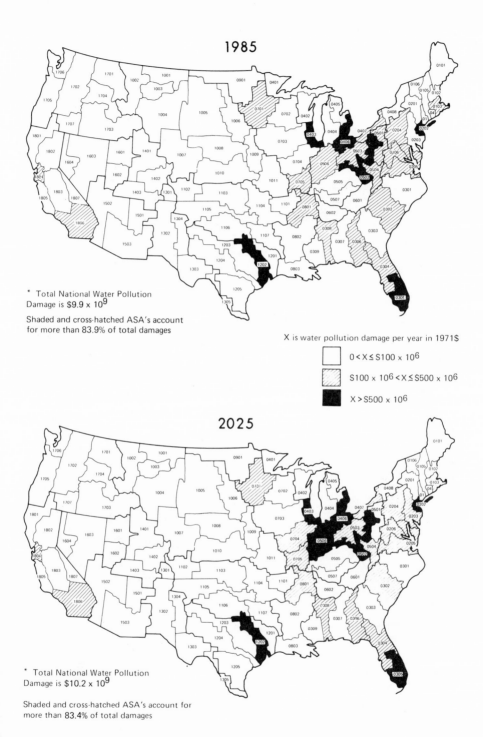

1985

* Total National Water Pollution Damage is 9.9×10^9

Shaded and cross-hatched ASA's account for more than 83.9% of total damages

X is water pollution damage per year in 1971$

$0 < X \leq \$100 \times 10^6$

$\$100 \times 10^6 < X \leq \$500 \times 10^6$

$X > \$500 \times 10^6$

2025

* Total National Water Pollution Damage is 10.2×10^9

Shaded and cross-hatched ASA's account for more than 83.4% of total damages

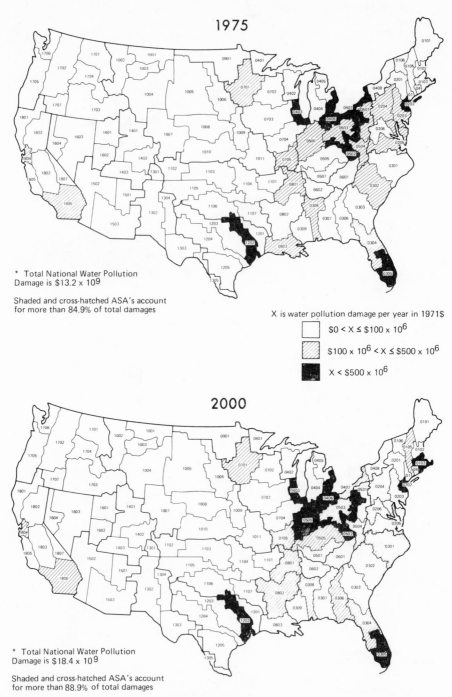

Figure 7–14. Regional water pollution damages under cost-minimizing enforcement, Scenario DH.

318

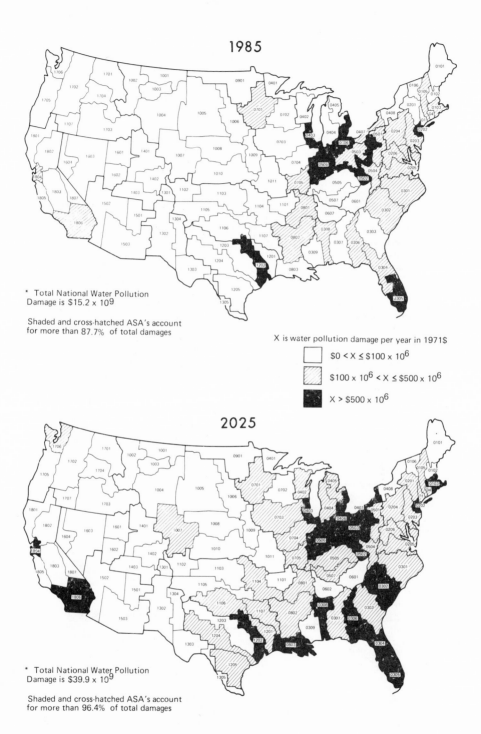

1985

* Total National Water Pollution
  Damage is 15.2×10^9

Shaded and cross-hatched ASA's account
for more than 87.7% of total damages

X is water pollution damage per year in 1971$

$0 < X \leq 100×10^6

$100 \times 10^6 < X \leq 500×10^6

$X > 500×10^6

2025

* Total National Water Pollution
  Damage is 39.9×10^9

Shaded and cross-hatched ASA's account
for more than 96.4% of total damages

319

Table 7–28. Air Quality Control Regions

No.	Name	No.	Name
1	Alabama and Tombigbee rivers	53	Augusta–Aiken
2	Columbus, Ga.–Phenix City, Ala.	54	Central Georgia
3	East Alabama	55	Chattanooga
4	Metropolitan Birmingham	56	Metropolitan Atlanta
5	Mobile, Ala.–Pensacola, Fla.–	57	Northeast Georgia
	S. Miss.	57	Savannah–Beaufort
6	Southeast Alabama	59	Southwest Georgia
7	Tenn. River Valley, Ala.–	60	Hawaii
	Cumberland Mountains, Tenn.	61	Eastern Idaho
8	Kenai–Cook Inlet	62	East Washington–North Idaho
9	Northern Alaska	63	Idaho
10	South Central Alaska	64	Metropolitan Boise
11	Southeastern Alaska	65	Burlington–Keokuk
12	Arizona–New Mexico S. Border	66	East Central Illinois
13	Clark–Mohave	67	Metropolitan Chicago
14	Four Corners	68	Metropolitan Dubuque
15	Phoenix–Tucson	69	Metropolitan Quad Cities
16	Central Arkansas	70	Metropolitan Saint Louis
17	Metropolitan Fort Smith	71	North Central Illinois
18	Metropolitan Memphis	72	Paducah–Cairo
19	Monroe–El Dorado	73	Rockville–Jamesville–Beloit
20	Northeast Arkansas	74	Southeast Illinois
21	Northwest Arkansas	75	West Central Illinois
22	Shreveport–Texarkana–Tyler	76	East Central Indiana
23	Great Basins valleys	77	Evansville–Owensboro–Henderson
24	Metropolitan Los Angeles	78	Louisville
25	North Central Coast	79	Metropolitan Cincinnati
26	North Coast	80	Metropolitan Indianapolis
27	Northeast Plateau	81	Northeast Indiana
28	Sacramento Valley	82	South Bend–Elkhart–Benton
29	San Diego		Harbor
30	San Francisco Bay Area	83	Southern Indiana
31	San Joaquin Valley	84	Wabash Valley
32	South Central	85	Metropolitan Omaha–Council
33	Southeast Desert		Bluffs
34	Comanchee	86	Metropolitan Sioux City
35	Grand Mesa	87	Metropolitan Sioux Falls
36	Metropolitan Denver	88	Northeast Iowa
37	Pawnee	89	North Central Iowa
38	San Isabel	90	Northwest Iowa
39	San Luis	91	Southeast Iowa
40	Yampa	92	South Central Iowa
41	Eastern Connecticut	93	Southeast Iowa
42	Hartford–New Haven–Springfield	94	Metropolitan Kansas City
43	New Jersey–New York–Conn.	95	Northeast Kansas
44	Northwestern Connecticut	96	North Central Kansas
45	Metropolitan Philadelphia	97	Northwest Kansas
46	Southern Delaware	98	Southeast Kansas
47	National Capital	99	South Central Kansas
48	Central Florida	100	Southwest Kansas
49	Jacksonville–Brunswick	101	Appalachian
50	Southeast Florida	102	Bluegrass
51	Southwest Florida	103	Huntington–Ashland–Portsmouth
52	West Central Florida	104	North Central Kentucky

(continued)

Table 7–28 (continued)

No.	Name	No.	Name
105	South Central Kentucky	156	Southwestern Mountains–
106	Southern Louisiana–Southeastern		Augustine Plain
	Texas	157	Upper Rio Grande Valley
107	Androscoggin Valley	158	Central New York
108	Aroostook	159	Champlain Valley
109	Downeast	160	Genesee–Finger Lakes
110	Metropolitan Portland	161	Hudson Valley
111	Northwest Maine	162	Niagara Frontier
112	Central Maryland	163	Southern Tier East
113	Cumberland–Keyser	164	Southern Tier West
114	Eastern Shore	165	Eastern Mountain
115	Metropolitan Baltimore	166	Eastern Piedmont
116	Southern Maryland	167	Metropolitan Charlotte
117	Berkshire	168	Northern Coastal Plain
118	Central Massachusetts	169	Sandhills
119	Metropolitan Boston	170	Southern Coastal Plain
120	Metropolitan Providence	171	Western Mountain
121	Merrimack Valley–Southern	172	North Dakota
	New Hampshire	173	Dayton
122	Central Michigan	174	Greater Metropolitan Cleveland
123	Metropolitan Detroit	175	Mansfield–Marion
124	Metropolitan Toledo	176	Metropolitan Columbus
125	South Central Michigan	177	Northwest Ohio
126	Upper Michigan	178	Northwest Pennsylvania–
127	Central Minnesota		Youngstown
128	Southeast Minnesota	179	Parkersburg–Marietta
129	Duluth–Superior	180	Sandusky
130	Metropolitan Fargo–Moorhead	181	Steubenville–Weirton–Wheeling
131	Minneapolis–Saint Paul	182	Wilmington–Chillicothe–Logan
132	Northwest Minnesota	183	Zanesville–Cambridge
133	Southwest Minnesota	184	Central Oklahoma
134	Mississippi Delta	185	North Central Oklahoma
135	Northeast Mississippi	186	Northeastern Oklahoma
136	Northern Piedmont	187	Northwestern Oklahoma
137	Northern Missouri	188	Southeastern Oklahoma
138	Southeast Missouri	189	Southwestern Oklahoma
139	Southwest Missouri	190	Central Oregon
140	Billings	191	Eastern Oregon
141	Great Falls	192	Northwestern Oregon
142	Helena	193	Portland
143	Miles City	194	Southwest Oregon
144	Missoula	195	Central Pennsylvania
145	Lincoln–Beatrice–Fairbury	196	South Central Pennsylvania
146	Nebraska	197	Southwest Pennsylvania
147	Nevada	198	Camden–Sumter
148	Northwest Nevada	199	Charleston
149	Central New Hampshire	200	Columbia
150	New Jersey	201	Florence
151	Northeastern Pennsylvania–	202	Greenville–Spartanburg
	Upper Delaware Valley	203	Greenwood
152	Albuquerque–Mid Rio Grande	204	Georgetown
153	El Paso–Las Cruces–Alamagordo	205	Black Hills–Rapid City
154	Northeastern Plains	206	South Dakota
155	Pecos–Permian Basin	207	Tennessee–Southwestern Virginia

(continued)

Table 7–28 (continued)

No.	Name	No.	Name
208	Middle Tennessee	226	Valley of Virginia
209	Western Tennessee	227	Northern Washington
210	Abilene–Wichita Falls	228	Olympic Northwest Washington
211	Amarillo–Lubbock	229	Puget Sound
212	Austin–Waco	230	South Central Washington
213	Brownsville–Laredo	231	Allegheny
214	Corpus Christi–Victoria	232	Central West Virginia
215	Metropolitan Dallas–Forth Worth	233	Eastern Panhandle
216	Metropolitan Houston–Galveston	234	Kanawha Valley
217	Metropolitan San Antonio	235	North Central West Virginia
218	Midland Odessa	236	Southern West Virginia
219	Utah	237	Lake Michigan
220	Wasatch Front	238	North Central Wisconsin
221	Vermont	239	Southeastern Wisconsin
222	Central Virginia	240	Southern Wisconsin
223	Hampton Roads	241	Casper
224	Northeastern Virginia	242	Metropolitan Cheyenne
225	State Capitol	243	Wyoming

Table 7–29. Aggregated Subareas

No.	Subarea	No.	Subarea
	New England Region (1)	0402	NW Lake Michigan
0101	Northern Maine	0403	SW Lake Michigan
0102	Saco–Merrimack	0404	Eastern Lake Michigan
0103	Massachusetts–Rhode Island Coastal	0405	Lake Huron
		0406	St. Clair–Western Lake Erie
0104	Housatonic–Thames	0407	Eastern Lake Erie
0105	Connecticut River	0408	Lake Ontario
0106	Richelieu		Ohio Region (5)
	Mid Atlantic Region (2)	0501	Ohio Headwaters
0201	Upper Hudson	0502	Upper Ohio–Big Sandy
0202	Lower Hudson–Long Island–North New Jersey	0503	Muskingum–Scioto–Miami
		0504	Kanawha
0203	Delaware	0505	Kentucky–Licking–Green–Ohio
0204	Susquehanna	0506	Wabash
0205	Upper and Lower Chesapeake	0507	Cumberland
0206	Potomac		Tennessee Region (6)
	South Atlantic–Gulf Region (3)	0601	Upper Tennessee
0301	Roanoke–Cape Fear	0602	Lower Tennessee
0302	Pee Dee–Edisto		Upper Mississippi Region (7)
0303	Savannah–St. Marys	0701	Mississippi Headwaters
0304	St. Johns–Suwannee	0702	Black–Root–Chippewa–Wisconsin
0305	Southern Florida		
0306	Apalachicola	0703	Rock–Mississippi–Des Moines
0307	Alabama–Choctawhatchee	0704	Salt–Sny–Illinois
0308	Mobile–Tombigbee	0705	Lower Upper Mississippi
0309	Pascagoula–Pearl		Lower Mississippi Region (8)
	Great Lakes Region (4)	0801	Hatchie–Mississippi–St. Francis
0401	Lake Superior	0802	Yazoo–Mississippi–Ouachita

(continued)

Table 7-29 (continued)

No.	Subarea	No.	Subarea
0803	Mississippi Delta	1303	Rio Grande–Pecos
	Souris–Red–Rainy Region (9)	1304	Upper Pecos
0901	Souris–Red–Rainy	1305	Lower Rio Grande
	Missouri Region (10)		Upper Colorado Region (14)
1001	Missouri–Milk–Saskatchewan	1401	Green–White–Yampa
1002	Missouri–Marias	1402	Colorado–Gunnison
1003	Missouri–Musselshell	1403	Colorado–San Juan
1004	Yellowstone		Lower Colorado Region (15)
1005	Western Dakotas	1501	Little Colorado
1006	Eastern Dakotas	1502	Lower Colorado Main Stem
1007	North and South Platte	1503	Gila
1008	Niobrara–Platte–Loup		Great Basin Region (16)
1009	Middle Missouri	1601	Bear–Great Salt Lake
1010	Kansas	1602	Sevier Lake
1011	Lower Missouri	1603	Humboldt–Tonopah Desert
	Arkansas–White–Red Region (11)	1604	Central Lahontan
1101	Upper White		Pacific Northwest Region (17)
1102	Upper Arkansas	1701	Clark Fork–Kootenai
1103	Arkansas–Cimarron	1702	Upper/Middle Columbia
1104	Lower Arkansas	1703	Upper/Central Snake
1105	Canadian	1704	Lower Snake
1106	Red–Washita	1705	Coast–Lower Columbia
1107	Red–Sulphur	1706	Puget Sound
	Texas–Gulf Region (12)	1707	Oregon Closed Basin
1201	Sabine–Neches		California Region (18)
1202	Trinity–Galveston Bay	1801	Klamath–North Coastal
1203	Brazos	1802	Sacramento–Lahontan
1204	Colorado (Texas)	1803	San Joaquin–Tulare
1205	Nueces–Texas Coastal	1804	San Francisco Bay
	Rio Grande Region (13)	1805	Central California Coast
1301	Rio Grande Headwaters	1806	Southern California
1302	Middle Rio Grande	1807	Lahontan–South

Source: U.S. Water Resources Council, *The Nation's Water Resources: 1975–2000,* vol. 3:*Analytical Data Summary, Second National Water Assessment by the U.S. Water Resources Council* (Washington, D.C., 1979).

References

Borko, B., M. DeBolt, T. Piwowar, and B. Stokes. 1978. "Water Residuals Update for Non-Energy Sectors: Methodology and Data Book," Mitre Working Paper WP-13026 (McLean, Va.).

CEQ. See Council on Environmental Quality.

Cooper, B. S., and D. P. Rice. 1976. "The Economic Cost of Illness Revisited," *Social Security Bulletin* DHEW publication no. (SSA) 76-11703 (Washington, D.C., GPO).

Council on Environmental Quality (CEQ). 1976. *Environmental Quality: 1976* (Washington, D.C., GPO).

EPA. See U.S. Environmental Protection Agency.

Gianessi, L. P., and H. M. Peskin. 1978. "Estimates of National Water Pollutant Discharges by Polluting Sector: 1972" (Washington, D.C., Resources for the Future) app. B-1.

————, ————, and E. Wolff. 1977. "The Distributional Implications of National Air Pollution Damage Estimates." Discussion paper D-5 (Washington, D.C., Resources for the Future).

Heaney, J. P., W. C. Huber, M. A. Medina, Jr., M. P. Murphy, S. J. Nix, and S. M. Hasan. 1977. *National Evaluation of Combined Sewer Overflows and Urban Stormwater Discharges* EPA-600/2-77-064 (Cincinnati, Ohio, EPA).

Heintz, H. T., Jr., A. Hershaft, and G. C. Horak. 1976. *National Damages of Air and Water Pollution.* Report to the U.S. Environmental Protection Agency (Rockville, Md., Environmental Control, Inc.).

Luken, R. A., D. J. Basta, and E. H. Pechan. 1976. *The National Residuals Discharge Inventory* (Washington, D.C., National Research Council).

Midwest Research Institute. 1975. *Cost and Effectiveness of Control of Pollution from Selected Non-Point Sources* (Kansas City, Mo., Midwest Research Institute).

National Commission on Water Quality (NCWQ). 1976a. *Staff Report to the National Commission on Water Quality* (Washington, D.C., GPO).

————. 1976b. *Report to the Congress by the National Commission on Water Quality* (March 18, 1976) (Washington, D.C., GPO).

Thaler, R., and S. Rosen. 1973. "The Value of Saving a Life: Evidence from the Labor Market." Paper presented at the National Bureau of Economic Research Conference, Washington, D.C., Nov. 30, 1973.

Truitt, J. B., A. C. Johnson, W. D. Rowe, K. D. Feigner, and L. J. Manning. 1975. "Development of Water Quality Management Indices," *Water Resources Bulletin* vol. 11, no. 3 (June).

U.S. Department of Agriculture (USDA). 1975. *Control of Water Pollution from Cropland* vol. I (Washington, D.C., USDA Agricultural Research Service).

————. 1978. "1977 SCS National Erosion Inventory Estimates" (December) (Washington, D.C., USDA Soil Conservation Service).

U.S. Environmental Protection Agency (EPA). 1974. *The Cost of Clean Air: Annual Report of the U.S. EPA to the Congress of the United States* document no. 93-122 (Washington, D.C., GPO).

————. 1973. *National Emissions Report* (Research Triangle Park, N.C., EPA).

Wade, J. C., and E. O. Heady. 1976. *A National Model of Sediment and Water Quality: Various Impacts on American Agriculture* CARD report 67 (Ames, Iowa, Center for Agricultural and Rural Development, Iowa State University).

Waddell, T. E. 1974. *The Economic Damages of Air Pollution* EPA-600/5-74-012 (Washington, D.C., EPA).

Water Resources Council (WRC). 1974a. *1972 OBERS Projections, Regional Economic Activity in the U.S. Air Quality Control Regions* (Washington, D.C., USDA Economic Research Service).

————. 1974b. *1972 OBERS Projections, Regional Economic Activity in the U.S.: Aggregated Subareas* (Washington, D.C., USDA Economic Research Service).

8

Other Environmental
Concerns

The last chapter was concerned with calculating an economically efficient level of control for several of the important and most common pollutants of air and water. Effective control of those pollutants cannot assure a clean and safe environment, however. Other, often more complex, factors may have a larger impact on environmental quality than the mass pollutants. Ideally, one should perform the same kind of benefit–cost analysis for every residual, separately and in combination, but the huge body of data necessary for such detailed analysis does not exist and will not exist in the near future. It is clear, however, that in spite of our ignorance, there are many environmental issues that must be resolved in the next fifty years because the consequences of ignoring them could be serious. This chapter will describe the present state of knowledge about the more critical of these issues and, where possible, will characterize their scale, severity, reversibility, and cost of control.

Future actions to alleviate burdens on the environment should concentrate on the most critical problems, but the number and variety of environmental threats seem to be unlimited. It is possible to classify these issues in several useful ways. The geographic extent of an environmental disturbance affects our perception of its severity. The effects of the pollutants discussed in chapter 7 usually are limited to individual watersheds or airsheds, but some other problems, notably climate modification, will have international or global effects. The duration of environmental impacts also ranges widely, from a few minutes for noise pollution from airplanes to the many thousands of years for the damaging radiation produced by even brief operation of a nuclear power plant.

It is also helpful to think of environmental problems in terms of the gravity of their consequences in order to judge how urgent it is to solve them. At the lowest level of urgency are losses of amenity caused by such annoyances as congestion of recreational facilities. Disruptions of this kind are increasingly common and contribute a great deal to the general impression that the quality of life is deteriorating. Far more serious are the pollutants that affect human health. Many of the common air and water pollutants discussed in chapter 7 are in this category. More menacing yet are those pollutants that cause genetic damage. These threaten not only the health of individuals but also the health of the human species. The many carcinogenic and mutagenic chemicals found in water supplies are particularly worrisome in this regard. The worst environmental destruction imaginable would be a large-scale failure of the natural life support systems of the earth, which might conceivably be triggered by extreme changes in ecological and atmospheric systems. Avoiding such disasters is obviously of the highest urgency, although the likelihood of their occurrence is not known.

Additional important characteristics of environmental impacts are their reversibility and predictability. Many pollutants, if not released in exceptionally large quantities, are absorbed and assimilated by the environment. Other residuals, such as junked autos, may accumulate but be retrievable at some later time, usually at large cost. Some cumulative pollutants may cause such complex and little known permanent changes in natural systems that eventual consequences are unpredictable. For example, our ignorance of the complex workings of the atmosphere is so great that we cannot predict with any certainty the future climate changes natural causes will bring, and we are even less able to predict changes caused by pollution. Only extensive research can explain the effects of our past and future actions, but the consequences of those actions may be seen long before they are understood. Many environmental problems must be dealt with before they are completely understood in order to avoid the possibility of irreversible changes to natural systems.

The first section of this chapter discusses the availability of land to support population and economic growth and the amount of land that will be degraded by waste disposal, excessive erosion, and extraction of minerals. The next section calculates the increasing demands that will be made on already strained water resources and the possibility that continued use of water as a medium for disposal of a wide variety of wastes will further diminish its quality. From these problems, which are essentially regional in impact, we turn to global issues, many of which are associated with energy production and use. The third section discusses the possibility that burning fossil fuels may alter the characteristics of the atmosphere enough to modify future climates. Thereafter, we discuss the practical and ethical issues associated with the nuclear fuel cycle. The chapter concludes with a brief evaluation of the implications of these diverse environmental issues for national growth.

Land Resources

Although the United States is a relatively land-rich country, growth in population and GNP in the next fifty years will place increasing demands on this finite resource. In 1975 this country had 10.8 acres of land per capita (9.1 acres excluding Alaska and Hawaii). By 2025 there may be only 6.2 to 8.5 acres per capita (5.2 to 7.2 acres per capita excluding Alaska and Hawaii), depending on which population series is assumed. Although these figures represent a significant change, they remain large in comparison to present ratios for some other areas; for example, in 1975, Europe had 2.6 acres of land per capita and Japan only 0.8 acres per capita. Although we will not even approach such high population densities by 2025, some problems of land adequacy may arise because of the large variations in climate, topography, and population density across the country.

Although land use problems are usually local, some may have more general consequences; in particular, the growth of cities may devour cropland and recreational land. The simple national projections of land use shown in table 8–1 address this issue. Built-up areas, such as cities, roads, and airports, are assumed in the table to grow in proportion to population growth.[1] Although this area almost doubles by 2025 in scenario DH, it is still only 6.3 percent of the area of the conterminous states. Thus the feeling that land will be paved over in alarming amounts seems to be unfounded. The countryside will become more difficult to reach as cities expand, but rising personal incomes and leisure time should ensure its accessibility to most people.

---

[1] During the period 1959–69, growth in this land use category was about 20 percent slower than population growth (USDA, 1973). Urban land use grew more than twice as fast as population in the same period, reaching a level where it was half of all the built-up area, but land used for transportation, farmsteads, and farm roads fell slightly.

Table 8-1. Major Uses of Land, Alternative Scenarios
(millions of acres)

Land use	1969	1985 EL	1985 DH	2000 EL	2000 DH	2025 EL	2025 DH
Built-up areas[a]	70	80	82	89	95	100	120
Public facilities[b]	27	27	27	27	27	27	27
Cropland	472	472	484	472	519	472	555
Used for crops[c]	(333)	(339)	(376)	(345)	(411)	(353)	(447)
Idle[d]	(51)	(45)	(20)	(39)	(20)	(31)	(20)
Used for pasture	(88)	(88)	(88)	(88)	(88)	(88)	(88)
Range and grassland	604	599	589	590	553	580	506
Forests[e]	723	716	710	709	688	700	654
Designated recreation land[f]	81	94	98	106	114	121	147
Other land[g]	287	276	274	271	268	264	255
Total	2,264	2,264	2,264	2,264	2,264	2,264	2,264
(Conterminous states)	(1,897)	(1,897)	(1,897)	(1,897)	(1,897)	(1,897)	(1,897)
Total acres per capita	11.2	9.6	9.3	8.6	7.9	7.5	6.2
(Conterminous states)	9.3	8.0	7.8	7.2	6.6	6.2	5.2

Source: 1969 data from U.S. Department of Agriculture, Economic Research Service, *Major Uses of Land in the United States: Summary for 1969* (Washington, D.C., GPO, 1973).

[a] Includes urban areas, highways, railroads, airports, farmsteads, and farm roads. Projected increases are proportional to population increases. New areas are assumed to come from cropland and grassland.

[b] Includes military bases, federal industrial land, and state institutions.

[c] Projections of harvested cropland from table 6–7 plus 35 million acres for crop failure and cultivated summer fallow. Harvested cropland amounted to 286 million acres in 1969, including 10 million acres of new irrigated land in 2025, taken from the category called other land.

[d] Includes soil improvement crops and abandoned cropland.

[e] May be used for grazing, lumber production, recreation, or watershed management.

[f] Includes state and federal parks, wildlife refuges, and wilderness areas. Projected increases are proportional to population increases. New areas are taken from forests and other land.

[g] Includes marshes, sand dunes, bare rock, deserts, and tundra.

Currently available cropland appears adequate to meet the needs of the base-case population through 2025. In contrast, scenario DH, with its higher population growth rate and higher agricultural exports, may require 83 million acres of new cropland by 2025. Although there is certainly ample forest and grassland of reasonably high potential productivity available for conversion to cropland, preparation of new lands for cultivation can cause environmental problems. Especially serious is the fact that most of these new lands have a high potential for erosion. Some of the new agricultural land will be developed by irrigation or drainage projects, which could aggravate problems of water adequacy, salinization, and loss of wildlife habitat. The smooth growth in demand for cropland shown in table 8–1 ignores short-term fluctuations, which could have significant environmental consequences. For example, the high food prices of 1972 to 1976 brought virtually all of the 51 million acres of cropland idle in 1969 back into production by 1976, and much of it was unprotected by adequate erosion controls (Crosson and Frederick, 1977). If grasslands and forests are used to relieve the land pressures caused by expanding farms and cities, the projected loss of these lands is small in scenario EL, but in scenario DH 16.2 percent of the grasslands existing in 1969 and 9.5 percent of forestlands would be converted to built-up uses by 2025. Output of livestock and forest products could be affected in the difficult case if highly productive forest or pasturelands are converted to cropland.

Compared with most other high-income countries, the United States is well endowed with lands appropriate for recreational purposes. The large amount of land set aside in table 8–1 for such purposes reflects the assumption that demand for recreation will grow rapidly as incomes and leisure time increase. In addition to land designated specifically for recreation, much of the land in the forest and miscellaneous categories is available for recreational use. A substantial portion of all this land is located far from population centers—more than half of all forest and miscellaneous other land is located in Alaska and the sparsely populated Rocky Mountain region, for example—but increased income and leisure will allow people to reach these areas. Meanwhile, the value of recreational experiences near densely populated areas may deteriorate because of crowding.

If we restrict our view to national figures on amounts of available land of different characteristics and future needs for it by major functional categories, there will be no major problem of land adequacy in the next fifty years, especially in the base case. Even for the difficult case, in which substantially more agricultural land will be needed to accommodate a larger population and higher food exports, the problem is the cost and potential environmental problems of land use, not the physical quantity of land available. This is in sharp contrast with land-supply limitations in other countries. Viewing the situation nationally, however, implicitly assumes that population and economic activities can move among regions at little or no cost. This is seldom the case. High-quality mineral deposits and good agricultural land cannot be moved, for example, because of encroaching urbanization, and costs of minerals and food could rise substantially as producers turn to deposits and land of lower quality. Similarly, costs of electricity could increase substantially if power plants are not located close to consumers, fuel, and adequate water for cooling purposes.

Public perception of land-use problems will be more influenced by the organization and quality of land uses in particular localities than by considerations of overall adequacy. Local controversies, especially those caused by locating objectionable but necessary facilities nearby, will become more prevalent in the future. To illustrate the general nature and extent of such regional problems, we consider the land requirements for power plants, solid waste disposal, and mining, and conclude with a brief discussion of erosion problems.

Power Plants

In all scenarios, the number of electric power plants in the United States will increase dramatically by 2025, as shown in table 8–2. The total number will increase between 320 percent and 580 percent, depending on the scenario, compared with the projected 253 to 450 percent increases in the GNP.[2] Except in the case of a nuclear moratorium (DHNU), after 1985 the majority of plants will be nuclear powered. In 1975, nuclear plants provided 10.6 percent of all electric power; by 2025, they will provide 63 percent in the base case and 73 percent in the difficult case on a gross basis.[3]

[2] All plants are normalized to a 1,000 megawatt electric [MW (e)] size with a capacity factor of 70 percent.

[3] The percentage for 1975, 10.6 percent, is calculated using the model. In 1975 nuclear power plants actually provided about 9 percent of all electric power on a gross basis (EEI, 1977). The percentage share of nuclear plants in total power plants is higher than their share in gross electric power production because each nuclear plant accounts for relatively less energy throughput compared to a fossil-fueled plant; so there are relatively more nuclear plants for a given gross output of electricity.

Table 8–2. Numbers of Electric Power Plants, by Type, Various Scenarios

Scenario and plant type[a]	1975[b]	1985	2000	2025
EL				
Fossil	243	382	309	395
Nuclear	34	90	390	794
DH				
Fossil		457	291	453
Nuclear		107	656	1,435
DHNU				
Fossil		457	824	1,790
Nuclear		107	102	0
DHP1				
Fossil		456	290	444
Nuclear		107	649	1,382
DHP2				
Fossil		409	339	430
Nuclear		110	499	1,385
DL				
Fossil		419	252	354
Nuclear		99	590	1,210
FH				
Fossil		448	268	307
Nuclear		107	615	1,102
FL				
Fossil		421	234	231
Nuclear		100	557	930

[a] All plants are 1,000 MW (e), operating at 70 percent of capacity.

[b] The numbers for 1975 are calculated by using the model.

The probable locations of these plants are shown in figures 8–1 and 8–2 for the base case. With some exceptions, these future power plants are assumed to be concentrated near heavily populated areas in order to minimize transmission losses.[4] The projections for the base case in 2025 include, for example, thirty-two nuclear power plants operating in the Delaware Valley. Because of the need for cooling water, these plants are

[4] Estimates of electricity-generating capacity at the aggregated subarea (ASA) level are made by applying regional shares or percentages to national capacity estimates. The regional shares are based on Federal Power Commission estimates of capacity allocations to the year 1990 (FPC, 1971). After 1990, shares are adjusted to reflect differential regional growth in accordance with Stevens and Trainer (1976). In some cases, special adjustments were required. For example, because of risk of damage by earthquakes in coastal areas, an increasing amount of nuclear generating capacity in California is assigned to interior areas where seismic activity is lower and cooling water is available. Another special adjustment is fossil fuel-fired capacity in Texas, where generating capacity declines after 2000 because of the increasing shortage of natural gas and petroleum for utility boilers. This is supplanted by increased capacity on the lower Mississippi River (in ASA 802), where barged coal and cooling water are available.

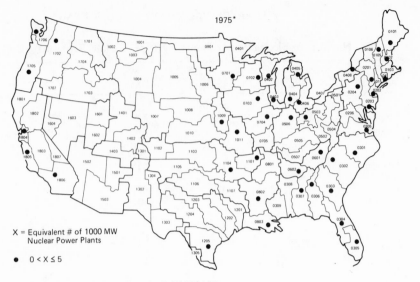

1975*

X = Equivalent # of 1000 MW
Nuclear Power Plants

●   0 < X ≤ 5

*   Total National Nuclear Capacity is 34,000 MW

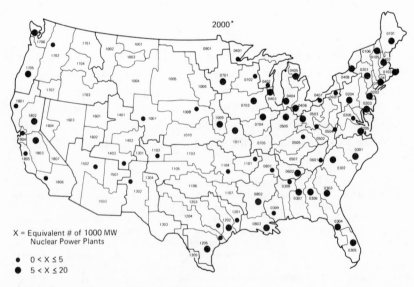

2000*

X = Equivalent # of 1000 MW
Nuclear Power Plants

●   0 < X ≤ 5
●   5 < X ≤ 20

*   Total National Nuclear Capacity is 390,000 MW

Figure 8–1.   Number of nuclear power plants in the United States for base case in selected years.

1985*

X = Equivalent # of 1000 MW
Nuclear Power Plants

● 0 < X ≤ 5

* Total National Nuclear Capacity is 90,000 MW

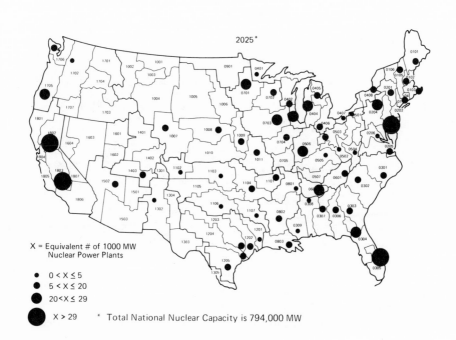

2025*

X = Equivalent # of 1000 MW
Nuclear Power Plants

● 0 < X ≤ 5
● 5 < X ≤ 20
● 20 < X ≤ 29

● X > 29   * Total National Nuclear Capacity is 794,000 MW

333

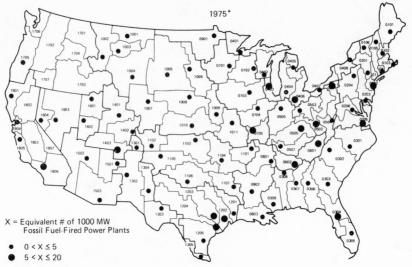

1975*

X = Equivalent # of 1000 MW
    Fossil Fuel-Fired Power Plants

●   0 < X ≤ 5

⬤   5 < X ≤ 20

* Total National Fossil Fuel-Fired Capacity is 243,000 MW

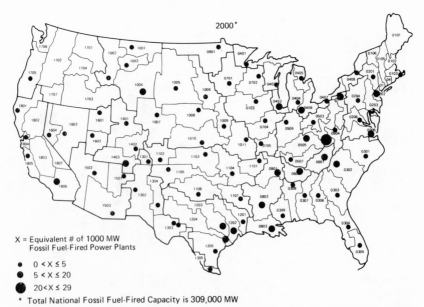

2000*

X = Equivalent # of 1000 MW
    Fossil Fuel-Fired Power Plants

●   0 < X ≤ 5

⬤   5 < X ≤ 20

⬤   20 < X ≤ 29

* Total National Fossil Fuel-Fired Capacity is 309,000 MW

Figure 8–2.   Number of fossil-fueled power plants for base case in selected years.

334

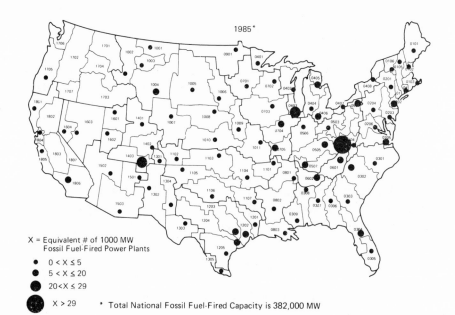

1985*

X = Equivalent # of 1000 MW
Fossil Fuel-Fired Power Plants

- 0 < X ≤ 5
- 5 < X ≤ 20
- 20 < X ≤ 29
- X > 29   * Total National Fossil Fuel-Fired Capacity is 382,000 MW

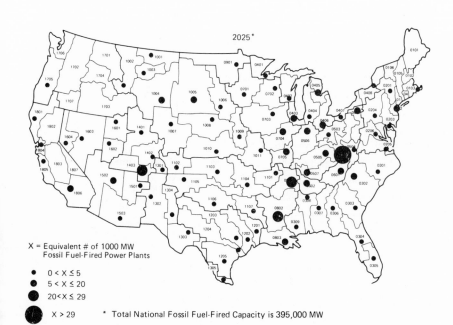

2025*

X = Equivalent # of 1000 MW
Fossil Fuel-Fired Power Plants

- 0 < X ≤ 5
- 5 < X ≤ 20
- 20 < X ≤ 29
- X > 29   * Total National Fossil Fuel-Fired Capacity is 395,000 MW

335

likely to be located along the river. If they were distributed evenly, there would be one reactor every 9 miles. If the high growth case, scenario DH, were to occur, an even distribution would mean one reactor every 5 miles. While it is more likely that such plants will be clustered into a smaller number of sites, acceptance of these plants by the local population is likely to be difficult to obtain. The Ohio River Valley is likely to be disproportionately burdened with coal-fired power plants because of closeness to both coal and industry. In scenario DHNU, 818,000 MW(e), or 55 percent of all coal-fired capacity is concentrated in the Ohio, Colorado, and lower Mississippi river valleys.

Given the public sensitivities about nuclear plants and the thermal, visual, and air pollution impacts of fossil-fueled plants, it will be far from easy to find appropriate sites for all these plants. In a nuclear accident, the radioactive cloud is most dangerous immediately after release; it then decays and dissipates quickly. Populations in areas immediately downwind of the nuclear plant receive the highest doses of radioactivity, but dangerous isotopes can be transported many hundreds of miles to cause latent cancers and genetic defects (NEPSG, 1977). In order to minimize the effects of such accidents, plant locations should be planned with local population distribution and meteorology in mind, in addition to the many other necessary physical and institutional considerations. For coal-fired plants also, the concentrations of various pollutants are usually higher in the immediate vicinity of the plants; however, the large concentration of coal-fired power plants in the Ohio and Tennessee valleys may lead to serious impacts in the Northeast because the prevailing westerly winds can carry sulfates and nitrates long distances. In any event, total damages could be reduced by careful plant siting, but in the past these problems have not been fully recognized. As a result, some nuclear and many fossil power plants are placed very near heavily populated areas or concentrated in regions where persistent winds can transport pollutants over long distances to heavily populated regions.

Solid Wastes

Like power plant siting, disposal of solid wastes is a familiar land use problem. Generation of urban solid wastes, shown in table 8–3, will increase faster than population but at a rate slower than the GNP will grow. Location of disposal sites will continue to be a problem because the amount of acceptable land near cities is limited. In later years, as concentrations of heavy metals and other highly toxic chemicals build up, more

Table 8–3. Production of Solid Wastes, by Type, Various Scenarios (millions of tons annually)

Scenario and type of waste	1975	1985	2000	2010	2025[a]
EL					
Urban	228.0	303.1	435.3	531.0	712.5
Lime-sulfur sludge[b]	0	74.4	115.3	127.2	0
DH					
Urban		321.4	489.3	643.2	968.0
Lime-sulfur sludge[c]		156.1	145.4	142.3	0
DHNU					
Urban		321.3	490.2	644.6	964.8
Lime-sulfur sludge[c]		156.1	453.9	491.3	0
DHP1					
Urban		319.2	467.3	612.7	914.2
Lime-sulfur sludge[c]		155.3	133.8	126.8	0
DHP2					
Urban		326.7	507.0	672.3	998.3
Lime-sulfur sludge[c]		130.6	135.7	148.8	0
DHRE					
Urban		320.2	488.4	647.0	971.2
Lime-sulfur sludge[b]		97.8	103.5	121.0	0
FH					
Urban		321.4	481.9	603.1	811.1
Lime-sulfur sludge[c]		153.3	133.7	117.4	0
DL					
Urban		300.6	437.2	550.2	790.2
Lime-sulfur sludge[c]		142.2	125.0	117.4	0
FL					
Urban		305.4	435.1	521.2	686.8
Lime-sulfur sludge[c]		143.0	115.8	97.3	0

Sources: Urban wastes are calculated by the solid waste–recycling module of SEAS/RFF. Coefficient of waste production by lime scrubbing for 3.5 percent sulfur coal is taken from R. J. Evans, *Potential Solid Waste Generation and Disposal from Lime and Limestone Desulfurization Processes*, Bureau of Mines Information Circular 8633 (Washington, D.C., U.S. Department of Interior, 1974). Oil is assumed to be 1.06 percent sulfur.

[a] In 2025, all coal-fired power plants use low-BTU gasification and need no scrubbing.

[b] For scenarios with trend environmental standards, one-half of all high-sulfur-coal-fired plants have scrubbers by 1990 and all coal- and oil-fired plants have scrubbers by 2015.

[c] For scenarios with strict environmental standards, all coal- and oil-fired plants have scrubbers by 2010.

careful, sophisticated waste management practices will be necessary to prevent leaching and runoff to the surrounding environment.

In 1971 industries produced about eighteen times as much solid wastes as did nonindustrial urban activities (NCMP, 1973), but typically, industrial wastes are more uniform, and hence easier to handle, than urban wastes. An exception may be the residues from lime stack scrubbers installed in fossil-fueled power plants to reduce their emissions of sulfur to the air.[5] As they are now designed, these scrubbers produce a wet lime-sulfur sludge with an unstable chemical composition. As indicated in table 8–3, sludge generation by power plants in 1985 may amount to 25 to 50 percent of urban wastes, but this percentage falls thereafter in most scenarios, as nuclear power and low-BTU coal gasification become more prevalent. In scenario DHNU, however, the amount of sludge generated in 2000 is almost equal to the amount of urban solid wastes. Sludge disposal will require isolating its toxic sulfur compounds to prevent locally severe pollution of surface streams and groundwater. Because this sulfur-scrubbing technology is relatively new, processes other than lime scrubbing may be developed that allow recycling of sulfur as a useful by-product. Unless further developments are made soon, however, widespread use of limestone scrubbing will cause a major disposal problem.

Mining

The amount of land disturbed by mining in any year depends on many economic and geologic variables that are not easily predictable. In the simple model we used for calculating disturbance levels, many of the variables are assumed to remain constant or to vary in highly simplified ways.[6] The demand for most minerals was taken from the calculations in chapter 4. Additional projections were made for stone, clay, sand, and gravel, but a number of relatively insignificant minerals like mica, olivine, and garnet, which accounted for 4.3 percent of land disturbance in 1971, were omitted. These data were combined with land disturbance values for 1971 estimated by Paone, Morning, and Giorgetti (1974), first assuming

---

[5] Lime scrubbing produces less sludge than limestone scrubbing and appears to be superior in sulfur-removal capability and efficiency (Evans, 1974). Values shown in table 8–3 are for lime scrubbing.

[6] Mining techniques and the fraction of demand met by recycling are assumed to remain the same as in 1971. Production lags and additions to stockpiles are assumed to be negligible. Net imports are assumed to remain a constant fraction of consumption, as in chapter 4. Relevant data were compiled from three government sources: Bureau of Mines (1970, 1973, 1976b). More detailed predictions were available for fuel minerals. Rough assumptions were made about the split between eastern and western coal and between underground and surface-mined coal. Coal mined in the East falls from 91 percent of production in 1971 to 50 percent in 2025. Seventy-five percent of eastern coal is taken from underground mines in 2025, compared to 53 percent in 1971. All western coal is assumed to be mined by surface methods in 2025. A series of uranium ore grades was taken from (ERDA, 1975), so that for this fuel the amount of land disturbed per unit mined changed over time. As in other parts of this study, no recycling of nuclear spent fuel was assumed. A hypothetical land use coefficient for shale oil is calculated from data in Hittman Associates (1975).

no reclamation and then assuming prompt reclamation of all land.[7] This provides us with the two extreme values in table 8–4 for land disturbed by mining. Reclamation is now required by law, so the maximum disturbance case will not be permitted. The assumption that all land can be reclaimed promptly is also unrealistic. According to one estimate (NAS, 1974), 11 percent of western lands can never be revegetated, and all revegetation of arid lands will be slow; exposure to toxic materials, such as the sulfur compounds common to eastern coalfields, will also make revegetation difficult or impossible in some areas.

If there is no reclamation, the amount of land disturbed in 2025 in the base case will be eleven times the amount disturbed in 1975,[8] but if there is prompt and complete reclamation, the quantity of land disturbed would increase 100 percent, and in intermediate years the amounts would actually be less than the number of acres in 1975. Because coal mining disturbs far more land than uranium mining, scenario DHNU will have 40 percent more land disturbance for fuel mining than scenario DH in 2025, contributing to the 104 percent increase in land disturbance in DHNU for 2025 over that of 1975, even with complete reclamation in 2025. Although alternative assumptions about population and economic growth lead to significant differences in amounts of disturbed land, holding policies constant, it is clear that changes in policy dominate and will be the principal determinants of land disturbance during the next fifty years.

Yearly reclamation costs for mined land were calculated using costs per acre for coal taken from Goldstein and Smith (1975); they should be regarded as very rough estimates. Reclamation costs per acre are assumed to remain constant and to be similar for different minerals.[9] Reclamation

---

[7] Mining of a tract of land is assumed to continue for three years, and reclamation to take an additional three years to complete, so that there is a six-year lag between mining and reclamation. All land disturbed before 1971 is reclaimed by 1977 in the minimum disturbance case, which implies that public money was provided.

[8] Both numbers shown in table 8–4 for 1975 are hypothetical. Some reclamation was carried out in 1975, so the actual land disturbance was somewhere between the maximum and minimum values listed.

[9] Three coefficients ($250 per acre for eastern open pit mines, $1,588 for western open pit mines, and $2,582 for eastern contour stripping) were taken from Goldstein and Smith (1975), using the average if a range of values was given. It was assumed that these coefficients for coal will also apply to other minerals. A composite coefficient for each mineral was calculated from the three coal coefficients and the general topography and location of mining in 1971 (Bureau of Mines, 1973), and it remains constant for all later years. Any future shift in mining location between arid and humid areas will not be captured here. The treatment of coal was different in that the shift from eastern to western reserves was included in the calculations.

Table 8–4. Land Disturbed by Mining, by Mineral Mined, Various Scenarios (millions of acres)

Scenario and mineral	1975[a]		1985		2000		2025	
	Max[b]	Min[c]	Max[b]	Min[c]	Max[b]	Min[c]	Max[b]	Min[c]
EL								
Fuel	0.9	0.6	1.7	0.5	2.9	0.5	5.5	0.7
Nonfuel[d]	0.6	0.3	1.1	0.3	2.0	0.4	4.1	0.5
Other[e]	1.1	0.5	2.5	0.6	5.2	1.0	12.5	1.8
Total	2.6	1.4	5.3	1.4	10.1	1.9	22.1	3.0
DH								
Fuel			2.0	0.6	3.8	0.8	9.2	1.5
Nonfuel[d]			1.1	0.3	2.2	0.4	5.3	0.7
Other[e]			2.6	0.7	5.6	1.2	15.9	2.5
Total			5.7	1.6	11.6	2.4	30.4	4.7
DHNU								
Fuel			2.0	0.6	4.3	1.0	11.9	2.1
Nonfuel[d]			1.1	0.3	2.2	0.4	5.3	0.7
Other[e]			2.6	0.7	5.6	1.2	15.9	2.5
Total			5.7	1.6	12.1	2.6	33.1	5.3
DHP1								
Fuel			2.0	0.6	3.7	0.8	8.6	1.4
Nonfuel[d]			1.1	0.3	2.2	0.4	5.2	0.7
Other[e]			2.6	0.7	5.5	1.2	15.6	2.5
Total			5.7	1.6	11.4	2.4	29.4	4.6
DHP2								
Fuel			1.8	0.5	3.0	0.5	8.1	1.6
Nonfuel[d]			1.1	0.3	2.5	0.4	5.3	0.7
Other[e]			2.6	0.7	5.6	1.2	15.9	2.5
Total			5.5	1.5	11.1	2.1	19.3	4.8
DHRE								
Fuel			1.9	0.6	3.7	0.8	8.7	1.4
Nonfuel[d]			1.1	0.3	2.2	0.4	5.3	0.7
Other[e]			2.6	0.7	5.6	1.2	15.9	2.5
Total			5.6	1.6	11.5	2.4	29.9	4.6

(continued)

here means that the land has been restored to nearly its original contour, stabilized, and revegetated. The resulting cost estimates, reported in table 8–5, seem affordable; they amount to 1.2 percent of the output of the mining industry in both the base case and the difficult case in 2025. Even if we had chosen the highest reclamation costs reported by Goldstein and Smith rather than the average, our estimates would rise to only 1.9 percent of mineral output in 2025 for scenario EL. These calculations show that, on a national scale, the cost of keeping land disturbance to tolerable levels is moderate.

But here again, national figures may conceal severe local problems. In order to suggest some of these problems, a simple regionalization scheme was used to predict mining locations in the future for seven im-

Table 8–4. (Continued)

Scenario and mineral	Level of disturbance							
	1975[a]		1985		2000		2025	
	Max[b]	Min[c]	Max[b]	Min[c]	Max[b]	Min[c]	Max[b]	Min[c]
DL								
Fuel			1.9	0.6	3.5	0.7	8.0	1.2
Nonfuel[d]			1.1	0.3	2.1	0.4	4.6	0.6
Other[e]			2.5	0.6	5.2	1.1	13.6	2.0
Total			5.5	1.5	10.8	2.2	26.2	3.8
FH								
Fuel			1.9	0.6	3.7	0.8	8.1	1.2
Nonfuel[d]			1.1	0.3	2.2	0.4	4.7	0.6
Other[e]			2.7	0.7	5.9	1.2	13.8	2.0
Total			5.7	1.6	11.8	2.4	26.6	3.8
FL								
Fuel			1.9	0.6	3.5	0.7	7.2	1.0
Nonfuel[d]			1.1	0.3	2.0	0.4	4.2	0.5
Other[e]			2.5	0.6	5.1	1.0	11.9	1.6
Total			5.5	1.5	10.6	2.1	23.3	3.1

[a] For minimum land disturbance, 67 percent of land disturbed before 1972 has been reclaimed.

[b] Assumes no reclamation, for maximum estimate of land disturbance, including 572,000 acres disturbed before 1972 by mining fuels and 422,000 acres disturbed before 1972 by mining selected nonfuel minerals (see table footnote d).

[c] Assumes prompt and complete reclamation of all mined land six years after it is disturbed. All land disturbed before 1972 is reclaimed before 1978.

[d] Includes iron ore, aluminum, copper, manganese, nickel, tungsten, molybdenum, titanium, sulfur, and phosphate rock. Fractions mined underground are assumed to remain the same as in 1971 and to cause no land disturbance.

[e] Stone, clay, sand, and gravel.

portant minerals.[10] Figures 8–3 and 8–4 show the results of this exercise for the base case in 1971 and 2025. The values shown on the maps include all minerals before 1971 (Paone and coauthors, 1974) and seven major minerals after 1971.[11] Although our regionalization method is very rough, it seems clear that large increases in the quantity of land disturbed by mining will occur in some western states, especially in Wyoming, Colorado, and New Mexico, because of increased mining of fossil and nuclear fuels. Eastern coal-mining states, although they continue to supply a

[10] Total production was divided among regions according to their shares in the base year. When a region's resource is exhausted, the pattern is broken and a new region is brought into production immediately. It is assumed that foresight is perfectly capable of predicting needed capacity. If more than one region is needed, several may be started at once. A new pattern is thus established and followed until another region's resources are exhausted. For aluminum and uranium, ore quality influences the choice of new regions, but most depend only on size of the resource. Information on resources was adapted from many sources: Bureau of Mines (1970, 1976a), Averitt (1975), ERDA (1976), NRC (1976), Bennett (1973), Everett and Bennett (1967), and Blue and Torries (1975).

[11] Coal, shale oil, uranium, iron ore, copper, aluminum, and phosphate rock.

Table 8–5. Reclamation Costs for Mined Land, by Mineral Mined, Various Scenarios
(millions of 1971 dollars annually)

Scenario and mineral	1975[a]	1985	2000	2025
EL				
Fuel	237.7	111.6	106.6	176.4
Nonfuel[b]	88.0	36.0	47.0	65.2
Other [c]	111.3	89.2	145.2	270.9
Total	437.0	236.8	298.8	512.5
DH				
Fuel		133.3	186.9	395.3
Nonfuel		38.9	58.5	103.7
Other		94.7	168.9	392.0
Total		266.9	414.3	891.0
DHNU				
Fuel		133.3	243.8	536.8
Nonfuel		38.9	58.5	103.7
Other		94.7	168.9	392.0
Total		266.9	471.2	1,032.5
DHP1				
Fuel		132.4	182.8	368.0
Nonfuel		38.9	57.7	101.4
Other		94.7	166.7	383.4
Total		266.0	407.2	852.8
DHP2				
Fuel		133.8	113.0	408.8
Nonfuel		38.9	58.5	103.7
Other		94.7	168.9	392.0
Total		266.9	340.4	904.5
DHRE				
Fuel		129.2	181.9	355.3
Nonfuel		38.9	58.5	103.7
Other		94.7	168.9	392.0
Total		262.8	409.3	851.0
DL				
Fuel		130.4	176.0	304.7
Nonfuel		36.1	51.5	76.1
Other		88.4	148.9	319.3
Total		254.9	376.4	700.1
FH				
Fuel		125.2	169.5	315.5
Nonfuel		38.9	56.2	81.1
Other		95.5	164.2	299.9
Total		259.6	189.9	696.5
FL				
Fuel		125.5	162.2	253.1
Nonfuel		36.4	49.4	66.6
Other		89.2	143.1	246.4
Total		251.1	354.7	566.1

[a] Includes cost for reclamation of a sixth of the land disturbed before 1972. The corresponding values for a single year only are $100.4 million for fuels, $29.2 million for nonfuels, $71.2 million for other minerals, and $200.8 million for the total.

[b] Includes iron ore, aluminum, copper, manganese, nickel, tungsten, molybdenum, titanium, sulfur, and phosphate rock.

[c] Stone, clay, sand, and gravel.

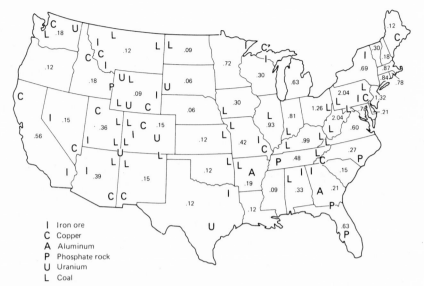

Figure 8-3. Percentage of total U.S. land area disturbed by surface mining, 1971.

Figure 8-4. Percentage of total U.S. land area disturbed by surface mining for Scenario EL, in the year 2025, with and without reclamation. Note that percentages include all minerals up to 1971 and major minerals, as listed, after 1971. Percentages not in parentheses assume no reclamation; those in parentheses assume complete and prompt reclamation.

Figure 8–5.   Percentage of total U.S. land area disturbed by surface mining for Scenario DH, in the year 2025, with and without reclamation. Note that percentages include all minerals up to 1971 and major minerals, as listed, after 1971. Percentages without parentheses assume no reclamation; those in parentheses assume complete and prompt reclamation.

significant fraction of national demand for energy, will have no more, and in many cases, less disturbed land in 2025 compared to 1971 if complete reclamation can be accomplished and the base case prevails. A few states with major deposits of nonfuel minerals, notably Arkansas, Florida, and Arizona, will bear larger burdens of disturbed land in 2025 than in 1971. The states with the largest percentages of disturbed land in 2025 will be Kentucky, Florida, West Virginia, and Ohio; the states with the largest amounts of disturbed land will be Arizona, Colorado, Florida, and Kentucky. The amount of disturbed land rises dramatically in many of these regions when we switch from scenario EL to DH or DHNU. In the eastern coal-mining states, the minimum disturbance figures in 2025 would be greater by 70 to 90 percent and in the western energy-producing states by 40 to 170 percent if scenario DH prevailed rather than EL (see figure 8–5). If instead, scenario DHNU prevailed, these figures would be 230 to 280 percent greater in the eastern coal-mining states and 100 to 180 percent greater in the western energy-producing states than in scenario EL.

   Although this state-by-state breakdown demonstrates that land disturbance is not evenly distributed across the country, the values shown on the maps are still too generalized to illustrate the specific local problems that will arise. The 128,000 acres of land in Florida devoted to phosphate mining in 2025 in the base case, for instance, may seem small in comparison to the total area of the state, but they will be concentrated in two fairly small areas in the central and northern parts of the state, with devastating effects on the landscape of those areas. Many such local areas will suffer in supplying the national demand for minerals. On a national scale, however, disruption can be kept within reasonable bounds if a vigorous reclamation program is carried out and if our optimistic assumptions about reclamation in arid lands are correct.

Erosion

Although it appears that adequate land is available in this country for most purposes during the next fifty years, this vast resource could be degraded by careless use. Repeated irrigation, for example, can reduce crop yields significantly by increasing salt concentrations in the soil. Problems of soil salinity are common throughout the irrigated area of the western states and are especially severe in the Colorado basin (Crosson and Frederick, 1977).

Of particular concern throughout the United States is the loss of valuable cropland by excessive erosion. Erosion is a natural process, but it is greatly increased by human activities, especially agriculture. Soil is lost from agricultural lands much faster than it is replaced by natural processes. The relationship between soil loss and productivity loss is not known, and it probably varies widely depending on local conditions. One estimate for the central Corn Belt is that productivity will be reduced from 10 percent to 30 percent if most topsoil is lost, depending on management practices, fertilizer use, and the nature of subsoil material. National average crop yields have not been reduced yet by loss of topsoil, apparently because the use of fertilizers and pesticides has increased. The U.S. Soil Conservation Service estimates acceptable annual rates of soil loss at 1 to 4 tons an acre, but it is not clear what "acceptable" means (Crosson and Frederick, 1977). Average yearly losses are now variously estimated at 9 to 12 tons an acre (Carter, 1977) and 7.5 tons an acre (USDA, 1977).

It is clear that such soil losses cannot be sustained indefinitely without hurting yields or requiring ever-greater compensatory inputs of other factors. Effective soil conservation methods are known, but past efforts to encourage their use have not been successful (Comptroller General, 1977). One particularly promising soil conservation method is minimum tillage, which could reduce soil loss by 50 percent or more and is likely to be adopted widely for economic reasons as well (Crosson and Frederick, 1977). If political or practical barriers prevent adopting effective conservation practices, loss of cropland productivity may become a reality on a national scale within fifty years. This possibility must be included as an important qualification to our previous conclusion that available cropland is more than adequate for our future needs in most scenarios.

Water Resources

The adequacy of water supplies to support projected economic and population growth is of fundamental concern. Although the United States in general is endowed with large quantities of high-quality runoff, this water is very unevenly distributed in time and space. Moreover, its distribution bears no relationship to the distribution of high-quality soils and mineable ores and little direct relationship to the distribution of population and economic activities. Water supplies and economic activities can be moved from one region to another, but typically only at high cost. Accordingly, adequacy should be defined by comparison of water supply and demand at a regional level. The water resource regions used here are seventeen large river basins or groups of basins defined by the Water Resources Council and illustrated in figure 8–6, plus Alaska and Hawaii.

Water supply is so variable that any estimate must be accompanied by its probability of occurrence. Streamflow varies daily, seasonally, and yearly, and in some areas maximum flow may be as much as 500 times minimum flow. In general, the greatest yearly variation occurs in those regions where the average flow is lowest. We have chosen annual natural runoff expected in 90 percent of years (Water Resources Council, 1968) as our estimate of water supply.[12] Because these estimates are annual averages, they are likely to be considerably larger than the amount of flow actually available on a hot August day, when demand tends to be highest for many uses. In the western regions, where groundwater makes a sig-

[12] Natural runoff is defined as surface runoff with no evaporation from stream channels or reservoirs, no human consumption, and no imports from other regions. The annual average may be considered the amount theoretically available if maximum storage facilities were built, with no increase in evaporation. The actual amount of available water will be reduced by evaporation from streams and reservoirs, lack of suitable dam sites, upstream consumption, and inability to capture peak flows.

Figure 8–6.   Water resources regions in the United States.

nificant contribution to water supplies, the sustainable yield from ground-water is added to runoff.[13]

Our water supply estimates are higher than the estimates by Woll-man and Bonem (1971) of present dependable regulated flow and lower than maximum dependable regulated flow in the East. In other words, small deficiencies in the eastern regions could be overcome by increases in storage. In the arid West, however, the estimates of both present and maximum regulated dependable flow are similar because most practical reservoirs have already been constructed. Our estimates are generally higher than Wollman and Bonem's present regulated flow in the West because annual averages ignore evaporation from storage of seasonal flow. For the western regions, then, if any deficits occur, they can be met only by decreasing consumption or increasing imports from other regions.

[13] Although it is possible to mine groundwater by withdrawing more water than is recharged to the underground reservoir as a temporary measure, we have included only sustainable yields from groundwater in the six western regions where it is now an important resource. The assumed values are 2.3 billion gallons a day (BGD) in the Great Basin (Eakin, Price, and Harrill, 1976), 3.6 BGD in the upper Colorado basin (Price and Arnow, 1974), 1.4 BGD in the lower Colorado basin (Water Resources Council, 1968), 4.1 BGD in the Texas–Gulf region (Baker and Wall, 1976), 2.0 BGD in the Rio Grande basin (West and Broadhurst, 1975), and 10.0 in the California region (Thomas and Phoenix, 1976). The values for the Rio Grande and California regions are our estimates based on very limited data from the references.

The demand for water is also highly variable and difficult to predict. We have chosen here to use a set of current demand coefficients that are likely to hold only if no special efforts at conservation are made. They are based for the most part on data presented by the Water Resources Council in its First National Assessment of the nation's water resources (Water Resources Council, 1968). The amount of water used for irrigation and for domestic and industrial uses was adjusted to conform generally to the population and economic projections of our scenarios.[14] Water use in energy was calculated using the power plant location projections described earlier in this chapter and assumptions about power plant water demand. Current water-use coefficients for the various cooling technologies were used with projections of their level of use in later years.[15] Water consumed in manufacturing synthetic fuels is assumed to be very efficient, because many of the plants will be built in the arid west.[16] Water demand is omitted for those plants assumed to use sea water for cooling, because for our purposes the water resources of the ocean may be considered infinite.

Water requirements for all scenarios are shown in table 8–6. Withdrawals, or the gross use of water, are the cumulative amount of water removed from streams. Some fraction of withdrawals is returned for additional withdrawal downstream, so withdrawals exceed actual requirements. The water returned to the stream usually is reduced in quantity or quality, however. The part of withdrawals not returned to the source is consumption. This water is evaporated or incorporated into a product, so it is lost for all downstream use. Actual water requirements include not

---

[14] The following values for withdrawal in 1980 and 2020 were taken from the Water Resources Council (1968) and used directly: municipal and domestic demand (148–166 GPD per capita), industrial demand (.05–.03 GPD per dollar of GNP), and irrigation demand (399–431 GPD per acre of harvested land).

[15] Nuclear plants using once-through cooling withdraw 1,589 cubic feet per second (cfs) and consume 19 cfs. Plants using cooling ponds withdraw 494 cfs and consume 20 cfs. Plants using cooling towers withdraw 35 cfs and consume 29 cfs (calculated by Ramsay from AEC, 1974). These include only on-site consumption and neglect downstream evaporation of heated discharge. Fossil-fueled plants use 40 percent less water because of their higher thermal efficiency.

In 1971, the following cooling technologies were used: once-through cooling with salt water (21.5 percent of capacity), once-through cooling with fresh water (47.7 percent), cooling ponds (7.3 percent), cooling towers (12.9 percent), and combinations of ponds and towers (10.6 percent) (FPC, 1975). The projected uses in 2025 are 40 percent once-through with salt water, 5 percent once-through with fresh water, 15 percent with cooling ponds, and 40 percent with cooling towers.

[16] Coefficients of water demand as taken from Probstein, Goldstein, Gold, and Shen (1975). Thirty-seven gallons of water per million Btu (mBtu) are required to convert coal to gas, 29.6 gallons per mBtu to convert coal to liquid, and 28.4 gallons per mBtu to extract oil from shale.

Table 8-6. Demand for Water in the Conterminous United States, Various Scenarios

(billions of gallons daily)

Scenario	1970		1980		2000		2025	
	With-drawals[a]	Con-sump-tion	With-drawals[a]	Con-sump-tion	With-drawals[a]	Con-sump-tion	With-drawals[a]	Con-sump-tion
EL	333	99	347.1	95.0	407.0	115.0	545.7	144.5
DH			377.1	101.7	508.8	140.7	802.4	200.3
DHNU			377.1	101.7	489.6	138.9	734.5	191.2
DHP1			377.1	101.7	496.1	137.2	737.4	184.1
DHP2			370.1	101.3	491.1	138.1	789.8	201.0
DHRE			372.8	101.6	504.0	140.4	795.9	199.6
FH			371.4	100.0	475.8	131.2	616.3	161.7
DL			364.4	101.0	473.8	138.0	699.9	188.7
FL			362.5	99.5	445.7	128.9	558.4	154.6

Source: 1970 data from C. R. Murray and E. B. Reeves, *Estimated Use of Water in the United States in 1975*, U.S. Geological Survey Circular 676 (Washington, D.C., USGS, 1972).

[a] Excluding salt water used for cooling.

only consumption but also evaporation from reservoirs and marshes and sufficient river flow to support aquatic life, to dilute pollutants, and to maintain navigation. Preventing saltwater intrusion in estuaries also requires an unknown amount of fresh water outflow. Thus, the correct value for water requirements lies somewhere between withdrawals and consumption. Wollman and Bonem (1971) calculate that flows required to maintain good water quality (defined as 4 mg per liter dissolved oxygen) are generally larger than consumption, even at high levels of effluent treatment. Considering their figures, we might conservatively estimate requirements as twice consumption.

In spite of this ambiguity in defining water requirements, some conclusions can be drawn from table 8-6. Water withdrawals increase by 60 to 140 percent between 1970 and 2025; the largest increase occurs in scenario DH because of its high population and economic growth rates and its dependence on nuclear energy.[17] Comparison of scenarios in 2025 shows that withdrawals and consumption are related more closely to population than to GNP. In the base case, about half of the projected increase stems from increases in water used in the production of energy. The greater use of electricity and synthetics, both large withdrawers of

[17] Scenario DH has higher withdrawals than DHNU because the latter supposes fewer nuclear reactors, which use 67 percent more cooling water than fossil-fueled power plants.

water, contributes to this increase. Withdrawals of water for irrigation, which were about equal to withdrawals for energy in 1970, grow much more slowly than those for energy so that in 2025 irrigation withdraws only 70 percent as much water as energy.[18]

Consumption in all scenarios increases at a slower rate than withdrawals, 50 to 100 percent in the period from 1970 to 2025, and remains far below the 810.7 billion gallons per day of estimated runoff. Most of the increase occurs because the switch from once-through cooling to cooling ponds and towers raises water consumption for energy production 3,400 percent. Actually, consumption in earlier years is artificially low, because the consumption estimates do not include offsite evaporation of heated discharges; the switch to cooling ponds and towers by 2025 moves this consumption on site, so that it then is included in our estimates. Consumption by municipal and industrial users and consumption for irrigation all increase slightly. At the national level, then, more than enough water is available for our future needs.

The prospects for water adequacy are different at the regional level, however. For the base case, shown in table 8–7, withdrawals exceeded supplies in four western regions in 1970 and in seven by 2025; in the high-growth cases, DH and DHNU, withdrawals would exceed supplies in eleven regions in 2025, including several eastern regions. Table 8–7 must be interpreted with care, however. It only identifies regional withdrawals, which overestimate actual requirements because some withdrawn water is returned; further, the water supplied does not include all available water but only that added by runoff. Thus, table 8–7 indicates relative water shortages among regions but does not indicate absolutely that a region will necessarily be in short supply. For example, although the table shows that for scenario DH withdrawals will exceed supplies in the Great Lakes region in 2025, the very large amount of water stored in the lakes will alleviate any supply problem as long as consumption (including evaporation) does not exceed runoff in the long run.

The comparison of consumption with supplies, shown in table 8–8, does yield very clear indications of future water supply problems. In three regions in the southwest—lower Colorado, Rio Grande, and California—

---

[18] As indicated in table 8–6, the basic data for these projections comes from Murray and Reeves, 1972. Since then, the Water Resources Council (1978) has published the Second National Water Assessment, which presents substantially different numbers, particularly for withdrawals. In 1975 the WRC indicates that total, irrigation, and steam electric withdrawals were 398, 159, and 89 billion gallons a day, respectively; comparable figures from Murray and Reeves (1977) are 420, 140, and 190.

Table 8–7. Withdrawals of Water in Scenarios EL and DH and Water Supplied (billions of gallons daily)

Region	Water supplied[a]	1970[b]	2000		2025	
			EL	DH	EL	DH
1. North Atlantic	123.0	55.0	47.7	62.8	68.3	107.0
2. South Atlantic	131.0	35.0	29.8	38.4	49.9	77.6
3. Great Lakes	63.0	39.0	31.4	36.9	45.0	64.6*
4. Ohio	80.0	36.0	34.5	41.3	44.0	65.5
5. Tennessee	28.2	8.0	13.9	18.3	19.0	29.9*
6. Upper Mississippi	36.4	16.0	21.3	30.3	30.7	50.1*
7. Lower Mississippi	29.7	13.0	13.3	16.4	25.2	34.6*
8. Souris-Red-Rainy	2.6	0.3	1.4	1.5	1.2	1.4
9. Missouri	29.9	24.0	30.0*	37.8*	36.2*	51.9*
10. Arkansas-White-Red	44.3	12.0	20.3	25.3	25.0	36.1
11. Texas-Gulf	19.9	21.0*	29.7*	35.5*	35.3*	52.9*
12. Rio Grande	4.6	6.0*	8.3*	10.1*	9.7*	13.4*
13. Upper Colorado	12.4	8.0	9.8	11.9	12.7*	18.8*
14. Lower Colorado	2.5	7.0*	8.6*	10.3*	9.0*	12.4*
15. Great Basin	5.4	7.0	6.7*	7.9	5.9*	7.7*
16. Columbia–North Pacific	154.0	30.0	56.3	69.2	73.6	100.4
17. California	43.8	48.0*	44.3*	55.0*	54.9*	78.1*
(Conterminous states)	(810.7)	(365.0)	(407.0)	(508.8)	(545.7)	(802.4)
18. Alaska	580.0[c]	0.2	0.7	0.8	1.2	1.6
19. Hawaii	13.3[c]	3.0	2.9	3.5	4.4	6.1
All states	1,404.0	368.5	410.6	513.1	551.3	810.1

Note: * indicates withdrawals larger than supplies.
[a] Natural runoff available in 90 percent of all years [Water Resources Council, *The Nation's Water Resources* (Washington, D.C., Water Resources Council, 1968)] plus sustainable yield from groundwater in six regions (see footnote 12).
[b] From R. C. Murray and E. B. Reeves, *Estimated Use of Water in the United States in 1970*, U.S. Geological Survey Circular 765 (Washington, D.C., USGS, 1972).
[c] Average runoff.

Table 8-8. Consumption of Water in Scenarios EL and DH and Water Supplied (billions of gallons daily)

Region	Water supplied[a]	1970[b]	2000 EL	2000 DH	2025 EL	2025 DH
1. North Atlantic	123.0	1.8	4.3	5.4	7.5	11.4
2. South Atlantic	131.0	3.4	4.6	5.7	7.8	11.5
3. Great Lakes	63.0	1.2	3.6	4.6	6.3	9.8
4. Ohio	80.0	0.9	2.7	3.7	5.6	9.3
5. Tennessee	28.2	0.2	1.3	1.7	2.1	3.4
6. Upper Mississippi	36.4	0.8	2.0	2.8	3.8	6.3
7. Lower Mississippi	29.7	3.6	4.0	4.8	6.3	8.4
8. Souris-Red-Rainy	2.6	0.1	0.5	0.6	0.6	0.7
9. Missouri	29.9	12.0	13.2	16.1[d]	14.4	19.3[d]
10. Arkansas-White-Red	44.3	6.8	9.1	11.0	10.0	13.4
11. Texas-Gulf	19.9	6.2	9.1	10.9	9.7	13.2[d]
12. Rio Grande	4.6	3.3	4.2[d]	5.0[e]	4.3[d]	5.6[e]
13. Upper Colorado	12.4	4.1	2.9	4.2	4.3	7.2[d]
14. Lower Colorado	2.5	5.0[e]	3.8[e]	4.6[e]	4.0[e]	5.2[e]
15. Great Basin	5.4	3.2[d]	3.0[d]	3.6[d]	2.8[d]	3.6[d]
16. Columbia–North Pacific	154.0	11.0	19.6	23.8	25.9	34.1
17. California	43.8	22.0[d]	27.2[d]	32.3[d]	29.1[d]	37.9[d]
(Conterminous states)	(810.7)	(85.6)	(115.0)	(140.7)	(144.5)	(200.3)
18. Alaska	580.0[e]	—	0.2	0.2	0.2	0.2
19. Hawaii	13.3[c]	0.8	1.0	1.2	1.4	1.8
All states	1,404.0	86.4	116.2	142.1	146.0	202.3

[a] Natural runoff available in 90 percent of all years [Water Resources Council, *The Nation's Water Resources* (Washington, D.C., Water Resources Council, 1968)] plus sustainable yield from groundwater in six regions (see footnote 12).
[b] From C. R. Murray and E. B. Reeves, *Estimated Use of Water in the United States in 1975*, U.S. Geological Survey Circular 765 (Washington, D.C., USGS, 1972).
[c] Average runoff.
[d] Indicates consumption is more than one-half available water.
[e] Indicates consumption is more than available water.

consumption is close to or greater than supplies in 2025 in every scenario. Even in 1970, consumption exceeded supplies in the lower Colorado region. This deficit is met now by imports from the upper Colorado region. A ten-year average flow from the upper to lower Colorado basins is set by law at 6.7 BGD, which is more than the 5.2 BGD estimated for consumption in 2025. The only way these regions can cope with their projected water shortages is by reducing demand or increasing supplies. However, most of the regions in the Southwest are close to maximum regulated flow already (Wollman and Bonem, 1971), and imports from other regions, except upstream regions, are usually far too expensive to be practical on a large scale. So it seems likely that future consumption must be less than the unconstrained demand we have calculated in these three regions. Reductions might be achieved by improving efficiency of water use or by shifting to less water-intensive industries, and rising water costs will encourage both. Our demand calculations are based on current demand coefficients, and they are certain to be modified by changing conditions in the future.

It is important to emphasize here that this exercise is very generalized and cannot produce reliable results for specific localities. The great geographic variety within each of the nineteen regions will cause local problems that differ from those of the region as a whole. For example, tables 8–7 and 8–8 show that region 10, which includes the basins of the Arkansas, White, and Red rivers, is one with plenty of excess runoff to meet future demand. Some areas in the region are likely to have severe water supply problems, however. The western part of the region lies in the high plains of Texas, New Mexico, and Oklahoma, where runoff and groundwater recharge are negligible and the present thriving irrigated farms are supported by groundwater mining. Eventually this supply will be depleted, causing loss of irrigated farmland beginning around 1990 (Frederick, 1977). In the central part of the region, a large volume of water is available, but it is so polluted by heavy sediment loads and salt drainage from oil fields and natural salt marshes that this area's cities also must rely on groundwater. In the Ozark and Ouachita Mountains of the eastern part of the region, large quantities of high-quality runoff are available, and flooding is the major water problem (Water Resources Council, 1968). Similar detailed information must be used to qualify our conclusions about other regions as well.

Current water management practices do not encourage efficient use of water. For example, the objective of water projects of the U.S. Bureau of Reclamation has been to promote irrigated agriculture rather than efficient use of water (NWC, 1973). In general, public water supply agencies are committed to providing water to their customers at the lowest possible price. There can be little doubt that a change in these practices would improve substantially demand–supply balances in many regions. Higher water prices would encourage the use of dry cooling towers, which consume less water but are more expensive than any of the wet cooling methods. On-farm efficiency of water use, now estimated at 50 percent, could rise to 70 percent if conservation practices were adopted (Water Resources Council, 1968). Conveyance losses, now 15 percent of withdrawals for irrigation (Murray and Reeves, 1972), could also be significantly reduced. A modest improvement in the efficiency of water use in irrigation, the largest water use in the dry western regions, would go far to ease projected deficits. Per capita consumption of municipal water is now much higher in the West than in the East, partly because of more irrigation of lawns, an arguably frivolous use of water, which could be restricted if necessary. Rising water prices could ease the burdens of water supply in some areas by causing water consumers to move to less arid regions. Relocation of water-consuming industries to more humid areas, although impractical in the short run, could occur in our time period to the extent that water-intensive industries in dry areas are not based on natural resources found there.

Rising water prices, in addition to depressing demand, may make some supply technologies economically feasible. For example, recirculating water from sewage in coastal cities may become competitive with withdrawing fresh water. Desalinization of brackish or salt water, now far more expensive than withdrawals of fresh water, will become more attractive as the price of fresh water rises. The availability of water to support economic growth in the future is not assured, especially in the Southwest, but available water can be augmented substantially if consumers are willing to bear the costs and institutions are able to adjust to the very different circumstances of the future.

We are left with a feeling of cautious optimism in considering future water supplies and shortages. If higher prices encourage efficiency in water use, water supplies are likely to be adequate in most regions in most years. The most important qualification to this already guarded conclusion is that water quality may be lower. Any future growth in water consumption, even if far below the available amount in rivers, will reduce the amount of water available for dilution of pollutants and other instream uses. Although the quality of water is not assured, it seems likely that more efficient use of existing resources can prevent serious long-term shortages, even in the arid West.

Climate

The air pollutants described in chapter 7 and a number of other residuals released into the atmosphere, in addition to their effects on human health and property, may have indirect effects on human welfare through their influence on climate. It now seems possible that man-made changes in global climate could cause major disruptions of human and natural systems in the next fifty to hundred years. Although the uncertainties involved in predicting climate are immense, the possible consequences of climatic changes are so large that the issue must be addressed.

One approach to understanding future climate is to examine the record of past climates. The most important lesson of climatic history is that climate is variable on many time scales. Major changes, such as the onset of glacial conditions, can occur very rapidly, on the order of one hundred years. The causes of these variations are not known, but there is no reason to suppose that climate will be less variable in the future than it has been in the past. Between 1930 and 1960 climatic conditions were exceptionally favorable, and world population grew rapidly. Since that time many observers believe that climatic variations have increased significantly in many parts of the world. Such increased variations could become a more important threat to future food security than a change in the average temperature of one or two degrees. Climatologists cannot predict whether this trend is temporary or continuing. If it continues, regional fluctuations in food supplies and energy consumption could be significantly increased.

The global climate is the product of complex and incompletely known interactions among the atmosphere, oceans, land, and biota. Because the workings of the atmosphere under natural conditions are not well known, the effects of any man-made disturbances are very difficult to predict. Some attempts have been made, however, to predict the influence of residuals on future climate. In general, these predictions rely on crude atmospheric models that hold many important variables constant. The interactions between the atmosphere and the oceans, polar ice, and the land surface, which determine much of its behavior, are generally neglected. These models, though crude in comparison to the way the atmosphere really works, now use the entire capacity of the largest existing computers, so they cannot be extended easily to include the neglected factors.

Some attempts have been made, using the current generation of crude climate models, to predict the influence of various residuals on global temperatures. A variety of residuals are suspected of altering global temperatures, including particulates, nitrogen compounds, (N_2O, NH_3, HNO_3), sulfur dioxide, halocarbon aerosols, water vapor, carbon dioxide, and heat. Particulates may raise or lower temperature, depending on their size, composition, and time aloft, but anthropogenic particulates can be controlled at a relatively small cost. Other residuals, such as nitrous oxide, methane, ammonia, and sulfur dioxide, could contribute to the greenhouse effect,[19] raising the average temperature by 2025 about half as much as it will rise because of carbon dioxide (Keeling and Bacastow, 1977). The effects of each chemical are additive but may be modified in unknown ways by chemical reactions in the atmosphere. Halocarbons, now used in spray cans and refrigerating units, also will raise temperatures significantly by the greenhouse effect if they continue to be used at present rates.

Halocarbons and nitrous oxide also are suspected of attacking stratospheric ozone. Ozone destruction could lower average temperatures, but somewhat less than they are raised by the greenhouse effect of the two chemicals (Keeling and Bacastow, 1977). A more serious consequence of ozone destruction is that it may allow an increased amount of damaging ultraviolet radiation to reach the earth. This possibility has led to a ban on manufacture of halocarbon propellants, which account for about 30 percent of all U.S. halocarbon emissions (Smith, 1978). The cost of this ban will be slight, but use of halocarbons in refrigeration and solvent manufacture will be more costly to reduce. Nitrous oxide presents more serious problems because its release into the atmosphere may be related to the use of nitrogen fertilizers, which will continue to increase worldwide.

The direct release of heat to the atmosphere also may affect climate, but it now occurs at such low levels that it exerts only a local influence. Averaged over the continents, artificial heat input was about 0.1 percent of solar heat flow in 1970 (SMIC, 1971) and will rise to 0.4 percent in 2025. Effects on climate should be negligible. However, artificial heat input is unevenly distributed and may approach or exceed solar heat flow in industrial cities in cold climates (SMIC, 1971). This energy and the effect of surface alterations now contribute to urban weather anomalies, including warmer temperatures and more rainfall than would otherwise occur. As urban areas expand in the future these alterations in local

---

[19] The greenhouse effect of atmospheric gases and particles is their tendency to warm the atmosphere by trapping outgoing heat and radiation.

climate will affect large areas. It is not known whether such scattered, but widely occurring, variations will have any effects on future climates on a global scale.

The atmospheric contaminant expected first to affect climate significantly is carbon dioxide (CO_2). Almost all (98 percent) of the CO_2 added to the atmosphere by industrial processes is the product of combustion of fossil fuels (Keeling, 1973). Deforestation is an additional source, which is of unknown magnitude. This additional CO_2 enters the complex and incompletely known global carbon cycle and its ultimate fate is uncertain. Historically, about half of the added industrial CO_2 has remained in the atmosphere; the rest must have been absorbed by the oceans and terrestrial organisms. The airborne fraction, which depends on the transfer rates between the atmosphere, oceans, and land plants, is likely to increase in the future.

The capacity of the oceans to absorb CO_2 depends on a number of chemical and physical parameters that are not firmly established, but recent calculations indicate that only part of the CO_2 not remaining in the atmosphere could have been absorbed by the oceans. The rest had been assumed to be incorporated into land plants. However, calculations by terrestrial ecologists tentatively indicate that deforestation has been so widespread that land plants have been releasing, not absorbing, CO_2 (Woodwell, 1978). Though this discrepancy has not yet been resolved, it is generally agreed that current fractions of CO_2 absorbed by the oceans and land plants are likely to decrease in the future because the capacity of both to absorb CO_2 is limited. In contrast to the other gaseous residuals, the very slow absorption of CO_2 by the oceans will leave high levels of CO_2 in the atmosphere for hundreds of years even if all fossil-fuel burning were stopped.

If we ignore these complexities and simply use the approximate historical value of 50 percent for the fraction of industrial CO_2 retained in the atmosphere, CO_2 in the atmosphere will rise by the percentages shown in table 8–9 over the preindustrial value of 295 parts per million (ppm). In all three world scenarios, concentrations in 2050 will be about twice the preindustrial levels. The values shown in table 8–9 may be considered extremely uncertain but possibly conservative. Keeling and Bacastow (1977) and Nordhaus (1977) have made more sophisticated calculations that deal with the terrestrial, marine, and atmospheric carbon reservoirs separately. Keeling and Bacastow calculate that CO_2 concentrations in 2050 will be more than three times the preindustrial level, assuming fossil-fuel consumption is similar to that of our global low-growth case.

Table 8–9. Percentage Increase of Atmospheric Carbon Dioxide
Concentration Over Preindustrial Levels

Growth assumption	1974	2000	2025	2050
Standard world case[a]	12.1[b]	27.9	54.1	104.2
High-growth case[c]	12.1	29.3	63.0	128.1
Low-growth case[d]	12.1	27.0	52.3	90.9

Note: It is assumed that 50 percent of the carbon dioxide released remains in the atmosphere.

[a] From table 6–9.

[b] From C. D. Keeling, quoted in C. F. Baes, Jr., H. E. Goeller, J. S. Olson, and R. M. Rotty, *The Global Carbon Dioxide Problem*, ORNL-5194 (Oak Ridge, Tenn., Oak Ridge National Laboratory, 1976).

[c] High-growth rates for GNP and population.

[d] Low-growth rates for GNP and population.

In principle, it is possible to reduce industrial CO_2 emissions by removing CO_2 from stack gases. But storing the massive quantities involved would be a major problem and no economically feasible way to do so has yet been demonstrated. Short of reducing combustion itself, the only potentially feasible solution may be a massive, global reforestation program. Fortunately, such a program would have other benefits as well. It is expected that doubling the CO_2 concentration will cause a rise in global temperatures by the greenhouse effect, but the size of the increase is not known. According to Schneider (1975), the average temperature rise will most probably range from 1.5° to 3.0°C, although estimates range from 0.7° to 9.6°C. These values are calculated using climate models of varying complexity, all of which neglect many important factors that are difficult to model. One omitted factor is that higher temperatures increase evaporation rates, which leads to more cloudiness and less incoming heat. But higher temperatures also reduce the capacity of the oceans to absorb CO_2. The relative sizes of these and other neglected feedback effects are not known. Schneider (1975) believes that taking neglected factors into account could modify the temperature-change estimates by several times in either direction, so that the true value could be as high as 10°C or as low as 0.5°C for each doubling of CO_2 concentration.

The possible effects of a temperature increase are even more uncertain than the size of the increase, but some speculations have been made (Baes and coauthors, 1976). A temperature rise of several degrees or more will reduce the fitness of organisms that function most efficiently at existing temperatures. This might cause profound changes in the distribution of many species, a matter of particular concern for crop species that are cultivated over very large areas. Warmer weather will increase evaporation and shift storm belts to different areas, drastically changing hydrologic regimes and local weather patterns with further adverse effects on agriculture. Total productivity of ecosystems may decrease because of increased respiration rates on land and weakened ocean circulation. The projected temperature increase will not be distributed evenly, so its effects will be highly variable among different regions. The largest temperature change will be in polar regions, the smallest in the tropics. Although melting of polar ice and the resulting rise in sea level are important eventual consequences of higher temperatures, it is likely that melting will occur so slowly that sea-level changes in the next fifty years will be quite small (Baes and coauthors, 1976). If the lower temperature estimates are correct, the consequences could be trivial, but the higher temperature change would cause severe disruptions to human and natural systems.

In our present state of ignorance, it is not possible to predict climate change with any degree of certainty. The need for more information is clearly acute and urgent, because nuclear power, the major substitute for fossil fuel, will also cause numerous environmental problems. Only further research will show if climate modification will be trivial or catastrophic in the next fifty years.

Radiation

In 1975 nuclear power provided 9 percent of all electricity generated in the United States and, in the absence of a nuclear moratorium, is projected to supply more than 60 percent in 2025. Other countries are enthusiastically adopting nuclear energy because of its economic advantages and greater security of supply compared with fossil fuels. This established and rapidly growing technology has been the target of vociferous opposition both here and in Europe, however. Some experts and a significant part of the general public question the safety and desirability of nuclear power. Radiation is easy to suspect: it is unfamiliar and impossible to see or feel, and its effects extend to future generations, who have no say in today's decisions (Hohenemser, Kasperson, and Yates, 1977). In addition, any description of nuclear safety issues is necessarily technical, complex, and subject to differing interpretations. The possible adverse consequences of depending on nuclear power are so serious that understanding these issues is essential.

The dangers of nuclear power generation are of four kinds: small amounts of radiation are released during normal nuclear plant operation; there is a small, but nonzero, probability of a reactor accident that releases large quantities of radiation into the atmosphere; radioactive spent fuels must be safely stored for thousands of years; and there are security problems associated with nuclear power because small amounts of fuel, particularly plutonium required in fast breeder reactors, can be used to produce weapons.

The effects of radiation on living matter are very difficult to estimate. Although radioactive isotopes decay most rapidly immediately after their formation, they can continue to emit particles for an extremely long time, often millions of years. They are released at high speed, but their energy is dissipated when they collide with other matter. When living matter absorbs radiation, its molecules are ionized, which produces physical and chemical changes that can cause immediate or delayed death to the organism and genetic mutations in future generations. But the nature and extent of these effects vary, depending on the isotope in question, the level and duration of the exposure, the pathway by which the radiation enters the organism—for example, whether through skin, stomach, or lungs—and the way biological processes eliminate it from the body or concentrate it in specific organs. Most estimates of the effects of radiation use data gathered from nonhuman populations—for example, from experiments with mice to acquire information on genetic disorders. Though some data on humans have been collected from situations in which large doses have affected small populations, it is situations where small doses affect large populations that are more relevant.

Moreover, estimates of the extent of emissions from normal operations, the probability of major accidents, and the extent of emissions resulting from such accidents are based on extremely limited empirical evidence. Although there have been no major accidents in the 200 reactor-years of operations so far experienced, there have been some near misses like the Three Mile Island incident, and there is no guarantee that we will continue to be so lucky during the next 20,000 to 33,000 reactor years projected by 2025 (see table 8–10). Of course, there is no empirical basis at all for weighing the risks associated with storage and security problems.

Table 8–11, which presents estimates of expected deaths resulting from power plant operations, goes about as far as is possible to quantify these risks. As it indicates, about one death per reactor year can be expected from the normal operation of a nuclear power plant. This figure can be compared to values for a coal-fired plant that range from one to

Table 8–10. Accumulated Reactor Years of Operation of Nuclear Power Plants, Various Scenarios

Scenario	1975	1985	2000	2025
EL	200	858	4,608	19,465
DH	200	954	6,951	33,058
DHNU	200	954	2,519	3,953
DHP1	200	954	6,896	32,248
DHP2	200	963	5,725	28,838
DHRE	200	930	6,786	32,388
DL	200	910	6,323	28,858
FH	200	949	6,618	28,264
FL	200	913	6,069	24,941

Table 8–11. Expected Deaths Related to Power Plant Operation (deaths per plant year)[a]

Cause of death	Light-water reactors	Coal-fired power plants With sulfur scrubbing	Coal-fired power plants With new source performance standards	Coal-fired power plants Without scrubbing, using 3 percent sulfur coal
Physical accidents[a]	0.23–0.41	1.10–1.85	1.10–1.85	1.10–1.85
Normal releases of toxic substances[b]	0.36–0.77	0.04–10.00	0.40–25.00	2.00–100.00
Total for normal operations	0.59–1.18	1.14–11.85	1.50–26.85	3.10–101.85
Reactor accidents[c]	0.02–10.00	—	—	—
Total for normal operations and accidents	0.61–11.18	1.14–11.85	1.50–26.85	3.10–101.85

Note: All plants are 1,000 MW(e), operating at 70 percent of capacity.

Source: Data are compiled from Nuclear Energy Policy Study Group, *Nuclear Power Issues and Choices* (Cambridge, Mass., Ballinger Press, 1977).

[a] Accidents in construction, mining, and transportation.

[b] For light-water reactors, includes only cancer deaths at 180 deaths per million man-rem for public and occupational exposures during mining, milling, transporation, and reactor operations, excluding plant decommissioning, fuel recycling, and waste management and disposal. Deaths from exposure to radon and carbon 14 more than a century after operation are not included. Coal-fired power plant data for health effects of sulfur compounds calculated by the Nuclear Energy Policy Study Group (*Nuclear Power Issues*) from the North–Merkhofer model used in National Academy of Sciences, *Air Quality and Stationary Source Emission Control*, Senate Committee on Public Works, 94 Cong., 1 sess. (Washington, D.C., 1975). Deaths from black lung are excluded.

[c] Cancer deaths and prompt deaths. The lower value is the average rate of loss from the Rasmussen report (Nuclear Regulatory Commission, *Reactor Safety Study: An Assessment of Accident Risks in U.S. Commercial Nuclear Power Plants*, WASH-1400 (Washington, D.C., Nuclear Regulatory Commission, 1975) and the higher value is a pessimistic, upper limit calculation by the Nuclear Energy Policy Study Group (*Nuclear Power Issues*).

one hundred, a range that reflects the great uncertainties about the health effects of air pollutants, the containment method employed, and the type of coal used. When an estimate for major accidents is added, there is somewhat more overlap with the range for coal, but the impression remains that nuclear power plants are safer—or at least no worse—than coal-fired plants.

This conclusion must, however, be qualified in a number of ways. First, the data for deaths associated with sulfur compounds from coal are taken from a single model; other models show higher and lower values. In fact, the lowest suggested value is zero deaths, because severe effects of sulfur emissions at low doses have not been conclusively demonstrated.

Second, the values for light-water reactors include deaths attributable to carbon 14 and radon for only the first hundred years after power generation, even though these isotopes and their radioactive decay products persist for many thousands of years. This hundred-year cutoff may be reasonable for carbon 14 because most of it is likely to be absorbed in the oceans as carbon dioxide within a century, but it is not appropriate for radon, which is released from uranium mill tailings. The total number of deaths from exposure to radon and its decay products over all time may be from ninety to seven hundred deaths from a single year's operation of a power plant (Ramsay, 1978). But in order to interpret the significance of these figures, a decision must be made about the comparative value of a death this year and one ten thousand years later. The values shown in table 8–11 incorporate the assumptions that deaths that occur one hundred years from now are as important as deaths that occur today, but that deaths that occur thereafter are not important.

Third, a recent assessment of the data on nuclear risks concluded that the "error bounds" on estimates of the type included in table 8–11 should be increased (National Regulatory Commission, 1978). Although no quantitative estimate is given of how much they should be increased, any significant increase would result in substantially more overlap with the range for coal. We can only conclude that nuclear plants are safer than coal-fired plants by focusing on the midpoint of these ranges.

Fourth, it must be remembered that a comparison of averages of this sort, even if they are complete and reasonably reliable, is an insufficient basis on which to draw conclusions about the relative safety of nuclear power plant operations. An accident that happens once in one hundred years and kills a thousand people is perceived very differently from a process that kills ten people during every one of the same one hundred years, although their average rates of loss are identical (Ramsay,

Table 8–12. Accumulated Nuclear Spent Fuel for All Nuclear Plants,
Various Scenarios
(thousands of tons)

Scenario	1971	1975	1985	2000	2010	2025
EL	3.5	6.6	28.4	152.4	308.6	643.7
DH			31.1	229.5	496.9	1,092.8
DHNU			31.1	82.9	112.3	130.3
DHP1			31.1	228.1	487.8	1,066.4
DHP2			31.4	188.9	405.6	953.2
DHRE			30.3	224.0	485.8	1,070.6
FH			31.0	218.4	456.4	934.3
DL			29.7	208.7	444.9	953.9
FL			29.8	200.3	413.0	824.4

Note: Estimates are based on the light-water reactor coefficient; 33.07 tons per plant-year, from Nuclear Energy Policy Study Group, *Nuclear Power Issues and Choices* (Cambridge, Mass., Ballinger Press, 1977).

1978). Marginal impacts, such as those for coal air pollutants, are easier to accept because they are less obvious and less dramatic. Thus more opposition to nuclear power can be expected than the data in table 8–11 would justify.

Finally, these estimates are for deaths only. They do not include injuries and illnesses, which result from both nuclear and coal operations. Nor do they include genetic damage to future generations arising from nuclear operations.

So far as storage and security risks are concerned, little of a quantitative nature can be said. The quantities of spent fuel likely to accumulate in the next fifty years are not large, amounting to no more than one million tons by 2025 (see table 8–12); projected costs are relatively modest, probably no more than $3 billion a year or 1.4 percent of the value of the electricity generated in 2025 in scenario DH; and the NEPSG (1977) believes that spent fuel can be stored safely and retrievably (in case it is needed for reprocessing) in geologic formations.[20] But no practical methods have yet been developed, and the cooperation of far-off future generations will be needed to guard and monitor both fuel disposal and decommissioned nuclear power plant sites. To date, no spent fuel has been permanently disposed of. Since reprocessing is unlikely to be permitted in the near future and as a consequence stocks of spent fuel are building up rapidly, decisions on permanent storage will have to be made soon.

[20] The total cost of disposal is estimated at $100 per kilogram by the NEPSG (1977).

Even less can be said about the risks of theft, sabotage, and diversion into weapons. Such problems are not unique to nuclear energy. A ban on nuclear power in the United States alone may not reduce these risks; indeed, if such a ban meant that the United States imported greater amounts of petroleum or exported less coal, it could force other countries to move more heavily in the nuclear direction. Such risks are not unique to nuclear energy. For example, the possibility of diverting highly toxic chemicals and viruses for release into water supplies and into urban air poses similar threats. A number of safeguards against diversion into weapons have been proposed. An international security force for monitoring inventories and safeguarding nuclear materials in transit would help. Controls on the export of sophisticated manufacturing techniques required to produce the relatively pure plutonium or highly enriched uranium needed for a powerful bomb—but not needed for light water reactors—would at least slow down the spread of such capability. The development of the breeder, which produces plutonium, would worsen the situation. The development of fusion and solar technologies that reduce the need for other nuclear systems would improve the situation.

This is clearly an area of great ignorance, risks, and uncertainty. A substantial amount of time and creative effort will be required to find political, institutional, and technological solutions.

Toxic Chemicals and the Oceans

The variety of toxic chemicals released to the environment seems to be unlimited. The diversity of their characteristics makes a general description impossible. Included in this category are the heavy metals, such as mercury and arsenic, which occur naturally but can be concentrated to more toxic levels by industrial processes. At the other end of the spectrum are the complex synthetic molecules, such as the PCBs (polychlorinated biphenyls), which are created in laboratories and can be extremely toxic at very small concentrations.

The chemical and biological properties of these numerous chemicals, though widely variable, often include persistence in the environment and high toxicity to many organisms at low exposures. Some of them are concentrated by biological processes, often building up to high levels at the top of food chains although their original concentration in air or water was very low. The concentration factor, or ratio between the concentrations in organisms and their surrounding media, can be as high as several million. The ecological effects of toxic chemicals are unpredictable because of their diverse characteristics and their different effects on various organisms. For example, a chemical that is more toxic to a predator can have more serious ecological effects than one that is more toxic to its prey, because predators are less numerous.

The large and growing number of new synthetic chemicals with diverse chemical and biological characteristics contributes to the difficulties in controlling emissions of toxic chemicals. The necessary actions to test and regulate these chemicals are just beginning, and effective control of many toxic chemicals remains far in the future.

Annual use of pesticides, the most publicized group of toxic chemicals, is projected to rise very slightly in scenarios EL and DH and to rise 23 percent in scenario DHRE (see chapter 6). The environmental consequences of continued use of pesticides are not likely to remain the same, because different kinds of chemicals will be used in the future. Recently, the use of insecticides (the largest group of pesticides) has shifted away from the persistent organochlorines, such as DDT, to the more degradable organophosphorus and carbamate compounds. The environmental effects of DDT, which is now banned in the United States, are by no means well known, although it has been studied much more thoroughly than the organophosphorus and carbamate insecticides. In general, compounds in these two groups are less persistent and more immediately toxic. This suggests that their long-term effects might be less serious than the effects of organochlorines, but this cannot be determined in our present state of ignorance (Crosson and Frederick, 1977). The three widely used groups of insecticides are toxic to a wide variety of species, which causes problems of inadvertent poisoning of nontarget organisms, but it also makes them relatively cheap to develop and use.

More specific methods, including the use of sexual attractant compounds, release of sterilized males, and introduction of predators, have been used successfully to control individual species of pests. These biological methods have far fewer side effects than the broad-spectrum insecticides, but they require more expensive research to develop. The eventual solution of completely enclosed, pest-free agriculture is not likely to be implemented in the next fifty years, and the expense of research on biological control methods will limit its widespread use. Further research into the effects of conventional insecticides on ecosystems and human health may uncover more serious consequences of their past and current use.

The most serious consideration with persistent chemicals is their possible effects on the oceans. A large part of the toxic chemicals in the environment enter the oceans from freshwater runoff or rainout from the atmosphere. The slow circulation of ocean waters keeps these chemicals in the biologically productive upper layers for hundreds of years. Their effects on aquatic ecosystems and the fisheries that depend on them are unknown, but the continuing discharge of highly toxic wastes into the oceans is certainly cause for concern.

The oceans are most productive near shore where they are also most vulnerable to pollution. Seemingly harmless actions may have drastic effects on aquatic organisms, especially in estuaries. For example, variations in freshwater flow caused by river damming and upstream water consumption can so alter the salinity and turbidity of estuaries that species composition is affected. Destruction of salt marshes by bulkheading is particularly damaging to fisheries because it destroys the habitat of the young of many ocean-living species.

The effects of oil spills vary with the amount and type of oil and the location of the spill; in some cases, toxic effects have been observed several years after the spill occurred. In 1975, 21 billion gallons of oil were spilled in U.S. waters in 8,700 separate incidents (CEQ, 1976). It is likely that this amount will grow as oil imports and offshore drilling increase. If oil spills are proportional to oil imports, a 400 percent increase in oil spills over 1975 can be expected in the year 2000 in scenario DHP2. The effects of mining and waste disposal on the deep ocean floor, if they are feasible at all, are not known because so little is known about bottom-dwelling organisms. Exploitation of marine resources will undoubtedly bring new environmental quality problems, which could make the vast resources of the ocean useless to us.

Common Characteristics

Threats to the environment are extremely diverse in their causes, effects, methods of control, and potential seriousness. Setting aside the less serious ones, the majority have several characteristics in common that distinguish them from the mass pollutants discussed in chapter 7.

First, most of these environmental pressures are likely to grow over time as population and economic growth continue. Indeed, if the more pessimistic estimates associated with some of them are correct or if they act in concert with each other, these pressures may grow at accelerating rates and a few may reach truly critical levels within our time frame.

Second, these pressures may manifest themselves in a variety of subtle and disconcerting ways. Frequently, their damages are diffuse and separated by space and time—perhaps even by generations—from the causal events. In some cases, there have been no damages yet; all one can point to is the buildup of factors—CO_2 concentration, quantities of nuclear materials, loss of topsoil—that are likely at some point to cause damages. In still other cases—increasing population densities relative to resources in general but especially to land and water—the growth of environmental pressures means increasing regulations, conflicts, and the closing off of life-style options.

Third, control and regulation of these pressures are typically very difficult. In some cases—CO_2 for example—the problem is technical and practical. In others—water allocation and erosion control—adequate institutions and incentives have not been developed. In still other cases—ocean pollution and nuclear proliferation—the difficulties are compounded by the need for international agreements. Many of the more serious problems are associated with energy production and use, in particular the production of electricity from coal and nuclear fuel, and it is not out of the question that some day we may find that the only way to contain these pressures is to restrict combustion and use of coal and nuclear power.

Finally, our ignorance about most of these problems is profound and worrisome. We frequently do not know what the environmental consequences of past human actions have been, let alone what present or future human behavior might bring. Nor do we know how long we may have to solve some problems before passing a possibly critical ecological threshold. For example, we do not seem to have reached the point today at which we need to restrict the use of some forms of energy, but we may not know until after the fact that we have reached that point. If less environmentally damaging forms of energy—solar, fusion—come into use rapidly enough, we may never reach that point.

In large part, the growth of these environmental pressures means living with increasing uncertainties and risks. This is an area in which population and economic growth, coupled with partial scientific insights, appear to be throwing up problems faster than technological and institutional innovations can cope with them. There is no way to change this situation without altering the relationships among these growth rates.

References

Atomic Energy Commission (AEC). 1974. *Nuclear Power Facility Performance Characteristics for Making Environmental Impact Assessments,* WASH-1355 (Washington, D.C., AEC).

Averitt, P. 1975. *Coal Resources of the United States, January 1, 1974,* United States Geological Survey Bulletin 1412 (Washington, D.C., USGS).

Baes, C. F., Jr., H. E. Goeller, J. S. Olson, and R. M. Rotty. 1976. *The Global Carbon Dioxide Problem,* ORNL-5194 (Oak Ridge, Tenn., Oak Ridge National Laboratory).

Baker, E. T., Jr., and J. R. Wall. 1976. *Summary Appraisals of the Nation's Ground-water Resources—Texas–Gulf Region,* U.S. Geological Survey Professional Paper 813F (Washington, D.C., USGS).

Bennett, H. J., L. Moore, L. E. Welborn, and J. E. Toland. 1973. *An Economic Appraisal of the Supply of Copper from Primary Domestic Sources,* Bureau of Mines Information Circular 8598 (Washington, D.C., U.S. Department of Interior).

Blue, T. A., and T. F. Torries. 1975. *Phosphate Rock,* Chemical Economics Handbook Report (Menlo Park, Calif., Stanford Research Institute).

Bureau of Mines (BOM). 1967. *Potential Sources of Aluminum,* Bureau of Mines Information Circular 8335 (Washington, D.C., U.S. Department of Interior).

————. 1970. *Mineral Facts and Problems,* Bureau of Mines Bulletin 650 (Washington, D.C., U.S. Department of Interior).

————. 1973. *Minerals Yearbook 1971: Volume I* (Washington, D.C., U.S. Department of Interior).

————. 1976a. *Commodity Data Summaries 1976* (Washington, D.C., U.S. Department of Interior).

————. 1976b. *Mineral Facts and Problems,* Bureau of Mines Bulletin 667 (Washington, D.C., U.S. Department of Interior).

Carter, L. 1977. "Soil Erosion: The Problem Persists Despite the Billions Spent on It," *Science* vol. 196 (April 22).

CEQ. See Council on Environmental Quality.

Comptroller General. 1977. *To Protect Tomorrow's Food Supply, Soil Conservation Needs Priority Attention* (Washington, D.C., U.S. General Accounting Office).

Council on Environmental Quality (CEQ). *Environmental Quality—1976* (Washington, D.C., GPO).

Crosson, P. R., and K. D. Frederick. 1977. *The World Food Situation: Resource and Environmental Issues in the Developing Countries and the United States,* Research Paper R-6 (Washington, D.C., Resources for the Future).

Eakin, T. E., D. Price, and J. R. Harrill. 1976. *Summary Appraisals of the Nation's Ground-Water Resources—Great Basin Region,* U.S. Geological Survey Professional Paper 813G (Washington, D.C., USGS).

Edison Electric Institute (EEI). 1977. *Statistical Yearbook of the Electric Utility Industry: 1976* (New York, EEI).

ERDA. See U.S. Energy Research and Development Agency.

Evans, R. J. 1974. *Potential Solid Waste Generation and Disposal from Lime and Limestone Desulfurization Processes,* Bureau of Mines Information Circular 8633 (Washington, D.C., U.S. Department of Interior).

Everett, F. D., and H. J. Bennett. 1967. *Evaluation of Domestic Reserves and Potential Sources of Ores Containing Copper, Lead, Zinc, and Associated Metals,* Bureau of Mines Information Circular 8325 (Washington, D.C., U.S. Department of Interior).

————. 1975. *Steam-Electric Plant Air and Water Quality Control Data: Summary Report* (Washington, D.C., GPO).

FPC. See U.S. Federal Power Commission.

Frederick, K. D. 1977. "Water Uses and Misuses: A World View," *Resources* no. 55 (April–June).

Goldberg, E., and S. Holt. 1977. "Whither Oceans and Seas." Paper delivered at Second International Conference on the Environmental Future, Reykjavik, Iceland.

Goldstein, M., and R. S. Smith. 1975. "Land Reclamation Requirements and Their Estimated Effects on the Coal Industry," *Journal of Environmental Economics and Management* vol. 2, no. 2 (December).

Hittman Associates. 1975. *Environmental Impacts, Efficiency, and Cost of Energy Supply and End Use: Final Report, Volume II* (Columbia, Md., Hittman Associates, Inc.).

Hohenemser, C., R. Kasperson, and R. Yates. 1977. "The Distrust of Nuclear Power," *Science* vol. 196 (April) pp. 25–34.

Keeling, C. D. 1973. "Industrial Production of Carbon Dioxide from Fossil Fuels and Limestone," *Tellus* vol. 25, p. 174.

————, and R. B. Bacastow. 1977. "Impact of Industrial Gases on Climate," in *Energy and Climate* (Washington, D.C., National Academy of Sciences).

Murray, C. R., and E. B. Reeves. 1972. *Estimated Use of Water in the United States in 1970,* U.S. Geological Survey Circular 676 (Washington, D.C., USGS).

———— and ————. 1977. *Estimated Use of Water in the United States in 1975,* U.S. Geological Survey Circular 765 (Washington, D.C., USGS).

National Academy of Sciences (NAS). 1974. Environmental Studies Board, National Academy of Sciences and National Academy of Engineering, *Rehabilitation Potential of Western Coal Lands* (Cambridge, Mass., Ballinger Press).

————. 1975a. *Air Quality and Stationary Source Emission Control,* Senate Committee on Public Works, 94 Cong. 1 sess. (Washington, D.C.).

————. 1975b. *Mineral Resources and the Environment* (Washington, D.C., NAS).

————. 1977. *The Potential Contributions of Research,* World Food and Nutrition Study (Washington, D.C., NAS).

National Commission on Materials Policy (NCMP). 1973. *Material Needs and the Environment Today and Tomorrow* (Washington, D.C., GPO).

National Water Commission (NWC). 1973. *Water Policies for the Future* (Washington, D.C., GPO).

NEPSG. See Nuclear Energy Policy Study Group.

Nordhaus, W. D. 1977. "Strategies for the Control of Carbon Dioxide," Cowles Foundation Discussion Paper No. 443 (New Haven, Conn., Cowles Foundation).

NRC. See Nuclear Regulatory Commission.

Nuclear Energy Policy Study Group (NEPSG). 1977. *Nuclear Power Issues and Choices* (Cambridge, Mass., Ballinger Press).

Nuclear Regulatory Commission (NRC). 1975. *Reactor Safety Study: An Assessment of Accident Risks in U.S. Commercial Nuclear Power Plants*, WASH-1400 (Washington, D.C., NRC).

————. 1976. *Final Generic Environmental Statement on the Use of Recycle Plutonium in Mixed Oxide Fuel in Light Water Cooled Reactors* (Springfield, Va., National Technical Information Service).

————. 1978. *Risk Assessment Review Group Report to the U.S. Nuclear Regulatory Commission* (Washington, D.C., NRC).

Paone, J., J. L. Morning, and L. Giorgetti. 1974. *Land Utilization and Reclamation in the Mining Industry, 1930–71*, Bureau of Mines Information Circular 8642 (Washington, D.C., U.S. Department of Interior).

Price, D., and T. Arnow. 1974. *Summary Appraisals of the Nation's Ground-Water Resources—Upper Colorado Region*, U.S. Geological Survey Professional Paper 813C (Washington, D.C., USGS).

Probstein, R. F., D. J. Goldstein, H. Gold, and J. Shen. 1975. "Water Needs for Fuel-to-Fuel Conversion Processes," *American Institute of Chemical Engineers Symposium Series* vol. 71, no. 151.

Ramsay, W. C. 1979. *Unpaid Costs of Electrical Energy: Health and Environmental Impacts from Coal and Nuclear Power* (Baltimore, Md., Johns Hopkins University Press for Resources for the Future).

Schneider, S. H. 1975. "On the Carbon Dioxide-Climate Confusion," *Journal of the Atmospheric Sciences* vol. 32, p. 2060.

SMIC. See Study of Man's Impact on Climate.

Smith, R. J. 1978. "Government Takes Partial Step to Protect Ozone Layer," *Science* vol. 200, no. 4338 (April 14) p. 187.

Stevens, B. H., and G. A. Trainer. 1976. "Distribution of Population and Economic Activity Among the BEA Regions of the United States in the year 2025," Resources for the Future working paper (Washington, D.C.).

Study of Man's Impact on Climate (SMIC). 1971. *Inadvertent Climate Modification* (Cambridge, Mass., MIT Press).

Thomas, H. E., and D. A. Phoenix. 1976. *Summary Appraisals of the Nation's Ground-Water Resources—California Region*, U.S. Geological Survey Professional Paper 813-E (Washington, D.C., USGS).

U.S. Department of Agriculture (USDA). 1973. Economic Research Service. *Major Uses of Land in the United States: Summary for 1969* (Washington, D.C., GPO).

————. 1977. Economic Research Service. *Food and Agriculture*. Report prepared for Resources for the Future (February) (Washington, D.C.).

U.S. Energy Research and Development Administration (ERDA). 1975. *Uranium Industry Seminar* (Grand Junction, Col., ERDA).

————. 1976. *National Uranium Resource Evaluation, Preliminary Report* (Grand Junction, Col., ERDA).

U.S. Federal Power Commission (FPC). 1971. *The 1970 National Power Survey: Part I* (Washington, D.C., GPO).

Water Resources Council (WRC). 1968. *The Nation's Water Resources: The First National Assessment of the Water Resources Council* (Washington, D.C., WRC).

————. 1978. *The Nation's Water Resources: The Second National Assessment by the U.S. Water Resources Council, Summary Report* (Washington, D.C., Water Resources Council, March).

West, S. W., and W. L. Broadhurst. 1975. *Summary Appraisals of the Nation's Ground-Water Resources—Rio Grande Region*, U.S. Geological Survey Professional Paper 813-D (Washington, D.C., USGS).

Wollman, N., and G. W. Bonem. 1971. *The Outlook for Water* (Baltimore, Md., Johns Hopkins University Press for Resources for the Future).

Woodwell, G. M. 1978. "The Carbon Dioxide Question," *Scientific American* vol. 238, no. 1 (January) pp. 34–43.

9
Summary and Prospects

The principal goal of this study has been to assess the resource and environmental consequences for the United States of major domestic and international developments likely to occur during the next half-century. Our approach has been to develop assumptions about each of the major factors, particularly population and economic growth, that will determine these resource and environmental consequences and to build them into scenarios. Computer models and more conventional studies of special problem areas were then used to analyze the economic, resource, and environmental implications of these scenarios.

Previous chapters have presented the results, along with methods and assumptions, from specialized viewpoints—the national economy, the agricultural sector, energy, and so on. In this chapter, we fit these partial results together, emphasizing those issues that crosscut specific areas of interest. We begin by focusing on just one scenario and present as comprehensive a picture of results for that case as we can. The second section of this chapter considers how these results differ for different scenarios. The final section is concerned with some broader implications of our analysis.

Base Case

The most useful scenario for this comprehensive review is the base case (along with the standard case for the rest of the world). This is a scenario in which U.S. population growth continues its slow decline and reaches zero (apart from immigration) a decade or so after the end of our time horizon and in which the rate of improvement in labor productivity recovers only modestly from its slow pace of recent years. The most important policy assumptions of this case are that (1) world oil and gas prices remain at their 1975 levels in real terms for the next thirty years or so, while domestic energy prices rise to world levels by 1985; (2) no special efforts are made to restrict petroleum imports or to develop a strategic stockpile; (3) pollution controls are applied with some slippage from strict enforcement of existing regulations; and (4) population and economic growth in the rest of the world continue but at slower rates than during the last quarter-century. In common with other scenarios, only modest changes in tastes and technology are introduced.

Population and the GNP

In this case, world population increases from 3.8 billion in 1972 to 6.4 billion in 2000 and to 9.4 billion by 2025; in the same years, GNP per capita grows from $1,000 to $1,700 and $2,600.[1] These figures represent a modest slowdown in rates of both population and economic growth compared to the fifties and sixties. The decline in population growth rates results from a simple continuation of recent trends and assumes no breakthroughs in family planning programs. The long-term decline in economic growth rates arises from a variety of factors: the elimination of the technological gap between developed countries that has allowed countries like Japan to grow more rapidly than the United States; the emergence of structural problems, comparable to those faced by the United States, in a growing number of countries as they approach U.S. per capita income levels; continued problems, especially in less developed countries, in adjusting to high energy prices; and so on. These growth rates, despite their deceleration, are sufficient to allow for substantial improvement in material well-being throughout the world. Indeed, they imply that most Latin American countries emerge from the less developed class, though the poorer countries of South Asia remain far from this goal, even after fifty years of growth.

The U.S. population grows from 209 to 304 million during this period, with the annual growth rate approaching zero by the end of the period. At the same time, the population becomes substantially older; the proportion 65 and over will grow from 11 to 16 percent, while that less

[1] All dollar figures in this chapter are in 1971 prices except where otherwise stated.

than 20 falls from 35 to 28 percent. Fortunately, these shifts allow the working age population to remain roughly constant as a percentage of the total, though some cycling of these percentages occurs as the baby-boom generation works its way through the age groups. Once that generation is fully absorbed in the labor force and the secular shift toward increased female labor-force participation is completed, the excessively rapid increases in the labor force experienced in recent years should come to an end, and unemployment rates should drop.

At the same time, the GNP per employee, after an initial spurt as the economy approaches full employment, progresses at a slower rate than the 2.4 percent a year considered the norm during the 1948–68 period: approximately 1.9 percent between 1980 and 2000 and just under 1.8 percent between 2000 and 2025. Such a deceleration arises in this case because of changes in the age, education, and sex composition of the labor force; shifts in the composition of output (in particular the end of the exodus of labor from agriculture); and several judgmentally determined shifts downward in the trend to reflect such factors as more-rapid-than-trend declines in the energy intensity of the economy.

With growth in both the labor force and its productivity decelerating, the annual growth in GNP also slows down, from 3.6 percent per year in the fifties and sixties to 3.2 percent during the first half of our fifty-year time horizon and 2.3 percent during the second half. Nevertheless, the momentum of the economy is sufficient to make it nearly quadruple in size, from $1.1 to $4.2 trillion between 1975 and 2025, while per capita GNP and consumption increase by a factor of three.

Given our assumptions, the composition of output does not change very dramatically. There is some movement toward services and away from construction, especially public construction, but the most significant change is toward higher rates of investment in equipment—a consequence, among other things, of efforts to meet environmental regulations and adjust to the higher energy prices existing after 1973–74. These increased investment requirements, particularly in the eighties, are large by historical standards and may prove difficult to finance without inflation and a slowdown in economic growth rates. After the turn of the century, however, aggregate investment requirements appear to settle down to more manageable rates.

This analysis does not include any estimate of feedbacks from economic or environmental to demographic variables. One in particular should be mentioned because it represents a potentially important qualification to our concern about a possible capital shortage. It pertains to the likelihood of substantially increased immigration rates, illegal if not legal, once full employment is reached. This is likely to occur in the context of an overheated economy, not just because of the added attractiveness of the U.S. labor market, but also because of pressures on the part of employers to allow more immigration and difficulties on the part of unions whose members are fully employed in arguing against it. If there were a single labor market, a greater influx would relax an important constraint on the rate of growth of the GNP by allowing an increase in investment without necessarily cutting significantly into other uses of output. The fact that there are many groups of domestic laborers with whom immigrants cannot compete complicates the situation and reduces its importance, but the net effect should be in the same direction. Thus, we cannot say for certain whether the increased investment requirements of the eighties will lead to a reduced rate of economic growth, as it might if our initial population assumptions hold and if monetary and fiscal policy cannot bring about a sufficiently high savings rate, or whether they will lead to an increased rate of economic growth because of induced increases in the labor force. Clearly, this is a topic requiring additional study.

A second possible feedback is from environmental pressures to mortality rates. As chapter 6 indicates, emissions of the common mass pollutants are projected to decline over time because of increasingly strict controls; emissions of many trace chemicals and carcinogens should decline in conjunction with the reduction in mass pollutants because they are normally filtered out by the same control processes. Mortality associated with these pollutants, therefore, ought to decline. On the other hand, the amount of radioactive materials in the environment will increase with the spread of nuclear power plants. So far as other environmental threats are concerned—possible climate changes and ocean pollution, for example—there is certainly no reason to believe that mortality rates, to whatever extent they are associated with these threats, will decline. These crosscurrents and the absence of data make it impossible to suggest what the net effect might be.

Nonfuel Minerals

Shifts in the composition of output are not dramatic, but they are sufficient, along with the technological changes built into this analysis, to reduce the mineral intensity of this output at least for the majority of the minerals analyzed in detail in chapter 4. The principal exceptions are lighter metals, such as aluminum, and cement, plastics, and glass, which are the beneficiaries of the substitution processes projected for the next several decades. The consequence is a further slowdown in the rate of growth in demand for many important metals and minerals. Our estimates probably understate the extent of this slowdown because we have assumed a constant recycling rate though there is reason to believe this rate will increase over time and because we have incorporated only a few of the many technological changes and substitutions that are likely to occur on the demand and supply sides of the markets. Our analysis of the supply side has been limited largely to efforts to estimate prospective reserves, the assumption being that, in the long run, problems of producing from these reserves will be solved. These estimates are, if anything, on the low side because "speculative" and frequently also "hypothetical" resource estimates are left out, as well as estimates of any kind for some continents.

Just because of these biases in our estimation techniques, we feel confident about our conclusion that nonfuel mineral prices in general are unlikely to rise in real terms as a consequence of depletion. In the case of some specific minerals, commercial grades in the United States will be depleted during the next half-century if imports remain constant, but worldwide supplies are generally sufficient to satisfy demands. The exceptions are lead, tin, tungsten, and perhaps fluorine and mercury, for which real prices will have to rise somewhat. But in all these cases, the gap between long-run demand and supply can be closed with only modest increases in these prices, probably no more than a doubling during our fifty-year time span. There are a few minerals, most notably those associated with deep-sea nodules, that could well fall in price if expectations for this technology prove correct.

There are, of course, influences other than depletion that may cause the relative prices of nonfuel minerals to rise over time. The costs of environmental controls and of energy for mining, beneficiation, reduction, and refining tends to be greater per dollar of output for these minerals than for other economic activities. There may be added restrictions on land use for mining purposes in the future. Acquiring sufficient water for mineral processing may prove to be a problem in some areas. Efforts to impose environmental and land use controls in the United States and to gain more local control over company operations and profits abroad may be increasing uncertainties and risks, and this could reduce the flow of investment into minerals production unless offset by higher profit rates. Further, the tendency of developing countries to process their own minerals a stage or two forward, as well as the existence of nationalist investment policies and local turmoil, may be diverting investments into lower grade deposits.

In the long run, these factors are unlikely to raise nonfuel minerals prices very much. Environmental controls, restrictions on land use, and water shortages are likely to affect U.S. production costs more than those in the rest of the world; if U.S. costs are increased for these reasons, imports will rise, holding down domestic prices. The situation with respect to the cost of energy used to produce minerals is different, because these costs will increase universally as ore grades decline or energy prices increase. But the percentage of energy used in mining and beneficiation, as opposed to reduction and refining, is small and, at least according to one estimate, not likely to increase significantly when lower grade ores come into use.[2] It is not clear that efforts to gain more local control over company operations signals the beginning of a long period of disruptions that will continue to inhibit aggregate investment, that is, investment by public as well as private enterprises. It is just as likely—indeed, perhaps more likely—that we are in a transition period that will not last for more than another five to ten years and that once the new rules of the game are fully established and accepted, uncertainties—and hence reluctance to invest on this count—will recede. Nor is it clear that more investment is diverted into lower grade deposits today than was the case in the past; costs of transport and of acquiring information have generally fallen over time and it is difficult to say whether local disturbances are greater or less than in the past.

The combined effect of all these factors on long-run prices could be of some significance, but given the fact that the minerals sectors constitute a small and diminishing portion of the whole economy[3]—.42 percent today and .38 percent in 2025—it would take very large price increases indeed before any measurable effects on aggregate economic growth would be observed.

What the national economy cannot absorb with equanimity are sudden disruptions in supply, disruptions which come upon purchasers so rapidly and unexpectedly that there is no time to adjust. But such disruptions for a period long enough to do substantial harm are unlikely

---

[2] Goeller and Weinberg (1976) point out, for example, that mining and beneficiation of iron ore requires 5 percent of the energy that goes into steel production. Even more significantly, they find that in no case investigated was the energy required to produce metals from essentially inexhaustible sources more than 60 percent greater than the energy required to win the metals from high-grade ores.

[3] Iron ore, copper ore, other nonferrous ores, stone and clay mining, and chemical fertilizer mining.

because of the diversity of suppliers, the difficulty of forming effective and aggressive cartels for these commodities—in contrast to petroleum—and the substantial stockpiles held by the U.S. government.

Energy

Whatever the problems in nonfuel minerals, they are likely to be minor compared to those of the energy sector. But even here the problems stem less from an insufficiency of resources than from their distribution, from their environmental consequences, and the transition in moving from one energy regime to another. Indeed, in terms of *usable* energy resources, vastly larger quantities are available today than were present in 1972, prior to the OPEC price rise; if real energy prices increase again in the future, even larger quantities, including virtually inexhaustible sources like solar energy and biomass, will become economically viable.

On the demand side, as with nonfuel minerals, we can look forward to a long period of declining rates of increase. In this case, the deceleration in demand is somewhat more rapid because of efforts at conservation induced by the 1973 embargo and subsequent price increases. This can be seen most clearly in our projections of the energy intensity of output. For the United States, the ratio of Btu per dollar of GNP declines by a third, from substantially higher than the world average—though far from the highest—to below that average in 2025. This relatively rapid decline occurs because the composition of output in this country is shifting away from energy-intensive sectors while that in many poorer countries is still moving in the opposite direction. Our already high per capita energy use is leading rapidly to saturation in many consumer markets, and we have a greater ability than less developed countries to accommodate technologically to a regime of higher prices. Other developed countries will also experience significant declines in energy intensity, but less rapidly than in the United States because their domestic energy prices were already higher and their Btu/GNP ratios substantially lower than ours prior to 1972. In contrast, developing countries are likely to experience increasing intensities of energy use as they industrialize, modernize their agriculture, and shift from noncommercial to commercial fuels. Despite this increase, the net result for the world, according to our projections, is virtually no change in the energy intensity of global output between 1975 and 1985 and thereafter a slow decline, amounting to 14 percent between 1975 and 2025.

Our projections on the supply side show a rapid expansion in the use of coal (1975–90), nuclear power (especially between 1990 and 2010), and synthetic oils and gases made from coal, shale, heavy oils, and tars (after 2015). The early expansion of coal and nuclear power results from phasing out oil and gas in the production of electricity plus continued increases in the percentage of energy consumed in the form of electricity. Solar sources of energy remain unimportant until after the turn of the century. In large part, this is because energy prices do not increase significantly before 2010, but it is also because technological improvements are not expected to lower costs significantly, except in the area of solar electricity and then only late in our period. Geothermal energy becomes about as important as hydroelectric power, but the latter does not expand much during the projection period.

Four significant conclusions follow from these, plus related, considerations. First, even if energy prices do not rise significantly, there is no danger of seriously depleting any of the world's energy resources, other than petroleum and natural gas, within the next half-century and probably well beyond given the assumptions of this scenario. A possible qualification must be added for uranium because estimates of its resource base are so uncertain, but even if it is overestimated, there are extensive possibilities for improving efficiency in use or substituting other fuels and processes (various forms of plutonium recycling including the breeder, laser enrichment, the thorium fuel cycle, and fusion). Even petroleum and natural gas are likely to remain important sources of energy throughout our fifty-year time horizon. In the standard case, 85 percent of the petroleum resources believed to be recoverable today with only modest increases in price or improvements in technology are used up by 2025, and production does not fall to insignificant levels until after 2020.

Second, if there were no constraints imposed on production or sale from any of the world's sources and if the price were not to fall below its present level, production of petroleum could keep up with the growth in demand until some time after the turn of the century. At that point, the price would have to rise, unless, of course, alternate sources of liquids become available at competitive prices before that time, an unlikely possibility without timely and significant government intervention. In the standard case in which we assume no such intervention, the price begins to rise in 2010, reaches a peak some 60 percent above the present level, but returns to within 10 to 15 percent of that level by about 2040, when the capacity to produce synthetics has expanded sufficiently. For gas, this transition to a synthetic world begins a decade later and does not last as long.

If there are constraints on production or sale from available supplies, the price will begin rising earlier. Given one plausible set of constraints the model indicates that oil prices would begin rising in 1987. But because petroleum reserves would be stretched out and production of synthetic fuels would begin sooner, the model also indicates that the price rise would be limited to a maximum of 40 percent above present levels and would be relatively slow and orderly. To obtain a more significant increase in price, one that is more in line with today's conventional wisdom, it was necessary to assume in addition that technological improvements do not come along to lower the cost of substitutes, that the price elasticity of demand for petroleum is lower than that used in the base case, and that income elasticity is higher. Although the price would begin rising immediately in this case, it would still increase relatively slowly, by no more than 2.2 percent a year in real terms to a peak in 2025 of 2.7 times present levels.

A final conclusion from this case pertains to import dependency. If no special efforts were made to speed up the rate at which substitutes for petroleum and natural gas from conventional sources come on-stream, dependence on imported oil would increase from 41 percent in 1975 to 77 percent in 2000; even in 2025, when the United States is producing substantial synthetic fuels, 69 percent of the oil consumed would have to be imported. It is only in the decade after 2025 that synthetic capacity would expand sufficiently relative to demand to eliminate imports altogether and perhaps even to make exports a possibility.

Although the balance of payments problems of this scenario could be difficult,[4] the political and security problems associated with it are far more worrisome because of U.S. vulnerability to oil production shortfalls and embargos. Indeed, given the likely sequence of exploitation of major fields, this vulnerability is likely to grow worse by the turn of the century. Although global production of petroleum may become somewhat less concentrated in the coming decade as non-OPEC sources come on-stream, efforts to reduce import dependence are likely to lead to rapid exhaustion of these sources. Thereafter, production from remaining major fields will become increasingly concentrated in a few hands, first the OPEC coun-

---

[4] It is not certain that they would be, however. Much depends on what happens in the world market for food grains, in which the United States is in about the same position vis-à-vis other countries as Saudi Arabia is in oil—and the way in which the international monetary system works to recycle petro-dollars, to mention only two important factors.

tries and later the Communist countries (assuming that the latter eventually solve their production problems and that our estimates of regional resources are reasonably correct). Until the United States develops its capacity to produce adequate substitutes, this concentration could prove to be a serious political liability. Many other countries are used to much higher dependency ratios than the United States will ever experience, but they are not used to the degree of geographic concentration of suppliers or to the growing vulnerability of the principal status quo power in the world.

There is, of course, a great deal of uncertainty in all this. Political difficulties in the Middle East may result in chronic production shortfalls or the failure of capacity to grow as rapidly as assumed. The recently discovered Yucatan fields of Mexico may prove much larger than believed at the time the petroleum resource numbers of chapter 5 were assembled. Solar and synthetics may develop more rapidly than assumed in this scenario. Nuclear power may develop more slowly. The prospect of tapping the vast deposits of heavy oils has not been factored into this analysis. And there are a host of environmental problems associated with energy. Our point here is a limited one: that growing shortages of energy resources and rising world energy prices are not the central problems we face in the next half-century; rather, we face transitional problems—adjusting to dramatically higher energy prices than existed just a few years ago and bringing new energy sources on-stream in an orderly fashion— and problems associated with changes in the distribution of the world's energy resources and resulting shifts in the balance of power.

Agriculture, Forestry, and Fisheries

In the world as a whole, the quantities of land and water appropriate for food production appear to be adequate to meet likely demands during the next half-century. But this land and water, plus the know-how, institutions, capital, and proper incentives necessary to achieve decent levels of productivity are not distributed in the same way as the world's population. Given differential population and economic growth rates, these disparities could well grow over time. The result could be a continuation of the slow increase in per capita output for the world as a whole, and a decline for some regions—most notably South Asia. International movements in food will have to grow substantially if per capita consumption in these regions is not to fall.

The United States plays a key role in this global picture because of its vast surplus available for export, but serious doubts have been raised recently about the ability of the United States to continue expanding this surplus without substantial increases in prices. Our analysis, particularly given the base-case assumptions, does not support this prospect. Largely out of prudence, we have assumed a substantial slowdown in the rate of growth of agricultural productivity in this case—from an average of 1.7 percent a year during the last quarter-century to 0.9 percent a year during our projection period. But the rate of growth of U.S. food consumption, even without increased prices, can be expected to fall even more, fairly quickly approaching the growth rate of population, which itself is falling. The result is an increase in exportable surplus compatible with our assumptions about global developments.

On net, no new land need be converted to cropland in this case, and the rate of growth in use of fertilizers, pesticides, and energy slows down appreciably during this period. Domestic energy prices and environmental control costs do rise somewhat, but not by enough to appreciably affect production costs until close to our time horizon. Fertilizer prices could well fall during the next decade or so as recent worldwide efforts to increase productive capacity come on-stream. Beyond 2025, this situation could change; and it is definitely different in other scenarios. But at least within our time horizon and for this base case, there seems no reason for significant increases in real prices.

Though not treated in this study, the forestry and fisheries sectors deserve mention because of two unique features that contrast rather sharply with agriculture. First, the current level of global exploitation is probably excessive in the sense that, with current technology, yields cannot be sustained. There are some unexploited, nontraditional marine species that can be used, especially for livestock feed, but most analysts seem agreed that the traditional fish population is not sustainable without some cutback in the catch. If ocean pollution grows over time, consumption will have to be reduced even further to protect the population, though there are no good numbers to indicate the magnitudes involved; the same holds for freshwater fisheries. Forests too are threatened. Twenty-five years ago, forest covered one-fourth of the world's land surface—it now covers one-fifth; if recent trends continue, this fraction will fall to one-sixth in 2000 and one-seventh in 2020. Most of this deforestation will occur in the developing countries, where population growth will increase subsistence needs significantly. In richer countries, reforestation projects, more intensive cultivation, and a growing range of substitutes for wood may keep price increases within reasonable bounds.

Second, in contrast to modern agriculture, these industries—particularly fishing—are still in the hunting and gathering stage and production technologies could change quite dramatically in the next half-century. Once they emerge from this stage, when fish and trees are routinely cultivated, sustainable yields could take a substantial jump upward, as happened in the case of agriculture. To accomplish this on a large scale poses many technological, financial, and institutional problems, but there is probably time to forestall major shortages if proper incentives are provided and if these tasks are approached with some degree of urgency.

The Environment

Present and prospective environmental issues are so many and diverse that some clustering is necessary for this brief summary. It is useful to start with those environmental problems that are currently being controlled or that pose no new control problems: the mass pollutants, solid waste disposal, and routine radiation emissions from power plants. All other problems and issues are discussed in two categories: those that are or may be severe at the local level though they are not severe nationally (for example, power plant siting and water shortages), and problems that may be serious nationally or globally (for example, erosion, global climate effects, nuclear proliferation, and ocean pollution). With the partial exception of this last category, the emphasis here is on the United States, the implicit assumption being that other countries will learn from U.S. experience and not allow erosion and climate problems to become so severe that repercussions are felt beyond their borders.

RELATIVELY WELL CONTROLLED PROBLEMS. If the percentage of residuals emitted into the environment were to remain constant in the future, emissions would quickly rise to intolerable levels as the economy grows over time. But emission controls are slated to increase even in the base case, which assumes some relaxation from currently legislated standards. Though far from optimal, these controls are sufficient to reduce emissions of ten of the eleven mass pollutants studied, the exception being nutrients in 2025 (nitrogen oxides, suspended solids, and dissolved solids are higher in the mid-eighties but lower thereafter). As a consequence, our estimate of damage costs from these pollutants falls from $35.4 billion to $20.4 billion between 1975 and 2025, despite the much larger economy and number of units at risk to damage. Annualized control costs, of course, rise from $17.3 billion in 1975 to $181 billion in 2025. But even when we include costs of controlling other pollutants—solid wastes, non-point sources, sulfur sludge, land reclamation, and radiation—they amount to only 1.1 percent of GNP in 1975 and 2.0 percent in 2025. Nevertheless, implementing these controls will cause problems, among other reasons, because these costs are not spread smoothly over time and across sectors. The extent of the slippage from legislated standards built into this case represents our estimate of the environmental impact of these problems.

The situation with respect to solid wastes from urban sources and radiation emissions associated with normal operations of power plants is similar: rapidly growing amounts to be controlled and increasing costs of doing so. The costs will not be so large as to interfere significantly with aggregate economic growth, however. In the case of solid wastes, for example, costs per unit of control are likely to rise as distances to acceptable sites increase over time and as more sophisticated procedures are applied in later years to avoid leaching and runoff that could become dangerous because of the buildup of heavy metals and highly toxic chemicals. Controls on radiation emissions associated with normal power plant operations are being built into plant design in increasingly sophisticated ways and (in contrast to other nuclear problems) should not pose serious problems in the future.

POTENTIALLY SEVERE PROBLEMS AT THE LOCAL LEVEL.   These include conflicts over land use (including siting of power plants, land disturbance by mining, and sulfur sludge disposal), water shortages, reactor accidents, disposal of spent nuclear fuel, and local weather modification. These problems differ in two ways from those in the first category. First, the technologies and institutions for controlling many of them are not as well worked out. Reclamation can keep the land disturbed by mining at any one time within reasonable limits for affordable costs in most areas, but water shortage in arid regions, where much future mining activity will have to be located, poses special problems not yet solved. There is considerable room for improving the efficiency with which water is used and in the process avoiding shortages and excessive contamination, but the institutional mechanisms for doing so are not adequate in most of the critical regions. The probability of reactor accidents and escape of radiation from waste disposal sites cannot be reduced to zero, any more than can probabilities of accidents in coal mines, but the additional fears associated with nuclear power make the problem of finding acceptable sites far more difficult. Standard procedures for managing solid wastes are inadequate for handling sulfur sludge from coal-fired power plants. All these problems are likely to prove solvable, but until solutions are found, we can expect associated pressures on the environment (along with siting and water allocation problems) to mount as local population and economic growth proceeds. This contrasts rather sharply with what we expect in the case of most mass pollutants.

Second, though these problems may have some social and economic consequences at the national level, their principal impacts, especially their environmental impacts, will be felt at the local level. Compared to most other high-income countries, the United States is still a land- and water-rich nation and is likely to remain so during the next half-century. This country is not in danger of "paving over" a large fraction of farmland during that time, spoiling large tracts of highly valued recreational land, or consuming an excessively large proportion of available water supplies. Nor is the total number of acres required for nuclear power plants, mines, synthetic energy production, and so on very large in relation to the number of acres potentially available for such purposes. Thus, if the distributional problems can be solved, the requirements of this scenario clearly can be met.

But that may prove to be a rather large "if." A number of regions will have to change character quite dramatically in the next half-century. The Delaware River Basin may have to accommodate an inordinately large number of nuclear power plants—thirty-two in the base case in 2025, which means an average of one every nine miles.[5] The Ohio River Valley will be excessively burdened with coal mines, coal-fired power plants, and eventually synthetic fuel plants. The Southwest will have to make water available for mining and synthetic fuels production, which will mean less for agriculture. Florida will have to permit the area devoted to phosphate mining to expand. In the process, some people and economic activities will have to move to make way for others. The extent of such movements may not be great. There is a good deal of room for other forms of adjustment, for example, getting used to living in more densely populated areas, making a serious effort to conserve water—which among other things means raising its price substantially and allowing reallocations among users—and living among more areas of restricted access. But few regions in the United States have the traditions and institutions required to bring about such adjustments quickly and equitably. Judging

---

[5] This may be a misleadingly difficult picture because these plants could be clustered in a few large centers.

from past history, conflicts, sometimes bitter and protracted, are likely, particularly in those regions with a confluence of desirable characteristics.

The overall effect of this local turmoil is difficult to judge. If efforts to prohibit the establishment of seemingly dangerous, dirty, or simply distasteful economic activities in one's region become sufficiently widespread, aggregate economic growth could be affected. On the other hand, the need for jobs and the desire for profits could win out, as they have in the past. Our guess is that as incomes continue to rise, preferences for environmental amenities will continue growing relative to desires for still more income. This adds to our list of reasons for believing that the lower rate of per capita economic growth incorporated into this base case is more likely than the higher rates incorporated into other scenarios.

PROBLEMS THAT MAY BE SEVERE NATIONALLY OR GLOBALLY.   Frequently mentioned concerns falling into this category are loss and deterioration of soils, loss of genetic variability, effects on global climate, ozone depletion, release of radon from uranium mill tailings, proliferation and buildup of toxic chemicals in food chains, ocean pollution, and nuclear proliferation. Judging from recent history, this list will change considerably in coming decades.

For a variety of reasons, virtually all the problems in this category are unlikely soon to be controlled effectively. In some cases, control is extremely difficult on technical and institutional grounds. Ultimately, for example, the spread of nuclear weapons depends on the spread of requisite knowledge; the worldwide growth of nuclear power plants—which itself may be impossible to control—may only affect the timing, and then perhaps only marginally. The concentration of carbon dioxide in the atmosphere may be controllable but only by Herculean efforts involving global agreements to capture it from stack gases, reverse the trend toward deforestation, and, in the end perhaps, reduce combustion itself. Methods of controlling soil loss and deterioration, though well known, are difficult to apply because of incentives on the part of farmers to maximize short-run production and, if necessary, compensate for soil and soil fertility losses by using more fertilizer, adding marginal lands, and reducing fallow periods.

These difficulties frequently are compounded by gaps in knowledge upon which to base judgments as to whether controls are needed at all and, if so, how strict they should be. Does carbon dioxide (CO_2) have to be controlled, or can we wait, hoping that alternatives to combustion, perhaps solar energy and fusion, will come along before the problem becomes acute? What level of risks are we really subjecting ourselves to when we allow increased nuclear plants to be built, and how do these risks compare with those we accept in other fields and with those we subject ourselves to in the absence of nuclear power? Then too, it is difficult to mobilize support for corrective actions. This is particularly the case if effective action requires international agreements, for even faced with the same facts, countries at different income levels will assess the risks and net benefits of a given action quite differently. This difficulty in reaching agreement also exists within countries because of differences in preferences and ethics, for example, in how much weight to give to the interests of future generations.

As a consequence, and in contrast to the mass pollutants discussed in chapter 7, these environmental pressures can be expected to increase with population and economic growth. Whether they will become so severe during the next half-century as to limit growth is an open question. They could if the more pessimistic assumptions about CO_2 and risks of nuclear power are justified or if a number of pressures act in concert to overload ecological or social systems. But little confidence can be placed in these—or any other—assumptions. Our guess is that during our time frame most of these pressures will manifest themselves as increased risks of major damages, not actual damages. Thus, on environmental grounds, we judge this scenario to be feasible, but because of the mounting uncertainties and risks not necessarily desirable.

Other Scenarios

The Difficult Case

Suppose the United States attempts to reduce these energy and the environmental risks by alleviating the need for energy imports, maintaining a strategic stockpile of petroleum, and imposing more strict environmental regulations. At the same time, suppose these actions are taken in the context of increased agricultural exports and higher rates of population and economic growth in the United States, such that by the year 2025 population would be 21 percent larger, GNP 46 percent greater, and agricultural exports 18 percent larger than in the base case. Is this scenario, with or without a significant increase in world petroleum and natural gas prices, feasible? What would be its consequences?

So long as only the U.S. growth rate increases by these magnitudes, global impacts on resources and the environment are not likely to be significant. For nonfuel minerals, the dates of hypothetical exhaustion (that is, dates when exhaustion might occur if prices were not to rise) are likely to average four to five years earlier (excluding those minerals for which these dates are a century or more away). For petroleum and natural gas, the impact is even less because of the offsetting effects of U.S. efforts to substitute domestic energy sources for imports. If growth rates in all countries were higher than this scenario assumes, the impacts would be greater, of course, but still they would be less than one might imagine. For example, our global petroleum market model suggests that if the global GNP in 2025 should be 50 percent greater than in the standard case, the world price of petroleum would begin rising just five years earlier and peak no more than 30 percent higher. Substantially more energy of all kinds would be consumed, however, and atmospheric concentrations of carbon dioxide might be 16 percent greater in 2025 and 23 percent greater in 2050.

The consequences of a shift from the base to the difficult case for the United States are more significant. On the positive side, there are four main effects: the United States would achieve a higher standard of living; it would build up a strategic stockpile of petroleum, which should provide substantial protection from threats of embargo; it would have a lower level of pollution emissions and damages; and it would be modestly less dependent on imported oil and gas.

A fifth possible benefit could be more rapid development of a synfuels industry based on coal, shale, heavy oils, or tar sands. In the difficult case, the equivalent of more than 1.7 million barrels a day of oil or high-Btu gas or both would come on-stream as early as 1985 rather than in 2010 as in the base case. Whereas dependence on imported oil would be 61 percent in 1985 and 77 percent in 2000 in the base case (about 65 percent in the difficult case without production subsidies), it would be 58 percent and 44 to 50 percent, respectively, in the difficult case (the smaller percentage would result if world petroleum and natural gas prices increase over time as in DHP1). The costs of this emphasis on synfuels include subsidies equivalent to between 0.4 and 0.6 percent of GNP (the larger percentage in DHP1) a year and somewhat greater environmental risks and costs. An additional long-run cost, which could be quite serious, is the risk that the United States would find itself prematurely locked into high-cost technologies and production facilities before research has a chance to select the best technologies to bring costs down to more reasonable levels.

One's judgment of the benefits of this scenario depends on the importance accorded to the reduction in import dependence. Because the worst features of this dependence can be mitigated by developing a strategic stockpile, the benefits of being less dependent on oil imports appear to us to be rather modest and probably not worth the costs so long as lower priced foreign fuels are available. It seems to us that a better policy would be one that, in addition to maintaining a strategic stockpile, subsidizes research and development, including perhaps the development of a few pilot plants, and emphasizes conservation (through both price and legislative measures) to contain balance of payments problems and provide more time for the research and development efforts to bear fruit.

There are five other significant consequences of the difficult case, all clearly negative. First, total investment requirements would average about 1 percentage point more than under the base-case regime, a consequence mainly of additional energy and environmental requirements; this would make it that much more difficult, particularly in the eighties, to contain inflationary pressures without reducing the rate of economic growth. Second, this scenario uses up U.S. energy sources somewhat more quickly. Although the effect on coal and shale can be ignored because these resources are plentiful, the implications for petroleum, natural gas, and uranium might be more significant. In 2025, 86 percent of petroleum resources would have been consumed in contrast to 72 percent in the base case; comparable figures for natural gas and uranium are 77 percent instead of 69 percent, and 69 percent instead of 35 percent. The relatively small differences between the two cases for petroleum and natural gas result from the substitution of synfuels; the relatively large difference in the case of uranium is a consequence of the assumption that the breeder reactor and other forms of recycling are not used in the difficult scenario.

Third, the composition of fuels would change in ways detrimental to the environment. In particular, by 2025, 62 percent more coal would have to be produced than in the base case, and 81 percent more nuclear power would have to be used, to say nothing of shale and tar sands, which are not used at all in the base case until after 2010. Here again, it is not the mass pollutants that are of major concern—the more stringent environmental controls this scenario incorporates generally hold emissions and hence damages to lower levels than in the base case, despite the much larger quantities of residuals that must be treated. But a number of other problems would grow in importance and potential seriousness. In contrast to the base case, by 2025, 15 percent more fossil fuel plants and 80 percent more nuclear plants would have to be in operation; more than a million tons of spent nuclear fuels would have to be stored safely in perpetuity rather than 640,000 tons; and conflicts over allocation of water in states producing significantly increased quantities of energy would be greater. Oil spills, if proportional to imports, would be only 12 percent smaller during the first twenty-five years but, because of the larger economy, would be nearly equal during the second twenty-five years, despite efforts to reduce imports.

Fourth, land and water requirements would be substantially more difficult to meet. By 1985, 11 million acres and, by 2025, 82 million acres of noncropland must be converted to cropland in contrast to zero net requirements for conversion in the base case. At that rate, all nonagricultural land considered to be of high agricultural potential would be in use by 2029, and land of more moderate quality—lower fertility, higher erosion potential, and higher conversion costs—would have to be added thereafter.[6] This, plus other needs for land, would result in significant declines in range and grassland between 1969 and 2025 (from 604 to 506 million acres compared with 580 in the base case) and in forestland (from 723 to 654 million acres compared with 700 in the base case). Aggregate water consumption requirements would be more than 50 percent greater under DH than under EL in 2025, and if we assume that shortages begin to appear on a regional level whenever consumption becomes more than half the available water supply, seven regions, instead of four, out of the nineteen studied, will face shortages in that year (table 8–8).

Finally, by 2025 the net result on the agricultural sector of these and other changes is to raise the farm-gate price of food, relative to other prices, by at least 25 percent. This figure is probably too low, because the costs of land conversion and effects on productivity may have been underestimated, and in any event, there can be no doubt that substantially greater price increases would occur after 2025 if the assumptions of this scenario continued to hold.

Is the economic growth rate incorporated into this scenario feasible? In the purely physical sense, it probably is. That is, this nation possesses sufficient natural resources and environmental carrying capacity, trained manpower, capital, and technical and organizational know-how to pull it off. But on social and political grounds serious doubts can be raised. Higher economic growth rates in the United States would increase many

---

[6] These figures overstated conversion requirements inasmuch as they assume no additional substitutions of fertilizer, pesticides, capital, and labor for land than are incorporated into the base case, despite the increasing cost of land. They understate conversion requirements in that they do not take into account the additional acreage required to replace cropland converted to nonagricultural purposes.

of the uncertainties and risks we would have to live with, especially if they stimulate higher growth rates in the rest of the world, as they typically do; it would be more difficult to mobilize the savings necessary to meet investment requirements, particularly during the eighties; and local conflicts over water use and siting of power plants, mines, and the like would surely grow more severe. Taken together, these factors could easily inhibit or retard investment activities to a degree that makes the high economic growth rates of this case impossible. Certainly, there is little in the events of the last five years to warrant arguing the reverse.

Nuclear Phaseout

This scenario adds to the difficulties of the previous case by phasing out the use of nuclear power, a possibility frequently discussed as a way to reduce the dangers of a nuclear world. To simplify the task, we have assumed that coal-fired electric power generation would replace nuclear and that there is no reduction in the total amount of electricity produced. Environmental control expenditures would be increased sufficiently to contain environment-related damages associated with the increased use of coal. These assumptions bias upwards our estimates of coal requirements and the costs of shifting from nuclear fuel to coal.

Despite these biases, the resource base is more than adequate to support this case. Only 10 percent of U.S. coal resources would be consumed in 2025 compared with 6 percent in the difficult case and 4.5 percent in the base case. Water requirements would be about the same, if not slightly less, and land requirements for mining would be about 10 percent greater in 2025, a consequence of the fact that the amount of earth that must be moved is only slightly larger for coal than for uranium per unit of electricity generated.

The additional economic costs, though significant for those regions of the country that would have to substitute coal for nuclear power, are surprisingly small for the country as a whole. In 2025 investment requirements as a percentage of the GNP would be half a percentage point more than if nuclear power were not phased out, and per capita consumption and government expenditures would have to be $55 billion, or $150 per capita, less. These costs could be considerably less if we had permitted some substitution of other forms of energy for electricity, if environmental standards were not so stringent, or if this phaseout were applied to scenarios requiring less nuclear power—for example, to the base case, which requires 55 percent less nuclear power than the difficult case. Thus, in economic terms, this case is only modestly more difficult than scenario DH to which it is applied; if that difficult case proves to be feasible, this one is likely to be also, at least on economic grounds.

A potentially important qualification pertains to the speed with which coal production and consumption must be increased: by 5.6 percent a year during the first twenty-five years and 4.4 percent during the whole period, compared to an average of 3.2 percent in the difficult case and 2.2 percent in the base case during the fifty-year period. Unfortunately, we have no clear judgment to offer as to the feasibility of such rates. Obviously, we could not gear up to such rates very rapidly, but after a five- or ten-year period of concerted effort, it is difficult to say what rate might be sustainable. Then, too, if it proved necessary, coal exports (assumed to run at about 5 percent of production) could be reduced and nuclear power could be phased out more slowly.

This leaves us with the trade-off between the dangers of nuclear power and the environmental costs of coal. Given the dearth of knowledge about these issues, anything said on this topic must be highly speculative. If no major accidents occur, nuclear plants are probably safer than coal-fired plants of equal size, even if the latter used advanced sulfur scrubbers or low-sulfur coal. If the possibility of accidents is added in and the most pessimistic of available estimates of loss from such accidents are compared, the expected loss of life from a nuclear plant is about the same as that from a coal-fired operation. There are, however, major differences in the way such fatalities would come about. In contrast to coal, most nuclear-related fatalities would be bunched together into quite rare but near-catastrophic events, while others would occur only after very long periods following an accident. These differences make comparisons difficult and help explain the common perception that nuclear power is far more dangerous than coal.

In addition, nuclear power generation entails serious dangers of sabotage, theft, and diversion of nuclear materials into weapons, a set of dangers that has no counterpart on the coal side of the ledger. Unless present research indicates that we face a CO_2 problem, it might be worth forgoing the use of nuclear power forever if it would substantially reduce the danger of such misuses. But this is not likely to be the case if the United States alone should initiate such a policy.[7] The best that might

---

[7] Indeed, if the United States were not to substitute coal for nuclear power on a one-to-one basis but substantially increased its imports of petroleum and natural gas and decreased its exports of coal, other countries might be forced to expand their nuclear power capacity even faster.

happen would be a temporary slowdown in the spread of nuclear power, a purchase of time that would be valuable in the long run only if used to develop safer forms of energy for countries presently without adequate alternatives to nuclear power.

Thus, though we do not yet know whether we can live with nuclear power, this scenario suggests that the United States, and probably any country with adequate fossil fuels, could live without it. But it is not at all clear that in the long run we would be that much better off for having done so. The unknowns in this area are too large to say more.

Other Policies

The remaining scenarios can be viewed as efforts to determine the consequences of relaxing one or more of the difficulties incorporated into the difficult case. Although a number of such sensitivity tests were discussed in previous chapters, we shall review just four such scenarios here; the two in this section pertain to petroleum and environmental control policies, and those in the next section summarize the effects of lower population and economic growth rates.

A DECLINE IN WORLD OIL PRICES.   Suppose a means could be found to force the price of petroleum down, or to keep it from rising with inflation for a period, so that between 1980 and 1985 it would fall in real terms to half its present level. What would be the impacts?

Between 1980 and 2000, the world would experience much higher levels of petroleum consumption and a spurt of economic growth.[8] But the transition from a petroleum to a synthetics world would then prove to be much more difficult. The price of oil would start rising some ten years earlier, reach a peak of nearly $40 a barrel, and not settle down to the long-run cost of synthetics production until perhaps 2050. In these circumstances, economic growth rates would decline and perhaps become negative for countries without adequate feedstocks to produce synthetic liquids.

These results strongly support the conservationist contention that a slower rate of growth of petroleum production and consumption would be beneficial for the world. But three caveats are needed to interpret this

---

[8] One indication of this is that, in the U.S. model, this case leads to a substantial fall in the share of GNP devoted to investment after 1980 and, as a consequence, a small but observable increase in consumption per capita between 1980 and 2010.

conclusion properly. First, it should be remembered that a slower rate of growth is beneficial, not because the world is running out of energy, but because it allows more time for an orderly phasing in of alternative energy sources. Second, this conclusion should not be used as a justification for OPEC policies. To do so is to ignore the impacts of OPEC's actions on the world's distribution of income and wealth, impacts that cannot be favorable for the vast majority of the world's population, which resides in poor, energy-deficit countries. A tax on petroleum consumption, the revenues from which are allocated according to an international agreement in which all countries had some say, would be, at least in principle, far more equitable than OPEC control of prices and production. Finally, these results are quite sensitive to assumptions about technology, costs, planning horizons, and the speed with which new production facilities can be brought on-line. This sensitivity, plus the inadequacy of knowledge about these factors, makes this another area in which uncertainties and risks are large.

ENVIRONMENTAL POLICY.   If environmental controls were kept at their 1975 levels, pollution emissions and damages resulting from them would increase rapidly as economic growth continues (see figure 9–1). For this reason, the difficult case incorporates a set of increasingly strict controls, which become increasingly expensive over time. Suppose these strict environmental controls are relaxed to a modest extent, the only kind of relaxation we can envision that would not allow damages to rise over time to unacceptable levels. What difference would it make?

As can be seen in figure 9–1, a shift from strict to relaxed controls would reduce control costs in all periods. This would make something of a difference in the economic pressures the difficult case imposes. In 2025, for example, it would reduce total annualized abatement expenditures from 3.1 to 2.1 percent of GNP and total investment requirements from 19.4 to 18.9 percent of GNP. But damage costs would be substantially higher in all years. If these are weighed against the saving in control costs, it appears appropriate to follow the strict policy during approximately the first twenty-five years and to shift to the relaxed policy thereafter.

There are several qualifications to this conclusion, however. First, the damage costs are average or expected values. An additional benefit of the more strict controls, which has not been quantified in monetary terms, is the reduced probability of instances when damage costs rise above these average values. Second, this analysis is restricted to comparing overall results of two policy packages. When the analysis is done in terms of individual pollutants as is done in chapter 7, one finds that in any given year

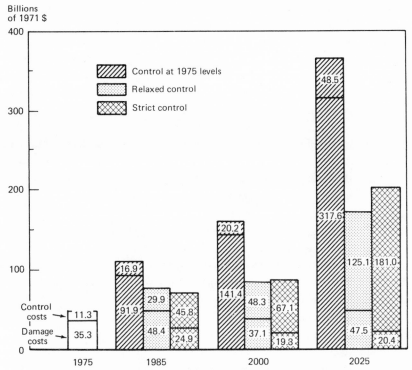

Figure 9–1. Pollution control and damage costs for alternative environmental policies, Scenario DH.

the package contains controls that are too strict for some pollutants and too lax for others. A related qualification pertains to the fact that these policies assume uniform national standards; substantial savings should be possible by tailoring standards to regional conditions. Finally, these conclusions are quite sensitive to assumptions about a number of parameters. In the case of water pollution, for example, the selection of a different, but still plausible, set of parameters would shift the whole thrust of policy away from point sources to nonpoint sources. Better information than is currently available is needed to resolve such uncertainties.

Lower Population and Economic Growth Assumptions

The final scenarios we shall review here differ from each other only with respect to their assumptions about population and per capita economic growth rates.[9] These scenarios are useful to indicate the extent to which lower growth rates for either or both of these factors would reduce economic, resource, and environmental pressures; they also help us examine the importance of population and economic growth relative to each other and to the set of policy assumptions we have investigated.

The principal future economic pressure we have identified is a rapid increase in investment requirements, particularly in the 1980s. But that period is too close to the present for changes in population or per capita economic growth to have much effect. Beyond that period, these variables do have significant effects on the required level of investment, but they also affect the level of output, and apparently by roughly the same extent. As a consequence, the investment share of the GNP remains relatively stable across scenarios that differ only with respect to population and per capita economic growth assumptions. There is a slight tendency in later years for this share to decline as population growth declines, and a corresponding tendency for the share devoted to consumption to increase; but the effect is small, seldom much more than half a percentage point. The effect on investment of a decline in per capita economic growth is smaller yet and is not systematic over time or across scenarios. Other changes—higher energy prices, import substitution policies for energy, and environmental policies—appear to influence the size of the investment share more than population and economic growth rates. Thus, within the range investigated, lower growth rates are unlikely to ease any tendencies toward capital shortages during most of the time period under consideration.

A second area of concern is the increasing dependence on imported petroleum and natural gas. Here, it appears that the size of the economy is important: the smaller the economy, the slower it uses up domestic sources and the smaller the dependence on imports. But again, the effects are small, varying by only a few percentage points in 2025,[10] and certainly small relative to the effects of policies aimed directly at influencing the energy sector. The separate effects of population and per capita economic growth are difficult to determine because of the small effect of each individually.

The effects on resources of differences in population and economic growth can be judged in several ways. In terms of annual demands, the

---

[9] More accurately, assumptions about population and labor productivity growth rates. For simplicity, the latter are referred to here as economic growth or per capita GNP growth assumptions.

[10] One reason for this small effect is that the capacity to produce synthetics is assumed to increase with the size of the economy. Thus, the smaller the economy, the less rapid is the development of import substitutes.

effects depend on the date on which they are observed. As one would expect, the effects of both population and economic growth grow over time. In addition, the impact of population on resources, which is initially smaller than that of per capita GNP, increases more rapidly and eventually surpasses the latter. In 2000, for example, the series F population is 12.3 percent less than the series D population, and domestic use of energy is 6 percent less; by 2025, however, when the F-series population is 28 percent lower than in the D series, the saving in energy consumption is 23.5 percent (see the first column of table 9–1). In contrast, a 13.7 percent smaller GNP per capita in 2000 results in an 11 percent saving in energy; by 2025, when GNP per capita in scenario DL is 21.0 percent less than in scenario DH, the saving is 17.3 percent (second column of table 9–1). This same pattern can be observed for the effects of population and economic growth on consumption of nonfuel minerals, the only exceptions being phosphate rock, potash, and sulfur—all feedstocks for fertilizer production—for which the impact of changes in population is always greater.

In assessing resource adequacy, cumulative demands are more important than annual ones. Judged this way, all the impacts are considerably smaller, and, again with the exception of the fertilizer feedstocks, differences in assumptions about per capita GNP are slightly more important than those about population, at least until 2025 and within the range we are considering. Table 9–1 provides numerical illustrations of this statement.[11] This result occurs because the impact of changes in population assumptions becomes greater than that of per capita GNP only in the last few years. Had our time horizon been extended another twenty-five years, the situation would have been reversed.

None of these results makes much difference for hypothetical exhaustion dates. For most U.S. mineral resources (assuming no recycling and no imports), these dates are postponed by two to four years. For global petroleum resources, it takes the combined impact of a decline in U.S. population and economic growth rates to postpone this date by two years.

So far as land and water requirements are concerned, a decline in population growth clearly has a larger effect than a decline in per capita

---

[11] The insignificant differences recorded for petroleum and natural gas production result from the fact that domestic production will be determined mainly by supply considerations, with differences between supply and demand being filled by imports. Other energy sources are not listed because they are assumed to grow at maximum rates in all scenarios.

Table 9–1. Percentage Reduction (Increase) in Selected Indexes, Comparison of Scenario DH with Others, 2025

Index	DH to FH	DH to DL	DH to FL
Population	27.9	0	27.9
GNP per capita	(6.4)	21.0	13.7
GNP	23.3	21.0	37.9
Resources			
Annual requirements			
Total energy	23.5	17.3	36.0
Aluminum	25.0	20.8	40.8
Iron in ore	25.6	21.1	41.8
Copper	25.5	21.2	41.5
Zinc	24.9	21.3	41.0
Phosphate rock	20.1	4.8	20.6
Cumulative requirements, 1975–2025			
Coal	11.5	12.2	20.3
Petroleum production	0.5	0.7	0.5
Natural gas production	2.0	3.6	3.9
Uranium	10.2	13.6	22.7
Oil shale	13.5	15.2	25.7
Aluminum	14.6	16.7	29.0
Iron in ore	12.5	15.7	26.5
Copper	11.5	15.5	25.3
Zinc	12.2	16.2	26.4
Phosphate rock	13.1	5.6	13.5
Cropland[a]	18.0	1.5	...
Water			
Withdrawals	23.2	12.8	30.4
Consumption	19.2	5.8	22.8
Environmental indexes			
SO_x emissions[b]	23.3	20.9	38.0
BOD emissions[b]	24.3	8.1	29.7
Radionuclide emissions[b]	23.6	16.2	36.0
Spent nuclear fuel, cumulative	14.5	12.7	24.6
Solid wastes	16.2	18.4	29.0
Land disturbed by mining	12.5	13.8	23.4
Number of electric power plants	25.0	17.2	38.5
Number of nuclear power plants	23.2	15.7	38.5
Pollution costs per capita[b]	(5.9)	15.9	12.3
Control costs[c]	(9.0)	13.3	8.0
Damage costs[d]	19.1	37.5	48.0

[a] Figures for first column are the percentage difference between two base case scenarios, the first incorporating the population and GNP series of DH and the second of EL (see table 6-10).

[b] Expected values assuming strict environmental controls.

[c] Total, comparable to materials in table 3–9.

[d] For pollutants covered in chapter 7.

economic growth, and the difference in these two effects grows over time because the income elasticity of demand for food falls. But the impact of population changes on farm output is less than proportional because of the offsetting effects of higher per capita income and lower prices when population growth is lower. The price difference is significant because it affects foreign as well as domestic demand. If in 2025 the U.S. population were 28 percent smaller, the GNP per capita would be 6 percent greater and the farm price index 19 percent lower. In our model, this results in a 3 percent increase in exports and hence only an 18 percent fall in farm output. In contrast, the impact on output of even a 20 percent decline in GNP per capita in 2025 would be negligible.

The shift from the higher to the lower population growth assumptions is particularly important in the case of land because it is the difference between having to convert over 50 million acres of nonfarm land into cropland and not having to use all of the presently available cropland. The reduction in water requirements, though substantial in the aggregate, is unlikely to ease pressures significantly in those regions where water problems are already severe.

With regard to environmental impacts of population and economic growth we must again distinguish between the mass pollutants, for which adequate control policies exist, and other environmental threats. Figure 9–2 provides two illustrations that summarize the situation with respect to mass pollutants. The full height of the bars indicates the amounts of residuals that would be generated if they increased in proportion to the GNP, the height of the striped bars indicates the residuals projected by our model, and the solid portion shows emissions under a strict control policy. The level of residuals our model projects could have been lower or higher than the GNP-related level, depending on changes in technology and the composition of output; as it turned out, for most mass pollutants, these changes generated significantly less than proportional increases in residuals. The impact of differences in population and economic growth on residuals, both over time and across runs, is fairly significant, but when we look at emissions, assuming any of the abatement policies we have experimented with, the picture changes dramatically. As can be seen by the height of the solid bars, a strict policy brings emissions down substantially below their 1975 levels, and differences in population and economic growth have virtually no effect.

Of course, to accomplish these improvements, control costs must increase over time. Indeed, these costs tend to increase somewhat faster than GNP, and they are quite sensitive to changes in population and economic growth rates. But in no case do they become an intolerably large percentage of the GNP. In 1975, on an annualized basis, they amounted to 1.1 percent of the GNP; in 2025, they would grow to 3.1 percent in scenario DH, 3.1 percent in FH, and 3.4 percent in DL, assuming a strict enforcement policy in all cases. Under the relaxed policy, these percentages and the differences among them are even smaller.

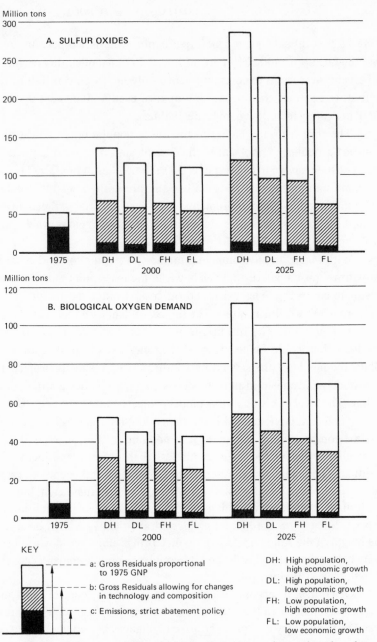

Figure 9–2. Sulfate residuals and biological oxygen demand under alternative scenarios and a strict abatement policy. *A*, sulfur oxides; *B*, biological oxygen demand. From Ronald G. Ridker, "Resource and Environmental Consequences of Population and Economic Growth," in Philip Hauser, ed., *World Population and Development: Challenges and Prospects* (Syracuse, N.Y., Syracuse University Press, 1979) p. 118.

For environmental problems less subject than mass pollutants to control but important at the local level, the impacts of lower population and economic growth are more visible. Examples in table 9–1 are numbers of power plants and land disturbed by mining. It is difficult to say just how significant these differences might be, for example, whether local conflicts would be appreciably less.

For problems important at the global level, the effects of lower population or economic growth rates in the United States or both tend not to be significant. It is not that the United States is a small contributor to such environmental concerns—quite the contrary, given the percentage of resources this country uses. Rather, the range of likely population and economic growth rates for the United States is sufficiently narrow compared with growth rates in the rest of the world that the effect of differences among rates is small. This is the same phenomenon we observed when considering the global impact of differences in U.S. resource consumption.

Scenario Comparisons Using an Index of Economic Welfare

A useful way to summarize our results is to attempt to indicate which scenario is preferable. Ideally, for this purpose, we should translate all the changes observed over time and between scenarios into a single common denominator of welfare. This is impossible, of course, given the diversity of results and their questionable relationship to welfare, but we can take a step in this direction by applying a simple measure of per capita *economic* welfare.

In common with most economic approaches to measuring welfare, we start with personal consumption expenditures per capita in constant prices and modify this measure in a variety of ways (compare with Nordhaus and Tobin, 1972). First, we eliminate categories of expenditures that are intermediate or instrumental in the sense that they are not desired for their own sake but because they facilitate the derivation of utility from other activities. Cases in point are commuting expenses, uniforms, advertising, repair services, and a few more controversial items such as medical services and drugs (on grounds that they are more like repair and maintenance expenditures than they are like recreational expenditures).

Second, we have made adjustments for consumer expenditures that are more like investments than like consumption. These expenditures should be subtracted and replaced by estimates of the value of the services they render within a given time period. The principal categories here are housing, durables, and education. Fortunately, the largest item, housing, is already taken care of, because the model follows the national accounting procedure of treating purchases of housing as investments and including in consumption an imputed value for rental services on owner-occupied dwellings. In the case of durables, we have included only an estimate of the service flows they yield, based on simplifying assumptions about the size of the stock in the base period, average rates of replacement, and yields on capital. Ninety percent of educational expenditures are assumed to be investments in human capital and are, therefore, excluded; but in this case, no imputation of returns is added back in, because these expenditures lead to higher labor productivity, already taken into account.

To the extent that government expenditures, either on current or capital accounts, directly yield utility to consumers, they also should be added in as consumption items. Most government expenditures are instrumental in nature, however, and the remainder is quite small in comparison to consumption expenditures, so little is lost by leaving out all government expenditures. The only exception we have made is for government educational outlays, for which we assume that 10 percent is more appropriately described as consumption than as investment.

A fourth adjustment pertains to environmental pressures. Chapter 7 presents dollar estimates of pollution damages. These estimates, plus direct consumption expenditures for abatement, are subtracted from consumption per capita. The much larger portion of pollution control expenditures paid for directly by businesses has already been taken into account, because these expenditures reduce the portion of output that can go to consumption.

A final adjustment is made for changes over time in leisure. This is done by increasing consumption per capita (adjusted in the above ways) by an amount reflecting the additional goods and services that might have been produced had there been no increase after 1975 in the proportion of time spent in leisure. In a free market, the value of the increased leisure must be worth at least that amount for it to occur.

These procedures are admittedly very crude and open to substantial criticism, but they have the advantage of summarizing many consequences of the scenarios we have developed, and some interesting conclusions do emerge (table 9–2). First, welfare is projected to increase substantially over time in all scenarios. This is due in large part to the continued increase in material goods and services, plus increases in leisure; both result

Table 9–2. Indexes of Per Capita Economic Welfare for Various Scenarios

Scenario	No adjustments for leisure				Adjusted for leisure[a]					
					1985		2000		2025	
	1975	1985	2000	2025	A	B	A	B	A	B
EL	1.00	1.26	1.81	2.89	1.27	1.31	1.88	1.99	3.39	3.75
DH	1.00	1.34	1.95	3.36	1.36		2.03		3.89	
FH	1.00	1.43	2.17	3.75	1.44		2.25		4.45	
DL	1.00	1.21	1.68	2.67	1.24	1.27	1.75	1.86	3.08	3.41
FL	1.00	1.31	1.89	3.14	1.32	1.35	1.96	2.07	3.73	4.12
DHNU	1.00	1.34	1.95	3.33	1.36		2.03		3.84	
DHP1	1.00	1.33	1.91	3.25	1.35		1.99		3.77	
DHP2	1.00	1.37	2.04	3.40	1.39		2.13		3.92	
DHRE	1.00	1.30	1.94	3.41	1.32		2.02		3.93	

[a] Columns A assume 0.3 percent a year decline in work hours. Columns B assume 0.6 a year decline in work hours. This latter assumption is assumed to be compatible only with scenarios incorporating lower rates of growth in labor productivity.

from a continuation of economic growth although at a somewhat slower pace than in the past.

Second, in all scenarios, this welfare index increases faster than does unadjusted consumption per capita. For example, in the base case (EL) in 2025, an index based on 1975 unadjusted consumption is 2.86, while the welfare index adjusted for leisure stands at 3.39; even if no adjustment for leisure is made, the index is 2.89. The principal reason for this result is the fact that per capita pollution damages are expected to fall over time as increasingly strict legislative standards are slowly achieved. In addition, the services of durables are projected to increase at a slightly faster rate than many other consumption items. These two adjustments appear to offset other downward pressures on the index, even not adjusted for leisure.

Third, the differences among scenarios are more or less in the directions one would expect. Other things equal, more rapid economic growth and less rapid population growth lead to increases in economic welfare.[12] But the impact of a difference in population assumptions declines over time.[13] This result occurs largely because the immediate impact of a lower population size is only on the denominator of the welfare per capita ratio, whereas the longer run impact results in a smaller labor force and hence output, the principal determinant of the numerator of this ratio.

The impact of the nuclear moratorium is small and occurs only in later years (compare DHNU with DH). The impact of higher energy prices, scenario DHP1, is also small. Scenario DHP2 is preferable to DH even in later years when petroleum prices increase, because the capacity, built up in earlier years, to sustain higher levels of consumption has not yet been whittled away. As expected, relaxed environmental controls produce slightly worse results in earlier years and slightly better ones in later years than more strict controls.

Finally, although differences in the welfare index over time are sizable, differences across scenarios, even in 2025, are surprisingly small. Moreover, if there is anything to the notion of diminishing marginal utility associated with the ownership of materal goods, either by oneself or by

---

[12] This is true whether we assume that the difference between the low and high economic growth scenarios is accounted for by differences in worker-hour productivity (columns A in table 9–2) or in labor hours per worker (columns B in table 9–2).

[13] For example, the shift from DH to FH in 1985 is associated with a 6.7 percent increase in per capita welfare (unadjusted for leisure) with a 5.3 percent decline in population, or an elasticity of approximately −1.3. A similar shift yields an elasticity of −0.9 in 2000 and −0.4 in 2025.

others (on the latter see Hirsch, 1976), the true differences in welfare will be narrower yet. A person suddenly transported from one scenario to another in 2025 would not feel substantially better or worse off.

These conclusions are subject to a number of qualifications. Other important dimensions of environmental pressures—those associated with density and size of city, land disturbances, and increased risk of accidents and ecological disruptions—have not been factored in. An index that gives some weight to these pressures would certainly fall below the values shown in table 9–2, and the larger the economy, the lower the index would be. No adjustment for expenditures on crime prevention and safety has been included, although some believe they will grow over time also. No weight has been given to the utility associated with different family sizes implied by the population assumptions of the varous scenarios. And no weight has been given to developments in other parts of the world that could be quite destabilizing in some scenarios. In other words, these conclusions are based on a welfare index dominated by fairly conventional economic concerns. We presume that a more complete index would not indicate such large gains over time as economic growth continues, but we cannot say just how much difference it would make.

Some Broader Considerations

The preceding summary of implications of alternate scenarios constitutes our main conclusions, but these results also permit us to speak to several broader, more qualitative issues.

The United States in the Next Fifty Years

Assuming no major catastrophies occur, all the scenarios we have investigated appear to be feasible during the next half-century. Problems will arise, more rapidly under high than under low growth rates, but the United States has the physical, technological, and managerial capabilities to resolve them without serious losses in economic welfare. This country is amazingly rich. If we cannot mine a resource, we can import it, find a substitute for it, design around it, or just consume a small amount less of it. If pollution emissions cannot be tolerated, we can change production processes, improve treatment, separate polluters and their victims, treat the symptoms, or simply produce less of the commodity causing the pollution. We can handle congestion during commuter hours by restricting the use of private cars, increasing the use of mass transit, and staggering work hours. We can alleviate congestion at recreation sites by building additional facilities, managing those we have better, encouraging substitutes (for example, foreign travel), and, if necessary, by staggering vacation periods. If water deficits threaten a particular part of the country, we can choose among raising charges to reduce consumption, transferring population and economic activities to other regions, and building longer and larger canals. We can even handle agricultural land shortages, given sufficient lead time, through shifts in locations and methods of production. None of these adjustments raises specters of dramatic downfall and collapse.

Though these scenarios are feasible for the United States in these terms, they may not be desirable or feasible on social and political grounds. It is true that all lead to increasing levels of per capita economic welfare, as we have measured it, and this improvement should not be dismissed lightly. But they also lead to a variety of pressures on the society that may be increasingly burdensome to live with: significantly higher investment requirements and inflationary pressures in some periods; increasing quantities of land dedicated more or less permanently to unsightly and sometimes dangerous uses; more and more local conflicts over land and water use; increasing dependence on foreign resources; potentially dangerous, resource-related shifts in the global distribution of wealth and power; and increasing use of ecologically and militarily dangerous technologies, especially in the energy sector. If ways to contain these problems cannot be found, society may decide, by opposing specific development projects, to restrict economic growth.

Coping with Uncertainties and Risks

What alternatives are there short of drastic cutbacks in economic growth rates? First, and most important, reducing the risks we have listed requires research to fill in the abysmal gaps in our knowledge about the environmental consequences of human actions, past as well as future. In particular, research in basic sciences, such as climatology, is required. So are intensified efforts to monitor environmental and ecological change, to provide us with something of an early warning system in this area. Technological and institutional research that improves society's ability to control difficult environmental problems is also needed. There is no more fundamental way to reduce uncertainties and risks.

Second, we might adopt a cautious, conservative approach to resource and environmental problems, playing it safe with nature wherever the opportunity arises. Where costs do not mount excessively, pollution standards can be set a bit more strictly than required to minimize expected costs as we now understand them. Larger safety margins than conventionally used can be built into nuclear plants. The price of fossil fuels can be raised to encourage conservation and the search for alternatives. Global reforestation programs, which would help nature absorb pollutants such as carbon dioxide, reduce flooding and soil erosion, provide an alternative source of fuel, and enhance supplies of some raw materials, could be pushed more rapidly than now seems to be the case. At a minimum, such actions provide a hedge against the possibility that new knowledge will indicate that the problem is more severe than we think today.

Prudence also calls for substantial efforts to develop alternative technologies in advance of need. Solar electric power, perhaps fusion, small-scale, decentralized energy systems, controlled environment agriculture, and aquaculture may all be cases in point. Such research should be undertaken not only for possible use in the United States, but also for potential use elsewhere. Indeed, after all is said and done, we may find that the only practical way to contain nuclear proliferation is to develop and provide energy-deficit countries with economical alternatives to fission and breeder reactors. Some of the technologies so developed may never become economical, but it is appropriate for a society to purchase knowledge about them in case of need in the same way that it purchases insurance or military protection that it hopes it will never have to use. Finally, new institutions and decision-making mechanisms are needed. We must improve our capability for long-range projection, for control and regulation of human uses of the environment, and for collective international action.

Such actions are required to cope with the uncertainties and risks we currently face. They can only become more important in the future as population and economic growth continue.

Role of Population and Economic Growth

The driving engine behind all the changes this analysis has pointed to, both positive and negative, is population and economic growth. How much difference would a slowdown in growth from these two sources make?

As we have seen, the differences both in per capita economic welfare in the terminal year and in dates when the same levels of resource and environmental pressures would be felt are relatively small for the range of assumptions we have used. Unless these differences involve crossing some critical thresholds that we do not know about, there would appear to be little reason to choose one set of growth rates over another. Moreover, in cases in which methods exist for attacking problems directly, such direct attacks are generally superior to across-the-board cuts in population and economic growth rates or both. A dramatic example of this fact is provided by figure 9–2, but the point holds for many other problem areas we have covered.

One explanation for these small effects is the narrowness of the range of population and labor productivity growth rates we have selected. Had we compared a continuation of past trends with no growth at all during the next fifty years, the impact would obviously have been more dramatic. But in this time frame it does not appear likely that population and economic growth rates, especially for the United States, will in fact fall outside the relatively narrow range we have specified.

A related explanation is that we have not projected far enough into the future. Had our time horizon been seventy-five or one hundred years, perhaps the differences between the high and low population growth rates would have been more significant. Perhaps. But the point can be argued either way.[14] In any event, we can only speak about the next fifty years. It is practically impossible to project that far into the future with even a modicum of confidence; it would be meaningless to push the time horizon further yet, when we have no conception of what might happen to technology and tastes, not to mention population and economic growth themselves.

Another explanation is that our focus has been primarily on the United States, a country capable of adapting in a variety of ways to practically any resource or environmental constraint that threatens. In poor countries with less capacity to adjust, the linkage between population and

[14] Differences in resource requirements and environmental pressures are likely to grow (though such growth is not certain if saturation with material goods becomes more widespread) and we are more likely to hit some critical threshold or discontinuity. But if Simon (1977) is correct, differences in capacity to cope with these requirements and pressures might also grow in the long run, increasing as the population increases.

economic growth on the one side and resource and environmental pressures on the other is more rigid. Their lower incomes, in addition, quite properly lead them to assess the risks and net benefits associated with resource and environmental policies differently than we do. These differences dictate caution about generalizing the conclusions of this study to countries significantly different from the United States in income, technological and managerial capability, or resource base.

Yet another possibility is that our methodology and assumptions have led us to understate the differences that various growth rates might make. The differences would have been greater, for example, if there were a constraint on the aggregate savings rate, if this rate varied inversely with population size, or if time lags involved in bringing new energy sources on-stream were longer. But the differences would have been smaller if hours of work varied inversely with income per capita, if the rate of innovation increased with the population growth rate, or if we had assumed economies of scale. There is no way to determine how these offsetting possibilities might balance out.

There is, however, one way in which our methods clearly have led to an understatement. Our quantitative analysis has not captured all the resource and environmental consequences of population and economic growth; attempts to resolve resource and environmental problems frequently create other social problems of a more subtle, qualitative nature.

First, slow but irreversible changes in life-style are forced upon us. Restrictions on energy imports, conservation of water resources, preservation of wilderness areas and animal life, restrictions on pollution emissions, limitations on fertilizer and pesticide use, and safeguards for nuclear installations all require public regulation. It seems inevitable that permits, licenses, fees, red tape, computers, and bureaucrats will intervene in daily life to an increasing extent. Population and economic growth can only intensify such interventions.

Second, efforts to resolve fundamental social problems are likely to be postponed because top priority must be given to such activities as finding necessary resources, building ever larger reservoirs and mass transit systems, and determining whether CO_2 is or is not a serious problem during our time horizon. For similar reasons, we are forced to introduce solutions to problems before their side effects are known. It might be far better environmentally to postpone the introduction of the breeder reactor until the inherently cleaner fusion reactors are developed; it certainly would be preferable to know more about the expected benefits and costs of water treatment programs before spending billions on such programs.

Slower rates of growth will not automatically change this situation, but at least a bit of the urgency—the crash program character of much of what we do—would be eliminated.

Finally, continued growth closes off options. There is less land per person, less choice, less room for diversity, less margin for error. Technology must advance; life-styles must change. Some may prefer this emerging world, but for those who do not, there will be fewer alternatives.

Because our quantitative analysis cannot take these consequences of growth into account, there is a tendency to understate the resource and environmental impacts of alternate growth rates. A useful way to characterize the overall impact is to say that a decline in growth rates purchases not only time, but also resources and additional options: time to search for solutions, resources to implement them, and additional freedom of choice in deciding how we want to live.

At this level of generality, both population and economic growth have similar impacts. The principal difference is that although the resource and environmental impacts of population growth take somewhat longer to be felt than those of economic growth, there is a more rigid linkage between these impacts and population growth, each additional person bringing along an additional packet of resource and environmental pressures. In contrast, economic growth can be used for different ends than it is put to now. Although it adds to problems that need solution, it also adds to the capacity to solve problems. It is difficult to find similar offsetting advantages from additional population growth at this stage in U.S. history.

References

Goeller, H. E., and A. M. Weinberg. 1976. "The Age of Substitutability," *Science* vol. 191, no. 4228 (February 20).

Hirsch, F. 1976. *Social Limits to Growth* (Cambridge, Mass., Harvard University Press).

Nordhaus, W., and J. Tobin. 1972. "Is Economic Growth Obsolete?" in Milton Moss, ed., *The Measurement of Economic and Social Performance* (New York, National Bureau for Economic Research).

Simon, J. 1977. *The Economics of Population Growth* (Princeton, N.J., Princeton University Press).

Appendix

The SEAS/RFF Model

The principal computerized model used in this project (the SEAS/RFF system) is a series of interdependent models developed for assessing future economic, resource, and environmental consequences for the United States of alternate assumptions about population growth, economic growth, technology change, environmental policy, energy prices, energy supply, and minerals policy. Structurally, the system consists of a number of special-purpose models linked to INFORUM, the University of Maryland's 185-sector, dynamic, macroeconomic-cum-input–output model of the U.S. economy.

The SEAS/RFF system develops national U.S. economic forecasts through 2025 based on an exogenously specified set of demographic, macroeconomic, energy price, environmental policy, and resource policy assumptions. In turn, these forecasts form the basic economic inputs used by other models in the system to develop their more specialized forecasts. Forecasts are made at both national and regional levels.

The National System

A generalized overview of the SEAS/RFF national system is presented in figure A–1. The dashed-lined box encompasses the six special-purpose models that have been integrated with INFORUM into a common model: PRICE, which uses relative energy prices and price elasticities to alter energy demands, capital requirements, and Gross National Product (GNP) growth; TECHNOLOGY, which uses technology change assumptions to alter current and capital account flows; INSIDE, which provides greater detail on industrial output; ABATE, which calculates costs for abating pollution and sector purchases for abatement; ENSUP-

411

SEAS/RFF NATIONAL SYSTEM

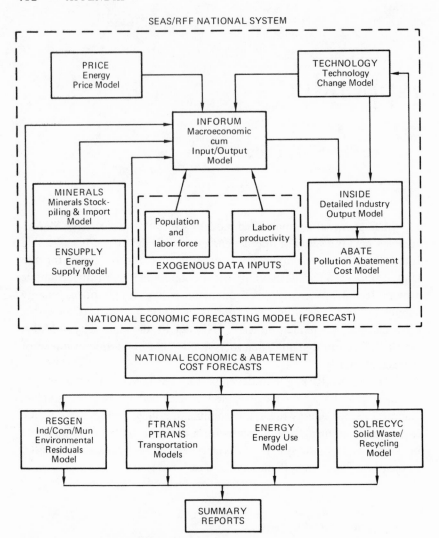

Figure A–1.   SEAS/RFF national system.

PLY, which uses assumptions about fuel availability and energy supply
technology to determine energy supply and demand mixes; and MIN-
ERALS, which allows exogenous specification of stockpiles and import
levels for selected minerals. Together, these seven models form the national economic forecasting model (FORECAST) for the SEAS/RFF
system. Linkage among all of the models allows population growth,
energy price effects, technology change, abatement, energy supply con-

straints and stockpiling/import constraints for minerals to be reflected in SEAS/RFF economic forecasts.

The national economic forecasting model, by generating annual economic and abatement cost forecasts through 2025, provides input data for five other special-purpose models:

RESGEN.   Estimates the annual national tonnage of pollutant residuals from industrial and commercial sources and municipal incineration.

PTRANS.   Estimates national passenger vehicle miles traveled and residuals by mode.

FTRANS.   Estimates national freight vehicle miles traveled and residuals by mode.

ENERGY.   Develops Btu forecasts of national energy consumption, domestic production, imports, and exports.

SOLRECYC.   Estimates the national tonnage of solid waste and recycled materials.

Output from these models and the national economic model are collected for presentation in summary reports.

The Regional System

A generalized overview of the SEAS/RFF regional system is presented in figure A-2. The major function of the regional system is to determine impacts on regional environmental quality as they stem from the national scenarios. Two sets of calculations are performed. The first results in the regionalization of environmental residuals from various sources. The second set of calculations measures regional environmental impact. This is done in two ways: first, by estimating ambient air and water quality and, second, by estimating regional dollar damages from air and water pollution.

The specific models used in the SEAS/RFF regional system are:

REGION.   Applies dynamic regional shares to the RESGEN and ABATE outputs to determine regional industrial, commercial, and municipal incineration residuals, and regional abatement costs.

PTRANS and FTRANS.   Estimates regional residuals from passenger and freight transportation, respectively.

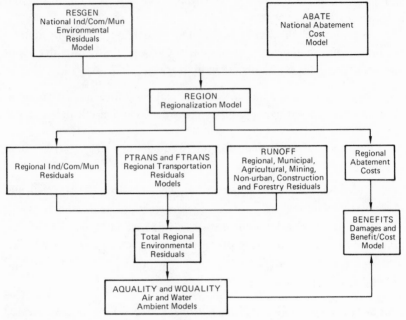

Figure A–2.   SEAS/RFF regional system.

RUNOFF.   Estimates regional residuals from municipal runoff, agriculture, mining, nonurban construction, and forestry.

AQUALITY and WQUALITY.   Uses simplified dispersion models to estimate regional air and water ambient concentration levels, respectively.

BENEFITS.   Uses regional damage functions to calculate dollar damages and pollution control benefit–cost ratios.

The Models in Detail

A detailed description of the major functions performed by each of the SEAS/RFF models is presented below. Because documentation already exists for the original SEAS system (EPA, 1974a, 1974b, 1974c), emphasis is given to the modifications RFF has made to that system.

The National Economic Forecasting Model (FORECAST)

The FORECAST model projects future total demands for the outputs of 185 economic sectors and allocates these demands to the specific markets, or buying sectors, to which these products are sold. Thus, the model differentiates between intermediate and final demands. Intermediate demands are generated by sales from one sector to other producing sectors. Final demands are developed from government expenditures, exports, imports, consumer purchases (including consumer purchases of pollution abatement equipment), changes in inventory, changes in mineral stockpiles, equipment investment, and construction. The sum of these final demand components is the GNP. Figure A–3 is a flow diagram of the FORECAST model. The column of boxes on the far left denotes factors that are specified outside the model. The boxes marked by an asterisk are RFF additions to the original INFORUM model.

The solution procedure begins by coupling a trial value of disposable income with relative prices and final abatement purchases in order to determine personal consumption expenditures. Then, total consumption is used with estimates of public abatement expenditure, number of households, and interest rates to determine residential and public construction. These aggregates are then broken down to sector purchases by applying the C-matrix coefficients. In a similar manner, nine different types of government expenditures are estimated for each year, some exogenously and others based on disposable income per capita and population projections. The G matrix breaks these aggregates down into purchases from individual sectors. The D matrix determines capital-account purchases of abatement equipment from the 185 economic sectors; these purchases revise the B matrix—the capital coefficient matrix—so that it translates both normal and abatement investment levels into purchases from the 185 sectors. Similarly, the E matrix determines current account or operation and maintenance purchases for abatement from the 185 economic sectors and revises the A matrix so that it tracks both abatement and nonabatement intermediate flows.

The energy-supply technology assumptions determine energy-supply capital requirements, which are fed to industry construction and equipment investment. Fuel availability assumptions are used to alter personal consumption of energy and intermediate energy flows through the A matrix. Technology change assumptions affect investment in industrial equip-

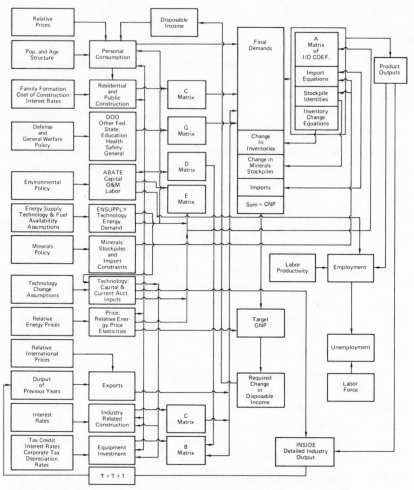

Figure A–3.   Flow diagram of the FORECAST model.

ment and construction, intermediate flows (via the A matrix) and detailed industry output (from INSIDE). Assumptions about relative energy prices affect industrial equipment and construction investment, intermediate energy flows (via the A matrix), and the level of GNP. Outputs of previous years, assumptions regarding the costs of capital and relative international prices are used to forecast exports, investment for pollution abatement, and normal equipment investment and construction by industry. The B and C matrixes then determine total industrial equipment and construction purchases from each of the 185 sectors. At this point, total final demands have been determined and the input–output coefficients in the A matrix fully revised to reflect exogenous assumptions.

The A-matrix coefficients then convert final demand to total product outputs for each of the 185 sectors. Inventory changes, net imports, and stockpile changes are computed simultaneously. The latter two depend upon exogenously assumed levels for stockpiles and mineral imports. Labor productivity is based upon forecasts for specific sectors made by the U.S. Bureau of Labor Statistics and upon the aggregate labor forecasts discussed in chapter 2. Employment is determined by dividing the product outputs by labor productivity. Unemployment is then calculated as the difference between the projected labor force and the calculated employment level.

Final demands are the sum of consumption, investment, construction, government, and export demands. These demands are added to inventory change, stockpile change, and imports (with a negative sign) to estimate GNP. The calculated GNP is then compared with a target GNP. If there is disagreement, the level of disposable income is changed and the calculations begin anew.

With this overview of the FORECAST model in mind, a more detailed description of the internal structure of each of its parts is now given. These components, referring to Figure A–3, are PRICE, TECHNOLOGY, INFORUM, ABATE, INSIDE, ENSUPPLY, and MINERALS.

Inforum

INFORUM is a consistent dynamic forecasting model that bridges the gap between aggregate GNP forecasts and the markets in which products are sold. INFORUM determines industry outputs year by year based on forecasts for *all* product markets, the building of sufficient capacity to produce those outputs, and the availability of labor. The entire accounting framework can be expressed as a single set of equations, as follows for the ith industry.

$$\text{Output } i = \text{Consumption}_i \tag{1}$$
$$+ \text{ Investment}_i$$
$$+ \text{ Government}_i$$
$$+ \text{ Net foreign trade}_i$$
$$+ \text{ Inventory change}_i$$
$$+ \text{ Stockpile change}_i$$
$$+ \text{ Intermediate sales}_i.$$

All of these demands, except intermediate sales, are final demands and fall into the familiar GNP accounts categories.

Most of the final demand components are based on econometric equations derived from regressions on historical time series (Almon and coauthors, 1974). Past levels of personal consumption expenditures are regressed against levels of disposable income, changes in disposable income, relative prices, time trends, and levels of consumption from previous years. Actually, two types of equations are used for estimating personal consumption expenditures. The first of these reflects consumption by "impulse." The impulse equation suggests that per capita expenditures c on a commodity i in a given year t are determined by the level of per capita disposable income in that year y_t, the change in the level of per capita disposable income since the last year $(y_t - y_{t-1})$, the relative price of the commodity P_{it} and the point in time t. The impulse equation has the form

$$c_{it} = b_1 + b_2 y_t + b_3(y_t - y_{t-i}) + b_4 P_{it} + b_5 t. \tag{2}$$

In this equation and those that follow, the $b_1, b_2, b_3, \ldots$ refer to parameters estimated by regressions on historical data.

The second personal consumption equation used estimates consumption by "habit." In this form, per capita consumption of a commodity in the previous year $c_{i,t-1}$ replaces the time variable; that is,

$$c_{it} = b_1 + b_2 y_t + b_3(y - y_{t-1}) + b_4 P_{it} + b_5 c_{i,t-1}. \tag{3}$$

Most of the personal consumption expenditures are estimated using the "impulse" equation form. In the case of direct energy consumption, the econometric equations have been overridden by exogenous consumption levels consistent with assumptions for fuel availability and relative energy prices. Other variables have been introduced to reflect judgments about the validity of economically determined coefficients for long-run projections. Some items, for example, are assumed to approach saturation levels, and growth in these demands are restricted accordingly.

Equations 2 and 3 estimate per capita consumption. Total consumption is calculated as the product of per capita consumption and population or age-adjusted population. Categories of public construction, except as they are impacted by abatement, are calculated by time trends or specified exogenously.

The equation used to estimate residential construction is

$$(I/H)_t = b_1 + b_2(C/H)_t + b_3 D_{t-1} + b_4 P_{t-1} - b_5(S/H)_{t-1}, \qquad (4)$$

where I is the construction level, H is the number of households, C is consumption expenditures, D is an interest rate differential, and P is the rent/cost ratio for housing, and S is the stock of housing.

Of the nine government expenditure categories, five are federal and four are state and local. The largest federal category, defense, is calculated as

$$\text{DEF}_t = \text{DEF}_{71}(\text{GNP}_t/\text{GNP}_{71})^{0.9}. \qquad (5)$$

Equation 5 is based upon the assumption that the growth rate in defense expenditure will be slightly less than the GNP growth rate. State and local expenditures are estimated using per capita disposable income y and affected population. The general equation form is

$$\text{Type of Expenditure/Affected Population} = b_1 + b_2 y. \qquad (6)$$

The parameters b_1 and b_2 are estimated by regression analysis.

Imports I and exports E are functions of domestic demand D, the ratio of foreign to domestic prices P, price elasticity n, and the output of the previous year Q_{t-1}. The fitted equations are

$$I_t = (b_1 + b_2 D_t) P_t^n, \qquad (7)$$

and

$$E_t = (b_1 + b_2 Q_{t-1}) P_t^n. \qquad (8)$$

In the case of minerals policy simulation, the econometric import equations have been overridden by exogenous levels, consistent with assumptions on mineral import levels.

Industrial construction is estimated on the assumptions that the stock B of existing buildings depreciates and that new construction NC is positively related to industrial output X. For some types of industrial construction, consumption levels and interest rates are used in place of output to explain industrial construction. The general equation used in estimating industrial construction is

$$NC_t = b_1 + b_2 X_{t-1} - b_3 B_{t-1} - b_4 B_0 (0.98)^t, \qquad (9)$$

where $(0.98)^t$ reflects a 2 percent a year demolition rate for old buildings.

To estimate equipment investment, it is assumed that the additions to capital Δk desired by an industry are determined by change in outputs Q and change in the cost of capital r, such that

$$\Delta K_t = \left(\frac{Q_t - Q_{t-1}}{Q_{t-1}} - \sigma \frac{r_t - r_{t-1}}{r_{t-1}} \right) K_{t-1}. \tag{10}$$

In this relationship, σ is econometrically estimated. However, the actual net investment called forth by changes in output and capital cost is not spent immediately but is spread over six years. The equation which does this has the form

$$N_t = b_1 + \sum_{i=0}^{5} W_i \Delta K_{(t-1)}, \tag{11}$$

where N_t is observed net investment and W_i is the fraction of capital spending which occurs in the ith year after the capital was first desired. Replacement investment is calculated as depreciation on the existing capital stock. The sum of net and replacement investment is total investment by the ith sector.

The above structural relationships determine expenditure levels. It is necessary to use several bridge matrixes to translate some of these into demands for the output of the 185 sectors. Intermediate sales from one industry to other producing industries (or alternatively purchases by other producing sectors) are represented by the A matrix. Each A-matrix coefficient represents the share of one industry's total output that comes from another industry. For example, if 10 percent of the automobile industry's costs are purchases of steel, then the A-matrix coefficient located at the point where the steel "row" and automobile "column" intersect would be 0.10. Sales to ninety categories of capital equipment are reflected by the B-matrix coefficients. A coefficient along the automobile row would reflect investment in automobiles by a particular buyer of capital equipment. Similarly, sales by each industry to construction and federal and state government are reflected by the C- and G-matrix coefficients respectively.

Total sales by industry i, X_i, may be illustrated mathematically as

$$X_i = \sum_{j=1}^{185} a_{ij} X_j + \sum_{k=1}^{90} b_{ik} K_k + \sum_{q=1}^{28} c_{iq} S_q + \sum_{m=1}^{9} g_{im} G_m$$
$$+ E_i - I_i + \Delta V_i + \Delta SP_i + C_i. \tag{12}$$

The first righthand term is sales to intermediate demand. The second is sales to each purchaser of capital equipment where K_k is total equipment investment by industry k. The third term is sales to construction, where S_q is total amount of construction type q. The fourth term is sales to government, where G_m is total expenditure by government category m. The other terms are exports E_i, imports I_i, change in inventories ΔV_i, change in stockpiles ΔSP_i, and personal consumption C_i. Simultaneous solution of 185 equations of the form illustrated by Equation 12 determines output levels for 185 economic sectors consistent with final demand and consistent with all assumptions including those for environmental and minerals policies, energy supply, technology change, and relative energy prices.

PRICE.   The PRICE model provides a mechanism whereby exogenously specified price assumptions for resources can influence the other models (prices for consumer goods are taken care of in the consumption functions). However, this model is currently specified only for energy prices. In this form, it performs three functions: it affects final and intermediate energy demands, it alters investment flows for energy production, and it determines full employment GNP consistent with energy use impacts on productivity. The PRICE model is critical for analyzing impacts of energy prices on demand and on the economy. Its specific assumptions and implications are discussed in chapter 5.

TECHNOLOGY.   The TECHNOLOGY model uses assumptions about technology change to alter current capital account flows within INFORUM and to alter technology splits within INSIDE. Its role is best explained by example. Consider a scenario in which it is assumed that nuclear energy grows from 0 percent of electric energy output in 1971 to 75 percent in 2025. The TECHNOLOGY model would increase IN-FORUM investment flows to reflect the higher capital requirements of nuclear generating stations, change the A-matrix coefficients over time so that appropriate current account flows of coal, oil, natural gas, and nuclear core material are purchased by the electric utilities sector, and alter the electric generating technology split within INSIDE so that appropriate levels of environmental residuals are calculated by RESGEN and appropriate levels of abatement costs are calculated by ABATE. It operates in this fashion for each of the technology change assumptions within the scenarios run through the FORECAST model. A description of the procedures used in making technology forecasts is found in Shapanka (1978).

Table A–1. Coverage of the INSIDE Model

Sector	Number of side equations	Units
Agriculture	12	Bushels, tons, cwt.
Municipal sewage and solid waste	20	Gallons, tons
Mining and drilling	14	Tons
Food processing	25	Tons
Fabrics and textiles	15	Tons
Pulp, paper, and wood products	20	Tons
Chemicals	71	Tons
Paints and soaps	10	Gallons, tons
Petroleum products	12	Barrels, tons
Rubber, leather, clay, and glass	18	Tons
Cement and stone	7	Tons
Ferrous industries	26	Gallons, tons
Nonferrous industries	30	Flasks, tons
Electric utilities	19	Btu, tons
Gas utilities	3	Btu
Cleaning	3	Dollars
Industrial combustion of fuel	34	Btu
Commercial/residential/institutional fuel combustion	7	Btu
Total	346	

INSIDE. The INSIDE model is a series of 346 side equations for dealing with product- and technological-mix problems. They are described in table A–1. The objective of the INSIDE model is to estimate the subsector output levels used in forecasting residuals and abatement costs.

Product-mix problems occur because different products of an IN-FORUM sector have significantly different residuals-generation and demand trends. Technology-mix problems deal with alternate processes for making the same material or product.

An example of a product-mix problem is emissions from nitric acid production. INFORUM sector 55 (the industrial chemicals sector) is responsible for a large share of the nitrogen oxide emissions from industrial processes. It would be possible to relate the future output of nitrogen oxides from the chemical industry to the economic activity of sector 55. However, there are several hundred major chemicals within sector 55, and the manufacture of nitric acid generates the vast majority of nitrogen oxide emissions that this industry produces.

About 80 percent of the nitric acid manufactured is sold to fertilizers (sector 59) and miscellaneous chemicals (sector 61), whereas sector 55 sells more than 50 percent of its total volume of products to plastics, non-cellulose fibers, cleaning and toilet preparations, miscellaneous chemicals, and paints. The growth rate of nitric acid does not parallel the aggregate growth of all major chemicals in sector 55. Thus, relating the nitrogen oxide emissions and abatement costs to nitric acid demand rather than to the aggregate of sector 55 gives a more accurate projection of nitrogen oxide emissions and abatement costs.

An illustration of a technological-mix problem is that of steel production by the competing processes of the electric arc furnace, open hearth furnace, and basic oxygen furnace. Side equations allow the pollution coefficients and abatement costs to be linked with the particular type of steel production rather than with steel production as a whole (sector 83).

The side equations serve to disaggregate INFORUM sector outputs X_j to the subsector level Z_k. This is done by determining from published data the sales by a subsector k to the 185 INFORUM sectors and to the other subsectors as well. Coefficients reflecting the sales by subsector k to INFORUM sector j (the a_{kj}) and other subsectors q (the b_{kq}) are applied to the respective sector and subsector outputs X_j, Z_q to determine intermediate sales by subsector k:

$$S_k \text{ (intermediate)} = \left(\sum_{j=1}^{185} a_{kj}X_j + \sum_{q=1, q \neq k}^{n} b_{kq}Z_q \right) \Big/ W. \tag{13}$$

Because the allocation of the sales by subsector k to the outputs of specified industries $X_j + Z_q$ does not always account for 100 percent of the outputs of these industries, a weighting factor W is used to compensate for truncation errors. If the truncation error is large ($W < .8$), then another method may be used. This method treats GNP as a miscellaneous sector. Coefficients W_k are derived that relate purchases from subsector k by unidentified industries to the total value of GNP. Thus, division by W is replaced by $W_k \times$ GNP.

Total output for a subsector k is determined by adding final demands to the intermediate demands. The final demands include exports by the k subsector E_k and consumer purchases F_k. Imports I_k are subtracted. Thus, the equation for total outputs by subsector k becomes

$$Z_k = S_k + E_k - I_k + F_k. \tag{14}$$

The coefficients and data inputs are usually constructed so that the side equation outputs are in physical units rather than dollars of output.

Side equation coefficients a_{kj}, b_{kq} are constructed by a two-step process. Initially each equation is constructed with static (base-year) coefficients. This is performed by finding for a base year the quantity of output from industry k sold to sectors j (sectors in INFORUM) and to sectors q (sectors derived from the side equation). Then each a_{kj} coefficient is trended by an index approach or by using trends from the A matrix. In the index approach, the base-year coefficient is multiplied by an index providing a coefficient for year t. The other technique allows any side equation coefficient to grow at the same rate as an associated A-matrix coefficient.

Technology mix is determined by specifying dynamic fractions for dividing total sector output into output from competing technologies or processes. The following are representative examples of some of the technology mixes considered in the energy sector in the SEAS/RFF system:

> Coal
> > Underground coal mining
> > Surface coal mining
> > > Western
> > > Eastern
> Electric power generation by fossil fuel
> > Coal
> > Oil
> > Natural gas
> Nuclear power generation
> > Fission
> > Breeder
> > Fusion

Coefficient trending and forecasts of technology mix are based upon expert judgment.

ABATE. The ABATE model estimates the investment costs and the operating and maintenance (O&M) costs associated with pollution control for the 131 abating sectors described in table A–2. It also determines feedback to INFORUM of consequent increases in consumption, investment, construction, government expenditure, intermediate sales, and employment. These feedbacks allow INFORUM to rebalance dynamically its forecasts of economic activity and produce consistent estimates of such macrostatistics as total consumption and investment, as well as interindustry demands and outputs.

The following data were developed for input to the ABATE model for abating sectors other than municipal wastewater treatment.
1. An inventory of plants. This includes a size distribution of the total capacity of the abating sector for a base year as determined from one

Table A–2. Abating Sectors

Type	Number
Agriculture	6
Food processing	16
Textiles	6
Pulp, paper, and lumber products	6
Chemicals	6
Petroleum	12
Rubber and leather	4
Ferrous metals	8
Nonferrous metals	9
Cement, asphalt, and asbestos	8
Machinery and equipment	6
Miscellaneous industry	3
Steam electric[a]	16
Municipal sewage treatment	7
Solid waste and incineration	1
Commercial and institutional heating	1
Industrial fuel combustion	10
Transportation	6
Total	131

[a] Includes abatement for air, water, thermal and radiation residuals.

or more of the following sources: trade associations, directories of periodic publications, government research reports, researchers' files.

2. Capital costs and O&M cost functions. These were estimated for each pollution standard mandated by the federal government—State Implementation Plans (SIP), Best Practicable Technology (BPT), Best Available Technology (BAT), and New Source Performance Standards (NSP). Cost functions were developed for sectors involved in water pollution abatement, for both full in-plant treatment and pretreatment options. (Pretreatment is partial cleanup by firms before wastes are dumped into municipal systems for additional treatment.) The general form of the cost equations is:

$$\text{Cost} = A_o (\text{Capacity})^a \tag{15}$$

The parameters A_o and a are determined by regression analysis or by applications of engineering principles. The key data sources used to estimate these cost parameters are Associated Water and Air Resources Engineers, Inc. (1973) and Battelle (1974). Some abatement costs, for example, costs for transportation control plans (extra bus lanes, vehicle inspection programs, and so on), are specified exogenously. Major sources for exogenous costs are the annual reports of the Council on Environmental Quality and various studies of the Environmental Protection Agency.

3. Feedback vectors for capital and O&M costs. The capital feedback vectors constitute the D matrix and contain the percentage allocation of total abatement investment as purchases from each of the 185 economic sectors and the 28 construction sectors. An example is total abatement investment for controlling air pollution from open hearth furnaces. If 40 percent of this investment is purchases from sector 19 and 60 percent is purchases of construction category 5, then .4 and .6 would be in the nineteenth sector row and the fifth construction row within the capital feedback vector for the open hearth sector. The feedback vectors for O&M costs are specified in a similar manner and constitute the E matrix. Gutmanis and Shapanka (1972) are the major source of data for specifying the feedback percentages.

4. Compliance years for each standard. These are specified according to the abatement policy being simulated. Air abatement costs are keyed to SIP standards and more stringent NSP standards. In the electric utilities sector, under a strict control policy, it is assumed that a SIP standard for sulfur dioxide discharges must be met by 1977 and an NSP standard must be met by all new capacity and replacement capacity for which construction is started after 1975. The ABATE model calculates the cost of meeting SIP standards for all capacity started before 1980. Higher costs for meeting NSP standards are calculated for capacity added after 1975. The model also keeps track of capacity by vintage so that capacity which originally had SIP costs is upgraded to NSP costs when it is replaced. Water abatement costs are keyed to BPT standards and more stringent BAT standards and are calculated in a similar fashion.

5. The number of years over which capital expenditures for each standard is spread and the fraction of expenditure for each year. This allows investment for abatement to start in advance of the year when standards are to be met and abatement capital to build up to the level needed for meeting the standards.

6. The average life of abatement equipment. This allows replacement of abatement capital as it wears out over time.

7. The year for increasing control efficiency and abatement costs in order to maintain environmental quality as the economy grows. In early runs of the system, abatement costs and control efficiencies approached NSP and BAT levels. But these were not sufficient to main-

tain environmental quality over time because growth in capacity finally exceeded growth in removal efficiencies, resulting in a relatively rapid rise in residual discharges. To avoid this problem, the ABATE model was modified so that after some specified year, NSP and BAT capital is replaced by abatement capital, which allows higher removal efficiencies. For most abating sectors, this begins to occur in the period between 2000 and 2010 and takes as long as twenty-five years to complete. The increase in control costs and efficiencies is keyed to the environmental policy being simulated.

8. For water abatement sectors, the percentage of total capacity in each size class for which pretreated wastewater is dumped to municipal systems. Each water abating sector has the option of fully treating its discharges or pretreating and dumping discharges into municipal systems. These percentages allow segmentation of capacity so that appropriate cost functions can be applied.

The ABATE model uses the following data to calculate costs for municipal wastewater treatment:

1. Population served and per capita wastewater flow by year.

2. Capital and O&M cost functions for primary, secondary, and tertiary treatment. These functions have the same form as Equation 15. Estimates of cost parameters are based upon data in Smith (1975).

3. Percentage of wastewater flow to each treatment type (primary, secondary, or tertiary) and the average plant size in each type.

4. Percentage of total population whose wastewater needs are either replacement or upgrading from primary to secondary and from secondary to tertiary, by year.

5. A similar collection of factors, percentages, and cost functions for sewer systems and combined sewer overflow systems.

6. Wastewater flow by industries that divert their wastewater to municipal facilities for treatment.

The ABATE model uses these data and cost functions in a straightforward manner to generate abatement costs for each industry and for municipal treatment facilities. The model starts by using growth rates calculated from the corresponding INFORUM sector or INSIDE subsector to forecast capacity. This capacity is distributed among plant-size classes, and capital and O&M costs are calculated for the average plant, depending upon the year and whether the plant must meet SIP or NSP standards, or BPT or BAT standards. The model then sums cost across classes to get total costs for the year. For water abatement costs, the model derives the costs using both the pretreatment and full-treatment cost functions, depending on the fraction of capacity using municipal facilities in each plant-size class. It also calculates costs for replacement capacity according to the abatement standards in effect. In addition, ABATE calculates the total volume of wastewater discharged to municipal facilities from sectors that pretreat.

Most of the costs calculated by ABATE are end-of-pipe abatement costs. But because it is linked with technology by INSIDE, ABATE does account for abatement cost reductions that occur as a result of technology switching. The steel industry is an example. Electric arc furnaces have relatively low end-of-pipe abatement costs, and open hearth furnaces have high costs. When electric arc capacity increases and open hearth capacity declines over time, ABATE uses capacities in each of these two technologies to calculate correctly end-of-pipe abatement costs for the steel sector.

The municipal portion of ABATE calculates costs associated with building and upgrading treatment facilities, with laying interceptor and collector sewer lines, and with controlling combined sewer overflows. The wastewater flow needing treatment in any year is based on incremental flow from industrial dischargers to municipal systems and that part of the nonindustrial flow that needs replacement or upgrading. This flow is allocated to treatment type (primary, secondary, and upgrading to tertiary). Average plant sizes by type are then used to determine the number of new plants to be constructed. Capital and operating cost functions are used to determine total cost based on plants to be constructed and their average size. The amount of this cost fed back into INFORUM is adjusted by a factor indicating the proportion of this total not already accounted for in the INFORUM baseline. A similar procedure is used to determine costs for interceptors and collectors and to correct combined sewer overflow using incremental cost functions for these categories.

The costs calculated by ABATE for a given year create a demand for resources that is reflected through feedbacks that modify the output levels from the affected INFORUM sectors. In turn, these changed output levels result in different sector growth rates, from which the abatement costs are calculated during the next year.

The procedure described above determines point estimates of abatement costs keyed to specific abatement policies. But to determine cost-minimizing control it is necessary to have costs over a range of control levels. To accomplish this, initial capital costs have been scaled by

$$F_{ij} = [\ln\{100/(100 - (PR_{ij} + \Delta PR_{ij}))\}/\ln 100/(100 - PR_{ij}))]^{b_{ij}},$$

(16)

where PR_{ij} is the percentage removed of pollutant i for source j when costs are at their initial levels. Equation 16 is an engineering relationship, based upon well-known principles of particle migration theory. For $b_{ij} = 1$, $F_{ij} = 2$ whenever the percentage removed is increased by the initial percentage applied against the percentage not controlled. For example, assume that initial point costs correspond with 80 percent removal. Applying 80 percent removal to the remaining 20 percentage points would raise the overall percentage removed to 96 percent (80 percent + 16 percent) and would, according to Equation 16, double costs. The idea here is that if you have two devices in tandem, each removing 80 percent of whatever enters it (and therefore two devices of equal size and capacity), then costs must be double the cost of a single device. For $b_{ij} > 1$, costs would be more than doubled, and for $b_{ij} < 1$, cost would be less than doubled. Values for b_{ij} are determined by fitting Equation 16 through costs and percentages that correspond to relaxed and strict enforcement of environmental standards or are based upon reported engineering values. The other category of abatement costs, O&M costs, are scaled in proportion to the amounts of residuals removed.

ENSUPPLY.   ENSUPPLY calculates capital requirements for supplying or generating energy and fixes the mix of fuels that can be supplied to the national economy over time.

The calculations for energy technology are based upon expert analyses of the rates at which various energy supply technologies can be developed. The following energy supply technologies are among those considered: fission reactors, breeder reactors, fusion reactors, coal conversion to natural gas, coal conversion to petroleum liquids, use of geothermal resources to generate electric energy and solar space heating. The outcome of this analysis is implemented in the FORECAST model by procedures established by the TECHNOLOGY model (see that discussion).

The analysis of fuel availability is also based upon expert judgment; details are found in chapter 5. Once the fuel mix is established it is used to alter direct fuel demands and intermediate demands so that the supply pattern is met. Final energy demands are established by overriding energy consumption functions. Intermediate energy demands are established by altering A-matrix coefficients. Similar procedures are used by the PRICE model. The difference is that the PRICE model is used to determine *total* energy demand as a function of energy prices and the ENSUPPLY model determines the fuel demand *mix* for this total demand as constrained by fuel availability and energy supply technology.

Energy availability is determined at the national level for these major fuels or energy sources: coal, oil, natural gas, uranium, natural gas from converted coal, petroleum from converted coal, shale oil, geothermal resources, hydropower, and solar energy; and for these major energy consumers—industry, the commercial sector, the residential sector, transportation, and electric generation.

The most important feature of the ENSUPPLY model (in conjunction with the PRICE model) is that it imposes an energy balance. Demand is matched by supply in physical terms for each type of energy. This occurs with the given energy prices and supply technologies.

MINERALS. The MINERALS model establishes stockpiles and exogenous import levels for selected minerals. Stockpiles are established by entering stockpile change into each sector's demand equations. Data used to do this are timing and rate of build-up of stockpiles and the ultimate levels of the stockpiles or equations for calculating those levels. Import levels are established by overriding the normal import equations. Both stockpile changes and exogenous imports are entered into the INFORUM model in a way that correctly preserves the simultaneous solution for product outputs, imports, and stockpile and inventory changes.

The FORECAST model has now been completely described. It is useful at this point to make some observations about its strengths and weaknesses. First, this model is very ambitious in the sense of attempting to represent the entire economy and to project some fifty years into the future. Many of its limitations stem from this fact. Obviously, confidence decreases the further out in time one goes. Furthermore, even a model with 185 sectors is probably too aggregated to capture comprehensively the ramifications of every policy one might want to simulate. Nonetheless, the FORECAST model comes fairly close (we think) to providing at least a framework or mechanism that, in principle, allows comprehensive modeling.

Table A–3. Sources and Residuals in RESGEN

Source and residual	Number of sources
Air residuals	
Particulate matter	100
Sulfur oxides	65
Nitrogen oxides	53
Hydrocarbons	74
Carbon monoxide	58
Radionuclides	4
Water residuals	
Biochemical oxygen demand	110
Chemical oxygen	63
Suspended solids	156
Dissolved solids	116
Nutrients	22
Acids and bases	19
Oils and greases	43
Thermal loadings	4
Pesticides	24
Total	911

Most large-scale economic models depend upon econometric relationships fitted by using historical time-series data. This is true of IN-FORUM taken by itself. The problem in this is that changes in relative prices, technology, consumer tastes, and so on may make future economic relationships quite different from current or past relationships. Consequently, a model calibrated to historical time trends may give, at best, only a poor picture of future change. The models coupled with INFORUM within the FORECAST model (PRICE, TECHNOLOGY, ABATE, EN-SUPPLY, and MINERALS) all are designed to help INFORUM overcome this weakness. Each of these models either augments or overrides INFORUM econometric relationships in an attempt to capture future change more comprehensively.

The Industrial/Commercial/Municipal Environment Residuals Model (RESGEN)

RESGEN estimates the annual national air and water pollutant residuals associated with industrial, municipal treatment, and electric utility processes. As table A–3 indicates, RESGEN makes more than 900 individual calculations of emissions in any given year.

RESGEN does not estimate transportation emissions, storm water runoff residuals, or emissions from nonpoint sources of pollution, such as urban runoff, agriculture, forestry, mining, and construction associated with land use activities. Transportation emissions are estimated by PTRANS and FTRANS; urban and agricultural runoff, and residuals from mining, forestry, and nonurban construction are calculated by RUNOFF.

For the emission sources it covers, RESGEN initially forecasts the gross pollutant emissions that would occur if no abatement activity had occurred pursuant to the 1970 Amendments to the Clean Air Act or the 1972 Amendments to the Federal Water Pollution Control Act. Then, it estimates the net emissions, assuming that some specified level of pollution abatement activity is occurring. The differences are the captured residuals, which include recyclable wastes. RESGEN also estimates significant secondary residuals resulting from the pollution treatment processes themselves such as air pollution from combustion of municipal sewage sludge.

The level and timing of residual removal RESGEN uses corresponds directly with the level and timing used by ABATE to calculate abatement costs.

The primary data source used to develop coefficients for air residuals was a set of industry reports prepared by Battelle Columbus Laboratories for the Environmental Protection Agency (Battelle Laboratories, Inc., 1974). Supplementary material was developed from the *Cost of Clean Air* reports (EPA, 1974d) and EPA report AP-42 entitled *A Compilation of Air Pollutant Emission Factors* (EPA, 1973a). Two major bodies of data were used for water pollutant: EPA development documents (both draft and final versions) on the effluent guidelines proposed for industrial point sources, and industrial reports prepared for the National Commission on Water Quality as part of its study on the costs and capabilities of water abatement technology (listed in NCWQ, 1976). Additional information was extracted from other EPA reports, including *The Clean Water Report to Congress* (EPA, 1973b), *Economics of Clean Water* (EPA, 1973a) and studies conducted by private industry (for example, the National Canning Fruits and Vegetables Industry). The NCWQ reports measure the amounts of secondary sludges occurring as a result of waste treatment; other secondary residuals were estimated from information obtained from industrial treatment handbooks. Thermal and radiation residual coefficients were obtained from a recent federal government report on energy supply alternatives (University of Oklahoma, 1975).

The Transportation Models (PTRANS and FTRANS)

The two transportation models, PTRANS and FTRANS, use annual forecasts of vehicle miles traveled by automobile, bus, truck, rail, commuter rail, and airplane to estimate passenger transportation vehicle air pollution emissions in five categories: hydrocarbons, carbon monoxide, nitrogen oxides, sulfur oxides, and particulates.

For a given calendar year, the PTRANS model uses the disposable income forecast by INFORUM and the population forecast to determine the number of new vehicles on the road. It uses data from the 1974 National Transportation Study for vehicle miles traveled by transportation mode and occupancy ratios to distribute the VMT forecast between intracity (auto, bus, rapid transit, rail transit) and intercity (auto, air, bus, railroad) transportation modes.

Then it uses EPA emissions factors to forecast gross and net residuals for the year. Gross residuals are those which would have occurred if EPA had not placed further regulations on motor vehicle emissions after 1971. Net residuals are those which occur after compliance with post-1971 regulation of motor vehicle emissions. In the case of automobiles, PTRANS also uses input data indicating the on-the-road distribution of cars by model year to forecast these residuals. Both stringency and timing of regulation can be altered to simulate different control policies.

The FTRANS model computes freight ton-mile projections by applying INFORUM growth rates for freight sectors to base-year data drawn from Department of Transportation studies. Modal splits and occupancy ratios are then applied to develop forecasts of vehicle miles traveled by truck, rail, water, air, and pipelines. In turn, pollutant emissions are estimated by applying emission factors to each mode.

The initial analysis in both PTRANS and FTRANS is done at the state level. National estimates are obtained by adding across states.

The Energy Use Model (ENERGY)

ENERGY estimates energy use in Btus by fuel category based on INFORUM annual output forecasts for the 185 economic sectors. For each fuel category, it also reports whether the fuel is used for combustion or as a raw material feedstock. In addition, ENERGY estimates conversion losses. This is particularly important for electric generation and the

Table A–4. Sectors and Fuels in ENERGY

Sector and fuel	Number of sectors
Industrial	
Natural gas	19
Petroleum	17
Coal	10
Electricity	9
Transportation	
Natural gas	1
Petroleum	17
Electricity	2
Commercial	
Natural gas	8
Petroleum	15
Electricity	14
Residential (four fuel sectors)	4
Electric generation	
Coal	1
Converted coal	1
Petroleum	1
Natural gas	1
Fission	1
Breeder	1
Fusion	1
Hydropower	1
Geothermal	1
Shale oil (four consuming sectors)	4
Solar (three consuming sectors)	3
Converted coal (four consuming sectors)	4
Total	136

synthetic fuel industries. Table A–4 outlines the coverage of the ENERGY model.

Because the energy forecasts are based on the INFORUM annual outputs, the supply and demand constraints caused by relative price adjustments (from the PRICE model) and energy supply adjustments (from the ENSUPPLY model) are introduced into the forecasts. In general, ENERGY is sensitive to all the policies being simulated by the FORECAST model.

The ENERGY model uses a set of base-year energy coefficients (in units of 10^{12} Btu per \$1 million), which are modified over time. These are applied directly to associated INFORUM sector flows (in units of \$1 million) to calculate energy flows. The base-year coefficients change over time in step with changes in A-matrix coefficients, or when it is not possible to do this, in line with policies being simulated by an indexing procedure. The rationale for changing the base-year coefficients follows.

Table A–5. Material and Product Categories

Material	Product categories
Paper	Newspaper
Paperboard	Writing/printing
Plastics	Tissue and other paper
Glass	Packaging/container
Aluminum	Construction
Zinc	Other paperboard products
Copper	Household durables
Lead	Electrical/electronics
Ferrous metals	Furniture
Wood	Other consumer goods
Textiles	Autos and light trucks
Rubber	Other transportation
	Other plastics
	Other glass products
	Other textile products
	Machinery
	Other metal products
	Batteries
	Apparel
	Tires

Assume that energy use is being forecast for 1985 and that technology and prices have changed so that by 1985, the A-matrix coefficient for coal into steel falls by 20 percent. In effect, this means that *per unit* of steel output, coal input whether measured in constant dollars or energy units, falls to 80 percent of its base-year value. Thus, the correct energy coefficient for 1985 in this case is 0.8 times the 1971 value. This corrected coefficient is then applied to total steel output for 1985 in order to forecast total coal use in steel for 1985.

The sources of data for the 1971 energy coefficients are the U.S. Bureau of Census (1972), several other government reports, and publications of trade associations.

The Solid Waste/Recycling Model (SOLRECYC)

The SOLRECYC model estimates the annual national tonnage of solid waste from nonindustrial sources and recycled materials from both industrial and nonindustrial sources. The materials tracked include aluminum, copper, ferrous metals, glass, lead, paper, plastics, rubber, textiles, wood, zinc, paperboard, and miscellaneous construction matter. The model keeps a running inventory of these materials as they are embodied in twenty different product categories (see table A–5). Each product has its

Table A–6. Sample of Chains Related to Purchasing Sectors

Automotive and truck transportation	$(a_{87,133} + a_{87,97} \cdot a_{97,133} + a_{87,117} \cdot a_{117,133})X_{133} +$ $(a_{87,140} + a_{87,95} \cdot a_{95,140})X_{140} \ldots$
Packaging and containers	$a_{87,92}X_{92} + a_{87,97} \cdot (a_{97,25}X_{25} + a_{97,31} \cdot X_{31})$ $+ a_{87,101}a_{101,25}X_{25}$
Durables	$a_{87,116}X_{116} + a_{87,123}X_{123} + a_{87,120} \cdot a_{120,123}X_{123}$

The a_{ij} are A-matrix coefficients attached to the following sectors:

87—Aluminum	92—Metal cans
133—Motor vehicles and parts	25—Canned and frozen foods
97—Metal stampings	30—Alcoholic beverages
117—Machine shop products	31—Soft drinks and beverages
140—Trailer coaches	116—Service industry machinery
95—Structural metal products	123—Household appliances
101—Other fabricated metal parts	120—Motors and generators

own distribution of lifetimes. Then, as products wear out and are discarded as solid matter, the model calculates the amounts that become solid waste and the amounts recycled. A large amount of recycling also arises from the materials discarded during the manufacturing process, for example, aluminum scrap resulting from stamping operations. This is calculated in the SOLRECYC model by applying recycle fractions to estimates of the materials entering various products. The levels of recycling are set so as to be consistent with the policy assumptions for each scenario simulated by the FORECAST model.

The matrix of materials, by product, prior to 1971 is based mainly upon Bureau of Mines and trade association reports. Thereafter, the macroeconomic forecasts and input–output flows of the FORECAST model were used to estimate materials, by product, using the following equation:

$$M_{ij}(t) = M_{ij}(1971) \frac{[\text{Purchasing Chain}_i(t)]X_j(t)}{[\text{Purchasing Chain}_i(1971)]X_j(1971)}, \qquad (17)$$

where M_{ij} is the amount of material i flowing into product j, and X_j is the total dollar output from sector j. Equation 17 states that the amount of material i flowing into product category j is proportional to the rates of dollar flow as projected by FORECAST from industry i to industry j in year t divided by the flow given in 1971.

An example of the purchasing chains is given in table A–6. The material is aluminum [INFORUM sector 87], and the end products are: automobiles and trucks [INFORUM sector 133]; packaging and containers [INFORUM sectors 92, 25, 30, 31]; and durables [INFORUM sectors 116, 123, 120]. Table A–6 shows that a product like aluminum is purchased directly by automobile and truck manufacturers and indirectly through purchases of metal stampings and structural metals products. In general, for each material and product, the SOLRECYC model calculates the important direct and indirect material flows.

The Regionalization Model (REGION)

The REGION model allocates national pollution residuals from RESGEN, national abatement costs from ABATE and national economic output from INFORUM and INSIDE to the following regional levels:

Regional units	Number
Standard Metropolitan Statistical Areas	254
Air Quality Control Regions (AQCR)	243
Bureau of Economic Analysis Regions	173
Major river basins	19
Minor river basins	221
Aggregated Subareas (ASA)	101
States	51
EPA federal regions	10

In its application of the REGION model, the SEAS/RFF Regional System distributes national air residuals and abatement costs to AQCRs and national water residuals and abatement costs to ASAs (see figure A–2). AQCRs and ASAs are designed, in principle, to be nearly self-contained air- and watershed regions, respectively.

The REGION model contains sixteen sets of regional fractions (SHARE), which are applied to the national estimates to determine regional quantities. Eight of these are for regionalizing outputs of and abatement costs to any of the eight regional levels. The other eight are for regionalizing pollution residuals to any of the eight regional levels. The most involved part of the REGION model is in constructing the SHARE values:

E-SHARE$_{ij}(t) \equiv$ the fraction of economic and abatement activity associated with sector i located in regional unit j in year t.

P-SHARE$_{ij}(t) \equiv$ the fraction of pollution associated with sector i located in regional unit j in year t.

Embodied in the above definition of the P-SHARE is the assumption that allocation of pollution to a regional level is independent of the residual.

An attempt has been made to remedy this problem by establishing for certain selected sectors (for example, particulate and sulfur dioxide discharges from fuel combustion) a SHARE file which is *dependent* upon the residual category:

P-SHARE$_{ijk}(t)$ = the fraction of residual k associated with sector i located in regional unit j in year t.

The SHARE files are constructed by finding the best information on a county level that can be used to regionalize residual or economic data. For example, plant capacity data or employment is often used as a way of allocating pollution or economic information, the assumption being that pollution and economic output is equivalent to capacity and employment or both.

Once a complete inventory is found, the shares are constructed. A SHARE is constructed for the base year (1971) by summing the county values for those counties within the regional unit and dividing by the national total:

$$\text{SHARE}_{ij}(1971) = \sum_c V_{im}(1971)/ \sum_n V_{im}(1971), \tag{18}$$

where V_{im} (1971) is the capacity for sector i in county m for 1971, c refers to all counties within regional unit j, and n refers to all counties within the nation.

The SHARE values are extrapolated into the future by applying growth factors determined from Office of Business and Economic Research (OBERS) regional reports. The OBERS growth factor (OG_{ij}) is:

$$OG_{i'j}(t) = \text{OBERS}_{i'j}(t)/\text{OBERS}_{i'j}(1971), \tag{19}$$

where OBERS $_{i'j}$ is defined as the industry earnings associated with each two-digit Standard Industrial Code (SIC) manufacturing sector i' in regional unit j. For each FORECAST sector i included in the OBERS sector i', the future SHARE values are calculated as

$$\text{SHARE}_{ij(t)} = \text{SHARE}_{ij}(1971) \times \text{OG}_{i'j}(t). \tag{20}$$

Then, as a final step, these SHARE values are renormalized so that their sum over all regions for sector i is 1.

The major sources of data used by the REGION model are the OBERS regional reports and the Economic Information System (EIS). EIS, which provided the basis for calculating most of the base-year

SHAREs, consists of employment data for 115,000 industrial establishments by name and address, state and county, and four-digit SIC. This includes a reasonably complete coverage of all plants in the continental United States with more than twenty employees. There are no disclosure limitations because the data are derived entirely from public sources. In some cases, accurate regionalization of pollution requires more detail than the four-digit SIC level provides. Whenever more detailed inventory data could be found, it was used instead of EIS to calculate pollution shares.

The Regional Transportation Residuals Models (PTRANS and FTRANS)

The general outlines of the PTRANS and FTRANS models have already been presented. Recall that PTRANS and FTRANS calculate passenger and freight transportation residuals initially at the state level. Within the SEAS/RFF regional system, these state residuals are allocated to AQCRs on the basis of population shares. Population shares for 1970 are used for every year on the assumption that growth rates for AQCRs *within states* will not change appreciably over time. The source of data for the population shares is the *City and County Databook* (1970 data).

The Regional Municipal Agricultural and Mining Runoff Model (Runoff)

The RUNOFF model calculates nonpoint source water pollution for urban runoff, mining, agriculture, nonurban construction, and forestry; and point source discharges from ore, coal, and mineral mining, and from acid mine drainage. The RUNOFF model also calculates pollution control costs for urban runoff sources. A model developed by Heaney and coauthors (1977) is used to estimate urban runoff and runoff control costs for 248 separate urbanized areas. Urban runoff depends upon acreage and population density in the three different zones—areas with combined sewers, those with storm sewers, and unsewered areas—and upon the type of activity within these zones—residential, commercial, industrial, or other. Costs of controlling runoff depend upon the mix of the different sewered zones and upon cost tradeoffs between size of treatment facility and storage for delayed treatment. Estimates for future years are made by assuming that gross runoff and control costs are proportional to population growth in each urbanized area. Population growth by urbanized area is based upon U.S. Water Resources Council (1974d).

For agriculture, the RUNOFF model estimates sediment, chemical fertilizer, and pesticide runoff for major crops over time. The Midwest Research Institute (1975) composite erosion factors (tons of soil per acre lost to water) are used in these calculations. Regional discharges are scaled (in effect adjusting the sediment delivery ratios) so that the aggregate national estimates agree with the U.S. Department of Agriculture gross and net erosion estimates as derived from the cropland forecasts presented in chapter 6.

To estimate residuals from mining the RUNOFF model develops base-year emission coefficients for point source discharges from mining associated with iron, copper, uranium, aluminum, and eastern and western coal. This is done at three levels of treatment—raw waste or no treatment, best practicable control technology, and best available control technology —using national discharge totals taken from Gianessi and Peskin (1978) and 1973 economic activity levels for these sectors. These coefficients are applied to projections of activity levels by state and by ASA, which are derived from the land use model described in chapter 8.

Sediment runoff from these mining sectors begins with estimates of land disturbed by mining prior to 1971 plus projections for the future derived from the land use model. These figures are then converted to tons of sediment delivered to water by applying two factors: gross tons of sediment per disturbed acre and tons of sediment delivered to water per gross ton. The first term is derived from the Universal Soil Loss Equation, which determines regional gross soil loss as a function of rain runoff potential, soil properties, slope length and steepness, cover, and management practices (USDA, 1975). The second term, known as the sediment delivery ratio, is a proportion based mainly upon educated guesses; it is usually considered to be a less reliable factor than the first term. Our composites of these two factors (for each ASA), taken from a recent study of sediment runoff (Midwest Research Institute, 1975), are adjusted so that they give the same national totals in 1973 as reported by Gianessi and Peskin (1978). In effect, this scales the MRI sediment delivery ratios to produce estimates for 1973 which are considered to be reasonable. To make projections, these adjusted factors are then applied to regional estimates of acres disturbed in future years.

Point discharges from other ore mining (lead, zinc, gold, silver, and ferroalloys) are based upon Gianessi and Peskin (1978). To make projections for future years, Gianessi and Peskin's regional discharge estimates are scaled by appropriate sector output levels taken from SEAS/ RFF. Gold and silver, exceptions to this, are kept constant over time because there is no firm basis in SEAS/RFF for projecting outputs for these two erratic sectors. Regional shares for any given ore are kept constant over time because all regional mining activity is scaled in proportion to aggregate national activity levels. This procedure and the one for nonurban construction, explained below, are the only ones in which regional shares were kept constant. The discharge levels from the mining of lead, zinc, gold, silver, and ferroalloys are relatively small and location of activity is relatively stable in our time frame; it is unlikely, therefore, that the use of constant shares generates errors of any significant amount.

Sediment from nonurban construction is estimated by applying regional shares to an estimated national sediment total. The latter is derived by taking a national estimate for 1973 of sediment runoff from all construction (Midwest Research Institute, 1975), subtracting from it (to avoid double counting) sediment runoff from urban construction (as estimated by Heany and coauthors, 1977), and then scaling this result in proportion to dollar estimates of highway construction taken from SEAS/RFF. Regional shares, taken from Midwest Research Institute (1975), are held constant over time. Most nonurban construction is for highways and is probably related to population. Population shares by ASA do change over time and judged on the basis of that, we have probably placed too much of this sediment over time in regions of the country where population is dense now and too little where population densities are growing. At a national level, this would tend to overstate pollution damages attributable to nonurban construction, and the error would become larger the further out in time we go.

Acid mine drainage from abandoned coal mines is estimated by assigning national discharges to ASAs, using shares and treatment levels taken from Gianessi and Peskin (1978).

Air and Water Ambient Models (AQUALITY and WQUALITY)

The AQUALITY model uses the following equation (a modified rollback equation) to estimate ambient air concentrations for each of 243 AQCRs:

$$C_{ij}^* = \left[\frac{\sum_k P_{ijk}^* E_{ijk}^*}{\sum_k P_{ijk} E_{ijk}} (C_{ij} - b_j) \right] + b_j. \tag{21}$$

The variables with an asterisk (*) are for future or forecasted values. C_{ij} is ambient concentration in region i of pollutant j; the P_{ijk} are source-receptor interaction factors in region i for pollutant j and source k; the E_{ijk} are emissions in region i of pollutant j from source k; and b_j is the background concentration of pollutant j.

The source-receptor interaction factors are estimated by

$$P_{ijk} = D_{ijk}G_i. \tag{22}$$

The D_{ijk} are the relative contributions of source k to exposures of pollutant j from all sources in region i. The Ds take cognizance of the fact that all emissions may not contribute equally to the ambient pollution levels because of different source-receptor arrangements. In effect, the Ds are proxy values for emission height and location variables, meteorological variables, and emission patterns. The G_i are factors measuring relative frequency of stagnant air conditions to sources; higher values for G_i reflect higher stagnation frequencies.

Average per capita exposure to air pollution is estimated by

$$X_{ij}^* = \sum_k P_{ijk}^* E_{ijk}. \tag{23}$$

Substituting this into Equation 21 and rearranging gives

$$X_{ij}^* = \frac{C_{ij}^* - b_j}{C_{ij} - b_j} X_{ij}. \tag{24}$$

Thus, forecast exposure equals base year exposure scaled in proportion to the ratio of above background, forecast concentrations to above background, base-year concentrations. Exposures (and therefore damages) from man-originated activity are zero whenever forecast concentrations equal background concentrations.

Base-year measures of C_{ij} and b_j are from the EPA (1973d). But not all AQCRs report ambient concentrations for the five pollutants being analyzed. For regions where base-year concentrations are not available, above background concentrations per weighted ton from known regions are assigned to these regions, for use in Equation 1, based upon judgments as to the similarity among regions. In the case of hydrocarbons, no regional concentration estimates are reported, so Equation 21 cannot be applied. The ambient quality indexes reported for hydrocarbons are from Equation 23 with 1971 set equal to 100. The D_{ijk} are based on data in

Krajeski, Kertz, and Bobo (1972), and Lewis (1971). The G_i are based on Holzworth (1972).

The WQUALITY model estimates ambient water quality and average per capita exposures as

$$
\text{PDI}_i^* = \frac{\sum\limits_j \sum\limits_k E_{ijk}^*}{\sum\limits_j \sum\limits_k E_{ijk}} \text{PDI}_i.
\tag{25}
$$

The PDI_i are base-year prevalence–duration–intensity index values. The PDI index is a crude, but in principle comprehensive, measure of ambient water quality. It is supposed to reflect impingement upon human activity as well as the degree of pollution concentration. Higher values indicate lower water quality. It is used to assess environmental quality (instead of pollution concentrations), because water pollution concentration data are fragmentary and of suspect quality and because dispersion modeling of water residuals is more difficult than in the case of air. Also, assessment of the relationship between water quality and impacts on human activities—whether or not they are based upon the PDI index or some other procedure—almost always rely upon subjective judgments of the type required in using the PDI index (Truitt and coauthors, 1975). The source of the base-year PDI values is Lake and coauthors (1976).

The Damages and Benefit–Cost Model (BENEFITS)

The BENEFITS model calculates air and water pollution damages, control benefits, and pollution control benefit and cost comparisons. For air pollution, calculations of damages and control benefits are performed for each of the 243 AQCRs and then summed to obtain national estimates. For water pollution, residual damages and pollution control benefits are calculated for each of 101 ASAs and then summed to obtain national estimates.

Air pollution damages and control benefits are estimated separately for five air pollutants—particulate matter, sulfur oxides, nitrogen oxides, hydrocarbons, and carbon monoxide—and for four major sources of emissions—electric utilities, industry, residential and commercial sources, and transportation. Water pollution damage and control benefits are calculated *in total* for the following pollutants—biological oxygen demand, chemical oxygen demand, suspended solids, dissolved solids, nutrients, acids, bases, oil, grease, heavy metals, and pesticides. These are then allocated to seven major sources—electric utilities, industrial point sources, municipal sewage treatment, urban runoff, agricultural runoff, mining, and other nonpoint sources.

The BENEFITS model uses 1971 damage estimates for the five major air pollutants and all water pollution to estimate corresponding per capita regional damage functions having the following properties:

Regional per capita damages are a function of regional pollution exposures.

The sum of regional total damages in 1971 equals the exogenous national damages supplied to the BENEFITS model for 1971.

Each regional damage function has the same *relative* rates of increase or slopes as exhibited by the few existing specialized empirical damage functions. Thus, if damages per capita quadruple along the empirical function as exposures go from their 1971 median level to twice that level, then each regional damage function also quadruples damages per capita as exposures go from their 1971 median to twice the median, and so forth. The major implication here is that our best knowledge about relative response rates is that displayed by empirical damage functions, and thus our best estimate of future damages is one that uses this information.

For any year beyond 1971, the BENEFITS model then uses these functions to calculate both regional pollution damages and control benefits.

To forecast damages and pollution control benefits, the BENEFITS model uses gross and net residuals generated by the REGION, PTRANS, FTRANS, and RUNOFF models. Gross residuals assume no pollution control; net residuals are residuals corresponding with specified control levels and timing of standards implementation. Gross and net residuals are converted to effective concentrations or exposures and then mapped into the regional per capita damage functions. The resulting per capita damages are multiplied by regional population and a regional income–environment elasticity multiplier to obtain gross and net regional damages for scenario-dependent control levels and timing. Pollution control benefits are calculated by subtracting net damages from gross damages.

The BENEFITS model calculates damages and benefits on an annualized basis and control costs on either an annualized or actual basis and also discounts control costs, damages, and benefits over specified planning horizons. The values can be either most likely levels or expected (that is, probability-weighted) levels. The planning horizon can extend as far as the year 2030. Options allow the discounting period to be divided between a current and future generation so that potential intergenerational conflicts can be analyzed.

TECHNICAL SPECIFICATIONS. Average per capita exposure to air pollution, as calculated by Equation 24, is used to estimate per capita base-year damage for each region according to

$$\frac{AD_{ij}}{Pop_i} = \frac{(X_{ij}/m) \cdot \lambda_j}{\sum (Pop_i(X_{ij}/m)\lambda_j} NAD_j. \tag{26}$$

AD_{ij} is air damage in region i from pollutant j; Pop_i is population in region i; NAD_j is national air damage from pollutant j; m is the median exposure over all regions in the base year; and λ_j are scalars related to X_{ij}/m in such a way as to make damages a concave upward function of exposure. If λ_j equaled 1 for all values of X_{ij}/m, Equation 26 would assign national damages to region i in proportion to its share of total exposures. In comparison, a strictly concave upward relationship assigns proportionately more national damages to regions with high exposures and proportionately less to less polluted areas. The values of λ_j are chosen to accord with the few existing empirical estimates of damage functions.

From Equation 26, a regional function for forecasting per capita damages is derived as follows:

$$\frac{AD_{ij}^*}{Pop_i^*} = (X_{ij}^*/m)\lambda_j MD, \tag{27}$$

where MD are damages per capita in the base year for the region with the median exposure.

Equation 27 follows from Equation 26 in the following way. In the base year, $(X_{ij}/m)\lambda_j$ for the region with the median exposure equals 1. Therefore, its damages per capita are

$$\frac{AD_{ij}}{Pop_i} = \frac{NAD_j}{\sum_i Pop_i(X_{ij}/m)\lambda_j}. \tag{28}$$

Substituting Equation 28 into Equation 27 gives:

$$\frac{AD_{ij}^*}{Pop_i^*} = (X_{ij}^*/m)\lambda_j \frac{NAD_j}{\sum_i (Pop_i(X_{ij}/m)\lambda_j}. \tag{29}$$

That is, forecast damages per capita equal forecast exposures (normalized and scaled) times damages per exposure for the base year. Using Equation 27, or its equivalent Equation 29, and summing, it can be seen for the base year that damages over all regions equal national damages. Also, Equation 27 (plugging in a range of values for X_{ij}) gives linear segments whose slopes (relative to the median exposure value) are the same as those of a few selected empirical damage functions.

One additional adjustment to Equation 27 is made for years beyond the base year. An income–environment elasticity multiplier is applied:

$$\frac{AD^*_{ij}}{Pop^*_i} = (X^*_{ij}/m)\lambda_j \cdot MD \cdot Z^*_t, \tag{30}$$

where $Z^*_t = ((DI_t/DI_{t-1} - 1)L_t + 1)Z^*_{t-1}$. In this equation, DI_t is average national disposable income per capita in year. L_t is the demand elasticity for environmental quality taken with respect to disposable income per capita or, in other words, a factor applied against the percent change in disposable income to reflect changing valuation of the environment with respect to per capita income.

The elasticities L used in this study are based, in part, upon Harris, Tolley, and Harrell (1968). Harris and coauthors measured the willingness of individuals at different income levels to pay higher prices for residential lots and found an income elasticity of demand for neighborhood amenities in the range of 2.5 to 4.0. There are two reasons why these elasticities cannot be used directly in this study. The first is that the "amenity" captured in the Harris estimates—the amenities associated with the immediate environs of one's residence—may not be perceived and evaluated in the same way as air and water amenities in the more general environment. Consequently, in this study an elasticity no larger than one-half the average of the Harris estimates is used to measure the willingness to pay for cleaner air and water. Second, the Harris estimates refer to a given point in time. But in this study income continues to rise over time and environmental quality with respect to mass pollutants (as measured by emissions and concentrations) generally improves. Therefore, one might expect elasticities to decline over time because the utility of further improvements in environmental quality diminishes. Consequently, this study uses declining income elasticities: for the period from 1975 to 1985, it uses an income elasticity of 1.6; between 1985 and 2000, an income elasticity of 0.67; between 2000 and 2010, an income elasticity of 0.3; and between 2010 and 2025, an income elasticity of 0. Consistent with this, Z^*_t reaches a maximum value of 2.3 in the year 2010.

Table A–7. Estimated National Water Pollution Damages
(billions of 1971 dollars)

Damage category	Estimate
Outdoor recreation	6.3
Aesthetic and ecological	1.5
Health[a]	1.6
Production (including municipal, industrial, agricultural supplies, commercial fisheries, and materials damage)	1.7
Total	11.1

[a] Starts with the estimates provided in Heintz and coauthors (1976), but adds costs of $1 billion a year for health care and forgone income as a result of increased cancer incidence. A study by Page, Harris, and Epstein (1976) indicates that about 5 percent of cancer incidence could be attributed to carcinogens in drinking water obtained from surface water sources. Costs for all cancer as measured by health care costs and forgone income is about $20 billion a year (Cooper and Rice, 1976).

Similar procedures are used to calculate regional and national water pollution damages. In this case PDI_i^*, as calculated by Equation 25, is the estimated exposure.

Sources of data are as follows: (1) national air pollution damages and national water pollution damages for the base year 1971 are taken from Gianessi, Peskin, and Wolf (1977) and Heintz and coauthors (1976), respectively (these are shown in tables A–7 and A–8); (2) population estimates for AQCRs and ASAs are based upon Water Resources Council (1974a and 1974b), respectively; (3) the scalars λ_j are based upon data in Ahern (1974), Dornbush (1973), and upon judgment. Damage functions for the base year, 1971, derived using the methods just described, are shown in figure A–4.

Table A–8. Estimated National Air Pollution Damages
(billions of 1971 dollars)

Pollutant	Estimate
Particulate matter	5.9
Sulfur oxides	8.3
Nitrogen oxides	3.1
Hydrocarbons	2.7
Carbon monoxide	0.25
Total	20.2

Source: L. P. Gianessi, H. M. Peskin, and E. Wolff, "The Distributional Implications of National Air Pollution Damage Estimates," in F. T. Juster, ed., *The Distribution of Economic Well-being* (Cambridge, Mass., Ballinger, 1977).

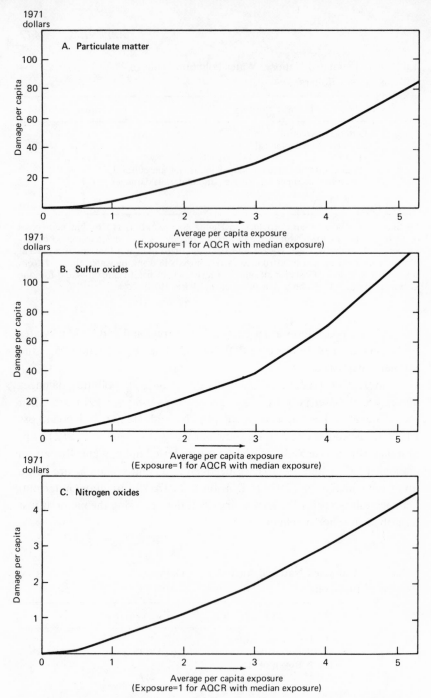

Figure A–4.   Damage functions for selected pollutants, 1971. *A*, particulate matter; *B*, sulfur oxides; *C*, nitrogen oxides; *D*, hydrocarbons; *E*, carbon monoxide; and *F*, water pollution.

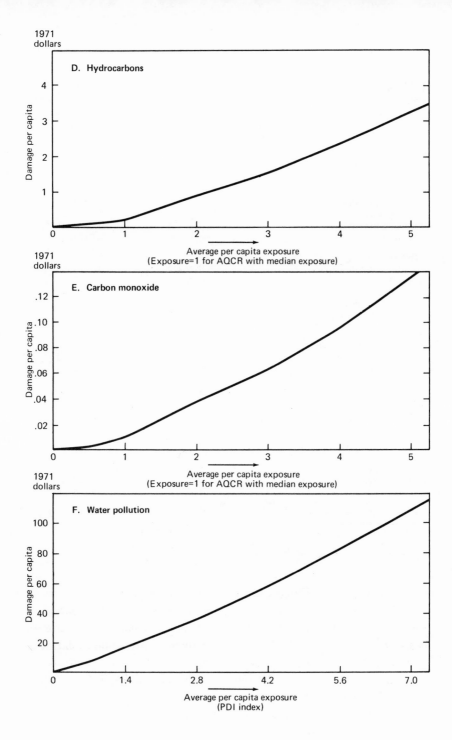

D. Hydrocarbons

1971 dollars

Damage per capita

Average per capita exposure
(Exposure=1 for AQCR with median exposure)

E. Carbon monoxide

1971 dollars

Damage per capita

Average per capita exposure
(Exposure=1 for AQCR with median exposure)

F. Water pollution

1971 dollars

Damage per capita

Average per capita exposure
(PDI index)

449

Table A–9. Confidence Ranges for Damages and Costs, by Source and Pollutant

Source and pollutant	96 percent confidence ranges[a]	
	Damages	Control costs
Electric utilities		
Particulate matter	0.5–2.5	0.75–1.45
Sulfur oxides	0.5–3.0	0.75–1.45
Nitrogen oxides	0.5–1.7	0.75–1.45
Hydrocarbons	0.5–1.7	0.75–1.45
Carbon monoxide	0.5–1.7	0.75–1.45
Water pollution	0.5–1.7	0.8–1.4
Industry		
Particulate matter	0.5–2.5	0.75–1.45
Sulfur oxides	0.5–3.0	0.75–1.45
Nitrogen oxides	0.5–1.7	0.75–1.45
Hydrocarbons	0.5–1.7	0.75–1.45
Carbon monoxide	0.5–1.7	0.75–1.45
Water pollution	0.5–1.7	0.8–1.4
Residential and commercial sources		
Particulate matter	0.5–1.7	0.75–1.45
Sulfur oxides	0.5–1.7	0.75–1.45
Nitrogen oxides	0.5–1.7	0.75–1.45
Hydrocarbons	0.5–1.7	0.75–1.45
Carbon monoxide	0.5–1.7	0.75–1.45
Water pollution[b]	0.5–1.7	0.8–1.4
Transportation		
Particulate matter	0.5–1.7	0.75–1.45
Sulfur oxides	0.5–1.7	0.75–1.45
Nitrogen oxides	0.3–3.0	0.75–2.0
Hydrocarbons	0.3–3.0	0.75–2.0
Carbon monoxide	0.3–3.0	0.75–2.0
Urban nonpoint sources runoff	0.3–2.5	0.8–1.4

[a] Numbers shown are factors applied to most likely values.
[b] Includes damages and control costs associated with municipal waste water treatment plants.

To estimate *expected* costs and risk avoidance, it is necessary to have frequency distributions. Table A–9 contains 96 percent confidence ranges for pollution control costs and damages. Damages and control costs are distributed according to the frequency distributions shown in figures A–5 and A–6, respectively. Ranges and distributions are based upon data in AWARE (1973), Battelle Laboratories, Inc. (1974), Waddell (1974), and judgment.

Expected damage costs (EDC) are calculated as follows:

$$EDC_j = \sum_{i=1}^{9} D_{ij}P_i \quad j = 1, \ldots, 10, \tag{31}$$

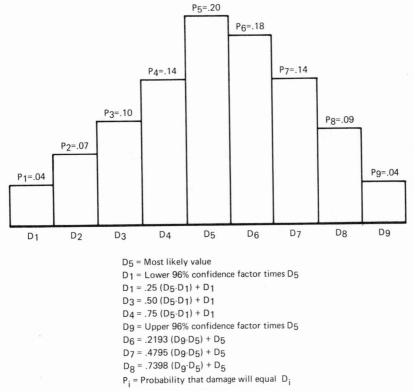

D_5 = Most likely value
D_1 = Lower 96% confidence factor times D_5
D_1 = .25 (D_5-D_1) + D_1
D_3 = .50 (D_5-D_1) + D_1
D_4 = .75 (D_5-D_1) + D_1
D_9 = Upper 96% confidence factor times D_5
D_6 = .2193 (D_9-D_5) + D_5
D_7 = .4795 (D_9-D_5) + D_5
D_8 = .7398 (D_9-D_5) + D_5
P_i = Probability that damage will equal D_i

Figure A–5.   Frequency distribution for damages.

where D_{ij} are damages at probability level i and control level j; and P_i is the probability that damages will equal D_{ij} (see figure A-5).

Expected total costs (the sum of probability weighted control and damage costs) are calculated as follows:

$$\text{ETC}_j = \sum_{i=1}^{9} (D_{ij} + C_{10-i,j})P_i, \tag{32}$$

where $C_{10-i,j}$ are control costs at probability level $10 - i$ and control level j (see figure A-6).

Risk avoidance is calculated as the probability over time that damages will not exceed their 1975 most likely levels. This is expressed as follows:

$$\text{Prob}_{j,t} = \text{Cumulated Prob}_{j,t}(\text{Dam}_{j,t}), \tag{33}$$

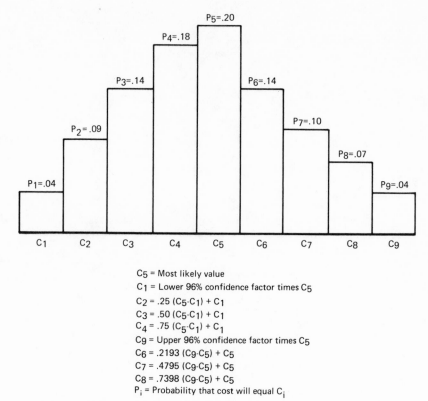

C_5 = Most likely value
C_1 = Lower 96% confidence factor times C_5
C_2 = .25 $(C_5\text{-}C_1)$ + C_1
C_3 = .50 $(C_5\text{-}C_1)$ + C_1
C_4 = .75 $(C_5\text{-}C_1)$ + C_1
C_9 = Upper 96% confidence factor times C_5
C_6 = .2193 $(C_9\text{-}C_5)$ + C_5
C_7 = .4795 $(C_9\text{-}C_5)$ + C_5
C_8 = .7398 $(C_9\text{-}C_5)$ + C_5
P_i = Probability that cost will equal C_i

Figure A–6.   Frequency distribution for costs.

where $\text{Dam}_{j,t}$ are damages at control level j in year t. Figure A-7 shows the general form of the cumulative distribution.

References

Ahern, W. R., Jr. 1974. "Measuring the Health Effects of Reductions in Automotive Air Pollution," in Henry D. Jacoby, *Clearing the Air: Federal Policy on Automotive Emissions Control* (Cambridge, Mass., Ballinger Press).

Almon, C., Jr., M. B. Buckler, L. M. Horowitz, and T. C. Reimbold. 1974. *1985: Interindustry Forecasts of the American Economy* (Lexington, Mass., Lexington Books).

Associated Water and Air Resources Engineers, Inc. 1973. *Estimating Water Pollution Control Costs from Selected Manufacturing Industries in the*

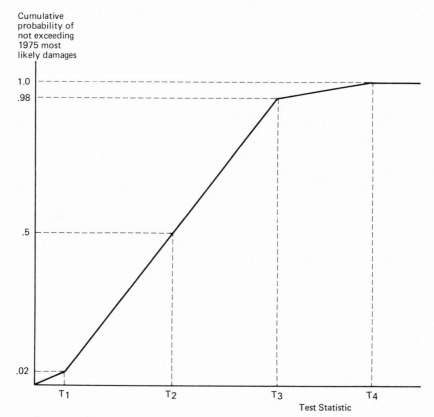

Figure A–7.   Cumulative probability distribution for damages.

U.S. 1973–1977. Report to the U.S. Environmental Protection Agency (Nashville, Tenn., AWARE).

Battelle Laboratories, Inc. 1974. Report to U.S. Environmental Protection Agency (Washington, D.C., Battelle).

Cooper, B. S., and D. P. Rice. 1976. "The Economic Cost of Illness Revisited," *Social Security Bulletin,* Social Security Administration, DHEW publication no. (SSA) 76-11703 (Washington, D.C., GPO).

Dornbusch, D. M. 1973. *Benefit of Water Pollution Control on Property Values.* Report to the U.S. Environmental Protection Agency.

EPA. See U.S. Environmental Protection Agency.

Gianessi, L. P., and H. M. Peskin. 1978. "Estimates of National Water Pollutant Discharges by Polluting Sector: 1972" (Washington, D.C., Resources for the Future) app. B-1.

———, and E. Wolff. 1977. "The Distributional Implications of National Air Pollution," in F. T. Juster, ed., *The Distribution of Economic Wellbeing* (Cambridge, Mass., Ballinger Press).

Gutmanis, I., and A. Shapanka. 1972. *Economic Costs Associated with Environmental Quality Alternatives in the United States, 1970, 1980, 1985: An Input–Output Analysis* (Washington, D.C., International Research and Technology Corporation).

Harris, R. N. S., G. S. Tolley, and C. Harrell. 1968. "The Residence Site Choice," *Review of Economics and Statistics* vol. 60, pp. 241–247.

Heany, J. P., W. C. Huber, M. A. Medina, Jr., M. P. Murphy, S. J. Nix, and S. M. Hasan. 1977. *National Evaluation of Combined Sewer Overflows and Urban Stormwater Discharges,* EPA-600/2-77-064, (Cincinnati, Ohio, EPA).

Heintz, H. T., Jr., A. Hershaft, and G. C. Horak. 1976. *National Damages of Air and Water Pollution.* Report to the U.S. Environmental Protection Agency (Rockville, Md., Environmental Control Inc.).

Holzworth, G. C. 1972. *Mixing Heights, Wind Speeds, and Potential for Urban Air Pollution Throughout the Contiguous United States,* AP-101 (Raleigh, N.C., EPA).

Krajeski, E. P., E. Kertz, and D. Bobo. 1972. "A Study of the Relationship Between Pollutant Emissions from Stationary Sources and Ground Level Ambient Air Quality" (Washington, D.C., EPA).

Lake, E., C. Blair, J. Hudson, and R. Tabors. 1976. *Classification of American Cities for Case Study Analysis,* vol. III. Report to the U.S. Environmental Protection Agency (Cambridge, Mass., Urban Systems Research and Engineering, Inc.).

Lewis, D. H. 1971. "Allocations of Air Pollution Control Research Funds on the Basis of Human Exposure" (Washington, D.C., EPA).

Midwest Research Institute. 1975. *Cost and Effectiveness of Control of Pollution from Selected Non-point Sources* (Kansas City, Mo., Midwest Research Institute).

National Commission on Water Quality (NCWQ). 1976. Staff Report to the National Commission on Water Quality (Washington, D.C., GPO, April 30).

Page, T., R. H. Harris, and S. S. Epstein. 1976. "Drinking Water and Cancer Mortality in Louisiana," *Science* vol. 193, no. 4247 (July 2) pp. 55–57,

Shapanka, A. 1978. "Long-Range Technological Forecasts for Use in Studying the Resource and Environmental Consequences of U.S. Population and Economic Growth: 1975–2025," Discussion Paper D-31 (Washington, D.C., Resources for the Future).

Smith, J. M. 1975. Unpublished data and analysis provided by the U.S. Environmental Protection Agency.

Truitt, J. B., A. C. Johnson, W. W. Rowe, K. D. Feigner, and L. J. Manning. 1975. "Development of Water Quality Management Indices," *Water Resources Bulletin* vol. 11, no. 3 (June).

U.S. Bureau of the Census. 1972. *Census of Manufactures* (Washington, D.C., GPO).

U.S. Department of Agriculture (USDA). 1975. *Control of Water Pollution from Cropland,* vol. I (Washington, D.C., USDA, Agricultural Research Service).

U.S. Environmental Protection Agency (EPA). 1973a. *Clean Water Report to Congress* (Washington, D.C., EPA).

————. 1973b. *Economics of Clean Water* (Washington, D.C., EPA).

————. 1973c. *The National Air Monitoring Program: Air Quality and Emissions Trends,* EPA-450/1-73-001-b (Research Triangle Park, N.C., EPA).

————. 1974a. *Users Manual for the Strategic Environmental Assessment System (SEAS)* (Washington, D.C., EPA).

————. 1974b. *Data Specifications for the Strategic Environmental Assessment System (SEAS)* (Washington, D.C., EPA).

————. 1974c. *Programmers Guide for the Strategic Environmental Assessment System* (SEAS) (Washington, D.C., EPA).

University of Oklahoma. 1975. *Energy Alternatives: A Comparative Analysis,* Science and Public Policy Program (Norman, University of Oklahoma).

Waddell, T. E. 1974. *The Economic Damages of Air Pollution,* EPA-600/5-74-012 (Washington, D.C., EPA).

Wade, J. C., and E. O. Heady. 1976. *A National Model of Sediment and Water Quality: Various Impacts on American Agriculture,* CARD Report 67 (Ames, Center for Agricultural and Rural Development, Iowa State University).

Water Resources Council (WRC). 1974a. *1972 OBERS Projections, Regional Economic Activity in the U.S.: Air Quality Control Regions* (Washington, D.C., USDA Economic Research Service).

————. 1974b. *1972 OBERS Projections, Regional Economic Activity in the U.S.: Aggregated Subareas* (Washington, D.C., USDA Economic Research Service).

Epilogue

Events during 1979 have so altered perceptions about the future that it is useful to comment on how their inclusion would have affected our results. The most dramatic of these events are the nuclear near-catastrophe at Three Mile Island, the doubling of world petroleum prices during the last twelve months, and the turmoil in Iran following on the expulsion of the Shah.

Three Mile Island and its aftermath make a slowdown in the expansion of nuclear power virtually inevitable during the next two decades and enhances the likelihood of a nuclear phaseout or moratorium. On the assumption that a complete phaseout does not occur, it now appears that nuclear power, which provided 2.8 quads of energy (primary fuel equivalent) in 1979, will not account for more than 10 quads in the year 2000. This contrasts with a figure of 20 quads for the year 2000 that was built into scenario EL and even higher projections made by others a few years ago.

The turmoil in Iran and the possibility of its spilling over to other Middle Eastern countries raises with more force than heretofore the specter of sudden, dramatic shortfalls in petroleum supplies. This makes it all the more imperative that the United States reduce its dependence on Middle Eastern supplies. So far, efforts to do so by developing a strategic stockpile have not succeeded, in part because of resistance by potential suppliers. This turmoil, plus the 1979 run-up in petroleum prices, forces us to consider more severe, politically imposed constraints on production than those incorporated into scenario DHP1 (see page 179). While this latest price increase does not invalidate our conclusion that, in the absence of such constraints, the price could have remained at $12 per barrel (1975$) for the next couple of decades, it certainly reduces its relevance for analysis of current problems.

Two other developments should be mentioned here. The first pertains to the growth of the U.S. economy, which has been roughly tracking the slow growth path of scenario EL. There is no reason to believe that a higher growth rate is likely to occur in the near future. The second factor involves a more rapid decline in the Btu/GNP ratio than that anticipated during the period from 1971 to 1975. This decline leaves our figures about 6 percent too high for total energy consumption between 1975–79.

What consequences would follow the introduction into scenario EL of higher petroleum prices, accompanied by constraints on imports and nuclear capacity, if EL were adjusted to reflect lower energy consumption for 1975–79?

We must start by incorporating the 1979 rise in the world price of petroleum from $12 to $20 per barrel (1975$). If full production in Iran were to resume in 1980, there could be some softness in this price for a few years; on the other hand, if exports from Iran were to cease, another round of dramatic price increases would result. For our present purpose, we will use an intermediate case which assumes that OPEC constrains production so that the price of oil increases to a level just below the long-run cost of producing substitutes; in the text we estimated this to be $24 per barrel and that still seems reasonable.[1]

Even in the absence of constraints on production and imports, such price increases (which we assume will be passed through to consumers in the next few years) will have significant effects. The most direct impact will be a slower rate of growth in energy consumption and, as a consequence, a further dampening of economic growth in the United States and other energy-importing countries. A second effect would be a more pronounced tendency toward a capital shortage in the 1980s. If the savings rate cannot be increased sufficiently to accommodate the increased investment requirements, a further fall in the long-run economic growth rate is likely. These two factors could easily press down the annual growth rates for the GNP that have been incorporated into scenario EL (2.6 percent between 1980–85 and 2.9 percent between 1985–2000) by a full percentage point, with somewhat more of a decrease during the next five years and somewhat less thereafter.[2]

This slowdown, plus the price increase, would substantially reduce energy consumption. Instead of energy consumption growing from 80.2

---

[1] Schurr and coauthors (1979, p. 263) indicate that liquids from coal can be produced for a price in the range of $15 to $19.80 per barrel, that shale oil produced by conventional means should be available for $24 to $38.40, and that gas from coal could be produced for $9.60 to $30.60 depending on its heat content and the process used (all prices in 1975$). Heavy oils appear already to be profitable, judging from the fact that they are beginning to be used in significant quantities.

[2] See pages 28 and 68–69 in this volume, and Ridker, Watson, and Shapanka (1977) for assumptions entering into this estimate.

quads in 1979 to 107 quads in 2000 (scenario EL adjusted), a more likely range for the year 2000 would be 84 to 89 quads. In this environment, petroleum imports, even without import quotas or greatly intensified public programs to develop domestic substitutes, are likely to grow very slowly during the eighties. Indeed, they may be no greater than 19 quads in 1985, as compared with the 17.8 quads expected in 1979, and by 2000 they may be substantially lower, possibly in the range of 15 to 16 quads, instead of 35 quads projected in the adjusted version of scenario EL.

If, in addition, there are constraints on nuclear power (5 quads in 1985 and 10 quads in 2000) and imported petroleum (a maximum of 18 quads), pressure would be placed on other domestic energy sources, especially coal. While the economic costs of such a shift to coal would not be very large except in a period of transition and in those areas where nuclear power is significantly cheaper than coal-fired electric, the environmental impacts are likely to be much more significant (see the discussions in various chapters of scenario DHNU); and transport and equipment bottlenecks, local resistance to mining operations, and bureaucratic delays could easily result in a constraint on the speed with which coal can expand. What would happen if, in addition to the other constraints, such problems result in production levels no greater than 15.8 quads in 1985 and 30 quads in 2000, still implying a fairly rapid rate of increase?

Between 1980–85, there would be little additional effect since the price increases that would occur, even in the absence of these constraints, are sufficient (given the response elasticities discussed on page 187) to hold demands for various fuels within bounds. Thereafter, things become increasingly difficult. By 2000 the delivered price (in 1975$) for 1 million Btu of coal could rise to $2.00 (compared with $1.19 in scenario EL); oil and natural gas could cost $6.40 ($38.40 per barrel) and $5.70, respectively; and electricity could be $10.60 (compared with $8.98 in scenario EL and $9.58 in scenario DHNU). Energy consumption could decrease by an additional 5 quads, with proportionately less electricity being used, with liquids being reserved for transportation and chemical feedstocks, and with various forms of solar expanding much more rapidly than assumed in other scenarios and being used, along with gas, for space conditioning. The economic growth rate might decline by an additional half to one percentage point. Per capita economic growth—in particular the growth of per capita consumption—would still be positive but not far from zero.

This outcome greatly depends on our ability to raise the domestic savings rate and to attract foreign savings. Much also depends on the speed with which substitutes in production and consumption can be developed, in particular on the future of the coal and nuclear industries in this country. All these factors can be significantly influenced by policy. If they are managed well, with a little luck a reasonable degree of economic growth could resume again after a period of transition. Otherwise, 1979 could signal the beginning of an era of economic stagnation.

It must be remembered that this scenario is based on a perception of the future formed in the last few months. Events appear to be changing so rapidly that yet other scenarios are likely to be appropriate in another few months. The best we can do is to reemphasize the point made in chapter 1, that studies such as this must be repeated many times, and that what is required is an ongoing process aimed at continually improving our ability to clarify the longer-run consequences of current actions.

References

Ridker, Ronald G., William D. Watson, Jr., and Adele Shapanka. 1977. "Economic, Energy, and Environmental Consequences of Alternative Energy Regimes: An Application of the RFF/SEAS Modeling System," in Charles J. Hitch, ed., *Modeling Energy–Economy Interactions: Five Approaches* (Washington, D.C., Resources for the Future).

Schurr, Sam H., Joel Darmstadter, William Ramsay, Harry Perry, and Milton Russell. 1979. *Energy in America's Future: The Choices Before Us* (Baltimore, Md., Johns Hopkins University Press for Resources for the Future).

Index

ABATE model, 251–254, 424–429
Aggregated subareas, 322–323
Agriculture, 221–222, 381–382
  and cropland requirements, 240–244, 328, 382, 390
  and domestic food consumption, 230–233
  and domestic output, exports, and prices, 233–235, 245–246
  and energy use, 245, 247
  and environmental policy, 230, 231, 239–240
  and farm prices, 245, 247–248, 390
  and fertilizer and pesticide use, 225, 245, 246, 382
  and foreign demand, 226–230, 235, 237–238
  input requirements, 240–245
  and population and economic growth, 235–237, 328, 329, 398–399
  and productivity, 222–226, 237, 238, 245
  and public policy assumptions, 52
  and world food prices, 50–51
Air quality control regions, 320–322
Aluminum, 122, 126–128, 143, 144, 153
Antimony, 152
AQUALITY and WQUALITY models, 441–443
Asbestos, 150

Barium, 150
Bauxite, 122, 127–128
BENEFITS model, 433–444
Biochemical oxygen demand, 256, 262, 264–265, 279, 400
Boron, 150–151
Bureau of Census, 17, 20–21
Bureau of Mines, 103–104, 154

Capital shortage, 68–69, 457–459
Carbon dioxide emissions, 357–359, 386–387. *See also* Pollution.
Chemical oxygen demand, 262, 265, 279
Carbon monoxide emissions, 261, 264, 267, 269, 274–276, 283, 284
Chemicals, toxic, 337, 364–366, 384
Chromium, 109, 114–115, 143, 144
Climate, 225–226
  and residuals, 355–359
Coal
  consumption and production by sector, 205, 207
  production, 184–185, 208–210, 338n, 389
  and world resources, 158, 164–165
  See also Environmental issues; Pollution.
Cobalt, 117, 121, 122n, 125, 144, 153
Communications technology, 37
Construction sector, 35–36
Consumer expenditures, 31–32
Copper, 39–40, 99–100, 117n, 122, 124, 143, 144, 153
Crop yield. *See* Agriculture.

Deep-sea mining, 117, 121–122
Dissolved solids, 259, 263, 265, 279

Economy, national
  and abatement investment for environmental control, 68n, 84–92, 402
  cutbacks to growth, 406–407
  general characteristics, 58–69
  and GNP growth rate, 58–64, 390–391
  and government expenditures, 59, 61–62, 402
  and import dependency, 73–78, 93
  and investment expenditures, 64–69, 71, 81n, 93–94

Economy, national (*continued*)
  and nuclear power, 78–81, 93
  and oil prices, 81–84
  and personal consumption expenditures, 59, 61–62, 64, 71
  and population and labor productivity, 69–72, 93
Economy, world, 42–47
Electricity, 190, 204–206
Energy
  distribution by fuels and sectors, 204–211
  and GNP. *See* Gross National Product, and Btu–GNP ratio.
  and other U.S. energy consumption projections, 198–199
  and projected total demands, all scenarios, 201–204
  cumulative demand and resources, all scenarios, 211–216
  environmental considerations, 378–381
  extraction, 37–39
  and labor productivity, 28
  and nonrenewable resources, 158–166
  and renewable resources, 166–168
  and U.S. demand and supply projections, 378–381
    consumption by sectors, 194–195, 197, 200–201
    methodology used, 186–188
    price assumptions, 188–193
  and world consumption projections, 168–174, 175
  and world demand, supply and price projections
    natural gas, 181–184
    other energy forms, 184–185
    petroleum, 174–181
    production constraints, 179, 380, 457–459
ENERGY model, 433–435
ENSUPPLY model, 429–430
Environmental issues, 52, 325–327, 366–367, 383–387, 394–395, 405–406. *See also* Land resources; Pollution; *specific pollutants.*
  climate and residuals, 355–359
  and erosion, 224, 345–346
  and land disturbed by mining, 338–345
  and land use problems, 327–330

  and power plant siting, 330–336
  and radiation, 359–364
  scenarios for, 372–373, 387–391
  and solid waste disposal, 336–338
  and toxic chemicals and the ocean, 364–366
  and water resources, 346–355
Erosion, 224, 345–346
Expenditures
  government, 53, 59, 61–62, 70–71
  investment, 64–69, 81*n*, 93–94
  personal consumption, 59, 61–62, 64, 71

Feldspar, 151
Fertility rates, 17–20
Fertilizer. *See under* Agriculture.
Food
  and U.S. price indexes, 233–235
  and world prices, 50–51
  See also Agriculture.
FORECAST, 415–417, 430
Forestry sector, 382
FTRANS, 433, 439
Fuel sources. *See specific sources.*
Fusion, controlled, 168

Gas. *See* Natural gas.
Geothermal energy, 167–168, 184–185
Gross National Product (GNP)
  and average annual growth rate, 58–64
  and annual growth rates per employee, 28–29
  and Btu–GNP ratio, 27–29, 169–174, 193, 197, 378
  and government expenditures, 59, 61–62, 70–71, 402
  and imports, 73–78
  and investment expenditures, 64–69, 70–71, 81*n*, 93–94
  and personal consumption expenditures, 30–32, 59, 61–62, 64, 70–71
  and population and labor productivity, 69–72, 93, 373–375
  and world population, 42–47

Hydrocarbons, 258, 260, 264, 266, 268–269, 283, 284
Hydroelectric potential, 166–167, 184–185

INFORUM model, 31, 417–421, 431, 434
Imports, and import dependence, 51, 73–78, 93, 209, 396
INSIDE model, 422–424
International Bauxite Association, 127
Instrument requirements, 64–69, 93–94, 374, 389
Iron, 117n, 128–130, 143, 144, 153

Labor force, 21–23
    productivity, 23–30
Land resources
    disturbed by mining, 338–345
    and erosion, 345–346, 386
    and land use problems, 327–330, 384, 390
    and power plant siting, 330–336, 384
    and solid waste disposal, 336–338, 384
Life-style, and personal savings, 30–31
Lead, 130–132, 143, 144, 146, 153

Manganese, 109, 117, 120–121, 122n, 143, 144, 153
Materials substitution, 40
Mercury, 148, 152
Metals, primary, 39–40
Methodology of study, 1–13
MINERALS model, 430
Minerals, nonfuel
    consumption as a function of GNP, 106–107, 130
    and demand growth rates and GNP, 140–142, 152–154, 375–376
    ferrous, 152
    and hypothetical exhaustion dates, 143–148, 388
    and methods developed to project demand, 104–107
    nonferrous, 151–152
    and other resource demand and supply estimates, 152–154
    price changes of, 96–102, 127–128, 148–149, 376–378
    reserves, 98–100, 102–104
    resource adequacy, 97–98
    resources defined, 100–102
    shortages of, 96
    and role of various demand determinants, 140–148
    and stockpiling of, 109, 117, 122, 135, 137, 140
    and world price of, 50

world projections, 105–107
    See also specific minerals.
Mining, 338–345
Molybdenum, 103n, 109–111, 117n, 143, 144, 153

Natural gas
    import dependency, 73–78, 388
    and public policy assumptions, 51
    world demand, supply, price projections, 181–184, 214–215
    world resources of, 158–159, 167, 389
    See also Energy.
Nickel, 117, 123, 143, 145, 152, 153
Nitrogen oxides, 258, 260, 264, 266, 268, 274–276, 283, 284, 356
Nonfuel minerals. See Minerals, nonfuel.
Nuclear power
    consumption and production by sector projected, 205, 207
    and national economy, 78–81, 93
    projected development of, 184, 385
    and public policy issues, 52, 78–81, 391–393
    See also Power plants; Radiation.

Oil. See Petroleum.
Oil shale, 159–162, 166, 185

Petroleum
    import dependency, 73–78, 207–210, 388–389
    and public policy assumptions, 51
    world prices of, 47–50, 81–84, 174–181, 388–389
    world resources of, 158–159, 165–167, 214–216, 389
    See also Energy.
Phosphate rock, 109, 118–119, 143, 145, 146, 153
Platinum, 152
Pollution, 250–251, 296–297
    and abatement investments, 68n, 84–92
    air and water emissions studies, 298–301, 394–395
    benefit–cost analysis of, 274–291
    control cost studies, 300–305
    control and damage costs, by scenarios, 291, 294–296, 383–384, 399
    damage estimates, 252, 270–273
        by region, 306–323

Pollution (*continued*)
emissions levels
for air and water sources, 260–263
and ambient concentrations, 266–270
national, 256–259, 261, 264–265, 270
and expected total costs
for alternative policies, 281–289, 290
for electric utilities, 276–277, 278
for transportation sources, 274–276
for urban nonpoint sources, 280–282
for water discharges from industrial sources, 277–280, 281
federal control standards assumptions, 52
procedures used in analysis of, 251–257
and sensitivity of water pollution results, 289–291, 292–293
and urban runoff and runoff control costs, 280–281, 305–306
See also specific pollutants.
Population
geographic distribution, 32–34
and labor productivity, 23–30, 69–72, 93, 373–375
projections, 16–21, 42–46, 372–375, 395–405, 407–410
world, and GNP projections, 42–47
Potash, 109, 116, 143, 145, 153
Power plants, 271, 272, 276–277
siting, 330–336
PRICE model, 421
PTRANS model, 433, 439

Radiation, 336, 359–364, 384. *See also* Power plants.
Reclamation, 339, 341–342, 384
REGION model, 437–439
RESGEN model, 431–432
Resource and environmental pressures
and personal savings, 30–31
and population projections, 16–21
previous studies on, 9–11
and primary metals production, 39–40
and public policy assumptions, 51–53
and resource base, 40–41
and summary of scenarios on, 53–55
and technological change approach, 34–35

and transportation, 36–37
and world population and GNP projections, 42–47
and world prices, 47–51
Risk avoidance, defined, 254–255
RUNOFF model, 439–441
Runoff. *See under* Pollution, urban runoff.

SEAS/RFF model, 6–9, 251
national system, 411–413
regional system, 413–414
See also specific models.
Solar energy, 166, 168, 184–185, 206–207
Solid waste disposal, 336–338, 384, 385
SOLRECYC model, 435–437
Stockpiling
of food grains, 226
of natural gas, 51
of nonfuel minerals, 109, 117, 122, 135, 137, 140
of petroleum, 51, 388
Sulfur, 132, 133, 145, 153
Sulfur oxide emissions, 258, 260, 264, 268, 276–277
Suspended solids, 262–263, 279
Synthetic fuels, 176–179, 193, 388

Talc, 151
Tar sands, 159, 160, 166
TECHNOLOGY model, 421
Tin, 103n, 132, 134–135, 143, 153
Titanium, 109, 112, 143, 153
Toxic chemicals. *See* Chemicals, toxic.
Transportation sector, 36–37
pollutants from, 274–276
Tungsten, 135–137, 143, 145, 148, 153

Unemployment. *See* Labor productivity.
U.S. Geological Survey, 100, 101, 103–104
Uranium resources, 162–164, 213–214, 389

Vanadium, 109, 113, 117n, 143, 145, 153

Water resources
and management practices, 353–354, 384
pollution of, 277–281
requirements for, 348–353
supply of, 346–347
Welfare indexes, 401–405

Zinc, 137–140, 143, 145, 153

Library of Congress Cataloging in Publication Data

Ridker, Ronald Gene, 1931–
    To choose a future.

    Includes index.
    1. United States—Economic policy—1971–
2. United States—Economic conditions—1971–
3. Economic forecasting—United States—
Mathematical models.   I. Watson, William D.,
joint author.   II. Title.
HC106.7.R42   333.7   79-3643
ISBN 0-8018-2354-4